THE GENERATIONS OF CORNING

Dear Fellow Employees,

Whether you've been with this company 50 years or 50 days, whether you work in upstate New York, or in a Corning facility elsewhere in the world, you are connected to an incredible heritage—a heritage shaped by the Houghton family. Few people can claim to be part of a company that is 150 years old. Fewer still can avow connection to a company whose inventions have transformed society with products such as electric lights, television and optical fiber. The fact that we were honored with the National Technology Medal of Honor attests not only to our long list of important inventions; it also reflects the fact that, to remain innovative, our company has reinvented itself repeatedly throughout our 150 years. Our history is indeed rich, and it grows richer every day.

It is apt that so many metaphors for history relate to glass, the material from which Corning has melted ideas into realities throughout our 150 years. History is a *window* through which we see clearly into our past. It is a *mirror* that reflects images back to us in ways we may not otherwise have seen. It is a *lens*, ground and polished to help us extract wisdom from our past and prepare for our future.

This history, in all its richness, is ours. Because you are a part of Corning, it belongs to you. And because you are a part of Corning, you are now shaping its future chapters.

We are grateful for the leadership of our founders and forebears. We are honored to be part of this company. And we are thrilled that you have chosen Corning as the place to spend and grow your talents. We look forward to working alongside you to create a future that continues to honor our company's rich history.

With deepest thanks,

Roger G. Ackerman, Chairman   John W. Loose, CEO

Board of Directors
June 2001

THE GENERATIONS OF

Corning

The Life and Times of a
Global Corporation

. . .

DAVIS DYER

DANIEL GROSS

OXFORD
UNIVERSITY PRESS

2001

OXFORD
UNIVERSITY PRESS

Oxford   New York
Athens   Auckland   Bangkok   Bogotá   Buenos Aires   Calcutta
Cape Town   Chennai   Dar es Salaam   Delhi   Florence   Hong Kong
Istanbul   Karachi   Kuala Lumpur   Madrid   Melbourne   Mexico City   Mumbai
Nairobi   Paris   São Paulo   Shanghai   Singapore   Taipei   Tokyo   Toronto   Warsaw

and associated companies in
Berlin   Ibadan

Published by Oxford University Press, Inc.
198 Madison Avenue, New York, New York, 10016

Oxford is a registered trademark of Oxford University Press

Library of Congress Cataloging-in-Publication Data
Dyer, Davis
The generations of Corning : the life and times of a global corporation /
Davis Dyer, Daniel Gross.
p. cm.   Includes bibliographical references and index.
ISBN 0-19-514095-8
1. Corning Incorporated.   2. Conglomerate corporations—United States.
I. Gross, Daniel, 1966–   II. Title.
HD2796.C66 D94   2001   338.766'0973—dc21   00-067091

Book design and composition by Mark McGarry,
Texas Type & Book Works
Set in Monotype Dante and Linotype Syntax

Permissions for illustrations can be found on page 508

9 8 7 6 5 4 3 2 1
Printed in the United States of America
on acid-free paper

*To the Houghton family to honor their remarkable vision, wisdom, passion,
imagination, and leadership in guiding the Corning company,
generation after generation.*

*To the employees of Corning
who have contributed to the success of the company
and made the world a better place to live.*

Contents

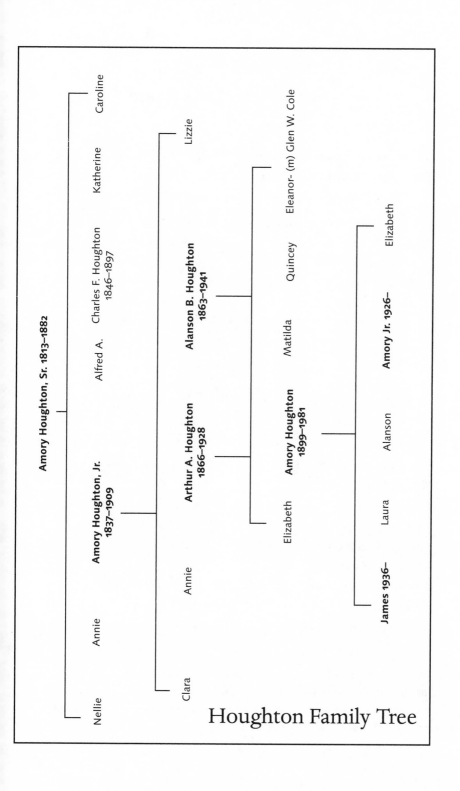

Houghton Family Tree

Chairmen of the Board

The company began using the title formally in 1919. Before that, the president served as chair of board meetings.

Alanson B. Houghton, 1919–1928
Alexander D. Falck, 1928–1941
Amory Houghton Sr., 1941–1961*
William C. Decker, 1961–1964

Amory Houghton Jr., 1964–1983
James R. Houghton, 1983–1996
Roger Ackerman, 1996–2001

*Amory Houghton Sr. was on leave as U.S. Ambassador to France, 1957–1961.

Presidents

CORNING FLINT GLASS WORKS
Amory Houghton Sr., 1868–1870
Joseph F. Hill, 1870–1875

CORNING GLASS WORKS
Amroy Houghton Jr., 1875–1909
Alanson B. Houghton, 1910–1918
Arthur A. Houghton, Sr., 1919–1920
Alexander D. Falck, 1920–1928
Eugene C. Sullivan, 1928–1930

Amory Houghton Sr., 1930–1941
Glen W. Cole, 1941–1946
William C. Decker, 1946–1961
Amory Houghton Jr., 1961–1964
R. Lee Waterman, 1964–1971
Thomas C. MacAvoy, 1971–1983

CORNING INCORPORATED
Roger G. Ackerman, 1990–1996
John W. Loose, 2000

There was no president during the tenure of the Management Committee (Six Pack) between 1983 and 1990. Between 1996 and 2000, there were co–chief operating officers of Corning, John W. Loose as president of Corning Communications and Norman E. Garrity as president of Corning Technologies.

Foreword

In 1851, my great-great-grandfather, Amory Houghton Sr. bought a stake in a small glassmaker in Somerville, Massachusetts. From that tiny seed has grown today's Corning Incorporated. This 150-year-old enterprise has one of the longest continuous records for manufacturing companies—but it has never been old-fashioned about its products or their use.

Throughout its century-and-a-half history, the company has continuously re-invented itself, shedding the old to concentrate on new opportunities as they arise.

I'm fond of saying that very few companies can claim to have made inventions which have spawned brand new industries that profoundly change the lives of mankind. Corning has made several in related materials, but three in glass stand out. Our seminal contributions to the Lighting, Television, and now the Optical Communications Industries were and are vital to their success.

Common to them all was light.

The creative response to the potential of light has been a constant theme for Corning. In the nineteenth century, the company manufactured red and green lenses for railroad signal lights and incandescent lamp envelopes for Thomas Edison's first light bulbs. Today the range extends from illumination to space exploration, from optical glass to cathode ray tubes for television, and flat glass for liquid crystal displays, from Steuben crystal to optical fibers. Light, and its reflectance, manipulation, and transmission, remains an essential resource for Corning.

The Generations of Corning traces the story of Corning Incorporated over its first 150 years. The book certainly describes the company's business strategies, operations, organizations and products, but the story is fundamentally one about people and their manifold contributions.

The title expresses well the point, in two respects. First, as successive generations of people moved through and took responsibility for the company, they constantly rose to the ever-changing challenges of particular eras—of developing superior capabilities in research, development, engineering, and manufacturing; of building businesses; of modernizing and automating facilities; of managing through wars and depressions; and of expanding our horizons to establish worldwide leadership—so especially important in today's information—intensive, global economy. People from a wide range of backgrounds and experiences continually make this happen. The continuous long line of outstanding employees has passed the company to the current generation, which does us all proud. It bears testimony to our belief that, in the end, people are our only competitive advantage.

Second, many employees have long-standing multigenerational ties to Corning. What is true of the Houghtons is no less true of numerous other families whose sons, daughters, and grandchildren have proudly followed their forebears to help shape Corning's future. These ties are an important "glue" in the company's long history and prominent position in Corning, New York, and the other communities in which it maintains operations. The bonds between the company, its employees, and its communities constitute a real and enduring strength.

This volume and its companion, *Corning and the Craft of Innovation,* are works of history, but they are not just monuments to the past. Rather, they tell stories that explain and put into perspective who we are. The volumes identify and chart the evolution of Corning's core values and capabilities, and provide lessons to guide, and hopefully inspire, future generations of employees. The first 150 years provide a solid foundation on which we will build a luminous future.

James R. Houghton

Preface

In 2001 Corning Incorporated marks the 150th anniversary of its founder Amory Houghton's investment in glassmaking. Corning's longevity makes it one of the oldest capitalist enterprises in the world, yet it displays few signs of age. In its anniversary year, the company more symbolizes the new, information age economy than an industrial past. In mid-2000 the company's stock traded at an all-time record high and the business press repeatedly hailed Corning as a driving force in the new economy. This book explains how it all happened, from the Houghton investment in 1851, to the high tech, highly valued materials company Corning is today.

The book explores several major themes in the story. These themes are described at length in Chapter 1, but three bear note here. First, evident from the title, is a distinctive generational pattern of change in the company. Five generations of Houghtons led the company between its founding and 1996. Tenures of chief executives and their close associates atop the company typically lasted many years. Significant changes in organization and operation accompanied each change of generation, and within recent generations, each change of leadership. This pattern of organization development is unusual among large companies, and surely is connected with Corning's remarkable ability to prosper over the long haul and to produce in generation after generation breakthroughs in materials technology. Which introduces the second major theme of the book: Corning's long and continuous history of working wonders with glass and related materials. The company is responsible for many innovations in its industry, including three that fundamentally shaped modern life: the light bulb, television, and fiber-optic communications. The book details these innovations and others and considers broadly how this one company has made its way from the industrial to the post-industrial economy while working with one of the oldest materials known to humankind. And third, as evident from the subtitle, this book sets Corning's story in wider contexts: of social, cultural, and political change in the United States, and of technological and economic change in the evolving global economy.

The Generations of Corning has an unusual provenance that bears on its scope and contents. In late 1996, Corning engaged The Winthrop Group, Inc. to produce three books to commemorate the impending 150th anniversary. The three books included a general corporate history of Corning, a history of innovation and R&D, and a pictorial history of the company, its products, and its hometown. Working with a steering committee consisting of Corning employees and retirees and two independent experts, the Winthrop authors designed the books not as a set but as separate and discrete volumes that each could be read without reference to the others. At the same time, the books were intended to inform and complement each other and their respective readers: the corporate history provides chronological and general corporate context around subjects considered in the innovation book; the innovation book provides insight and detail on many topics that receive relatively brief attention in the general corporate history; and the pictorial book looks at Corning's history from still another angle— its dominant products—and tests the old dictum that a picture is worth a thousand words.

The authors and research assistants on all three books decided collectively particular topics and themes to be covered in each book, collaborated in research and interviews, and read and commented extensively on outlines and drafts as they took shape. The authors of each book possessed freedom of interpretation. Each book touches on (and, we hope, is consistent with) topics and interpretations developed in the others. But each book also, we hope, stands on its own merits and provides a complementary angle from which to view growth and change at Corning. Having subjected manuscripts to its customary outside review process, Oxford University Press agreed to publish the general corporate history and the history of innovation and R&D as, respectively, *The Generations of Corning,* and *Corning and the Craft of Innovation.* The pictorial history is privately printed.

Authors incur many debts in writing books. We start by thanking Jamie Houghton, retired chairman and CEO, Roger Ackerman, chairman and chief executive of Corning Incorporated, and Marie McKee, senior vice president, for sponsoring our work. We wish also to acknowledge and thank the members of the History 150 Steering Committee at Corning Incorporated: Peter Bridenbaugh (formerly chief technical officer and a senior officer of Alcoa), W. Bernard Carlson (professor at the University of Virginia), Rob Cassetti (Steuben glass designer and senior manager of the Corning Museum of Glass), Cindy Demers (public relations, until her departure in 1999), Gus Filbert (retired scientist and R&D executive), Jack Holliday (retired Corning executive), Jamie Houghton, Eve Menger (retired scientist and R&D executive), Al Michaelsen (senior vice president and general patent counsel), Meleny Peacock (Director, Specialized Communications, who managed the 150th anniversary celebrations), and Stuart K. Sammis (History 150 project manager, former archivist, and presently project leader in knowledge management and organizational learning, science and technology division).

The History 150 Committee was present at the conception of the three books and endured through their long gestation, suggesting resources to consult, lines of inquiry to explore (and blind alleys to avoid), and commenting on outlines and drafts as the manuscripts materialized. As authors of this volume, we benefited greatly from rigorous critiques and vigorous discussion of our work in Committee meetings. We are also grateful for close readings of the manuscript from a variety of perspectives. We wish especially to thank Bernie Carlson for pushing us in the direction of developing the broader context of the story; Gus Filbert for helping to ensure that we dealt with technical matters correctly; Jamie Houghton for his deep understanding of and insight into the long history of the company and its connections with his family; Al Michaelsen for clarifying legal matters; and Stu Sammis for exceptionally careful reading of the manuscript in its stages of evolution. As supervisor of the entire effort, Stu invested countless hours in ensuring that we had the support we needed while keeping a large and multifaceted project barreling down the track.

More than 150 Corning employees, retirees, and directors gave generously of their time for oral and video history interviews, and this book could not have been written—or written confidently—without their contributions. Their names are too numerous to be listed here but the notes at the end of the book reveal just how essential the interviews are. The tapes and transcripts of them will be an invaluable resource to Corning for generations to come. Many interviewees also provided us access to documents, photographs, publications, and memorabilia in their possession. We thank particularly Roger Ackerman, Bill Armistead, Don Bonnell, Carole Herrlich, Jamie Houghton, the late Frank Hyde, Jack Ludington (Dow Corning), Chuck Lucy, John MacDowell, and Pierre-Louis Roederer. We are also grateful to many present and former Corning and joint venture employees and officers of the American Flint Glass Workers Union who facilitated research in Corning, New York, Hickory, North Carolina, Midland, Michigan, Martinsburg, West Virginia, State College, Pennsylvania, and Wilmington, North Carolina.

Most of the documentary research for this book was conducted in Corning's Department of Archives and Records Management, where several major collections constitute an essential foundation for understanding the company's history. The Houghton Family Papers are an essential source for understanding the connections between the company and its founding family. Many of the company's own historical materials have been organized serially in earlier efforts to write its story. A manuscript by George Buell Hollister, an executive in the 1920s (and a Houghton in-law) provides an excellent overview of the company's early development. In the 1950s, Corning commissioned Ralph L. Epstein, an economics professor at the State

University of New York at Buffalo to write the company's history. Epstein fell ill and was unable to complete the project, but notes and transcripts of his interviews remain, along with his extensive files of original sources. Otto Hilbert, another executive, later served as the company's unofficial historian, gathering primary and secondary sources into a score of notebooks and writing many informative short memos about particular topics. The archive also houses a nearly complete series of the company magazine, *Corning World*, and its predecessors *Gaffer* and *Cullet*. Among secondary sources, we found especially helpful the work of Warren Scoville and Pearce Davis on the glass industry; Thomas Dimitroff and Lois Janes on the history of Corning and Painted Post; Mary Jean Madigan on Steuben Glass; Joseph Morrone on the company's diversification and contraction; Jeff Hecht on fiber optics; and Regina Lee Blaszczyk on Corning's consumer products. Full references are available in the notes at the end of this book.

Many Corning employees and contractors assisted us in researching this volume. Gerry Orr and Cheryl Quinn provided outstanding administrative support, arranging research trips, scheduling interviews, and coordinating the day-to-day effort. In the Department of Archives and Records Management we are grateful for the assistance of Michelle Cotton and Tony Midey. Kristine Gable and Gerry Orr rose to the formidable challenge of examining thousands of photographs and images and identifying the best ones for display in all three books. Timothy Shaddock brought his considerable technical expertise to the series of video history interviews. Stu Sammis also participated in most of these interviews and contributed countless good questions and suggestions. Jane Shadel Spillman of the Corning Museum of Glass read the manuscript carefully and suggested important corrections and improvements.

Throughout the research and writing of this book we enjoyed and profited from close collaboration with Margaret B.W. Graham and Alec T. Shuldiner, authors of *Corning and the Craft of Innovation*. We hope that we gave as much as we got. In addition to Meg and Alec, current and former colleagues at Winthrop who supported our work include Sandra Densmore, Kathleen McDermott, Lygeia Ricciardi, George David Smith, and Suzanne Spellman. From their base in nearby Ithaca, independent researchers Rachel Maines and Garrel Pottinger helped identify important records at Corning and at Cornell University.

Herb Addison, our editor at Oxford University Press, read the manuscript in two iterations with patience and care and made numerous and significant suggestions for improvement. We are grateful also for the comments of two anonymous reviewers at the press. Helen Mules shepherded the manuscript through production with high professionalism and Chrisona Schmidt served ably as copy editor. We are also grateful to the rest of the Oxford team, Ellen Chodosh, Peter Ginna, Amy White, Liz Hartman, Brian Hughes, Chris Critelli, and Ben Lee, for their contributions to the publication of our book. Marianna Stewart prepared the index.

Finally, and most of all, we thank our families—Janice McCormick and Ricky and Bella Dyer; Candice Savin and Aliza Gross—for their patience and understanding during the stretches when we were away and the long days in front of the computer when we might as well have been absent. Writing books exacts a high personal toll and it is only the love and support of others that make it sustainable.

D.D.   D.G.
Cambridge, Massachusetts   New York, New York
June 2000

CHAPTER ONE

Corning and Glass

THIS BOOK EXPLORES the relationship between Corning and glass, the material from which it (as well as its forebears) has wrought its livelihood since 1851.

One hundred and fifty years is a long time. It is twice the span of the average American's life, and many times that of the average company's. The most august and well-known names in American commercial history —Ford, IBM, Motorola, to name a few—are less than one hundred years old. A very few, like Du Pont and Procter & Gamble, can trace their origins farther back. But longevity without purpose or significant accomplishment is not particularly meaningful. To be sure, Corning's long history has been filled with significance—for the small city that it has called home since 1868, for the generations of its employees, and for the family that founded, owned, and managed the company for virtually its entire history. But Corning's significance has been almost as great to people and companies whose connection to the company is less direct. Very few companies have made inventions that have affected humankind profoundly. Corning has been involved with at least three: electric lighting, television, and fiber-optic communications. Glass is the hidden but essential material that makes all three work.

Most people take glass for granted. It is everywhere, even in unexpected places. It is used in windows, containers, mirrors, lightbulbs, telescope mirrors and lenses, cameras, high-tech optical systems, eyeglasses, coffeepots, fiber-optic cable, TV picture tubes, flat-panel displays, and all manner of works of art. In modified forms it appears in lubricants, sealants, insulation, cookware, missile nosecones, and pollution control devices. All these glass products are integral to the lives of families and businesses the world over. Ancient yet preternaturally modern, glass is an industrial, consumer, and artistic material par excellence. Frequently overlooked (perhaps because it often is transparent), glass is an indispensable material of modern life.

For an old, familiar friend, glass is full of surprises. Formed by the happy marriage of sand, heat, and other additives, it has been called "a frozen liquid."[1] It can be blown, bent, pressed, twisted, and molded into an astonishing variety of forms: from twenty-ton blocks to strands of cable the width of a human hair, from a honeycombed ceramic cocoon to a fiber with the consistency of wool; from a fluid silicone (a material formed from silicon and organic compounds discovered by Corning) to ultrastrong glass that can resist thousands of pounds of pressure and corrosive substances; from delicate crystal to glazed windows that can withstand the heat of a spacecraft's reentry to the atmosphere; from extraordinarily durable dishes to TV picture tubes. Glass can be sufficiently porous to filter liquids and sufficiently airtight to form a diving bell. Transparent or opaque, strong or sensitive, rigid or flexible, glass can allow sunlight in or keep it out. It can change color when exposed to light and retain its strength under a wide range of temperatures and conditions.

The partnership between Corning and glass has yielded numerous innovations with profound technological and economic consequences. That is justification enough for a history of the company and its material. But this history is also part of the larger story of the evolution of American industry. Corning has participated in the major trends that have transformed American manufacturing: the harnessing of energy; the organization and interactions of managers and workers, scientists, and engineers; the race to develop new products and processes; the push to cultivate markets around the world; and the application of new information technologies to streamline operations and erode boundaries between companies and their customers and suppliers. The history of Corning is also the history of its changing times and contexts, as it grew from a regional to a national to an international business, and as it moved from an agrarian to an industrial to a knowledge-based economy.

In this book, we trace Corning's long story chronologically, from its roots in the 1850s to the present. Certain themes echo throughout the decades and provide a framework for understanding the company's history and its distinctive character. These themes include (1) the interconnections among the founding family, the company, and the city it calls home; (2) a generational pattern of organizational change and development; (3) glass as a specialization; (4) glass as science and art; (5) life on the brink; (6) the nearly constant search for the next big hit; (7) leveraging capabilities with partners; (8) people and values; and (9) occupying a wider stage.

A Family, a Company, and a City

For most of its 150 years, Corning has been a family-owned and operated company based in Corning, New York, the small city in upstate New York from which the company draws its name. Five generations of Houghtons served as chief executives between 1851 and 1996, although the line was broken several times for brief interludes. Generally, the male descendants of the founder, Amory Houghton Sr. (1813–1882), went into the family business after graduating from college. In an unstated policy of primogeniture, the eldest son in the direct line was groomed for the top, although in each generation leaders worked in teams with their relatives and trusted colleagues. (There are no direct descendants of the most recent Houghton chairmen, Amory Houghton Jr. and James R. Houghton, presently working in the company. Their nephew, Carter Houghton, joined in 1999 and represents the sixth generation of his family in the business.)

A hardware merchant, Amory Houghton Sr., first invested in glassmaking in 1851 in Somerville, Massachusetts, because he recognized its value as a building material. He bought another glass company in Brooklyn in 1864 and then moved it to Corning four years later. His sons, Amory Jr. (1837–1909) and Charles (1846–1897), turned the firm into an ongoing concern. In the long years of their partnership, they began Corning's tradition of scientific inquiry and development of specialty glass products. Amory Jr.'s two sons, Alanson (1863–1941) and Arthur (1866–1928) institutionalized research by founding the company's laboratory and brought automation to its lightbulb envelope and glass tubing businesses. The fourth generation of Houghton leadership consisted of Alanson's son Amory Houghton (1899–1981) and his cousin Arthur Houghton Jr. (1906–1990), who guided the company through the Depression and World War II, and into the postwar era, with Arthur playing a particularly significant role at Steuben Glass. Amory Houghton's sons, Amory Jr. (1926–) and James R. Houghton (1936–), together led the company from the 1960s until the mid-1990s, overseeing the company's diversification and refocusing, as well as the development of major new businesses in ceramic substrates, fiber optics, and photonic components, which split, combine, and amplify optical signals.

Corning first sold its common stock to the public in 1945, with the Houghton family interest gradually dwindling to less than 5 percent of the ownership. Roger Ackerman, chairman and CEO since 1996, has no connection with the Houghtons beyond friendship. Although the founding family no longer has a direct say in the company's operations, its indirect influence will linger for many years.

The family connections and values account for much of Corning's character and culture. Its physical location adds another important dimension. The company is by far the biggest employer in Corning, New York, a city of approximately 10,000 inhabitants, situated on the Chemung River in the "Southern Tier" of New York state, about 275 miles northwest of New York City. The city has the feel of a small town: people are friendly and informal. Typically they know their neighbors well, address shopkeepers (and are addressed by them) by name, and greet leading officials of the company and the city by their first names.

Although the company built operations outside of the Chemung Valley in the 1910s and later set up joint ventures and new plants all over the United States and, ultimately, the world, it remains firmly rooted in Corning.

Despite all the changes and expansions and periodic natural disasters, the company never gave sustained consideration to moving its headquarters elsewhere. Rather, it has continued to invest locally, building up a community of scientists, business managers, and production workers who interact frequently and informally to the benefit of the whole enterprise. To nourish these interactions, the company has invested not only in constructing its necessary facilities but also in local institutions and services. The city bears many signs of the company's presence, both directly in the factories, offices, and parking lots, and indirectly in the services, amenities, and cultural institutions and activities rarely if ever matched elsewhere in communities of comparable size.

A Generational Pattern of Organizational Change and Development

During most of Corning's history, Houghton family members led the company in collaboration with colleagues from more or less the same age bracket and for typically long tenures. The first Amory Houghton Jr. worked closely with his brother Charles Houghton and Henry Sinclaire; Alanson B. Houghton shared power and responsibility with his cousin Arthur Houghton Sr., Alexander Falck, and Eugene Sullivan. Their successors have continued this pattern through the present administration of Roger Ackerman and his colleagues John Loose and Norm Garrity. The result was consistent direction and stable management teams.

The theme of generations connotes organic growth and periodic rejuvenation, a pattern that applies particularly well to Corning (and perhaps other family companies). Corning grew steadily by developing its original business and branching out; at the same time, generational shifts in leadership coincided with important business transitions. The transitions seldom involved immediate significant shifts in strategy because the new leaders participated in high-level planning and decision making years before they took over. Rather, the transitions often betokened a burst of fresh energy, a willingness to entertain new ideas, and consider major changes in operations. The first Amory Houghton Jr. and his brother Charles invested in understanding the chemistry of glass in ways that their father had failed to appreciate. Amory Jr.'s sons, Alanson and Arthur (Sr.), invested in automation, process technology, and foreign markets at levels the previous generation deemed unnecessary. Under the second Amory Houghton Sr., Corning opened up wholly new areas (architectural glass, fiberglass, and silicones) through joint ventures and eventually placed a winning bet on TV glass. The second Amory Houghton Jr. led the company's diversification, aggressive expansion overseas, and investments in new areas such as environmental products, fiber optics, and biotechnology. His brother James presided over deep and thoroughgoing changes in management and operations, especially through his indefatigable championing of Total Quality Management. And the generation headed by Roger Ackerman is reshaping the company through massive commitments to fiber optics, photonics, and other telecommunications products.

Not all of these transitions, of course, signaled a new generation's willingness to depart entirely from the ways of their predecessors. Each generation of Corning's leadership not only embodied a new era in the family and the company but also reflected broader social and economic trends in the world around them. The second generation (Amory Houghton Jr. and Charles Houghton) brought science to glassmaking at a time roughly coinciding with similar developments in the electrical and chemical industries, and their story partly illustrates that larger movement. Similarly, the fifth generation (the modern Amory Houghton Jr., Jamie Houghton, and their close associates Bill Armistead and Tom MacAvoy) in some respects typify the generation that came of age after World War II during the optimistic, expansionist era of the twenty-five-year "American century" and then was obliged, in its maturity, to confront a different world of energy shortages, wide oscillations of economic fortunes, promising but problematic new technologies, and intensifying global competition.

Specializing in Glass

Corning took off in the post–Civil War years and persevered through rapid industrialization, the reforms of the Progressive Era, the challenges of the

Great Depression, the maelstrom of World War II, the postwar boom, the go-go expansionism of the 1960s, the crises (manmade and natural) of the 1970s, and the grueling cycle of expansion, reinvention, and restructuring of the 1980s and 1990s. Each era presented daunting challenges to Corning and its employees. In each generation, the company's scientists, managers, and workers responded by finding new and innovative uses for their endlessly malleable material—glass, glass ceramics, and ceramics.

In the late nineteenth century, as rival glass companies plunged into what were essentially commodity businesses—bottles, jars, drinking glasses, windows—Corning chose instead to focus on specialty products made by craftsmen and requiring more than ordinary skill. The first such application was railroad signal glass, in which colors had to be uniform, highly visible, and impervious to weather. Another was blown glass bulbs for Thomas Edison's system of electrical lighting; these required unusual resistance to heat and breakage, as well as precise standardization of form and suitability for mass production.

Throughout its 150 years, Corning's best businesses, from railroad signal glass to lightbulb glass to Pyrex and Corning Ware to TV picture tube bulbs to ceramic substrates to optical fibers and photonic devices, have resulted from its ability to tailor glass for particular applications.[2] The company developed a remarkable capability to engineer the properties of glass— strength, temperature resistance, weatherability, resistance to breakage (or controlled pattern of breakage), color, transparency, purity, electrical characteristics, and optical characteristics. By arranging and combining these properties in certain specific ways, Corning multiplied the uses of glass in industrial and consumer products.

Glass as Science, Glass as Art

Corning's success as a manufacturer of specialty products depended on its profound understanding of glass as a material. Starting with the first Amory Houghton Jr. in the 1850s, Corning's executives have taken a particular interest in research and development. As early as the 1870s, Corning was working with outside scientists to help develop new products and processes.

In 1908, it became one of the first American companies to set up its own research and development laboratories. In this facility, generations of scientists and engineers were given the freedom to wander down paths where their inquiries and talents took them, although they were also encouraged to stay in touch with developments in manufacturing and production. Many of the inquiries proved to be dead ends. But through the years, Corning researchers made hundreds of scientific breakthroughs and frequently developed their findings into commercial applications.

While many of the discoveries were the result of patient, systematic inquiry, others were the result of serendipity, luck, happy coincidences, and interactions among different sets of talents residing in the laboratory, the factory, the executive suites, the community, and an extensive network of professional contacts and associations. The company, time and again, displayed an ability to take advantage of opportunities that presented themselves. Discoveries in one generation frequently led to breakthroughs in another. The development of better railroad signal lights set into a motion the chain of events that led to Pyrex; a laboratory accident resulted in the discovery of a material that the company used to produce both missile nosecones and Corning Ware.

Aside from making progress in materials, Corning developed breakthroughs in processes. In the 1920s, it introduced the Ribbon Machine, which could blow lightbulb envelopes with machine-gun rapidity. Seventy-five years later, it still stands as the state of the art. Other innovations have included improved machinery for melting glass and making glass tubing; spinning glass into coffee pots and TV picture tube funnels; pressing glass into dishes, pans, and panels; forming perfectly smooth sheets of glass; extruding ceramic materials to form substrates; gathering deposits of fused silica, the purest form of glass; and drawing glass blanks into miles of optical fiber. The stunning panoply of products and processes that Corning has produced over the years is as much a testimony to the ingenuity of researchers, engineers, marketers, and workers as it is to the enormous flexibility and potential of glass.

While bringing the full power of science to bear on the composition and manipulation of glass, Corning has always had an appreciation for the ancient tradition of using glass as a medium of artistic expression. The company's original product—lead glass blanks—was used by artists and artisans to make vases, bowls, and other objects. Steuben, the prestigious art glass company, has been a unit of Corning since World War I. Although it has never accounted for more than a small fraction of the company's business, Steuben manifests a disproportionate impact on the company's image and reputation. Its standards, class, and abiding faith in the artistic possibilities of glass convey an important symbolism. The Malcolm Baldrige National Quality Award (which Corning itself won in 1995) is made of Steuben glass. In the same vein, the Corning Museum of Glass, established by the company in 1951 and expanded several times since then, constitutes one of the greatest collections of art glass, glass jewelry, and other glass objects in the world. The museum also houses a world-class library on glass and glass objects. Near Corning's headquarters complex, it is a living symbol of the coexistence of art and science, of craft and industry, and the company's profound belief in the inexhaustible wonders and mysteries of glass.

Living on the Brink

In successive generations Corning has faced potentially devastating setbacks and challenges, from forces both natural and manmade. A quote attributed to Amory Houghton Jr., who ran the company from 1875 to 1908, has been repeated like a mantra by his descendants: "Every day of my business life I feel I'm walking along the edge of a precipice. At every step I must be careful that I don't fall in." Indeed, a sense of the tenuousness of the company's existence has been a recurring theme. In the early 1870s, just a few years after moving to Corning, the company went bankrupt, a painful circumstance that left an indelible mark on the Houghtons. And in a dozen instances (most recently in 1972), the company suffered from devastating floods of the Chemung River.

Corning also saw manmade threats recur in different generations. For example, many of its breakthrough products—railroad signals, Pyrex, black-and-white television, Corning Ware, and optical fibers—attracted fiercely competitive rivals. Corning frequently faced the possibility that its biggest customers would decide to eliminate it as a supplier and make their own glass. In the early 1900s, Corning competed with and also supplied General Electric, the world's biggest manufacturer of lightbulbs. When television was being developed in the 1950s and 1960s, Corning fended off competition from RCA, the leading television manufacturer, which periodically threatened to make its own glass bulbs. (Later, RCA made good on the threat and triggered an involuntary retrenchment at Corning.) In the 1970s, Corning tackled the auto industry on its own turf by devising ceramic substrates for pollution control devices. And in the 1970s and 1980s, it challenged huge, wealthy, and politically connected telecommunications companies the world over in the race to develop optical fibers from glass. In every generation, then, there was a palpable tension between working with customers and competitors on the one hand and engaging in often sustained efforts to tackle them head-on in new arenas on the other. Balancing this tension was crucial for the company's long-term survival on the brink.

Throughout its life, Corning maintained the balance by remaining an essentially conservative company in areas of governance and finance. Although it has been a publicly held company since 1945, Corning maintained an investment horizon that extended well beyond the next quarter's, or even the next year's, performance. It avoided excessive levels of debt, and the Houghton family retained effective voting control of the company's shares for many years after the initial public offering. This independence allowed it to undertake risky, long-term endeavors and to take substantial risks with research and technology. It plowed significant resources into the development of the Ribbon Machine and its predecessors, and it spent heavily on efforts that were commercially marginal but psychologically crucial, like the mirror blank for the Mount Palomar telescope. Employing "patient money," Corning funded the development of optical fibers between 1966 and 1983, before it broke even at the operating margin line. It took many more years to recoup all the cash invested in the business before earning a return. Corning's ability to be fiscally conservative and simultaneously to take prudent risks has been the key to its remaining independent and profitable for 150 years.

The Search for the Next Big Hit

Corning's solid foundation would have proved insufficient if the company had not been able to continually find new breakthroughs. For most of its life, Corning executives and scientists have been engaged in a search for the next big breakthrough—the discovery of a proprietary formula, product, or process that would sustain the growth of the company through another generation. Once again a sequence is clear, starting with railroad signal glass and proceeding through products for lighting, housewares, television sets, transportation, and telecommunications. Each of these big hits was the result of proprietary research and patient investment, and each emerged from collaboration between scientists and engineers, manufacturing and marketing personnel, managers and production workers.

In most instances, the search for new breakthroughs originated in technology and capabilities the company already possessed or was in the process of mastering. On occasion, however, the search led Corning into areas only tangentially related to glass: nuclear power, semiconductors, home appliances, industrial biotechnology, and medical equipment and services. Some of these forays succeeded, at least for a time, while others failed miserably. But the search always continued and continues to this day, with the recent doubling in size of Corning's science and technology organization and a major corporate bet on photonics—using photons (pulses of light) rather than electrons to transmit information.

Leveraging Capabilities with Partners

To bring the next big hit to market and ensure its survival, Corning sometimes sought to leverage its capabilities through associations and partnerships with other institutions. Although it was rooted and based in a small city in upstate New York, the company in each generation made efforts to expand its markets and reach across the United States and throughout the world. In the early generations, it did so by establishing patents on its products and processes and by licensing competitors in areas such as lightbulb envelopes.

In the early decades of the twentieth century, Alanson Houghton and Arthur Houghton Sr., leaders of the third generation, discovered the advantages of association in cooperative ventures to control production of glass-making machinery and refractories. Although antitrust problems eventually forced the Houghtons to retreat in some areas, they remained wedded to the concept of collaboration as a means of leveraging the company's resources and capabilities. They took minority equity positions in their European licensees, for example, to establish beachheads in foreign markets. The head of the next generation, the second Amory Houghton Sr., pushed the concept farther. In areas where it was unsure of itself or lacked the capabilities or resources to proceed alone, Corning sought a compatible partner for a long-term marriage. The first of its longstanding fifty-fifty joint ventures, Pittsburgh-Corning, was formed in 1936 to make and market architectural glass—an area in which Corning believed that Pittsburgh Plate Glass had complementary experience and expertise. And that was followed by ventures such as Dow-Corning (silicones), Owens-Corning (fiberglass), Ciba-Corning (medical diagnostic equipment), and Genencor (industrial biotechnology), among others. Corning's leaders didn't let corporate ego get in the way of an opportunity: the company's name almost always came last. Yet as its successful ventures became powers in their own right, Corning maintained its ownership interest and profited immensely. (And also bore attendant risks and liabilities. Dow-Corning's forced bankruptcy because of litigation over silicone breast implants in the mid-1990s hit Corning's balance sheet and income statement hard. Corning executives believe, however, that as Dow-Corning reemerges from bankruptcy its value will again become evident. See chapter 14.)

Beginning in the 1960s, Corning used joint ventures to open new markets overseas as part of a conscious effort to become a multinational corporation. It cooperated with Asahi Glass, one of its major competitors in Japan, to make sealed beam headlights for Japanese automobiles and an array of consumer products for the Japanese public. Later, it linked up with other Asian partners, and Samsung-Corning (its Korea-based joint venture to produce TV glass) has proved a remarkable and enduring success. Corning also formed alliances with local partners in Europe, including once forbidden countries like Romania, Poland, and Hungary. The process continued through 1980s and 1990s, and today Corning is a truly global company with major equity investments in every region of the world, including Russia and China.

People and Values

From its earliest generation, Corning has understood that its people constituted its great competitive advantage. This understanding reflected not only the gentlemanly beliefs of the founding family but also an unmistakable business reality. In the nineteenth century, glassmaking was a highly skilled occupation, and the company gained much of its competitive advantage by treating its employees well—lower turnover, greater consistency, and the wisdom and know-how of experienced and loyal people. Over time, the company's informal personnel policies evolved into a more systematic and progressive approach to workforce management. By the 1920s Corning offered attractive (for the industry) compensation and frequently sought ways to improve working conditions and reward loyalty. It sponsored clubs, athletic leagues, and other activities, including an annual service dinner at every location to honor long-time employees. Although Corning resisted unionization until World War II, it did not employ illegal tactics or draw the ire of government officials. Since recognizing the American Flint Glass Workers Union ("the Flints") in 1943, Corning has worked closely with the union in most of its businesses and has experienced few grievances and work stoppages. The company has enlisted employees, and has listened to them, in many initiatives ranging from product and process improvement to total quality management to managing the growing diversity of the workforce.

Corning's personnel and industrial relations policies are consistent with its overarching goal of achieving superior performance on a consistent basis over time, as well as its overriding values. Management has sought to make Corning an attractive place to work and to secure an enduring commitment from highly qualified people. The company emphasizes fair treatment, integrity, innovation, pride in accomplishment, and room to grow. At the same time, Corning has invested heavily to improve working conditions in its factories and offices and in providing a stimulating cultural environment outside of work.

On the Wider Stage

With each successive generation, Corning came to play a larger role in American economic, industrial, social, and political life. As the family business grew into a Fortune 500 company, the actions of its executives and workers naturally took on a larger significance. But over the years, many of Corning's executives, particularly the members of the Houghton family, figured prominently in the realms of business, science, politics, diplomacy, philanthropy, education, and the arts.

Alanson Houghton spent nearly as much time in the diplomatic service as he did as Corning's chief executive. A two-term congressman, he was the first Ambassador to post–World War I Germany and was Ambassador to England in the 1920s. His son Amory was a high-ranking economic official during World War II, a confidant of President Eisenhower, and served as Ambassador to France in the late 1950s. *His* son Amory Jr., has represented the Corning district in Congress since 1986—the seat once held by his grandfather. Arthur Houghton Jr., the longtime leader of Steuben who served as a curator of rare books at the Library of Congress, was a driving force behind the creation of Lincoln Center and a prominent backer of educational institutions, from Harvard University to Corning Community College. James Houghton, who retired as chief executive in 1996, serves as a member of the executive board governing Harvard University and as chairman of the Metropolitan Museum of Art—a post his cousin Arthur once held. The Houghtons over time also served on prestigious corporate boards such as those at Citicorp, IBM, Met Life, Exxon, J.P. Morgan, and Procter & Gamble.

Many top executives of Corning have occupied leadership positions in industry associations, government advisory boards, philanthropic and educational institutions, and economic development agencies. In different eras, the modern Amory Houghton Sr. and Tom MacAvoy, president of the company between 1971 and 1983, served as national head of the Boy Scouts of America. Scientists such as Arthur Day, Eugene Sullivan, J. Franklin Hyde, Donald

Stookey, and the team that developed optical waveguides—Robert Maurer, Donald Keck, and Peter Schultz—played leading roles in national scientific, technical, and industrial associations and received numerous prestigious awards and honors. In 1994, the company itself received the National Medal of Technology for its contributions to American life. In some areas of specific concern to the business community—total quality management and managing a diverse workforce, for example—Corning employees have served as spokespersons and leaders on a national level.

These activities and endeavors were not merely pursuits of company personnel in their spare time. Rather, they were an explicit dimension of their leadership of the company. For Corning has long been possessed of a wide-ranging public-minded spirit. It has projected a sense of its responsibilities as a company, not just to shareholders, workers, and customers, but also to the many communities in which it had a presence, and to those in which it did not. In wartime, Corning's resources were fully devoted to working with the government and military. In peacetime, it was involved with projects ranging from the Mount Palomar telescope to the space shuttle. On the social level, the company has long been involved with improving conditions in Corning, New York, and in the other locations where it maintains operations.

The disproportionately high profile of the company and its personnel in business, scientific, public, and civic affairs has attracted individuals of outstanding national reputation to its managerial and technical ranks and its board of directors.

The chapters that follow proceed chronologically, tracing 150 years in the life of glass. It starts from the Houghton family's initial investments in glassmaking in the bustling streets of Somerville, Massachusetts. Throughout these different eras, or generations, the march forward in time provides the animating spirit of the story. But the themes discussed above will resonate, time and again, in the following pages. Some themes became evident in the company's earliest days, when the first Amory Houghton encountered a glass industry in flux, and his company teetered on the edge of failure.

I

FIRST GENERATION

CHAPTER TWO

Founding and Foundering, 1851–1875

IN THE SPRING OF 1868, residents of a small town in upstate New York witnessed a momentous event in the life of their community. In early June, canal boats that had started their journey days before on the thriving wharves of Brooklyn, floated gently to a dock on the south bank of the Chemung River, in Corning. In a narrow valley, workers unloaded equipment never before seen in this area: glassmaking molds, clay pots, parts of furnaces, and blowing rods. Along with a vast number of locally made bricks, these components would prove the basis of the Corning Flint Glass Works, which would begin operation a few months later on this riverside site.[1]

The arrival of a well-established industry such as glassmaking was an occasion for great celebration in this twenty-year-old town, where agriculture was the predominant source of commerce. A few weeks before, the *Corning Journal* noted, the factory's owners "were led to entertain a proposition to remove their entire machinery, moulds, and business to Corning, in order to save largely on coal and the expenses of the living of the workmen." The glassmaking equipment wasn't the only new arrival. Accompanying a few dozen glassworkers who made the arduous trip from downstate were the factory's owner, Amory Houghton Sr., and members of his family.

The small-town paper had greeted the news of the company's impending arrival with boosterish, Victorian exuberance. "The establishment of the Glass Works here is an important event in the history of Corning," trumpeted the *Journal*. "It will be an era from which its future prosperity may be dated, as aside from the signal advantages to be reaped from employing such a large number of operatives, it will inspire confidence generally, and unquestionably lead to the introduction of other mechanical or manufacturing interests, and thus give accumulative power to industrial pursuits in this village." Couched in language that appears ponderous and antique to the twenty-first-century ear, this statement nonetheless proved prescient beyond the editors' wildest imaginations.[2]

While it would prove monumental in time, the Houghtons' decision to relocate their glass company to Corning in 1868 was one of a series of events and actions—some related, many unrelated—that combined to turn the town into a center of glass manufacturing: "Crystal City," as it would come to be called at the turn of the twentieth century. And their decision, in turn, was the result of more than a century of interrelated developments in three different spheres. First, descendants of an old English family, the Houghtons had been laboring in the New World for more than 200 years but were brought to this region by a series of financial and strategic considerations. Second, craftsmen had been making glass since antiquity, yet glassmaking boomed in the middle decades of the nineteenth century and rode the wave of post–Civil War industrial growth in the northern United States. Third, the Corning area, inhabited by Indians for several centuries, had been settled by Americans in the late eighteenth century but grew by leaps and bounds with the development of mid-nineteenth-century transportation networks and the efforts of enterprising boosters.

On that spring day, the United States was less than 100 years old, and industrialization was still in its relative infancy. The move came several years before the invention of the telephone and the electric lamp, and decades before the automobile—industries in which the glass-based products of the Houghtons' little company would come to play an important role.

The Founders and the Business

The United States, then as now, was a nation of immigrants. And the Houghtons, then as now, were old-timers by comparison. Their presence in the colonies dates from 1635, when John Houghton and his brother, Ralph, came to New England aboard the ship *Abigail* and helped settle the town of Lancaster, northwest of Boston. As was the case with many towns in New England, Lancaster was named after the town or region in England from which its settlers hailed. The Houghtons were descendants of an ancient Anglo-Saxon family that had lived in and around the village of Hoghton, in Lancashire, since the time of the Norman Conquest, but without notable distinction. "The earliest Houghtons probably lived in thatched huts and painted themselves with blue mud," mused family historian Arthur A. Houghton Jr. To this day, there stands in Hoghton a minor sixteenth-century castle, Hoghton Tower (the *u* was apparently added on this side of the Atlantic). According to Arthur, "The lands have never left the possession of the Hoghton Family."[3]

For several generations after their arrival, the Houghtons were an unremarkable clan. As Arthur put it: "For over 200 years the Houghtons accomplished but little, spending their lives in New England as farmers or as merchants in small towns." Amory Houghton, born in 1813, the tenth of Rufus and Abigail's thirteen children, gave every indication of being another in the long line of such merchants and farmers. He spent his early childhood on his parents' farm in Bolton, Massachusetts, and at the age of twelve went off to school in Lancaster. After serving as an apprentice to a carpenter, he went into business for himself, founding companies specializing in building contracting and dry-goods trading. An inveterate entrepreneur, Amory had something of a checkered history. He was described in documents between 1846 and 1854 variously as a trader, coal dealer, and wood and coal dealer, and he was also active in real estate along with his brother, Francis Houghton, and a local businessman named John P. Gregory. "He made and lost many fortunes. At one time he was worth $400,000, a tidy sum for those days," Arthur A. Houghton Jr. wrote. In the early 1830s, he married Sophronia M. Oakes and they began to have children. Amory

Houghton Jr., born in Boston in 1837, was the first of eight. Charles F. Houghton, the fourth, was born in 1845.[4]

In the 1850s, Amory Houghton Sr. began to take an interest in yet another business: glass. Little did he know that it would involve the next five generations of his descendants. In 1851, Amory bought an interest in Cate & Phillips, a small glass firm in Somerville, Massachusetts, a town adjacent to Cambridge; Cate & Phillips changed its name to Bay State Glass the same year. Three years later, Amory, who befriended a British glassmaker called "Gaffer" Teasdale, helped organize a new firm, the Union Glass Company, which was incorporated on January 21, 1854, and based in Somerville. Amory Houghton owned two-thirds of the company and served as treasurer. Francis was president and owned a one-sixth share, while John Gregory owned the remaining share.[5]

In the nineteenth century, the craft and art of glassmaking were already ancient. From its origins, glass was a material that was blown and molded into sturdily utilitarian and purely ornamental forms. At Roman, Greek, and Mesopotamian sites, archaeologists have unearthed quotidian glass storage and drinking vessels and exquisite pieces of glass jewelry. Glassmaking was also a trade that had been practiced in the American colonies from the very origins of settlement. In 1608, the London Company sent a group of eight Dutch and Polish glassworkers to the fledgling settlement at Jamestown. In 1621, the company sent a second group—six Italian glassworkers—to make glass beads for trade with the Indians. Throughout the seventeenth century, glassworks popped up sporadically in the colonies—Philadelphia, New Amsterdam, and in Massachusetts—but few of these concerns lasted for more than a few years. Old World methods of glassmaking persisted in the New World. Raw ingredients—sand, mostly, with smaller portions of soda ash, manganese, lead, and iron—were heated in a crucible made of clay or other heat-resistant material. The molten material was then gathered at the end of a hollow rod. By blowing through it and manipulating the metal—as the molten glass was known—the gaffer would give shape to the mass. As it cooled, the material could be rolled out and flattened to form window glass. To produce more contoured products, glassmakers would blow the gob of molten glass into a hinged mold that gave the inchoate mass a complex shape, such as that of a bottle. Once the glass cooled into shape—be it a bottle or drinking vessel—craftsmen would use mills to "cut" the glass and create intricate designs.[6]

The first truly successful commercial glassworks on the Atlantic's western shores was founded by German immigrant Caspar Wistar in Salem Country, New Jersey, in 1739. The Wistarburgh Glass Works made window glass, bottles, and green tableware until 1777, when production ground to a halt—probably due to the incipient revolution. Several Wistar workers set up their own glass works in a nearby town in 1774, which came to be called Glassboro. Throughout the eighteenth century, other immigrants from Germany—long a center of glassmaking—brought their skills across the Atlantic, setting up shop in New Jersey and Maryland.[7]

By 1800, glass historian Warren Scoville estimated, there were no more than ten glass houses in the United States. The consumers of the young nation, whose economy was largely based on agriculture and natural resources, generally relied on glass products imported from Europe. But that began to change in the early nineteenth century. As the United States began to assert itself, and as it continued to wage a grueling set of trade and military wars with Britain, a domestic industry finally began to take root. In 1807, the firm Bakewell & Company was founded in Pittsburgh. The company, which distinguished itself in cut glass, heralded the origins of the industry in western Pennsylvania. By 1820, there were only thirty-three glass houses in the United States. But between 1820 and 1840, spurred in part by the enactment of a protective tariff in 1824, nearly seventy glass factories were started; twenty-five were designed primarily to fashion glassware for table or domestic use. Most of those were small enterprises, employing twenty-five to forty workers and producing $12,000 to $30,000 of glassware annually.[8]

Glass factories were growing larger, especially those on the eastern seaboard. Whereas the New Jersey and Pittsburgh glass houses were founded largely by German and other immigrants, those that sprouted up in Boston and New York were staffed primarily by skilled Irish and British immigrants. In 1792, the Boston Crown Glass Company built a factory on Essex Street in Boston. But it was the area across the Charles River—Cambridge—that would emerge as a glass center in the early decades of the nineteenth century. In 1814, Boston Porcelain and Glass Co., was founded,

with capital of $200,000, at Lechmere Point in Cambridge, near the termi-
nus of the newly completed Canal Bridge. When the company failed in
November 1817, the works were taken over by the New England Glass Company—a firm whose historic importance would rise as much from its
lengthy run as for the innovations and commercial offshoots it spawned. [9]

New England Glass's two flint furnaces and twenty-four steam-operated
glass-cutting mills turned out a wide variety of products: lamps, chemical
ware, globes, decanters, and dishes. Its massive chimneys, 325 feet high,
dwarfed the nearby Bunker Hill monument. By the late 1820s the firm had
agencies in New York, Philadelphia, and Baltimore. Aside from producing
glass through conventional means (i.e., by blowing and molding it) employees at New England Glass helped engineer a third, enduring method: pressing. Pressing refers to a process in which molten glass was poured into a
mold and then pushed up against its walls by a plunger, or press. Presses
were used in producing tableware such as dishes and bowls. In November
1826, two New England Glass employees, Henry Whitney and Enoch
Robinson, obtained a patent for an improvement in pressing glass knobs
that used a "bench press." In the next few years, New England Glass also
developed a machine press.

In the following decades, Cambridge and Somerville (which split off to
form its own town in the 1840s) became a center of light manufacturing.
The boom picked up pace in the 1840s after the completion of the Fitchburg
Railroad, which ran west from Boston through the two towns. In the 1850s,
New England Glass, with 500 employees, a yearly payroll of nearly $200,000,
and annual output of $500,000, was one of the largest enterprises in town.
But it had company. In the 1850s, two new glass companies appeared in East
Cambridge and Somerville. Combined with the older New England Glass
Company, they would employ at least 631 people by 1855.[10]

Amory Houghton Sr. had a hand in both of those new concerns. He was
a director at Bay State Glass, whose factory stood at Bridge and North
Fourth Street, and he was the proprietor of the Union Glass Works. Established in 1854 with a capital of $60,000, Union Glass Works was much
smaller than New England Glass, although its product mix was largely similar. Its works were adjacent to the Fitchburg Railroad, fronting fifty feet
along Webster Avenue at the intersection with Prospect Street. Primarily a

wholesaler, the company employed 100 people and produced about $120,000 of ware in 1855. "The first two years of operation were so successful that the capital was raised from $60,000 to $200,000," historian Lura Woodside Watkins wrote. But business soured after the panic of 1857, and the works began to encounter financial difficulty.[11]

As Amory Houghton Sr. began to focus more on glass, so did his oldest son, Amory Jr. But the younger man's temperament differed from that of his entrepreneurial father. "He never uttered a word as a child and his family believed that he was a mute. At the age of six, at the breakfast table, he opened his mouth and said, "The Mexican Situation is fraught with interest, is it not?" his grandson, Arthur A. Houghton Jr., wrote. "Grandfather never could abide idle chit-chat."[12]

Amory Jr. was educated at a private school in Ellington, Connecticut, and graduated from the high school in Cambridge in 1854. The family lived in a house at 47 Prospect Street in Cambridge. He worked for three years at Lawson Valentine, a dealer in paint oils and varnishes, where he likely learned the rudiments of chemistry. Amory Jr. joined Union Glass in 1857 and in 1860, at the age of twenty-three, he married Ellen Bigelow, whose family ran a successful jewelry store in Boston. The Bigelows were less than pleased by the union, as they looked down on the less-well-off Houghtons.

In the mid-nineteenth century, the notion of corporate research and development was nonexistent. Research was still largely a cottage industry, conducted by enterprising individuals and largely detached from the world of manufacturing. But Amory Jr. took a step to unite the two disparate fields. At the Union Glass Works, he set up a small laboratory to experiment on the fundamentals of glassmaking. Starting on October 26, 1859, he would periodically make notes in a battered notebook. These notations continued through 1897. The jottings bear witness to Amory Jr.'s meticulous approach to business. Just as important, they compose a document that stands as an evolving testament to the growing sophistication of his (and his company's) understanding of the properties of different kinds of glasses and to the interplay between the science of chemistry and the art of glassmaking. The book would ultimately contain over 500 different compositions. (Not all were related to glass, however; one detailed the specifications for cooking up Boston brown bread.)[13]

Sitting as it did astride the Fitchburg Railroad, the Union Glass Works symbolized the way industry grew up around the nation's burgeoning infrastructure network. In 1860, just as the Civil War was about to rend the fabric of the nation, the United States were becoming more closely tied together—economically, politically, and culturally—than they had ever been before. A transportation grid composed of layers of interlocking toll roads, canals, natural waterways, and railways, which connected the densely populated eastern seaboard to the expanding and vast interior, was helping to create an integrated continental economy—one in which it wouldn't be uncommon for a Boston merchant to conduct business and maintain an office in New York City. Indeed, in November 1860, the Union Glass Company announced that it had leased "the large and eligible Warehouse at 73 Hudson St., N.Y." The proprietors promised that the five-story wholesale outlet in lower Manhattan "will be kept well stocked with an extensive assortment of their manufactures, also of such trimming as the lamp trade require." The works commended themselves to the "Crockery Trade, Lamp and lantern trade, stainers and dealers in druggists' and chemical glassware, gas shades, castor bottles, and fancy glassware." A man who had been working in Somerville with the improbable but portentous name of G. E. Light moved to New York to head up the store.[14]

An Industry, a Business, and a Family Grow Together

With the establishment of the New York outlet, the Houghtons of Massachusetts began to devote more of their attention to the booming financial and commercial center on the Hudson. Amory Houghton Sr. first appeared in the 1862 New York directory as an agent of the Union Glass Company. New York (or more particularly, Brooklyn, which was until 1898 an independent and thriving city) was also a center of glassmaking. "Brooklyn and its environs became the seat of an extensive glass-cutting business, whose output consisted mainly of decanters and glasses, lamps, lamp globes, prisms for lamps, chandeliers and girandoles, and other lighting appurtenances," wrote one glass historian.[15]

The first known glass works in Brooklyn opened in 1754. But it was a veteran of the New England Glass Company who came to be associated with the growth of the city's glass industry. John Gilliland, an Irish immigrant, left Cambridge in 1820 with Richard Fisher to set up a factory on the West Side of Manhattan—near what is now 47th Street and 11th Avenue. In 1823, Gilliland paid $7,000 for a plot of land in downtown Brooklyn, bounded by Atlantic Avenue and State Street, Hicks St. and the East River. On May 1, 1823, he laid the cornerstone for the Brooklyn Flint Glass Works amid a public celebration that included the firing of artillery. (Flint glass refers to the variety of glass that uses lead oxide to strengthen the molten material.) From his base at 50 State Street and a warehouse at 30 South William Street in Manhattan, Gilliland ran the business for about thirty years, making blanks for local glass cutters and globes for gas lanterns. By 1850, he employed 100 workers, whose skill and quality products were recognized across the Atlantic. At the London Crystal Palace World's Fair in 1851, Gilliland received the only prize given to an American glassmaker for the best flint glass metal (metal being a commonly used term for molten glass). The *London Art Journal* called the product "absolutely free of all colour, of remarkable purity, and standing pre-eminent for brilliancy." But Gilliland faced a series of financial difficulties in the early 1850s, and the Brooklyn Flint Glass Works failed before going through a series of short-term proprietorships.[16]

Gilliland wasn't alone in Brooklyn. Christian Dorflinger, born in Alsace in 1828, came to the United States in the mid-1840s and set up shop on Concord Street in 1852 to make flint glass blanks. He prospered as Gilliland floundered, and in 1860 he created a third factory, the GreenPoint Glass Works. By 1865, he employed eighty-five workers and sold $300,000 of ware. Anxious to retire to the country, Dorflinger leased the factory to an outside firm, Hoare & Dailey, between 1858 and 1865. A few years later, Hoare & Dailey would move their works upstate and play an important role in the development of Corning's glass industry.[17]

New York began to exert a pull on the Houghtons. "As a matter of business too you ought to take a look at N.Y.—see the N.Y. Branch Warehouse, go around in the stores of the trade and see others goods &c &c," G. E. Light wrote to Amory Jr. in May 1861. "The effect of making such visits would be good on you for the home concern and good on customers for the N.Y branch." While business in New York was slow in general, Light assured his colleague that "our sales are rather increasing than decreasing, weekly, so far, owing to weekly additions to our list of customers."[18]

Amory Jr. evidently took Light up on the offer several months later. In February 1862, he visited Charles at school in Connecticut and then traveled to New York to visit the Oakes family and check on business. "If the weather improves, I mean to go to Brooklyn and go through Dorflinger's this p.m," he wrote to his wife, Ellen, whom he affectionately called "Nellie Dear." "Business is rather quiet at the N.Y. branch and probably will be for two or three weeks."[19]

While Amory Sr. owned the business and made the larger strategic decisions, Amory Jr. was deeply involved with the firm's efforts to produce glass that could compete with domestic and foreign products. G. E. Light in early 1864 wrote Amory about a customer who preferred German ruby glass. "He has a firm opinion too that the foreign are less brittle than ours and will stand more knocking round," Light noted. To win this client's business, Union Glass would have to make a higher quality product. "Please take special pains with this order and notice the color of sample sent," Light advised.[20]

After several years of shuttling back and forth between New York and Boston, the Houghtons apparently concluded that Brooklyn offered a more hospitable locale for glass manufacture than did Cambridge. And the continuing struggles of the Brooklyn Flint Glass Works seemed to have presented an opportunity. In October 1864, Amory Houghton Sr. sold his interest in Union Glass and purchased the Brooklyn Flint Glass Works. Soon after, he moved to Brooklyn and into a house at 12 Sidney Place, where his son Charles lived as well. Amory Jr. also moved to Brooklyn, taking up residence at 252 Hicks Street in Brooklyn, just a few blocks away from the factory. (His profession in *Lain's Brooklyn, New York, Directory* was listed as "chemist.") Amory Jr.'s home included his growing family: Alanson B. Houghton, born in 1863, and Arthur A. Houghton, born in 1866.[21]

The Houghton family's circle of business associates was expanding. A certificate of incorporation from 1865 lists the officers of the Brooklyn Flint Glass Works—capitalized with $100,000—as Amory Houghton, president and treasurer, with Austin Stevens as secretary. The board of trustees included Houghton *père et fils*, George Bradford, William Thomas, and

Josiah Oakes, brother of Amory Sr.'s wife, Sophronia. At a meeting in March 1866, Henry P. Sinclaire, who was married to an Oakes sister, was elected secretary. The presence of Amory's well-off in-laws as officials of the company underscored the nature of their relationship, for his wife's family members supplied Amory with capital and sponsorship. In 1864, a correspondent for Dun's, the credit-rating service, noted that Josiah Oakes "will guarantee his honesty and straightforwardness in all business transaction." For the most part, they left the running of the business to him. "AH also acts as treasurer and has full control of all departments," a Dun's correspondent noted in May 1866.[22]

The company set about expanding. In March 1866 it agreed to buy the Union Glass Company's warehouse at 73 Hudson Street, for $45,200. But the business encountered obstacles to its growth, and just a few years after the Houghtons became involved with it, the Brooklyn Flint Glass Works teetered on the brink. In the fall of 1866, a Dun's correspondent reported that the company "is in a bad way" and that Amory was in a great deal of debt. A fire ripped through the plant and destroyed it on December 3, 1866. The owners decided to rebuild (it is unclear whether the Houghtons had insurance on the property) and in late 1867 the firm proudly announced that it was again open for business. "The subscribers would respectfully inform you that their WORKS having been rebuilt and greatly enlarged, they are now prepared with increased facilities to furnish all kinds of Rich Cut, Plain Blown, and Pressed Glassware," an advertisement proclaimed. In addition, the company offered cane glass "suitable for button making," thermometer, barometer vial, and gauge tubing drawn to order, as well as druggists' and chemical glassware. "Having had many years' experience in the glass Business, we feel confidence in being able to execute orders promptly and in a manner calculated to please," the company announced.[23]

The expanded property was described by Charles Houghton in a January 1867 letter to Amory Jr.: "Supposing that you would like to hear from home, I will send you a few lines, although nothing of importance has [illegible] since you left. The office building is roofed and the clerks in N.Y. will move over here today. The factory and liers are roofed and the glory hole, between the two furnaces, on the west side has been rebuilt." The missive also included more frivolous news. "I held a ticket for the 'Cooper Union

Lottery' and went over to see the drawing, but did not get the $10,000. All are well and send love. Your aff. Bro, Chas."[24]

As the Houghtons were settling in Brooklyn and expanding their business, they were about to confront enormous change. The late 1860s would bring great transformations and upheavals to all areas of the country. The close of the Civil War ushered in the tumultuous era of Reconstruction and a series of economic booms and busts. Meanwhile, the nation's center of gravity was continuing to shift westward. The U.S. population tripled from 12.9 million in 1830 to 38.6 million in 1870, with much of the expansion occurring in the interior.

The glass industry too was undergoing substantial change in this decade. Entrepreneurs responded to the demand of the rising populace, especially for pressed tableware, by starting some seventy-two new glass houses between 1846 and the outbreak of Civil War. But the glass industry's center of gravity was also shifting westward and away from Boston, Brooklyn, and New Jersey. Pittsburgh grew vastly in stature, in no small part because it was closer to the supplies of fuels that fired glassmaking furnaces: coal and, increasingly, natural gas. In fact, in the 1860s, Pittsburgh became the site of the glass industry's semiannual trade show.[25]

Among those departing the seaboard for the interior in the 1860s was the Leighton family. In 1863, William Leighton Sr. and William Leighton Jr. left New England Glass to join J. H. Hobbs, Brockunier, and Company, in Wheeling, West Virginia. The family patriarch, Thomas Leighton, had come to America from Ireland in 1826 and had managed New England Glass. Upon his death, his son, William Sr., became superintendent and ran the plant until 1858, when William Jr. succeeded him.

Soon after his arrival in Wheeling in 1864, William Sr. made an important breakthrough. By substituting bicarbonate of soda for poor grades of soda ash and by perfecting the proportions, he concocted a new and intriguing composition of crystalline glass. The new composition produced glass that looked much like lead (or flint) glass. It was almost as brilliant but differed in important ways. It was lighter in weight, was less resonant, and reflected more light. Most importantly, lime glass, as it came to be known, could be produced at about one-third the cost of flint glass. It soon replaced flint glass in most American glass houses, especially for use in making pressed pattern tablewares. The new mix had another attribute that helped pave the way for the industrialization of glass: it hardened more quickly. Thus glassmakers had less time to mold, shape, and press the glass. This property pushed them to develop better processes for producing ware of all sorts and helped push the ancient craft farther along the road toward becoming a modern industry.[26]

Meanwhile, powerful forces were spurring industrialization in glass, as well as in other sectors. With the improvements in transportation, the rise of coal and natural gas, and the growing population in the West, communities whose livelihood had previously arisen from agriculture and harvesting natural resources like timber aspired to build or attract industry. Local businessmen, bankers, and boosters in towns all over the country sought to lure and attract factories of all sorts.

One such booster was Elias Hungerford, a banker and businessman in the upstate New York town of Corning. In 1866, he came up with and patented a concept for a glass window blind—movable slats of green glass attached to a window pane—that could open or close to allow light into a room. Since there were no local glassmakers capable of manufacturing the product, he began to seek out distant companies, including the Brooklyn Flint Glass Works. Apparently there was some interest. "We cannot leave here at present. Would like to see you here on Monday if possible—the proposition looks favorable," Amory Houghton Sr. wrote him by telegraph on December 8, 1866.[27]

Hungerford's window blind never became a commercial product. But the discussions between the businessmen led to something far more crucial. The Houghtons were facing difficulties in Brooklyn of an unspecified nature. In the absence of direct commentary on the situation by the earliest executives, it's necessary to rely on the conjecture of historians. George Buell Hollister, a top Corning Glass Works executive in the early twentieth century and company historian, refers to "serious labor troubles" and "other embarrassing complications." Other scholars have pointed to the high fuel costs and threat of fire posed by Brooklyn's urban setting. While there is no evidence of labor agitation at the works, labor unions *were* becoming more active in the New York area at that time. Moreover, it is undoubtedly true that the cost of everything from labor to raw materials to real estate were higher in Brooklyn than in Corning.[28]

There is evidence to support an alternate explanation. Amory Houghton, who had already built and lost a few fortunes in his busy life, was struggling in 1867 and 1868. Although he had assets of about $80,000 and was the titular head of the company, "he has been repeatedly embarrassed in bus[iness] and it is presumed that everything belongs to his wife," Dun's correspondent noted in March 1868. Sophronia Oakes in 1867 indeed owned the company, having assumed all its debt. Worse, the company had no established credit "and banks refuse to deal with them." Although Amory Houghton knew a great deal about the glass business, he wasn't a particularly reliable businessman. "The co. is not looked upon as desirable and caution is necessary in dealing with them."[29]

Given this state of affairs and his propensity for striking deals, it is apparent that any opportunity that offered Amory a fresh start—a chance to reestablish himself in business independent of his wife's family—must have seemed compelling. So Houghton made a proposition: if Hungerford and other Corning businessman could come up with a sum of money to invest in a new factory, he would establish a new glass works in Corning.

The Allure of Corning, New York

Corning, at the time, was an unlikely setting for a traditionally urban industry such as glassmaking. With a population consisting mostly of farmers, millers, and small-town merchants, the town had about 7,000 residents in the late 1860s. Its economy was highly agricultural and depended on natural resources for its prosperity and growth.

The area had been inhabited for centuries. The Chemung Valley, like the rest of the United States, was dominated by Native Americans until the late eighteenth century. At the point where the Chemung is formed by the confluence of the Conhocton and Tioga Rivers, there stood a hewn oak tree painted with Indian symbols. Called by various names in Indian languages, the landmark was known in English as Painted Post. The Andaste Trail, a network of pathways that hooked up with the Great Warrior Path and the Susquehanna River, wound through the area and provided a route for the Iroquois and Delaware tribes, as well as for European explorers and settlers.

The first European to document the region was Etienne Brule, a French explorer who came in 1615.[30]

An important battle was fought in the area during the Revolutionary War. The Senecas, who supported the British, joined forces with Tories to harass American settlers in the frontier regions of Pennsylvania. In early 1779, Congress authorized a campaign against the Indians. Under the leadership of General John Sullivan, about 5,000 troops headed up the Susquehanna River. They reached Tioga on August 11. On August 29, they engaged a force of Indians and Loyalists just outside the Indian village of Newtown (about six miles southeast of present-day Elmira). Although three Americans died, the colonists succeeded in driving off their opponents. Sullivan pursued his foes throughout the region, destroying cornfields, orchards, and gardens. "This victory practically settled the fighting of the whole campaign, for the Indians did not make another stand," wrote New York state historian Alexander Flick.[31]

The longer-term effect of the military campaign was to drive hostile Indian tribes away from this part of the vast American frontier. In the years after the war, vast tracts of lands in upstate New York were purchased by New England businessmen and other land speculators. As early as 1789, surveyors began to lay out townships on a grid six miles square. Drawn by cheap and fertile land that could support cash crops like tobacco, by the massive stands of timber, and by abundant game, settlers began to trickle into the area. The formal organization of towns wouldn't come about for a few decades, with most of the towns being named after the individuals who bought large tracts of land. Colonel Arthur Erwin bought a chunk of land west of present-day Corning, which was later incorporated as Erwin. A second buyer of land was Colonel Elezaer Lindsley, who brought seven slaves with him in 1790 and settled south of Erwin's holdings. The town named after him was organized in 1838. The town of Painted Post was formally organized in March 1826.

In the spring of 1789, Frederick Calkins, Caleb Gardner, Ephraim Patterson, Justus Wolcott, Peleg Gorton, and Silas Wood purchased the area that would become Corning. Calkins received 140 acres of land in what is now part of the business district, while Gorton took land that would become South Corning. In 1805, Ansel McCall built a grist- and sawmill along the river, and the area of present-day Denison Park came to be known as The Mills.[32]

The Chemung River was a natural highway of commerce: products could be floated down the river to the Susquehanna and ultimately to the Chesapeake Bay. But the area was also well positioned to take advantage of the internal improvements being built. In the early decades of the nineteenth century, American leaders realized that new modes of transportation would be required to develop the nation's vast interior. "Foreign commerce may cooperate in creating flourishing Atlantic cities," New York's visionary governor, DeWitt Clinton, proclaimed in a famous speech. "But internal trade must erect our towns on the lakes and rivers, and our inland villages; and internal trade must derive its principal aliment from the products of our agriculture and manufactures." At Clinton's prompting, the state approved a risky and daring venture: the construction of a 353-mile canal running from the Hudson River across the Mohawk valley to Buffalo, connecting the Great Lakes, the Finger Lakes, and the Hudson in one thruway. Work began in July 1817 on the controversial—and expensive—Erie canal, which was completed in 1825 at a cost of $6 million.

The completion and success of the Erie Canal set off a ditch-digging boom. Canals encouraged economic development by lowering transport costs and creating new jobs in quarrying, lumber, and agriculture. In 1817, the average rate for freight shipments between Buffalo and New York via overland wagon and the Hudson River was $.1912 per ton-mile. After the completion of the Erie Canal, it declined further to just $.0168 per ton-mile. The development of canals had a similar effect on glass. To ship a hundredweight of glass overland from Pittsburgh to Philadelphia in 1800 cost about $10; after the state's canal system was completed, it cost just $1.25. By 1840, some 3,000 miles of canals were built, and by 1860, there were more than 4,200 miles in twenty-three states, built at a cost of $188.2 million.[33]

With the success of the Erie—which ran about sixty miles north of the Chemung Valley—local boosters began agitating for a canal. In 1826, James Geddes, a surveyor, proposed digging a canal that would run from Elmira to Seneca Lake and a thirteen-mile feeder connecting Chimney Narrows to Horseheads. That would allow Chemung River water traffic to reach the Erie Canal through Seneca Lake and hence to Albany, New York City, and points beyond. Construction on the canal began on July 4, 1830. Completed in October 1833, it was one of the most economical canals ever built in the state. The cost of the forty-mile project was $314,395.51, or $8,504.96 a mile. Just four feet deep, it was forty-two-feet wide on the surface and had fifty-three locks.[34]

At about the same time, another mode of transportation began to link the region to the larger world, one that would eventually make the canals obsolete. The first railroad was built in the Baltimore area in the late 1820s, with horses pulling the cars along the tracks. But with the advent of steam engines, railroads gained momentum. Track mileage in the United States grew from 3,000 in 1840 to more than 9,000 in 1850. One of the earliest lines was the Blossburg Railroad. Completed in 1839, the fifteen-mile railroad connected Blossburg, a coal town across the Pennsylvania border, to a bend in the Chemung River, where the product could be loaded onto canal boats and floated to its final destination.[35]

The first major railroad to transverse New York state began to take shape in the 1830s, running roughly parallel to the Erie Canal. One of its early investors was a prosperous Albany businessman named Erastus Corning. Born in 1794 in Norwich, Connecticut, this son of a Revolutionary War veteran eventually settled in Albany, where he owned a hardware store and invested in both the Albany Nail Factory and Albany Iron Works. Corning also served several brief terms as mayor of Albany and was president of Albany City Bank. For this busy entrepreneur, land speculation was but one of many business interests. But it's the one for which he is most remembered.

In 1835, he joined with Hiram Bostwick, Thomas Olcott (an officer at the Mechanics and Farmers Bank of Albany), and six other men to form the Corning Company. Between November 1835 and July 1844 the company bought close to 2,000 acres of farmland and forest in the region at an average price of $30.10 per acre. The company began to carve up the forest land into lots. In 1836 a two-story wooden tavern, the Corning House, was built. Soon after, a bridge was laid out over the Chemung and a road cleared through town. The Bank of Corning was formed by Hiram Bostwick on January 12, 1839, with capital of $78,500. Thomas Olcott's sons, Alexander and Theodore, moved to Corning and set up the Payne & Olcott foundry.

Meanwhile, the Corning Company set up a public square—now known as Courthouse Square—and helped organize School District no. 14 on September 2, 1839.

Given Corning's remote location from the eastern seaboard, transportation improvements were key to its growth. In 1835, construction began on the Erie Railroad, which would connect Lake Erie to the Hudson River by way of the southwestern tier. But it quickly ran into financial problems. In 1845, however, the state legislature finally passed a measure that guaranteed the completion of the Erie. For its part, Corning gave over 34.5 acres of land to the railroad for right-of-way. To inaugurate the 483-mile line in 1851, President Millard Fillmore and Secretary of State (and famed orator) Daniel Webster rode the rails in a specially outfitted train, stopping frequently for tub-thumping speeches. Webster, eager not to miss the scenery, sat on a chair nailed down to a flatbed car, fortifying himself against the chill spring air with frequent swigs from a bottle of rum.[36]

The completion of the Erie Railroad signified Corning's arrival as a railroad hub, and it presaged the role it would play in the future development of the railroad industry, and vice versa. By rail and by water, Corning was now in direct contact with both the Atlantic seaboard and the Great Lakes. In 1848 Corning was the third largest shipping point in New York. And in 1850, 1,116 boats poled their way down the canal, sending soft coal, lumber, tobacco, grain, and whiskey to markets far and near.[37]

With the transportation infrastructure in place, area residents took steps to lay down a legal and social infrastructure. The original town site was on the south side of the river, where the population stood at 1,746 in 1846. After successfully petitioning the state to become a village, the area was incorporated as a town on October 25, 1848. Dickinson House on Pine Street Square, Corning's most enduring landmark, was built in 1850 by Hiram Bostwick and Andrew Dickinson. The area was officially named Corning in 1852, according to Hiram Bostwick, "only to flatter the vanity and induce liberal aid to the enterprise there projected by Erastus Corning."[38]

In 1855, the first census in which the town of Corning was counted, the population stood at 6,334 people, of whom more than 20 percent were foreign born. Many of the immigrants had worked on the canals and railroads and decided to settle in the area. Of those, 59 were from Canada, 95 from

England, 31 from Scotland, 201 from Germany, and 978 from Ireland, with a handful each from several other European countries. Most were farmers specializing in hops, grain, dairy, and apples. In all of Steuben County in 1855 only one man reported himself a glassmaker.[39]

There was a diversity in religion as well as in country of origin. Baptists, Methodists, and Episcopalians all had their own churches in the 1840s. The largest single group of newcomers were Irish Catholics. In February 1848, the Catholics of Corning were officially recognized in the congregation of St. Mary's by John Timon, first bishop of Buffalo. Their first pastor, Thomas Cunningham, arrived in March 1854. Generally poor, refugees from not only the potato famine but also the poverty of New York, they settled in shacks on the edge of town, near the church, which came to be called "Irish Hill" or "Catholic Hill."

The growing diversity came to reflect many of the tensions building in American society at the time. In the 1854 election, Corning pulled 612 of its 902 votes for the nascent Know-Nothing Party, whose platforms were generally anti-immigrant and anti-Catholic. After the flood of Sunday, November 11, 1857, in which the Irish Catholics suffered disproportionately, the Ladies' Benevolent Society held a meeting to organize relief efforts. The society passed a resolution saying "that the Catholics of this village should not receive any of these donations, but Protestants helped."[40]

Periodic floods of the Chemung weren't the only natural calamities afflicting the fledgling town. On June 30, 1856, a fire that began in the Payne & Olcott foundry quickly raged out of control and ripped through seventy-eight buildings. As the townspeople rebuilt, they forsook the local wood and turned instead to less flammable materials like brick and stone.

Like virtually every other town in the Union, Corning was caught up in the Civil War. Company C and Company D (known locally as the Irish brigade) of the Sixtieth Regiment of the state militia were headquartered in Corning. Another local armed force, the Eighty-Sixth regiment, also known as the Steuben Rangers, saw action at Bull Run, Manassas Gap, Fredericksburg, Wilderness, Gettysburg, and Appomattox. In the 1864 election, in the midst of the war, the area gave a small majority to McClellan Democrats.[41]

As the nation began to shift its focus from making war to making products, the period after the Civil War brought great strides in industrialization.

During these decades, the American manufacturing powerhouse began to take shape as craftsman, entrepreneurs, and, increasingly, professional managers, used technology, growing sources of power, and innovation to create large industrial enterprises. In the postwar period, Corning too began to undergo a transition from a transportation hub for locally harvested agricultural and natural resources, like coal, timber, and tobacco, to a center of manufacturing.

Corning's industrial future would be dictated largely by glass. In 1866, when Elias Hungerford began to think about marketing his window blind invention, he approached several glass companies. But as Hungerford learned more about the glass industry, it struck him that his town would make a good locale for the industry. It was a well-established transportation hub, so bringing in raw materials and shipping finished products would be easy. In addition, the materials needed to make glass—coal to fuel the furnaces, sand, and other ingredients—were available nearby.

Amory Houghton Sr. soon became convinced of the same. Houghton agreed to bring his enterprise (and $75,000 in capital) to Corning if local businessmen could raise $50,000 to invest in the works. Hungerford enlisted support from the *Corning Journal*, which on April 30, 1868, urged local boosters to kick in. By May 1868 they had raised the money, including $10,000 each from Joseph Fellows, Erastus Corning, and Theodore Olcott.[42]

An agreement was quickly reached. At its May 18 meeting, the trustees of the Brooklyn Flint Glass Works concluded that because "it has been deemed expedient for some time past to remove the manufacture of glass from this city to some point in the country where coal was cheaper and rent and expenses less" and because Corning had made an attractive offer, the company would soon move. A few days later, the *Corning Journal* trumpeted the agreement. "On Tuesday [May 19] the papers were signed, and the Trustees named for one year, as follows: Geo. T. Spencer, C.D. Sill, B.W. Payne, Theodore Olcott, of Corning, A. Houghton of Brooklyn, and A. Houghton, Jr., of Brooklyn, and Charles R. Maltby, of Corning." The decision was greeted with great joy in Corning. "When the works are in full operation, they will employ about two hundred men," a huge number given the local population. [43]

The article also noted that Amory Houghton Sr., the president of

Brooklyn Flint Glass Works, "intends to remove here and give his personal attention to the business. His son, Mr. A. Houghton, Jr., who also comes here, is regarded in New York as unsurpassed for his skill in the preparation of the mixture for forming the Glass."[44]

On May 30, 1868, stevedores loaded up furnaces, pots, blowpipes, molds, and other equipment onto canal boats at the Brooklyn wharves. From there, they were towed up the Hudson River to Albany by steamers and then poled west along the Erie Canal to the Seneca Canal. Heading south toward Geneva, they entered Seneca Lake and emerged at its southern tip in Watkins Glen. Floating into the Chemung Canal, which took them south to Horseheads, they maneuvered onto the Feeder Canal to Gibson. From Gibson, they poled upstream to Corning and docked at Pine Street. The material was unloaded directly on the two-acre site on the Chemung's south bank. The Houghtons brought with them nearly 100 employees, some of whom had moved from Somerville to Brooklyn just a few years before.[45]

On Monday, June 8, 1868, work started on the foundations, which consisted of a pair of two-story buildings made of stone in the form of a T, one 110 feet by 40 feet, and the other 112 feet by 60 feet. Above them towered two chimneys, about 100 feet high and 30 feet at the base. Their construction required over 600,000 locally made bricks. At the base of chimneys stood furnaces, one with ten pots and the other with eight. The works also included a sixty-foot-long brick oven in which the products were annealed (strengthened by heat treatment). The factory wasn't the only substantial construction work occurring in town. Amory Houghton Sr. bought the residence of a Dr. Dartt on First Street for $3,400. "He intends to remove the projecting front and improve materially the main building," according to a contemporary account.[46]

After the Corning Flint Glass Works plant began manufacturing on October 22, 1868, it drew crowds so large that the company had to start issuing visitor passes in early November. The locals simply marveled at the enterprise. The *Corning Journal* noted that "no description can give a correct idea of the ease with which the ductile metal is wrought, and the novel modes of making the various articles." The furnaces were kindled with a ton of Blossburg coal, and with both chimneys in operation, the works were projected to consume 4,000 tons of coal a year. Inside the factory, workers made the same products they had in Brooklyn: everything from goblets to globes, jars, fruit dishes, lamp chimneys, and tumblers, along with glass blanks for other companies.[47]

Corning had a captive customer for the blanks. Hoare & Dailey, the cut glass firm that had occupied space in the Brooklyn Flint Glass Works, had also decided to move to Corning. It set up shop on the second floor of the factory and employed fifty people. One of them was Thomas Hawkes, an Irishman. After coming to New York City in 1863, he signed on with Hoare & Dailey and moved to Corning in 1870. Hawkes would later start his own glass-cutting firm and emerge as a major citizen of "the Crystal City."[48]

For its part, the Corning Flint Glass Works did indeed employ about 200 people. On November 12, 1868 the *Elmira Advocate* estimated that the factory's payroll would "require the expenditure of $200,000 per year for labor." But the impact of the works on the local economy was more than a matter of dollars and cents. "The tall chimneys are a standing advertisement to the traveler of the important industrial interests of Corning. It is the pioneer for other extensive manufacturing establishments," the *Corning Journal* noted.[49]

In and Out of Bankruptcy

But the scenario was actually far less rosy than that described by the *Journal*. Soon after the Corning Flint Glass Works lit its furnaces, the newly founded company was in danger. In its first years in Corning, the glass works faced a series of financial, technical, and competitive difficulties that would ultimately drive it into bankruptcy and force the company's founder out of the glass business. In the late 1860s and early 1870s, the national economy was in the midst of a period of uncertainty, recession, and occasional panic that lasted several years. To make matters worse, the works were plainly on the wrong side of a shift in the glass industry—from lead flint glass to lime glass. With the Pittsburgh companies, which had switched to lime, making greater strides in producing in volume, the glass blank business was growing more competitive and less profitable. This development had an even greater effect on the pressed tableware business.

Given the economic situation, a company with few financial problems would have had difficulty weathering these years. Unfortunately for the Houghtons and their investors, the financial footing of the Corning Flint Glass Works was anything but sound. Its financial predicament can be seen through the cash book, which covers the years 1868–1872. The works plainly owed money to creditors in New York. Adding to their financial woes, the Houghtons had not been able to sell the Brooklyn plant.

In Brooklyn, the Houghtons had engaged in the common practice of selling three-month notes against their receivables to raise short-term cash. They continued to do so after moving upstate. In November 1868, the company began selling notes against revenues yet to be collected to local bankers such as Quincy Wellington and J. N. Hungerford and to distant financiers like Nathan Cushing of Boston. The money raised through such debentures—$2,000 or $3,000 at a time—was immediately applied to expenses such as payroll and raw materials. More often, however, the funds went to pay down other notes that were coming due. Meantime, sales were insufficient to cover the expenses for supplies and labor. On February 11, 1869, for example, the company recorded the sale of two proof glasses for $1.00 and received a $46.49 check from a corporate client.[50]

The works also faced technical problems. The raw materials in the area —whose abundance and relative cost were apparently factors behind the move from Brooklyn—were not of sufficient quality to make flint glass. What's more, the design of the new furnaces didn't function well with the kind of coal available from the adjacent coalfields. As a result, Corning's glassmakers had a difficult time keeping the furnace at the right temperatures. And less than a year after its assembly, the newly constructed plant literally began to fall apart. In April 1869, the *Corning Journal* noted "that business was much delayed or impeded by the giving way of the crowns of the arches in the chimneys and consequent destruction of pots in which the metal is fused." Now that new equipment had been brought in from New York, the arches were repaired and "the establishment is in full blast." But the structural problems had more far-reaching financial implications. "The unexpected expense of construction and loss incident to the delays has necessitated an increase of working capital, and that is forthcoming, so that the prosperity of the concern is certain."[51]

That increase in capital came with the issuance of $50,000 in mortgage bonds. The bonds were evidently discounted by Quincy Wellington's bank, for the cash book on May 14, 1869, notes the influx of $37,500 in cash for bonds from Wellington. Much of this cash flowed out the door immediately: $10,000 went to the Fall Brook Coal Company, and another $2,500 to retire a bills receivable note. With the weekly payroll running at about $2,500, the new funds dissipated quickly. By May 29, just two weeks after the infusion, the works showed a balance of just $2,572.[52]

Indeed, at the end of 1869, the company showed that, despite the investments, it was piling up significant liabilities. An annual statement dated January 1870 lists capital stock of $127,570 and total liabilities of nearly $111,000 —$50,000 in mortgage bonds and $60,815 in sundry accounts. The need for cash evidently led the Houghtons to enlist other local businesspeople in the management of the firm. The statement lists Corning resident J. F. Hill as president, with Amory Houghton Jr., C. D. Sill, and George T. Spencer as trustees. Indeed, Hill emerged as both an investor and a source of credit for the company. On August 8, 1870, for example, Hill wrote a check to pay a $3,000 note in New York. The absence of Amory Sr.'s name from the document suggests that he had already begun to remove himself from the firm's operations.[53]

Throughout 1869 and 1870, the firm's financial situation continued to deteriorate. Its expenses, which included interest on debt, raw materials, payroll, and supplies, far outweighed its sales. Eventually the firm's many creditors were no longer willing to sustain the struggling company. In September 1870, the *Corning Journal* reported that Judge Hall, sitting in Rochester, had appointed Alexander Olcott to be receiver for the struggling company, in effect signifying its descent into bankruptcy. Olcott provided the cash to meet the $2,720 payroll that week. For the next several months, Olcott paid the interest on the works' mortgage bonds and assumed other liabilities.[54]

The financial plight of the works—and its continuing efforts to provide glass products to customers—elicited a mixture of deep disappointment and stubborn local pride. In most bankruptcy proceedings, holders of equity capital stock had to cede their interests to creditors. And in the fall of 1870, the *Journal* predicted that the inevitable restructuring of the firm would likely "wipe out all of the stock subscribed for in 1868, by our citizens, to secure the construction of the Glass Works."[55]

Still, the works, struggling as they were, were viewed by some as a credit to the region. "The glass works is the only firm in the United States that makes exclusively the first quality of lead glass," the *Corning Journal* noted on April 27, 1871. "They are also the only works that manufacture a copper ruby glass for colored lanterns for signal purposes that surpasses any made." Even though the factory had difficulty meeting its payroll, it employed "about one hundred hands" while Hoare & Dailey employed another thirty-five.[56]

For better or worse, the works had spurred local employment and raised the town's economic profile. In December 1870, a year that saw Susan B. Anthony speak to an eighty-person crowd at Corning's Washington Hall, President Ulysses S. Grant placed a $1,000 order for glassware. Meanwhile, Corning was shipping blanks to distant cutters such as Meriden Silver Plate Company in Connecticut. It also sold thousands of globes to Dane, Westlake, and Covert of Chicago, which used them to make railroad lanterns. The relationships were slightly more complicated than the usual supplier–customer ones. Managers at firms such as Dane Westlake and Cover would send samples to Corning and ask the craftsman to make molds for these products.[57]

Frustrating as the Works' travails must have been for the local investors, they likely weighed more heavily on Amory Houghton Jr. and his brother, Charles, who were, for the moment, in charge. By December 1870, Dun's correspondent wrote, "the Corning Glass Co. has practically failed and as soon as it can be brought around a copartnership will be formed to continue the business partnership. The business is now being transacted by A. Houghton, Jr." The brothers faced a seemingly endless succession of woes, financial and otherwise. When a fire in late March 1871 damaged several homes and properties in town, a barn and tenement house owned by Amory Jr. each suffered $200 worth of damage but were insured for only $100 each. The next month, the Houghtons were mystified by the production of defective glass. It seems that young workers who had to work on Saturday afternoons "conceived the idea of spoiling the crucible of glass, and thus gaining a holiday" by throwing nails into the batch. "A week since they spoiled one mass worth about three hundred dollars." The saboteurs were found out and brought to justice.[58]

Throughout the latter half of 1870 the cash book shows a marked decrease of activity—a function of either inattentive bookkeeping or a massive slowdown in business. Whereas each week in 1868 and 1869 took up an entire page in the ledger, the activity between February and December 1871 is confined to a single page. The book ends abruptly in January 1872, showing a balance of just $16.75. It's possible that a new set of books (now lost) were started. An equally plausible explanation is that Amory Houghton Sr., who seems to have kept the books, was no longer engaged with the business.[59]

Amory Houghton Sr.'s connection was severed entirely in late 1871, when it was clear that the struggling entity would undergo a change in ownership. One of the creditors interested in taking charge of the works was Boston financier Nathan P. Cushing, who had loaned cash to the Houghtons in 1868 and 1869. He visited Corning in September 1871 and was soon followed by his lawyer and agent, A. B. Pomeroy. As a result of a series of financial and legal maneuverings in late 1871, Cushing refinanced the mortgage bonds and thus gained control of the works. The building in Brooklyn that had once housed the Brooklyn Flint Glass Works also passed into Cushing's ownership.[60]

By 1871, Amory Houghton Sr.'s long career as an entrepreneur was essentially over. He left Corning and moved to his farm in North Castle, New York, in Westchester County and ultimately returned to Brooklyn. His reputation and his fortune were shattered. His youngest son, Alfred, who had enrolled in Harvard University in 1869, had to leave after his first year. For the next several years, Amory Sr. managed the Brooklyn industrial property that he once owned, collecting rent and sending it to Cushing in Boston.[61]

Unwilling to move from Boston to supervise the Corning works, Cushing faced a choice—liquidate and close the factory or find a new manager to run them. When he opted for the latter, Amory Houghton Jr. was the logical choice to head the operation. Unlike his father, Amory Jr. had a great knowledge of the nuts and bolts of glassmaking. And he had a growing reputation as a reliable businessman. "He is a young man of good habits and character and owns house and lot," a Dun's correspondent wrote in 1871. "Think him good for any contracts he enters into." His ability, reputation, and attention to detail likely figured in Cushing's decision to name him manager of the Corning Flint Glass Works.[62]

Even as the firm encountered financial difficulties, Amory Houghton Jr. continued to try to refine the company's products and processes. To do so, he corresponded with other glass industry experts. In January 1871, H. C. Fry wrote him from Pennsylvania advising on the best place to obtain clay mills and their prices. From Boston, Nathan Cushing wrote about a supplier of soda ash.[63]

Amory Houghton Jr. also swapped formulas with other glassmakers. Henry Libbey in the summer of 1871 notified him of the batch he was using for stemware. "Please try this and I think you will like it—but let us two interchange ideas in true friendship and keep results to ourselves," Libbey wrote. Sending a sample of the lead glass he was making that day, Libbey complained of the slack demand for light opal glass and notified his friend of a new form of red glass being produced in England. "Don't let my Bro. Know I gave you this receipt, but I think the trade is large enough for both."[64]

Amory Jr. was also in touch with John Leighton, a member of the now famous Leighton family in Wheeling although still himself living in Cambridge, Massachusetts. In return for describing how Corning Flint Glass Works made opal glass, Amory Jr. received Leighton's explanation of how to make "gold stone." Leighton provided minute details on the ingredients that went into the batch—including copper. "With these hints and some perseverance on your part I have no doubt you may arrive at what you desire," Leighton wrote.[65]

Ownership of the works wouldn't stay in outside hands for long. By May 1872, Amory Houghton Jr. and Charles Houghton had scraped up enough cash to buy the plant back from Cushing, who was apparently eager to be rid of the property. This time, the townspeople who had invested in the original works did not have (or take) the opportunity to obtain shares. There seemed to be some remaining bitterness over the failed initial venture. In May 1872, at a fifteenth (or crystal) anniversary party thrown by banker Quincy Wellington for his wife, the local gentry presented valuable gifts of glassware. "Henry Sherwood had his joke in contributing ten shares of the original stock of the

Corning Glass Works, costing actually one thousand dollars, but now worth no more than a Confederate bank note," the *Corning Journal* reported. (The year marked another important transition. In late 1872, Erastus Corning died. Although his holdings in the area were valued at about $200,000, he had never visited the town named for him, as far as is known.)[66]

Despite the problems, the works maintained their employment level of about two hundred in 1872, and in that year two buildings were added to the physical plant. The Glass Works wasn't the only local enterprise expanding. In March 1873, John Hoare announced his intention to bring workers from his shop in Brooklyn to Corning. "He advertises in this paper for a dozen dwellings for the use of the coming employees," the *Corning Journal* noted on March 28, 1873.[67]

Meanwhile, the Houghton brothers began to plant deeper roots in the community. Starting a tradition that would outlast the family's run at the glass company's helm, the Houghtons became involved in local Republican politics. In August 1872, Charles Houghton was selected as a delegate to the Republican State Convention. Calling him a "zealous Republican," the *Corning Journal* noted that "last year he entered on the campaign with such earnestness as inspired courage in others." He must have ultimately won an office because local papers referred to him henceforth as the Hon. C. F. Houghton. Members of the family also became involved in local church affairs. At a January 1872 benefit for the Episcopal Church fund, the *Corning Journal* noted, "Mrs. Houghton played the piano admirably."[68]

After a few years of operating on a shoestring, Amory and Charles Houghton evidently became sufficiently confident in the enterprise to again seek outside investors. In 1875, the company was reorganized and incorporated as the Corning Glass Works, with $50,000 in capital. The Corning residents who had invested in the company in 1868 were no longer involved in the ownership. Virtually all the top positions were again held by family members. Amory Houghton Jr. was president and treasurer, and Charles F. Houghton was manager of sales. Their uncle, Henry P. Sinclaire, was secretary. Joseph J. Tully, the superintendent of production, was not related to the Houghtons. (However, his son, William, would ultimately marry Amory Jr.'s daughter.)[69]

In 1875, the plant was expanded again to include a third furnace. The works now comprised a larger compound, including a three-story brick building on the south of the blowing room. The ground floor contained finishing, inspection, and packing operations. The second floor housed the offices, and the third floor was the domain of J. Hoare & Co. A separate building contained the powerhouse and cooper's shop.[70]

A Crucial Change of Direction

The arrival of the works in Corning, Amory Houghton Sr.'s departure from the scene, and the reorganization of the company—these events marked the first real transition in leadership from Corning's first generation to its second. For the works to recover from their disastrous first few years in Corning, this second generation of management would not only have to take the reins but also find a new generation of products.

In the mid-1870s, Amory Jr. and Charles made a strategic decision. Concluding that it was fruitless to try to compete with the Pittsburgh area producers in the manufacture of lime glass, they decided to return to their roots: lead glass. After all, the company had built up a great expertise in the material, as Amory Jr. had continued to build on the research he had started in Brooklyn and Somerville. Moreover, since the material was highly refractive and elastic and since the use of lead allowed for the fusion of materials at low temperatures, the material was ideal for creating specialty glass products.

Over the coming years, the reconstituted company would use its expertise to produce specialty glassware: railway signal glasses, semaphore lenses, lantern globes, thermometer tubes for medical suppliers, and tubing for chemists and druggists. By the middle of the turbulent 1870s, Corning was transforming itself into a producer of low-volume, high-profit specialty glassware. It was this focus on research and specialty glassware that would carry the company through its next generation and give it the means to weather the periodic crises that lay ahead. [71]

II

SECOND GENERATION

CHAPTER THREE

The Rise of Corning Glass Works, 1875–1908

UNDER its first generation of leadership, the Houghtons' peripatetic glass company had found difficulty establishing itself as a profitable, going concern. With Amory Houghton Sr. essentially retired, it fell to a second generation—his sons, Amory Jr. and Charles—to attempt to revive the bankrupt company. Fortunately, the brothers would prove to be shrewder operators than their father had been. Over the course of the next three decades, they would build Corning Glass Works into a powerful, profitable company. They would do so by creating new glass compositions for railroad globes, by establishing themselves as a leading producer of lightbulbs for the growing electric industry, and by developing proprietary methods of creating specialty glassware like tubing. As the nineteenth century gave way to the twentieth, the Houghtons' family concern would plant its roots deeper in the soil of the small town that was quickly developing into a center of glass manufacturing.

Under new, more energetic management, Corning Glass Works quickly

recovered from the crisis that had brought it—and Amory Houghton Sr.—
down. As Dun's correspondent reported tersely in January 1875, "Have a
well established and profitable business and are believed making money."
Within a year, the reorganized company was on sound footing, with a
steady flow of orders from companies like Meriden Silver Plate Company.
In October 1875 Meriden ordered 20,000 dozen caster bottles, at $.80 per
dozen, and $20,000 worth of dishes, pickle jars, wine bottles, toilet sets, and
vases, for a total of $36,000. Indeed, the works were generating enough cash
to allow Amory Jr. to pay off the debt held by Nathan Cushing. The last of
the debt was retired on December 13, 1875.[1]

But as soon as the company had gotten back on its feet, it suffered
another in the series of disasters that would periodically strike the
Houghton family's enterprise. In the early morning of October 4, 1876, a
fire broke out in the factory's main building, probably in packing material
on the ground floor. The flames blazed out of control before volunteers
arrived with their hand pumps. When the smoke cleared, the packing and
finishing rooms, the second floor office, and part of the third floor were
charred. The roof collapsed. "It was said that bystanders looking through
the window openings could see the shelves of the cutting shop, ladened
with cut glass ready for the Christmas trade, drop with their loads into the
fire," wrote George Buell Hollister. Corning's losses were estimated at
$35,000, while those of J. Hoare & Co. were estimated at $20,000.[2]

As their father had in Brooklyn nearly a decade before, Amory Jr. and
Charles Houghton quickly set about rebuilding the factory, this time with a
larger ten-pot furnace. The reconstructed works would return to prosperity
on the strength of two products: copper ruby glass and the inner corrugated railway signal lens. Both were the result of proprietary research, the
first of many efforts by the company's owners to marry craft to science.
And both were intended for the railroad market—one that would expand
rapidly in the coming decade. Over the next three decades, the company's
relationship with the railroad industry would lead to a series of developments and innovations that would power the company's growth and bring
key personnel to upstate New York.

In the 1870s, virtually all railroads employed red signals—known as semaphores—to let engineers know when to stop or slow down. But companies

had great difficulty making glass that held a consistent, deep red tint—an important effort, given the potentially disastrous outcomes if railroad engineers failed to heed a signal to stop. The Houghtons, and many other glassmakers, produced red glass infused with copper, but it varied in color, lacked range, and wasn't reliably visible in rain and fog. But Amory Jr. was a relentless tinkerer with glass compositions. His meticulously maintained batch book was filled with dozens of formulas and hypothetical mixtures for new types of glass. In 1874, through such dogged experimentation, he "was able to produce a glass based on the Copper Ruby principle which was so much better than other similar glasses then in use that it was widely adopted by the railroads for signal lights and in marine service for ship lights." The introduction of this product allowed Corning to gain a significant competitive advantage.[3]

At the same time Amory Jr. was developing a new composition for glass semaphores, Charles Houghton was tinkering with their design. Blown "bull's eye" lenses (or "bull's eyes") contained optical systems that were controlled by corrugation (i.e., the lens had fresnels [ridges] traditionally on the outside). But this design allowed for dust to build up and had limited range, and hence it proved a safety hazard. After consulting with Ward W. Willits, president of the Adams & Westlake Company of Chicago—a major customer—Charles Houghton designed a bull's eye with the corrugation on the *inside*, leaving a smooth, rounded surface on the exterior. After molding a solid piece of glass into a concave form, he noted in a January 9, 1877, patent application, "I form, by means of suitable molds or by grinding-tools…a series of concentric corrugations, or alternate elevations and depressions."[4]

To ensure that the design was viable, Charles Houghton consulted with a professional scientist. Fortunately, his efforts came in a period when such expertise was becoming more widely available to American industry.[5] The 1860s and 1870s brought a rapid expansion of American universities specializing in science. In 1861, the Massachusetts Institute of Technology was founded in Boston. And in 1872, Johns Hopkins University, the first American university specifically modeled after German institutions, with strong graduate programs in physical and biological sciences, opened its doors. Hopkins's success sparked the upgrading of graduate programs at universities such as Harvard, Yale, Princeton, and Cornell.[6]

Cornell University had been founded in 1865 in Ithaca, a town about fifty miles north of Corning on the shores of Cayuga Lake, by telegraph magnate Ezra Cornell. Among the professional scientists on Cornell's faculty was William Anthony, a physicist who had built one of the first electric generators made in the United States. After the Houghtons initiated correspondence with Anthony, he designed a lens that was corrugated on the inside. Anthony quickly passed on the work to one of his colleagues, George Sylvanus Moler, a physicist who was also a skilled mechanic.

The relationship between the Corning Glass Works and Moler would last for several decades. Typically, Charles Houghton would obtain specifications for lenses from Corning's railroad and marine clients, draw up preliminary sketches, and send them to Ithaca. Moler would craft blueprints and send them back to Corning, where machinists would make iron molds in which they would press the lenses. "Please give me a drawing for a plano convex lens or bulls eye just 4 in [sic] in dia. With focus 2½ inches," Charles Houghton wrote Moler on October 29, 1885. A few days later, Moler sent back the designs, which were satisfactory. "Drawing such OK. Herewith chk 2.00." Charles Houghton would also ask Moler to consider theoretical questions and make special calculations essential to successful lens design. "Semaphores we have a range of 100 yards. What would be the relative values of two different illuminated lenses at that distance say one of the lenses is 4 in. dia and the other 6 in. in dia. Please give me a formula by which I can determine the comparative value of any two lenses at any range, charging for same of course," he wrote on April 16, 1888.[7]

Thus by 1879 Corning had introduced successful new products. More importantly, in establishing relationships with scientists Moler and Anthony, it had identified a new means of building competitive advantage. This set of attributes placed the firm in an excellent position to participate in one of the greatest technological developments of the nineteenth century: Edison's lightbulb.

The Birth of Commercial Electricity and the Lightbulb

The rise of professional scientific research was an important trend in American economic history. In the 1870s, however, most innovations still came from their traditional source: inventor/entrepreneurs. In fact, two of the biggest breakthroughs of the 1870s, which created industries in which Corning's glass products would play a key role, came from just such individuals: Alexander Graham Bell and Thomas Edison.

In 1873, Bell, a Scottish immigrant who had taught deaf students, began experimenting with a multiple-message telegraph. On February 14, 1876, Bell filed what would become the controlling patent for the telephone—the ability to transmit voice through wires by transforming sound waves into electrical signals. The following year, he and his backers organized the Bell Telephone Company, which ultimately evolved into AT&T. Nearly a century after Bell's breakthrough, Corning would introduce a product—optical waveguides—that would revolutionize the telecommunications industry.[8]

Edison's incandescent electric light had an immediate impact on the Corning Glass Works. Throughout the nineteenth century, European and American inventors and scientists had been exploring the phenomenon of electromagnetism. Eventually, they developed dynamos, which turned mechanical energy into electrical energy. With the invention of Herman Sprengel's mercury vacuum pump in 1865 and improvements of the dynamo in the 1870s, electric lighting began to develop into a commercial product. In June 1879, using inventions by Charles F. Brush, the California Electric Light Company in San Francisco built the first American arc lighting system powered by a central station.[9]

But Brush had rivals. Chief among them was Thomas Edison. Like Bell, Brush, and the Houghtons, Edison was a self-taught entrepreneur/inventor. Born in Milan, Ohio, in 1847, he left home at sixteen to work as a telegraph operator. After patenting several inventions relating to the telegraph, including a stock ticker, he set up shop in Menlo Park, New Jersey. There, the autodidact evolved into a prototypically eccentric American folk hero as he churned out a string of discoveries, developments, and innovations that resulted in the lightbulb, the phonograph, and moving pictures.[10]

As he worked to perfect the incandescent lightbulb, Edison began to order supplies from Corning. On September 13, 1879, he sent tubing samples to Corning (which must have been made of lime glass) and asked if the works could duplicate them. The company responded, "We cannot fill your order for we only make lead glass. It is tough and elastic and could be drawn to any distinctions if it would answer your purpose. We return samples by this mail," came the prompt response.[11]

About a month later, on October 21, 1879, Edison produced the first successful incandescent electric light—a filament that sustained a brilliant light when heated by an electric current. When trying to develop an envelope that could house the filament structure, Edison asked his staff members for help. William Holzer, a glassworker who joined Edison's firm in the winter of 1880, eventually married the sister of Edison's wife. Holzer was familiar with the glass works in upstate New York and likely suggested contacting Corning again. The company dispatched a representative to Menlo Park in June 1880, probably Charles Houghton.[12]

Although accounts differ, it is likely that William Meadowcroft, an Edison assistant, visited Corning in 1879 or 1880 with a sketch of the bulb he wanted. As he met with a shop staffed by James Lear and Joe Lear, who had come from Brooklyn with the Houghtons in 1868, Edison's representative watched a boy blowing a glass bubble. (Subsequently, three people—Joseph Baxter, Frederick Deuerlein, and James Goggin—each claimed to have been that boy.) "The first bulbs were blown 'free hand'; that is, without a shaping mould." Throughout the day, workers drew tubes of glass with closed outer ends, reheated the ends and then put them on a gaffer's bench and rolled them back and forth while a boy blew into the opposite end. "There were 165 bulbs satisfactory to Mr. Edison made on that first day, and the record states that 'it took all day to make them.'"[13]

Regardless of how the initial contacts occurred, it is most likely that the crucial events took place in the spring or summer of 1880 rather than 1879. For in May 1880, Edison ordered 485 pounds of glass tubing for $198.70, "to be used for electric light." In the summer and fall of 1880, Edison requested a variety of products from Corning and proved a demanding customer. "We received bill from you also bill laden on NY Lake, Erie & Western RRC dated Sept. 13 but have failed to receive goods. Will you please advise us in regard to this," he wrote on August 3, 1880. It wasn't until the late fall of 1880 that Edison placed his first order for lightbulbs. On November 17, 1880, Corning sent 307 dozen bulb blanks to Edison, along with 819 pounds of glass tubing. The total bill was $311.97: $119.17 for the tubing and $112.80 for the bulbs, or about three cents each.[14]

The modest order evidently convinced Edison that Corning could become his sole supplier of bulb blanks. (Bulbs, or blanks, were the empty glass envelopes in which Edison's workers installed the filament structure, thus creating what were called electric lamps.) On November 27, responding to a Census Office question as to whether he was going to start a factory to make lamps, Edison responded, "We buy tubes and bulbs of the Corning Glass Works and make them up into lamps by table blowing." In its first year, 1880, Corning made 3,684 bulbs for Edison, marking the beginning of a product line that would drive Corning's growth for the next several decades. Corning was plainly a thriving concern. "[They] pay cash for everything and carry a large cash surplus," Dun's correspondent reported in June 1881. "Are not borrowers, but lenders of money."[15]

Corning's early efforts to produce bulbs for Edison represented a crucial breakthrough, something it would achieve time and again throughout the next century. The works had come up with a new application for glass as an indispensable, though frequently overlooked, industrial material. And the lightbulb would prove to be the first of many products that Corning would transform from a handmade specialty product into a machine-made commodity.

A New Industry Organizes

In time, lightbulbs would prove a lucrative product for Corning Glass Works and some of its competitors. But in 1880, the vast majority of the nation's 169 active glass works were making the same kinds of products they had been making for decades. Together, they employed 24,000 people and produced $21 million worth of goods. That means the average works employed about 142 people and had revenues of $124,000. By 1880, the Corning Glass Works had 278 workers, making it about twice as large as the average American glass firm. The industry's center of gravity was continuing to shift westward, with a majority of the factories in Pennsylvania, Ohio, and West Virginia.[16]

Corning and the other glass companies in the 1880s did not make any great strides in technology. As Hollister wrote, "the old crude melting in hand-fired coal-burning furnaces was continued, the use of hand labor for the manufacture of all types of ware persisted." In fact, virtually every competitor in 1880 used the old coal-fired pot furnaces; there were 280 of them in the United States. But in Europe, important industrial developments were afoot. In 1856 Frederic Siemens patented the principle of regeneration —a process by which waste heat from burning gases was used to preheat fuel. Eventually, he applied the principle to pot furnaces, the precursors of more efficient continuous tank furnaces—furnaces divided into three compartments, with separate portions for melting, refining, and purifying glass. Siemens patented a continuous tank furnace in 1870, and in 1879, a glass factory in Poughkeepsie became the first American firm to adopt the technology. Most U.S. glass companies, Corning icluded, continued to use coal because it was cheap and plentiful. Still, by 1880, twenty-one domestic producers (about 12 percent) were using gas, an energy source that was subject to more precise temperature control than coal.[17]

Despite this trend, U.S. glassmakers still faced intense competition from European rivals, largely because of higher American labor costs and the less advanced technology employed here. To assist domestic producers, the U.S. government maintained stiff tariffs on imported glass. In 1880 the duties collected on all dutiable glass imports amount to almost 55 percent of their value. Duties on bottles and jars were between 35 percent to 40 percent, up to 57 percent for unpolished windows and between 30 percent and 40 percent on pressed and blown glassware. The Houghtons naturally supported such measures. As Harlo Hakes wrote of Amory Houghton Jr., "In politics he's a Republican and essentially a protectionist."[18]

The growth of glassworkers unions was one force that helped contribute to higher labor costs. The American Flint Glass Workers Union was organized in 1878 as one unit of the Knights of Labor, a confederation that included skilled workers in a range of industries. The AFGWU—better known as "the Flints"—had several departments representing glassworkers in areas such as lamp chimneys and pressed tableware. Union officials engaged in collective bargaining with producers and set wages on a regional basis. As they won important concessions, union shops also began to standardize working procedures and wages. By the mid-1880s, unions negotiated an almost universal work stoppage annually from June 30 to August 12, essentially codifying the long-standing practice of shutting down for a few weeks during the hottest part of the summer.[19]

The Flints first attempted to unionize workers at Corning in 1880 and again in July 1883. The effort was led by James Smith, who had attempted to organize workers at the Houghtons' Brooklyn glass works. Smith made a small amount of headway. The company responded as most other similarly situated firms did: it fired the three most active union agitators. And when the Houghtons refused to rehire them, eighteen glassblowers walked off their jobs. Those who walked off represented a small part of Corning's workforce, which numbered nearly 300. And since there were no other glass companies in town, the situation was quickly resolved. Corning would remain an open shop for another sixty years.[20]

The failure to gain representation notwithstanding, Corning's skilled and experienced glassworkers made major contributions to the company's growth. They often generated key ideas and innovations in process. In the 1880s, for example, workers developed a new technique for making bulbs. The workers formed the glass in hinged wood or cast-iron molds that had been soaked in water and were coated with a thin film of paste. Gatherers would shape the glass and hand the gob to a master blower, who would blow it into the paste mold. The use of labor-saving and time-saving devices like molds was important because the demand for bulbs increased as the availability of electricity expanded in the early 1880s. Edison built his first central power station, which provided power to businesses and street lights, on Pearl Street in lower Manhattan in 1881. Corning was his main supplier. By 1882, Edison reported that "the Corning people make the best glass in the world; it is perfectly reliable and we never have any trouble."[21]

Edison had competitors, and many of them became Corning customers as well. Chief among them was the Thomson-Houston Company of Lynn, Massachusetts. Elihu Thomson, born in 1853, grew up in Philadelphia. After graduating from Central High School, where he took courses with physics teacher Edwin J. Houston, he worked at a chemistry lab in town and taught. Following a ritual of American scientists, he went to Europe in 1878 to research electrical developments. He returned the following year and built a new lighting system with Houston. In 1880, Thomson joined American Electric in New Britain, Connecticut, as an electrician. American Electric adopted a strategy of selling equipment to central stations, installing twenty-eight lighting systems, in hotels, theaters, and textile mills, mostly in Connecticut, between July 1880 and September 1882. In 1883, a group of Lynn, Massachusetts-based entrepreneurs bought the company and moved it there, and it was renamed Thomson-Houston. Doubtless aware that Corning supplied Edison with bulb blanks, Thomson-Houston also became a customer of Corning's glass.[22]

The growth of electricity stimulated demand for bulbs. After assembling 130,000 lamps between November 11, 1880, and April 11, 1882, at his lamp works in Harrison, New Jersey, Edison made 216,000 in 1883, 396,000 in 1884, and 700,000 in 1886. That was good news for Corning, whose business grew rapidly. A January 1882 report in Dun's noted that it "continues prosperous as ever. Believed making money rapidly and established with over $100m ask very little cr[edit] and are prompt." In October 1885, the correspondent reported, the Corning works business was "as good as ever, composed of first class men in every way, and bus very successful." As Edison and Thomson-Houston grew (and would ultimately merge), Corning would parlay its early contacts with these companies into lucrative, long-term relationships that would help secure its future.[23]

The Houghtons and Corning

With the establishment of the Corning Glass Works as a growing concern, the Houghtons began to plant their roots more firmly in town. In 1878, Amory Houghton Jr. purchased the residence of banker George W. Patterson Jr. at Pine and Third Streets for $10,000, a princely sum for the time. The same year proved eventful for Charles Houghton too. He was elected to the New York State Assembly as a Republican to represent the second assembly district, Steuben County. At the age of thirty-two, he married Helen Hall, a daughter of Judge Benjamin Hall of Auburn. The groom's parents were unable to attend. "Of our wedding I can say but little as I hope to see you all before very long and tell most of it myself," Helen Hall Houghton wrote to her mother-in-law the day after the wedding, as they headed west for their honeymoon. "One thing I can say though, and that is that I regret more than anyone can ever know that you and your Brooklyn household were missing at the ceremony." Declining health may have been the cause for the absence of Amory Houghton Sr. and his wife, Sophronia, who died in 1880. And on February 20, 1882, Amory Houghton Sr., who had continued to manage the Brooklyn Steam Power Works as an agent for Nathan Cushing, died in his home at 259 Sixth Avenue in Brooklyn.[24]

In Corning, the Houghton brothers started a tradition that would last for more than a century: participation in local Republican politics. Charles served as an elector for Republican presidential candidate James Garfield in 1880. Temperance was a major force in the area in the 1870s and 1880s. In February 1881, Amory Houghton Jr. ran as a no-license candidate for the excise board but lost. Entering politics on the Temperance slate was perfectly in keeping with Amory Jr.'s personality. Exacting, sober-minded, and meticulous, in business and in personal habits, Amory Jr. seemed to define himself in opposition to his less reliable father.

Of course, most of the brothers' energies were devoted to the company. Although they shared responsibilities, Amory Jr. was clearly the senior partner. "For nearly a quarter of a century he was the dominant personality in the organization," as George Buell Hollister put it. As the primary manager, he supervised the batch mixing personally and ran the firm with a stern hand. "Mr. Houghton was a little quick tempered and in [superintendent] Mr. Tully's absence, if he saw the boys on his shops loafing or fooling around, he was known to have fired them all on the spot," one anonymous early worker recalled. Of course, Joseph Tully would usually hire them back the next day.

Indeed, Amory Jr. was a formidable presence, occasionally to members of his own family. His grandson, Arthur, remembered him as "crusty." And he had a problematic relationship with his youngest brother, Alfred, who was the maternal grandfather of actress Katharine Hepburn. In her memoir, she charged that "Amory fired him from the glassworks because he was always late." Charles Houghton, nine years younger than Amory Jr., was clearly the junior partner to his older brother. Although he did not enjoy traveling, Charles was in charge of sales and spent a great deal of time on the road. He had a natural ability, "aided by a very attractive personality" as Hollister put it, and established valuable trade connections.[25]

The town the Houghtons lived in was changing in shape and size. In 1878, the feeder from the Erie Canal was closed, but the railroads continued to expand. New stations were built in 1880 and 1881, when the Lackawanna, which ran from Binghamton to Buffalo, with a branch to Rochester, reached town. The residential portion of the city, largely confined to Third Street, began to expand as houses popped up on Fourth Street, farther up the hill. In May 1882 about 100 homes were under construction in Corning. To commemorate his father's role in the development of town, Erastus Corning Jr. helped fund the construction of a clock tower in the center of town. It was completed in late 1883, and, with its 1,400 pound bell, became a highly visible and audible symbol of the growing town.[26]

Just as Irish immigrants had settled in Corning after working on the canals and railroads, another group of immigrants—the Italians—stayed on after completing their labors on the Lackawanna. Many settled along the Erie Railroad yards and Water Street on the South Side, contributing to the town's growing Catholic presence. In 1882, work was started on St. Peter's School. And in January 1886 Father Colgan bought the old Salvation Army barracks on the southwest corner of Market Street and Steuben Street, which became the site of St. Patrick's, a second Catholic parish.[27]

Many of the new arrivals found work at companies that were incubated and spawned by the Corning Glass Works. Cut glass and art glass grew more profitable and gained popularity as gift items. And in the 1880 census, the town counted forty cutters, of whom twenty-one came from England or Ireland. Most were affiliated with the Glass Works or J. Hoare & Co. In 1881, George Abbott, who was married to Amory Jr.'s youngest sister, Nellie, bought a stake in the firm. That year, however, Thomas G. Hawkes, a foreman at J. Hoare, left to form his own company, the Hawkes Rich Cut Glass Works. An Irish immigrant who had come to Corning in 1870 to work for Hoare, Hawkes quickly became a steady customer for Corning. On April 30, 1880, for example, he bought $105.41 worth of dishes and tumblers, one of a number of purchases for the year. And Hawkes enjoyed a deeper relationship with the Houghtons. H. P. Sinclaire Jr., the son of Corning's plant manager and a corporate officer, joined the Hawkes firm as a bookkeeper. In 1882, Hawkes leased the upper two stories of a newly completed three-story brick building west on Market Street and Walnut. Hawkes quickly developed a reputation for producing quality, high-end merchandise. In September 1885, he filled an order for fifty dozen pieces of table glassware for the White House.[28]

Hawkes's fifty-employee factory was the site of the first serious labor strife in town. In October 1886, some workers who had been affiliated with the Knights of Labor walked out of Hawkes's shop to protest the extensive use of low-wage apprentice workers, a practice that held the payroll down. Hawkes successfully resisted the union, and the strike was settled in his favor in March 1887. But it engendered lasting enmity between him and the Flints, as the union was known. Meanwhile, John Hoare & Co. continued to grow. It set up a shop in town in 1882, and John Hoare Jr. came into the business in 1887. This was "one of the largest cut glass concerns in the country," according to glass historians Farrar and Spillman.[29]

Like Hoare's firm, Corning Glass Works was very much a family business. As was typical of most nineteenth-century firms, only the sons went into the family business. Charles and Helen Houghton had two daughters. But Amory Jr. and his wife, Ellen, had five children—Elizabeth, Alanson, Arthur, Annie, and Clara. Both of Amory's sons would enter the company in their twenties and would come to constitute the third generation of Corning's leadership.

The eldest son, Alanson B. Houghton, born in 1863, was educated in a sequence that would recur for later Houghtons. He attended Corning Free Academy and public schools in Corning and St. Paul's School in New Hampshire. From there, it was on to Harvard, where he made a lifelong friend in fellow classmate George Santayana and displayed an interest in writing. He was an editor at the *Harvard Crimson* and was elected to Phi Beta Kappa. "I shall have a twelve or fifteen page article on 'Omar Khayyam' (a Persian physician and poet) in the next *Monthly*, and I have spent so much care on it that I am anxious that people should like it," he wrote to his father in 1885.[30]

The serious literary efforts betrayed a dry wit. "I presume he is studying to be a civil engineer," Alanson wrote of George Patterson, the son of the Corning banker, who attended MIT. "He can get to be an engineer easily enough, but unless he has changed considerably from his former self, he'll find great difficulty in becoming a civil engineer." Alanson would also see other Corning natives in Boston. "The Wellingtons start for New York tomorrow. Addie is quite recovered from her sickness. Charlie and I called on them yesterday at the Brunswick where they are stopping, but did not find her at home," he wrote in the same letter. "Addie" was Adelaide Wellington, the daughter of banker Quincy W. Wellington, whom he would marry six years later.[31]

At Harvard's June 1886 graduation, Alanson read a twenty-four-verse poem he had written, which was chosen as the class poem. "The poem is by far the strongest literary productions written by a Harvard undergraduate for many years. Besides its polished form and graceful diction, there is depth of thought and feeling in it which is remarkable," the Boston Daily Advertiser wrote. Although Harvard president Charles Eliot wanted to keep Alanson on the faculty, he was eager to continue his education abroad. For the next two years, he studied history, government, and economics at the University of Paris, and the Universities of Berlin and Göttingen. He began to pen scholarly works such as "Italian Finances from 1860 to 1884," which appeared in the January 1889 Quarterly Journal of Economics. While in Europe, he traveled extensively. Amory Houghton Jr.'s personal cash book shows shipments of money to his son in Germany, Prague, and Vienna. In 1888, at his father's insistence, Alanson abandoned dreams of becoming a scholar and returned home for good. He joined the company and went to work under his uncle Charles.[32]

Arthur Houghton also attended St. Paul's and joined the company in 1887. "His first work was in the Shipping department. He reported daily at seven o'clock in overalls and worked the long hours that were then customary. No favors were asked or given and he worked for next to no pay," according to one biographical sketch. Soon he became assistant to his father in the management of the factory, and he was entrusted with the company's secret glass formulas and given supervision over mixing.[33]

Growth of Electricity and Growing Pains

The company that Amory Jr.'s sons joined was growing. In 1886, electric lights were installed at the works, and by 1888, it included two more furnaces with 104-foot chimneys. The capacity was needed to cope with the growing demand for lightbulbs, which was fueled by the success of Edison and other companies in building electrical lighting systems. By mid-1886, Edison had installed fifty-six central city-wide power stations with a combined capacity of 150,000 lamps. A year and a half later, the number of stations had climbed to 121. George Westinghouse entered the field in 1886 with an alternating-current system. His sales rose from $180,000 in 1886 to $4.7 million in 1890. And Thomson-Houston continued to build systems all over the country, including one in Corning, where the erection of light poles started on March 18, 1890.[34]

For several weeks in the summer, the Glass Works and other glass companies would shut down. But in the early and middle 1880s, Corning continued to make glass bulbs during the summer months and stockpile them. By the late 1880s lightbulbs accounted for more than 50 percent of the works' production volume, with railroad orders accounting for 17 percent and other specialty glass products accounting for the rest. In 1889, electric lamp products accounted for 76 percent of output, up from 48 percent in 1886. While numbers are unavailable for Corning from this period, the Edison Lamp Company estimated that it produced around 4,000 bulbs a day in 1888, compared with the 11,000 manufactured by all other companies. The price of the completed lamps was falling, however. In 1880, it cost Edison $1.21 to produce each lamp. By 1883 the cost fell to $.30 and would fall to $.22 in 1890. Edison's growing companies were reorganized in 1889 by financier Henry Villard, who created Edison General Electric Company, capitalized at $12 million.[35]

Even as the bulb business grew, it remained vulnerable to existing and potential competitors. The firms that actually produced the finished bulbs could always choose to make their own glass blanks instead of buying them from Corning or other glass companies. Apparently George Westinghouse was considering doing just that—a prospect that alarmed the Houghtons. "My idea is to meet W. with you and discuss the matter of glass manfr. with him, making him understand he is undertaking a job that is likely to fail. He is already two thirds persuaded and the influences are all against the enterprise," Charles Houghton wrote to his brother from New York on July 12, 1889. He saw Westinghouse's gambit as a negotiating plea. "Agree on a cost that will bear criticism and yet leave us a good margin. Then we will try to get him to agree for a long term."

Apparently, however, Charles's personal charm failed to impress West-inghouse, for in November 1889, the brothers were still concerned. "If W. starts a concern I predict that Edison will for he has always been in favor of it," Charles wrote. Westinghouse also seemed to express some concern that Corning's works weren't large enough to meet the current demand and that it was losing business as a result. "If our money had gone into pot arches and furnaces...it would have been worth in the present crisis many times the value of what we have," he wrote. "We would have run everything all summer and had a stock of goods and experienced help to carry us along now." The brothers decided to expand the capacity two days later. "Wouldn't it be a good idea to construct #6 fur[nace]...?" Charles wrote Amory. By 1890, Corning Glass Works sported eight chimneys, and the blowing room was extended fifty-four feet, making its total length 356 feet.[36]

Meanwhile, in 1890, the glass industry was in the midst of yet another transition. The center of gravity of the industry continued to shift farther west, with a new center emerging on the shores of Lake Erie in western Ohio. New England Glass, founded in Cambridge back in 1819, began to face increasingly serious problems in the 1870s and 1880s. A strike shut down the company in 1877, and it faced serious competitive disadvantages, since the fuel that it used came from a great distance. By contrast, factories in Pennsylvania and Ohio could tap into nearby energy sources, which were much cheaper. The price of natural gas, a newly discovered and utilized fuel, fell from $2.75 per thousand cubic feet in 1878, to $2.25 per in 1883, to $1.25 in 1888. "This one factor more than any other figured largely in the causes that finally led the company to abandon the industry in Cambridge," historian Lura Woodside Watkins wrote.[37]

When the New England Glass Company was put up for sale in 1877, gen-eral manager William L. Libbey bought it. And when he died in 1883, his son, E. D. Libbey, took over. Although he had success with "Amberina," a patented flint glass product into which he mixed a solution of gold, Libbey was losing money. In the face of a strike organized in 1888—in which work-ers in the West demanded that eastern glassmakers raise their wages to equal those paid in the West—Libbey shut down New England Glass and pulled up stakes. He settled upon Toledo, a city on the banks of Lake Erie, because it was close to power sources and because city businessmen came up with money to pay for factory land. There, in 1888, he formed the Libbey Glass Company, which would lead the way in automation and create a center of glass production to rival Corning and Pittsburgh.[38]

Corning Glass Works would also soon encounter serious labor difficulties. In the summer of 1889, as union activity began to heat up again, the Houghtons were monitoring the situation closely. "I had heard of the early Sunday meeting and shall hope for a full report when I return, having arranged...to attend in case such a meeting was called," Charles wrote Amory Jr. in July 1889. Officials of the American Flint Glass Workers Union (AFGWU), including vice president John Hinckley and organizer Barney Cahill, had come to town to meet with workers. "I suppose Hinkley will report to Smith fully and Smith will decide whether to pass us by or have some fun with our boys—probably pass," he predicted. And he recommended a stern reaction. "The only thing McGovern can digest is a club and kindness impedes his alimentation completely. If Barney Cahill should cheek it and walk into our place he should be led out by the ear," Charles wrote on July 31, 1889.[39]

Evidently union officials weren't scared off. According to a later account, the workers had several complaints. Wages were stuck at between $1.25 and $2.20 a day, and skilled workers received raises for neither seniority nor higher skill levels. Workers who had asked for time off to attend a funeral for a coworker were denied permission. And appeals to Amory Houghton Jr. were largely ignored. Although most of the older workers weren't interested, "we managed to get about fourteen of the young men together and organized a local," AFGWU vice president John Hinckley reported to the AFGWU convention in 1890. On December 31, the AFGWU Corning Local 108 called a strike. Out of 780 men, 135 bulb blowers and assistants threw down their tools and walked out. From the company's perspective, the timing was awful. Demand for bulbs was at an all-time high. "Not only did it badly disorganize production, but, what was far worse, it started a period of bitterness and disorder which finally spread to the city itself."[40]

Both local papers supported the company, which offered to reinstate people who would return within three weeks. Many, including Yank Hultzman (a later recipient of an 80-year service pin) and his brother Jake, returned to work. And the works began to run advertisements to recruit replacement workers. In town, union workers began to antagonize replacement workers and colleagues who crossed the line. Street brawls were common. "Even the local police force seems not to have been able to keep order, and things went from bad to worse."[41]

The AFGWU offered relief payments and helped workers leave Corning to find work elsewhere. Some did so without the knowledge of their parents. In late January, teenager John Higgins caught a train for Findlay, Ohio, where he hoped to find a steady job with a better employer. "It was the promise of higher wages that induced me to go out there," he later said. With the help of the union, which paid his train fare, he found work as a gatherer at a glass factory in Findlay at $2.50 a day. But the boy's irate father, Michael Higgins, went to see a union official named Hollingsworth, who told him where his son had gone. He then tracked his son down in Ohio and dragged him back home.[42]

With workers like John Higgins returning to work and an adequate supply of replacement workers, the strike didn't have the intended effect. Not everything was running smoothly, however. "Now, for the usual tale of woe," Charles wrote to Amory Jr. from New York on June 10, 1890. "Aikman says he ordered two months since 6 inch ruby fresnels and has never heard from them again that Porter and he have been borrowing from each others stock because they could not get orders filled at Corning and when both were out of goods they lost the bus—sending customers away. That their spring trade has been very poor because we paid no attention to their orders and they have suffered serious damage. They propose to hunt up competition for us and not depend upon us alone in future."[43]

In the summer of 1891, when John Finnigan, a correspondent for the *Elmira Telegram*, visited the works and received a tour from Amory Houghton Jr., the striking workers were not missed. "Their places have been filled with other workmen, and the company is now every day in receipt of applications from striking employees who want to return to work."

Finnegan's tour of the works provides a detailed view of the company's operations. Five hundred people worked at the sprawling complex, which, as a 1891 company document showed, represented an investment of $99,230, excluding machinery.

Embarking on their tour, Finnigan and Amory Houghton Jr. first walked through a long low wooden building that stood across the tracks—a storehouse for swale grass, used in packing. Then they entered a two-hundred-foot-long melting building, where "several bare-footed men were industriously trodding upon masses of raw, soft clay, packed in wooden bins" to get the air particles out. After hastening through the boiler and engine room, the coal shed and mold room, they entered the factory's center—the blowing room, 450 feet long and 65 feet wide. "Four hundred men are toiling perspiringly over red hot glass and around eight fiercely blazing furnaces kept continually at a temperature of 3,000 degrees Farenheit." He also went through tube sheds, where glass was drawn in hollow tubes, 100 feet long.[44]

The cash book from the late 1880s and early 1890s shows a healthy and thriving concern. In 1889, Corning spent about $6,500 every two weeks on its payroll. Orders and cash came in regularly from companies like Edison and went out just as regularly to members of the Houghton family. In January 1890, for example, Thomson-Houston paid more than $20,000 for orders. On May 28, 1890, there was an $11,000 payment to Amory Houghton Jr.[45]

Amory Houghton Jr. plowed the cash into safe investments, which he documented in a precise and meticulous hand in a large ledger. It began in 1885, counting assets of $240,617. These include either a loan to or his stake in Corning Glass Works, $14,909; $13,382 in an account with Brewster Cobb & Estabrook in Boston; $15,000 in City of Toledo bonds; and $17,487 owed to him by his brother Alfred. Total assets as of July 1, 1885 were $334,818. Over the years, he would invest his money in municipal bonds. By July 1, 1889, he had total assets of $607,863. By July 1, 1892, his assets topped $1 million. He also purchased interests in some mines, listing a stake in the Butler Mine Company in 1894 at $109,735. By that time, his assets had grown to 260 different items, and he was buying municipal bonds in chunks of $50,000. He was by any standard a very wealthy man, and a prominent figure about town. Young Thomas J. Watson Sr. of Painted Post drew inspiration from seeing Amory Houghton Jr. traveling about the county in a grand horse-drawn carriage and vowed to live as well himself. Decades later, as head of International Business Machines, Watson would realize his goal.[46]

The spring of 1891 was a time of joy for the Houghtons. On June 25, 1891, Alanson married Addie Wellington, with his brother Arthur serving as best man and several other Glass Works executives on hand as guests. After the wedding reception at the bride's parents' house, the newlyweds left on a Delaware, Lackawanna, and Western train for a month's honeymoon. Upon their return, they took up residence in a new house on Pine St. that Amory Jr. built for them.[47]

In that summer of 1891, however, tragedy struck. About fifty of the striking glass workers who left town to find work found employment at a glass works at Findlay, Ohio. In early July, when the Findlay plant shut for its summer break, forty-four of the workers chartered a railcar to return to Corning. The car was attached to the back of an Erie passenger train that stopped at the crossing of the Erie Railroad with the Cleveland & Pittsburgh in Ravenna, Ohio. At 2:30 A.M., a fifty-car freight train carrying meat east plowed into the back of the train. The wooden car burst into flames, and by the time the smoke cleared on the morning of July 3, seventeen of the forty-four passengers were dead, with thirteen burned beyond recognition.[48]

Seizing on the emotions sparked by the train wreck, the AFGWU on July 23, 1891, announced it would hold a convention in Corning the following year and erect a monument to the workers. And, according to the *Corning Journal*, they announced plans to raise funds and build their own plant to compete with Corning. The prospect never materialized, but in July 1892, a raucous union convention convened in Corning at a building called the Wigwam. To undercut this activity, local businessmen persuaded the Erie to cancel the lease of the property on which the Wigwam stood on the excuse that it was needed for a new freight house. A week after the convention started, the meetings were abandoned, largely ending the union's drive in Corning. The following year, on September 16, 1893, a monument was placed in St. Mary's Cemetery. The black slab listed the names of the workers who had died in the fiery train crash. Beyond the personal toll it took, the strike would have a more far-reaching and unanticipated effect on Corning's bulb business.[49]

Corning Enters the Age of Big Business and Consolidation

The stakes of the bulb business were growing larger as the customers grew larger and more powerful. Between 1883 and 1892, Thomson-Houston's capitalization rose from $125,000 to $15 million, its profits from $93,000 to $1.5 million, and its payroll from 45 to 3,500. For its part, Edison General's growth continued so that by 1892, its facilities included a large machine works at Schenectady, a lamp factory at Harrison, New Jersey, and a plant in New York City. Incandescent lighting caught on, with the number of lamps in use growing from 250,000 in 1885 to 3 million in 1890. But the growth of the electrical industry, as well as the growing sophistication and size of its competitors, would pose a threat to the Corning Glass Works. Not for the last time, the company would face the threat of losing its core business to a competitor or of having its powerful customers decide to try to make the products themselves.[50]

Spurred by the desire for greater operating efficiencies, growing professional management, concerns over excess capacity and the force of bankers like J. P. Morgan, industrial leaders began to consolidate into larger corporations and trusts in the early 1890s. One of the factors driving such combinations was the control of patents. With technology and processes so crucial to competitive advantage, firms with rival or competing patent claims would often pool their interests in an effort to forestall competition and obviate litigation. Since Edison General owned Edison's crucial patents, along with several related to electric railways, while Thomson-Houston also possessed key lighting patents, the two firms decided to merge and form the General Electric Company. Engineered in part by Boston banker Henry L. Higginson, GE was formed on June 1, 1892, and capitalized at $50 million with 10,000 workers. Most of the top management came from Thomson-Houston, with Charles Coffin serving as president.[51]

In the 1890s, to meet soaring demand, glass companies also began to develop more effective ways of manufacturing bulbs. In the 1890s, Toledo became a locus of many innovations in a variety of areas of glassmaking— bottles, windows, tube drawing, and, most importantly, lightbulbs. During the Corning strike, representatives of the AFGWU approached E. D. Libbey in Toledo and suggested he start making bulbs for Edison. The union further offered to supply blowers. In 1891, Libbey began making bulbs in nearby Findlay, and his plant manager, Michael Owens, quickly began devising a means to make bulbs more efficiently. In 1894, he patented a semiautomatic bulb machine that would revolutionize the glass container industry. After gathering glass on the end of blowpipes, workers would place them upright on an arm of a circular rotating machine. The machine used compressed air to blow the glass in carbon-coated iron molds. Of course, it still required the labor of ten people to run smoothly—three gatherers, one man to place the pipes on the machine, and six boys to take the bulbs out of the molds. But since the process eliminated the need for skilled blowers, it both increased productivity and allowed glassmakers to save on labor costs. The machines were also adapted to making tumblers and lamp chimneys. To develop the technology, in 1895 Owens helped start the Toledo Glass Company, to which he assigned the patents.[52]

Short of merging, glass companies sought other means to rationalize competition. Often the leading firms in a given area would enter agreements to carve up the market among them. Such agreements, whose legality was at best questionable following the Sherman Antitrust Act of 1890, were often kept secret. Corning entered its first such agreement in the 1890s regarding railway signalware. "To control the market for these goods, the Houghtons entered a series of clandestine trust agreements with managers at the Macbeth-Evans Glass Co. and the Libbey Glass Co." As a result of the agreement, between 1895 and 1905, Corning would sell 76 percent of the lenses, while Libbey and MacBeth would sell 17 percent and 7 percent, respectively. In the same period, Corning sold 57 percent of lantern globes, while Libbey and MacBeth sold 20 and 23 percent, respectively.[53]

A more important set of agreements related to bulb production. The patents surrounding bulb production had become a source of dispute between Corning and Libbey. On September 27, 1894, Corning and Libbey reached an agreement to assign to a trustee all rights under their patents. The companies further agreed to provide data on sales of bulbs and tubing and to pay money equal to the excess of agreed-upon selling prices to the trustee. The Phoenix Glass Co., which owned some patents for glass molds and incandescent lamp bulbs, became a signatory to the agreement in October 1894.[54]

Meanwhile, other steps were taken to rationalize the market. With certain crucial Edison patents set to expire in 1894, GE entered into an agreement with its chief competitor, Westinghouse, and fifteen other producers that fixed prices and allotted a share of the business to each company. GE took 50 percent of sales and Westinghouse 15 percent, with the remainder split among the smaller companies.[55]

GE, in turn, moved to rationalize its relationships with the firms that supplied it with blanks. On September 28, 1895, it reached an agreement with Corning, Libbey, and the Phoenix Glass Company. Each was given a code name: Corning was "England," Libbey was "Canada," and Phoenix was "Vicksburg." For ten years, GE promised to buy bulbs from the three parties, with Corning and Libbey each receiving 40 percent of the volume, and Phoenix receiving the remaining 20 percent. In return, the glassmakers guaranteed prices to GE that were lower than those paid by other customers. GE's price for the standard P17 clear bulbs was $21 per 1,000. This set of agreements helped ensure stability among the competing companies and locked Corning into a leading role in bulbs for a decade. In the meantime, however, Corning would work to develop new products and technology.[56]

Corning: Growing Businesses in a Growing Town

The 1890s saw the rise of a third generation of Corning glass cutters—entrepreneurial craftsmen who invested their savings, sought financial backers, and set up shops in town. After all, Corning was a nonunion town with plenty of skilled craftsmen. Between 1894 and 1896, three glass companies were founded. Frank Wilson, founder of Frank Wilson & Sons, had cut glass for Hawkes. So had Thomas Taylor Hunt, who in 1895 set up Hunt & Sullivan, with the backing of local businessman Daniel Sullivan. Oliver Egginton, born in 1822 in England, had come to Corning in 1873. He had managed the Hawkes works and ultimately built a factory at 5th and State Street. In the late 1890s, these firms flourished. By 1898, Egginton had fifty-two employees. The growth was fueled by an influx of skilled glassworkers, largely from Bohemia and England. In addition, women began to enter the workforce as well; virtually every shop employed at least some female workers. In 1896, there were 181 cutters and four engravers in the town directory. By 1895, Corning was so identified with glass that it was being referred to in the *Corning Daily Journal* as "Corning–the Crystal City—The Birth Place of some of the Largest Enterprises on the Face of the Earth."[57]

The new glass-cutting shops weren't the only new additions to the town's landscape. In 1892, the Episcopalian congregation, to which the Houghtons, Hawkes, and Hoares all belonged, purchased property at the corner of Cedar and First Streets for $60,000. The cornerstone of the large, Gothic sandstone church was laid in November 1893, and construction was completed on February 3, 1895. With a seating capacity of about 800, the newly completed Christ Church was one of the largest structures in town.

The Houghton family's mark was evident on the church, where Amory Jr. served on the vestry for thirty-four years. The narthex running across the front consisted of tile made and donated by the Corning Glass Works. Inside, the family donated a Louis Comfort Tiffany-designed stained glass window depicting the resurrection. And, as a local newspaper noted, "the organ will be presided over by Mrs. Amory Houghton, Jr., who is a talented musician."[58]

Such buildings—the growth of local industry and of the town—were the pride of locals who had left town for larger cities. Among them was Mark "Brick" Pomeroy, a journalist and an editor who got his start in Corning and went on to a prominent career in New York City. In 1895, he wrote a letter to the *Corning Journal* that stands as a wonderful example of the florid, polemical style popular among Victorian journalists.

> Gracious! How Corning is growing. In 1850 when I landed in your then quiet village, just after the biggest fire the place has ever had to mark its history, there was no Street or Electric Railway, nor thought of one....Then, Monkey Run was a tearer, and the flats across the river were the Delectable land where lovers wandered Sundays in the dandelion time. Then Knoxville and Painted Post were foreign corporations, and Centreville and Suckerville were far, far away. Now look at Corning! No pent-up Utica nor sleepy Elmira contracts her powers. For miles in different directions, from hill top to valley, Corning is a city; and the numerous outlying villages are the bumpers that keep the outer world from hurting her expanding sides...She

has her head in the lap of Hornellsville, her left shoulder resting on Bath, her right feeling for a lodging place in Caton, and her heels playing Devil's Dream on the stomach of Elmira, as she is settling down to the work of Corningizing the entire country for miles in either direction.[59]

A Third Generation of Corning Management

Throughout the 1890s, even as Amory Houghton Jr.'s sons began to take on greater responsibilty, the Houghton brothers maintained their partnership. Amory Jr. was still the senior and decisive executive. Charles was genial and approachable, popular among workers and customers. But his ebullience masked anxiety. Charles disliked traveling and feared riding in horse-drawn carriages and eating food prepared by others. In the 1880s and 1890s, he suffered a series of personal setbacks. In 1888, his seven-year-old daughter, Florence, died of typhoid. Four years later, both his sister Annie and his brother, Alfred, passed away. (Alfred plainly suffered from what would now be called depression and shot himself.) One day in late March 1897, Charles left his office at the works in the morning and didn't return. The next morning, searchers found his body in a sand shed at the Glass Works. Apparently, he had committed suicide.

Upon Charles's death, Alanson took over responsibility for sales. Although Alanson possessed some of Charles's gifts for personal relationships, he had a temperament that differed significantly from that of either his father or uncle. Scholarly, gentlemanly, and worldly, Alanson, though raised in the nineteenth century, was a man of the twentieth century. "He was particularly skillful and clearheaded in his handling of important negotiations on which depended the stability of the Company's most vital products," as Hollister wrote. "Because of his contacts, and his education, he was more receptive to increasing development in broad field of scientific research."[60]

Meanwhile, Arthur A. Houghton was making his place in the company too. Anna Haar, who started wrapping at the works at the age of fourteen in 1902, compared the two brothers. "Arthur was a little more gruff than Mr. A.B." Although he wasn't as educated as Alanson, "Father was far from

being an uneducated person," his son Arthur Jr. recalled. "He was the perfect example of a self-educated man. His knowledge was astonishingly
broad and deep. His particular love was that of the English language."
Standing five feet ten inches, sporting a well-clipped mustache, and wearing
suits from Wetzel in New York, he was Mr. Inside to Alanson's Mr. Outside.
"He was in the factory more....In the early days he knew every man and
boy in the factory by name and among them found many congenial spirits."
Arthur would also go out fishing with one or two of the men when the season opened.[61]

As they assumed more responsibility, the brothers began to replicate the
relationship of the second-generation Houghtons. The two brothers would
go for walks together in the country, to talk over the business. While he was
on the road making sales calls, collecting orders, gaining feedback, and generally hob-nobbing with clients, Alanson would write his brother frequently. "Railroad business is in fine shape," he wrote on October 16, 1897.
"Hanolan will forward me on here an order for 24 cases of globes or Willets
also will give an order Monday." When Willets, the long-time head of the
Adams Westlake Company, was getting married, Alanson asked Arthur to
have Hawkes make a an ice-cream set with a salad bowl, fork and spoon,
and so on. "What I have in mind is something elegant, and yet not enough
to seem as if I were overdoing the matter."

While taking orders, Alanson had to be sure not to violate the agreements. As he sent in an order from Hanolan for a carload of flint globes on
October 17, 1897, he noted that the order included no colored globes and
recommended they be sent to Libbey and MacBeth, which had been lagging
behind in their production quotas. But there were other competitors out
there. On December 11, 1897, he reported from Chicago that the Baltimore
and Ohio were using Sneath lenses. "This wouldn't have happened if I had
gone down there sooner," he said.[62]

Alanson and Arthur Houghton differed from their father and uncle in an
important manner. Both were more well-traveled and more forward looking. Children of the electrical and industrial age, they were conversant with
and comfortable with the sweeping changes that were transforming industry at home and abroad. Consequently, the brothers were increasingly pre-
occupied with innovation. The ultimately revolutionary developments

taking place in Toledo threatened to pass Corning by. Throughout the 1890s, it made few, if any, serious efforts, to automate its processes, although it was still trying to expand its basic operations. In 1896, the factory was enlarged with the addition of two more furnaces. While on the road, however, Alanson continually gathered intelligence on the machines that their rivals and partners were making. And he was aware of the success of Libbey's machine. "Mac [George MacBeth] says the Rochester people paid Libbey $100,000 for the right to use his machine in their line. Whew! What is your tube machine worth?" he wrote in 1897.[63]

By "your tube machine" Arthur was referring to Corning's first real effort to automate production. In the late nineteenth century, craftsmen the world over made tubing by drawing out an oblong blank into tubing horizontally, parallel to the floor. As it was being elongated, workers would rotate the blank. But this resulted in spiraling—an intolerable defect for some precise applications such as thermometer tubes.

In 1896, Arthur Houghton, assisted by Charles Githler, one of the most experienced tube makers in the plant, began to work on a new method of drawing thermometer tube. Taking inspiration from processes he had seen on a trip to England, Arthur reasoned that drawing the tube *vertically* would allow them to avoid the fatal twisting. Together, they built a sixty-foot-high tube tower adjacent to the A Factory furnaces. Inside the tower, they rigged a movable frame that would hold the blank, which could be raised or lowered with a rope and pulley. By drawing the blank vertically, they eliminated the negative effects of twisting. This technique proved successful, resulting in improved quality and greater yield. Arthur received a patent for the process on November 16, 1897. And the experiments were so successful that the glass works in 1913 built a 187-foot tubing tower. This tower, upon which the company later stenciled the image of Little Joe, the iconic lightbulb blower, became an addition to the city's modest but distinctive skyline. Moreover, it stood as a symbol of the company's commitment to developing specialty glass products through the steady application of scientific observation to craft.[64]

Around the turn of the century, the Houghton's work, social, and family lives were contained in a an area bounded by several city blocks. Amory Jr. and Ellen Houghton continued to live in the large brick house at Third Street and Pine Street that they had bought back in the 1870s, filled with cut glass. Clustered around the streets on the slope above the Glass Works, other members of the family began to raise a fourth generation of Houghtons in Corning. "Your grandson Amory arrived this morning both Adelaide and boy doing finely," Alanson wrote to his father on July 27, 1899.[65]

Earlier that year, on April 19, 1899, at the First Presbyterian Church in Rutherford, New Jersey, Arthur A. Houghton married Mabel Hollister. Her family had lived on Remsen Street in Brooklyn, New York, near where the Houghtons had lived previously. They sailed to England on their honeymoon on a ship whose passengers included Andrew Carnegie, a prodigy pianist named Melanie Schram, and a half dozen opera singers, including Silli Lehman Kalisch. On their trip, they bought a grandfather clock that they installed in the main hall of their house at 22 W. 3rd Street, which Amory Jr. built for them at a cost of $37,924. Every day, Arthur would walk up the hill from the Glass Works at noon for lunch, have a nap, and then return to work. Mabel Hollister's parents moved to Corning, where they lived in a small house on the north side of East Fifth Street.[66]

The Use of Science at the Dawn of a New Century

At the turn of the century, Corning, the Glass Works, and the other enterprises it housed, were thriving and growing along with the Houghton family. The United States had experienced booming industrial growth since the time Amory Houghton Sr. loaded up his belongings and his factory onto canal barges in 1868. Between 1869 and 1901, the U.S. gross national product soared from $9.1 to $37.1 billion, while per capita income tripled. The nation's population rose from 40 million in 1870 to 76 million in 1900, and in the same period, Corning's population grew from about 7,000 to 11,000. More Americans were concentrated in cities. In 1870, 10 percent of the population lived in fourteen cities having over 100,000 residents. By 1890 that percentage had doubled, and the number of cities of that size had nearly tripled. The number of railroad tracks had risen from 75,000 miles in 1875 to 200,000 in 1900. The glass industry grew along with the rest of the economy. By 1899, 391 pot furnaces and 192 continuous tank furnaces were in operation in the United States. Sales at the Corning Glass Works had risen steadily "until in 1902 they were nearly ten times as great as they were in 1875." That year, some 18 million incandescent lamps were in use.[67]

Corning Glass Works had already participated in some of the large trends sweeping business and society—battles with organized labor, a new era of big business in which larger firms reached agreements to rationalize competition and pool patents, and automation. In the first decade of the twentieth century, Corning would lead the way in another larger economic trend: the growth of scientific and industrial research.

In the decades after the Civil War, a number of companies began to hire employees with scientific training to design products and installations, analyze materials, and rationalize procedures. These disciplines became even more important in the early twentieth century. In 1890, Congress passed the Sherman Antitrust Act. As the government began to enforce it seriously after 1900, agreements such as those that had guaranteed Corning market share in lightbulbs would be deemed illegal and terminated. Firms that were forced to compete with one another more directly therefore sought other means for competitive advantage. One of the means for gaining such advantage was through proprietary, company-owned scientific research and development.

Around the turn of the century, large U.S. companies took steps to institutionalize such efforts. General Electric, for example, employed engineers in laboratories at the factories, including the standardizing laboratory at Schenectady, which was started in 1896. In the fall of 1900, Charles Proteus Steinmetz, GE's chief consulting engineer, suggested creating a company-owned research lab. To head it, the company hired MIT faculty member Willis Whitney, who had studied chemistry at MIT and went to Germany for postgraduate work at Leipzig. Whitney hired four scientists from MIT and they set to work on electric lighting. By 1904, the laboratory had a budget of $60,000 and employed forty people. By 1908 the lab would help create the rugged, high-efficiency filaments that ensured GE's domination of the market for years to come.[68]

Although it was the product of an independent evolution, GE's lab, as Leonard Reich put it, "brought to America a type of research institution pioneered by the German chemical and pharmaceutical industries several decades before." It was set apart from the production facilities, staffed by people trained in science and advanced engineering, and somewhat insulated from immediate demands but responsive to firm's long-term needs. It was this model that other firms, including Corning, would follow and use to great advantage in the coming decades.[69]

Even before its laboratory gained critical mass, GE was a center of power in its industry. It provided about half of the orders for the 50 million lightbulbs made by the three main bulb makers between 1900 and 1902. By 1900, 23 million lightbulbs were sold in the United States, and the business accounted for 40 percent of Corning's $822,100 in total sales.

In August 1901, Corning and GE extended their contract for three years, guaranteeing GE a price of $18 per thousand for the standard sixteen candlepower bulbs, while other companies would pay $21 per thousand. The agreement also gave GE the right to order bulbs for sale in foreign markets from the Fostoria Bulb and Bottle Company, of Fostoria, Ohio, which was a subsidiary of National Electric Lamp Company, if the signatory companies weren't willing to make them at the price GE wanted. In return, Phoenix, Corning, and Libbey agreed not to make incandescent lamps in the United States. The three parties agreed that Fostoria could make 1.5 million bulbs annually, plus half of all production above 32 million annually—until it reached 15 percent of the total production of all four companies.[70]

Even as it entered new agreements to hold its share of the bulb market, Corning began investing in research to create new and improved proprietary products. After all, it could not take any of its markets for granted. As railroads continued to grow in size and complexity, they demanded better lenses that would maintain consistent colors and that wouldn't crack when exposed to the elements. Although Corning had a long and impressive list of clients, it felt its products weren't all they could be. As Alanson told Arthur in early 1899, "we are in a bad mess," for "instead of getting better, our lenses get worse."[71]

Of particular concern were the company's red ruby lenses, which were losing out to those made by Nicholas Kopp of Swissvale, Pennsylvania. To produce the lenses, Corning employed a flashing technique, which involved pressing a lens, coating it with copper ruby glass, and heat-treating it to bring out the color. Since the color was unreliable and inconsistent, Charles

Houghton had started working on an improvement in the 1890s. After Charles died, Arthur Houghton began to experiment with glasses containing selenium and cadmium. Since these mixes posed complex chemical problems, Arthur sought the advice of Joseph A. Deghuee, a Columbia Ph.D. and staff member of the New York City Health Department who consulted part-time. By shipping samples and formulas back and forth, they developed a lead glass containing selenium. After pressing the lenses, they heated them in small kilns to bring out the color. The process, perfected in 1900, was called "cerise," and it had better range and uniformity.[72]

Meantime, a separate set of issues surrounding color and railroad signals soon occupied the Houghtons and the outside scientists with whom they worked. Throughout the nineteenth century, each railroad had its own color system, employing various shades of white, green, red, blue, and purple to tell of conditions ahead. Corning's glassmakers were thus forced to produce some thirty-two different shades of green, for example.[73]

Even the most basic color—white, which was often used as an all-clear signal—was a source of problems. White lights were becoming very common due to electrification. In 1898, an engineer on the New York, New Haven, and Hartford railroad, known as the Old Colony, was guiding the train through Whittenton Junction, Massachusetts. He mistook the white lantern on a highway crossing for a clear signal and drove the train into another, causing a severe accident. As one observer noted, "The number of deaths or injuries among railroad employees caused by faulty appliances had reached critical dimensions by the 1890s." And the number would continue to grow so that in 1904, 10,017 people were killed and 83,871 were injured in railroad accidents.[74]

Like so many other industries in this period, the railroads were moving toward standardization. Engineers in the 1890s set up groups to coordinate standards for measurement and terminology in all fields. And in 1895, the railroad industry founded the Railway Signaling Club, which later became the Railway Signal Association. It was primarily concerned with researching new products, creating specifications, and working with manufacturers to design standards.

Alanson Houghton began to think about developing standardized railway signal colors after attending a November 16, 1899, meeting of the New

York Railroad Club. There, he heard Yale University professor Edward Wheeler Scripture give a paper on color blindness. Scripture was looking for ways to find methods to measure acuteness of vision and color perception, and he had crafted a color sense tester that railroads were using to devise new color schemes. Scripture complained that his task was made more difficult by the fact that the signal glasses made by different manufacturers weren't uniform.[75]

In October 1902, Alanson retained one of Scripture's graduate students, William Churchill, to conduct a two-year study of signal color and glasses at Yale. In the summer of 1903, Churchill traveled to Europe for Corning to study glassmaking techniques and retrieve samples. Eventually, in July 1904, Churchill moved to Corning, where he assumed the directorship of the Glass Works' newly established optical lab—a fancy name for a one-man department. Churchill, an alumnus of the University of Leipzig, represented a new type of hire for the company. Comfortable in the laboratory and the club dining room, he was a scientist well versed in the art of sales. With his top hat and Yankee demeanor, he cut an elegant figure. Once settled in Corning, Churchill reported mostly to Arthur Houghton and took responsibility for a wide variety of tasks. He was charged with improving production methods, creating glasses that matched color standards, and upgrading the physical characteristics of signal lenses. His arrival, and the use of scientists in general, was not a subject of universal agreement among the company's management. According to family lore, Amory Houghton Jr., in particular, was skeptical about the utility of such new hires. An essentially conservative man, the self-taught chemist was skeptical that professionally trained scientists unschooled in the craft of glassmaking could add value. "Grandfather felt that only glassmakers could make glass. Father and uncle Alan thought scientists could help,"[76] Author Houghton Jr. wrote.

When Churchill arrived at the works, it was far from a scientific enterprise. Craftspeople still dictated the pace at the factory, much as they had thirty years before. But to make standardized products more efficiently, Churchill would have to change manufacturing processes and bring more efficiency to the factory floor. In 1904, Churchill helped roll out the production of a series of improved lenses for long-time kerosene burners. Pleased with his work, the Houghtons signed Churchill to a five-year contract in

October 1905, paying him $2,750 a year for the first three years and $3,000 for the next two years.[77]

Churchill wasn't the only scientist laboring for Corning. Joseph Deghuee, the New York–based chemist whom the Houghtons had engaged to do research on "cerise," remained on the company payroll for several years. Typically, Corning would send him samples for examination. On March 20, 1903, Dughuee wrote to Arthur Houghton, "Enclosed please find certificate of analysis of the piece of red glass sent to me. You will see by the results that it is practically a zinc soda glass...I have not as yet quite satisfied myself in regard to the cause of the red color but all indications at present point strongly to selenium." A few days later, he submitted a $50 invoice for the work. The chemist would also do work of a personal nature. "You are perfectly safe in using the water for all household purposes," he wrote to Arthur A. Houghton in 1907, after having subjected it to a battery of tests. The work of Deghuee, Churchill, and the others would bear fruit in the coming years.[78]

The Crystal City's Growing Cast of Characters: Frederick Carder

Corning was blessed with an influx of scientific and glassmaking talent and skill in the first decade of the twentieth century. Between 1900 and 1905, sixteen new glass firms sprang up in Corning, "like mushrooms in a night," as Hawkes put it, so that the 1905 directory listed 490 glass cutters in a population of 13,500. In 1901, James O. Sebring, a lawyer who had come to town in 1891, opened the Corning Cut Glass Company in Riverside. The following year, Corning Glass Works sued Sebring over his use of the name. The suit dragged on until 1911, when Sebring ultimately won. Glass engraving was a growing business too. Joseph Haslebauer, a Bohemian immigrant who came to Corning in the early 1870s to work for Hoare, left Hawkes in 1904 with H. P. Sinclaire, who set up his own shop. Several of Haslebauer's countrymen, many from the town of Meisterdorf, arrived in Corning in the following years.[79]

The most important addition to the growing roster of glass cutters came from England. Frederick Carder was born on September 18, 1863, in

Staffordshire, England. As a boy, he went to work in his father's pottery factory. At nights he studied art, as well as chemistry, electricity, and metallurgy. In 1880, after seeing the Portland Vase, he began his career at Stevens & Williams, which made art glass. Carder also bought a small furnace and started "to test every known and unknown material that I could get my hands on." He made goblets, molds, and original glass designs in a variety of colors, and he was an early practitioner of the cameo technique.

A spirited young man—he climbed the Eiffel Tower the year it was completed—Carder developed into a prize-winning designer. After he started an arts school, the South Staffordshire county council in 1902 sent him to Europe to report on glassmaking in Germany and Austria. The council found the report so valuable that it asked him to undertake a similar mission to the United States. It proved a fateful assignment. Leaving Liverpool in February 1903, Carder journeyed to New York, Pittsburgh (where he met Andrew Mellon), Washington, D.C., and finally, Corning, New York. This last destination necessitated an arduous journey through "the dreary brown landscape" that included a three-hour layover in Elmira. There, he fell into conversation with an "old chap with white hair," who rode from Elmira to Corning with him. It was Mark Twain, on his way to lecture in Rochester.[80]

Arriving in Corning in March 1903, Carder met Alanson Houghton at the Corning Glass Works, which he called "Smokestack University." Then he met with T. G. Hawkes, to whom Carder had already sold some blanks. Hawkes had a proposition for the visitor. "Mr. T.G. Hawkes was anxious to make their own glass instead of buying from others. We had quite a session, and I was persuaded to come back to the U.S. and start a factory in Corning, New York," he recalled. According to historian Jane Spillman, however, it wasn't the first contact between Carder and the Hawkes firm. "In the spring of 1902, Samuel Hawkes interrupted a trip to England to visit Frederick Carder and ask him to manage a new glassworks in Corning," she wrote. "Only when he reached Corning, ostensibly on a fact finding trip for his County Council, was the new company announced." In any case, Hawkes and Carder filed papers for the newly created Steuben Cut Glass Company on March 9, 1903, with Hawkes as president and majority stockholder and Carder as minority stockholder. Rather than name their glass concern after its hometown, Carder and Hawkes decided to name it after their home county, Steuben—after revolutionary war hero Baron Von Steuben.[81]

Reluctant to leave home, Carder was lured in part by what he had found in Corning. "I found that the Americans were taking all the best mechanical devices which the Contintent produces," he told a British newspaper before leaving. Moreover, he was moving to a genuine Crystal City, with 400 glassmakers in one factory, 200 in another, and 80 in a third, "so that in this city alone are engaged many more cutters than in the whole of the Stourbridge district." Of course, all things being equal, Carder would have preferred to stay in England, which, contrasted with the "wild rugged character" of upstate New York, seemed to him "like a well laid-out garden."[82]

Carder returned to Corning for good in July 1903. He and Hawkes converted the Payne Foundry Building and adjacent space on West Erie Avenue into a factory with a ten-pot furnace that began producing crystal blanks in October 1903. Carder later boasted that in the first year of operation, he "bought the materials, built the glass furnace, and retired 40 per cent of the $50,000 indebtedness." It wasn't all smooth sailing, though. While in England Carder had arranged for fifteen English glassworkers to come along with him. But in October 1903 the workers were detained in Montreal because the union objected that they violated the Alien Contract Labor Law. Carder argued that the glass he was going to make couldn't be made by Americans. On December 23, 1903, the U.S. Department of Commerce and Labor ruled that Carder had failed to try to find labor in the United States and deported the men. In Corning, Carder hired a Swedish glassblower named Henning Overstrom, who had worked at Dorflinger's in White Mills, Pennsylvania. Overstrom got in touch with other Swedes and brought them to Corning.[83]

Despite the rocky start, Steuben quickly became a success, producing luxury crystal with brilliant colors. Carder invented Gold Aurene—a gold glass—in 1904 and succeeded with Blue Aurene, which employed cobalt, the following year. In 1905, Steuben began to make Verre de Soie, an iridescent glass with greenish and bluish tints. His designs proved popular, and Steuben pieces sold briskly through department stores like Altman's in New York, Marshall Field's in Chicago, and Gump's in San Francisco. Between 1903 and 1932, the company would turn out some 7,000 varieties of vases, bowls, goblets, candlesticks, and other items. And Carder, with his high forehead, hair swept back in a part, slightly crooked nose, and bushy moustache, would become a fixture in town. He bought a house at 249 Pine Street, down the street from Amory Jr., where he would live for nearly sixty years.[84]

Investments in Infrastructure and Technology

Corning Glass Works was growing and investing in new infrastructure to become more self-sufficient. In 1903, it built a thousand-ton coal shed near the Chemung River. It also installed a self-contained electrical system. To handle the increased demand of the lightbulb business, the company in 1904 built a new factory—B Factory—west of the main factory. This time, the blowing room floor was built on the second story to avoid the episodic ravages of the Chemung River. The factory's most distinctive features were its three sixteen-pot furnaces that relied on natural gas rather than coal.[85]

Once up and running, the B Factory furnaces posed a problem. For decades, operators had judged the intensity of the fires from the roar of the fire or by the feel of heat. But the gas furnaces were silent and their heat fluctuated greatly. This made it harder to gauge the temperature, which caused numerous production problems. Once again, in December 1904, the company turned to an outside expert: George Buell Hollister, a Yale graduate who had worked at the U.S. Geological Survey and was Arthur Houghton's brother-in-law. One of Hollister's colleagues at USGS was Arthur Day, who had received undergraduate and Ph.D. degrees at Yale, where he had taught physical geology. An expert on heat control and commercial melting, Day had developed an apparatus to help control the furnaces, which he provided to Corning. As a result of this quantum leap in the manufacturing process, Day was hired as a research consultant. "It is of interest to note that the Corning Glass Works was the first industry in the United States to adopt this type of temperature control for its furnaces."[86]

Day's other contribution was to spur the Glass Works toward new discoveries in the area of tougher glasses that could withstand great fluctuations in heat. Initially, Day sought to develop a hard glass that could be used for arc lamps used in street lights. (The stresses created by the hot carbon arc and changing weather conditions caused such globes to break frequently.) He had worked with quartz glass, which had a low coefficient of expansion (i.e., it was less affected by temperature changes). But quartz glass was tough to melt and handle because of its high silica content. Adding various oxides, he reasoned, could make it better. For an example, he looked to Germany, where Otto Schott and Ernst Abbe had started making systematic studies of glass in the 1880s. In the early 1890s, Schott discovered high temperature–resistant borosilicate glass, which had started to find use in inner arc globes for street lights in Europe. Ironically, the Houghtons were familiar with the crucial ingredient in borosilicate glass—borax—but had dismissed its value. Amory Houghton Jr.'s batch book contains his judgment on the chemical. "I do not think it of any use in the making of Flint Glass" he concluded.[87]

Drawing on the Germans' work, Day helped Corning develop high-temperature glasses from silica and boric oxides. While they turned out to have limited applications for street lights, the company quickly realized that such glasses could have an application for another set of longstanding customers, the railroads. In 1906, Churchill and Hollister began building on Day's hard glass research to create better lantern globes for railroad clients. By 1908 they succeeded in producing a lead borosilicate glass suitable for lantern glass. To test the globes, Corning scientists would heat the lamp frames and then plunge them into ice water.[88]

In April 1908, Alanson and Churchill went on the road to visit major railroad hubs to demonstrate the product. By August 1908, they had shown it in St. Paul and Chicago, and following a "whirlwind of acceptances," they planned trips to Altoona and Baltimore. By the fall of 1908, the Glass Works was making heat-resistant globes for stock in anticipation of large orders, and in early 1909 the firm would begin marketing these globes under the trade names CNX or Nonex, for Corning nonexpansion glass.[89]

At the same time, Corning's scientists were evangelizing for the new, improved color schemes. William Churchill gave papers to the Railway Signal Association in both 1905 and 1906, urging the association to adopt a signal system based on colors he made for Corning. His plea drew a great deal of attention from the industry. As Churchill later said, "Corning soon became the mecca of the railroad engineers." Between 1905 and 1908,

Churchill, who was as proficient in selling as he was in science, worked with RSA members to create ideal hues. In 1908, the RSA published the photometric specifications of Corning colors as its national standard. The same year, further cementing the progression from laboratory discovery to sales process, Churchill was named assistant sales manager for Corning. By 1910, many railroads had abandoned their unique color systems for Corning's RSA-sanctioned colors.[90]

In the wake of these improvements, sales of globes and lenses grew dramatically. In 1904, Corning sold $237,536 in globes and $82,425 in lenses. But as new products caught on, sales skyrocketed so that by 1907 Corning sold $406,343 in globes and $280,866 in lenses. Overall, the company's sales rose from $900,000 in 1904 to $1.275 million in 1906 and $1.8 million in 1907.[91]

Despite these hot new products, Corning's biggest business remained lightbulbs. For twenty years bulb sales had been increasing and "had become by far the most important single item of our sales, equaling in value the sales of all our other lines combined," Hollister wrote. In 1906, Corning sold $503,900 in bulbs, or 40 percent of its total sales. But a 1903 photograph of the factory lays out the problem the bulb business faced. It depicts three men—Alvin Wendel, David Wasson and Paul Wendel—one of 300 three-man hand shops, which worked ten hours a day and made 648 bulbs a day.[92]

Bulbs were a huge—and labor-intensive—business. Niles & Niles, a New York–based CPA firm that audited Corning in 1906 and 1907, found that Corning produced 19,735,894 SS#19 bulbs—its main bulb product—at a cost of $14.64 per thousand. The accounting broke down the costs as follows: $1.92 per thousand for mixing materials, $8.13 for direct labor, $2.25 for indirect labor, $1.61 for factory expenses, and $.73 for repairs and depreciation. In other words, 55 percent of the total cost of making the bulbs came from "direct labor."[93]

Corning's competitors, such as those in Ohio, were increasingly relying on machines to produce bulbs en masse. With the machines available for licensing, and with the exclusive arrangements with General Electric poised to expire, other companies could theoretically enter the field. Once again, the company's core business stood on the brink of extinction. Although Alanson and Arthur Houghton were very concerned about the competition posed by bulb-making machines, Amory Jr. was skeptical. "When his sons showed him some MacBeth lantern globes made on an Owens bottle machine, the elder Houghton scoffed, declaring that the youngsters had been hoodwinked—and that the chimneys were handmade."[94]

The attitude frustrated the younger generation, especially because Amory Jr. began to spend less time at the works. He suffered from gout and frequently found it difficult to move around. "He didn't come into the office every day," Anna Haar recalled. But he maintained his stern demeanor, which masked a sense of humor. As his grandson Arthur Jr. recalled, he didn't like it when people asked if they could borrow umbrellas. But he was happy to lend them because he had them stencilled in large letters, "Stolen from Amory Houghton, Jr."[95]

So convinced were Arthur and Alanson of the need to automate bulb production that they decided to support research into a new bulb-making machine and engaged Day in the effort. In late 1906, Day enlisted Benjamin D. Chamberlain, a mechanical technician in Day's Washington laboratory, to work on preliminary design, as well as Orin A. Hanford, a machine designer based in Rochester. They began to pursue the subject, but it would be three years before they could create experimental machines for trial. In 1909, Arthur and Alanson would use their own funds to create the Empire Machine Company, an entity to pursue further research on bulb-making machines.[96]

This venture, along with their sponsorhip of Day and Churchill, indicated the third generation's faith in innovation. In 1908, they persuaded their father to set up a laboratory devoted to chemical research. Day convinced a friend of his, Eugene Sullivan, to head it. Sullivan had attended the University of Michigan, received a Ph.D. from the University in Leipzig in 1899, and then returned to teach chemistry at his alma mater. As a staff chemist at the USGS, Sullivan had built up a great expertise in silicate chemistry.

After signing on with Corning in 1908, he quickly assumed several main responsibilities, which included heading up the mixing department. But he also needed a quiet space away from the factory floor where he could study glasses and devise new formulas. He set up shop in 1,200 square feet of space on the fourth floor of the factory building and hired an assistant, William C. Taylor, a graduate of the Massachusetts Institute of Technology.

From these humble and modest origins, Sullivan would supervise a laboratory that would spawn many generations of products.[97]

By 1908, the, Corning Glass Works was more than a successful industrial enterprise. Although it faced serious competitive issues, it had well-established positions in several large markets, proprietary products that were recognized as superior in the marketplace, and a growing wealth of employee talent. Amory Houghton Jr. had built the company from a bankrupt shambles into a healthy, well-capitalized firm that could deal on its own footing with massive corporations like General Electric and Westinghouse. By 1908, he and his sons had put into place the processes, infrastructure, personnel, and business practices that would stoke the fires of a third generation of products and leadership.

III

THIRD GENERATION

CHAPTER FOUR

Pyrex, the Ribbon Machine, and a Wider World, 1908–1928

AMORY HOUGHTON JR. spent the summer of 1909 in Robbinston, Maine, as he had for several years, and returned to Corning around September 1. Bedridden for a few weeks, he died at his home in early November, at the age of seventy-two, and was buried in the family plot at Hope Annex Cemetery. More than the four children and eight grandchildren he left behind, or the civic positions he held in the city and his church, or his multimillion-dollar estate, Amory Houghton Jr.'s true legacy was the Corning Glass Works, the struggling company he and his brother Charles had transformed into a leading competitor in the glass industry. At his death, the works maintained exclusive contracts with the largest customers in its two main lines of business—railroad glass and electric lighting products. The company had annual sales of $1.5 million and employed several hundred workers, making it six times bigger than the average American glassmaking firm. And it turned profits every year, having paid dividends consistently since 1880.[1]

Upon the death of Amory Jr., Alanson B. Houghton, his oldest son, was named president. Alanson's long-planned ascendance completed the transition that had been developing in recent years. Alanson and his younger brother Arthur were now in control—legally and managerially. Over the next twenty years, the two brothers would maintain a close working and personal relationship, despite the different paths their careers would take. In the early 1900s they bought land in South Dartmouth, Massachusetts, near Buzzard's Bay, on which they built adjacent summer homes. The compound, which they called "the Meadows," would serve as a retreat for family members for many years.

The smooth transition of power from the second generation of glass-making Houghtons to the third differed markedly from the more abrupt succession that had taken place in the early 1870s, when Amory Houghton Sr. left his thirty-three-year-old son in charge of a bankrupt company. Alanson and Arthur, both in their forties, took the helm assisted by an experienced crew of managers and scientists. With the help of recent and new arrivals like Eugene Sullivan, Arthur Day, and William Churchill, they would guide Corning to growth and prominence in an era of expanding horizons.

The small-town company would be forced to grapple with strong new forces in the coming years, for this was an era in which large enterprises grew in both scale and scope. The automobile and the plane evolved from curious inventions to commercial products and helped add dynamism to society. Powered by electricity and boosts in engineering, factories like Henry Ford's complex at River Rouge became models of industrial efficiency. Increasingly, mass production and automation replaced craft. In this era of mobility and fluidity, Corning could no longer rely solely on established agreements to divide crucial markets with competitors. It would have to compete on the basis of its proprietary knowledge of materials and processes. In the coming twenty years, Corning's scientists would create entirely new product lines by developing new glass compositions, its mechanical experts would invent powerful automatic bulb-making machines, and its managers would find opportunities to sell the company's products across the Atlantic. Most importantly, perhaps, the self-image of this quintessentially small-town company would become less parochial as the Corning Glass Works and its executives found new roles on the national and international stage.

In the short term, however, the works faced several serious challenges.

The first was the dilemma of the company's patented hard glass, Nonex. As it caught on, the sturdy glass proved a boon to railroad customers. Between 1906 and 1909, for example, customers reported a 60 percent reduction in breakage. While the reliability of the lanterns helped Corning increase its share of the railroad glass market from 57 percent in 1905 to 69 percent in 1910, Nonex's durability had a significant downside. Fewer broken lanterns meant less repeat business. Between 1906 to 1909, Corning shipped 43,951 dozen clear globes a year to a group of seven big rail customers that included the Burlington, the Great Northern, and the New York Central. Between 1910 and 1913, Corning would ship 68 percent fewer globes to these lines. With approximately one-third of the company's annual revenues at stake in 1910, this was a troubling development. It was a cunundrum Corning executives would face time and again. Designing products and materials that didn't break helped the company gain market share and boost sales. But it obviated the need for frequent repeat business. Accordingly, Corning's scientists would begin to work on new applications for borosilicate glasses. This effort set into motion a chain of events that would lead to the invention of the wonder material Pyrex. And as the company proved willing to go where glass led it, Corning rolled out a product line that appealed to an entirely new group of customers—female homemakers.

The second challenge was to improve the efficiency of bulb manufacturing. Bulbs were becoming a huge business for Corning—electrical products brought in $960,000 in sales in 1910. And while the long-term contracts between the company, General Electric, and other lamp manufacturers guaranteed a certain amount of stability, the business was in flux. In, 1911, General Electric began making some of its own bulbs, a development Corning's managers had always feared. The following year, GE introduced the long-lasting tungsten filament, which took the market by storm; within two years, GE bulbs accounted for 71 percent of the market. Another constraint on Corning's bulb business was the persistence of traditional methods of production. Craftsmen continued to produce bulbs just as they had that first order for Edison back in 1880—by hand. And the seemingly insatiable demand for electricity overwhelmed the works' human capacity. The lack of a bulb-making machinery didn't necessarily hinder growth and profits—the works enjoyed profit margins of 20 percent or more in the early 1910s. But it did make the company vulnerable to potential competition. After all, glass-makers were growing more proficient at making and perfecting automatic and semiautomatic machines. By 1910, the Owens Bottle Machine Company, which had introduced the Owens bottle machine in 1903, directly controlled 77 of the 191 such machines in operation and reaped revenues from the sale and licensing of the rest to other companies.[2]

Another development threatened the stability of Corning's bulb business. In the first two decades of the twentieth century, the federal government began to put some teeth into the antitrust legislation that had been enacted in the 1890s. Increasingly, arrangements like those between Corning and its fellow lightbulb makers to divide the market between them would become unworkable. If Corning were to survive in this new age of automation and competition, it would have to revolutionize its lightbulb business through automation. Since 1906, the Houghton brothers had quietly funded the development of bulb-making machines—largely against their father's wishes. Benjamin Chamberlin, the Washington-based consultant whom the brothers had retained in this regard, noted significant progress in March 1908: "I am pleased to be able to report at last that I have a bulb machine designed, and have submitted the design to Mr. Dorsey who seemed to think it quite safe to go ahead." Vernon Dorsey, the Houghtons' Washington-based patent lawyer, was as much involved in the whole process as the engineers. And his role highlights the way Corning was competing based on knowledge, since patents were a means of keeping knowledge out of rivals' hands. Chamberlin and his associates pressed on until in the fall of 1909, when Arthur Houghton showed his ailing father a sample bulb made on a machine the mechanics had developed. After looking at it, the once skeptical Amory Jr. pronounced, "Well, Arthur, I did not think you would be able to do it." In November 1909, a few weeks after Amory Jr.'s death, Chamberlin wrote, "Here is a picture of my completed machine—i.e. one arm is completed ready to try."[3]

The Competition to Develop a Bulb-Making Machine

In an effort to institutionalize the research and protect any patents that might arise from it, the Houghton brothers formed the Empire Machine

Company in 1909. In early 1910, Chamberlin traveled to Corning to negotiate terms under which he would "take charge of the work of the Empire Machine Co." He griped about the salary offered—$3,000—and about the company's practice of docking salaries for time lost on holidays and vacations, and he asked for a guaranteed raise and a month's paid vacation. Evidently the parties agreed on acceptable terms, for within a couple months, Chamberlin had moved to Corning and was supervising a dozen mechanics and workers at the Empire Machine Company, which rented space on the first floor of A Factory. Chamberlin's arrival betokened an important shift in the company's attitude. Amory Houghton Jr. jealously guarded the craft secrets he had amassed in his little brown book and would have not tolerated bringing in outsiders and entrusting them with crucial tasks. His sons, by contrast, took a more expansive view.[4]

With the arrival of Empire and the growth of the bulb business, the works were fairly bursting at the seams. In 1912, as the tests on the machine progressed, Corning built a third factory—C Factory—which had three eighteen-pot gas-burning furnaces. It was situated immediately to the west of B Factory, with its blowing room and working floor at the same level of its counterparts in B Factory. This design allowed for the easy movement of products and materials through both factories. In 1913 Corning added a 187-foot tower onto C Factory to facilitate production of greater volumes of tubing.[5]

Chamberlin's machine design, which slowly began to take shape, called for workers to hand gather glass on an iron and place the iron on an arm that swung to assist in the elongation process. The machine also included a plate against which the bulbs were marvered. The designers suffered a great many false starts and setbacks before they developed a viable machine that would pass the muster of the patent authorities. As Day wrote Chamberlin, with typical pessimism, in 1911, "Whether dividends are in sight, as you suggest, I do not feel the same certainty about....The point is that we have got to master this job. If it afterward brings dividends, so much the better, but we have got to make good on the job now to save our self-respect."[6]

The mechanics developed successive prototypes, each labeled with a letter: A, B, C, and D. By 1912 and early 1913, however, Empire was ready to move forward with trials of the fifth prototype, the E Machine. With three working arms to which workers attached hand-gathered glass, it permitted one skilled and two unskilled workers to make over 400 bulbs an hour. By contrast, two skilled and one unskilled worker could at best turn out 150 bulbs an hour using the customary hand method. "I can now report to you five machines, or the entire lot, making good bulbs," Chamberlin wrote Alanson Houghton in June 1913. "One is yet to be given what I have intended giving to all of the lot, that is, a ten hour straight run after being adjusted to do good work." Within a few years, several E Machines would hum for ten-hour runs, day in and day out.[7]

The Pyrex Breakthrough

As the mechanics at the Empire Machine Company labored to perfect the E Machine, Corning's scientists were simultaneously continuing their investigations of basic glass chemistry. Indeed, while the third generation of Corning managers was acutely aware of the need to improve automation in the manufacture of bulbs, they were also more than willing to invest resources to mine the potential of glass. That involved recruiting new personnel. The Houghtons tried to entice Arthur Day to join Corning full-time in 1911, but he was reluctant to leave his comfortable and prestigious position at the Carnegie Institution.[8]

Corning had an easier time recruiting Henry Phelps Gage, a Cornell Ph.D. whose father, Simon H. Gage, was a Cornell professor of optics. "I write to offer you a tentative position on our staff for a period of not less than three months, with the probability of its extending over a year and perhaps leading to a permanent position," Churchill entreated him in the summer of 1911. The salary was $25 a week, or $1,250 a year. Gage accepted, and shortly after joining the works, he developed filters that improved the quality of light given off by electric lamps in daytime. Like many scientists and executives before and after him, Gage found his temporary stay in Corning evolve into permanence. He would rise into laboratory management and remain with the company until his retirement in 1947.[9]

In a memo written in 1912 or 1913, Gage laid out the potential for increased business in optical glass and chemical glassware, sounding a theme that would be echoed frequently by managers of the rapidly growing company. Companies around the country were following the gospel of Frederick Taylor, a consultant who conducted time and motion studies of manufacturing processes and recommended techniques for improving efficiency. In Detroit, Henry Ford was developing an intricate assembly line to produce the popular Model T. Corning, however, remained largely aloof from such trends. The works' 1,000 workers, most of them devoted to making bulbs, by and large adhered to the old craft traditions. The works' productive capabilities were so devoted to keeping up with the unebbing demand for lightbulbs that there was little time or energy left for rationalization efforts. Gage believed the "cost of production might be reduced by more carefully systematizing the work." To his dismay, however, there was poor coordination between the scientists, managers, and production supervisors. "No one seems to be definitely in authority over any particular branch of the work, and hence much delay and needless expense is involved because of lack of responsibility." The way the facilities had grown, with one factory essentially tacked on to another, was doubtless one of the factors contributing to this problem.[10]

And the company did take steps to improve its physical layout. When he came to Corning in 1908, Eugene Sullivan had been promised a new laboratory. In 1913, Corning finally tore down an old structure between the A and B factories and replaced it with a four-story, 5,400-square-foot chemical and laboratory building. This strategically located edifice, designed by Sullivan, connected the two factory buildings and afforded room for mixing, laboratory space, and mold storage. More importantly, it provided the scientists, who had previously been scattered throughout the plant in the separate optical and chemical labs, a single, central location in which to work and share results and ideas.[11]

The interaction between scientists would help propel Corning's next crucial scientific development and lead to its next big hit: Pyrex. In 1912, with sales of railroad globes falling rapidly, Eugene Sullivan and William Taylor began to focus their energies on developing products for a borosilicate glass that resisted both heat and corrosion. Intent on finding a new use for this glass, Corning cast its creative net beyond its usual network of scientific and industrial contacts. It solicited ideas from others in Corning for possible uses for the material. And the suggestions that came back included a line of housewares—pots and pans, nursing bottles, griddles, and the like. People believed the transparency of glass would be attractive to consumers who were increasingly concerned with hygiene. Although the lantern glass was low expansion and heat tolerant—thus making it a good candidate for such use—it absorbed water too readily for household cooking use.

Turning this material into a new product would require a greater understanding of its physical properties than the company's chemists possessed. Accordingly, Sullivan convinced the Houghtons to set up a physical laboratory to investigate the potential of the glass and hired University of Michigan physics professor Jesse T. Littleton to head it. Soon after Littleton arrived, in June 1913, his wife, Bessie, overheard a conversation between her husband and his colleagues on the need to develop new products. She had recently been disappointed when an earthenware casserole fractured in the oven, and she asked her husband to bring a piece of more durable material home from work. Littleton dutifully brought home two sawed-off battery jars made of Nonex. She whipped up some batter and made a spongecake in the ware, which he brought to work. The scientists observed that it was "very well cooked" and was a "remarkably uniform shade of brown all over." Over the next few weeks, Bessie Littleton used the low-expansion glass to make a variety of foods, including steaks, french fries, and cocoa.[12]

Based on Bessie Littleton's informal experiments, Corning scientists believed that the durable, transparent glass would make an appealing baking material. But since the battery jar glass, which contained lead, could theoretically poison food, they began to perform more experiments to devise a safer formula. "This was done in an atmosphere charged with pessimism and we cautiously explored further the preposterous notion of using glass utensils in an oven," as Eugene Sullivan noted. The works enlisted longtime consultant Joseph Deghuee to test some prototypes, but they also turned to new experts, like Mildred Maddocks, who ran the Good Housekeeping Institute. In December 1913, she confirmed that the glass would indeed make good material for casseroles, baking dishes, and combination baking and serving dishes, especially because she found that it radiated heat better and more efficiently than metal. Over the course of 1914, Corning produced experimental teapots, cups, and tumblers, and its scientists perfected a lead-free borosilicate composition—G 702 EJ. Since the first dish made from this formula was a pie plate, Churchill suggested calling it Pyright. Corning eventually changed the name to Pyrex, to rhyme with CNX and Nonex, and filed applications for the patents in 1915.[13]

Corning had not only a new material on its hands but also a new line of business. The company realized that Pyrex would be sold to a different class of customer and through a different set of distribution channels than its industrial products. As a result, it cast a wide net for expertise and advice on how to bring Pyrex to the public. In a move that doubtlessly would have upset Amory Houghton Jr., who was conventionally conservative when it came to women's role in society, the company contacted Sarah Tyson Rorer, a nutritionist who was an editor at *Ladies' Home Journal*, wrote a column in *Good Housekeeping*, and had founded the Philadelphia Cooking School—a sort of Martha Stewart for the early twentieth century. "She replied that the idea of putting glass into an oven didn't appeal to her at all, but she would make a baking test if we insisted," Sullivan recalled. Rorer subjected the ware to various tests, including a successful stab at making Baked Alaska. She eventually met with company executives to discuss the optimal sizes and shapes for the ware, and Corning hired her as a consultant—the first woman to play a formal role in the Corning business.[14]

Rorer helped the male executives at the works understand the needs and concerns of housewives and simultaneously served as an effective conduit through which to introduce Pyrex to its target audience. She traveled to far-flung cities like Omaha, Nebraska, and Salt Lake City, Utah. "I have had such good success in this state and Indiana, that I am sure when you are ready to place the goods on the market you will find the ladies quite ready for them," she wrote in January 1915, while in Ohio. In the spring of 1915, she conducted public demonstrations at department stores in large population centers like Boston and New York. "The demonstration in Boston at Jordan Marsh was a great success from the point of view of the attendance," William Churchill wrote Alanson Houghton in late May 1915. "On Tuesday about eight hundred were present and Wednesday, although it rained very heavily and the newspaper advertisement was insufficient there must have been at least five hundred present." Most women seemed to buy one piece at a time, with the large baking dish and pie plate proving the most popular items. In June, Rorer staged similar public events at Gimbel's in New York City.[15]

The launch of Pyrex was backed by an aggressive print advertising campaign—a first for the Glass Works. "Bake in Glass!" urged a large advertisement in the October 1915 issue of *Good Housekeeping*. "Away with the drudgery of scouring and scrubbing, the fruitless and endless efforts to clean things which seem to resist all cleaning! Away with slow, tedious baking! Away with unsightliness in the kitchen and sore trials to the temper!"" (Prices for a baking dish and cover were $1.75 and $.25 for the 3.5-inch custard cups.) The early advertising also highlighted Pyrex's scientific origins. "A New Material Has Come Into the World," one broadside trumpeted. Still another promised that bread would bake an inch higher in Pyrex than in metal ware.[16]

With such advertisements, historian Regina Blaszczyk has recently argued, Corning aimed to align Pyrex with the prevailing ethos of the Progressive Era—cleanliness, efficiency, perfection. "These attributes particularly made Pyrex a white middle-class product, appealing directly to phobias about germs and dirt," Blaszczyk wrote. Whatever its appeal, Pyrex caught on. After selling $38,545 worth in the last few months of 1915, Corning saw its Pyrex sales soar to $286,424 in 1916, so that they constituted about 8 percent of total sales. Pyrex sales leapt to $460,353 in 1917.[17]

A small percentage of the Pyrex sales came from products that were not pitched toward housewives. For in 1915, Corning began to sell a complete line of flasks, beakers, apparatus, and test tubes forged from the new material. The market for these goods had generally been dominated by glass produced by German companies, especially after a 1913 tariff reduction. But the imports from Germany had ceased abruptly with the outbreak of World War I in 1914. This opening for Pyrex was one of many ways in which the Great War would create opportunities for, and place new demands on, the growing glass company in the Chemung Valley.[18]

The Impact of World War

World War I disrupted a global economy that was growing increasingly interdependent. As the Atlantic Ocean became a dangerous thoroughfare for commerce, trade between Germany and Austria and the United States plummeted from $160 million in 1914 to $1 million in 1916. Some components of the German trade were crucial glassmaking ingredients, such as potash, manganese, and clay. Corning, and the rest of the $123 million U.S. glass industry, immediately strained to find local suppliers for these commodities. And Corning's scientists worked to develop a non-potash glass that employed borax and nitrate. To complicate matters, prices for glassmaking supplies that had a wartime application—lead, for example—soared rapidly. Between 1914 and 1917, the price of sand would rise 45.4 percent, raw lime 27 percent, soda ash 48.7 percent, and natural gas 80 percent.

On a deeper level, however, the Great War proved a stimulus to the glass industry and the other cogs of the American industrial machine. In 1914, the United States was a net importer of goods. But as American trade with the Allies rose from $285 million in 1914 to $3.214 billion in 1916, the country became a net exporter of goods—including glass.[19]

The Corning Glass Works faced pressure on several fronts after 1914. The company, which produced about half the bulbs made in America annually, found demand rising rapidly. World War I was the first major war powered by electricity. And the availability of reliable lighting allowed factories that produced goods for the war to run around the clock. As the tungsten filament lamp caught on, bulb sales would grow by about 40 percent annually until 1920, becoming a mass consumption product. In 1914, Corning's bulb sales were $949,554, or 54 percent of its $1.745 million in total sales. Bulb sales alone soared to $1.7 million in 1916 as total sales leaped to $3.9 million—up more than 100 percent in just two years.[20]

Faced with escalating orders, Corning formed new bulb shops, recruited glassmakers form Pennsylvania and Ohio, and built new furnaces. By 1916, Corning's workforce had practically doubled in five years to nearly 2,000 employees. But simply hiring more labor was difficult and expensive. In 1916, labor costs constituted about 40 percent of the total value of all glass made in the United States; for lamp chimneys the number was 52.4 percent —not all that much less than the ratio the Niles & Niles accounting firm measured at Corning in 1907. Moreover, prices for labor rose rapidly in the early years of the war, as did those for virtually every other commodity. Between 1914 and 1917, blowers' average weekly wages rose from $28.36 to

$34.56, up 21.86 percent; gatherers' wages rose 31 percent; and batch mixers' pay rose 41 percent. In 1916, Corning granted all its employees a 15 percent bonus to cope with higher wartime prices for food and other staples.[21]

Fortuitously, the long-awaited semiautomatic E Machine, which would allow Corning to save greatly on labor costs, was ready to be placed in production. In 1915, the first year for which commercial production figures on the E Machine are available, Corning used them to produce about 12 million bulbs, a small percentage of the total. With demand continuing to explode, Corning decided to build a new plant equipped solely with the E Machine. But there was comparatively little room available in the strip of land between the Chemung River and the growing town. And given that installing several machines at the works would have displaced a great deal of hometown labor, the logic of finding a second site located outside the Crystal City became more compelling.

In Wellsboro, Pennsylvania, a small town about forty miles to the south, the former Columbia Window Glass Company lay vacant. In 1916 Corning purchased the works, revamped the furnaces, and charged William Woods with getting the plant up and running. Woods, one of three glassworking brothers from Pittsburgh, had come to Corning in 1898 as a nineteen-year-old bulb blower. The onetime boxer, who had worked at Westinghouse, quickly rose to foreman. In Wellsboro, he recruited eighty local farm boys, who had no experience with glassmaking. Together with a few experienced Corning workers, he trained the new recruits to gather glass and place them in the twenty semiautomatic E Machines installed there—a capacity of 8,000 bulbs per hour. In November 1916, the machines were first fired up at Wellsboro. In the next thirteen months, the factory would produce 30.26 million bulbs. Since the refractories then in use for tank melting could not accommodate the high volume of lead-alkali glass needed to feed the voracious machines, William Taylor quickly developed a new lead-free soda lime composition for bulbs. Some 40 years after the Houghtons' company shifted from producing lime to lead glass, Corning in a sense returned to its roots in glass chemistry.[22]

In 1917, as sales soared to $6.69 million, Corning made 113.4 million bulbs. Its next largest competitor, the Libbey Glass Company of Toledo, made 80.6 million. The following year, Corning made 123 million bulbs, about 41 percent of the 296 million produced in the United States that year. The Glass Works' employees perceived their output as an important contribution to the war effort. "We make more bulbs than anything else, and because we have always made them we may not think of them in relation to the War," wrote an anonymous editorialist in the *Cullet*, the magazine started by and for Corning's workers in its inaugural October 1918 issue. "War goes on day and night and on cloudy days as well as bright ones. Munition factories work at night. Ships sail at night....Signals must be flashed at night."[23]

Impressive as the increases were, Corning's bulb production still had ample room for improvement. Corning always lived with the possibility that its largest customers would simply decide to eliminate their suppliers and make bulb blanks themselves. With the growing reliability of bulb-making machinery, this threat became a reality. In 1917, General Electric purchased the rights to the Westlake machine, an automatic bulb machine that had been developed by August Kadow of the Libbey Glass Company. GE installed the Westlake machines at some of its plants and began making its own bulbs. "It did what generations of hand blowers had never believed possible," historian John Hammon wrote, "it produced symmetrical, moulded bulbs of glass automatically."[24] Corning was not interested in licensing the Westlake machine because it was counting on the engineers at the Empire Machine Company to develop an even better machine.

At the time, Empire's staffers were working on a fully automatic successor to the E Machine, called—predictably—the F Machine. Between 1912 and 1916, Chamberlin and machine designer Robert Canfield developed a machine that relied on a rotating series of molds. But they had difficulty developing a device that would feed the glass continuously into the molds. In 1916, Eugene Dorsey and Canfield visited the Fairmont, West Virginia, factory of the Hartford-Fairmont Company, a mid-sized glassmaker, and were impressed by the paddle feeder employed there. In June 1916, Corning and Hartford-Fairmont agreed to join forces. By forming the Hartford-Empire Company, the Houghtons' first joint venture, Corning effectively gained the rights to the paddle feeder. The same year, however, GE expressed interest in developing the F Machine, Canfield moved the work to a GE facility in Harrison, New Jersey. It would be several years before Corning was actually able to put the F Machines to work in its own factories. But these agreements represented an important step in the company's evolution. For the first time in this era of knowledge-based competition, it was cooperating with and sharing innovation with other firms.[25]

Aside from pushing companies to redouble efforts to automate, the war placed stresses on the glass industry by cutting off the supply of specialty and technical glass previously imported from Germany. The American glass industry was not particularly well-equipped to pick up the slack. A 1916 investigation of 245 glass factories found that "only a few of the largest companies had employed a chemist, that the batch and the application of chemical principles had been neglected, and that the most important detail of successful manufacturing, a scientific knowledge of the glass itself, was lacking."[26]

In the years after 1914, when the United States was not yet militarily involved in the war, the government tried to compensate for American companies' relative backwardness. A series of successive public-private agencies ultimately developed into the War Industries Board, an overlapping set of committees composed of heads of large corporations, government officials, and financiers like Bernard Baruch. Their efforts intensified after the United States formally entered the war in April 1917, a date also marking the first large-scale government efforts to manage the American economy. Organizations such as the Emergency Fleet Corporation took over shipbuilding, the War Trade Board licensed foreign trade, and entities sprung up to manage railroad and labor issues. For its part, the War Industries Board ranked industries in order of their importance to the war effort, and attempted to dictate production and pricing policies to certain industries.[27]

The efforts extended to the glass industry. No longer able to look to Europe for high-quality glass, the government set up a school at Rochester where mechanics were trained to make optical glass. Companies such as Bausch & Lomb Optical and Pittsburgh Plate Glass received assistance from outfits like the U.S. Geophysical Lab to make optical glass for government use. And the military stimulated demand for glass products. "The total number of orders placed by the Government amounted to more than $50 million, of which about $15 million went to the Navy," Bernard Baruch wrote.[28]

Arthur Day, the prickly Corning consultant, was among those who helped organize the national effort to produce optical glass for military applications. After Day and his colleagues from the Carnegie Institution visited companies like Bausch & Lomb, Eastman Kodak, and American Optical, he reported to Alanson Houghton in March 1917, "I am fully convinced from such inquiries as I have made, and the information the National Research Council is gathering, that you in Corning know more about glass at this moment than any other firm in this country."[29]

At the time, Corning was already making products for the war effort. These included colored glasses for marksmanship used by naval gunners, glass for aviators' goggles, sextant glasses, X-ray shields, clinical thermometers, and vials for typhoid toxins. When American forces started their fateful drive to Chateau Thierry, the *Cullet* noted with pride in October 1918, American divisions had 100,000 maps of the territory—blueprints made on a machine for which Corning provided the glass cylinders. The timing of the Pyrex introduction was excellent, as the material turned out to make excellent chemical tubing and proved useful as vials for typhoid toxins. By 1918, the Glass Works could well boast that it was "the world's largest manufacturer of technical glass."[30]

During the war, Corning officials frequently corresponded with military officers. In the fall of 1917, the works sent samples of its specialty glasses to the chief signal officer of the Army. Through the fall of 1917 and the spring of 1918 men from the Army asked Churchill and others in Corning for information about glasses for reflectors and searchlight beams. In 1918, as the war edged toward its close, Corning was working with the office of the director of aircraft production and members of the National Research Council to produce landing-strip lights and headlamps for tanks and other vehicles. It is unclear how many of these products found their way into wartime use, given the U.S. Expeditionary Forces' relatively short sojourn in Europe.[31]

To manage the rapid growth and the expanding sphere of operations, the Houghtons hired new executives and created new managerial positions. This represented yet another step in the company's evolution. Although it had long hired scientists and engineers to manage technical operations, it had not relied on non–family members to manage important segments of the business. In 1916, Will Hedges was tapped to oversee Pyrex sales, long-time employee Charles Githler was elevated to production manager, and Frederick Cameron supervised marine- and railroadware sales. The following year, the Houghtons again tried to coax Day to return to Corning full-time to help with their continuing problems in keeping up with demand. "I like your problem," Day wrote to Alanson Houghton, "and more bluntly I like you. I can think of no two people I would more like to argue with than the two of you." But he resisted. To begin with, the Houghtons offered him a salary of $6,600, when Churchill, the head of sales, was thought to be making between $30,000 and $40,000. And he again expressed frustration that the Houghtons had been unwilling to allow him to buy shares in the company to which he had contributed so much. In addition, Day enjoyed a certain status by virtue of his position at the Washington, D.C.–based Carnegie Institution, which he was unwilling to give up. Finally, he was reluctant to leave the cosmopolitan city of Baltimore, where he and his family lived, for the small town of Corning.[32]

While companies like Corning benefited from the demands created by the war, other glassmakers suffered. One of them was Steuben. It was difficult to make fine crystal blanks without German potash. And once the War Department declared cut glass a nonessential product, Steuben had difficulty obtaining other raw materials. As the war ground on, Samuel Hawkes faced the unenviable prospect of shutting down the factory and throwing his 270 employees out of work. To compound matters, Frederick Carder's twenty-five-year-old son, Cyrill Carder, was killed in the war in July 1918—one of thirty-one Corning boys who didn't make it back from Europe. So in 1918 Corning took over the Steuben plant, which was comparatively small, and began making lightbulbs there. In 1918, the Steuben factory accounted for $293,813 in sales—as compared to nearly $7.8 million for the Glass Works.[33]

When World War I, thought to be the war to end all wars, finally ended in November 1918, it left a world scarred, damaged, and irreversibly altered. The traumatic events had reached from the killing fields of the French forests to small towns like Corning. In an era when technological advances like the car, the radio, and the telephone were improving the general standard of living, the world had witnessed similar advances in technology and

LEFT Amory Houghton Sr. made and lost several fortunes by the time he decided to enter the glass business in 1851. He owned glass operations in Somerville, Massachusetts and Brooklyn and Corning, New York. The latter was bankrupt when he retired in 1870.

RIGHT Amory Houghton Jr. proved a creative glassmaker, as well as an astute businessman. Together with his brother Charles, he presided over the resurgence of the Corning Glass Works in the late 19th century. Amory Jr. understood the importance of glass composition, while Charles worked with scientists at Cornell University to develop new products.

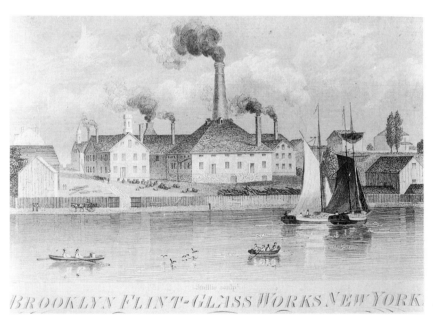

BROOKLYN FLINT-GLASS WORKS, NEW YORK.

In the 1850s, the Brooklyn Flint Glass Works won prestigious international awards for the quality of its glass. By the time Amory Houghton, Sr. acquired it in 1862, however, it was veering toward collapse. Enticed by new investors in Corning, Houghton and his sons looked forward to a fresh start.

Charles F. Houghton

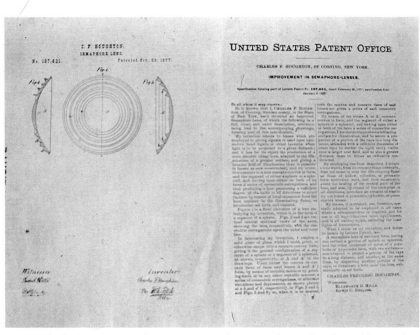

Among Charles Houghton's achievements was this patent for a railroad signal lens with a smooth convex exterior. The design kept the lens free of grime and dirt while also improving visibility. In the late 19th and early 20th centuries, the railroads were major customers of the Glass Works.

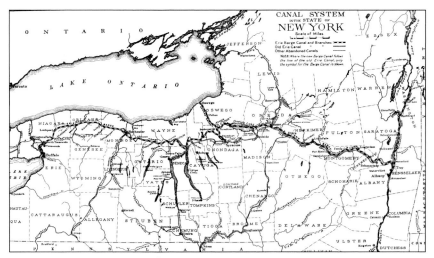

This map of the canal system in New York State shows the route taken by the Houghtons, their employees, and equipment on the move from Brooklyn to Corning: up the Hudson River to Troy, across the Erie Canal to Syracuse, then through smaller canals and Seneca Lake to Corning.

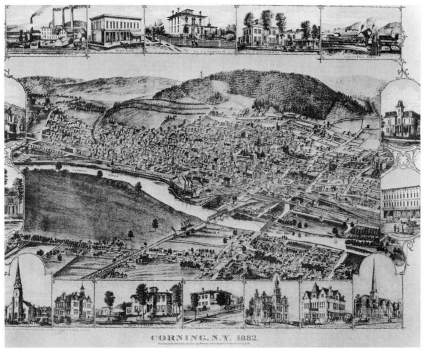

The Glass Works (center, featuring four smokestacks, along the river) was by far the biggest employer—and landmark—in Corning by the early 1880s.

In the 1880s, Corning supplied glass envelopes for Thomas Edison's electric light bulbs. Gaffers blew individual bulbs into molds and sometimes achieved rates of several hundred bulbs per day—an impressive feat but one that limited production and the spread of electrical lighting across the United States.

Alanson B. Houghton and Arthur Houghton Sr. (sons of Amory Jr.) constituted the third generation of family leadership of Corning Glass Works. The brothers led the company into a new era of automation and negotiated its first foreign ventures. The urbane Alanson later served as a member of Congress and a U.S. ambassador in Europe in the 1920s. Arthur stayed close to home and was responsible for important innovations in mixing glass and drawing tubular shapes.

Frederick Carder joined the Steuben Glass Works in Corning in 1903 and helped to make it one of the brightest ornaments of the Crystal City.

The steady expansion of the Glass Works in the late 19th and early 20th centuries made it seem a permanent construction site as new tanks were added and new processes installed.

Corning Glass Works, Corning, N. Y.

The dominant feature on Corning's skyline after 1912 was the 187-foot tower used for making thermometer tubes by the vertical up-draw process. Pictured here three years after it was built, the tower remains the tallest structure in the city today.

Under the leadership of research director Dr. Eugene Sullivan, Corning became a world leader in glass chemistry and technology. Sullivan also served as Corning's president between 1928 and 1930 before returning again to the laboratory.

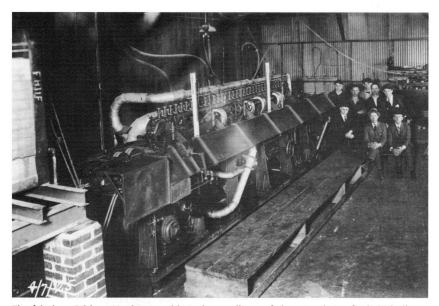

The fabulous Ribbon Machine could produce millions of glass envelopes for light bulbs each year, making electric lighting affordable to the masses. Pictured here: the development team for the ribbon machine. William Woods, the originator of the idea for the machine, is seated at the center, wearing a hat, next to David Gray, chief engineer.

The partnership behind Pyrex: Young physicist Jesse T. Littleton joined Corning's R&D lab in 1913 and began working on applications of a new heat-resistant glass called Nonex. His wife Bessie (called Becky in the family) used a sawed-off battery jar of the glass to bake a cake, thus inspiring the Pyrex line of cookware.

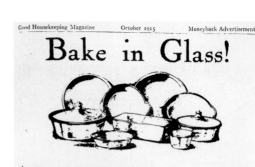

Pyrex proved a hot product in the 1920s and its success later prompted the Glass Works to consider renaming itself as the Pyrex Corporation. Pictured: the first advertisement for Pyrex as it appeared in 1915 in Good Housekeeping.

science put to use in the creation of nerve gas, chemical propellants, machine guns, and air warfare.

The Corning Glass Works emerged from the war a far different company than it had been in 1914. In 1918, of its total sales, electric bulbs accounted for $4.377 million or more than half. Other lines contributed heavily to the bottom line. Pyrex and chemical ware—two lines that were nonexistent or insignificant before the war—brought in $589,000 and $355,379, respectively. Railway ware had fallen to just 12 percent of sales. To meet wartime demands, the company had been forced to expand beyond the boundaries of the Crystal City, acquire another company, and introduce automation in its production. In the ten years after the Armistice, Corning would build on the boost the war had provided.[34]

The Postwar Roller Coaster

In the spring of 1919, with Woodrow Wilson lecturing the participants at the Paris Peace Conference about the Fourteen Points, the United States was assuming a central role on the world stage. The United States had not only helped provide the decisive margin of victory for the Allies, but it had also emerged as an economic powerhouse. In 1914 the United States was a debtor nation; American citizens owed foreign investors $3 billion. By the end of 1919 the United States was a creditor nation, with American investors holding $3 billion dollars in foreign debt.[35]

Throughout the 1920s, a decade of prosperity fueled by the growth of the automobile, electrification, and a booming stock market, U.S. companies would flex their muscles abroad. In the 1920s Corning would expand into Europe by striking joint ventures with European firms and licensing its patented products like Pyrex for sale on the Continent. In addition, Corning's top executive, Alanson Houghton, would come to occupy a central role in the affairs of Europe, parlaying his successful election in 1918 to Congress into ambassadorial appointments to Germany (from 1922 to 1925) and Great Britain (from 1925 to 1929).

Corning's long-standing support of science stood it in good stead in the emerging competitive industrial environment. Between 1900 and 1920, the eighteen industrial companies with the greatest number of scientists would see their roster of Ph.D.'s rise from 4 to 172. The percentage of papers in the *Physical Review*, a major physics research publication, written by scientists in industrial laboratories rose from 2 percent in 1900 to 22 percent in 1920. In the previous decade, Corning's scientists had won forty-eight patents. Thirty-two of those related to articles of manufacture, eleven related to glass compositions, and five to manufacturing methods and apparatus. Such patents were indeed growing more valuable. In 1919, Corning spent $350,000 to acquire the rights to the Danner tube drawing machine.[36]

Companies, especially glass companies, were consolidating and getting larger. In 1914, the average glass company had 226 employees, $353,000 in output, and $442,000 in capital. In 1919 the averages had risen to 264 employees, $826,000 in output, and $680,000 in capital. After the war, then, with about 2,000 employees and $8.3 million in sales, Corning ranked as one of the biggest glassmakers in the United States.[37]

With the growth and continued profitability of the works throughout the 1910s, the Houghton brothers had seen their personal wealth grow. Still in their forties, Arthur and Alanson led lives typical of wealthy industrialists. They both traveled a great deal with their families and would typically spend much of the summer playing golf together at a country club near the Meadows. During the winter, Arthur would occupy a suite at the Plaza Hotel in New York City for weeks at a time. Or the brothers would travel with their families, help, and cars, to the Hampton Terrace or Bon Aire Hotel in Augusta, Georgia.

Yet the brothers constituted something of an odd couple. Arthur's passport photo from this period shows a chubby, balding, middle-aged man with close-cut gray hair, a prominent nose, and brown eyes with bags under them. Alanson, with his trademark wire-rimmed glasses and double-breasted suits, struck a more cosmopolitan and scholarly figure. In 1916, Alanson commissioned architect Howard Greenley to design a large mansion to be built on the hill south of Corning. One of the central features of the "Knoll," as the family home was called, was a two-story library, "which he liked best of all the rooms he had ever owned" and housed Alanson's extensive book collection.[38]

After the war, the brothers would soon relinquish day-to-day control over the company—Alanson would pursue a political career and the ailing Arthur would retire. As already noted, the Houghton family had been active in local and state Republican politics since the 1870s, soon after their arrival in Corning. Alanson had been a delegate at various state and national Republican conventions, as well as a donor to the party. In 1918, he ran successfully for the region's congressional seat. He took up residence in an apartment on Connecticut Avenue in Washington, D.C., and sat on the Foreign Affairs and Ways and Means Committees.[39]

Upon his election to Congress, Alanson assumed the position of chairman of the Glass Works. After having one chief executive for thirty-seven years—Amory Houghton Jr.—and a second for nine years, the Corning Glass Works would have four presidents in the next twelve years. First, Arthur Houghton was named president in February 1919, at the age of fifty-two. But he fell ill soon after Alanson left and, having worked in the family business for thirty-three years, retired in the spring of 1920. He moved with his family to New York, kept up on company affairs, and pursued other interests. A story from the August 1921 *Cullet* described a fishing excursion "Sword Fishing in Buzzard Bay," in which Arthur took several Corning managers out on his seventy-two-foot schooner, the *Rhodos*. The lengthy story concluded with the capture of a twelve-foot-long fish that weighed more than 400 pounds.[40]

In the spring of 1920, for the first time in fifty years, the Corning Glass Works installed a non-Houghton as chief executive: Alexander Falck. Born in 1878 in Elmira, Falck attended Williams College and Columbia Law School and then joined an Elmira law firm. As a partner in Stanchfield, Loveil, Falck, and Sayles, he became a trusted legal counsel to the Houghtons. He helped to organize the Empire Machine Company, for example. Falck first came to work at Corning in 1918 as general counsel and assistant to president, and he was named president in March 1920. Despite his title, Falck was not an autonomous chief executive. The Houghton brothers controlled virtually all the company's stock and made virtually every important decision. For much of the 1920s, the firm was run by an executive committee composed of Falck and the Houghton brothers. And by the mid-1920s, it was clear that Falck would only remain in the post until Alanson's son, Amory Houghton, had gained enough experience to take over as president.[41]

The company Falck led faced an array of potentially overwhelming problems. "The matter of internal organization has given me grave concern during the last week," he wrote to the Houghton brothers in early 1920. Lacking faith in his ability to supervise every aspect of the business, and without a partner, he felt that the company needed a more highly developed organizational structure and that each line of business should have a vice president or general manager. Indeed, as Falck assumed the presidency, the works underwent a major reorganization. Rather than a revolution, this represented an evolutionary step. Since the mid-1910s, the Houghtons had moved to compartmentalize the business and assign professionals to run different units. Falck hired Hanford Curtiss as his assistant, named John Thomas to the post of treasurer, and elevated George Buell Hollister to the position of vice president and sales manager.

One of those notably missing from the executive lineup was Arthur Day. Day had come to Corning full-time in 1919, after finally acceding to the Houghtons' repeated offers. But Falck was reluctant to share power with the difficult Day. And when Falck wouldn't carry through on what Day perceived to be a promise to let him buy or have stock, Day returned to the Carnegie Institute. He did, however, retain his title as vice president of Corning, with the concomitant salary and benefits. Following Day's departure, Eugene Sullivan took the post as vice president for manufacturing, even as he continued to oversee the company's research efforts, which were also growing and being rationalized. By the end of World War I, the laboratories consisted of three components: the optical laboratory, led by Gage, the chemical laboratory, led by Taylor, and the physical laboratory, led by Jesse Littleton. The Laboratory Committee, with members from the different units, met monthly.[42]

Despite his constant demands and barbed personality, which shines through in memos and correspondence, Day remained a valuable asset to the Glass Works. In August 1920, he submitted a development plan that neatly spelled out the challenges facing Corning in the postwar years. Corning's manufacturing capacity had not kept up with its sales, which was nearly eight times what it had been in 1910. Also, because of the location of the plant on a narrow, completely enclosed strip of land between the city and the Chemung River, growth in Corning would have to be "intensive rather than extensive." In the race to ramp up production, the research and the mechanical development shops had ceased doing original work and were instead "fully occupied with the detail required for the competent daily operation of existing facilities." The factories were poorly organized, with insufficient storage space and inadequate automation, as workers still trucked bulbs around by hand when they could have been moved by conveyer belts. Moreover, even though Corning had built a new power plant in 1918, its power capacity was woefully overtaxed. The average daily horsepower used nearly doubled between June 1919 and June 1920, from 651 to 1105.[43]

But the most serious problems Day found were human rather than mechanical. "When all is said about economy and percentage efficiency, we still confront an underlying and uncompromising fact, namely, that the chief limitation upon Corning as a place of manufacture is the absence of an adequate labor supply," he wrote. By 1920, Corning was running flat out but still couldn't keep up. And the lack of automation was the main culprit. "We are in a very bad situation for bulbs," Falck wrote Arthur A. Houghton in February 1920. "We had been promised an "F" machine in December.... We will be over two million bulbs short for February; over 500,000 of which are due Westinghouse and they are in a rather nasty mood because of this shortage, which will continue for at least several months. It is the first time we have failed to live up to our contract with them since October, 1918."[44]

Day concluded that the company needed to expand its bulb-making capacity but would have to do so away from Corning. "Some two years ago, by common consent, though without making it a matter of positive record, a policy was adopted for the Corning Glass Works of limiting the growth of the present plant in Corning and providing for such extension as might follow future development by the erection of branches in other places where conditions of labor or the availability of raw materials might indicate special advantages," Day wrote. His main recommendation was that the company build new tanks to expand capacity at Wellsboro.[45]

Corning had already dealt with a similar problem with its Pyrex production. Pyrex was a difficult material to work with, in part because it required an exceedingly high melting temperature. That placed stress on Corning's furnaces. "On my return to Corning I find that we have been unable to make Pyrex glass at all for most of this week," George Buell Hollister reported to Arthur Houghton on January 31, 1919. "Of our two small tanks which were running, one is out of commission for temporary repairs and the other one started up yesterday after being idle nearly a week." The problem wasn't just volume (Corning sold more than 4.5 million pieces of Pyrex in 1919) but variety. Aside from the baking dishes, Corning, which had a Pyrex sales office on 5th Avenue in New York City, sold chemicalware like beakers, flasks, apparatus, test tubes—about forty-seven different products in all. The capacity constraints were sufficiently critical, Hollister concluded, that "I am not at all sure that we should not consider building an additional tank or possibly a Pyrex unit factory, aside from our present plant." Management took Hollister's memo seriously. Subsequently, in the summer of 1919, Corning paid about $10,000 to buy the Edgewood Arsenal from the War Department in Kingsport, Tennessee, and quickly refitted it to produce Pyrex. Production started there in early 1920, with Dr. Frederick F. Shetterly as plant manager.[46]

Several months after the Kingsport plant came on line, the economy slid into a quick but deep postwar recession. The works' first quarter sales plunged from $2.96 million in 1920 to $1.786 a year later—a 40 percent decrease. In 1920, sales of Pyrex were $3 million, or about one-fourth of Corning's total sales, but they would fall to $6.7 million in 1921. In response to the sharp slide in business, Corning was forced to slash its payroll from 2,771 in November 1920 to 1,139 in April 1921. And the employees who remained worked fewer hours. The works' payroll fell from $95,620 in November 1920 to $30,497 in April 1921—a 68 percent reduction. To cut costs further, Corning reduced its laboratory and mechanical forces, suspended publication of the *Cullet*, and shuttered the Kingsport plant.[47]

A Broadening Perspective

To combat the drop-off in Pyrex sales, Corning in the 1920s redoubled its marketing efforts. In January 1922 a sales brochure trumpeted the fact that "there are now 100 shapes and sizes in Pyrex." It cut prices to 1918 levels and rolled out new products like nursing bottles and teapots. Corning spent hundreds of thousands of dollars advertising in magazines like *Good House-keeping, Farm Journal, Modern Priscilla, Ladies Home Journal, Farmer's Wife,* and *McCall's*—magazines with a combined circulation of 15.65 million people. And the company was conscious of appealing to different market segments. A 1922 primer for salespeople noted that aside from offering saving fuel and being easier to clean, "Pyrex is 'kosher.' This interests the Jewish trade."[48]

In the early 1920s, Corning took other important steps to expand the market for Pyrex. These new efforts highlighted the ways in which Corning's executives had adopted a more cosmopolitan worldview. For in 1921, Corning joined forces with French glassmaker St. Gobain and created a joint venture, Société Le Pyrex, which was licensed to make and sell Pyrex in France, Belgium, Holland, Spain, Portugal, Italy, and Switzerland. The same year, Corning also licensed James A. Jobling & Company to make Pyrex in England. In the 1920s, Germany, though in a continuing state of crisis, was beginning to reenter the world economy. And in 1924, Corning reestablished the dialogue it had started with the technologically advanced Schott & Genossen works in Jena before the war. The two companies negotiated a deal for that firm to sell Pyrex in Germany. Just as it had with General Electric and Hartford-Fairmont, Corning displayed a willingness to leverage its technologies and capabilities by working with a potential rival. These associations, established in the 1920s, not only helped the company expand its reach in the near term but proved to be crucial for its long-term growth. [49]

It's unclear what role, if any, Alanson Houghton played in the negotiations with Schott & Genossen. But he was certainly in a position to help. For after serving two terms in Congress, Alanson was tapped in the spring of 1922 by Secretary of State Charles Evans Hughes for the delicate assignment of serving as the first postwar U.S. ambassador to Germany. On March 17, 1922, the works staged a going-away ceremony for its former president. At 11:45 A.M, when the factory whistles blew, all employees who could step away from their work came into the yard. A committee that included George Miles, Frank Hultzman, and Fred Deuerlein presented Alanson with an American flag for use in the embassy. "It is a wonderful thing that you have done for me," Alanson said. "I don't mean the gift of this beautiful flag which signifies so much to every American....Two weeks from to-morrow I sail—on April 1. And I am glad to go because I firmly believe in this instance, as in so many others, that the longest way round is the shortest way home. Home to Corning, home to the Glass Works, to live and die among the men and women I care for and really love."[50]

When Alanson arrived in Germany, he found a country in crisis. Germany's domestic economy was in a shambles from a combination of the ruinous war and the intentionally punitive settlement imposed by the Allies on Germany at Versailles. The American embassy, which had stood empty since the nation's entry into the war, suffered from horrible neglect. The building was in such bad shape that, by his estimate, Alanson spent $150,000 of his own money to upgrade the property into livable condition. Alanson served during a tumultuous period that saw several changes in government, Hitler's unsuccessful putsch in Munich, and continuing efforts to settle Germany's debts. Soon after his arrival, he offered a plan to cancel Europe's debts to the United States in exchange for disarmament. And he garnered criticisms for views that some critics regarded as excessively pro-German. As one student of his tenure in Germany wrote, "Houghton's influence was not great during his tenure as America's first postwar Ambassador to Germany. He failed to convince the Administration that Germany was the pivot of European affairs and that the Versailles Treaty was a disaster for Western civilization." He did, however, warn that Hitler was a potential menace.[51]

Although separated by an ocean from the company he owned, Alanson remained involved with the company's operations. Although Arthur had retired, he could rely on a loyal and sharp set of eyes to keep him abreast of developments in Corning: his son, Amory—another future Corning president and U.S. ambassador. Born in 1899, Amory attended St. Paul's and Harvard, just as his father did. After graduating from Harvard, he married Laura DeKay Richardson in Providence, on October 19, 1921, and moved into the Knoll. He started working in 1921 in the blowing room of B Factory for $25 a week. But his wages were supplemented by a $4,000 annual allowance he received from his father, and he was plainly being groomed for the presidency of the works. Along with his cousin, Arthur A. Houghton Jr., Amory Houghton would constitute the fourth generation of Corning leadership.[52]

Expanding Corporate Culture in an Era of Welfare Capitalism

Of course, Alanson could have afforded to pay his son a far greater allowance since the Corning Glass Works was a very profitable firm in the 1920s. Between 1911 and 1922, the company had retained earnings of $3.992 million. And in 1922, when it tallied sales of $7.6 million and profits of $1.2 million, the firm paid dividends of $591,125 on common stock and $223,621 on preferred stock. (The Houghtons held all but a tiny fraction of both classes of stock.) Due to a change in tax law, the company decided to retire the preferred stock it had issued in 1920 by selling $2 million in bonds, at a favorable 5.5 percent rate, through Estabrook & Company in December 1922. Holders of the preferred shares—mostly the Houghton family— received $112 for each share.[53]

Throughout the 1920s, Amory—"Am" to family members—would write his father to update him on the progress of various projects, and on general business conditions. While he was certainly involved in major decisions, Alanson seemed comfortable allowing Falck and the other executives to operate with a fair amount of autonomy. "I spent the entire morning here yesterday with John Thomas and Amory on the final details prior to inaugurating the health and accident insurance plan," Falck wrote to Alanson in 1923. "I presume Amory has written you that we have determined to establish this plan, insuring with the Metropolitan Company." Insuring the company's 2,400 or so employees would cost about $11,000.[54]

The effort by Corning to establish health insurance reflected a trend among many big corporations in the 1920s later dubbed "welfare capitalism." Moved by impulses including paternalism, growing government regulation, a desire to forestall union organizing, and the incipient influence of industrial psychology, companies in a variety of industries developed new programs aimed at improving their workers' welfare and making them feel more positive about their jobs. Companies labored to improve worker safety, built cafeterias and clinics for the workers, sponsored recreational activities, and in some instances provided housing and transportation. In 1923, U.S. Steel reduced its workday from twelve hours to eight. In 1927, Ford Motor Company adopted a five-day work week. The same year, International Harvester began offering workers two-week paid vacations.[55]

Such policies were made possible by the growing profitability and productivity of American industry during the booming 1920s. The percentage
of industry that was electrified rose from 30 percent in 1914 to 70 percent in
1929. Between 1921 and 1929, the nation's industrial production index rose
from 58 to 110, while the number of people working in manufacturing
remained stable. Perhaps most important to workers, the real earnings of
laborers, which were essentially unchanged between 1890 to 1918, rose
quickly in the 1920s.[56]

As the Corning Glass Works generally prospered in the postwar decade,
it was part and parcel of this movement. The works in 1918 established the
Cullet to promote a feeling of community among the company's workforce.
The same year, it organized the Corning Glass Works band, providing uni-
forms and instruments. While remaining unalterably opposed to unions,
management made efforts to involve workers in decision making. In 1921,
Corning established the Production Club, a group that met to discuss plant
conditions, brought in guest speakers, and held annual outings. Each year,
starting in 1921, the company held service awards dinners to honor long-
time employees. Workers who had been with the company for fifty years
(calculated as active service plus years in retirement) received a $1,000 check
—a practice continued to the present. The company also sponsored field day
meets and a company baseball league, with teams of Calcites, Penmen,
Blowers, Builders, Mechanics, and Scientists. And in the early 1920s, Corning built a company hospital and clinic.[57]

Judging from a 1927 investigation by Dr. Wade Wright of the Metropolitan Life Insurance Company, however, Corning's factories left a great deal
to be desired. Investigating the works, probably as part of the underwriting
process, Wright found a range of health hazards. Litharge, lead, arsenic,
and other potentially toxic materials like hydroflouric oxide were not
always properly managed. "Quite recently they had a case of extensive and
serious disfigurement of the face due to a severe burn from this substance,"
Dr. Wright found. The floors in the factory were rough, with pools of
standing water, and lighting and ventilation were poor. "The toilet facilities
are, for the most part, extremely unsatisfactory," he continued. "The men
are not provided with lockers." With insufficient lunchroom facilities,
workers ate at their stations. "I was informed by the employment manager

that it has been a practice, which possibly does not prevail at the present time, for men to "wash" by rubbing over their hands the batch which is prepared for the melting pot," he noted in apparent horror. Wright concluded that the works "presents a very interesting collection of specific occupational health and accident hazards." He recommended changes, such as banning eating in the work room, installing modern drinking fountains, and upgrading the toilets.[58] In some ways, these conditions were more typical of a nineteenth-century factory than a modern industrial enterprise. Their persistence highlights the degree to which the craft methods and environment created by Amory Houghton Jr. survived as the works grew up around the original buildings. The company may have been using the most modern materials and processes known, but its working conditions remained less than exemplary.

At the time of Wright's visit, Corning had already taken significant steps toward improving the working conditions for its researchers and executives. In 1923 the laboratory was enlarged by 9,000 square feet, as the north wall of B Factory was pushed outward to house two small furnaces. And the following year, Corning built a five-story office building at the Walnut Street entrance of the plant to house various department heads, such as sales, treasury, purchasing, and their clerks.

Developments such as the expansion into Europe, the creation of employee benefits and welfare programs, and the increasing differentiation between administration and manufacturing meant that the Corning Glass Works was taking its place as a major industrial company. But it still lacked the one attribute that characterized the best manufacturers of this period: automation.[59]

The Revolution of the Ribbon Machine

Efficiency and automation were hallmarks of 1920s industrial culture. Henry Ford's River Rouge plant, which could turn a lump of iron ore into an automobile in forty-one hours, was opened in 1921, and stood for years as a paragon of large-scale integrated manufacturing operations. Although Corning had made great strides in improving the volume and efficiency of its lightbulb production in the 1910s with the introduction of the E and F Machines, bulb production was still far from fully automated. Indeed, those machines merely speeded up the traditional craft method of making bulbs. In the postwar decade, however, Corning's mechanical developers would produce a home-grown bulb-making machine—the Ribbon Machine—that would remain state of the art for most of the remainder of the twentieth century.

The country's seemingly insatiable demand for bulbs showed no sign of abating as the 1920s powered on. In 1922, the F Machine's second year in use, the works produced 9 million bulbs on the F Machine and 73 million on the semiautomatic E Machine. That year, however, Corning still made 34 million bulbs by hand—for a total of 126 million. The number was impressive, but Corning could not necessarily count on continuing domination of the market. General Electric, with its F Machines and Westlake Machines, had started to produce its own lightbulbs in great bulk in the 1920s. In 1924, a year in which its sales topped $300 million, GE made 143 million bulbs, compared with Corning's 154 million. While demand from GE must have decreased, Corning found other large customers. In 1924, for example, it sold more than 50 million bulbs—about a third of its production—to Westinghouse.[60]

Evidently, General Electric was content to let Corning continue to supply it with bulb blanks. For in 1924, GE sold its Central Falls, Rhode Island, plant to Corning. The facility featured three Westlake machines. Following the purchase, Corning decided to double the capacity. "We have come to a definite conclusion that we should install three more Westlake machines at Rhode Island as soon as possible," Falck wrote the Houghton brothers in August 1924. "Negotiations are underway for the purchase of three machines now at the Pitney plant of GE. These could be delivered to us in November."[61]

With the Central Falls plant, Corning was now operating three different automatic and semiautomatic machines—the E, the F, and the Westlake. But the E Machine, on which Corning made about 36 million bulbs a year until 1925, would no longer be relied upon as the workhorse. In 1925 and 1926, Corning made 40 million and 63 million bulbs on the F Machine, respectively, with the Westlake machines accounting for most of the rest. In 1925, the Wellsboro plant shut down temporarily, primarily because the F

Machines in Corning and the Westlake machines in Central Falls were so much more productive than Wellsboro's E Machines.[62]

For two years, the works ran its six F Machines in Corning and its six Westlake machines at Central Falls, which amounted to a large scale industrial experiment. Corning ran tests to determine whether to stay with the F Machine, try to improve it, or switch over all its bulb production to the Westlake machine. While the company found that the cost of the Westlake bulbs was cheaper than F bulbs by about 7 percent, the dilemma was mooted by the development of Corning's most remarkable process invention to date, a bulb-making machine that would make existing machinery of whatever type instantly obsolete. Like the other breakthroughs Corning made in this era, it was the result of applied science and whimsical experimentation, drawing on the creativity of professional scientists and self-taught craftsmen.[63]

In the spring of 1921, William Woods took a shovel with a hole in it and held it under the feed of the Danner tube drawing machine. Designed by Edward Danner of Libbey Glass, the Danner machine had mechanized the horizontal method of drawing tube. Molten glass poured into the machine was transformed into a continuous ribbon of tubing, which was cut automatically. As he suspected, a gob of molten glass fell through the hole and formed a sac. It was from this insight that the Ribbon Machine was born. Woods had very little formal education or training but had proven himself over and over, first in starting up the Wellsboro operation and then in figuring out how to draw clinical thermometer tubing vertically from a pool of glass. "As a result of his years of experience as a glassworker he had developed an almost uncanny insight into the possibilities of handling molten glass," wrote George Hollister.[64]

Woods thought that if he could flatten a gather of molten glass and then run it over a plate with properly sized holes, gravity would draw gobs of glass downward. With air pressure applied from above and molds catching the molten glass from below, this process would form bulbs automatically. By linking a series of such plates together to form an endless chain or belt and by feeding a river of molten glass onto it, one could make blanks continuously with virtually no hand labor. Woods, along with Charles Githler, who had assisted Charles Houghton in the development of the thermometer-drawing machine, and David E. Gray, an MIT-trained engineer, began to experiment with a single plate and plunger in 1922. Between 1922 and 1926, Corning committed $197,723 to the development of the new machine, which was carried on behind a walled-off section of the main factory in Corning. Customers and onetime collaborators like General Electric were not informed of the development. The level of secrecy was such that the developers destroyed the cullet produced from their experiments.[65]

When finally completed, the 399 machine—as it was first called—consisted of two metal drums or rollers between which the continuous stream of glass passed. The rollers flattened the glass into a ribbon, which was carried forward on a chain with holes in it. A series of plungers, arrayed in a row above the chain, applied compressed air to the river of glass. Below the chain, a succession of bulb molds closed around and controlled the shape and size of the blanks. These plungers and molds were carried forward by a second and a third endless chain, one above and another below. The entire process was completed while the chains went just a few feet. When the molds were opened and the finished bulbs tapped off, "they emerged in a veritable shower but a fraction of a second apart."[66]

In 1926, the machine seemed to be nearing completion. "Messrs. A.A. and A.B. Houghton saw the 399 machine in operation," Eugene Sullivan wrote in his daybook on March 25, 1926. They obviously liked what they saw. "Decision reached to start experimental operation of 399 at Wellsboro," Sullivan noted the next day. The machine was moved from Corning to Wellsboro, and on July 22, 1926, the works shipped 20,000 frosted 399 bulbs to Westinghouse. The 399 machine represented a quantum leap forward. In its early development the machine produced between 123 and 168 bulbs per minute. In March 1926, however, it was cranking out 300 bulbs a minute, or 18,000 an hour. For comparative purposes, bulbs were blown by hand at a rate of two bulbs per minute by a team of two men. "By eliminating the gathering operation and replacing the rotary motion by straight-line motion, it was possible to turn out about 15,000 bulbs an hour with one operator, four mechanics, one relief operator, and one transfer mechanic," Arthur Bright wrote. It is difficult to describe the wonder of the Ribbon Machine. In full operation, it is like a symphony, in which each instrument is perfectly harmonized: the deep-throated roar of the furnace, the rush of the molten glass, the relentless percussion of the chugging chain of molds, the brief blasts of compressed air. The rhapsody in glass culminates in a high-pitched finale: a tinkling glissando of completed bulbs.[67]

The development of the Ribbon Machine also led inadvertently to a new line of business for Corning. With the higher capacity and greater action associated with continuous tank melting, the company had to develop more durable refractories, the ceramic materials that lined furnaces and pots. In 1922, Corning began to work on a new refractory referred to by the code name "Adamant." Harrison P. Hood, a chemist from Cornell only recently arrived at Corning, and G. S. Fulcher, a physicist, eventually devised an electrically molded aluminum silicate refractory that became known as Electrocast. Using this new refractory in its melting units helped increase their life span by three to five times.[68]

Aside from resisting the corrosive effects of molten glasses, the new refractories also turned out to have an application for furnace linings in other industries. When Corning made the refractories available to other companies on a trial basis, it realized it had a potential new market segment. Corning decided to form a company to produce them for sale. Because Hartford-Empire held important patents relating to certain components of the process, the two companies set up a joint venture in 1927 and called it Corhart. Corhart bought land for a factory in Louisville, Kentucky, because of its central location to the desired markets and because the fuel and raw materials needed for production were nearby. The same year, to support sales of Corhart in France, St. Gobain and Corning organized a company, L'Electro-Refractaire, to sell Corhart materials in Europe. The rapid development of refractories from an in-house necessity to an international line of business neatly encapsulates the broad-minded way in which Corning's third generation of managers pursued business opportunities. The company's engineers and scientists devised a new process and material to solve a problem presented by automation and mass production. They leveraged their own capabilities by working closely with an outside firm. And once the Corhart refactory had been established in the United States, Corning quickly sought to make it an international product.[69]

A Transition for a Prominent Company
in a Decade of Prosperity

In 1925, Alanson Houghton was offered a new diplomatic posting as ambassador to the Court of St. James in London—a vitally important position in U.S. diplomacy. As the 1920s wore on, Alanson became an important and well-known public figure. He was featured on the cover of Henry Luce's *Time* magazine. And in 1927, when his daughter Mathilda married Chandler Parsons Anderson, who had been Alanson's attaché in Berlin, the event received prominent coverage in London and New York newspapers. When journalist Frederick Collins profiled him in a generally positive article in the *Companion* magazine, however, the portrait was less than reverential: "He labors under the delusion, so common among short, plump men, that he looks well in a double-breasted suit."[70]

Despite tending to diplomatic affairs, Alanson continued to serve as chairman of the Glass Works. On his trips back to the United States, he would visit Corning to discuss matters with works executives, including Alexander Falck, who remained in his post as president throughout the 1920s. Indeed, many of the same executives whom Falck had installed in 1920 remained with the company for much of the decade. Amory Houghton was named assistant to the president in 1926, the same year in which his first son, Amory Jr., was born. In the mid-1920s, Am would write his father dense, three-page or so letters every week. "Business is splendid," he wrote in October 1926. "September was large and October bids fair to being of approximately the same magnitude as October 1920 which, I think, was the biggest month we ever had."[71]

As it grew and expanded its horizons, the Corning Glass Works remained very much a family business. Amory Houghton and George Hollister were top executives. Glen Cole, who had come to work at the company as a laboratory assistant in the 1910s, married Alanson's daughter, Eleanor Wickham Houghton, and would rise to become a key executive. Ownership remained solidly in the hands of the family. The Houghton brothers and various trusts controlled more than half the stock, while the Charles Houghton estate owned a quarter, the Sinclaires—connected to the Houghtons by marriage—had about 10 percent, and the remainder was spread among other employees and investors. In the late 1920s, as companies continued to consolidate, the works considered buy-out offers from other firms, going so far as to ask Estabrook & Company, their long-time private bankers in Boston, to run some calculations in 1927. Estabrook placed a value of $17.5 million on the company's existing common and preferred stock. But the Houghtons decided against selling out. As Arthur (Sr.) put it, "We will not give up our opportunity to protect the Glass Works' employees by running the company in accordance with our principles." While the concern for the employees was genuine, it's more likely that the Houghtons preferred to maintain control of their family company because they enjoyed owning and running it.[72]

Such family connections also brought complications, however. In 1924, Falck sent Alanson a handwritten letter expressing displeasure with Hollister, citing the complaint of a senior Westinghouse executive that Hollister wasn't sufficiently responsive to customers' questions and needs. "We don't want Hollister to come here any more. He makes bad feeling every time he comes," Falck quoted the executive as saying. Although a clear successor was not readily available, Falck wrote, "in my judgement the Sales Dep't can no longer remain under Hollister's direction." But Falck didn't feel he could act unilaterally. "Because he is a vice-president but more because of the family situation I feel that the decision must be made by Arthur and yourself as to how far the change shall go." Apparently the Houghtons decided Hollister should remain in his post.[73]

One of the topics of the letters from Amory to his father in 1926 and 1927 was the declining health of his uncle, Arthur. In August 1927, Am informed Alanson that Arthur was thought to have about six months to live. In the ensuing months, Arthur, his wife, Mabel, and his children, Gratia and Arthur Jr., who was a student at Harvard, would continue moving between the Meadows, New York, and Corning. In the spring of 1928, Arthur Sr. grew significantly weaker and returned to the family's apartment in New York, where he died on April 29. His body was conveyed to Corning, where he was buried in the family plot at Hope Annex Cemetery. Amory Houghton relayed the news to his father in a poignant letter. "The last few days of his life he lost completely any fear of death and at the end he really wanted to go. There was no struggle—just a gradual fading out of life," he wrote. "He could not have gotten well...and it was a blessing and a truly merciful thing that he went so quickly."[74]

Four months after Arthur's death, Alexander Falck resigned as president of the Glass Works. Combined with Alanson's continuing devotion to public affairs, these events represented the passing from the scene of the third generation of Corning's leadership. Upon Falck's resignation, Eugene Sullivan was elected president and would serve as such until the twenty-eight-year-old heir apparent, Am Houghton, was deemed prepared to take the reins.[75]

The third generation of leaders were men of the nineteenth century who had brought the company into the twentieth century, shepherding it through sustained growth in a time of economic, technological, and social upheaval. The Corning Glass Works of 1928 was a large company, with sales of $10.6 million, more than 2,000 employees, operations in four states, and relationships with companies in Europe. In 1928, it spent nearly $400,000 on research and development. Yet the works, as ever, faced business challenges. Its bulb business was safe—for now. But sales of Pyrex had stagnated for much of the decade, hovering at about $1.5 million annually between 1922 and 1928. As a result, bakeware slipped from 20 percent of sales in 1922 to 14 percent in 1928. And although Corning in 1925 developed the updraw process to produce Pyrex in greater quantities at Corning's A Factory, its mechanical experts were still having difficulty producing large volumes of Pyrex cheaply. Meanwhile, the Steuben division, acquired in 1918 for its lightbulb capacity, had switched back to art glass and was racking up never ending losses.[76]

By 1928, Corning, more than a small-town company, was an institution with deep roots and far-flung operations. "Last week, as you know, we had our Sixtieth Anniversary celebration," Am wrote Alanson in 1928. "We had a dinner for all those employees who had been with us fifteen years or more, the total being 378." A great deal had changed in the previous twenty years. The Corning Glass Works was no longer confined to the strip of land along the Chemung.[77]

Corning was more broadly recognized in the world, and not just by executives in industries it had long served, like electric lighting or railroads. Rather, its Pyrex line was a household name. And Americans who kept an eye on public affairs were sure to be familiar with Alanson Houghton, who had evolved from a rather anonymous executive in 1908 into a sometimes controversial public figure. In the summer of 1928, after his brother's death, he returned to the United States, where he won the Senate nomination of the Republican party for New York. With the popular Franklin D. Roosevelt heading the Democratic ticket for governor in the state and former Democratic governor Alfred Smith carrying the Democratic banner in the presidential election, Houghton faced an uphill battle for the Senate seat. In an era before aggressive, media-intensive campaigns, Houghton made one whistle-stop tour of the state and then returned to England to await the results. When he lost by a narrow margin, he simply resumed his diplomatic duties.

As the decade raced to a close, the future seemed bright indeed. With the memory of brutal war fading rapidly, progress seemed inevitable. Corning's ability to exploit and undertake research in glass chemistry and glassmaking had been institutionalized and had become a core mission of the company that drove its growth. Efforts to improve the manufacturing processes had borne substantial fruit. The bulb-making machines allowed the company to increase its production dramatically while maintaining steady employment levels. The company, and the economy, were thriving. In December 1928, President Calvin Coolidge declared, "No Congress of the United States ever assembled, on surveying the state of the Union, has met with a more pleasing prospect than that which appears at the present time."[78]

But the next decade would bring a fresh series of challenges for a fourth generation of Corning leadership. It would strive to find new uses for its homegrown materials and would labor to devise more efficient means of production. More seriously, though, it would grapple with the general malaise that afflicted the United States, and much of the developed world, for nearly a decade. As resurgent and vibrant as the U.S. economy seemed in the late 1920s, a decade of depression was just around the corner.

IV

FOURTH GENERATION

CHAPTER FIVE

Surviving and Thriving
in the Depression Decade, 1928–1939

ON THURSDAY, September 13, 1928, about 400 people gathered for a festive dinner at the Masonic Cathedral in Corning—the only building in the city big enough to accommodate the crowd. The occasion marked the sixtieth anniversary of the arrival of the Glass Works in the city, but it also honored 378 employees of the Corning Glass Works with at least 15 years of service. Attendees dined on "an excellent roast turkey," plus pickles, celery, olives, fruit cocktail, dressing, mashed potatoes, glazed sweets, peas, combination salad, rolls, ice cream, cakes and coffee, with cigars and cigarettes available too. The master of ceremonies, 29-year-old Amory Houghton, drew a laugh by apologizing for his presence at the gathering. With less than ten years of service, he failed to qualify for an invitation. On the other hand, he pointed out, if ten-year employees had been invited, the gathering would have swelled to nearly twice its size and nearly 40 percent of the company's total workforce.[1]

The guests at the banquet were grouped by seniority, and three 50-year employees—Frederick Deuerlein, Frank J. Hultzman Sr., and William S. Rotsell—sat at the head table with Houghton and Corning's president, Dr. Eugene Sullivan. (A fourth 50-year veteran, George Miles, was too ill to attend. Alanson B. Houghton, whose association with the Glass Works stretched back 40 years, was still in England as U.S. ambassador to the Court of St. James.) The attendees formed a group so large that it took more than 30 minutes for Houghton and Sullivan to greet them in a receiving line. Each employee received a blue-and-gold lapel pin commemorating his or her service, with gold stars added for each five-year increment, rubies for 35 and 40 years, and diamonds for 45 years and beyond.[2]

Three speakers sounded common themes of appreciation and cooperation. Amory Houghton spoke first. The people present, he said, "have made Corning Glass Works one big family." Noting their skills, experience, and loyalty, he also praised the cooperative spirit in the company: "The individual prospers only as the company for which he works prospers, and each man helps himself best by helping his organization." Whiting Williams, formerly vice president of the Hydraulic Pressed Steel Company and more recently a noted author and lecturer on industrial relations, continued the theme.[3] Recalling a recent trip to Russia, he pointed out that officials and workers he met there were "tremendously interested in American industry" but attributed its success to machines and equipment. "They worship American industrial machinery. But the secret of American industrial prosperity is not the machinery, it is the wonderful cooperative relations which exist between the men who own and the men who run the machinery."

The final and featured speaker was Walter Cary, first vice president of Westinghouse, which happened to be Corning's biggest customer. Again, he hammered the evening's theme, drawing an appreciative response when he said "he liked to consider the glass works not as an outside company selling lamps to Westinghouse, but as the glass division of the Westinghouse Company." He went on to attribute Corning's success to the fact that

the owners have not been selfish. They have surrounded themselves with able associates, whom they have allowed to grow into the business, and whom they have promoted to positions of responsibility. The finances of a business may be raised in a short time and the buildings erected and machines installed with no great trouble, but an organization thriving on good will and cooperation is the work of a lifetime.

The occasion, which Dr. Sullivan had prompted in one of his first official acts as head of the Glass Works, proved the start of an annual dinner to honor long-time employees at each location. Later in 1928, similar service dinners were held in Wellsboro and Central Falls, and top company executives attended both. Amory Houghton pronounced himself very pleased with the dinner in Corning. Recounting the evening to his father, he observed that "the meeting went off extremely well and I think on the whole did more to help the esprit than any one thing we have done in some time."[4]

The service dinner was fraught with symbolism, some of it tellingly obvious: of harmony between labor and management, especially valuable in a small city like Corning and a craft-oriented business like specialty glass; of the interconnections between the company, the city, and families in the Chemung Valley, as evident not only by the owning families present (Houghton, Sinclaire, and Hollister) but also by the laboring Hultzmans, whose members at the banquet included not only the 50-year honoree but also Andrew F. Hultzman, 45 years of service, Francis L. Hultzman and John J. Hultzman, 25 years, and Fred J. Hultzman, 20 years; of the tight relationships between Corning and its customers in the electrical industry; of a company proud of its heritage and confident in its future; and finally, in the person of young Amory Houghton, of the rise of a new generation of leadership at the company.

Although Amory—Am, as most people called him—was not yet the executive head of the company, that responsibility would not be long in coming. The 56-year-old Dr. Sullivan would remain an influential figure at the glass works for decades longer, but it was widely understood inside the company that he was an interim president until the board deemed Am ready for the job. Whereas Alanson Houghton had accepted his obligations to the company reluctantly, his son proved eager to pour his talents into the business. He was also better suited temperamentally than his father to run a manufacturing company. To Anna Haar, a young secretary in the corporate office, Am seemed "much less formal than his father. His father was—oh, much more dignified." The younger Houghton, in contrast, was "more friendly and more of a mingler."[5]

At the end of 1928, Sullivan and Am Houghton believed that Corning Glass Works was poised on the threshold of a great burst of growth and opportunity. The Ribbon Machines at Wellsboro and Central Falls popped out lightbulb envelopes by the millions, as electrification spread across the country and households acquired more electric lamps and then expanded the market for replacement bulbs. Ovenware and baby bottles made of Pyrex still commanded premiums from consumers, while management continued to seek better ways to sell and distribute these products. There were also new markets to conquer in glass tubing, as the makers of radio sets and other electronic devices faced exploding demand. Finally, although their focus was on what they perceived as abundant growth opportunities, Corning's leaders also took care to defend their core businesses. One manifestation was a push to bolster its position in housewares before the Pyrex patents expired in the mid-1930s; another was an incipient probe into organic chemistry and plastics as a potential substitute for glass in many applications.

Temporary Optimism

The most pressing matter facing the leadership of the Glass Works in September 1928 was how to meet a sudden surge of demand for glass tubing. The company had fared well in recent years, riding the rapid growth of neon signs, one of the most visible symbols of the Roaring Twenties. Between 1924 and 1928, two Danner machines in C Factory yielded a steady output of about 350,000 pounds of tube glass per year. In the fall of the latter year, however, new orders began to flood in, and output surged to more than 850,000 pounds by the end of the year. Corning brought three more Danner machines on line in C Factory and arranged to buy surplus tube glass from GE's Bridgeville glass works, and still struggled to keep up with orders.[6]

The "major factor" behind the new business, wrote J. C. Hostetter, the manager responsible for tube and bulb production, was tubing for radio sets. He estimated that in 1928 there were more than 12 million radio sets in the United States and projected that "ultimately, there should be at least as many radio sets as there are automobiles registered" in the country—about 25 million, and very likely much more. Meanwhile, he pointed out, "television and other applications may still further increase the demand for radio tubes. With seven vacuum tubes in each radio and a third of these in need of replacement every year, he forecast a rosy future for tube production. And he found it "quite obvious" from this arithmetic that "additional production capacity is needed immediately." The choice facing Corning was to expand C Factory or build an entirely new plant.[7]

Hostetter himself was not convinced that building a new, specialized tubing plant was necessary, although he fretted about "bad operating conditions" in the congested tubing department in C Factory and the need to upgrade aging equipment: "It should not be overlooked that Westinghouse representatives have commented unfavorably on conditions in our tubing department." As a matter of pure cost, he believed, building a major addition on the south side of C Factory would be the most economical alternative. On the other hand, he argued that erecting a new, specialized plant to make tubing would have "a decided advantage primarily because every employee has but one interest and, in this particular case, this would be 'pounds of tubing packed per hour.'" He also saw organizational benefits in a specialized plant, including the opportunity to develop "a clean-cut organization reporting to one responsible head." This he contrasted with the less efficient decision-making structure of C factory, where mixing and melting operations reported to one executive, production and shipping to another, and inspection and packing to still another.[8]

In the end, Hostetter declared for a new plant, and the board of directors backed him up. The company purchased an abandoned railroad property about a half mile east of Main Plant on Tioga Avenue and allocated about $600,000 to begin construction. Ground was broken on December 12, 1929, with the first product—sign light tubing—shipped the following June. The new plant was christened Fallbrook after the name of the railroad that had previously used the site for its roundhouse and maintenance shops.[9]

The expansionist spirit expressed in the Fallbrook investment also animated Corning's other businesses at the end of the 1920s. In Pyrex, for example, the company continued its search for ways to boost lagging sales. Between 1924 and 1928, sales of Pyrex products had remained essentially flat at about $1.7 million per year.[10] Early in 1929, Corning retained Harvard Business School professor Melvin T. Copeland to carry out a market study of Pyrex ovenware. Author of several influential texts on merchandising and consumer marketing, Copeland proved well suited to the task.[11] After poring over market survey data provided by J. Walter Thompson, the company's advertising agency, Copeland concluded that "a large, undeveloped market for Pyrex ovenware exists." To tap it, he reasoned, Corning should proceed "not by means of any clever scheme, nor by means of premature price reductions, but by perfecting the coverage of its market, by revamping its advertising program, and by carrying out a series of experiments scientifically to ascertain the best way of handling its marketing job."[12]

Copeland's most important recommendation was to redirect sales from jobbers, who sold mainly to the hardware trade, to purchasing agents in department stores. Pyrex, he pointed out, was "essentially women's merchandise" and Corning needed to get its products in stores catering to women. As for advertising, Copeland recommended scrapping the existing "515" campaign—so named because the company packaged sets for $5.15 in an attempt to overcome price resistance—in favor of a new message to emphasize other Pyrex features: "serving especially well-flavored food and serving it hot; the pleasure of the craftsman in working with good tools;...the pride of having a kitchen equipped with Pyrex." The experiments that Copeland recommended consisted of formal evaluations of in-store baking demonstrations and tests of different regional advertising themes (e.g., "determining whether the Southern housewives can be induced to recognize the superior qualities of hot biscuits baked in Pyrex. Pyrex biscuits rise higher, brown better, and have an even texture which should appeal to all lovers of hot biscuits.")

Am Houghton, production manager Glen Cole, and sales manager Jim Peden greeted Copeland's work enthusiastically and proved eager to reposition the Pyrex line. As a first step, they recruited 30-year-old Charles D. "Lafe" LaFollette, a Harvard MBA and former student of Copeland's, as sales manager of the Pyrex housewares division. LaFollette had previously worked for publisher Bobbs-Merrill in Indianapolis, but was nonetheless deemed a bright prospect to sell glass ovenware. He joined Corning in November 1929.[13]

LaFollette was one of four young men (all with Harvard connections) to join the company in key managerial and technical positions in 1929 and 1930. A few weeks before LaFollette arrived, Arthur A. Houghton Jr., Am's cousin and a recent graduate of Harvard College, began his climb through the ranks, starting as a clerk in the Pyrex production department. The following spring, William C. "Bill" Decker, another Harvard MBA recommended by Copeland, was hired as a manager of the industrial sales department; and the following summer, at the behest of Sullivan, Corning recruited J. Franklin "Frank" Hyde, a young Ph.D in organic chemistry, who was just coming off a postdoctoral fellowship at Harvard. Together with other young executives and scientists, including Am Houghton and Glen Cole, these men would make major contributions to the company in the coming decade—but not before they were tested by fire.

The Depression Comes to Corning

"Needless to say," Lafe LaFollette later remarked of his hiring date in the fall of 1929, it was "not the most propitious time to become a sales manager."[14] At that very moment, the U.S. economy was teetering into a prolonged and extraordinarily bleak period of economic hardship. The Great Depression is frequently traced to Black Tuesday, October 29, 1929, which saw the biggest single-day plunge of stock market values since the panic of 1907. Yet the pain of this event was not fully apparent until many months later. 1930 proved a bad year, 1931 worse still, and 1932 worst of all. At its low point in 1932, U.S. GNP hit a level 30 percent below its peak in 1929. During these years, wholesale prices plunged 32 percent, national unemployment soared to 25 percent, and a disheartened nation witnessed more than 9,000 bank failures.

In the city of Corning, perception of the magnitude of the crisis developed slowly. For the city, the company, and the country at large, the late 1920s had been heady times. In the same week as Corning's sixtieth anniversary dinner in September 1928, for example, the city of Corning celebrated the opening of the Baron Steuben Hotel. More than a thousand people gathered for the official dedication. The six-and-a-half story structure featured 100 bedrooms (all with private toilet accommodations and most with either a private bath or shower), a large dining room (with Sunday dinner available for $1.50), and four large "sample rooms created for the accommodation of commercial travelers, who wish to display their wares to the business people of Corning." The half story on top housed the Corning Club, a suite of five wood-paneled rooms adorned with fixtures designed by Fred Carder and intended for the use of the city's business establishment. City fathers boasted that the hotel's economic impact on the city would rank with those of opening of the Chemung canal, the coming of the railroads, and the arrivals of Corning Glass Works and Ingersoll-Rand Company.[15]

The new hotel was one of a string of new buildings indicating the city's prosperity. A few months earlier, a J.C. Penney department store had opened on Market Street. The initialed competition soon followed: a J.J. Newbury in 1929 and, the year after, a W.T. Grant. The abandonment of streetcar service between Corning and Elmira in 1929 was hailed as a sign of progress, the replacement of an obsolete technology with a newer one— regular bus service.

Yet the optimism of the 1920s faded quickly with the coming of hard times. Just months after the opening of Grant's, local government officials recorded an ominous sign: the number of homeless men in the county poor house rose to 140 men, up from 94 in 1927. From there, matters only got worse. During the first seven months of 1931, the city of Corning spent a record $33,000 on relief, exhausting its annual budget. On Market Street, juxtaposed to the new department stores, a growing number of establishments boarded up their windows. At local banks, Christmas Club deposits began to shrink, and the banks announced that they could no longer afford to pay interest on these accounts. In December, the Painted Post National Bank failed. Teachers went unpaid. Local government employees took 10 percent pay cuts and still faced layoffs.[16]

Meanwhile, at the Glass Works, the downturn also manifested itself slowly but brutally. In 1929, the company recorded its best results ever, with gross revenues of $15.1 million, net income of $4.7 million, and more than 2,700 employees. In February of the next year, Sullivan asked to step down as president, relinquishing direction of the company to Am Houghton and assuming a new position as vice chairman. (Alexander Falck remained chairman of the board until 1941.) At the same time, Arthur A. Houghton Jr. became a special assistant to his cousin and joined the board of directors; Charles Githler became manager of manufacturing; Glen Cole (Am's brother-in-law and four years his senior), production manager; Harry Hosier, production superintendent of Main Plant; and Dr. J. C. Hostetter, director of research.[17]

Looking ahead, Houghton felt short-term concerns but long-term optimism. Dashing off a personal note to his cousin in August 1930, he commented briefly on the company's health. "Business I will tell you about when I see you. For the first seven months of 1930 it is 27% behind last year. All divisions except bulb and tubing are behind 22% and the bulb and tubing is behind 32.4%." Still, he did not seem particularly worried, bearing in mind that the company was coming off an exceptional year. Results for the first six months of 1930, he pointed out, "were a little bit ahead of 1928."[18] Indeed, the new team atop the company was still thinking about expansion. The new Fallbrook plant had just come on stream and was hiring. The laboratory was expanding and adding personnel, with a budget for 1930 nearly twice that of 1929.

But the reckoning could not be long delayed. By 1932, revenues had plummeted by 50 percent and employment by a third, although the company eked out a profit of $800,000—probably because the executive owners took home little pay themselves. Even in strong lines like tubing, employment at the new Fallbrook plant dipped from 123 to 110, and shipments dropped from 5.7 million pounds to 4.4 million. The Central Falls plant nearly closed. The Ribbon Machine shut down and only one Westlake machine remained in operation to make large bulbs and blue glass bulbs. Employment fell to just 50 people. At Main Plant, production of insulators for telephone and electrical lines simply ceased. Activity was so low that the company restructured working assignments from three eight-hour shifts to four six-hour shifts. Although that saved some jobs, the company was forced to cut wages by 10 percent in August 1932.[19]

Yet through the worst of times, several factors mitigated the crisis at the Glass Works. With its equity privately and closely held by a small group of people, most of them related to one another, and no debt, Corning was shielded from frantic investors and creditors. At the same time, Corning was fortunate that two of its core businesses—lamp glass and glass tubing—declined much less than many other industrial lines as people still bought lightbulbs and managed to scrape together enough money to buy radios to help take their troubles away. Corning played an essential role in this development. As some types of vacuum tubes could be produced on the Ribbon Machine, prices of components fell dramatically. Between 1929 and 1932, in turn, the average selling price of radio sets plunged from $133 to $35.[20]

Other Corning lines suffered more grievously during the depression. As personal income across the nation plummeted 42 percent, the population deemed purchases of upscale products like Pyrex housewares discretionary. Total volume of Pyrex sales dipped from $1.7 million in 1929 to about $940,000 in 1932—results that postponed a meaningful test of the new sales and distribution strategy Professor Copeland had prescribed.

Corning tried several tactics to turn the business around and reposition Pyrex as a product for the mass market. It sought to cut manufacturing costs by automating production, starting with small items such as custard cups and eventually graduating to larger pieces such as pie plates. At the same time, the company developed a more sophisticated understanding of consumer behavior. LaFollette extended the market research begun by Copeland and collected detailed information about household buying habits and houseware purchases at the point of sale. The company also hired its first fulltime home economist, Lucy M. Maltby. A Corning native with a bachelor's degree from Cornell and a masters from Iowa State, Maltby was teaching home economics at Mansfield State Teachers College in Pennsylvania in 1929 when she delivered an unsolicited critique of Pyrex ovenware to sales manager Peden. Pointing out that some Pyrex pieces came in awkward sizes and shapes, Maltby argued that Corning was not listening to complaints and ignoring actual users of the product. She urged Peden to follow the lead of some food and consumer products companies and apply research in home economics to product development. Peden was so impressed with Maltby's presentation that he engaged her to manage a new consumer service office. Her initial work involved answering complaints, corresponding with consumers, and preparing materials to educate them on the proper use of Pyrex products. As she settled into the job and gathered valuable intelligence from the field, however, her role expanded. In 1931 she established a test kitchen at headquarters to evaluate new designs and products before they hit the marketplace.

In combination, the efforts to automate production and make products better suited to customer needs could not prevent sagging sales as the depression wore on. Finally, in August 1932, after many dreary months of low sales, Am Houghton made the painful decision to cut Pyrex prices by up to a third. The price of a 9-inch Pyrex pie plate that had sold for $1 dropped to about $.70. The stratagem worked: in 1933, total sales volume began to climb, and as the economy recovered, Pyrex enjoyed a sustained upward ride that would continue unchecked until World War II. By then, Corning had successfully repositioned Pyrex ovenware as a product line for the masses.[21]

Climbing out of the Trough

The depression did produce one salutary effect on the Glass Works: it accelerated interest in new business. Indeed, the ownership of the firm and its young leaders viewed hard times as an opportunity to explore new markets in optical glass, art glass, and architectural glass. During the early 1930s, several projects gained impetus that may well have faltered in more prosperous circumstances. At the same time, Am Houghton and Dr. Sullivan challenged the R&D organization to extend their knowledge of the properties of glass and find new applications for the material. This work yielded significant dividends with the return of good times later in the decade.

The Giant Disk

During the early 1930s researchers at Corning tracked new developments in astronomy and telescopes with mounting excitement. Although the company had occasionally fabricated mirror blanks for telescope makers in the 1920s, much bigger projects were suddenly in the air. There were several reasons for the growing interest. The most important was a sequence of breathtaking astronomical discoveries that new reflecting telescopes made possible.[22]

During the 19th century, most new telescopes had been refractors—larger versions of the familiar "spyglass" used for generations aboard ships at sea. In simple terms, a user peered through a small lens at one end of a tube to view objects magnified through a bigger lens at the other. With construction of the 40-inch refractor at Yerkes Observatory in Michigan in 1897, however, refracting telescopes had reached their upper limits. The massive lenses for bigger telescopes would distort under their own weight, while also absorbing too much starlight to permit observation of faint objects. A better solution was a reflecting telescope, which used large, curved mirrors to capture and focus images of astronomical objects. Reflecting telescopes achieved no greater magnification than refractors but gathered much more light, permitting observation of very faint, and presumably very distant, objects. And unlike a lens, a mirror needed polishing on one side only and could be supported on the other to prevent sagging and distortion.

In 1908, George Ellery Hale, an entrepreneurial and wealthy astronomer, oversaw construction of the first big reflecting telescope in the United States, a 60-inch model at Mount Wilson near Pasadena, California. A decade later, Hale raised funds (from Andrew Carnegie, among others) for a 100-inch reflector, the Hooker telescope, also at Mount Wilson. Although the Hooker telescope proved exceedingly temperamental—it could be used only a few hours in each 24-hour period because temperature changes atop Mount Wilson affected the dimensions, and hence the sensitivity, of the mirror—it enabled significant discoveries. The most important stemmed from the work of Edwin P. Hubble, who demonstrated that many of the nebulae lying beyond the Milky Way were independent galaxies and that most of these galaxies were speeding farther away. Through observations enabled by the Hooker telescope, Hubble established that the universe was expanding at a constant rate—a finding with staggering cosmological implications and the source of enormous scientific interest and general fascination. During the 1920s and early 1930s, the Hooker telescope and other large reflectors also permitted important discoveries about the solar system, including the first pictures of Pluto, the ninth planet, whose existence had been predicted but never before confirmed.

In this heady environment, Hale set his sights on building a still larger telescope, a 200-inch reflector. With four times the light-gathering power of the Hooker telescope, the 200-inch model would greatly extend the limits of the known universe. To finance construction Hale received a $6 million grant from the Rockefeller Foundation. The telescope would be owned and operated by the California Institute of Technology, where Hale held faculty standing. It would also be the biggest and most expensive scientific instrument ever built.

Fabricating a 200-inch mirror, Hale knew, constituted an immense technical challenge. To begin with, it was fiendishly tricky to cast large masses of glass without causing bubbles and imperfections. Annealing (heating to remove stresses and strains followed by a long period of controlled cooling) of large pieces of glass presented other significant difficulties. The process could take many months and if not carried out precisely would result in cracks and distortions. And if glassmakers could manage to overcome these problems, still others remained. Conventional plate-glass formulations, such as the mirror blank for the Hooker telescope (cast by St. Gobain in 1904), were too sensitive even to minor temperature changes to permit round-the-clock use in such a delicate (albeit massive) instrument.

When specifying the 200-inch mirror in 1927, Hale opted for a mirror blank made of fused quartz. Although this material constituted the purest known form of glass and offered the desired thermal stability, it had only been produced in experimental quantities far below the amounts needed for the big disk. Nonetheless, Hale contracted with GE in 1927 to fabricate the mirror blank, and the renowned inventor Elihu Thomson took charge of the project. Meanwhile, Hubble's discoveries and publicity around the new telescope triggered a wave of observatory building at colleges, universities, and research institutions across the United States. And many telescope designers were interested in making the mirror blanks from Pyrex or borosilicate glass because of its low expansion and temperature resistance.

Early in 1929, Corning received an inquiry from the Yerkes Observatory about making mirror blanks of Pyrex. Noting this request and the apparent boom in observatory building, George McCauley, a physicist in Corning's optical glass department, persuaded Sullivan to fund casting of a 27-inch-Pyrex disk—a substantially bigger disk than the company had made previously—to demonstrate Corning's capabilities and serve as a promotional sales tool. A Ph.D. in physics from Wisconsin and a former staff member at the National Bureau of Standards, McCauley had joined the company before World War I. He was well aware of the 200-inch reflector project and believed that Pyrex could compete both with fused quartz and European optical glass as mirror-blank material—if Corning could learn to cast and anneal big pieces of glass successfully.

The fabrication of the 27-inch disk in the summer of 1929 proved full of tribulation, some of it comic. At one point before the pouring, workers used the mold as a temporary surface and stacked tools and other objects on it. The mold cracked and had to be patched with wet clay and cement. Later, after the mold was poured and set aside for annealing of the glass, the heat it radiated triggered automatic sprinklers in the factory. Technicians sprang into action and shut off the sprinklers and moved the mold to a safe location. When it had finally cooled and was freed from its mold, the disk betrayed its scars, with obvious imperfections tracing to the mold repairs and the interrupted annealing process. Nonetheless, the disk successfully demonstrated that Corning could cast big pieces of Pyrex and that these, moreover, could serve as telescope mirror blanks.

Despite McCauley's enthusiasm, his bosses were only vaguely interested in the telescope business. The high cost of the 27-inch disk remained a substantial obstacle to growth in a business that seemed unlikely ever to generate much sales volume. Most telescope builders in the United States continued to import optical glass from Germany, while watching eagerly for news from GE. And under Thomson, GE appeared at last to be making progress. In 1931, after many fits and starts, GE built up a nine-inch thick 60-inch blank of synthetic quartz. As McCauley later summarized it, Thomson's method involved "spraying grains of crystal quartz through a hydrogen-gas burner and fusing them in place on the face of the blank which was gradually formed by passing the burner repeatedly over the area of its surface." The achievement was marred in significant respects, however. The disk itself contained far too many flaws to be useful as a mirror blank. Worse, to Hale's mounting horror and depression, the cost to produce it vastly exceeded original estimates. In 1927, GE had projected that it would take two years and about $75,000 to produce a 60-inch disk from fused quartz. After four years and more than $600,000 in expenses, GE still had not made a usable disk. Worst of all, GE now refused to be pinned down on a cost or delivery schedule for the 200-inch disk, although it did forecast expenditures of at least another $750,000.[23]

Fortunately, back at Corning, McCauley and a handful of determined colleagues had pressed on in their search for ways to lower costs of Pyrex disks. Working some on their own time, the group sought to fabricate molds, furnaces, annealing kilns, cranes, and lifting equipment from materials on hand or available at low cost from commercial sources. Early in 1931, the group demonstrated that no big cash outlays would be necessary to proceed and that the company could offer competitive prices for Pyrex mirror blanks. In March, Corning took its first order for a Pyrex telescope blank, a large elliptical disk for use in an auxiliary telescope at the Perkins Observatory at Ohio Wesleyan University. Given the depressed fortunes of the company, executives were now happy for the business.[24]

A few months later, Hale wrote to his friend Arthur Day, at the Geophysical Laboratory at the Carnegie Institution of Washington, with a blunt question: could Corning cast Pyrex glass for the 200-inch reflector? Still close to Corning, Day replied, "I think now, as I have always thought that [Corning] could successfully make it." Once Hale and his associates terminated the contract with GE, Day arranged for them to meet with Corning technical representatives, including Hostetter and McCauley, in New York. By the middle of October, the basic terms were worked out. As GE had done before, McCauley proposed that Corning build up its capability in stages and incorporate learning by making successively larger disks. The company would start with a 26-inch blank and then proceed to cast 30-inch, 60-inch, and 120-inch disks before attempting the 200-inch blank. He estimated that the costs of all of the disks would fall in a range between $150,000 and $300,000 and stated that the final disk would be ready for delivery within 18 months of the start of work. If second pourings were necessary for each disk, the delivery date might stretch to 31 months. Corning would undertake this work on a cost-plus basis, with expenses paid as accumulated and an extra fee of 10 percent to be billed after the disks were ground into usable mirrors.[25]

The Corning group approached the first pour by experimenting with glass formulations, mold properties and designs, and casting techniques. To cut the weight of the larger disks and hasten response time to temperature changes, McCauley, in consultation with Hale, designed ribbed structures for the backs. The design required making special molds containing columns or cores of firebrick—a challenge McCauley compared to completing a jigsaw puzzle in three dimensions.[26] The challenge was further complicated by the need for new techniques to fasten the cores to the mold, lest they come unstuck under the extreme temperatures of molten glass and bob to the surface. Corning scientists, engineers, and technicians focused on developing heat-resistant cements and devising new mechanical approaches to holding the cores in place.

Corning's early pours showed encouraging progress, and lessons learned at one stage were applied during the next. In May 1932, a 30-inch disk emerged in excellent condition, and the company shipped it to Pasadena for grinding as a mirror blank and eventual use in an auxiliary telescope. Two months later, Corning was ready to pour a 60-inch disk. By then, McCauley's group had devised another casting innovation: domed ovens, or "igloos," over the molds to keep them hot during the protracted process of pouring a big piece of glass.

Analysis of the 60-inch disk by chemists Martin Nordberg and Harrison Hood revealed concerns about the "weatherability" of the glass—its ability to maintain specification after prolonged exposure to the elements. This analysis, in turn, led the chemists in December to recommend a different borosilicate formulation than conventional Pyrex. The new formula, 715F, possessed not only superior weatherability but also a coefficient of expansion 25 percent lower than the original formula. The disadvantage, however, was still higher working temperatures during casting.

During the early months of 1933, Corning cast more intermediate-sized disks and further refined and adapted its procedures. The cores inside the molds were secured with not only temperature-resistant adhesives but also cold-rolled steel rods. The lining of the glass tanks was steadily improved. Bigger molds were built with the pouring holes in new positions. Larger annealing kilns were developed. And the company's progress attracted notice. In June, Corning obtained orders for two 60-inch disks from Harvard University. In the same month, David Dunlap University in Toronto ordered a 76-inch mirror blank, and the University of Texas an 81-inch blank.[27]

Corning began pouring the 120-inch disk on June 24, a day on which work started at 5 A.M. and casting concluded 11 hours later. The mold was transferred to the annealing kiln at 4300C. There the glass was warmed to 5200C for 11 days, and then cooled at 1.60 per day for 140 days. When the mold was opened in late December, the glass blank featured a few bubbles but was pronounced satisfactory and suitable for grinding. Analysis of the pour revealed that making the cores hollow would permit faster cooling.

During the next several months, Corning cast disks for its growing list of observatory customers and readied to pour the 200-inch disk. By then, publicity about the project spurred repeated requests to permit the public to view the pouring. NBC radio newsman Lowell Thomas, indulging in hyperbole, pronounced the operation as "the greatest item of interest to the civilized world in twenty-five years, not excluding the World War." At first, Corning resisted admitting the public but at last acceded in the face of overwhelming demand. The Corning Club atop the Baron Steuben Hotel became a press center. Journalists covering the event hailed from as far away as London and ranged from seasoned veterans at the *New York Times*, *Wall Street Journal*, and *Time*, to 14-year-old cub reporter and photographer Donald Bonnell, present on behalf of the *Elmira Gazette*.[28]

The Corning Club also served as home base for dignitaries from Caltech, the Rockefeller Foundation, the U.S. Bureau of Standards, and other distinguished guests. What they, the journalists, and the estimated 6,000 viewers who streamed through Main Plant came to see was a casting operation on a monumental scale. The finished disk would be the biggest and most expensive piece of glass ever made. The final dimensions measured 202 inches across and 26 inches thick, with a gross weight of 20 tons. The mold featured three pouring holes, and inside 114 cores would form the rib structure of the back of the mirror. To fill the mold, more than 65 tons of glass was melted and heated to a temperature of 2700C—a process that itself consumed two weeks. Giant ladles, each holding 750 pounds of glass, were filled and positioned over the three pouring holes in the mold every six minutes. To maintain constant temperatures in the mold, only the first 400 pounds from each ladle was used, with the remainder returned to the melting tank for reheating.[29]

After years of work and months of intensive preparation, casting of the big disk finally began on Sunday, March 25, 1934, at 8 A.M. (The choice of day was deliberate to minimize disruption of regular factory operations.) The process proceeded according to plan until early afternoon. McCauley left the plant for a short period to speak on the phone with a reporter from England. When he returned, he learned that one of the cores inside the mold had come loose. He recognized the news as potentially disastrous and ordered the pouring to cease while technicians poked at the floating piece with metal rods to break it apart or submerge it. When that failed, he ordered pouring to resume, hoping that the problem was isolated and could be fixed later. The last ladle was poured at 6 P.M. By then, another 21 cores had broken loose and were bobbing inside the mold.

McCauley and his colleagues sought feverishly for ways to remove or submerge the loose cores, but everything they considered only increased the likelihood of more serious damage to the glass. Late at night, they finally conceded that this pouring would probably fail to yield a usable mirror blank. Amid great disappointment, they decided to transfer the mold to an annealing kiln, accelerate the annealing process, and see what they might learn down the road from this experience.

After two months, the disk was cool enough to remove from the mold. In addition to the imperfections that the floating cores had caused, it was found to have ten times the residual stress expected in a well annealed disk. But the good news was that in other respects the disk seemed fine. Corning could thus rightly assure Hale that "a 200-inch glass disk can be successfully made." Privately Amory Houghton notified the project sponsors that Corning would pour another disk.

The fate of the first 200-inch disk could easily have been misinterpreted and could have caused an embarrassment had it been widely disclosed. The company and its sponsors kept quiet for months while waiting for the results of annealing and deciding what to do next. In any event, Corning had at the outset acknowledged the possibility of casting a second disk if the first one proved unsatisfactory. The company came to consider what had happened in the first pouring as a necessary, if unhappy, learning experience. At one point in September, however, McCauley, who had grown fond of the limelight, indiscreetly discussed the disk's problems with a reporter and stated that it would be cheaper to pour a new disk than to fix the first one. Immediately, Alanson Houghton fired off a letter to his son:

> When I saw McCauley some months ago, I told him not to make the pouring of the first lens a failure but to explain that we had planned to pour two and possible three discs to make, in an experimental work of this magnitude, certain that we should get a good lens. I cautioned him in particular not to say that we poured another lens because the former lens was a failure. Obviously he has done precisely this thing.
>
> I do not know how much damage indirectly he has caused but I think you will find before the matter is concluded that he has seriously weakened our position. I suggest, therefore, that from now on any interviews or statements shall be made by you or someone in whom you have confidence and that McCauley be told to keep his mouth shut.[30]

During the summer and fall of 1934, Corning prepared for a second try at the 200-inch disk. A subdued McCauley oversaw many changes in the process. A new alloy resistant to temperatures as high as 8500C was used in the rods to anchor the cores in the mold. These pieces had to be cast with caps and stems because they could not be machined. The cavity in the hollow cores was enlarged and fitted with pipes to carry forced air for cooling. Technicians developed more efficient ways to move the ladles and hasten the rate of pouring.

At 8 A.M. on December 2, 1934, Corning cast the second 200-inch disk, this time before a more select group of onlookers. The pouring went smoothly, with no surprises, and finished in just six hours. That evening, the mold was moved to the annealing kiln. During the next several weeks, the temperature of the glass was slowly raised from 450 degrees to 5000C. On January 21, 1935, the cooling process began at a controlled rate of 0.80 per day.

Although the operation showed every indication of success and the annealing process appeared straightforward, the Chemung River introduced an unwelcome moment of high drama. In early July 1935, a torrential downpour produced rising water, which broke through the dikes next to Main Plant and flooded the area where the 200-inch disk was annealing.

Desperate employees called in the city fire department to pump the area but these frantic efforts failed to stem the inrushing water. The annealing kiln was situated above the high-water mark, but it was hardly out of danger, as electrical power to most of the plant went out. A technician managed to isolate and save a single transformer, which for three days became the only source of power to the annealing kiln. Even so, the temperature of the glass in the mold dropped from 3700C to 3000C, raising concern about complications from stress. Once power to the plant was restored, the glass was reheated to 3700C and held there for five days before the controlled cooling resumed.

In late October—ten months after the pouring and another tense period a minor earthquake in Corning—the disk had cooled sufficiently for McCauley to inspect it while still in the mold. He found three fractures in the surface that bowed metal in the kiln cover had caused, but these appeared to be wounds that would disappear in the grinding of the mirror. Nonetheless, in reporting to Hale and his associates, he recommended that the surface be ground to a thickness of 3 5/8 inches rather than the 4 inches originally specified. A relieved Hale accepted the recommendation and authorized Corning to ship the disk to Pasadena when fully cooled.

The shipment of an object as big and heavy as a 20-ton piece of glass proved itself replete with unusual challenges. Corning had to build a special padded and reinforced crate and work with the New York Central Railroad to customize a freight car to carry the disk. During this activity, the first 200-inch disk proved useful, allowing Corning to experiment with hoisting and packing techniques. Meanwhile, authorities in Pasadena planned a route from Corning that would avoid traffic, minimize encounters with uneven terrain and poor track, and bypass older tunnels and low bridges. Insured by Lloyds of London for $100,000, the disk left Corning on March 24, 1936—one day short of two years after the first pouring. The railroads took special precautions, restricting speed to 25 miles per hour and traveling only during daylight. As the train wended slowly across the country along advertised routes, curious onlookers in most cities and towns thronged the tracks for a glimpse.

The disk arrived in Pasadena on April 10. It proceeded to grinding and finishing operations while other parts of the giant telescope were fabricated and a new observatory complex was built on Mt. Palomar. Work was suspended during World War II and the telescope did not become operational until January 1948. By then, George Ellery Hale was long since dead and George McCauley on the verge of retirement. The honor of the "first light," however, passed to another legendary figure in the story, Edwin Hubble, whose work two decades before had helped launch the project.

In pure financial terms, casting telescope mirror blanks afforded little direct gain to Corning. An accounting by the company in 1938 concluded that it was entitled to a fee of approximately $30,000 on top of expenses of about $330,000—a modest sum collectible several years after it had performed the work.[31] Nor did the company do much better through sales of additional telescope mirror blanks. Correspondence between Alanson Houghton and Harvard's Shapley revealed that the Houghton family donated at least one 60-inch mirror to the university: "I have decided to give you the rough glass disc for the mirror you want," Houghton wrote, adding, "I must ask you, however, to keep my name out of the matter. You realize if I give a mirror to Harvard, I shall, undoubtedly, be afforded many opportunities to give other mirrors to other institutions of learning and these I should be glad to escape." In estimating the value of the gift for tax purposes, accountants at the company pegged the selling price of a 60-inch disk at $6,650, of which direct cost constituted $2,260, overhead added a similar amount, and the remainder was profit.[32] Selling a few such items each year thus could not have a material effect on Corning's finances.

But the big disk paid dividends in many other ways for Corning. During the depths of the depression, it and other telescope projects at the Glass Works kept scores of people employed, ensuring their loyalty and extending their capabilities on the company's behalf. The massive publicity surrounding the big disk also helped establish Corning's reputation for tackling difficult assignments and solving problems. At last, it seemed, the United States possessed a glassmaker whose technical abilities rivaled those of the leading European glassmakers. This reputation—and Corning's ability to engineer glass—would prove highly important when new technical challenges arose during World War II. Finally, the story of the glass disk became a central element of Corning lore. It was recounted often to illustrate the company's technical proficiency and perseverance, to attract scientists and engineers, and to inspire them to invest the extra commitment and effort essential to sustaining technical leadership. Public display of the first 200-inch disk reinforced these points. In this respect, the telescope mirror business had much in common with another small business that assumed disproportionate significance during the depression: Steuben Glass.

A Little Star in Corning's Crown

During the decade after World War I, the Steuben factory on Erie Avenue in Corning resumed hand production of art glass, in a variety of sizes, shapes, and colors for uses ranging from decorative items to everyday tableware. Virtually all of these pieces bore the imprint of Steuben's irascible founder, Fred Carder. As a maker of art glass, Steuben enjoyed an impeccable reputation; as a business venture, however, Steuben was perennially a shaky proposition. Carder himself was uninterested in administrative matters and contemptuous of people who were—although he remained friendly with some near contemporaries at the Glass Works, especially Eugene Sullivan, his Saturday golf partner for many decades. For their part, the top leadership of the Glass Works viewed Carder as a valuable asset, but one to be handled gingerly.

During the postwar recession, Corning bumped Carder into a new position, art director, and turned over leadership of the Steuben division to a series of young executives, including J. C. Hostetter and Glen Cole, who rotated through for a year or two and skirmished with Carder on their way up. During the next several years, the division eked by, seldom gaining or losing more than a few tens of thousands of dollars per year on revenues that bounced between $320,000 and $530,000.[33]

With at least some management controls in place, Corning acceded to Carder's wishes and reinstated him as general manager. Almost immediately, the move began to backfire. In 1926, Steuben embarked on an extended string of losses, as cheaper European art glass became popular with the American middle class and as pressed (mass-produced) tableware made in the United States became more fashionable. In short order, Steuben's products became perceived as outmoded and unduly expensive.

Meanwhile, sales of a once promising product line of decorative shades and bases for electrical table lamps also began to decline in the face of changing tastes and cheaper alternatives.[34]

With the onset of the Great Depression, Steuben's condition moved from serious to critical. To clear out a backlog of inventory and raise cash, the division held a special sale at the Baron Steuben Hotel. The sale netted modest proceeds but not nearly enough to cure Steuben's fundamental problems. A review of the division's operations in April 1931 depicted a mess: "Inefficient layout and plant conditions slightly less than deplorable...Morale very low...Sales assistance should receive most careful attention...Present cost system does not function as it should...Considera- tion should be given as to how the product can be best distributed and mer- chandised...Lack of co-operation on part of Steuben Division toward Corning Plant is very evident...No consistency in pricing different pieces in a line of similar shapes."[35]

In light of this dismal assessment, early in 1932, Corning took strong actions. It dislodged Carder again, moved Steuben production from the Erie Avenue factory into Main Plant, and installed a new general manager, John J. MacKay, formerly head of the company's sales office in New York. Amory Houghton also paired MacKay with a new consultant, industrial designer Walter Dorwin Teague. The combination of Teague and MacKay—with Teague very much the dominant party—would start Steuben on the road to enduring success.[36]

Teague's involvement with Steuben had originated with an unsolicited letter in November 1931. Teague had learned that Houghton admired his work, and so he wrote to offer his services to Corning to help with its "tableware, architectured glass, as well as the PYREX line." Teague believed that it would be possible "to introduce a new note into these wares," and he proposed to develop his ideas on a six-month renewable retainer arrange- ment. Houghton accepted the proposition and then passed Teague along to MacKay.[37]

Teague is not remembered fondly in Steuben history, primarily because his association with the business was brief and the designs he contributed never became popular.[38] Yet his consulting advice pointed the direction of the division's eventual turnaround in the mid-1930s. His most potent ideas included a new definition of the customer, a restricted product line, and a preference for working with clear over-colored glass. These ideas were interconnected, of course, and they originated in Teague's conclusion that it would be hopeless for Steuben to attempt to reclaim ground it had already lost. Rather than compete with makers of pressed tableware, he argued, Steuben should capitalize on its strengths in making glass by hand and its sustained reputation for design excellence and high quality. Rather than offer an extensive variety of unique, costly-to-make pieces, it should develop a few lines of distinctive glassware. Such a strategy would appeal not to the middle class customers Steuben had served in earlier years but rather to a smaller, wealthier, and more select group of customers—what Teague called the "smart market." This consisted of people who were "exceedingly eager to...have the right things" like Wedgwood china and Cartier jewelry, and they would pay any price for them. To succeed, Teague counseled, "we must establish Steuben as the finest glassware in America and worth all that we ask for it."[39]

The decision to work with a new glass formula reflected both business and artistic motives. As a cost-saving measure, MacKay was eager to reduce the number of glass formulas in the division's repertoire. Teague, for his part, was intrigued by a new crystal glass composition recently developed in Corning's laboratory. He used this formula in designing a line of drinking glasses, pitchers, decanters, and other glassware. The composition had originated in the lab's quest for an optical glass that transmitted rather than reflected ultraviolet light. Achieving this goal required raw materials of exceptional purity, as well as improved refractories to reduce contamination in melting. In the mid-1920s, "possibly coincidentally," Corning scientists discovered a new source of clean boulders and quartz in North Carolina. Starting with high-grade raw materials, Harrison Hood devised a froth flotation separation process to refine them further. The sand was then washed and, in a nice touch, placed in Pyrex pans for drying in a lehr oven. The glass eventually resulting from this material was similar to a soft crystal formulation already known to Steuben, wrote chemist William Shaver. "But the important small subtractions and additions as noted" gave it a remarkable brilliance, clarity, and character.[40]

As MacKay and Teague began to institute radical changes at Steuben, time was running out. In 1932, the division somehow managed to lose $145,748 on sales of $137,599—its seventh consecutive annual loss.[41] With bigger businesses in the Glass Works also struggling, this performance could no longer be tolerated and there was ample sentiment in Corning's board to close Steuben for good. At a meeting early in 1933, however, 26-year-old Arthur Houghton Jr. made a plea for a reprieve and volunteered to take over the business himself. The board accepted the offer, and shortly afterward, MacKay returned to selling Pyrex. Teague remained a consultant for nearly a year before his contract was not renewed. "It was months and months," Arthur Houghton later wrote, "before I realized he couldn't design a god-damn thing."[42]

Arthur Houghton came to view the revival of Steuben not as a business challenge but as an opportunity to reshape his career. Although his stake in the Glass Works virtually guaranteed him a senior executive position in the company if he wanted it, he was not temperamentally suited to the life and knew it. A contemporary who became friendly with him in the 1930s portrayed him as "brilliant, debonair, mercurial, possessed of a wit in turn charming and devastating, and, to those who didn't know him very well, aloof."[43] His real interests were intellectual and aesthetic. A bibliophile, he was already accumulating a trove of rare books, including an unsurpassed collection of writings, publications, and memorabilia associated with Lewis Carroll. Among the items he possessed were editions of *Alice in Wonderland* in virtually every known language, including Czech, Chinese, and Esperanto, as well as a locket of hair from Alice Liddell, the young girl who had inspired the tale. In later life he became a noted patron of the arts and benefactor to libraries and educational institutions. Steuben became the vehicle that enabled him to combine family obligations to the Glass Works and the city of Corning with his abiding passion for the arts and the cosmopolitan culture of New York City.

The reconstruction of Steuben began in October 1933, when the division was reconstituted as Steuben Glass Inc., a wholly owned subsidiary of Corning. Am Houghton served as president, with Arthur as vice president and general manager. (Arthur succeeded his cousin as president in 1937.) In practice, Arthur enjoyed wide latitude in running the business. One of his first steps was to establish a corporate headquarters in New York City. Next, he persuaded his childhood friend and fellow Harvard alumnus, John M. "Jack" Gates, to leave his promising career in a New York architectural firm to become Steuben's director of design. Gates, in turn, introduced Arthur to Sidney Waugh, a young sculptor who had trained as an architect and also developed an interest in art glass. Waugh agreed to design etchings and engravings for Steuben on a part-time basis.

The new group atop Steuben retained several key innovations of the previous regime, most notably the decisions to transform Steuben glass into a luxury item and to exploit the new crystal glass composition. But they also took matters considerably further. Interviewed together decades later, Houghton and Gates described their early, lofty ambitions. As Arthur summarized:

> ...[we] set ourselves the highest possible and the most rigorous standards [and] determined that we were going to attempt to make the finest glass that had ever been made in the history of the world and would accept no compromise on that, and if we lost out at least we'd go down with our colors flying.
>
> Jack and I also by mutual compact determined that we were going to have a happy organization, we might just as well have one that was a pleasant place; if we were going to work and spend our days and years working on Steuben that we were going to have a pleasant and happy time doing it...[44]

An early, controversial action taken by the group was to eliminate most of the remaining inventory of old Steuben pieces, which consisted primarily of Carder's colored-glass designs. After the hotel sale and other efforts to dispose of old glass, the factory still warehoused many pieces. None of these items was perceived to be especially valuable (they had been picked over on numerous occasions) and many were chipped or flawed. Arthur Houghton ordered the imperfect pieces smashed to bits. He led the destruction himself, sweeping pieces of glass off shelves and tables. It was a dramatic, theatrical gesture, deliberately intended to proclaim that the future would be different from the past. The episode certainly left an indelible impression on Steuben employees. It also left Carder an embittered man.

Although he remained on Corning's payroll for many more years (he finally retired in 1959 at the age of 98, two years before he died) and designed occasional pieces of art glass, he never forgave Arthur Houghton and took only a cursory interest in the progress of Steuben.[45]

The new leadership at Steuben reconciled lofty goals for artistic achievement with more modest and attainable goals for financial performance. They made no promise to Corning "that this thing would make any substantial amount of money." As Arthur explained, "Jack and I, as a matter of pride, wanted to operate [Steuben] so that it could be self-supporting, but...the greatest contribution we could make [would be to become] a little star in Corning's crown." If Corning was "the great technical glassmaker," Steuben, would be its complement. "We could...show the world that Corning, if it wished, could...utilize glass as a medium of the arts and make the finest glass of that sort that is presently being made and perhaps has ever been made."[46]

Houghton and Gates developed a three-part strategy, which they called "the trilogy," for guiding Steuben's resurgence. This consisted of "perfection in the quality of the material,...perfection in the quality of the craftsmanship, and perfection in the quality of design." The "perfect material" was the crystal glass formulation that Teague had already spotted. As Houghton and Gates put it, crystal was "a very challenging medium....With color, you can cover up a lot of mistakes. But by sticking closely to crystal and...by driving ourselves to explore further we've made breakthroughs of one sort and another....I know we've made far more progress than [we would have] if we'd made colored glass."[47]

As for perfection of craftsmanship, Houghton and Gates retained and recruited the most skilled gaffers they could find. They left factory operations in charge of production manager Robert Leavy in Corning. Leavy, in turn, relied on veteran gaffers and engravers such as Johnny Johnson and Joe Libisch. And to achieve perfection of design, Houghton and Gates sought another break from the past. They dismissed most of the design staff and built a new team of designers at Steuben headquarters in New York City. The prerequisite to join the group was architectural training. This decision was calculated: Houghton, Gates, and Waugh preferred architects to, say, graphic artists, because they believed that architects possessed more disciplined design training, as well as "a great understanding of the whole history of the development of style, starting with the classic orders in Greece." At the same time, architects were used to working spatially in three dimensions. All of these characteristics reflected the "strong belief" shared by Steuben's leaders that "the person with an architectural background will make a very skilled glass designer."[48]

The separation of the designers from the factory initially caused some problems. Fred Schroeder, a veteran glassworker who left behind a memoir of his career at Steuben, remembered widespread skepticism among the gaffers and their assistants during the early years of the new regime. Schroeder himself "was not so sure that we really knew what we were doing" in the field of design, citing Steuben's "fling" with Teague and wondering whether Houghton and Gates could possibly succeed. And, in fact, it took a period of adjustment for the designers and gaffers to work together. As Schroeder recalled:

> The workmen themselves at first had difficulty. There was a tendency still to inject their experience, their understanding into these new forms. In some respect that was absolutely necessary. In others, we found it became a handicap to the designer himself for it was easy for us to tell what we thought could or could not be made in glass by hand.

Eventually, however, "as our every day contacts with the designers became closer, and the designs themselves actually began to take real form," the men in the factory "could not help but find that activity the most interesting and intriguing part of the whole organization."[49]

On the demand side, Houghton and Gates abandoned sales through the network of diverse outlets of department stores and gift shops that Steuben had used traditionally in favor of more controlled distribution through company-owned retail stores and a handful of carefully vetted, upscale department stores. The first Steuben store opened in New York City near the new design studio on Fifth Avenue in February 1934. Subsequently, Steuben added stores in Chicago (1935) and West Palm Beach (1937). Each was tastefully designed and furnished to attract a wealthy, discerning clientele. Sales personnel in the stores consisted primarily of young women who hailed from well-heeled families, prestigious women's colleges, or both. These "Steuben Girls" wore elegant gray dresses and jewelry and were coached at all costs to avoid pressured sales tactics in favor of helping customers in understated ways.[50]

Steuben advertising matched the understated elegance of the product and its retail environment. The company placed discrete print ads in publications likely to be viewed by the customers it sought: *New Yorker, Town and Country*, and the like. But Steuben also relied on word of mouth to build demand. In an inspired move, Houghton and Gates chose to exhibit their first new pieces in London in the belief—correct as it turned out—that they would attract more notice there. This attention was magnified by the decision, made in concert with David Stelling, a British public relations executive, to declare that none of the pieces was for sale. This coyness produced the desired effect: the exhibit at the Fine Arts Society Gallery on Bond Street proved "a howling success" and "a mob scene." "It was a *succès fou*, recalled Arthur Houghton much later. "A *succès fou* is right," added Gates.[51]

During the mid-1930s, Steuben showed signs of attaining its desired status as a producer of high art for affluent, discerning customers, as well as stanching the flow of red ink. By 1937, Steuben could afford to move into expanded quarters, including a new design studio and retail shop, in Corning's new mid-town office building at 718 Fifth Avenue. But the significance of Steuben to Corning transcended that of a business turnaround. Under Houghton and Gates, Steuben burnished Corning's image and reputation for craftsmanship and making quality products of the highest order. Together with the 200-inch disk, Steuben helped to reinvigorate the company, make it more attractive and understandable to employees, and inspire them in the continuing quest to work wonders with glass.

New Areas of Opportunity

When the board of the Glass Works elected Eugene Sullivan as president in 1928 (and when it appointed him vice chairman later), it consciously made a bold statement about the company's faith in research and development in glass. By then, Sullivan had become not only a dominant force in the company but also a preeminent figure in the glass and chemical industries. And he believed strongly in the future of glass. In a 1929 article, he proclaimed his views that "it is only in recent years that the individuality of the members of the glass family is becoming known" and that "glass is a many-sided material" about which much had yet to be learned. Enriched knowledge of glass, moreover, would yield tangible benefits: "A more general recognition of the wide range of physical properties which are at our disposal in glasses would lead undoubtedly to special glasses developed for specific purposes, becoming useful additions to the materials now serving industry."[52]

The attitude among those at the top of the Glass Works reflected a growing interest in research and development generally in American industry, and in the chemical industry in particular. The period between the world wars saw a great flowering of chemical research in academia and industry. The most sensational breakthroughs came at Du Pont, where R&D under the vigorous leadership of Charles M.A. Stine evolved from the periphery of the company's operations to its vital center. Stine sponsored Wallace Carothers, a young organic chemist, whose work yielded valuable new materials such as nylon and other plastics and synthetic fibers.[53]

The more general trend was the "chemicalization" of the economy, as manufacturers recognized the advantages of working with refined rather than natural materials: uniformity, standardization, reliability, controlled availability, and significantly lower cost. In addition, manufacturers took advantage of increased technical knowledge about their businesses: a better understanding of basic chemical reactions allowed them to make dramatic improvements in products and processes and to open new areas for growth and diversification. Chemically controlled processes replaced traditional empirical methods in industry after industry: textiles, paints and varnishes, paper, printing, adhesives, perfumes, rubber, cement, asphalt, plastics, and glass.[54]

At Corning, these developments followed Sullivan's lead with a prolonged inquiry into the chemistry of glass with a goal of gaining not only a better understanding of the material but also new ways to tailor its properties for specific applications. Sullivan was also interested in how other engineered materials, especially plastics, might compete against glass in some of its traditional uses.

The first new technical challenge to the lab came from Sullivan and Am Houghton, soon after the latter assumed the presidency of the Glass Works. Houghton wanted researchers to engineer "strong" glass that would be less likely to fail and more controlled in breaking when it did. Houghton and Sullivan had several applications of strong glass in mind. Lantern globes, for example, faced hotter temperatures and more hazardous environments. There was also growing interest in developing stronger vehicle windshields that would break in predictable ways without causing further trauma to accident victims. More immediately, Corning wanted strong glass for stovetop cookware to extend its line of housewares and bolster its position for the coming competition after the Pyrex patents expired in 1936. Corning was also intrigued by the possibilities of making a glass tableware tough enough to withstand automatic production and everyday household use.[55]

William W. Shaver, a Ph.D. in physics, led Corning's research on strong glass in the 1930s and drew on the expertise of his colleagues, including glass chemists Harrison Hood and Martin Nordberg. Taking a cue from Houghton, Shaver adorned his lab in the old Steuben factory with a simple motto above the door: "Strong Glass." The new lab first focused on strengthening the mechanical properties of glass through various treatments. In the mid-1920s, for example, Corning had experimented with acid treatments to fortify glass. Frosted bulbs, for example, were strengthened by treatment with hydrofluoric acid, although this process also made the glass vulnerable to abrasions and scratches. Shaver continued investigations along these lines but also looked at new ways to temper glass with blasts of air and/or chemical baths.[56]

Although the lab worked on strong glass for lantern globes and windshields, it faced more immediate pressure to develop the stovetop cookware. In the 1920s, J. Walter Thompson had identified the need for a stovetop product line to complement the Pyrex ovenware line, a market opportunity also revealed in Lucy Maltby's correspondence with consumers. In the early 1930s, the need became more urgent as the expiration of the Pyrex patents approached. Pyrex glass itself could not be used in stovetop applications because when it was pressed to necessary thicknesses, its thermal capabilities changed and it could not reliably resist the shock of sudden exposure to a gas flame or hot electric burner. At the same time, when blown into shape—as with lab ware—Pyrex pieces were too weak mechanically for everyday kitchen use.[57]

Shaver's lab struggled for several years to adapt Pyrex formulations for the stovetop application. A composition labeled 702EJ, for example, showed promise when subjected to special thermal tempering. It appeared to work well in the company's test kitchens and was tried further in homes in and around Corning. After about three months of use, however, one unfortunate cook witnessed a 1.5-quart saucepan full of boiling potatoes abruptly shatter on the stove. Analysis revealed that the thermal tempering process had indeed strengthened mechanical properties and thermal shock resistance of the glass, but at the cost of lowering the stress (breakage) point by a significant amount.

The consequences of sudden failure of glass cookware, of course, were intolerable to Corning. As researcher Howard Kiehl put it, "The idea of cooking in glass was a new one to the housewife and her initial experiences with it could influence all future sales, even those of ovenware."[58] Recognizing that the lab had pushed Pyrex formulations farther than they could go, Shaver redirected research to the search for a new glass composition. Hood soon found encouraging results from an aluminosilicate composition identified as 172RM. This glass overcame the problems of its predecessors but posed others, including great difficulty in eliminating impurities that occasionally formed in melting. Another time-consuming challenge involved controlling the tendency of the glass to form "seeds" (imperfections in melting and handling.)[59]

By 1935, some technical issues with the aluminosilicate glass remained but it was faring well in field tests. More than 18,000 pounds of potatoes were boiled and fried in experimental saucepans and skillets, with good results. Accordingly, Corning prepared to launch a new line of stovetop ware under the name "Flameware." Lucy Maltby's home economists prepared companion literature and touted the convenience and versatility of the new line. Early sales results for Flameware were encouraging. When it appeared on the market, noted the *Gaffer*, "Mrs. Housewife became just as eager to possess it as she was to own 'Pyrex' ovenware." The aluminosilicate glass posed unusual difficulties in manufacturing, however, and the line did not become profitable until after World War II.[60]

In addition to its initiative in strong glass, Corning researchers explored other lines of investigation, including several that helped establish promising businesses in the short term. The first new inquiries involved architectural glass, an area closely related to Corning's work on strong glass and its ongoing search for new markets for Pyrex. In the early 1930s, moreover, opportunities seemed attractive due to the growing use of glass blocks and panels in construction, a development stemming from the spread of modernist architecture from Europe to the United States after World War I. Tough glass like Pyrex—less likely to chip or crack, more likely to endure the extremes of weather over many years—possessed obvious advantages as a building material.

In 1932 Corning began working with the architects planning Rockefeller Center commissioned sculptors Lee Lawrie and Attilio Piccirilli to design enormous glass panels for display above the entrances to three of the center's main buildings. The biggest was Lawrie's panel above the entrance to the RCA Building. It depicted the figure of Genius manipulating and interpreting cycles of light and sound. Measuring 15 by 50 feet and weighing 13 tons, the panel consisted of 240 separate blocks of Pyrex glass cast and installed by Corning. George McCauley, the company's expert in casting telescope mirror blanks, led the project, assisted by David Gray and Fred Carder. Corning subsequently produced architectural pieces for other buildings in Manhattan, including the company's own "House of Glass" on 5th Avenue, where the New York sales office and Steuben division were headquartered.[61]

Corning also explored production of glass blocks for construction. Pioneered in Europe where they were used primarily for decoration, glass blocks inspired American architects to designs that took advantage of their strength, fire resistance, and transparency. In 1935, Corning began making glass blocks from a soft Pyrex formulation. Test sites revealed serious drawbacks, however, including the tendency of the blocks to crack along the edges and difficulties in developing mortar and sealing compounds to bind the blocks together. Corning went to work on a different formulation, developing in 1937 a high alkali soft glass called Lumite that seemed highly promising. By then, the company was acutely aware of competition and began considering faster ways to develop the product.[62]

A venture farther afield was Corning's investigations into organo-silicon compounds—materials today known as silicones. Sullivan recognized that plastics were competing with glass in a growing number of applications, and he recruited organic chemist J. Franklin Hyde in 1930 to investigate whether Corning might develop new materials related both to glass and plastics. Hyde's work shortly paid dividends. Assigned to help with installing the Pyrex architectural panels at Rockefeller Center, he learned about the problems of sealing glass panels to each other and to the surfaces supporting them. In this instance, the cementing agent was a known organic material, but the episode opened Hyde's fertile mind to consider experiments with organo-silicon compounds as sealants and lubricants.[63]

In December 1934, William Taylor dispatched Frank Hyde to visit the Owens-Illinois glass fiber plant in Newark, Ohio. Taylor was specifically interested in the bonding agents and lubricants Owens-Illinois used to lubricate and protect glass fiber from breaking in handling and applications in which it could be woven, and he reasoned that organic compounds were the answer. "I'll never forget it," Hyde later said of the visit, recalling that he walked about a mile from his hotel to the plant in subzero conditions and suffered frostbite on both ears—a problem that lingered throughout his very long life. Hyde found that Owens-Illinois was also searching for solutions to the problem Taylor had identified.[64]

On his return to Corning, Hyde moved to Fallbrook, which was then attempting to make electrical and insulating tapes from glass fibers. Hyde focused on developing a stable varnish for the tape and was making headway when he learned of similar research efforts under way at the Mellon Institute at Pittsburgh.[65] By 1937, his work showed vast potential, but useful applications seemed distant.

Resuming Growth, Carefully

By the middle of the decade, the worst effects of the Depression were behind Corning and business picked up notably. Sales surged from $7 million to $20 million between 1932 and 1937, and net profits climbed from $808 thousand to $2.8 million over the same period. Most of the employees laid off during the lowest ebb in 1932 were back at work and cooperating with management through an "industrial council" chaired by Glen Cole, Am Houghton's brother-in-law.

Cole, said Corning's later vice president of industrial relations Harry Hosier, was "one of the best personnel men I ever knew." Am Houghton, meanwhile, declared that Corning "must have the best employee relations in the country." With Whiting Williams, a prominent national advocate of harmonious relations between management and workers as an adviser, Corning took pains to listen to employees and act on their concerns. As manager in charge of personnel, for example, Hosier met once a month with ten groups of equal numbers of supervision and employees from various departments of Main Plant. The industrial councils at the branch plants met frequently and delivered wages and benefits comparable to those emerging in collective bargaining elsewhere under the National Labor Relations (Wagner) Act. There was no sign of significant industrial unrest in Corning and the occasional appearances of the American Flint Glass Workers, which hoped to organize the company, made no headway. Meanwhile, Corning's industrial council delivered key benefits such as paid vacations and a credit union (1936) and guaranteed minimum wages and an insurance plan (1937). In 1937, Corning's board of directors authorized payment of $145,000 to erect a new personnel building to house Hosier and his assistants and to provide meeting space for joint labor-management committees.[66]

Tempered by the experience of the Depression, Houghton and his colleagues took a cautious approach to new business development. They continued to fund research in the R&D labs but also sought to leverage the company's resources through its own ingenuity and inventiveness, as well as through association with other parties. And in one instance—Macbeth-Evans—Corning bolstered its business through an acquisition.

The development of a new process for making glass tubes for fluorescent lighting illustrated Corning's engineering ingenuity. During the lingering months of the Depression, Corning had taken advantage of slow times to dispatch senior personnel to Europe to broaden their experience and scout for new opportunities. In March 1931, for example, Houghton sketched a proposition to his son: "I am wondering if it would not be a good plan to take advantage of what is probably the last quiet year for a while and send Glen [Cole] and probably someone else to look over the glass plants in

England, France and Germany? I think he might get something out of such a trip and in particular learn other methods in first rate plants."[67]

The company followed up on the suggestion, and in 1931 Cole and Jesse Littleton visited the French glassmaker, St. Gobain. There they observed an experimental tube-making machine developed by Leopold Vello, a naturalized Frenchman of Spanish birth. At the time, the Danner machines used by Corning made tubing by pouring molten glass over a rotating mandril. As the glass wound around the mandril, it formed a tubular shape and was pulled until it reached the desired dimension. The Danner process worked well to make narrow-gauge tubing but mechanical constraints—especially the size of the mandril and the rate at which the glass cooled—limited the size of the tubing and its throughput. The Danner machines also required a small crew of operators to attend them. Vello's machine, in contrast, was a simpler device that could be run by a single operator. Molten glass drained from a bowl through an orifice ring and into a stream of hot air emerging from a blowpipe. By adjusting the size of the orifice ring and controlling the airflow from the blowpipe, the operator could vary both the diameter and the wall thickness of the tubing. The Vello machine could make large-diameter tubes and pipes useful in a variety of industrial processes. Another intriguing application was pharmaceutical containers.[68]

The Vello machine impressed Cole and Littleton, and Corning arranged to obtain the blueprints from the inventor and passed them along to Edmund Wellech, a resourceful mechanical engineer at the Fallbrook plant. Wellech had come to the United States from Austria in 1924 by a remarkable set of coincidences, settling in Corning. In his home country, he had worked as a production manager in a factory that made glass wool for insulation. When he had decided to emigrate, he wrote to several American glass companies and got a warm response in German from Fritz Kraissl, Corning's Austrian-born salesman of pharmaceutical apparatus. As a further introduction to Corning, Wellech by happenstance met and struck up a friendship with Kraissl's brother just before leaving Austria. Once in Corning, Wellech briefly worked on machinery to make glass wool before being reassigned to the Danner tube machines. He exhibited an intuitive understanding of the machinery, sometimes briskly sketching ideas for improvement in chalk on the factory floor.[69]

Wellech's grasp of glassmaking technology proved valuable in assessing the new Vello process. Vello sought to license and install his machine for a fee of $135,000. After inspecting the blueprints, however, Wellech found that "some of [the design] was very ingenious, [and] some of it was very unpractical." Wellech thought that the design of the bowl and the channel feeding it were inadequate and believed that many of the components specified by Vello were unnecessarily expensive. As a result, Wellech recommended that Corning pay Vello $35,000 for the rights to build its own machine. If this machine should fail to work, then the company would pay Vello the entire amount.

Eager to please, Vello assented to the deal and agreed to visit Corning in 1932 to inspect the new machine. Under Wellech's direction, the machine was ready in due course, and Vello arrived shortly before the first full-scale test. When he saw what Wellech had done, he "was running around pulling his hair," cursing Wellech, and exclaiming that his invention had been ruined. Once the machine started up, however, Vello's attitude quickly altered. At the end of its first day of operation, recalled Wellech, "we had hampers full of saleable tubing...roughly twice what we got on the Danner machine. Vello nearly kissed me."[70]

Wellech never knew the final details of Corning's negotiations with Vello, but the process was an obvious success. Before long, the Vello machines were adapted to make glass tubing of different compositions and dimensions for a variety of applications. Soft glass compositions found their way into lighting, with fluorescent tubes a rapidly growing business later in the 1930s. Hard glass compositions were used for high-temperature applications in radios and other electronic devices, as well as in industrial pipes. Fallbrook shipped more than 10 million pounds of glass tubing per year by the end of the decade. In 1939, Corning established a separate bulb and tubing division to focus on these product lines.[71]

Corning's willingness to grow by forming associations with other parties was also evident in the late 1930s. As its work on glass blocks proceeded, managers realized that the company lacked the resources to establish distribution and a marketing presence to the building trades. However, the company had worked closely with Pittsburgh Plate Glass on technical matters since the 1920s, and discussions between Am Houghton and his counterpart at PPG resulted in the formation of a fifty-fifty joint venture, Pittsburgh Corning, in 1937. Each party contributed financing and its complementary capabilities: Corning's technology for making glass blocks and PPG's distribution channels and knowledge of the marketplace for construction. The corporate parents held equal positions on the board of directors and rotated chairmen, but PPG provided most of the management. The following year, Pittsburgh Corning erected a plant at Port Allegany, Pennsylvania and began producing glass blocks using Corning's Lumite composition.[72]

Pittsburgh Corning established several patterns that would become enduring aspects of Corning's joint ventures: the fifty-fifty ownership, which obliged the partners to work together rather than to fight for control; the tendency of Corning's name to appear second, because in negotiations, Am Houghton was reputed to have said, it is better to fight for concerns that really matter; and the involvement of the highest officers from both partners as board directors rather than as executives.[73] These patterns quickly recurred in another joint venture to develop glass fiber technology.

Corning had initially investigated making glass fibers in the 1920s (hence the hiring of Ed Wellech) but abandoned the work for several years. Learning of advances in the technology at Owens-Illinois, Corning resumed its investigations in 1934.[74] Then, in the following year, two things happened. First, Corning and Owens-Illinois signed an agreement to coordinate research and share results. Owens-Illinois had a three-year headstart, but Corning possessed better fundamental knowledge of glass. The partners faced a twofold challenge: to improve properties of the glass itself, and to improve manufacturing processes. Under the agreement, Corning paid an estimated $1 million to balance Owens-Illinois's research, development, and patent expenditures. Second, Corning built an addition to the Fallbrook plant to make glass fiber for electrical and structural insulation.[75] By 1937, Corning was selling more than $800,000 worth of glass fibers, with three-fourths of the output used for building insulation.

In 1938, with both Owens-Illinois and Corning under antitrust scrutiny as part of a government probe of the glass industry, the two parties decided, recalled one manager from the Owens Illinois side, "to stake the boy and put him on his own"; that is, to transform the technical exchange agreement into a formal joint venture. The Owens-Corning Fiberglas Company was incorporated in November 1938. Each parent owned 47.5 percent—with the remainder held by key executives—and contributed to a total working capital of approximately $1 million. In addition, $2.1 million of preferred stock split five shares for Owens-Illinois to one for Corning to balance the greater value of the Owens-Illinois plant and equipment turned over to the new company. Board membership was divided fifty-fifty. Most of the executives and employees came from Owens-Illinois, where the plant at Newark, Ohio, already employed 500 people. Only about 20 joined from Corning, which closed its glass fiber operation at Fallbrook.

The new corporation got off to a fast start, reporting $3.7 million in sales and a profit of $6,000, eked out by tight control of overhead. Owens-Corning faced an uphill climb to penetrate channels for building and electrical construction, but would be hugely aided by the outbreak of World War II.[76]

Corning also sought to grow during the late 1930s via acquisition. Late in 1936, it completed a merger with Macbeth-Evans Company of Charleroi, Pennsylvania, the largest producer of lamp glass and opalescent (opaque) glassware in the world. Corning was roughly twice the size of its new purchase, and the fit seemed a good one. The histories of the two companies bore many resemblances: each boasted a proud tradition of research, important achievements in areas such as lighthouse lens blanks, telescope mirror blanks, and optical glass. Macbeth-Evans had also sponsored research at the Mellon Institute in areas of interest to Corning, including organo-silicon compounds. Headed by George D. Macbeth, a third-generation descendant of the founder, Macbeth-Evans had recently developed automatic pressing machinery for making opalescent dinnerware. It also made architectural glass, including tiles for the Lincoln Tunnel and was experimenting with glass blocks for construction.

Interviewed three decades later, Macbeth explained that the merger occurred for two reasons. He "had known Amory Houghton for a number of years....as time passed they both understood one overwhelming fact. Macbeth-Evans had a consumer line [pressed tableware] which Corning did not have and did not have the capacity of really getting into. The second thing was that Macbeth-Evans had a considerable lighting business which Corning did not have." At the same time, the two parties considered including the Hocking Glass Company (later Anchor-Hocking), a leading supplier of consumer glassware but much weakened during the Depression, in the deal. However, due diligence by Corning treasurer Bill Decker revealed that Hocking was locked into several money-losing propositions and he argued for confining the deal to Macbeth-Evans alone.[77]

The merger took effect on December 24, 1936. In a move that he surely later regretted but was understandable in the aftermath of the depression, Macbeth insisted on payment in the form of preferred stock rather than common stock.[78] Macbeth stayed on as a director and officer (controller) of the glass works, where he overhauled and modernized the cost accounting system. Macbeth-Evans contributed other management talent, including several plant managers, and it also introduced Corning to the Pittsburgh law firm of Reed, Smith, Shaw and McClay and labor lawyer Nick Unkovic, who would become an important figure in Corning's industrial relations through the coming decades. Corning was most eager to get Macbeth-Evans's automatic pressing technology. In 1937, the board authorized an expenditure of $950,000 to build an automatic pressed ware plant in Corning, east of the Fallbrook plant. The new facility, Pressware, featured continuous furnace and production equipment and was run by personnel drawn from Macbeth-Evans. The first dishes came off the line on June 13, 1938.[79]

By the late 1930s, Corning had not only recovered from the Depression but was in a cautiously expansive mood. New products and product lines were emerging in a steady stream. One of these—silicones—resulted from the new collaborative relationship between Frank Hyde and his counterpart at the Mellon Institute, Dr. Rob Roy MacGregor. In 1938, Hyde synthesized the first silicone resins and immediately recognized their utility in making improved cements and lubricants. This work became in 1942 the foundation of another joint venture, Dow Corning.[80]

Hyde's discoveries were part of several innovations from Corning's labs and plants in the late 1930s that appeared to offer high potential. Gaffers in the bulb and tubing division, for example, were fabricating experimental bulbs for iconoscope tubes, oscilliscopes, and experimental television sets. Engineers in the same department found ways to make Christmas tree ornaments on the Ribbon Machine, the basis of an attractive, if seasonal, business. Research scientists Harrison Hood and Martin Nordberg developed a new, very pure form of glass called Vycor that had promising applications in lighting and industry. Corning also established a cooperative research program in optics with Eastman Kodak.[81]

Yet, for all their optimism, obvious concerns faced the company at the close of the decade. In December 1938, the Temporary National Economic Committee launched an investigation into the glass industry that appeared to target Corning's role at the center of collusive behavior. Although Corning was a relatively small competitor in the glass industry, the government argued that the company's and Houghton family's ownership of key patents gave it and them disproportionate influence in the industry. Of particular concern to the government was the role of Hartford-Empire—the maker of glassmaking machinery with roots tracing to investments by Alanson B. Houghton and Arthur A. Houghton Sr. in 1908—in restricting competition in the glass container industry. At the same time, the antitrust division of the U.S. Department of Justice mounted separate investigations of General Electric's dominant position in the electric lighting industry (an inquiry that extended into the intimate and intricate connections between the company and its key suppliers, including Corning), Hartford-Empire, Libbey-Owens-Ford, and Owens-Corning Fiberglas. All of these loomed on the horizon as growing threats to Corning.[82]

Also looming on the horizon was the much graver threat of world war.

CHAPTER SIX

Corning Goes to War, 1939–1945

THE 1939 World's Fair, which opened in New York City on April 30, 1939, seemed to herald the promise of a new era rich with technology and opportunity. Booths and exhibits set up by sixty countries, the League of Nations, and dozens of companies projected an almost uniformly optimistic worldview that bordered on the utopian. RCA gave the mesmerizing new medium called television its first large-scale public demonstration, and the Carrier Corporation presented the unimaginable luxury of air conditioning. Other products debuting at the fair included the diesel engine, color film, and Lucite. Corning Glass Works' imprint seemed to be everywhere on the sprawling fair grounds, in Flushing Meadows, Queens. Television, of course, had a glass heart—the cathode ray tube. An exhibit in the glass industries building showed how an electrical insulator made of Fiberglas™ —a material pioneered by Corning affiliate Owens-Corning—permitted small motors to deliver the same horsepower as motors twice their size. To memorialize the technology shown at the fair, Westinghouse buried a Pyrex-lined time capsule. Among its contents were a Mazda electric lamp and a Westinghouse Sterilamp, both fitted with Corning bulbs.[1]

The spirit of progress and improvement seemed to mesh nicely with the mood of a nation finally emerging from the Great Depression. Although a brief, sharp recession had occurred in 1938, the wholesale economic crises that had rocked the economy a decade earlier seemed more and more remote. And yet the cheery outlook of the fair masked the intimations of war brewing in both Europe and Asia. The aggressive military regimes of Japan and Germany had already started to threaten and, in some cases, attack and absorb neighboring territories. In September 1939, when Germany invaded Poland, World War II was formally under way. The war, which would slog on for nearly six years at locales ranging from the snows of Stalingrad to the jungles of the Philippines, would prove in many ways to be the twentieth century's pivotal event. It ushered in a series of violent and destructive—but ultimately transformative—political, social, economic, and technological changes. Most significantly for the Corning Glass Works, the war would sweep the United States, its citizens, and its industries into an unprecedented cooperative effort to battle the Axis powers.

The all-consuming war demanded, and received, the attention and energy of the citizens of Corning, the employees of the Glass Works, and its owners and executives. In previous generations, Corning and its managers had frequently lived on the brink of financial and business destruction. During the war years, however, the issues truly involved life and death. Between 1939 and 1945, thousands of employees left home to serve in faraway combat theaters. Their replacements at Corning worked overtime to keep the furnaces burning, scientists labored to bend glass in new ways to assist in the war effort, and the company's executives worked with, and in some cases for, the military. Corning's ability to apply its scientific methods to the production of specialty glass made it a valuable contributor to the war effort. In these eventful six years, Corning developed new uses for glass that would bear fruit in the postwar years, embarked on a profitable joint venture with the Dow Chemical Company, came to terms with the American Flint Glass Workers Union, struck new alliances in South America, and sold stock to the public. By the time V-J day arrived in August 1945, the Corning Glass Works had undergone a metamorphosis: it was unionized, publicly traded, and counted holdings stretching from Brazil in the south to Canada in the north. Its reported annual sales were three times greater than those of 1939. In other important ways, however, Corning remained substantially the same company it had been for nearly eighty years—rooted deeply in the soil of upstate New York, focused on developing, through internal research, new applications for glass, and under the firm control of a descendant of Amory Houghton Sr. and a coterie of veteran key executives.

War in Europe Affects the American Economy and Corning

In the months after the World's Fair the situation in Europe erupted into open war. Germany launched a blitzkrieg on Poland in September 1939, and within days Britain and France declared war on the Nazi regime. In April and May of 1940, Hitler's armies plowed through the Netherlands, Belgium, and France. At first, Corning was affected by the war in Europe only at the margins. Corning's researchers continued to pursue research projects that had started in the late 1930s, like developing 96 percent silicate glass stoveware and organo-silicon resins. "Business continues on at fairly good pace," Amory Houghton wrote to George Buell Hollister on the day in June 1940 when French troops evacuated Paris. "Our principal operating problem as you can well imagine is one of fuel. We are getting along insofar as keeping our units going is concerned but at a greatly increased cost." Such higher costs would cut into profits. Whereas in 1940 sales rose 24 percent, to $24.8 million (from $20 million in 1939), Corning's profits grew just 11.5 percent.[2]

By 1940, Houghton had a firm grip on the company's helm. The forty-year-old father of five had led the company through the travails and triumphs of the Depression. Although his father, longtime chairman Alanson Houghton, lived in Washington and devoted his time to public affairs, the former ambassador was still the company's controlling shareholder. Alanson had a complete and affectionate confidence in his only son. "I am making you a gift of 2,500 shares of Houghton Associates stock," he wrote Amory in June 1940. "I do this because I am proud of the manner you have carried on the family tradition at the Glass Works and assumed the responsibility for the family property...I feel very confident that our achievements in the coming years will bring me even greater satisfaction—difficult as the times may be."[3]

Amory, in turn, was concerned with the progress of the next generation of Houghtons, taking a particular interest in their education. His eldest son, Amory Jr., was attending the Arizona Desert School in Tucson. "Sending him back to you again is, I am completely satisfied in my own mind, the very best thing for the boy provided he really settles down and does good work," the occasionally stern but loving father wrote to headmaster Alan Lake Childsey. "He, like Hell, is paved with good intentions but the time must be here now when reasonable performance must be insisted upon in lieu of excuses."[4]

In its ownership, management, and style, Corning Glass Works was still very much a family company. Amory's brother-in-law, Glen Cole, was vice president in charge of production. He would be promoted to president in May 1941 and serve in that post for the duration of the war. Like previous non-Houghton presidents, however, his autonomy would be sharply constrained. Amory's cousin, Arthur A. Houghton Jr., continued to run the Steuben division. He maintained residences in Manhattan, at 130 E. 62nd Street, and on Wye Plantation, near Queenstown, Maryland. Aside from dealing with corporate responsibilities, Arthur was increasingly involved with pursuits relating to his lifelong obsession: rare books. In March 1940, Archibald MacLeish, the renowned poet then serving as Librarian of Congress, named the thirty-three-year-old bibliophile curator of the rare book collection of the Library of Congress, calling Arthur "one of the most distinguished American collectors of rare books and the owner of the largest collections of Keats, Spenser and Lewis Carroll in existence." Arthur was simultaneously working on his most lasting contribution to the world of rare books. In the summer of 1940, he pledged to Harvard 1,500 shares of Corning Glass Works common stock for each of the next four years if the university would build a library dedicated to housing rare books in Harvard Yard. He told Harvard treasurer William Claflin, "In my opinion the stock is worth $40 per share," which brought the commitment to some $240,000 plus projected annual dividends of $12,000. The estimated cost of the rare book library, which upon its completion was known as the Houghton Library, was $475,000.[5]

But Arthur was also concerned with the company's core glass business. After his appointment, he moved to Washington with his wife, Ellen Crenshaw Houghton, and three children, Jane, nine, Sylvia, seven, and Arthur III, who was born in May. One of his neighbors in the capital was George Moffett, a food company executive who had joined the War Resources Board. The board was a newly created agency composed mainly of businessmen and headed by Edward R. Stettinius Jr., the chairman of U.S. Steel. The goal of the group, as its name suggests, was to plan for the management of the economy in case of war. Moffett, who was concerned with food supplies, told Arthur that the Army would create a huge demand for canned food but that the supplies of tin available for canning were meager. "Geo. Moffett says if some glass company will only develop a strong, light weight container, the business is theirs, and enormous," Arthur wrote Amory.[6]

By the fall of 1940, when the Battle of Britain was raging over the skies of London, the war was no longer a hypothetical proposition and started to affect the lives of individuals. On October 16, 1940, all men between the ages of twenty-one and thirty-six were required to register for the nation's first peacetime draft. And in February 1941, the first Corning boys left for training at Fort Bragg. By the spring of 1941, the company was on a war footing. All factory gates except the one on Walnut Street were closed, and all employees were required to wear identification buttons. The stress apparently began to take its toll on some of Corning's executives. In the spring of 1941, Hanford Curtiss, the veteran vice president and secretary, suffered a nervous breakdown that colleagues attributed partly to increased workload and job stress. "Mr. Curtiss had a serious nervous break-down and is now at the New York Hospital in New York but all word that I get is encouraging and I am hopeful that it will not be too long before he will again be able to be back on the job and well again," Amory wrote to H. Kaye Martin.[7]

As 1941 wore on, the news from Europe and Asia grew worse. In June 1941, Hitler opened a second European front by declaring war on the Soviet Union. The delicate balancing act that U.S. and other diplomats, including Alanson Houghton, had tried to assemble in the wake of the devastation of World War I, had crumbled entirely, with no hope for a settlement. As Allied troops fought Axis forces on battlefields in Libya, Egypt, Greece, and Russia, the former ambassador to both Germany and Britain watched from Washington, increasingly discouraged. A prominent Republican, he had generally not been relied upon by the Roosevelt administration for advice and input. Yet he remained active and engaged in world affairs, having traveled to Germany as late as 1938.

On the morning of Sunday, September 16, 1941, Alanson Houghton died of a heart attack. Amid the tumult of Europe, with whose affairs he had been so intimately involved, Alanson's death received less public attention than it otherwise might have. "He was suavity personified," the *New York Times* noted in its obituary. "He seemed never to be in a hurry. He spoke in a measured and quiet way and radiated culture." Even his political enemies hailed him. His death "deprives us of a really great American and one of the wisest and most farsighted statesmen I have ever encountered in my four decades of dealing with public men here and abroad," wrote Oswald Garrison Villard, the left-leaning editor of the *Nation*. "It is a simple truth that no other American Ambassador to Berlin has ever achieved such success or won such tributes or expressions of heartfelt respect when he left." The funeral service was held in Corning and he was buried in Hope Annex Cemetery. Alanson Houghton's death marked the end of an era for the Corning Glass Works. Working with his brother, Arthur, he had helped ensure the company's survival by sponsoring the development of new processes like the Ribbon Machine and new materials like Pyrex. Just as important, he had entered alliances and cross-licensing agreements with customers and competitors. At the time of his death, this network of agreement was under attack by the U.S. Justice Department, and many of them would soon be invalidated. Still, the long arc of his career—as an executive, a politician, and a diplomat—helped define the Corning Glass Works in the public mind and set an example that successive generations of Houghtons and Corning managers would follow.[8]

Alanson's death weighed heavily on his only son. While Amory had developed confidence as Corning's chief executive, he relied heavily on his father's advice and, to a large degree, still lived in the shadow of his large public persona. In the fall of 1941, Amory Jr. wrote a note to his younger brother, Alanson Houghton, who was in his first term at the Arizona Desert School. "I don't want to tell you to do this and don't do that, Al, but I just want to tell you now that Grandfather has died, Daddy is terribly sad, so I think you and I should try to make him happier by doing well in school. Just go out and do the best job you can."[9]

Throughout the rest of his life, Amory would seek to follow his father's example, as an executive at Corning and in the public arena. In 1957, he left his post at Corning to serve as U.S. ambassador to France, just as his father had entered the ambassadorial ranks in the 1920s. (Amory Houghton thereafter was referred to as "the Ambassador.") Houghton's first involvement in public service came in the fall of 1941. Earlier in the year, President Roosevelt formed a group of federal bureaucracies, such as the Office of Production Management (OPM), the Office of Price Administration and Civilian Supply, and the Supply Priorities and Allocations Board. All were intended to ensure the continued smooth functioning of the American economy by monitoring prices and the flow of materials and finished goods. These committees were staffed by high-ranking executives from the ranks of labor and business who essentially volunteered their help as "dollar-a-year men."[10]

Houghton already had personal and business connections with many of the top dollar-a-year men, including Philip Reed, the General Electric executive whose wartime career Houghton's would closely track. In November 1939, when Reed was elected chairman of the board at GE, Houghton sent him a handwritten note. "I couldn't have been more tickled about the news of your succeeding Owen Young if it had been my own brother or son." By November 1941, Reed had already recruited Houghton to the OPM as deputy chief of the bureau of industry in the division of industry operations. "I am delighted to hear that you are coming down hereon the 1st of December and I hope I can help to make things run smoothly for you," wrote Marshal Dodge, one of Reed's assistants. On December 6, 1941, hardly knowing what was going to take place the next day, Houghton notified Boy Scouts president Walter Head that the OPM work would render him unable to attend board meetings and resigned his post on the BSA board of directors. This act foreshadowed the way in which the war would pull Houghton away from his family, corporate, and civic commitments.[11]

With supplies of everything from gas to rubber growing scarce, the government began to assign priorities to certain products so manufacturers of crucial goods could obtain the necessary materials. Corning Glass Works was, to a degree, fortunate, in that glass was used in many strategically important products—like cathode ray tubes. The fighting in Europe stimulated demand for many new products, such as the components of radar, the new technology that revolutionized warfare by allowing technicians to track the progress of planes and ships and fix the location of targets. These included cathode ray tubes, which had been developed for television. During the 1930s, Corning had made five-, seven-, and nine-inch picture tubes for television from one-piece blown borosilicate glass bulbs. Although commercial broadcasting was set to begin in the summer of 1941, it was delayed due to the war. The British government, however, had a great need for hard glass bulbs for radar equipment. So in late 1940 and early 1941, Corning began making them in volume in B Factory, sealing them in the apparatus department in main plant and returning them to B Factory for finishing work. By the end of 1941, Corning produced 60,000 cathode ray bulbs. These awkward production arrangements would continue until September 1943, when a new sealing department was erected in B Factory.[12]

Thus far, the war in Europe had proved a stimulus to American industry. Between January and December of 1941, munitions production in the United States rose 225 percent. Over the course of the year, spurred by the demand for cathode ray tubes, lightbulbs, Pyrex, and other products, Corning's sales soared 50 percent to $36.5 million. Due to the growth of products like cathode ray tubes, by December 1941, almost 30 percent of Corning's output had priority ratings. And the works was already seeking to establish new ties to military organizations that might need glass products. On December 4, Corning researchers T. J. Thompson and W. W. Shaver visited various senior officials at the ordnance division in Washington to discuss whether glass could be used as a substitute for metal in high-explosive bombs and hand grenades.[13]

In Washington as a Dollar-a-Year Man

In the early morning of December 7, 1941, without warning, Japanese planes bombed American ships and other installations at Pearl Harbor, Hawaii, destroying 188 planes and 19 ships, and killing 2,403 American citizens. The next day, Congress declared war on Japan, with President Roosevelt pronouncing December 7 a "date that will live in infamy." Three days later, Congress declared war on Germany and Italy, and World War II was officially joined. After the formal declaration of war, the economic shift to wartime footing accelerated. On January 16, 1942, Roosevelt created the War Production Board (WPB), which was intended to "exercise general responsibility" over the nation's economy and subsumed much of the infrastructure of the OPM, which had been deemed ineffective. In March 1942, the Second War Powers Act gave the WPB greater ability to allocate materials or facilities. The WPB was headed by former Sears, Roebuck executive Donald Nelson. As dollar-a-year-man J. S. Knowlson, president of the Stewart-Warner Corporation, described it, "the job of the War Production Board was really one of clearing away anything that interfered with the facilities or the materials needed by the services, and then to trust that these materials and these facilities would be used." In fact, Houghton would eventually work for Knowlson, who was head of the Division of Industry Operations, and whom he dubbed "a grand fellow."[14]

Houghton quickly settled into a new life in Washington. He occupied an office in Room 4006 of the Railroad Retirement Building. He relocated the family from Marion, Massachusetts, to a house at 1300 30th Street in Washington, D.C. In addition to his new duties, he found time to visit Corning and New York City for corporate matters, board meetings, and other occasions.[15]

Houghton's government work rested on a different set of assumptions than his other professional work. The effort was no longer to be concerned with profit and loss, but rather with life and death, victory and defeat. Many companies and sectors of the economy found this adjustment to be traumatic and abrupt, as the conversion to a military footing was one of the most wrenching economic transformations in the nation's history. Entire industries were effectively ordered to stop what they had been doing for decades and devote their resources to other endeavors. In February 1942, for example, the automobile industry was forbidden to make passenger cars and asked to make tanks and military vehicles instead. By April, production of household radios and electric refrigerators was ended as iron and steel were banned from use in consumer goods. To prevent the inappropriate use of materials, the government through June 1942 issued 277 limitation and conservation orders. As a result, by the end of June 1942, nearly a third of prewar production of consumer durable goods had ended. The government was now dictating terms to proud and powerful private sector companies and was inserting itself into the economic lives of American citizens as never before.[16]

The central dilemma that Houghton and his colleagues at the WPB confronted was that demand for products of all types was growing rapidly, while supplies of materials like steel, iron, and rubber were growing scarce and expensive. In May 1942, war appropriations and foreign orders for the year totaled $170 billion. Adding in the War Department's request for another $40 billion in goods, the war program "is much more than twice the national income we have ever attained in any previous year," OPM staffer Robert Nathan wrote to Houghton and Philip Reed. To keep up with demand, industry facilities had increased "without proportionate expansion in raw material production and a general tightening up of the slack in our national economy." As a result, he suggested, the government needed to develop a better and more comprehensive system for the control of the flow of materials, as well as to implement stronger conservation measures.[17]

The constantly evolving government/military bureaucracy presented challenges for companies struggling to maintain adequate supplies of crucial materials. Each quarter, Corning had to file production requirement plans. Managers in various Corning divisions gave their orders to buyers, who coded the items appropriately. Each purchase order bore Corning's distinct production requirement plan number, and each plant kept its own logs and orders. Managers buying production materials had to ensure that they didn't purchase too much of any specific material in the first or second month of a quarter, lest none be available for the third month. And those who wished to order machine tools or capital items had to fill out an entirely different set of applications.[18]

Corning and other companies seemed to be operating in an entirely different mode, as once routine requests from new customers took on supreme urgency. In the early months of the year, a Washington official called Corning with an urgent request for certain sizes of tubular boiler gauge glasses. When Otto Hilbert, a laboratory researcher, found that some were in stock, he jumped on the afternoon Lackawanna train to Buffalo and delivered them to an officer waiting at the platform. "We had no idea what this urgency call was all about until many months later," Hilbert recalled.

"The Japanese bombing of Pearl Harbor had destroyed the Navy's supply of gauge glasses which were urgently needed for boilers in the Navy warships in Hawaii. An Air Force officer was ordered to fly these gauge glasses from Buffalo to Honolulu."[19]

At his post in Washington, Houghton occasionally was asked to act in two capacities—as a government official and as a representative of Corning. In April, for example, three Corning representatives visited a Washington conservation official to advocate greater use of industrial glass piping. "They also expressed the thought that this product was not receiving the consideration due it by members of the War Production Board," the official, Harvey Anderson, wrote to Houghton. "I suggested that they determine whether or not a Corning man could be placed in this department on a loan basis, either part or full time....What is your reaction to this?"[20]

By the summer of 1942—just weeks after the U.S. Navy stemmed Japan's advance in the Pacific at the Battle of Midway—Houghton was anxious to return to Corning, where his family was spending the summer. "I have overstayed the period for which I agreed to come down and really should get back to my own knitting in Corning as we are doing so much war work," he wrote to a colleague John Sessions on July 1, 1942. "However, I am staying here from week to week or month to month, as long as it seems that there is an assignment here in which I can really help." Houghton's return to upstate New York would be put off for at least two months because of an impending promotion.[21]

The next week, Donald Nelson reorganized the WPB again under a new presidential directive that gave the body control over the Army and Navy Munitions Board and authorized it to act as a referee in sorting out disputes over crucial materials. As part of the reorganization, Nelson announced at a July 7 press conference that "all of the operational work—including the industry and material branches, appropriate bureaus, and the field organization –is brought together under a Director General of Operations." He continued, "This post has been given to Amory Houghton, formerly deputy chief of the Bureau of Industry Branches." Responding to the slew of congratulatory letters that streamed in from colleagues and friends, Houghton expressed some trepidation about the new post. "I feel very much as though I were jumping off of the Brooklyn Bridge, but I will enjoy it at least until I hit the water," he wrote to Irving Cary at Corning. And he told Edward Ryerson of Inland Steel, "I wish that somebody else had been drafted for it as it seems a Herculean and possibly suicidal task."[22]

Indeed, the new job entailed a great deal more responsibility than his previous post. "At least half the burden of surmounting the present production crisis rests on the shoulders of Amory Houghton," *Business Week* noted in its August 15, 1942, edition. "To get the program clicking again calls for plenty of high policy decisions—the balance between military and civilian, between arms plants and raw materials division." Adding to the anxiety, Houghton, whom *Business Week* had dubbed a "dark horse," was a controversial choice. "New Dealers, long concerned over the industrial monopolists in the WPB's lower ranks, are deeply disturbed by Houghton's elevation," *PM Daily* reported in its July 13, 1942, issue. As a business owner and a prominent Republican, Houghton was naturally suspect among ardent Democrats. And the company's ongoing antitrust problems further cast a cloud over his nomination in their eyes. *PM Daily* noted that Houghton had recently paid a $5,000 fine after being indicted as a participant in a conspiracy by GE, CGW, and two foreign firms to stop competition in glass bulbs and that he was a central defendant in a pending Hartford-Empire antitrust case.[23]

This antitrust activity would cut short Houghton's Washington career. The Hartford-Empire case had started when Thurman Arnold, the indefatigable deputy attorney general, filed suit in 1939. Congressional activity in the latter stages of the New Deal had encouraged the Justice Department to investigate and root out what it viewed as monopolistic practices in a range of industries. The glass industry came in for particular scrutiny. The suit filed in 1939 charged that nine companies and sixty-one individuals, including Amory Houghton, had conspired to monopolize the glass container business through long-standing licensing and production agreements. Arnold also pursued charges against the main players in other sectors of the glass industry, such as incandescent and fluorescent lighting, flat glass, and fiberglass. In each instance, Corning and companies such as General Electric and Owens-Corning were named as codefendants, as were the Houghtons. Attempts to negotiate a consent decree in the Hartford-Empire case failed and the case came to trial in March 1941. At trial, the Justice

Department essentially charged that the system of cross-licenses and patent agreements, dating back to 1916, which had been set up by Corning and its customers and allies, constituted an illegal conspiracy to divide up domestic markets, fix prices, and restrict access to technology.

On August 25, 1942, Judge Frank L. Koeb, of the federal district court in Toledo, found the defendants guilty of violating the Sherman Antitrust Act. The 138-page opinion concluded that the first agreement between Hartford and Empire in 1916, as well as all successive agreements, were illegal and that Corning and the other companies had conspired to allow Corning to monopolize the market for "laboratory, electrical, paste mold, signal, optical, oven ware, chemical-resistant and heat-resistant ware, and bulbs, tubing and cane." Hartford-Empire was forced into receivership. The judge decreed that Corning's glassmaking machinery patents should be made available to other firms and that future patents won by Corning should be licensed. This latter order was a potentially devastating decree, given that Corning's survival rested on the patents it held on glassmaking equipment like the Ribbon Machine.

Upon learning of the decision, Amory Houghton submitted his resignation from the WPB immediately. "My directors are insistent that I return home to take my part in the many necessary decisions affecting the operations of the business including those involved in an appeal, and to them and the employees I feel a compelling obligation particularly because of the extent of the war work in which they are engaged," he wrote. "Equally and perhaps more controlling is my conviction that I can best serve the country in this most critical hour by taking the step which will avoid any possible embarrassment to you and the War Production Board in the grand job you are doing." He was succeeded by Ernest Kanzler, a former head of production at Ford Motor Company and founder of Universal Credit Corporation.[24]

Before leaving the WPB, Houghton drafted a memo to Reed detailing changes he felt needed to be made. Much of the advice he offered may have stemmed directly from his nearly two decades as an executive at a scientifically-oriented manufacturing concern. The WPB needed to attract higher quality personnel "with whatever measures are necessary" and prevent poaching of nonclerical staff by other branches of the armed forces. He rec-

ommended creating a post of deputy director general for scientific operations, establishing a production engineering division to iron out bottlenecks, and setting up a more rational vertical means of allocating materials.
This last piece of advice was followed. On November 2, the WPB introduced a new controlled materials plan. Rather than have each firm submit
plans to the WPB for approval, as under the old system, prime contractors
would prepare and submit a breakdown of all materials required, and then
parcel them out to subcontractors.[25]

After Houghton's resignation, dozens of letters of sympathy poured in.
Nobody was more disappointed than Philip Reed, who had been sent to
London to work with Averell Harriman at the U.S. mission for economic
affairs. "Laura's letter just received," Reed wrote in a telegram. "Can imagine what you've been through and though supremely confident of your
judgment I grieve and deplore loss to WPB will return Nov. or December
expect you rested and ready discuss future." In fact, it would be more than a
year before Houghton joined Reed in London.[26]

Switching to Defense Production

The unfavorable antitrust ruling was but one of the challenges Houghton
and his colleagues faced. Corning ultimately appealed the decision to the
Supreme Court. The Supreme Court, while finding that an illegal trust had
indeed existed in the glass container market, ultimately overturned the
more draconian portions of the judge's decision, largely preserving Corning's patent ownership rights. In the short term, however, the works operated under an air of uncertainty. It also had to struggle to cope with the loss
of personnel, and with heavy demands placed on it by the war. More importantly, however, it was adjusting to the rhythms and methods of a new set of
highly demanding customers—the armed forces—which constantly
inquired about hypothetical products, expected large amounts of specialty
products to be delivered immediately, and asked that glass be put to heretofore unprecedented uses.

In prior generations, Corning had sought and found ways to work with
professionals and entities in distant areas and disciplines. During these years,

the company found new ways to leverage its capabilities with a new set of associates: the military. Throughout 1942, Corning's executives and scientists constantly met with Army and Navy officials, discussing products ranging from glass bullets to substitutes for asbestos mittens, from coated glass pipe for oil lines to glass containers for sea mines and depth charges. In March 1942, a Mr. Schwartz of the hand grenade section asked for a representative to visit him in Washington to discuss the use of glass in the design of land mines. In September 1942, Dr. Shaver visited Capt. C. A. Burress of the engineer board in Fort Belvoir, Virginia, who wanted experimental glass cones for use in demolition bombs. Sometimes the government requests were shrouded in secrecy. An official at the Naval Research Laboratory called on October 19 about special test glasses for a confidential purpose. "The application has to do with a device which is used under water and glass discs from 4 in to 15 in diameter and _ to 4 and ⅝ [inches] thick are required," Shaver noted. "If the experiments prove successful the quantities required will be in lots of 1,000 to 2,000 pieces, which would be obviously a hand pressed job."[27]

A document, likely from 1942, found that 41 percent of the work of key Corning executives and scientists was directly applied on articles to be used by the armed forces; 37 percent was devoted to articles to be used by other industries making national defense products; and 22 percent was spent on general research work that could theoretically result in direct application to national defense production. Even so, Corning's engineers and scientists managed to make progress on long-standing problems. In 1940, they had made a breakthrough in the manufacture of so-called multiform glassware. The new multiform molding technique enabled them to mass-produce odd-shaped pieces of glass—a capability refined and improved as the company produced glass insulators and other new items.[28]

Of course, there were advantages to dealing with customers like the Army and the Navy. For example, the only way for companies to expand or build new production facilities during the war was to have them sponsored by the government. Such was the case with Corning's wartime efforts to produce optical glass. The end of commerce with Germany stimulated a demand for domestically produced optical glass, just as it had in World War I. During the years after World War I, American companies again relied on foreign sources for optical glass. So when trade with the continent was cut off in 1939 and 1940, American glass firms, Corning among them, were deluged with orders for optical glass. In January 1941, Corning took orders for 100,000 pounds of optical glass a year for two years, at $3.47 a pound, from the Frankfort Arsenal. That was a huge amount, considering that the total national production of optical glass that year was 556,000 pounds. To produce this heightened volume, Corning built five new furnaces with platinum-lined pots. In the summer of 1941, Corning was requested to consider increasing capacity to 50,000 pounds per month, mostly to make M3 binoculars. Since doing so would have overwhelmed the already increased capacity, Corning asked the government to build a new optical glass plant at Parkersburg, West Virginia, which the company would design and operate.[29]

Investing Abroad

Even amid the war, Corning was casting a large and wider net for growth. Initially, Corning's first overseas markets had been across in the Atlantic. It signed licensing deals with British and French firms in the 1920s to make Pyrex and refractories. Now that doing business in Europe was an impossibility, Corning looked south rather than east, to South America. In the 1930s, the Houghtons had established acquaintances with glassmaking families in South America. In 1940, Arthur Jr. and Amory sent a crystal vase as a wedding present to Leon Fourvel-Rigolleau, the proprietor of Buenos Aires-based Cristalerias de Rigolleau. Fourvel-Rigolleau expressed a desire to visit Corning. "I always feel in my heart a kind remembrance of your dear father, when I had the pleasure of meeting him, in those happy days," he wrote Arthur Jr. The correspondent was the descendant of Gaston Fourvel Rigolleau, a French immigrant who founded the company in 1882. Its factory, based in Berazetegui, which came to be known as the Glass City, made bottles and lightbulbs.[30]

Instead, Corning executives trekked south to meet with Rigolleau. In 1941, Eugene Gentil, an executive who had been associated with French glass company St. Gobain, had traveled around South America and sent back reports from countries such as Bolivia and Ecuador about the glass industry, general economic conditions, and the climate for foreign investment. The following spring, Eugene Sullivan, Gentil, and two others went to South America. "We have made some progress in getting at the glass situation but no part of the picture is sufficiently complete yet to report on," Sullivan reported to Houghton in April 1942. (Although Cole was the president, Amory Houghton continued to be the ultimate decision maker.) "We have visited innumerable glass plants, mostly small and crudely operated and welcoming help. Santa Marina here is an outstanding exception. Except for semi-automatic machines working small fancy bottles it is completely mechanized. It has ample floor space. The set up for vertical tube-drawing is grand."[31]

Corning's first South American investment was in Rigolleau's firm. In November 1942, it invested $212,000 in cash and licenses valued at $182,000 for a minority stake. In addition, Corning agreed to transfer certain patents and to render technical supervision and collaboration for the utilization of patents. The investment was made through a newly formed subsidiary, Corning Glass Works of South America. Over the next three years, Corning would also invest in a Brazilian and Chilean glass company. In each instance, Corning opted to take a minority interest in an established firm and provide it with technical know-how and, if necessary, financing to sell Corning products like Pyrex in their home markets. This was one way to get around the trouble and expense of exporting to distant markets and dealing with tariffs in protected economies.[32]

A New Self-Image

Even as it dispatched executives to scout out new business opportunities in the Southern Hemisphere, Corning's self-image was changing. World War II was a war with many fronts, including the home front. It was a period in the nation's history when making products for war was viewed as the near equivalent of combat, when factories were a sort of battleground. Because of the many military applications of glass, Corning was seen as a possible target of German bombers and domestic saboteurs. In 1940, after the government told Corning to take security precautions, the works set up a plant police. First organized by World War I veteran Charlie Hammarstrom, the auxiliary military police were under the command of a U.S. Army officer. Armed with 30-30 Springfield rifles and pistols, they manned guard towers overlooking the flood wall at the edge of the Chemung River, the plant's northern boundary, and ensured that no unauthorized people entered the plant property, which was designated by military decree as a prohibited zone. The war brought no acts of fifth-column terrorism. But after the war it was revealed that a 1942 Nazi plan called for Luftwaffe planes to bomb twenty East Coast targets, including Corning Glass Works and the Bausch & Lomb Company in Rochester.[33]

Like valorous soldiers, industry workers received decorations for outstanding performance. Early in the war, the Army and Navy instituted the E Award for excellence to reward and inspire military contractors. Some 4,299 of the nation's war production plants and construction projects—or 5 percent—would earn the award. On February 4, 1943, the works held a rally to receive its first E Award, the first of fourteen awards its plants would win. At 1:50 P.M., nearly 4,000 workers began to assemble around a platform outside Main Plant Building No. 54 as the Corning high school bands played. Glen Cole welcomed Colonel Frank J. Atwood, chief of the Rochester Ordnance District, who presented the award. "We realize that a good war-production team has no star players; in that spirit, we perform our work," Cole said. "The man who accurately weighs and puts together batch materials, the man who supervises furnace temperature controls, the inspector, the packer, the blower, the pressman and the machine operator—all of us are members of a production team." An employee, Earl Cortright, formally accepted the award. "Over our heads in this factory building hangs a war-slogan which we have adopted. It says: 'DON'T FIRE OVER—FIRE ON!' That's glass-workers' language, it means—'DON'T STOP—KEEP WORKING!' And that is what we are going to do." An observer noted that the only time a crowd of comparable size had gathered at the plant "was when the great 200 inch telescope mirror was poured in 1934."[34]

The comparison with the telescope mirror is apt. Corning had always taken pride in the fruits of its research. Its institutional advertising campaigns had long sounded the theme "Corning Means Research in Glass."

Now, however, Corning took its greatest pride in the application of its productive and scientific efforts to the war effort. "War and Corning research have put glass in a lot of strange places," trumpeted an ad in *Time* magazine describing how glass piping was being used in place of alloys. Another advertisement highlighted all the ways in which glass was used in combat airplanes. Amory Houghton drove home a similar point in a March 28, 1943, radio address to armed services in Iceland, Ireland, England, and North Africa, which was part of a weekly series that related progress on war production and industrial developments. "You who are bombardiers, gunners, or photographers can be certain that the optical glass in your instruments has never been surpassed. Once America depended on Germany for optical glass…but no longer. We need it now no more than we need German wheat." Throughout the war years, the ability to come up with new products ranging from optical glass to silicones was as vital to the war effort as it was to the health of the company.[35]

New Ventures: Dow-Corning and Owens-Corning

In March 1942, Glen Cole traveled to Detroit to meet with Harold Boeschenstein, the head of Owens-Corning, W. H. Dow of Dow Chemical, and several other executives to discuss ways to increase production of a new glass-related product: silicon resins. In the 1930s, chemist J. Franklin Hyde, who had arrived at Corning in 1930, began using his knowledge of polymers to investigate the properties of organo-silicon oxides. Meanwhile, researchers at Owens-Corning, Dow Chemical, and General Electric were investigating the same materials. Silicones were quasi-liquid waterproof materials that had a high resistance to chemical attacks and heat, and maintained a uniform viscosity at temperatures ranging from -57C to 260C.[36]

Boeschenstein had convinced Hyman Rickover, chief of the electrical division of the Bureau of Ships, that silicone-glass combinations could be used as lubricants in electrical equipment like motors or for aircraft hydraulic fluids. "Other than these, no known markets existed for silicone products," Dow-Corning president W. R. Collings noted. In 1942, Dow made about 1,000 pounds of a silicon lubricant used for ignition systems as well as to seal water out of radar connections on aircraft. This product would prove the basis of an entirely new company.[37]

At the meeting in March 1942, the executives agreed to pool their resources to develop silicones further and made plans for a pilot plant. Once samples were made and pilot production runs completed, Dow and Corning formed a fifty-fifty joint venture, the Dow-Corning Corporation, in February 1943. At first, the company basically sold a single product, Dow-Corning sealing compound no.4, known as DC4. In the first six months of 1943, it produced 23,000 pounds of the material, which it sold exclusively to the U.S. armed forces. With demand escalating, the directors of Dow-Corning voted to build a plant in June 1943, which was a more complicated proposition in wartime. Companies had to receive government approval to make capital investments. Consequently, Dow-Corning executives lobbied government officials to support their request. "We are now applying to the War Production Board for authority to construct this plant," Collings wrote to the commanding general of the air service command. "This is being done with the aid of bureaus in the Navy Department which are primarily interested in the insulating resins for motors and panel boards. If you wish us to include increased capacity to produce Dow Corning No. 4 Sealing Compound, a letter addressed to the writer stating the importance to your command of having adequate supply facilities for the DC-4 ignition Sealing Compound would be helpful."

The lobbying effort was evidently successful. For in September 1943, Dow-Corning began constructing a plant in Midland, Michigan. In the fiscal year that ended May 31, 1944, Dow-Corning had sales of $1 million, with DC-4 accounting for 80 percent of sales. But the potential was much larger. General Electric, the only potential competitor at the time, had meager production capabilities. Dow-Corning officials told Collins that GE wouldn't have sufficient production to meet their own needs for between eight and twenty-four months, "and that in the interim they wish to use our materials.... They stated that they now could use twenty times their present production."[38]

Another Corning joint venture, Owens-Corning, experienced similarly rapid growth during the war. Its product, fiberglass, was flexible, ultralight, and incombustible; had a very high strength-to-weight ratio, and didn't shrink or stretch. The versatile material could be made on a spool like yarn or in clumps like wool. Accordingly, it found many applications for the war effort. Long before Pearl Harbor, large-scale production was started at Newark, Ohio, and Owens-Corning opened a new plant at Ashton, Rhode Island, in 1941. The company's main customers were the army and navy, which used fiberglass as heat and sound insulator on ships, as insulation for arctic shelters, and in navy diving suits. Tiny strips of fiberglass were also used as filters in the tubing of the portable apparatus used to give blood plasma transfusions. Owens-Corning sales, which were $3.7 million in 1939, rose to $11.845 million in 1941, more than doubled to $27.411 million in 1942, and surged to $56.244 million in 1944.[39]

The Home Front: Corning's Changing Labor Force

The seemingly inexorable rise of the sales of Owens-Corning and Corning Glass Works masked one of the greatest single challenges company managers faced during World War II. During the war nearly 11 million men and women left their peacetime pursuits to enter the armed forces or provide indirect support to the military effort. These included hundreds of Corning employees. As noted, Amory Houghton went to Washington to work for the war bureaucracy. But at every rung of the corporate ladder, Corning people were set into motion by the war. Physicist John Hicks was loaned out to the secret Manhattan Project in 1942. Arthur Houghton worked for the Office of Special Service (OSS). Hundreds of line employees enlisted in, or were drafted into, the marines, the army, and the navy.

Back at Corning, factories were running full tilt, and the workers who remained grew more productive. Between 1939 and 1945, the number of man days of labor rose 50 percent; in the same period, however, output nearly doubled. Over the course of the war, as more than 3,000 CGW employees left to serve in the army and an extra 4,000 workers were required at its various plants, the works had to find more than 7,000 new employees—a daunting task, especially given that most of Corning's facilities were located in rural areas with comparatively sparse population density. At Main Plant, for example, employment—based on a forty-hour week —rose from 428 in 1939 to 1,057 in 1942. During the war, total company employment soared to 10,000, more than twice the prewar level. In addition, new methods adapted for making new products required greater training. "Because the armed forces needed certain glass products which could be made only by hand, Corning Glass Works has tripled its hand shops since 1941," one Corning observer wrote. Consequently, the company's Corning payroll nearly tripled between 1939 and 1944, from $5.42 million to $15.374 million. The company's total wages paid grew from $20.975 million in 1943 to $22.657 million in 1945, or 47 percent of sales, up from 41 percent in 1943.[40]

One of the biggest changes in the labor force was the growing participation of women. Women had long been employed at Corning as secretaries and administrative assistants, and in the finishing and packaging departments. As the war ground on, however, female employees assumed more prominent roles. In the fall of 1943, the new Corning magazine, the *Gaffer*, ran a salute to soldiers of "the home front army," including Lorena King and Gladys Hazelbauer of the Fall Brook division, who worked in a vegetable garden in their spare time, CGW employees Verald Clark and Alice Riffle, who volunteered as nurses at Corning Hospital, and Katherine Morris and Stella Suita of Central Falls, Rhode Island, who made glass envelopes for thermos bottles. Pearl Gentile, a blind woman whose brother Larry had been killed in the Pacific in 1942 and whose youngest brother, Joe, was in the marines, worked six days a week packing flameware.[41]

The absent Corning Glass Works employees were a constant presence. The works erected a huge billboard in front of Main Plant, the "Corning Glass Works Honor Roll," which listed the names of all employees in the service. By May 1944 it counted 2,000 names, and those killed or missing had a gold star next to their man. Many families had multiple members working at the factory, and they sent them off to war. Antonio and Anna Maio both worked at Corning during the war. All five of their sons, who had been Corning employees, were serving abroad: Pfc. Louis Maio (apparatus), twenty-six, was building roads in India; his twin, Sgt. Carmen Maio (tubulating), was with the Army Medical Corps in England; Arthur (apparatus), twenty-one, was in the navy in the South Pacific; Cpl. Blaze Maio, thirty-one, was serving with a chaplain in England; Pfc. Joe Maio, twenty-three, was with engineers on the Italian mainland. Four other Maio children remained at home.[42]

Aside from the increased presence of women, the other major change among the company's workforce was its unionization. Following passage of the National Industrial Recovery Act in 1933, Corning had formed workers councils at each of its plants consisting of equal numbers of hourly and salaried employees but under the chair of senior executive Glen Cole. The lone exception was the Charleroi plant. Before the 1936 merger with Corning, Macbeth-Evans had recognized the American Flint Glass Workers Union (AFGWU, or, more commonly, "the Flints") at its Charleroi plant. Although the workers councils proved satisfactory both to the company and employees—at least insofar as industrial unions mounted no significant attempts to organize the company—these arrangements came under increasing scrutiny in the early 1940s. The Congress of Industrial Organizations (CIO) took a growing interest in the glass industry, having won its big battles in the automobile, steel, and electrical equipment industries. Federal law and enforcement seemed—at least momentarily—tilted in the unions' favor. The CIO adopted a no-strike pledge during the war and CIO president Sidney Hillman held high positions with groups like the OPM and WPB.[43]

In 1940 organizers for the United Electrical Workers (UE), an aggressive and left-wing CIO union, made an initial foray in Corning, New York. Although the organizers did not make much headway, the leadership of the Glass Works understood that the UE or another CIO union would soon be back. At the same time, George Macbeth and Nick Unkovic, the Pittsburgh labor lawyer who advised on Corning's relationship with the Flints at Charleroi, argued that the company faced a choice: it could wage a protracted, expensive fight against unionization—a course implemented successfully at such companies as Thompson Products and Pitney-Bowes—or agree to recognize a union in hopes of establishing a cooperative relationship and a better prospect of maintaining control. Given their generally positive experience at Charleroi, Macbeth and Unkovic urged that Corning consider recognizing the Flints in its plants. Harry Hosier, the company's personnel director, concurred.[44]

In the spring of 1943, Corning's top executives agreed to meet with representatives of the Flints, including President Harry Cook, in Corning. Facilitated by Unkovic, the talks took place in Corning during the week of May 24. The Flints were delighted at the prospect of gaining recognition without a fight and proved willing to trade. An agreement announced on May 29 featured several provisions favorable to management. Collective bargaining would occur plant by plant rather than on a company-wide basis. The Flints also agreed to negotiate a single contract for each plant, thus enabling the company to avoid separate negotiations for different classifications such as gaffers and pressers.[45]

Federal law governing representation elections gave employees the exclusive right to determine a bargaining agent of their own choosing, without interference from employers. The next step, then, was an employee vote on whether to authorize the Flints as their representative. The first election in Corning was scheduled for October. During the interim, the UE returned to the fray, pledging the strength of the CIO and mounting a vigorous campaign. In the end, however, a significant majority of employees chose the Flints, perhaps because a traditional craft-based union seemed more in keeping with company traditions than a militant industrial union. And although management was proscribed from influencing the election, its preference for the Flints was obvious.

The Glass Works and the AFGWU signed the first contract for the Corning-area plants on January 20, 1944. Meanwhile, employees at other Corning installations were beginning to unionize. "We have finally signed a contract both here and in Wellsboro," Glen Cole reported to Houghton in February 1944. "There is a five-cent increase across the board when, and if, the labor board approves." The first round of bargaining also produced significant new benefits to employees. A pension program effective January 1, 1944, provided annual retirement income for employees with more than five years of experience who turned sixty-five. Workers were also offered the opportunity to buy hospital and life insurance, purchase meals cheaply at a new cafeteria, bank at the credit union, and buy Pyrex and other Corning products at a discount.[46]

Returning to Government Service

Amory Houghton received word of the union election vote while he was in Buenos Aires, Argentina. "Flints won 60-40, ninety percent voted," Glen

Cole wrote him via telegram. The itinerary shows what an ordeal interna-
tional travel was at the time. On September 23, he left New York for Miami,
via railroad, where, on September 26, he caught the first of a series of Pan
Am flights that took him through Cali and Lima, and ultimately to Santiago,
Chile. The Corning contingent spent a week in Chile, thirteen days in
Buenos Aires, and two weeks in Rio de Janeiro, before embarking on a similarly long trip home. While at the Hotel Carrera in Santiago, Chile, on
October 8, Houghton received a telegram from his old friend Philip Reed in
London. "Consolidation of Lend Lease OEW and OFRRO in Washington
will be reflected in London setup. . .Your services as my deputy and partner
urgently required....When are you returning to United States and how soon
can you leave for London?"[47]

Reed was reporting, in shorthand, that he was about to succeed Averell
Harriman as the head of the newly reorganized industrial war bureaucracies in London. The Mission for Economic Affairs would represent a half
dozen Washington departments and war agencies and serve as the U.S. representative for the London offices of the Combined Shipping Adjustment
Board, the Combined Raw Materials Board, and the Combined Production
and Resources Board. Established in 1942, the powerful combined boards
were responsible only to Roosevelt and Churchill, and to the combined
Chiefs of Staff. The boards acted as supergovernment agencies in allocating
the world's resources, and expanding raw materials and finished goods production. By the end of 1943, these boards controlled 95 percent of the critical raw materials outside Germany and Japan, directed virtually the entire
shipping industry, and had at their command the productive facilities of
Britain, Canada, and the United States. Throughout 1944, they would also
be concerned with reconversion of economies from war to peace.[48]

Houghton returned to the United States on October 25, 1943, and five
days later, a press release announced he accepted the post of deputy chief of
the U.S. Mission for Economic Affairs. Unlike his previous government job,
this one carried a salary. In addition, he had to file civil service applications
and attach a note explaining his antitrust conviction. When Houghton
arrived in London (Reed had secured a room for him at Claridge's), he made
efforts to keep up with company activities. "Our shipments for the period
which ended last Friday seemed considerably greater than for the previous

period," Cole wrote him on December 6, 1943. "We miss you here, and I am hoarding scotch for your return. If I am able to get any substantial amount I will call on you for financial support." (The procurement of scotch was a recurring theme in his correspondence. "Knowing your dry situation, we worked it out with Seton Porter to try to get you some Scotch," William Levis wrote him from Toledo. "I hope delivery was completed satisfactorily.") Houghton's wife, Laura, who was living in Marion, Massachusetts, also helped expedite supplies that were in short supply in London. "Do you know of any way we could get a metal container and send some sealed butter to Mr. H?" Laura Houghton asked his assistant, Julia Peck.[49]

Alexander Falck, who had retired in 1941, performed the same correspondent role for Amory that he had for Alanson, when he was off serving as an ambassador in Europe twenty years earlier. "The annual meeting of stockholders passed off yesterday in the usual way," Falck wrote to Houghton in February 1944. The meeting was chiefly devoted to discussing the possibility of acquiring part of Brazilian glass firm Vidraria Santa Marina, which Houghton had visited the previous fall. Cole, Sullivan, and Curtiss—who had recovered enough to return to work and was serving as president of the South American subsidiary—all agreed that any investment would be risky and shouldn't be expected to generate strong returns in the short term. "There was a general feeling that you favored taking the gamble and that there was more or less of a definite commitment subject to the ironing out of certain conditions," Falck wrote. Santa Marina was a strong company, with estimated profits of nearly $400,000 in 1942. In August 1944, Corning injected more than $600,000 of cash into the company and provided $991,000 net funds through the sale of licenses. In addition, it granted the company the ability to use compositions like opal and borosilicate glasses, as well as production methods like the Turret Chain Machines, the Ribbon Machine, and the updraw machine.[50]

The Company in High-Gear: War Production

Amory Houghton came home in the spring in time for his children's spring vacation. He left London on March 30 by boat, arrived in New York on April

6, and eventually made his way home to Corning. Houghton now found himself in charge of a unionized company with far-flung operations, whose 10,000 employees were engaged thoroughly in the war effort—in the factory and in the laboratory. (Over the course of the war, Corning had some 174 research and development projects actively connected with the war effort.) One of the ways that it attempted to maintain a sense of community among all its workers was through a new magazine, the *Gaffer*, which had debuted in the spring of 1943. Issues were frequently sent to the men serving overseas. In response to a plea from a Corning worker serving in India, the *Gaffer* in September 1944 originated a new feature: *Gaffer's* girl of the month. The first was Sue Serdula, who had been nominated by her fellow employees of Main Plant's Department 02. She was photographed sitting cross-legged, looking into the camera like a Hollywood ingenue.[51]

To boost morale, the company sponsored a variety show on local radio station WENY, called the Corning Glass Works Radio Family Party. Hosted by "Smiling Bob" Smith, who would go on to fame as the creator of Howdy Doody, the program featured performances by the Corning Glass Works Glee Club. Curtis Oakley, a shipping clerk at Corning's Main Plant, wrote the theme song for the show, which went as follows: "Don't Fire Over, Fire on!/ While our troops are marching on! / We at home have work to do. / We have got to see it through. / While they fight for you and me—we must work for victory—so smile and sing while you work./ Don't Fire Over, Fire on!"[52]

Corning's employees were also attempting to aid the war effort in their spare time. The company plowed, harrowed, and fertilized the Houghton Plot, a 12.5 acre tract located just south of the Chemung, about a half-mile from Corning's main square. The land was quickly turned into victory gardens by more than 200 employees, who planted corn, potatoes and other vegetables. "Today, you could count on the fingers of one hand the number of square feet (out of the 654,000 total) that isn't producing its quota of vitamins for Victory," the *Gaffer* noted proudly in 1944. Corning workers also plowed their savings into the war bond campaigns and banded together to raise funds for a specific cause. Employees of Pressware in the spring of 1943 raised $1,492.80 to purchase and donate an ambulance. In late 1944, employees of all CGW plants "poured more than $300,000 into in the Sixth War Loan campaign last month to back up the armed forces in their fierce fighting against the powerful Nazi counter attacks and the stiff Jap resistance," the *Gaffer's* editors wrote, in the fighting language typical of the day. By May 1945, Corning employees would purchase 137,707 war bonds worth $3.478 million.[53]

But the heart and soul of Corning's patriotic efforts lay in the furnaces, the blowing rooms, and the packing areas of its factories. Throughout the war, the company sought ways to make products that used less vital material. In August 1944, the *Gaffer* reported that Corning devised a method to produce glass bulbs for vacuum tubes in a tin-plating process that required only a third of the tin needed in more conventional processes. Corning also made efforts to salvage everything from paper to steel. "In the three and a half years of salvage operations at Corning, 2,000 tons of scrap metal and 2,000 tons of scrap paper have been routed back to the mills to be reprocessed and remade into essential war materiel," the *Gaffer* reported. By 1944, Charleroi had collected and shipped fifty-one carloads of scrap paper and the Parkersburg optical glass plant had salvaged ten tons of scrap metal.[54]

In the summer of 1944, the city of 16,500 was abuzz with war-related activity that was spirited, if a little confusing to outsiders. A correspondent of the *Saturday Evening Post* visiting in the summer of 1944 found "a pucker and a huddle of buildings in which meticulous hand glass-blowing still abides alongside frighteningly prolific automatic machines." The magazine marveled at the array of products Corning could make from as many as 50,000 different glass compositions. "Last year, when the British called urgently for a special glass for a special war job, chemist Harrison Hood took two and one half hours to find the right formula, and that was considered very fast indeed."[55]

Corning also developed processes to make products it had once made by hand on a mass basis. During the war, the demand for cathode ray tubes grew unabated, as radar assumed a vital role. The bulbs consisted of two parts, the faceplate and the funnel, which had to be sealed together. E. M. Guyer, a veteran Corning researcher, developed a tool that used electricity to melt two pieces of glass together along a seam. The development of so-called electric sealing allowed Corning to make the products by machine. In 1943, it produced more than a million cathode ray tubes, many of them at the Charleroi plant, and by the end of 1944 it had made about 3 million.

In addition, Corning scientists were developing ways to produce optical glass in larger quantities. Dr. Charles F. DeVoe, who had joined Corning in 1936, was responsible for overseeing optical glass production. Although DeVoe and his crew had built more than twenty-four furnaces and a new factory had been built in Parkersburg, the company was still having difficulty keeping up with demand. DeVoe discovered that running an electric current through a bath of molten optical glass would allow them to produce high-quality glass more efficiently. "The first of the new continuous melting units was lighted in January 1945, and for the first time large volumes, up to 100 pounds per hour, of uniform quality optical glass could be continuously melted and delivered to automatic forming equipment," one expert later noted.[56]

Corning also continued to make its traditional products, but in larger, more heroic ways. In October 1944 Corning shipped to the American Bemberg Corporation in Elizabethton, Tennessee, "the longest sections of glass pipe ever made"—five 27-foot lengths. The Pyrex was to be used in a plant that made supply-parachutes and other materiel for the armed forces. Great Britain had asked the United States to construct a huge plant to process magnesium, the principal component of incendiary bombs. But the plans for the facility, to be built near Las Vegas, were sent over on a ship that went down in the Atlantic after being struck by a torpedo. So William H. Tomb Jr., a CGW salesman, traveled to Las Vegas to figure out the specifications for the plant's heat exchangers: 23.5 miles of 1.5-inch glass pipe.[57]

Corning also took pride in the role glass was playing in the increasingly deadly air and ground war. The *Gaffer* of May 1944 featured an article on elbow benders, six-inch glass tubes, "bent in the heat of a gas flame by a girl," that "play an important part in the daily bombing of Uncle Sam's enemies and in the gradual destruction of the Nazi Luftwaffe." The glass was the exterior section of the fuel line of expendable auxiliary gas tanks that allowed the tanks to break off cleanly without imperiling planes. The *Gaffer* also trumpeted Corning's production of ampules used in radio proximity fuses—a tiny, five-tube two-way radio that fit in the nose of a three-inch shell. When the shell passed within seventy feet of its target, impulses from the transmitter were reflected back to explode the shell. Workers at Fallbrook started making them in quantity in 1944 and produced 8,000 a day.

The antipersonnel shells were used to great effect in the Battle of the Bulge.[58]

But Corning's glass could heal as well as kill. During the war, Corning was the only producer of a glass, code-named 9741, which could transmit sufficient quantities of the ultraviolet rays capable of killing disease germs. Bulbs made of the glass were used to irradiate water stored on life rafts. In addition, "germicidal lamps now stand guard over blood plasma and penicillin in the vital steps of processing the life-saving fluid and 'wonder drug' on their way to our wounded fighting men on every front," the *Gaffer* noted. "From the time the blood is received from local Red Cross donor banks until the plasma is on its way to the front, the invisible death-dealing rays are on duty to destroy any germ-invader."[59]

Planning for Postwar Markets

In the spring of 1944, in one of the most dramatic single battlefield events, Allied forces successfully landed on the bloody beaches of Normandy. In the months after D-Day, as the Allies liberated Paris and began to press toward the Rhine, there was a sense that things were winding down. Throughout the fall of 1944, Houghton remained in London, trying to deal with the new issues posed by what seemed to be the beginning of the ending of the war. He was working on projects like getting supplies of soap from Britain to liberated areas, acquiring Spanish sweaters, doing financial planning for the Balkans, and obtaining horse meat from Argentina and Canada for relief purposes. While the war of the generals was far from over, the campaign of the logisticians and economic warriors seemed to be coming to an end.[60]

Eager to return home and prepare General Electric for the new postwar environment, Philip Reed resigned in November 1944. "It would be impossible for me to remain here through the post European war adjustment period, which I am sure you agree will require continuance here of the U.S. war agencies representation for a considerable time," he wrote to Ambassador John Winant. Houghton, impelled by the same sense of duty, resigned the same day. He left London on November 12, sailed from Glasgow the next day, and arrived in New York on the afternoon of November 19. Twelve days later, he traveled to Washington, D.C., where he formally submitted his resignation. "I sever my connection with very mixed emotions but, as you know, when I went to London, it was with the understanding that I could not remain under any circumstances more than a year—the year was completed this month—and it is now imperative that I return to my own business," he wrote.[61]

Back at Corning, Houghton paid tribute to the workers, writing an introduction to a simple small booklet with an American flag on its cover. Inside it listed the names of 2,159 Corning Glass employees, male and female, who had served thus far in the armed forces. "This is a powerful book. Yet all it contains is a list of names," he wrote. "American names of course and names of Italian, Swedish, English, Polish, Greek, Norwegian, French, German, Czech, Irish, and Scotch extraction....the men, the boys, the women of many origins who once proved that they could live in peace together in this community—who together helped build our strong and useful industry—who went off to war together to defend their country— and who, if we continue to give them the support they need, will come home to keep democracy working."[62]

While war production continued apace, the company was beginning to plan for the postwar world. During the war years, the company's recurring search for the next big hit had been largely suspended. But in the latter months of the war, the quest began to gear up again. On September 22, 1944, planners had assembled a checklist of tasks to be done in preparation for the introduction of a new consumer product: prepare the laboratory to provide several thousand skillets and prove consumer acceptability; have engineers design a pilot plant and a factory capable of making 1 million a year. By March 1945, Corning had also plotted a postwar television program, which involved building machinery for experimental work and making samples. With the ability to take a somewhat longer view, planners were suggesting possible pilot plant projects, working on proposals to improve efficiency through greater mechanization and better handling methods.[63]

Meanwhile, Corning was escalating its activities in South America. In the fall of 1944, Hanford Curtiss, William Taylor, Lawrence King (resident managing director for CGW of South America), and Eugene Gentil left for a two-month trip. Aside from visiting enterprises in Brazil and Argentina, they traveled to Chile to negotiate a deal with Chilean glass firm Cristalerias de Chile, which made bottles, tableware, and window glass. "We are confident that the southern hemisphere is due for a rapid industrial growth after the war which will mean an increased demand for glass products in industry, science and the home," Curtiss said upon his return. The investment in Chile didn't take place until October 1945, when the company essentially invested $350,000 in the form of shares and licenses. In addition to providing them with capital, Corning was providing its South American affiliates with technology. In 1945 it sent blueprints of the type C finishing machine to Cristalerias de Argentine, along with a copy of Corning's method for analysis of B2O3 glass. Corning also helped design and construct an opal glass tank for both the Argentine and Chilean companies, and a small continuous updraw tube tank for the Chilean firm.[64]

As American and Allied troops smashed their way across Germany in March 1945, the end of the war seemed ever nearer. Consequently, companies began to take concrete steps to prepare for the postwar world. The expansion of capabilities for research, development, and production was but one of the many necessities long deferred during the war. To be sure, Corning had expanded by investing in South American firms, by creating joint ventures like Dow-Corning, and by operating plants like Parkersburg for the government. But it had been largely unable to invest substantially in improving its existing plants. When it became apparent that resources might soon be freed up for nonmilitary applications, Corning's executives began to plot an extensive postwar expansion and retooling. In the spring of 1945, the company was already planning to buy and develop a plant to make Pyrex at Leaside, Ontario, and to build a new pilot plant in Corning. But retained earnings alone—$932,000 in 1945—were not sufficient to fund the ambitious postwar program.[65]

At the same time that the company projected the need for significant capital to fund postwar growth, it also sought to address its ownership structure. The Houghton family had borrowed considerable funds to settle the estate of Alanson B. Houghton and was eager to retire its loans. At the same time, the holders of the company's common stock had grown from two or three into the hundreds, as the heirs of the Houghtons, the Sinclaires, and other employee owners had their own children and grandchildren. Selling shares to the public would allow the shareholders to establish a market for their holdings and place an accurate value on them. Finally, Corning's executives and directors recognized a need for stock as an incentive for employees.[66]

In the spring of 1945, these factors converged in the decision to sell part of the Glass Works to the public. Enlisting the aid of investment bank Lazard Frères (Lazard Frères banker George Murnane was a long-time acquaintance of Amory Houghton), Corning in April 1945 sold 412,340 shares of common stock, representing 15 percent of the company's equity. At the same time, CGW borrowed about $5 million by selling preferred stock bearing a 3.5 percent interest rate.[67]

When Germany, utterly shattered by the Russian and Allied forces that had converged in Berlin, surrendered on May 8, 1945, it brought equal measures of relief and sadness. For as the Allied forces slogged their way through the forests and plains of western Europe, the death toll mounted on both sides. March alone brought the deaths of two Charleroi workers, Andrew Evanich Jr., twenty, infantryman Andrew Krupka, and two Corning-based workers Robert Blackman, twenty-one, and James Burd of Pressware—all in Germany. The same month, Sgt. Bernard Ladd of Main Plant hand bulbs, a B-29 gunner, was killed in the Pacific. That brought Corning's toll to 85 dead, 103 wounded, and 50 missing or taken prisoner. The *Gaffer* exhorted people to continue the work, since Japan was still fighting. "Confirmed reports of prison camp atrocities and privations combined with the warnings of our own CGW men returned from the fighting fronts and prison camps renew the challenge to all industrial workers to stick to their production jobs." Despite the fact that war production was grinding down, employment remained steady. The payroll on June 16, 1945 was 9,597 employees, down a bit from 9,881 on September 30, 1944.[68]

Victory over Japan in August 1945 brought news that was horrific and joyous at once. With the explosion of two nuclear bombs in Hiroshima and Nagasaki, on August 6 and August 9, respectively, the shell-shocked Japanese fighting machine was finally pummeled into submission. On August 10, 1945, Japan tendered an unconditional surrender. V-J Day was proclaimed, which brought great celebration to Corning; the Glass Works and the Ingersoll-

Rand factory closed for the day. Three weeks later, on September 2, when representatives of Japan's government and military signed the final articles of surrender on board the USS *Missouri*, World War II was officially over.

The war had indeed taken its toll on Corning. With the fall bringing a final casualty—Sgt. Eugene Scott of Pressware, a B-17 radio gunner who had been missing and was presumed dead—the number of Corning employees killed in the war rose to 108. There was little time for Corning and the rest of American society to mourn or to stop and savor the victory. The shift from peace to war had jolted the nation's productive capacities and forced American companies to serve new customers, abandon certain product lines, and devise methods to mass-manufacture new products. Just so, the abrupt shift back to peace would force them to turn on a dime again. "Now that Uncle Sam has stepped out of the picture as the biggest buyer in history, his nephews and nieces have taken over," noted a May 1945 *Gaffer* article, which depicted a stereotypically American family, Nancy and Pete Miller, and their son and daughter. "No one of them buys so very much, but there are 140 million of them, and together they buy plenty. That is, they will buy plenty—from the first company that offers them a good buy on a lot of things they've been waiting for." Such consumers, the article continued, are "our new bosses, the bosses of CGW employees and management, and of every wage earner in the nation."[69]

Reorienting the company toward a new set of customers was like trying to turn a battleship—a lengthy process rather than a discrete event. Over the course of 1945, production for military needs fell from 75 percent of capacity to less than 10 percent, and sales fell to $48.2 million from $52.4 million the previous year. Profits for the year would fall to just 4.9 percent of sales— about half the profit margin in the first years of the war. Even so, the consumer part of the business, which constituted about 25 percent of 1945 sales, seemed to be bouncing back. Glen Cole noted in October that "total company sales since V-J Day, according to preliminary reports, show only a moderate decline as compared with the corresponding period of 1944." By October 1945 the company reported substantial backlogs for Pyrex colored mixing bowls, bakeware, Christmas tree ornaments, and coffeemakers.[70]

"In taking stock of Corning's prewar and apparent postwar competitive situation, it is evident that in many respects our competitive situation is much less favorable," senior Corning executive noted in a memo. The successful prosecution of antitrust cases had sapped some of Corning's long-standing competitive advantages. During the war the company either discontinued or greatly curtailed production of Christmas tree ornaments, domestic tableware and tumblers, neon sign tubing, and Steuben. The lower output of civilian ware "enabled some competitors to make considerable gains in markets in which we had been leaders before the war, especially in the sale of consumer products." In addition, Corning had shared formulas and manufacturing methods for radar, electric sealing, and strengthening tumblers with other glassmakers. As a result of all these developments, Anchor Hocking and the McKee Glass Company were selling glass ovenware in 1945 for up to 20 percent less than Corning's offerings, and the Libbey Glass Company had been licensed to make toughened tumblers. Anchor Hocking, Sneath, and Inland were all producing coffeemakers, and "because of our inability to deliver, they obtained wide distribution." Meanwhile, the Wheaton Glass Company was considering installing Danner machines to make low-expansion tubing glass that would compete with Pyrex.[71]

To be sure, Corning still had strong market leadership in specialty products (it manufactured some 37,000 different items made of 450 chemically different glass compositions) and in automated lines like cathode ray tubes and incandescent lamps. Corning sold 45 percent of the lightbulb blanks made in the United States in 1945. Despite the adversity Corning faced, *Fortune* magazine noted, "it still has its research, its profound knowledge of glass, its bold management techniques, and its imperturbable Houghtons." In the coming decade, Corning would use these formidable assets to develop new products—like television bulbs—reinvigorate old lines like cookware, and expand into new geographic areas. With labor peace, a stable and experienced management team, and a strong balance sheet, Corning was well situated to ride the postwar boom.[72]

CHAPTER SEVEN

A Decade of Unbounded Opportunities,

1945–1954

THE END of fighting in Europe and Japan brought a relatively quick return to normalcy to Corning and the other towns that housed Corning Glass Works operations. Soldiers returned from abroad to resume educations, careers, and personal lives that had been suspended during the war as industry shifted gears to meet new demands. For the Corning Glass Works, and for many American companies, the conversion from wartime to peacetime was painful at first. But powered by technological advances and by a robust American economic engine that dwarfed the war-shattered economies of Europe and Asia, American businesses enjoyed rapid growth and low inflation for much of the postwar era. To be sure, the period between 1945 and 1954 brought war: a hot war on the Korean Peninsula and a Cold War throughout Europe and the developing world. And at home, a frequently reckless search for Communists and the budding civil rights movement in the southern states punctured the calm of postwar life. Still, the decade after the war was in many ways an extraordinary time for American business. The nation's industrial strength helped produce a growing middle class that was eager to buy new goods that used Corning products, ranging from Pyrex containers to televisions.

In this period, Corning would use its expertise in glass to create a new product that would revolutionize American culture and become a household staple: television. It also continued the decades-long tradition of providing specialty glass products for industrial and military use. The advent of the Cold War made it imperative for the military and industry to work together to develop new technologies. And Corning was able to leverage the associations it had forged during wartime to branch out into promising new business areas. The Glass Works generally thrived between 1945 and 1954; its sales nearly tripled and its stock soared. The company built new plants throughout the United States and struck new alliances abroad. All the while, its scientists in upstate New York continued to pursue the apparently endless potential of glass. While veteran executive Amory Houghton Sr. remained at the company's helm, William Decker and his cadre of managers, who would include Amory Houghton Jr., assumed increasing responsibility.

Postwar Transitions

In the months after V-J Day, the American private sector gradually broke free of its wartime shackles. It was a time of some dislocation and confusion, as companies that had cooperated were free to compete again as bitter rivals. Labor unions, liberated from wartime bans on strikes, began to flex their muscles. "In common with other business concerns, Corning Glass Works had to contend with crippling strikes in the coal and transportation industries, shortages of key materials and unpredictable problems resulting from the country's war effort," Amory Houghton Sr. noted in the 1946 *Annual Report*. While avoiding strikes itself, Corning raised wages twice, in January and October. Sales in that year climbed to a record $55.9 million, spurred in large part by a 35 percent jump in consumer products sales. But the collapse of large government orders threw certain business segments into chaos. For example, sales of optical glass fell from $700,000 in 1945 to $218,201 in 1946. And the rapid decline forced the company to take quick action. Demand for optical products shrank so severely that Corning in August 1946 purchased the Parkersburg plant from the War Assets Administration, tore out all the optical manufacturing features, and installed machinery to make Pyrex tubing.[1]

Corning's reconversion efforts were hampered by one of the Chemung River's periodic floods in May 1946. Big Flats was inundated, and a surging Monkey Run flooded businesses on Market Street and parts of Corning's A, B, and C Factories; the rising waters caused a 123-day shutdown of at least one manufacturing unit. Young recruit Forrest Behm recalls the flood clearly: it occurred on his first day in Corning. He had spent the night at the Baron Steuben Hotel. When he came down the next morning in the elevator, he overheard one man saying to another.

> "So you think the dike will hold?" I said, "What dike?" He said, "Oh, we are having a flood in the river. We have these floods regularly." So I immediately moved my beat-up old Ford up on the hill.
>
> I started to go in the direction where I was told I should go for A Factory. I met a man in hip boots coming along. It was pretty much a mess around there, water running in the streets. I said, "I'm looking for Jack Hanigan." He says, "I'm Jack Hanigan." I said, "Well, I'm Forrest Behm. I'm supposed to have an interview with you." He says, "This is not a very good day for you to have an interview. I have three feet of water in my factory." So I left. That was my first experience.

Despite the inauspicious first contact, Behm, a former all-American football tackle at the University of Nebraska who had attended Harvard Business School, decided to take the job.[2]

The conversion of the Parkersburg plant was but one component of an ambitious postwar expansion program. In 1946, Corning converted the old gas company building on the northern bank of the Chemung River into a Pilot Plant. A miniature factory, the Pilot Plant provided space where scientists and engineers could develop manufacturing methods, meet with customers without letting them into production facilities, and experiment without jeopardizing ongoing manufacturing. The Pilot Plant would assume a prominent role in Corning's postwar development. When compelling problems (or projects) arose, the plant would provide a dedicated space where the company could mass its substantial intellectual resources and bring together experts from a range of disciplines.

Most of the Corning-area residents who had served in the war returned home in 1945 but some continued to serve through 1946. Amory Houghton Jr. (known to most people around Corning as "Amo") had been admitted to Harvard in December 1944 but was deferred until he completed his military service. In the fall of 1946 the twenty-year-old freshman followed the path his father and grandfather had taken. In Cambridge, Amo received the extra attention befitting a freshman whose last name graced a library in Harvard Yard. As dean of freshmen Delmar Leighton wrote to Amory Sr., "Phil Hofer [a friend and classmate of Arthur A. Houghton Jr.] is looking after your boy."[3]

Like his father, Alanson Houghton, Amory Houghton Sr. would continue to run the company while devoting an increasing amount of time to public affairs and politics as he entered middle age. And just as Alanson had turned over increasing amounts of responsibility to trusted deputies—Alexander Falck and Eugene Sullivan—Amory Sr. would delegate an increasing amount of responsibility to Bill Decker. In October 1945, Decker, who had run the bulb and tubing division, was given the additional responsibility of the technical products division. The following April, Decker was promoted to president. "Well, I was tremendously surprised at the timing of it because, you see, having just gotten this new divisional job, I just couldn't understand the other thing happening so fast," he said. In his sixteen years at the company, the Harvard MBA had already shined in a range of managerial positions. And over the next fourteen years, Decker would prove a vital senior executive. Serving as a bridge between two generations of Houghtons, Decker established himself as an industrial statesman in his own right.[4]

There was a certain amount of continuity in the laboratories as well as in the executive offices. Work stemming from wartime breakthroughs, such as the multiform glassmaking process and optical glass, continued under the supervision of Eugene Sullivan and Jesse Littleton. But the scientists in Corning's laboratories were on the verge of exciting new discoveries. Since joining Corning in 1940, after having earned a Ph.D. at the Massachusetts Institute of Technology, chemist S. Donald Stookey had devoted much of his time toward investigating photosensitivity—the phenomenon through which glass changes color after being exposed to light. And in June 1947, Corning announced the development of photosensitive glass. It would be nearly twenty years before the company reaped significant revenues from the breakthrough. Nonetheless, by 1948, Corning's optical business had rebounded, as it sold more than $1 million of optical products, mostly single-vision lenses to customers like Bausch & Lomb and the American Optical Company.[5]

In 1947, with demand rising for several classes of products, the company issued $5 million in preferred stock and spent $5.3 million on plant expansion. The Corning Pressware plant, built in 1938, supplied Pyrex ovenware for the entire domestic market. But Corning's executives believed that a second plant in a different part of the country would allow the company to save a great deal on freight. "We compared different areas such as Mississippi, California, Washington, Illinois, and it became quite apparent that what we called the southwest...was the most promising," consumer products executive Stan Fairman later recalled. After inspecting sites in Missouri, Kansas, and Arkansas, Corning settled on Muskogee, Oklahoma, which afforded access to high-quality sand and cheap natural gas. Muskogee was familiar to Corning veterans. In 1920 Hanford Curtiss had written to the local chamber of commerce expressing preliminary interest in locating a branch plant there. Corning subsequently added capacity in other locations, but it did not forget about Muskogee. Ground was broken for the factory in March 1947, and production began in January 1948, mostly of Pyrex coffee percolators. "Muskogee operation looked very good to Bill Taylor and me," Decker reported to Am a month later.[6]

There was also new construction in Corning in the late 1940s. The watchtowers ringing the main plant were dismantled. On the north bank of the Chemung, apartment and housing developments such as Crystal Gardens and Meadowbrook were constructed for returning veterans. Veterans were also given preference to purchase the two-bedroom homes built on Houghton Plot—the former site of Victory Gardens. In the spring of 1947, nearly 1,200 people inspected a model on Pyrex Street. In anticipation of the town's centennial in 1948, the company donated 10.5 acres of land on the north river bank, which was dubbed Pyrex Park, and Corning subsequently ratified a bond issue to build a stadium that would stand as a memorial to veterans of World Wars I and II.[7]

The week-long centennial celebration started in September 1948 with a balloon parade through the streets of Corning, continued with the crowning of the Crystal Queen, and included an address by Erastus Corning 2nd, the descendant of the land speculator for whom the town was named, and the powerful, longtime mayor of Albany. The highlight, however, was the visit of retired Gen. Dwight Eisenhower, now the president of Columbia University. On Sunday, September 12, 1948, the one-time supreme commander of Allied Forces flew into the Big Flats airport on a Corning Glass Works plane, had lunch with Amory Houghton Sr. and his family at the Knoll, and then proceeded to the new Memorial Stadium. Wearing his five-star general's uniform, Eisenhower addressed an overflow crowd estimated at 10,000 people. His address was brief and to the point. "Corning has now witnessed 100 years of American history," he said. "It is fitting that it should celebrate this occasion by giving this fine stadium to the memory of the men and women who served in two great world wars."[8]

The visit was an important event for Corning and also for Amory Sr., who was forming a solid, enduring relationship with the former general. Amory Sr. wrote Eisenhower to thank him for attracting "the largest gathering by far in the history of the community....From a personal point of view Laura and I enjoyed tremendously having you with us. We were both disappointed that Mrs. Eisenhower could not be with you but hope that you know that whenever you or yours are in these parts or are moving west that a quiet stopping place with a warm welcome awaits you in Corning with us."[9]

A Television Pioneer Perseveres

The visit by Eisenhower, the dominant political figure of the decade, and Am's personal relationship with him, highlighted the degree to which the small town in upstate New York would be directly connected with the individuals and forces that would influence America's public life in the coming decade. For in this period, the Corning Glass Works also made major contributions to one of the most significant industrial and cultural phenomena of the latter half of the twentieth century: the television. Just as the introduction of electric light and radio had in prior generations, the advent of commercial television would forge a new medium and exert vast influence on journalism, entertainment, and consumer culture. And as it had done with the instruments that transmitted electric light and radio signals, the Corning Glass Works would provide the glass heart of this revolutionary new product.

Television as a product class first appeared in Corning records in 1939—the year David Sarnoff exhibited the futuristic technology at the World's Fair —with sales of $77,429. The war forestalled any further development. But after the war, broadcasting and manufacturing companies such as RCA, General Electric, Sylvania, and DuMont hastened to reintroduce television to an eager viewing public. Because crucial parts of the television, including the cathode ray tube and the bulb itself, were made of glass, television presented significant opportunities for the company. In previous generations, Corning had often worked with pioneers in industries such as railroads and incandescent lighting to help establish standards. But with about 100 manufacturers trying to establish market dominance based on proprietary platforms, it was difficult for components suppliers to ramp up mass production. Moreover, television was slow to catch on. In 1947, when the Federal Communications Commission reached a provisional decision on broadcasting standards, just over 200,000 American families had televisions.[10]

Corning's executives, always on the lookout for the next big hit, believed television could be it and immediately took steps to prepare for the expected breakthroughs. In 1947, Corning established a separate facility to make television bulbs and cathode ray tubes at the Charleroi plant. "Production of 10 inch television panels at Chareleroi is now much better," Decker wrote to Amory Sr. in February, 1948. "Selection averaged 2950 per day for the past 9.5 days compared with around 1300 on the preceding run." The following year, however, Corning decided to concentrate its TV-glass efforts at Pressware, in large part due to a more hospitable labor climate in the Chemung Valley. But centralizing development in Corning would also enable its scientists and engineers to work more closely on the manifold challenges presented by television. Corning placed a relatively recent hire, Forrest Behm, in charge of the effort.

In 1948, anticipation was building. First, one of Pressware's melting tanks was converted to make black-and-white television bulbs. The company quickly decided that it needed more production facilities dedicated exclusively to the new product. After negotiations with the union, Behm shut down the entire Pressware plant for six weeks in the summer of 1948 to iron out kinks, furloughing some 2,400 workers. And there were a great many kinks to be ironed out. By the late 1940s, Corning had substantial experience making cathode ray tubes. But it was less proficient with the requirements for television bulbs. As Behm put it, "We didn't know what we were doing." Television bulbs had three pieces—a faceplate, a funnel, and a neck. At first, Corning blew the funnels and pressed the faceplates, and then sealed them together. There were several bottlenecks in the process, however. The pressed panels (or faceplates), for example, had to be polished by hand. In the initial setup, some 800 people were employed in polishing faceplates, completing them at the rate of one per man-hour. This pace was much too slow for the volume Corning contemplated.[11]

For Corning to satisfy the anticipated demand, it would have to revamp the whole process from beginning to end, starting with the glass. Most early television bulbs used a 30 percent lead oxide formula, which had excellent electrical resistivity but was difficult to melt and form. John Sheldon, manager of the television department, reasoned that different parts of the bulb could be made from different formulas. The neck, the smallest and easiest part to make, required high electrical resistance and hence demanded lead. By contrast, the funnel and panel required just one-tenth the electrical resistivity as the neck. Using knowledge gained from working on opthalmic glass, research scientist William Armistead in 1948 developed a new formula, known as 9010, a 12 percent barium oxide glass for the faceplate and funnel. After months of trials in the Pilot Plant, the new formulas would enter full-scale production in 1949 and remain the norm until the mid-1970s.[12]

Developing the right glass composition was only part of the solution. The next challenge was sealing the three parts effectively. Sealing was a tough chore that involved lots of heat. At first, Corning workers sealed the parts together through a circular gas-fired torch, which was inefficient and potentially dangerous and contributed to the low selection rates. Under E. M. Guyer, Corning in 1949 would develop a technique for electric sealing that employed a combination of flames and electricity. The area to be sealed was preheated by a pinpoint flame that softened the glass and altered its electrical characteristics to the point where an electric spark could facilitate electric welding. This worked well but couldn't be automated.

As Corning's engineers and scientists struggled to rationalize the production of television bulbs, the company was confronted with a new obstacle that was potentially insurmountable. Decades earlier, when Corning supplied far larger companies like General Electric with large quantities of bulb blanks, it faced the unenviable prospect of having its largest customer simply decide to make the product itself. A similar dynamic recurred in the late 1940s with RCA. The giant electronics and broadcasting company accounted for about half of Corning's television business and utterly dominated the market. In 1947, RCA believed it could boost profits by eliminating Corning as a supplier and making its own bulbs. In 1948, RCA bought a government tube plant in Lancaster, Pennsylvania, which had been built during the war. There, it began producing glass bulbs with a slight wrinkle—they had a cheaper metal funnel. In addition, RCA offered its many licensees a new technical package that included the bulb, production equipment, and guidance.[13]

Suddenly, Corning's nascent television business was in peril. With RCA slashing orders, Corning's management faced a loss of revenue and a loss of credibility with employees. Just before Christmas 1948, a chagrined Forrest Behm was forced to lay off 800 employees, many of whom had recently been furloughed when Pressware was revamped. "I talked to all of them in groups. I told them what happened. My integrity was questioned, because I promised them something and I couldn't deliver....RCA lied to us. They had told us nothing. They had kept it absolutely secret."[14]

Faced with this challenge, Corning did what it had in the past: it turned to its homegrown talent for a new process. This time the hero was James Giffen, a prodigious inventor who, in the course of a 32-year career, helped Corning break in to several new product areas. In the tradition of Charles Githler and William Woods, Giffen was another largely self-taught mechanical genius whose talents were noticed, nurtured, and rewarded by the science-oriented company. A native of Iowa, Giffen had been hired in 1944 to work on mechanical development in the lab. Initially, Jesse Littleton assigned him to work on the centrifugal casting of casseroles. Centrifugal casting involved forming shapes by dropping a gob of molten glass into a spinning mold. A layer of steam prevented the glass from adhering to the mold, and as it spun the glass would form evenly and quickly into the desired shape. When Giffen went to the blowing room to work on this problem, however, he found that workers were having difficulty sealing funnels to television faceplates, whose edges were not sufficiently thin. Giffen, who had seen centrifugal casting at Owens-Corning, noted that shape of funnel molds should permit ideal centrifugal casting. Working with gatherer J. Overmeyer, he quickly set up a mold-spinning device and found that he could spin funnels in the existing molds.[15]

This was good as far as it went. But increasingly, customers required that the bulbs feature rectangular rather than round faceplates. And that shape seemed to pose particular problems to the principles that underlay centrifugal casting. So much so that Howard Lillie, a physicist in the R&D lab, claimed it was theoretically impossible to do so. Giffen took this as a challenge. As one contemporary put it, he "held all degrees—and especially the Ph.D.—in contempt." So the next day, he used a mold rigged with dams in the corners. The molten glass in the corners flowed around the dams before it could head up the sides, thus arriving at the same time as the slower glass nearer the center. Soon after issuing his report, Lillie was presented with a centrifugally cast rectangular television bulb.[16]

Giffen's ingenious tinkering, which combined the formation of the neck *and* the funnel in a single process, would ultimately make it possible for Corning to make bulbs more efficiently. But the breakthrough would have been for nought if RCA's engineers were as proficient. Fortunately for Corning, the television tube producers who switched to metal were finding that RCA's design didn't entirely overcome significant electrical interference problems inherent in the material. And Corning stood ready with an economical alternative. As Decker later put it. "Unless we could have developed machine processes for making television bulbs the way we did, we could never have knocked metal out of the picture."[17]

Giffen's centrifugal-casting process plainly worked. After tests in the Pilot Plant, he moved the equipment to A Factory. Studies were undertaken to ascertain whether it would provide a significant savings over the existing method. Centrifugal casting required glass to be about 20–50C higher than glass for pressing, which would require more energy. On the other hand, aside from eliminating the requirement of neck sealing, a ten-inch pressed bulb needed a 3.43-pound gob of glass, while a centrifugally cast one required just 3 pounds of molten material. A study conducted in April 1949 found that centrifugal casting would result in lower batch material, mixing, and blowing room expenses. And while it was slower than the automatic pressing method—producing eight per minute instead of twelve—the cast bulbs' selection rate was higher—90 percent compared with 80 percent for pressed bulbs. By the summer of 1949 Corning engineers were working on a twelve-head centrifugal casting machine for ten-inch and twelve-inch television funnel neck sections.[18]

The introduction of labor-saving devices for making television bulbs was crucial because television production was growing by leaps and bounds. Just as radio had caught on in the 1920s, the mesmerizing new medium spread rapidly. Between 1946 and 1950, the number of television stations rose from six to 105. As companies such as NBC and CBS linked stations together to form networks, programs such as Milton Berle's *Texaco Star Theatre* became national phenomena. One of the more enduring early programs, the *Howdy Doody Show*, debuted in 1947. It starred a puppet—Howdy Doody—and Buffalo Bob Smith, who had hosted wartime radios shows in Corning.[19]

By 1950, there were 10 million black-and-white televisions in American homes; U.S. production of televisions rose from 3 million in 1949 to 7.5 million in 1950. And while there were twenty tube makers, Corning was essentially the sole volume supplier of television bulbs. This led to constant demands by customers. At one point, DuMont promised lobsters to workers in Corning's A Factory if they could make 120 twenty-inch television bulbs in a day—an incentive that worked. But Corning continued to invest in developments to make black-and-white televisions more efficiently. In 1950, it opened a new television bulb plant in Albion, Michigan, as part of its further expansion westward. On the strength of increased television sales, Corning's sales exploded 59 percent in 1950, from $73 million in 1949 to $116 million. Earnings per share more than doubled, from $2.56 to $6.52. Television quickly became an extremely profitable line of business. And Corning's search for the next big hit seemed to have found a winner.[20]

Expanding Internationally

While work on television had been suspended during the war, another long-standing Corning goal—expanding internationally—had gained momentum in the early 1940s with a series of affiliations in Brazil, Argentina, and Chile. When the war ended, the company reestablished relationships with licensees and affiliates in formerly hostile countries like Japan and Germany and began to work more closely with affiliates in war-torn France and Britain. Corning's first act of postwar expansion, however, was closer to home. In June 1945, Corning paid $150,000 for a manufacturing facility in Leaside, Ontario, an industrial area about five miles northeast of Toronto. The 100,000-square-foot government-owned plant had been used by a Canadian firm to make optical instruments and radar equipment. Corning installed its own equipment and was soon producing Pyrex and glass ovenware for the Canadian market.[21]

Most of the international postwar activity took place in Western Europe. And whereas the company had expanded in Latin America by taking minority stakes in small, unsophisticated glass firms, Corning now decided to strike licensing deals with established European firms. In 1947, Corning reached agreements with its long-standing British and French licensees, Jobling and Le Pyrex, to supply them with the latest in borosilicate and opal production developments. The following year, Jobling built a pressware factory. In 1947, Corning also struck a deal to give Glass Bulbs Ltd. of England technical assistance in using the Ribbon and Turret Chain Machines. After the war, the U.S. government supported the reconstruction of Germany, which lay devastated. Corning had had contacts with the famous Schott & Genossen glassworks of Jena before World War I. At the close of the war, it was clear that Jena would fall in the sector of Germany controlled by the Soviet Union. To prevent the works from falling into Communist hands, the U.S. Army physically moved much of the glass plant across the border into West Germany. In 1951, the newly reconstituted works licensed the updraw tubing machine for use in Germany. And a few years later, Hans Schott would visit Corning.[22]

But Corning's international efforts had as many false starts as successes in these years. Corning aimed to continue its string of investments in Latin

America in April 1951 by exchanging know-how and trademarks for a 25 percent interest in Cristales Mexicanos, a Monterrey, Mexico–based firm that made bottles and tableware. But the proprietor of Cristales Mexicanos, Umberto Garza, proved to be something of a rogue. As Eugene Sullivan noted in 1952, "[Cy] Paquette thinks Garza irresponsible, insane, tricky." Garza would manipulate sales by moving products from the company to a warehouse in Mexico City, which was owned by a separate Garza-controlled corporation. And when Corning sent auditors from Price Water-house, he tried to kick them out. Meanwhile, a rival glass firm in Monterrey controlled by the Sada family had hired a former Charleroi employee who brought with him extensive drawings of Corning plants and technical infor-mation. In 1956, Corning rescinded its contracts with the Mexican firm.[23]

In addition, Corning decided *not* to pursue certain international alliances in the early 1950s. Philips, the Dutch electronics manufacturer, was interested in becoming a Corning licensee. But Corning, skeptical because Philips had little experience with glassmaking; turned the firm down. A sec-ond decision turned out, in time, to be an even greater missed opportunity. Asahi, the large Japanese glassmaker, had been licensing Corning's refrac-tory technology since 1930. Communications had been cut off during World War II, but later Asahi officials came to Corning with a check for royalty payments owed since the beginning of the war. In the early 1950s, Asahi also proposed a joint venture to make television cathode ray tubes. Decker, believing the devastated Japanese market was a long way from profitability, decided not to pursue a joint venture. Instead, he agreed to allow Asahi to make bulbs under a license in 1954. In time, and in ways unforeseeable, this would prove a fateful decision.[24]

Opening the Glass Center

Closer to home, Corning acted more decisively. The greater Corning area benefited from a large amount of public and private infrastructure invest-ment in the years after the war. After the 1946 flood weakened the aging Gibson bridge, Corning voters gave permission to rebuild it as a four-lane bridge and to build a highway through Denison Park. Governor Thomas

Dewey came to Corning on October 4, 1950, to dedicate the new bridge, and Erie Avenue was renamed Denison Parkway.[25]

The early 1950s also saw construction of important cultural infrastructure in Corning. In preparation for the centennial of Corning Glass Works —or at least the centennial of Amory Houghton Sr.'s involvement with the Bay State Glass Company in 1851—the Houghtons and Corning Glass Works decided to back an ambitious project. Arthur A. Houghton Jr., the longtime head of Corning's Steuben division, was a driving force behind the decision to build the Corning Glass Center. The center would include a museum, a science exhibition hall, the Steuben factory, an auditorium, and recreational facilities. Designed by architect Wallace Harrison, who was responsible for much of Rockefeller Center, the Corning Glass Center would provide space to exhibit some of the company's proudest achievements. In January 1951, the observatory in Centerway Square was dismantled so that the flawed 200-inch disc could be removed. (Because of its bulk, workers had to construct the new building *around* the disc.) [26]

Completed just twelve months after its conception, the center was a testimony to the power of glass. It was faced with sheets of photosensitive glass, plate glass, and glass block. The bridge from the Hall of Science and Industry to the Steuben blowing room was made of bent Pyrex tubing. Meanwhile, Arthur Houghton hired Thomas Buechner, a twenty-four-year-old employee at the Metropolitan Museum of Art, and gave him an ample budget to create a collection of historical pieces of glass objects. Like the thermometer tower and the cracked telescope disc, the Glass Center would become another widely recognized landmark in Corning.

New York governor Thomas Dewey officiated at the dedication of the Glass Center on May 19, 1951. At a celebratory dinner attended by 1,800 people, Amory Houghton Sr. reflected on the company's eighty-three years in Corning. With no small amount of pride, he recounted the company's contributions to the works' home base. In 1950 alone, Corning paid $27 million in wages in the area, about ten times the amount from 1921. And in the thirty years Am had worked for the company his great-grandfather had founded, Corning-area residents had earned $242 million of the company's $342 million payroll. Although Corning would build plants in other communities, he noted, "this in no way gives support to the utter nonsense that one occasionally hears that Corning Glass Works is moving away from Corning." Am closed by saying, "Corning is my home—Corning was the home of my forefathers and I hope will be the home of some of my children and grandchildren—Corning is your home—Corning belongs to all of us."[27]

Corning also belonged to the larger world, a fact of which the company's management was acutely aware. As part of the festivities, Corning and the American Council of Learned Societies planned a conference on life in the industrial age, to which they invited leading intellectuals, writers, and corporate executives to Corning for the weekend. Many of those invited had long been in the Houghtons' and Corning's circle. Participants included Harold Boeschenstein of Dow-Corning, Harry Cook, international president of the American Flint Glass Workers Union, Dean Donald David of the Harvard Business School, Eastman Kodak treasurer Martin Folsom, architect Wallace Harrison, anthropologist Margaret Mead, and RCA chief executive David Sarnoff. On Friday, May 18, participants convened in roundtable discussions on topics such as work and human values in industrial civilization, and leisure and human values in industrial civilization. A session on Friday night was devoted to comments from a panel of observers of the American scene from Great Britain, India, and Mexico. At the final general session, Saturday morning, two spokesmen from each roundtable presented brief commentaries on the conference theme.[28]

The building was opened to the public on May 30, and in its first year it attracted 384,366 visitors. By October 10, 1953, 1 million people had filed through the glass doors. Apart from attracting tourists and visitors, the Glass Center was a cultural and recreational center for the Corning community. It featured bowling alleys and billiards rooms, and the center's large auditorium was an ideal setting for summer stock theater. The first season opened in the summer of 1951, with actress Joan Blondell starring in *Happy Birthday*. It also hosted Shakespeare productions, concerts of the Corning Philharmonic, films, and visiting speakers and lecturers. Some of the performers and cultural personalities visiting in the early 1950s included Robert Frost and Am's friend, the Duke of Windsor. In 1954, to celebrate the seventy-fifth anniversary of Corning's first blown incandescent lamp bulb for Edison, the company lit a 75,000-watt bulb at the Glass Center.[29]

The centennial that Corning celebrated in 1951 signaled an end to the period of post war adjustment in many ways. Corning's factories were operating full tilt, and it had opened several new facilities. More significantly, the establishment of the Glass Center and the events surrounding its dedication signaled a broad, outward-looking posture that the company and its executives would maintain for the next several decades. While firmly rooted in the community of Corning, these efforts made clear, the Corning Glass Works viewed itself as inextricably linked to the world far beyond the Chemung Valley. By holding the conference and constructing the Glass Center, Corning attempted to involve itself more fully in public affairs and to involve the public more fully in its affairs.

Trial and Error in Managing Growth

Soon after the opening of the Glass Center, the Houghtons and Corning suffered a scare. In the fall of 1951, examinations revealed that Amory Houghton had a cancerous tumor in his tongue and that the cancer had spread to the lymph nodes in his neck. After spending thirty-three days in a New York hospital, Corning's chairman spent much of the winter of 1952 convalescing in Florida; he chartered an eighty-five-foot diesel yacht, *Scout*, which cruised up and down the coast. Amory Sr. continued to struggle with jaundice and evidently had a tough time taking it easy. "I have no doubt from your history that things were progressing well in Florida until you started to exercise again and to go back to more or less a routine dietary regimen," his doctor, Edgar Lawrence, told him. In August 1952, he was back in a New York hospital. "Forgive me for not replying to your note of September 11th before this," he wrote Eugene Gentil in October 1952. "But due to a reoccurrence of jaundice I have been pretty flat on my back since the first part of July. I am glad to say that now I am well on the road to recovery and come in to the office part time."[30]

Am's life-threatening illness and lengthy recovery signified something of a changing of the guard that was taking place in the early 1950s. To be sure, he would be actively involved in the affairs of the company throughout the decade. But his illness, his involvement in public affairs, and, ultimately, his service as ambassador to France in the late 1950s would leave much of the day-to-day operations to president Bill Decker and his cadre of managers. In addition, some longtime Corning fixtures had departed from the scene. Optics pioneer William Churchill died in August 1949. The following spring, Alexander Falck, the former chief executive, passed away at the age of 72. A few years later, Glen Cole died suddenly from a heart attack at age sixty.[31]

At the same time, important new figures were entering Corning's orbit. Walter Bedell Smith, Ike's chief of staff during World War II and director of the Central Intelligence Agency, was named to Corning's board of directors in 1950. His presence was indicative of the larger way in which the company would work more closely with government entities on major science-related projects. In the coming years, Smith would influence Corning's entry into nuclear-related fields. Just as important, the first member of the fifth generation of glassmaking Houghtons formally joined the company. Amory Houghton Jr., who graduated from Harvard in 1950 and married Ruth West almost immediately thereafter, came to work at Corning in 1952. "I saw Amo on Tuesday," Decker reported to Am. "He is very enthusiastic about coming to work. He will start here in Corning on August 1st in the Main Plant on some job in the factory."[32]

Amory Houghton Jr. quickly became established in the company. In 1953, Corning expanded its board of directors from thirteen to fourteen and named Amo to the board. As manager of appliance parts sales in the company's specialty products department, he worked earnestly to improve his skills. In 1954, for example, he went to the Lacy Sales Institute, where sales guru Jack Lacy instructed students on his 5W formula—Why, What Is It, Who Says So, Who Has Used It, What Does He Get. In addition, as part of what would be a twelve-year apprenticeship before assuming the chief executive post, he began to participate in the noncorporate activities that were so essential for executives at major industrial firms. Having been nominated by his father, Amo was admitted to the University Club in New York and became a member of the Manufacturers Club. In the coming years, Amo would assume many of the civic, social, and corporate posts held by his father.[33]

Meanwhile, Bill Decker and his colleagues were confronted with the difficulty of managing the rapid growth—and occasional rapid contractions—in the television business. In the previous eighty years, Corning had introduced a series of products whose sales grew rapidly: railroad semaphores, lightbulbs, and Pyrex. But none had grown into a large business as rapidly as television bulbs had. In a matter of three years, Corning's fortunes had become tied very tightly to television. In 1950, 61 percent of sales came from electronic and electrical products, while consumer goods accounted for just 14 percent and technical and other products accounted for about 25 percent —a ratio that held steady through the early 1950s. But the boom year of 1950 was followed by a bust. The Korean War, which broke out in July 1950, temporarily halted the production of television receivers, which required scarce weapons-grade materials. In addition, the FCC had ceased granting new television station licenses in September 1948 because it needed time to sort out conflicts over frequency allocation. Consequently, television production fell 28 percent. Corning's sales were flat for the year and earnings fell sharply, from $17.6 million to $10.14 million.[34]

As television production resumed, however, Corning's sales bounced back smartly, rising to $126 million in 1952 and booming another 18 percent to nearly $150 million in 1953. Meanwhile, Corning was plowing large sums of money into television development, investing more than $3 million alone in 1953, mostly on the nascent technology that promised to be the company's next big hit: *color* television. By 1953, Corning was producing millions of television bulbs each year. "During the first three weeks of this period, we shipped 397,000 bulbs, as compared with 386,000 for the first three weeks of Period 4," Decker wrote in May. In 1953, 7.3 million televisions were produced in the United States.[35]

But Corning was constantly forced to keep pace with its large and expanding television customers. For example, it was contemplating building a plant in Santa Barbara, California, to make television bulbs to supply western producers like Sylvania. Sylvania CEO H. Ward Zimmer and other executives constantly pressed Corning to reduce prices. "At Zimmer's request, we are making effective further price reductions on television bulbs to be effective on June 1st and retroactive to May 1st," Decker wrote Am in May 1953. "The 24 inch bulb will be reduced from $18 to $15; and the 27 inch bulb will be reduced from $22.5 to $20.5."[36]

Decker was also trying to expand Corning's electronics business. In addition to the booming television business, Corning had established profitable lines in electronic components like capacitors and delay lines, which were manufactured at the company's Bradford plant. But Decker was eager to build on that success. In March 1952, the company entered into preliminary discussions with Sylvania over a possible merger. But Corning, a veteran of numerous antitrust proceedings, believed any move would have to be approved by a federal judge and hence invite unwanted scrutiny. What's more, the Department of Justice had recently impaneled a grand jury to look into the television industry. "Under such conditions, Sylvania, and also Glen and I, think it would be most difficult for either Sylvania or ourselves to operate in a normal fashion," Decker wrote to Am.[37]

In May 1953, Decker asked investment banker George Murnane to look into two other electronics firms, Sprague Electric Company and P.R. Mallory & Company, Inc., as possible acquisition targets. Both were rather large—$44 million and $70 million in sales, respectively. But, as Decker remarked to Am, "we were unable to dig up any small company which seemed to offer possibilities with regard to the development of our electrical components: such as capacitors, resistors, and printed circuits." Neither acquisition materialized.[38]

Corning had more success with its tried and true method of expansion: building branch plants. In 1952, when Corning spent some $9 million on plant expansion, it opened a facility in Danville, Kentucky, to make lamp bulbs and tubing. The same year, it opened an optical plant in Harrodsburg, Kentucky. Harrodsburg quickly became the locus of a new and ambitious glass program: massive glass. Having established contacts with the military during World War II, Corning continued to respond to the requests and demands of the Cold War military. The Air Force needed huge, homogeneous optical glass castings for use in aerial and space photography and for wind tunnels. After signing contracts with the Wright-Patterson Air Force Base near Dayton, Ohio. Corning constructed several gigantic pieces of glass, the largest of which were fifty-two-inches in diameter and eight inches thick. Harrodsburg produced even larger pieces of glass to be used as atomic radiation shields. Measuring six by eight feet and weighing up to twelve tons, the windows were made up of a number of pieces of massive glass stacked together in a steel frame and were used at the Atomic Energy Commission's national reactor testing station near Idaho Falls, Idaho.[39]

In these years, as during the war, there was a symbiotic relationship between Corning and certain branches of the military. In direct contrast to the World War II period, in which the relationship helped spur Corning's sales and allowed it to build new plants like that in Parkersburg, the postwar relationship brought several complicating factors. Inevitably, government work was politicized. And the anti-Communist fervor that gripped many branches of the government and the public ensnared Corning and its top scientist—Edward Condon—in an ugly tug-of-war.

The Condon Affair

Within months of the German and Japanese surrender, the Soviet Union and communism had replaced Germany and fascism as the greatest enemy of the United States. In 1948, Winston Churchill first used the term Iron Curtain to describe the Soviet Union's domination over Eastern Europe. The Cold War intensified when it was revealed in September 1949 that the Soviet Union had successfully detonated an atomic bomb. In February 1950, when Klaus Fuchs, a British-employed physicist who had worked on the Manhattan Project in Los Alamos, was arrested for passing secrets to the Soviets, it added fuel to the fire of anti-Communist crusaders like Wisconsin senator Joseph McCarthy. In the early 1950s, McCarthy and his allies recklessly pursued suspected Communists in sensational public hearings. The vast majority of those who found their careers and reputations tarnished by the domestic hunt for Communists were innocent. One such victim was Edward Condon, Corning's research director.

Condon, a brilliant and controversial theoretical physicist, was hired in 1951 to succeed Jesse Littleton as research director. Born in 1902 in Alamogordo, New Mexico, he received a Ph.D. in physics from the University of California at Berkeley in 1924. After holding academic posts at Columbia University, the University of Minnesota, and Princeton University, in 1937 he took a research management post at Westinghouse. During World War II, he worked on uranium fission with J. Robert Oppenheimer and in 1943 became Oppenheimer's associate director at the secret Los Alamos lab. He spent the latter months of the war heading the theoretical physics division of the radiation lab at Berkeley. In 1945, Secretary of Commerce Henry Wallace asked him to direct the National Bureau of Standards. An outspoken figure, Condon quickly became involved in the debate over whether control of the nation's atomic program should rest with the military or should be under a civilian authority. Coming down squarely on the side of civilian control, he advised Sen. Brian McMahon, one of the authors of the McMahon–Douglas Bill, which in 1946 established the civilian U.S. Atomic Energy Commission.[40]

As early as 1945, Condon's opposition to military control of atomic development encouraged the wrath of powerful forces in Washington. "The day I started work as scientific adviser to Senator McMahon's special Senate committee on atomic energy in the fall of 1945, two colonels from the Army Corps of Engineers, Manhattan District, called on him to 'warn' him that I was a Communist," he recalled. There was no evidence that Condon was a Communist or had Communist sympathies. But Condon engaged in activity that, in retrospect, seems openly antagonistic to the excessively zealous anti-Communists. In 1945, he accepted an invitation from the National Council of American–Soviet Friendship (later branded as subversive by the attorney general) to attend meetings of the Academy of Sciences in the Soviet Union. General Leslie Groves, the commander of strategic weapons development and the top military officer at Los Alamos during the war, prevented him from going.[41]

When he was appointed to a commission to monitor naval atomic bomb tests at Bikini, the accusations grew louder. On March 1, 1948, the House Un-American Activities Committee, chaired by J. Parnell Thomas, a Republican from New Jersey who was soon to go to jail on corruption charges, labeled Condon "perhaps one of the weakest links in our atomic security." In the wake of a series of attacks on the Truman administration as being "soft on Communism," Truman in the spring of 1947 had issued an executive order calling for federal employees to be vetted through loyalty hearings. Under the order, anyone that was found to have even a "sympathetic association" with a "subversive" group could be dismissed. Condon was cleared by a Commerce Department loyalty hearing. The Atomic Energy Commission, which had suspended Condon's clearance in the spring of 1948, reinstated his clearance in July 1948 after the Federal Bureau of Investigation had interviewed more than 300 people. A second loyalty hearing held by the Department of Commerce resulted in a third formal clearance.[42]

Condon served without further incident until 1951, when he joined

Corning. Upon his arrival, he focused more on matters of science than politics. "When I first came to Corning in 1951 we had only the very crowded facilities of the old lab next to A factory with essentially no modern scientific equipment," he recalled. "There were 98 technical people, 8 clerical staff and 91 technical support people." (The company's second Pilot Plant, on Tioga Street, was nearing completion.) Condon felt that the company wasn't investing enough in fundamental research. At Westinghouse he had established research fellowships to allow young scientists to work on problems of their own choosing. He quickly set up a similar program at Corning and began to agitate for new and larger laboratory space.[43]

Soon after Condon joined Corning in October 1951, however, Navy security officers in Buffalo insisted that Condon undergo another clearance process. After all, Corning was engaged in work on massive glass and other sensitive projects. And many of the physicists who had been associated with Berkeley and Los Alamos in the 1930s and 1940s came under suspicion. J. Robert Oppenheimer's brother, Frank, also a physicist, had admitted to being a Communist in the 1930s. And Robert Oppenheimer had belonged to several radical groups at Berkeley in the 1930s. The physicist's opposition to developing a hydrogen bomb was taken as further evidence of unreliability. As a result, virtually all the scientists in Oppenheimer's orbit became suspect again.

In Condon's case, a renewed investigation began early in 1952 with the seizure of more than 1,000 pounds of his papers and documents. When Condon refused an invitation to appear voluntarily before HUAC, he was subpoenaed to a hearing in Chicago in September. The congressmen repeatedly badgered Condon about friends and associates who were suspected of being Communists. Condon, not shrinking from a fight, refused to budge an inch. Throughout this period, professionals named as suspected Communists were frequently discharged from sensitive jobs at universities, corporations, government agencies, and Hollywood studios. "From General Motors, General Electric and CBS to the New York Times, the New York City Board of Education, and the United Auto Workers, there were few, very few, public or private employees who did not fire the men and women who had been identified during a first-stage investigation," wrote historian Ellen Schrecker. Accepting the navy's unwillingness to grant Condon clearance, the company in April 1952 named a colleague to supervise business details of classified work. When reporters questioned Corning executives about Condon's status, public relations director Harlan Logan responded with a statement supporting Condon. Corning also worked closely with Condon's well-connected Washington legal team at Fowler, Leva, Hawes, and Symington. [44]

By 1953, as the McCarthy hearings raged on, Condon realized he was putting himself and the company in a difficult situation. According to notes that appear to be in Sullivan's hand, from January 1953, "Condon is happy at Corning and wants to....He remarked, however, that he realized it would be awkward to have a research director not permitted access to confidential work carried on in the laboratory." In the fall of 1953, Condon received yet another military security board. Always vague, the charges now bordered on the absurd. One alleged instance of proof of his unreliability was that "your wife was critical of the foreign policy of the United States and you did not reprove her."[45]

By early 1954, Condon was growing increasingly frustrated. "I am appalled at the waste of time that will be involved, and at the legal expense implied," he wrote to Am in January. On April 5 and 6, 1954—a month after Robert Oppenheimer lost his security clearance—Condon submitted to yet another two-day hearing in New York City before the Eastern Industrial Personnel Security Board (EIPSB). Three months later, it finally rendered a favorable verdict. Despite the outcome, Condon seemed somewhat distracted. In September 1954, according to Sullivan, Decker was "concerned over Condon not knowing what was going on when a certain laboratory project was mentioned—something [another colleague, illegible] had talked about with a Condon a few days [earlier]."[46]

Condon's clearance was made public on October 19, 1954. Two days later, however, Navy Secretary Charles Thomas again suspended Condon's clearance and asked the EIPSB to investigate Condon yet again. A few days later, Vice President Richard Nixon, whose political fortunes had risen with the increasing zeal of his anti-Communism, claimed credit for the reversal in campaign speeches in Butte, Montana, and Cheyenne, Wyoming. Decker and counsel Henry Fowler called on Navy Secretary Thomas. Thomas admitted that he hadn't even read the hearing record but told Decker that Corning would get no classified business as long as Condon was research director.[47]

The executives considered several options, including naming a temporary research director until Condon was cleared. It was also suggested that Amory Houghton appeal directly to Eisenhower and ask that a civilian board rule on Condon's clearance. But Condon had had enough. On November 24, 1954, Sullivan noted, "C now favorably inclined toward setting up as consultant, perhaps with CGW as chief client, in Berkeley, Calif...where he has a married daughter." Condon finally resigned from Corning just before Christmas, noting that he had been cleared over the years by the Manhattan Project, the Atomic Energy Commission, the Department of Commerce, and the military. "I now am unwilling to continue a potentially indefinite series of reviews and re-reviews. I have therefore withdrawn my application for clearance." He moved to Berkeley, consulted for Corning, and went on to teach at Washington University in St. Louis and the University of Colorado. Condon died in 1974. [48]

Condon's departure helped return a measure of stability to Corning's research department and ended the company's experience with a frustrating and ultimately shameful chapter in American history. But the ways in which this mid-sized glass company became caught up in national politics, and the complications created by Corning's involvement with government agencies, serve to illuminate some of the ways Corning had changed since the end of the war. By the end of 1954, Corning was again a company transformed. The firm that in 1945 had faced the postwar world with a mixture of anxiety and enthusiasm was unabashedly confident and exceedingly well positioned. The fruitful collaboration between its scientists and craftsmen had allowed Corning to establish a strong foothold in the most exciting new consumer product in a generation. Comfortably at home in its longtime base, Corning was connected to the world beyond the Chemung Valley in novel and intense ways. Under the solid leadership of veterans like Bill Decker, the company had confronted a series of daunting challenges and had managed impressive growth. In the next five years, the company would further develop its television business and reap the unexpected fruits of its decades-long quest to plumb the depths of the limitless potential of glass.

CHAPTER EIGHT

Ambitious Expansion: TV Glass, Pyroceram, and Corning Ware, 1954–1960

NEARLY A DECADE after the war had ended, deep into a period of prosperity and relative stability, Corning was nonetheless entering yet another period of transformative change. With its dominance of the black-and-white television bulb business, the works was in an enviable position. But in the years between 1954 and 1960, Corning would face substantial pressures to develop the next advances in the new medium: color television. In addition, the company's scientists would successfully probe glass for the next big hit—a tough new form of glass that would find applications in military *and* consumer markets. In these years, as befitted a company firmly entrenched in the nation's industrial establishment, Corning would continue to build new associations and relationships with entities far from the Chemung Valley. And its highest-ranking executive, Amory Houghton Sr., like his father before him, would move to Europe to serve as a diplomat. A confident company in a confident period, Corning entered the atomic age with a sense of purpose and urgency, intent on projecting its influence onto a wider stage.

Advances and Setbacks in Color Television

When Edward Condon finally left Corning, he recommended that Bill Armistead succeed him. Succeed Armistead did, serving first as director of research and then as vice chairman with a special focus on technology for the next three decades. When he first took over, Armistead recounted crisply, he had two immediate mandates: to keep Jim Giffen happy, and to bring color television to the market. At first, it was unclear which task would prove more difficult. Giffen, a mechanical genius, was somewhat temperamental and needed to be treated more like an artist than an engineer. Understanding his value to the company, Giffen continuously bargained for a better deal. Giffen, 51 years old, wanted to spend more time hunting and fishing at his second home in Florida. Decker and Armistead ultimately agreed to let him to go Florida six times a year, pay for plane tickets for Giffen and his wife, and send Giffen's colleagues to Florida when necessary.[1]

Bringing color television to fruition ultimately proved far more complicated. Color television bulbs would have to be different from black-and-white bulbs for several reasons: different electrical requirements mandated new glass compositions, which in turn mandated new production equipment and brought on new difficulties in sealing faceplates to funnels; the faceplates, moreover, had to be ground to much greater precision than black-and-white bulbs.

Meanwhile, the market for color bulbs was slow to develop. After the war, the competition resumed on the part of companies to win FCC approval of a color system. In 1948, the FCC approved a system developed by CBS. But it was incompatible—color shows couldn't be seen on black-and-white sets, even in black and white. For the next several years, RCA and other companies fought a legal and regulatory battle to establish new standards, thus forestalling any real progress.[2]

Color television bulbs were more complicated and expensive than black-and-white bulbs. In order to get a clear picture with the RCA tube—whose standards would ultimately win out over CBS standards—phosphor dots coating the inside of a color cathode ray tube faceplate had to be laid down with extreme precision. One way of doing this was to construct a stencil—an aperture mask pierced by millions of tiny holes in regular patterns through which the phosphor could be applied. Jesse Littleton believed glass could work as a material for the aperture and challenged his researchers with a seemingly impossible task: "We must find an economical way to drill a million holes in a plate of glass!" he said in 1947.

The first solution Corning had was rather impractical: seal together a million small glass tubes and then saw them into slices. But Don Stookey, the pioneer of photosensitive glasses, believed it might be possible to achieve the same ends through a different means. He immersed photosensitive opals in different chemical solutions to see if powerful acids and other abrasives could work their magic on glass. To his delight, Stookey found that glass made with barium disilicate was etched substantially by hydrofluoric acid. As the experiments continued, Corning's scientists realized they were able to produce glass that could be worked with chemicals, that is, it was photochemically machineable. They dubbed this new breed of glasses Fotoform. Once again, Corning had discovered a heretofore unseen dimension of glass. After all, for the last several thousand years, glassmakers had believed the only means of substantially altering glass was through the application of heat. Now they could essentially punch holes in glass through the application of chemicals. This new process held out a great deal of promise. By 1954, seven years after Littleton's challenge, Corning had developed the necessary technology to make the intricate glass screens with 200,000 holes "so small they cannot be threaded with a human hair." Just as important, these screens produced pictures that had far better definition than existing models. Screens were made from Fotoform and converted by a strengthening process to Fotoceram, a material two to three times stonger than the parent glass. "A miracle, I thought to myself. Another secret door had opened," Stookey later wrote.[3]

Corning seemed to have an innovation that lacked a ready market, for color television was slow to catch on. No major set manufacturer joined the CBS effort to sell incompatible color. Finally, in October 1953, at the request of the Federal Communications Commission, an industry-wide group called the National Television Systems Committee invited companies to exhibit their systems at the Waldorf-Astoria Hotel in New York City. A month later, the FCC formally adopted compatible color standards. And on New Year's Day, 1954, the Tournament of Roses parade in Pasadena,

California, was viewed on a handful of color sets. At the time, however, there were fewer than 10,000 sets in operation, and each cost about $1,000. Even though 100,000 sets would be produced in 1956, it would be nearly a decade before color television gained wide commercial distribution.[4]

While color television was developing slowly at home, black-and-white television continued to boom. In 1954, 7.3 million were sold in the United States, at an average price of $175. And the new phenomenon began to catch on abroad. As a result, Corning took steps to export its technology and know-how to the recovering economies of Western Europe and Japan. In 1954, both Schott & Genossen and Asahi Glass were licensed to manufacture television glassware. Corning's executives viewed licensing as a less risky and complicated means than forming a joint venture with, or taking a minority interest in, a German or Japanese company. (This was a decision that would, in time, prove fateful to Corning's television business.) In 1955, Corning expanded its minority interest in Le Pyrex—the joint venture with French glassmaker St. Gobain—to 32 percent. The venture was renamed Sovirel, an acronym for Société des Verrières Industrielles Réunis du Loin. That year, Sovirel built a television bulb plant in Bagneaux, south of Paris.[5]

A Town and a Company Grow Together

By the end of 1954, Corning had completed a massive $48 million, five-year program of plant construction, expansion, and modernization. With 12,250 employees and sales of $148 million, it had grown by 215 percent since 1945. But the company was merely pausing for breath. The 1954 *Annual Report* featured on its cover an architect's drawing of a new complex of buildings to be constructed on the north bank of the Chemung. The area, to be known as Houghton Park, would contain a nine-story office building, a three-story research headquarters, and a building for lab and development, which would more than double the space devoted to research.[6]

At the time, the town of Corning was in the midst of its own growth spurt. In October 1954, Gov. Thomas Dewey came to dedicate a new four-lane arterial highway—U.S. Route 17. Meanwhile, Corning's growing research and development departments brought an influx of well-educated,

In the 1930s, the triumvirate of Sidney Waugh, Jack Gates, and Arthur Houghton, Jr. (l to r) took the Steuben Glass division from bankruptcy to the pinnacle of fashion in art glass.

In 1934 Corning cast a mammoth disk of Pyrex as the mirror blank for the ambitious telescope program at Mt. Palomar Observatory. Shown here being readied for shipping, the disk endured a flood on the Chemung, and cross-country train trip that attracted thousands of onlookers, and a lengthy hiatus in funding before becoming operational in 1948. A disk from Corning's first attempt at casting the 200-inch behemoth is on display at the Glass Innovation Center at the Corning Museum of Glass.

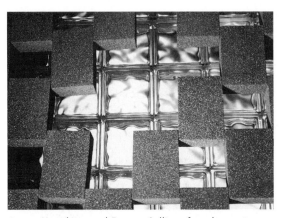

Amory Houghton and Eugene Sullivan found ways to leverage the resources of a relatively small company through joint ventures. In 1937, Corning joined with Pittsburgh Plate Glass to form Pittsburgh-Corning, a company devoted to making and marketing glass blocks and other glass products for the building trades.

Corning's work on fiberglass became the basis of another major joint venture with Owens Illinois in 1938: Owens Corning. These joint ventures were each 50/50, with Corning's name second. "Concede on the little things," Amory Houghton reportedly said, "but stand firm on what's important."

The 1930s was a fertile decade for innovation at the Glass Works. Organic chemist J. Franklin Hyde discovered silicones (the basis of the car wax he applies here, as well as a valuable joint venture with Dow Chemical Company), helped to pioneer fiberglas, and patented a process for making fused silica that the company later used to make optical fibers.

Amory Houghton (right), with his father Alanson B. Houghton. The third of four Amory Houghtons to run the company, this one served between 1930 and World War II. Following stints in Washington and London during the war, he returned as Corning's chairman until he followed his father's example by becoming U.S. Ambassador to France in 1957. Called "Am" by colleagues early in his career, he was later known as "the Ambassador."

In May 1943, the Glass Works recognized the American Flint Glass Workers—the Flints— as bargaining agent for its hourly employees in its U.S. plants. Pictured (l to r) are Charles Scheff, Harry Cook, Harry M. Hosier, and Joseph R. Palme, Sr. Cook was president of the Flints, and Hosier Corning's vice president of industrial relations.

To mark the hundredth anniversary of the first Amory Houghton Sr.'s investment in glass-making, the company established a philanthropic foundation and endowed the Corning Museum of Glass. Arthur Houghton Jr. (left) and Amory Houghton (right) flank New York Governor Thomas E. Dewey at the museum's dedication in 1951.

Bill Decker loved to play poker. A Harvard MBA, he served successively as president and chairman of the Glass Works in the 1950s and 1960s and bet the company by making big investments in TV glass in advance of demand.

Between the late 1940s and mid-1970s, TV glass was by far Corning's biggest and fastest-growing business. The company's experience with large glass bulbs originated in experiments in the 1930s but exploded during World War II as the company made thousands of cathode ray tubes for radar sets. After the war, Corning pioneered significant new processes for making black-and-white and color TV bulbs (pictured here).

The technical team that developed new glass-ceramic materials included (l to r) Ben Allen, Jim Giffen, Bill Armistead, and Donald Stookey. Stookey first discovered the new material, and Giffen, a mechanical genius, found ways to form it into the shape of a radome or nose cone for rockets and missiles. Armistead's tenure atop the R&D labs rivaled Eugene Sullivan's for length and significance. A promising research manager, Allen died soon after this picture was taken.

Corning first believed that glass ceramics would find many applications in aerospace and industry. Its most popular application, however, was Corning Ware—a miracle cookware that easily withstood temperature extremes in the kitchen—perfect for suburban housewives who could bake casseroles, freeze them, and reheat them without changing pans.

Amory Houghton's diplomatic connections resulted in a coup in 1961, when former Undersecretary of State Robert Murphy (center) joined Corning as head of its international operations. Assisted by Forrest Behm (left), formerly general manager of Corning's TV glass business, Murphy led rapid penetration of foreign markets. Pictured at right is Albert Lecron, president of Sovirel, Corning's associated company in France.

A former merchandising executive, Lee Waterman (seated) understood the value of glass ceramics for consumer cookware. The phenomenal success of Corning Ware assisted Waterman's rise to the presidency of the Glass Works. At the top, however, he worked for another Amory Houghton Jr. (standing). "Amo" served as Corning's chairman and chief executive for 19 years and launched the company toward global leadership in fiber optics.

well-paid employees to the region. "A survey in 1953 reported that income per household in Corning was 24 percent above the national average," according to town historians Thomas P. Dimitroff and Lois S. Janes. Corning's growth, and the demographic phenomenon known as the baby boom, would push local population from 17,931 in 1951 to 19,253 in 1957, and spur development in surrounding areas. A photo essay in the May-June 1955 *Gaffer* entitled "How Young Corning Lives" captured the spirit of the times. It described Corning employee Jim Evans and his wife, Alice, who had first come to Corning in 1952 and lived in an apartment. By 1955, however, they had moved with their children into a three-bedroom house on a half-acre plot on Brown Road in South Corning. It was one of many new developments in the hills and valleys ringing the town. "In one section, 26 children from 14 homes keep the noise and activity at a high point from morning until twilight," the *Gaffer* noted.[7]

Aside from expanding its physical presence, the Corning Glass Works was branching out into new business areas. With a confidence born of its successful efforts during the war, Corning took steps to work more closely with government units and with other private companies working on solutions to military problems. In 1954, for example, Corning set up an atomic energy department. The following year, Corning and seven other companies banded together to build a nuclear reactor. Walter Bedell Smith, chairman of the board and president of AMF Atomics, Inc. (and a Corning board member), was the driving force behind the venture, which was named Industrial Reactor Labs. Corning lore has it that a discussion between Amory Houghton Sr. and Smith during a golf game helped push Corning into the venture.[8]

At about the same time, Corning was responding to requests from the military for materials that could be used in nuclear reactors. In 1954, Hyman Rickover, who had worked with Corning during World War II and had pioneered the nation's nuclear submarine fleet, asked Corning to develop a ceramic cladding to protect uranium pellets. The metal cladding then in use couldn't resist the intense heat generated in the navy's nuclear reactors. Decker wrote to Am following a February 10, 1955, visit by Rickover, "he wants us to undertake the development of uranium oxides and uranium alloys as fuel for atomic power....He said he picked out Corning because he has been impressed with its research work and prefers to work with a company of our size rather than one of the giants."[9]

Corning felt it might be best to respond to Rickover's requests through a joint venture with Sylvania, the large New York–based electronics company that had long been a customer. Corning did have a small but growing electronics business based in the Bradford, Pennsylvania, plant. It made capacitors, resistors, and other passive electronic components. And the company had already made some important contributions to military technology. In the early 1950s, the Defense Department was constructing a series of radar installations in the northern parts of Canada, geared toward detecting Soviet missiles. The Distant Early Warning (DEW) system relied on ultrasonic delay lines, devices that acted as a sort of crude information storage system and let radar operators compare sequential scans. At first, the military used dangerous mercury-filled tubes. Searching for a better material, Chuck Lucy, a scientist at the U.S. Naval Air Development Center, became intrigued by the potential of using Corning's patented fused-silica vapor deposition techniques to make the delay lines. Lucy contacted Corning and learned more, and in 1952 the works hired him to be the company's liaison with the navy and tasked him to work on the project. Ultimately, Corning produced the electronic delay lines under a secret contract with the Signal Corps. More than twenty years after Franklin Hyde had patented the vapor deposition technique, the innovation found its first commercial application.

Sylvania's electronic capabilities were far greater that Corning's. With thirty-six domestic plants that made lightbulbs, tubes, and radio and television components, and 1955 sales of $307 million, it was nearly twice the size of Corning. But the companies' businesses were in many ways related, and in February 1955 Sylvania executives met with Decker and Corning's longtime investment banker George Murnane to discuss the possibility of a merger and other areas of possible cooperation. As their conversations continued, the two companies found that "the field of atomic energy is more promising than any other for common development by Sylvania and Corning." After all, Sylvania already had a plant devoted to atomic research and was developing reactor components. By combining Sylvania's nuclear expertise with Corning's ceramics knowledge, the companies believed they could meet some of Rickover's demands. Discussions continued through the summer of 1956 about setting up a new company devoted to nuclear research. Ultimately, Sylvania agreed to contribute the assets and personnel of its existing atomic energy division and $2.5 million in cash, while Corning would contribute $4.4 million in cash to the fifty-fifty joint venture. The company, Syl-Cor, opened shop in April 1957 with a research and development facility in Bayside, Queens, and a manufacturing plant in Hicksville, Long Island.[10]

Historical Landmarks and Labor Unrest

With new joint ventures like Syl-Cor, construction of the new headquarters building, and breakthroughs in color television, there was a great deal of activity at Corning. Indeed, the year 1957 brought a series of historic landmarks to the Corning Glass Works. Some of the landmarks involved individuals who had great historic significance to the company. Frank Hultzman had first come to work at Corning as a boy in 1876 and remained on the payroll for nearly eighty years. In 1956, Am presented him with a diamond-studded pin at a banquet in his honor. "Your eighty years of continued service with a single company—Corning Glass Works—is a record probably unique in American industry and an achievement deserving the highest praise," President Eisenhower wrote to Hultzman. In January 1957, Hultzman died. "I was greatly saddened Dutch to hear of your father's death," Am wrote to Hultzman's son. "My deep and affectionate sympathy goes out to you and your sister and all the family."[11]

Another event in the spring of 1957 also led some at Corning to think back to the nineteenth century. In April, workers at the Parkersburg plant went out on strike—the company's first strike since 1891. Throughout the 1950s, labor relations had generally been positive. In October 1955, for example, Corning and the Flints signed a contract that raised wages 12.5 cents an hour and increased other benefits. "The contract we have just signed represents the 13th consecutive year that the American Flint Glass Workers Union, AFL, and Corning Glass Works have negotiated successfully," said union president Harry Cook. "I am pleased that our talks were carried out in the same harmonious manner that has characterized our previous meetings with Corning Glass Works."[12]

The trigger for the Parkersburg strike was a disciplinary action against an employee. The episode took on much greater significance, recalled Tom Waaland, at the time Corning's vice president of labor relations, in the context of local union politics, where a handful of members sought to replace the Flints with a more militant industrial union. The strike lasted eight days and failed to spread to other plants. "The Parkersburg situation as of the moment is quiet," Amo wrote to Am on April 29, 1957. "The company took action after a good deal of deliberation to fire six employees and suspend four others." Amo, who had recently been promoted to executive vice president in charge of administrative functions, said the action was necessary because the union members viewed the company as weak "because of its long-standing ease in labor negotiations." He speculated that the causes of the strike included poor communication between management and hourly employees, laxity on the part of a previous plant manager, and cultural differences between the workers in Virginia and the managers in Corning. "It became quite apparent that the southerners, and they are individuals first and company employees second, as I have learned during the past few weeks, were not willing to take any tightening without proper explanation."[13]

Amo was writing to his father in Paris, where the senior Houghton had embarked upon an endeavor that harkened back to a previous generation. Like his father, Alanson Houghton, Am had been involved in Republican politics since his youth. In the postwar years, however, his activities intensified. Many of his friends and colleagues from the wartime agencies in which he served, like Philip Reed of General Electric, were among the primary backers of Eisenhower's campaigns. As these men grew in stature and prominence in the postwar years, Am also stepped out onto a wider stage. Am was a member of Eisenhower's informal circle of advisers. "When President Eisenhower really wants to relax, he invites a group of old and comfortable friends to join him for a Dutch-treat week end of golf, bridge, good food and congenial conversation," U.S. News & World Report said in 1955. This group included Am, Clifford Roberts (a New York investment banker and chairman of Augusta National Golf Club), General Motors executive

Albert Bradley, and tire magnate Leonard Firestone. In January 1955, Eisenhower invited Am to "an informal stag dinner" at the White House. "I shall probably wear a black tie, but a business suit will be entirely appropriate," the president wrote. And in September 1955, Eisenhower invited him for "a little fishing, trap shooting and barbecue at Gordon's Lake," a resort near Denver.[14]

Am worked to enlist the support of businessmen for Eisenhower's campaigns and contributed to various Republican campaigns, $5,000 in 1952 and $9,000 in 1956. "I know you did a lot of work in the recently concluded political campaign and that, in addition, you helped materially on the financial end," Eisenhower wrote Am after his 1956 landslide victory over Adlai Stevenson. "This note is merely to express my lasting appreciation of the personal compliment implicit in your action." Soon after, Eisenhower honored Am for his work by naming him to succeed C. Douglas Dillon as ambassador to France. The son of a diplomat, who had frequently visited his father in both Germany and Great Britain when he had served as American ambassador, entered foreign service at the age of fifty-seven.[15]

After being confirmed by the Senate on Thursday, March 14, Am formally asked for a leave of absence from his post at Corning and sailed from New York on the French liner *Liberté* on April 9. Like Alanson before him, Am would continue as the ceremonial chairman of the company. For the next four years, although he would not be involved in Corning's day-to-day operations, Am would remain the company's chief decision maker and most influential shareholder. In Paris, he quickly became caught up in the routines of diplomatic service, and both he and Laura took French lessons. "If you think the glass business is hard work, you're greatly mistaken," he wrote to Amo soon after arriving. "Your father, who at one time had a reasonable degree of freedom, has now fallen into a state of servitude and become a very obedient man. I start in the morning with an hour and a half of French, which, by the way, so far is almost completely removed from such French as I knew before."[16]

Amo Houghton served as his father's eyes and ears in Corning, much as Am had done for Alanson when he was abroad during the 1920s. And William Decker assumed the role Alexander Falck had played a generation before, albeit with substantially more executive authority than Falck possessed. Each week, Amo would send his father information on personnel and personal developments. "My job is terrific. I hope I don't fall flat on my face within the next few months," he wrote in April 1957. He would also send along other intelligence. "Enclosed, as I will send regularly on Monday mornings, is the *New York Herald* sports section and also the *New York Times* —with the idea that you possibly do not get as good coverage there."[17]

By 1957, Corning Glass Works was attracting increasing press coverage. In March 1957, a *Wall Street Journal* reporter visited Corning and expressed awe at the futuristic attitudes he found at this rural upstate New York "Idea Mill," where "an ancient art and a jet-age science flourish side by side." As countless other visitors to Corning had done before, he came away impressed with the seemingly endless potentials of glass. As Armistead put it, "There are solids, liquids, and gases....glass can be considered a kind of fourth state of matter, unlike anything else and not yet completely understood." The reporter ran through a checklist of Corning's many wonders: giant mirrors, screens for use in radar machines, electronic storage tubes, capacitors, and what Decker labeled "perhaps the most marvelous piece of glass ever made," chemically machineable glass. The article concluded by noting Corning's efforts to develop substances to be used in "jets, guided missiles and atomic reactors," and by hinting at a secret new discovery that Decker had tabbed "a revolutionary new type of material." The article, in a nutshell, managed to sum up the recurrent themes of the company's history: a relentless pursuit of the potential of glass, the ability to form new associations with customers and government entities to develop new products, and, most importantly, the unending search for the next big hit. The secret new discovery would be made public in the spring of 1957, and it did indeed prove to be revolutionary.[18]

From Pyroceram to Corning Ware

In the spring of 1957, anticipation was building in Corning for a variety of reasons beyond Decker's cryptic reference to a new material. The new research and administrative complex on the north side of the Chemung was nearing completion. In the days before the formal dedication on May 23,

1957, townspeople and workers toured the new offices. "Friday was plant Town Day and it seemed to me that all the employees from the branch plants made a bee-line for this office," Am's longtime assistant, Julia Peck, wrote. "When the public came on Sunday, there were 8,000 visitors in a 3-hour period." On Saturday morning, crowds began to gather for the ceremony, in which the research laboratories were dedicated to Corning's employees and named for Dr. Eugene Sullivan. Mrs. George Cunningham sang the national anthem. The Grey Saints Drill Team performed, and ceremonial keys to the complex were presented by Lou Crandall, chairman of the George A. Fuller Co. "It was a grand day for Dr. Sullivan and he seemed really affected," Peck wrote to Am.[19]

Aside from touting the glass works' near century of growth in the Chemung Valley, Corning executives used the occasion to trumpet the discovery of a "new basic material," Pyroceram (of which the ceremonial keys were fabricated). Discovered by Don Stookey, who, fittingly, was celebrating his forty-second birthday that day, Pyroceram was "lighter than aluminum, harder than high carbon steel, many times stronger than glass" and possessed "excellent electrical insulating properties, high deformation temperature and thermal shock resistance," Decker said. "No other material possesses this *combination* of desirable properties." And because the batch materials were cheap and could be forged through Corning's regular glassmaking process, the company could easily produce this new wonder material at low cost. Among the commercial forms in which Decker predicted the world could see Pyroceram were curtain walls, jet engines, chemical and oil-refining products, or "as a range top, with heat supplied from an electric-conducting coating." The introduction provided a jolt of excitement to the world beyond Corning. As Julia Peck wrote to Am, "as a result of the announcement of the development of Pyroceram, Corning's stock went on Friday, May 25, to a high of 94½, low 86¾, with 92½ at closing. This compared to a low of 57¼ for this year."[20]

Decker did not mention the most prolific and profitable use to which Pyroceram would be put in the following years: a line of cookware. In the spring of 1957, Corning Ware—one of the products that would embed the company in the popular consciousness—was conceived as a commercial product. And it could not have come at a better time. Sales of consumer products had inched up from $16 million in 1950 to just $17 million in 1955. "By 1956 the Pyrex Brand line growth had reached a plateau," said Lee Waterman, a veteran merchandiser hired to head Corning's consumer products division in 1955. "All future growth was predicted [sic] on the population explosion."[21]

What's more, Corning was encountering difficulties in other core businesses. "Although volume has been greater this year than last, we have been operating at a lower profit this year," Decker wrote to Am in July 1956. The business problems were several. General Electric had been purchasing some fourteen-inch bulbs from competitor Kimble. In addition, the long-awaited color television expansion wasn't coming to fruition. "RCA is getting very pessimistic about the outlook for color television," Decker wrote in July 1956. "They have asked that we postpone supplying them with 1,000 glass bulbs for a run of color tubes." That year, just 100,000 color televisions were produced, compared with more than 7 million black-and-white sets.

Of course, Corning was still investing considerable resources toward improving the production of color television bulbs and was making some progress. In the mid-1950s, Pilot Plant 2 was home to a high-powered set of Ph.D. chemists and engineers who were focusing on the challenge of sealing color bulbs effectively. Shipping the complicated color bulbs as a single completed piece would be more expensive and would risk greater breakage. So Corning aimed to develop glasses that would permit customers to assemble and seal bulbs at their own bulb plants. This would necessitate perfecting special sealing glasses that melted at a very low temperature. In 1956, Corning's scientists were hard at work developing just such a glass composition—a "frit," as it was known. One such frit, developed by researcher Stewart Claypoole, would prove an important asset when color television gained critical mass and took off in the early 1960s.

In 1956, however, color television's ascendance was still future. In response to the short-term challenges, Corning temporarily shut down Pilot Plant 2 and slashed salaried payrolls in the summer of 1956. On the year, sales edged up less than 4 percent to a record $163 million but profits fell. "Earnings were squeezed by the pressure of higher material and labor costs," the annual report noted.[22]

Waterman's mandate was thus to find a way to reduce Corning's reliance on the unpredictable television industry. And the experienced sales-man, who was cut from a different cloth than many of Corning's executives, possessed the skills necessary to do so. After graduating from Bates College in 1926, he went to work at W.T. Grant Company, starting as a floor man and rising to manage the chain's largest store. He then worked in merchan-dising at Montgomery Ward for seven years and returned to Grant's in 1941 as director of sales promotion. In 1951, he became president of Sloane Blabon Corporation, a subsidiary of Alexander Smith, Inc. His hiring was a significant step for the company. Along with Decker, who had worked his way up from Corning's corporate accountant in the 1930s to the post of president, Waterman was one of the few nontechnologists (and non-Houghtons) to rise to a high position within the company in the 1950s and 1960s. Their ascent and importance constituted a recognition that disci-plines such as finance and marketing could be as crucial to the success of the company as chemistry and physics.

Polished, personable, and possessing four decades' worth of experience in dealing with distributors, dealers, and consumers of hard goods, Water-man had a unique understanding of the forces roiling the marketplace and, just as important, he possessed the salesman's knack for optimism. He believed in the mid-1950s that Corning could double its sales of consumer goods with the right marketing program in place—an assertion widely dis-missed by his new colleagues. But Waterman would ultimately be proved correct. And it was his ability to marshal the company's scientists and exec-utives to focus on ways of developing new consumer products that would make him one of the more influential executives in the company's history.[23]

In the spring of 1957, Waterman was actively searching for a new prod-uct that could build on the long-standing success of the Pyrex brand line. Corning had an active twelve-person market research department run by R. L. Patey. The unit conducted about 200 surveys a year and tallied informa-tion gathered from some of the half-million people who visited the Glass Center annually. Surveys had shown there were two natural areas to expand upon the Pyrex franchise: range-top cooking and tableware. But, as Water-man later put it, "We had no material which would withstand the heat of range tops and no material which could be offered in competition to china or earthenware."[24]

In 1956, soon after Waterman arrived, Donald Stookey and William Armistead showed him just such a material. In 1952, while Stookey was heating a plate of preexposed Fotoform glass at 600C, something went wrong with the furnace's temperature controller. While he was away, the temperature rose to 900C—a level at which the glass was expected to melt. "Damn it, I've ruined a furnace!" was Stookey's first thought. But the chemist was in for a surprise. Although he expected to find a mass of molten glass inside, Stookey was astonished to find that the plate was intact. This state of puzzlement perhaps led to a second mistake. "I took it out of the hot furnace with tongs, but it fell on the floor with a clang like a plate of steel, and didn't break." Stookey examined the piece of glass with fascination. The glass was opaque, rather than clear, with a milky white appearance. "It must have crystallized so completely that it could not flow....And obviously it was much stronger than ordinary glass," he accurately noted. Stookey's remarkably felicitous series of mistakes led to yet another unexpected discovery about glass. He concluded that all types of glasses could theoretically be converted to crystalline bodies having new properties that depend on the nature of the particular crystals. In the years after this discovery, Stookey set out to patent this principle. He applied for the initial broad glass ceramic patent in 1956 and ultimately received it on January 12, 1960, as patent 2920971.

The discovery of this new material highlighted the role of serendipity in Corning's century-long romance with glass. For this material, which would prove an enduring component of the company's revenues and self-image, was the result of not one but two laboratory mistakes. Fortunately, Corning's scientists and executives proved willing to pursue the path of innovation.[25]

As Stookey and his colleagues continued to investigate the possibilities of this highly durable glass, they quickly realized that it wouldn't expand much when exposed to high temperatures and that it simultaneously had the ability to transmit high levels of certain types of radiation. Corning's scientists knew they had something big on their hands but were unsure where it would lead them. The company's deepening associations with government-sponsored research institutions provided the first indication.

The Johns Hopkins Applied Physics Lab, which was developing the Terrier and Tartar missiles for the U.S. Navy, needed a material for the nosecone that could withstand the tremendous heat and pressure of passing through a rainstorm at supersonic speeds. In the spring of 1956, under the direction of Dr. Ben Allen, Corning began making pilot radomes (as the products were called) from a material dubbed 9606 Pyroceram. Corning developed a spin-molding technique to make the glass. By 1958, radomes were deployed in missiles made by Convair, Hughes Aircraft, and Raytheon, although they accounted for a relatively small percentage of sales. Nonetheless, Corning's scientists generally believed that radomes would be the most immediate and profitable application of Pyroceram.[26]

But Lee Waterman and others within Corning foresaw greater application for Pyroceram as a consumer product. And as it did with black-and-white television, the company showed a willingness to throw all available resources at a promising project. In 1957, Corning refitted a full-scale production tank to make larger quantities of Pyroceram. "Suddenly, the research project changed from a low-key, one-man exploration to a recognized breakthrough, and every available glass composition researcher was enlisted to contribute his effort," Stookey recalled. By testing various compositions, members of the company's 350-strong research laboratory staff created a lithia-alumina-silica mix nucleated by titanium oxide that had a negative coefficient of thermal expansion: Pyroceram 9608.[27]

Waterman believed the material could be used in a new line of cookware that would tap into the changing habits of the American housewife. Pyrex, after all, couldn't be used on top of the stove, which was where 80 percent of the cooking was done in the 1950s. (Baking was no longer as popular as it had been in the 1910s, when Pyrex was introduced.) In addition, home habits were changing. Waterman believed people would go for a product that could be transferred directly from the freezer to the oven, and vice versa, thus allowing housewives to prepare foods in advance, freeze or refrigerate them, and heat them for dinner. Further, he believed Corning could own the market if it got there first. "If the patent Department can give us a three-year lead in the marketplace, no one will ever catch us!" he said.[28]

The Rollout of Corning Ware

Urged along by Waterman and Ray Voss, who led product development, the effort to make consumer cookware from the new material gathered critical mass in January 1957. On February 12, 1957, the first dish of the new material was pressed in the research lab. In the fall of 1957, having chosen the name Corning Ware, the company produced the first workable glass ceramic skillets and saucepans for home testing. The design featured a square bottom in a round shape, designed for heating packages of frozen vegetables, which was already used in the Pyrex Flameware line. Also, to ease handling of the product, Corning devised a detachable handle and metal cradle on which the hot ware could sit without burning the tabletop. In January 1958 the company decided to go ahead with production.[29]

Three months later, marketing executive Jim Bierer took about $1,000 worth of newly pressed Corning Ware to Rochester, New York, for two store sales tests, backed by television and newspaper advertisement support. Rolling out its first new product line in several decades, Corning was still operating under old assumptions. "We contracted for six television spots and two newspaper ads to support the market test in two stores. The test product was sold out before the newspaper ads were in print," said Lee Waterman, testifying to the newfound power of television.[30]

Corning hastened to set up a production run at A Factory in the summer of 1958. To make the ware more attractive, Corning added a blue cornflower emblem. (Consumer testing in the meantime had determined that a wheat decoration would be more attractive, but such was the firm's haste that it went ahead with the cornflower.) Corning next took its ware east to four New England cities—Boston, Hartford, Providence, and Springfield. The area was chosen because it was close to Corning and because "the consumer there is somewhat conservative in the acceptance of new products," Waterman said. But Corning wasn't content to merely run advertisements, as it had done in Rochester. In preparation for the fall 1958 introduction in those markets, Corning embarked on an education campaign geared toward the people who would buy and sell the product, not consumers.

In important ways, the rollout of Corning Ware would hark back to the introduction of Corning's first consumer product line in 1915. Just as it had relied on the expertise of columnist Sara Tyson Rorer to introduce Pyrex to female customers, Corning now deployed its staff of home economists and tried to influence newspaper and television columnists with access to large audiences of women. The company dispatched two salesmen and a home economist to the aforementioned New England cities in July 1958, outfitted with small combination stove-refrigerator-sinks and the entire product line: three saucepans, a skillet, four covers, and a handle. Holding court in hotel rooms, they talked with distributors and dealers one at a time, explaining and demonstrating the product. Over the course of forty days, they held seventy-five such meetings. "Lee Waterman and his troops literally captured New England on the first round of PYROCERAM. The distributors were most enthusiastic and bought, and the retail trade is coming through in great shape," treasurer Charles LaFollette wrote to Am in August 1958.[31]

On the Sunday after Labor Day, Corning Ware was introduced to consumers in New England. In November, the ware was formally introduced and placed on sale in New York City, upstate New York, New Jersey, eastern Pennsylvania, Los Angeles, and San Francisco. Corning angled to get free media pickups of the product by holding press luncheons in new markets and by mailing "do-it-yourself" press parties, including canned foods, a news release, and photos to newspaper, radio, and television editors in upstate New York and in eastern Pennsylvania. "Reports to date, for example, show that news on Corning Ware, based on receipt of these kits, was broadcast on fourteen radio and TV shows," the firm reported in December in 1958. Every Philadelphia and New York daily newspaper ran an article on Corning Ware. Sales of the ware—expected to be about $3.9 million in its first year—ran so far ahead of plans that on December 23, 1958, Corning simply ran out of stock.[32]

As it rolled out the product, Corning didn't take a uniform tack. Rather, it tried to learn something from every new area it entered. "The New England program was so successful that it was used as the basis for all that we have done since. We held a total of more than 140 of the one hour presentations for more than 7,500 people; and these 7,500 people are the most important people in the country in the distribution of our products," Waterman recalled in a speech given in July 1959. Corning staffers made house calls to people who bought the ware and packed questionnaires in 1,500 boxes of

Corning Ware, with some 62 percent of the customers responding. Corning found that 67 percent had received the ware as a gift, that 34 percent had bought it for gift giving, that 35 percent had bought for themselves, and that 75 percent said they planned to buy it for themselves. "This told us that we not only had a seasonal, gift-giving product, but one that would be a year-around top seller," Waterman wrote. By the end of 1958, then, Corning had introduced its first successful new line of consumer products in more than forty years. The seemingly unending search for the next big hit had yet again produced an unlikely and unexpected result.[33]

The formal introduction of Corning Ware continued until June 1, 1959, when it entered Seattle, the last major U.S. urban market. Working together, Corning's scientists, engineers, and marketing experts had turned raw Pyroceram into a strong consumer product in twenty-five months. "The experts say that the normal time cycle from scientific discovery to product marketing is from 5 to 7 years," Waterman later noted with great pride. "We are proud of the fact that we did this job in two."[34]

Waterman insisted that Corning Ware's impressive performance was just a beginning. In the summer of 1959, he announced that "the largest advertising campaign ever run on a line of cook-ware, and will bring us at least as much volume in its first full year as the "Pyrex" Baking Ware line which we have been building for 43 years." He noted that Corning was already looking into new uses for Pyroceram, displaying a new electric skillet slated to be test-marketed in the fall. But new products were added almost immediately, before the electric skillet. In the summer of 1959 at the housewares show in Atlantic City, Corning displayed six-cup and eight-cup coffee percolators.[35]

Corning perceived an obstacle in marketing its new product, however. As Waterman fairly exclaimed, "Think of a housewife who believes she owns all the pots and pans and serving dishes she needs, who doesn't know a radome from a radiator, who thinks of missiles only in terms of doom and destruction, who has become wary of product claims—and figure out how you are going to get her to plunk down twelve dollars and ninety-five cents for a cooking-serving dish she doesn't even know exists!"[36]

The answer to this challenge would lie in the new medium that Corning had helped pioneer: television. Advertising on television was to be the key, especially for skeptical New Englanders, who, Waterman (a New Englander himself) concluded, "must see to believe." The fall of 1959 saw the launch of a $1 million multimedia advertising program. It began with full-page ads in mass-circulation magazines such as *Life, Saturday Evening Post, Ladies Home Journal*, and *Reader's Digest*, reinforced by a four-week saturation of sixty-second television spots in all sixty-six of the nation's major markets—with an average of forty spots per market. In addition, advertisements appeared on the three networks' hit prime-time shows, including *Cheyenne, Sugarfoot, The Lineup, Five Fingers*, and *The Alaskans*. Finally, Corning oversaw the airing on 200 television stations of a fifteen-minute film narrated by Chet Huntley and entitled *American Women—Partners in Research*. Filmed in Corning, it traced the market research and home-kitchen testing that went into the development of the Corning Ware percolator.[37]

The print material highlighted the unique aspects of the product and of the times—the dawning space age. "The advent of Sputnik created high interest in space materials and made our story particularly timely," Waterman noted. One piece of corporate promotional literature showed a rocket blasting into the sky: "New Corning Ware Blasts Off." Another brochure read: "Rocketing into your daily life!...Corning Ware made of an astounding new missile material, Pyroceram—for all its beauty, it can't crack for heat or cold." Continuing a long tradition of selling with science, most advertisements featured a line identifying Corning Ware as "a product of Corning Research." Many others featured the now-famous fire-and-ice demonstration—a picture of a Corning Ware casserole dish, half of it stuck in a block of ice while the other half was licked by flames from a torch. Still another featured a man in an asbestos fire suit walking through flames with a piece of Corning Ware and plunging it into a barrel of ice water.[38]

Advertisements run by department stores in newspapers in 1959 reinforced the theme. New Orleans department store Maison Blanche ran an ad on April 3, 1959, in the *New Orleans Times Picayune* for Corning Ware under the line, "Toward the Golden Future," featuring a crescent moon. Wanamaker's in Philadelphia ran a full-page ad on "The Cookware That Came from the Moon." Sibley's Housewares in Rochester would go a step further, proclaiming in a March 27, 1961, *Rochester Times Union* ad for Corningware, "A New Triumph of Space Age Research! Never again will you have to give your dishes kid-glove handling." The department store had a glass booth on the fourth floor where customers could drop the product and test its durability. Even journalists got into the act. In her column in the *Cleveland Plain Dealer* on February 19, 1959, Marion Fisher Hill wrote, "Products of the space age are not limited to Cape Canaveral. The same super-strength ceramic Pyroceram that is used in missile nose cones is appearing in cooking utensils made by Corning Glass Works."[39]

The massive advertising and marketing programs spurred a demand so heavy that by late December 1958, Corning ran out of stock. Initially, the company sought to relieve the overburdened Chemung Valley production lines by renting a facility in Paden City, West Virginia. On October 13, 1959, at a luncheon attended by more than eighty community leaders, Corning announced its intention to build a factory in Martinsburg, West Virginia, a small town in the rural West Virginia panhandle. On a sixty-acre site, four miles south of Martinsburg, amid peach orchards and cornfields, Corning built a 244,000-square-foot plant that initially employed about 350 people. The plant, which opened in the spring of 1960, was a boon to the largely impoverished region; the only other local industry was Interwoven, a sock manufacturing company.[40]

The Martinsburg plant was managed by Bob Sanders, a Syracuse University–trained lawyer who had most recently been assistant to the manager of manufacturing for the consumer products division. Sanders was immediately tasked with overseeing the deployment of a revolutionary new forming machine: the Hub Machine. Like the Ribbon Machine, it was an invention that would alter the company's history. The animating force behind the Hub Machine was master machinery designer Jim Giffen, who had created the centrifugal casting process for television bulbs. Just as the Ribbon Machine did, the Hub Machine relied on a continuous stream of molten glass feeding into a series of molds. The hub itself was a large wheel studded with a series of molds. As the hub turned, it presented an empty mold into which a dollop of molten glass fell. As the machine continued to rotate, the glass was sucked into the mold and shaped. An automatic trimmer cut off excess glass, allowing the machine to churn out an endless stream of formed pieces. The Hub Machine allowed workers to cut different pieces of ware from a continuous sheet of hot glass—like cookies out of a sheet of dough. One author described it as "a flaming Ferris wheel" after seeing it in action and gaining an appreciation for the speed, heat, and power inherent in modern glassmaking. The first Hub Machine was first installed at Martinsburg in 1961 and would remain the basis of producing Corning Ware for the next forty years.[41]

Martinsburg offered an ample supply of labor, proximity to materials, and a low-cost operating environment. But it wasn't a transportation hub. Rather than use the plant as a distribution base, Corning decided to build a new facility to handle that function. On February 24, 1960, construction began on a 600,000-square-foot plant just outside Greencastle, Pennsylvania, about thirty miles north of Martinsburg and affording better access to new interstate highways. The distribution center initially employed 150 people.[42]

Corning Ware quickly became a big business. Although the company didn't release figures, estimates varied widely. "In 1959, its first full year on the market some $15 million worth of Corning Ware was sold," *Forbes* asserted in 1962. Duff, Anderson, and Clark speculated that sales of Pyroceram consumer products in 1960 "probably reached the $25 million level." The runaway success of Corning Ware brought a shift in attitude for a company that had heretofore relied on industry for most of its sales. In 1960, President Bill Decker concluded that Corning would be better off selling more of its products to the consumer. After all, industrial customers were harder to reach and more fickle than consumers. And by shrewdly using the all-powerful medium of television, Corning could reach large masses of customers easily. "I would like to see our consumer business greater than 50 percent of the total," Decker said. (In 1957, consumer products accounted for just 14 percent of total sales.) In 1960, $50 million of Corning's $215 million in sales were domestic consumer products. Between 1950 and 1960, sales of consumer products rose 325 percent, with most of the increase coming in 1959 and 1960.[43]

Struggles at the Verge of a New Age

The success of Corning Ware and its emergence as a potential big hit was crucial for the company, since Corning was encountering serious difficulties in the late 1950s. Once again, as in prior generations, Corning found itself dealing with the vagaries of seemingly maturing products, like black-and-white television and Pyrex, and the excitement of an entirely new line created by its proprietary technology. Between 1955 and 1958, sales barely budged, from $158 million to $159 million. Meanwhile, the company's employment costs per man-hour rose sharply, from $1.98 in 1955 to $2.45 in 1959—an increase of 24 percent in four years. And Corning was plowing larger sums of money into research and development. In 1958, research expenses rose 22.6 percent to $6.9 million, and the company spent $18.2 million on new plants and equipment—the largest amount for any year in its history. At the same time, customers constantly demanded price containment, especially in television. "As we will undoubtedly have to increase wages in November and as other costs are rising, we are studying the possibility of increasing prices wherever we can, including price increases on television bulbs," Decker wrote in late 1958. "It may be impractical to increase prices on television bulbs but we are going to make a strenuous effort to do so."[44]

Raising prices was impractical because television was again in one of its temporary slumps. In 1958, the production of televisions—at 5.05 million—was lower than for any year since 1949, and down 35 percent from 1955. As if to underscore the difficulties, in November 1958, Corning received an alarming message. An anonymous typewritten letter addressed to Amo threatened a bomb would explode at 1:55 P.M. on Thursday, November 13, at the Pressware plant. The plant was evacuated, and an extensive search failed to turn up anything. The same day, two unidentified men showed up at the Knoll, asking to see Amory Sr., who had left for Europe the day before.[45]

To aggravate matters, some of Corning's once-promising initiatives stumbled. In some ways, the Syl-Cor atomic energy joint venture was ill-fated from the beginning. In establishing it, the company violated one of its cardinal rules—of not setting up joint ventures with major customers or competitors. As a television manufacturer and a maker of electronic components, Sylvania was both a customer and a competitor. What's more, its products fell far outside Corning's core competencies in glass. To avoid potential conflicts, Syl-Cor was charged with avoiding electronics and glass-making—two important areas with large potential for government uses. By the time Syl-Cor set up shop, at least five other companies were supplying metallic elements to what had quickly become a buyer's market. In 1959,

Syl-Cor's main buyer, the U.S. Navy, canceled the contract. As a result, Syl-Cor racked up huge losses: $299,000 in 1957, $1.48 million in 1958, and $2.28 million in 1959. In 1961, Sylvania would offer to buy out Corning for $950,000. Corning accepted, even though this meant booking a loss on the project of almost $4 million.[46]

Despite such difficulties, Corning was plainly looking to a future built on glass and was intent on stepping out onto a wider stage. Nothing represented the company's aspirations and self-confidence better than the new building it began to construct in 1956. In the mid-1950s, Corning's New York quarters in the five-story building on the southwest corner of Fifth Avenue and 56th Street were growing crowded. In July 1956, the company purchased 717 Fifth Avenue, a site occupied by the Langdon Hotel that lay directly across the street. After issuing $16 million in mortgage bonds, the company started construction on a twenty-six-story glass tower designed by architect Wallace Harrison, who had designed the Corning Glass Center.

In the nexus of Manhattan's business and tourism district, four blocks north of Rockefeller Center and two blocks south of the Plaza Hotel, the tower would be an impressive testament to the centrality of Corning to American industrial life. The move across the street for Steuben, recalled Arthur's long-time associate Sally Walker, was "a marvelous idea because [the east side] was the right side of Fifth Avenue. The traffic between Tiffany's and Saks Fifth Avenue is probably one of the greatest, most lucrative stretches of retailing" in the world."[47]

Like the Glass Center several years before, the new building was a monument to the versatility of glass. The 359-foot skyscraper, sheathed in green-tinted heat-absorbing panels, was the first glass tower on Fifth Avenue. Glass was used throughout the relentlessly modern building—in partitions between offices, acoustical tile, illuminated ceilings, fiberglass insulation, and even door handles; the building featured six miles of fiberglass drapes instead of the usual venetian blinds. In Corning's second-floor reception room, the walls, ceilings, tables, and even the receptionist's desk, were made of glass. When it opened in March 1958, Corning and Owens-Corning occupied about one-third of the 345,000-square-foot building, and the ground floor featured a Steuben showroom. On the twenty-sixth floor, the officers of Corning set up a luncheon club, the Fifth Avenue Club.[48]

Many of the most exciting events of the thirteen years following the war —Eisenhower's visit, the Corning centennial, the company's centennial, and Am's ambassadorial appointment—had contained echoes of Corning's past. But the completion of 717 Fifth Avenue and the gradual introduction of Corning Ware pointed to the future. By 1959, Corning had laid the platforms for growth in the coming decade: a rejuvenated consumer products division, dominance in the black-and-white television business, and crucial advances in color television. Corning had also laid the foundation for more international expansion. In 1959, it set up a new subsidiary, Corning Glass International, SA, to sell Corning and Corhart refractories products abroad. Together, the technological and human infrastructure Corning built in the 1950s would provide the support for the company to grow into a truly diversified multinational glass house in the coming decade.

V

FIFTH GENERATION

CHAPTER NINE

Encountering Limits and Diversifying, 1960–1966

FOR LARGE American manufacturing companies like the Corning Glass Works, the early 1960s were, in many ways, the best of times. They entered the decade possessed of a strong, pervasive optimism—in technology, in their strong market position, and in the stability and economic and political might of the United States. And during the 1960s, Corning would expand from its strong domestic base into new foreign markets, becoming a true multinational. At home, it would use the profits generated by television bulbs and consumer products to rush headlong into new businesses such as semiconductors and electronics. And the company made efforts to bring a greater range of executive disciplines to bear on the problems posed by its rapid growth. The first half of the 1960s was marked by transition and expansion, fueled in large part by the success of Corning Ware.

New Leadership Takes Charge

Corning Ware wasn't the only homegrown product introduced in the late 1950s and early 1960s. Amory Houghton Jr., known to all inside and outside the company as "Amo," was emerging into the top leadership of the company. The grandson of Alanson Houghton and the great-grandson of Amory Houghton Jr., he would be the fourth generation of eldest Houghton sons to serve as chief executive of the Corning Glass Works. In 1957, he had been promoted to executive vice president in charge of administrative functions. To be sure, William Decker, who had grown into a highly respected executive, continued to exercise wide authority as the executive responsible for day-to-day operations. But as the heir apparent to Decker, Amo took on increasingly prominent roles within and without the company.

These roles emerged when Amory Houghton Sr. was abroad as U.S. ambassador to France between 1957 and 1961. The relationship between father and son was strong and respectful and neatly replicated that between Amory Sr. and his father, Alanson B. Houghton. Just as Amory Sr. served his apprenticeship while Alanson served in diplomatic postings in Europe during the 1920s, so Amo prepared to assume direction of Corning while his father served overseas. During Amory Sr.'s absence, Amo acted as his father's eyes and ears, writing him frequently about company affairs and calling on the telephone to discuss hirings and promotions. A typical letter was the following, dictated on July 14, 1960 (Bastille Day). "Several things I'd like to mention," Amo wrote. "Paul Perrot is now Director of the Museum. I have just split Art Weber's Engineering and Manufacturing staff into two areas, and the resulting groups will be Art as director of manufacturing services and Ben Allen as director of engineering." In addition to telling him about reconstruction work on the local church and a relative's financial troubles, Amo told his father of the announcement of the electric percolator and electronic skillet, products, he believed, that "are going to be a great thing for us."[1]

Amo also acted as his father's surrogate in watching over the progress of his brothers, especially the youngest, Jamie (born in 1936). Ten years younger than Amo, Jamie graduated from Harvard in 1958 and moved on to the Harvard Business School. It was an experience for which he later admitted being unprepared, and he took time off after his first year to complete his military service in the National Guard and then work for a year at Goldman Sachs. (Jamie's sister, Elizabeth, had married Sidney Weinberg Jr., whose father, Sidney Weinberg, was the senior partner at Goldman, Sachs and had worked with Am on the War Production Board.) While working on Wall Street, Jamie lived in an apartment on Manhattan's East Side, just around the corner from his cousin Arthur A. Houghton Jr., the longtime head of Steuben.[2]

In the fall of 1961, Jamie returned to finish his MBA at Harvard. In a foreshadowing of his future career path, he took several courses in international business. For a course in international economic relations, he submitted a dense, forty-page report, with partner Lawrence Coolidge, entitled "India 1961: A Report on India's Economic Development." To meet the requirements of his financial accounting course, he wrote a paper on the challenges that a company with subsidiaries in both Europe and Latin America faces in reporting the results of foreign operations. Just after completing his MBA in June 1962, Jamie married May Tuckerman Kinnicutt ("Maisie"), who had just graduated from Radcliffe, at Christ Church in Cambridge, Massachusetts. Soon after, Jamie joined the Glass Works, moving with his wife to Danville, Kentucky, to start as a production foreman.[3]

Amo was also beginning to follow his father's path in assuming positions of greater responsibility in civic and public affairs. In the summer of 1960, for example, he worked a shift in the temporary tourist booth at Centerway Square in Corning. He was also named a director of the New York Telephone Company, was initiated into the University Club in Manhattan, and joined industry groups such as the Manufacturers Club. Amo socialized with and entertained colleagues like David Rockefeller, the chairman of Chase Manhattan Bank, with whom he served on the board of B.F. Goodrich. In the summer of 1960, Rockefeller visited Corning, partially as a social visit and partially to convince Corning to do more of its banking business with Chase.[4]

Amo and his father also shared intelligence on what for several decades had been the Houghton family's second business: politics. In the summer of 1960, Amo handicapped that year's presidential race. "Kennedy had the thing sewed up before he even got to Los Angeles, and I feel he will be very difficult to beat in November unless something unusual develops during the ensuing months." Amo's prediction proved correct, although John F. Kennedy's victory over Richard Nixon was extremely close.[5]

With a Democrat about to enter the White House, Amory Houghton

Sr.'s tenure as ambassador to France came to an end. On January 24, 1961, the ambassador returned home to a large public reception. His plane was met at the Big Flats airport by a motorcade that proceeded to Centerway Square, where some 3,000 Corning residents waited in bitter subzero cold and storefronts were plastered with posters reading "Welcome Home" or "Soyez Les Bienvenus." Overwhelmed by the reception, the ambassador uncharacteristically choked up. "I was born here, I have lived here, and I propose to live here the rest of my days," he said. "All I want is to be allowed to play my part in the affairs of the community for which I have a deep and abiding affection."[6]

A Commitment to Education and the Arts

The company to which Amory Sr. returned in 1961 was much different than the one he had left in 1957, and not just because of the revitalization of its consumer products business. Rather, Corning was expanding rapidly in several directions at once. In 1960, the company purchased 400 acres of land in the nearby town of Erwin, New York. On this plot, which would later be enlarged substantially, the company would construct a large complex to house its research and development arms. The area was named Sullivan Park in honor of the founder of Corning's research laboratory in 1908 and its guiding spirit for decades. On August 1, 1961, the eighty-nine-year-old scientist helped light the tank at the Process Research Center, the first of several buildings to be constructed at Sullivan Park over the next forty years.

Corning's building boom extended beyond the Chemung Valley. In 1960, it enlarged its technical products plant at Muskogee, Oklahoma. The following year, it announced plans to build a plant in Raleigh, North Carolina, to produce electronics products such as resistors and capacitors, a new Corhart facility in Buckhannon, West Virginia, and a Vycor plant in Danville, Virginia. In 1960 and 1961, Corning spent more than $40 million on new facilities—far more than in any comparable period in its history.[7]

Aside from erecting new buildings, Corning also invested substantial resources in enhancing its image. Part of this impulse stemmed from the natural desire of any consumer products company to raise its profile with the broad American buying public. Just as powerful, however, was a sense among the company's executives that the Corning Glass Works, a small-town glass company for nearly a century, was in the midst of a more profound transformation. It was beginning to expand internationally, developing vital new product lines and undergoing a change in management. In April 1961, the sixty-year-old Decker was elected chairman and chief executive officer, and Amo succeeded him as president. In essence, Amo had become the chief operating officer of the company, while Decker continued to serve as a mentor and the company's public face until he was prepared to retire. At the same time, R&D head Bill Armistead acquired a new title—director of technical staff.[8]

These changes reflected a new mood of optimism, self-confidence, vitality, and engagement at the company. New initiatives included everything from sponsoring new institutions to developing a new logo. ("Corning Adopts 'New Look' with Modern, Solid Styling," the *Gaffer* trumpeted in July 1962. The new logo consisted of the word "CORNING" in capital letters) In conjunction with the American Council of Learned Societies, the works hosted the second Corning Conference from May 18 to May 20, 1961, on the theme of "the individual in the modern world." Like the Corning Conference a decade before, the series of seminars, discussions, and lectures brought together political figures, intellectuals, and industrialists. Those attending included theater critic Brooks Atkinson, novelist John Dos Passos, historian Merle Curti, French political theorist Raymond Aron, novelist John Hersey, labor leader George Meany, and executives like David Sarnoff, Harold Boeschenstein, and David and J. Stillman Rockefeller. John Brooks, the prolific *New Yorker* writer and author, published an account of it.[9]

The company's involvement with another cultural event the following year brought it far more attention. Arthur Houghton, the longtime head of Steuben, had been one of the prime movers behind the creation of Lincoln Center, a $142-million public–private development aimed at revitalizing several square blocks on Manhattan's West Side. In 1955, when the area was designated for urban renewal, both the Metropolitan Opera and New York Philharmonic decided to build new concert halls there. As president and chairman of the Philharmonic, Arthur was deeply involved in the planning for the complex. (While he was still responsible for Steuben, Arthur devoted much of his time to philanthropies. He also served as a trustee of the New York Public Library, the Pierpont Morgan Library, and the Metropolitan Museum of Art.)

The Houghtons' contributions to the center were many. Arthur served as a vice president of Lincoln Center, Inc., and made substantial personal donations. In March 1958, the Corning Glass Works Foundation donated $100,000. At about the same time an anonymous donor pledged a substantial gift toward the cost of a 1,000-seat chamber music hall. This donor was eventually revealed to be Alice Tully, the singer and philanthropist who was a daughter of Alanson Houghton's sister, Clara. Alice Tully, a professional mezzo-soprano who had served as a licensed pilot in World War II, was a Corning shareholder to whom Amo frequently sent advance copies of the annual report, as well as prototypes of products like Pyroceram skillets. (A large portrait of Tully, painted by Thomas Buechner, the longtime head of the Corning Glass Museum, hangs in the building's lobby.)[10]

President Eisenhower helped break ground for the project in 1959, and work began on a series of structures designed by an illustrious group of architects that included Philip Johnson and Eero Saarinen. Corning Glass Works sponsored the glittering September 1962 Lincoln Center gala opening night concert, which was aired nationally on CBS television. Arthur Houghton escorted New York City Mayor Robert Wagner to a special box, adjacent to seats occupied by dignitaries such as Governor Nelson Rockefeller, First Lady Jacqueline Kennedy, UN Secretary-General U Thant, and Secretary of State Dean Rusk. Leonard Bernstein conducted a program that included the Gloria movement from Beethoven's *Missa Solemnis*, Ralph Vaughan Williams's *Serenade to Music*, and the premiere of a new work by Aaron Copland. "In addition to the more than 3000 people in Philharmonic Hall that night, the opening was witnessed by an estimated 26 million television viewers throughout the United States," wrote Lincoln Center historian Edgar Young. "It was probably the largest audience, up to that time, to attend a single concert."[11]

Corning also sponsored institution building at the local level. Corning Community College (CCC) had opened in 1958 with 185 full-time students and a full-time faculty of eight in a building on East Fifth Street. Arthur Houghton, who divided his time between his New York City apartment and his Maryland eastern shore estate, Wye Plantation, donated his former home on East Third Street to the college. Two years later, CCC announced it would build a campus on Spencer Hill, two miles south of Corning. The four-building, $4.5 million project, which could accommodate 850 students, was funded by a $2.25 million grant from the Corning Glass Works Foundation and by the donation of land by Arthur Houghton.[12]

As part of a broader commitment to continuing education, Corning established a tuition assistance program that reimbursed 75 percent of tuition for employees who completed college-level courses. By the end of 1962, more than 350 students had enrolled in courses in 150 different subjects at twenty-five different schools around the country, with math and science courses being the most popular. One such employee was James Siner, a twenty-year-old father who worked the 4 P.M. to midnight shift in Muskogee's maintenance department. During the day, he attended Northeastern State College in Tahlequah, Oklahoma—some thirty miles away—and maintained a 3.4 grade point average.[13]

Chemcor: The Next Big Hit?

Corning's involvement with education and Lincoln Center helped reinforce its reputation as a progressive business. But in the early 1960s, Corning's continuing application of proprietary technology to new consumer goods, as well as its connections with the space program and a futuristic medium like television, gave substance to this effort. In a description that must have pleased Corning's public relations officers, *Forbes* opined in 1962 that "basically it is a technology company selling its scientific ability to use glass in solving a variety of industrial and consumer problems."

Indeed, Corning's commitment to technology grew in the early 1960s. Research and development costs rose from 2.9 percent of sales in 1956 to 5.4 percent in 1962, when the Works spent $14.3 million on R&D. Such an increase was possible because its revenues were rising rapidly—65 percent between 1958 and 1962. Partially as a result of the rapid growth fueled by the growth of Corning Ware, and partially because of its association with high technology, investors bid Corning's shares up to unprecedented levels. In

1961, when Corning had a book value of $146.9 million, it had a market capitalization of $1.1 billion. (At that point, the Houghton family still held over 50 percent of Corning stock.) In September 1961, the common stock, which had risen nearly twenty-fold since 1946, traded at about 165, or forty-seven times 1961 earnings—a stunning multiple for an established company.[14]

Investors were plainly betting on a bright future for the company. And Amo, then thirty-six, projected a youthful optimism. In yet another iteration of the company's historic habit of following glass wherever the mysterious material led, Amo told *Time* magazine in 1962, "Sometimes we start out with one objective and end up with something 180 degrees in the other direction." Noting that 25 percent of the company's sales stemmed from products introduced in the last five years, Amo marveled at prospects for the company and its chosen, malleable material: "It's sort of a wild dream, but I would like to feel that one day glass can be as important to our economy as steel is today."[15]

Comparing glass to steel—the nation's largest materials manufacturing industry—may have been wishful thinking. But at this time, Corning was about to introduce a glass material whose tensile strength could rival that of steel. Though not a technologist, Bill Decker had an appreciation for the potentials of glass (perhaps a finer appreciation than some of the scientists in the laboratory had) and a faith in the company's ability to mine its depths. In the late 1950s, he famously told Bill Armistead, "Glass breaks....Why don't you fix that?"[16] In response, Armistead kicked off a systematic effort to do just that. Calling the effort Project Muscle, Armistead asked his technical directors to investigate all known forms of glass strengthening. The most commonly employed method was the ancient technique of tempering —strengthening glass with heat. A second method was layering glasses that expanded at different rates when exposed to heat. When these glasses would cool, the reasoning went, they would create powerful compressive forces and strengthen the final material. (This process ultimately found use in Corelle Livingware. See Chapters 10 and 11.)

Project Muscle experiments through 1960 and 1961 combined both tempering and layering ultimately leading to a new ultrastrong glass material, which Corning's scientists dubbed Chemcor. Glass treated with the Chemcor process could withstand pressures up to 100,000 pounds per square inch, as compared with 7,000 pounds per square inch for ordinary glass. In one experiment, researchers dropped Chemcor-treated glass tumblers from the top of the Research Center onto steel plate. They remained intact!

By early 1962, Corning seemed yet again to have engineered a material that could prove to be a big hit. But the company lacked a ready application for it, unlike Pyroceram. So Corning took a somewhat unorthodox approach, broadcasting its findings to see if potential customers and partners would propose good ideas. In September 1962, the company's public relations department sent a seventy-two-second film clip to over 200 television stations. That month, Armistead and Amory Houghton Jr. touted the new glass at a press conference at Manhattan's Plaza Hotel. There, the company's scientists demonstrated Chemcor, bending, twisting, and banging panels of specially treated glass. But they emphasized that it was still experimental. "These new strong glasses have been made only in the laboratory," Armistead said. "We expect it will be some time before they are in commercial production."[17]

More than 100 magazine and newspaper articles about Chemcor were written and placed by Corning's public relations department. Meanwhile, George McLellan, Corning's coordinator of technical information, and scientists like Bill Shaver and Don Stookey spread the word through lectures to professional groups. But Chemcor didn't pay the sorts of short-term dividends that Pyroceram had. To be sure, by April 1963, the *Gaffer* reported, the company had fielded 2,000 inquiries about Chemcor and more were arriving at the rate of fifty per week. And within a year of the announcement, Corning had come up with over seventy potential uses for Chemcor, including windows for jails. Bell Telephone considered using glass strengthened by Chemcor for telephone booths, thinking they might be more resistant to vandalism, for example. But comparatively few of these speculative efforts made it into production, and none became a major product line.

The first commercial application of Chemcor came in Centura Ware, a new line of tableware launched by Corning in 1961. Corning's scientists layered Pyroceram with a glass laminate invented by researcher John MacDowell. The dishes were treated with the company's new chemcor process, and hence became ultra-strong. This adjunct to the wildly popular Corning Ware line was backed by an aggressive advertising campaign. Advertisements that

ran in 1963 and 1964 featured a half-ton Holstein bull wandering through a
china and glass shop; when it knocked over the objects lining the shelves, the
Centura Ware remained intact. While it proved a profitable addition to
Corning Ware, Centura Ware never developed the same commercial cachet
that its sister product did. Indeed, it was only after several years and a host of
frustrating, expensive developments that Chemcor would contribute significantly to Corning's bottom line.[18]

Electronics and the Space Age

While the company's rapidly growing consumer business boosted sales and
profits, an array of new products in areas such as electronics and aeronautics helped reinforce Corning's high-tech image. Since the invention of the
transistor at Bell Labs in 1948, scientists labored to develop new, more powerful electronic components and devices. Researchers at Bell Labs and elsewhere made great strides during the 1950s on semiconductors, materials
that possess properties intermediate between a conductor and an insulator,
such as silicon and germanium. By implanting transistors and diodes on
pieces of silicon crystal, researchers reasoned that they could essentially
place an entire integrated electronic circuit on a tiny piece of silicon. In
1959, a Texas-based researcher named Jack Kilby succeeding in doing just
that and received a patent for the integrated circuit—which was to become
an important subset of the semiconductor industry. The same year Robert
Noyce invented a scheme for interconnecting circuit elements that made
the integrated circuit practical. (Noyce would go on to found Intel Corporation several years later.) Throughout the 1960s, researchers would essentially double the number of active elements in a single integrated circuit
every year.

The rise of the integrated circuit was a threat to Corning's long-standing
business in passive electronic components. Mal Hunt, the energetic and
ambitious manager of Corning's electronics business, advocated an aggressive response. First, he convinced the company to move production of electronic components to a new facility. In 1961, the company announced plans
to build a plant to produce electronics products such as resistors and capac-

itors in Raleigh, North Carolina—an area that in the coming decades would grow into a center of technology and science.

But Hunt viewed the establishment of the plant as a beginning. Concerned that the laboratories in Corning lacked a commitment to electronics, he urged his colleagues to set up a research laboratory devoted to electronics in North Carolina. Such a step marked a significant departure. Over the last century, virtually all the major innovations developed by Corning had come out of the growing complex of laboratories in the Chemung Valley. And it was the proximity of physicists, chemists, and engineers bringing their talents to bear on complex problems that had been a hallmark of Corning's history of innovation. But Hunt and his influential allies within Corning, including Amo Houghton, believed that a sharper focus on niche areas of electronics would help the company take advantage of new opportunities. Hunt hired Charles Wakeman, a Ph.D. in electrical engineering, to set up and run the new lab, which would employ about fifty professionals by the mid-1960s.

Hunt also cast his eyes westward. In the early 1960s, dozens of established and newly formed technology companies, many of them clustered in the area southeast of San Francisco subsequently known as Silicon Valley, rushed to capitalize on the growth of semiconductors. They were spurred in large part by support from the U.S. government, which made grants to firms like AT&T, General Electric, RCA, TRW, Raytheon, and Fairchild. By 1962, the semiconductor industry racked up $571 million in sales, with integrated circuits accounting for $4 million.[19]

In 1961, four scientists at Fairchild left the larger firm to start their own semiconductor company, which they dubbed Signetics. Operating out of a small facility in Sunnyvale, California, it had about thirty employees and sales of about $250,000 in its first full year. Its main products were DTL (diode-transistor logic) circuits, which were used in computers. In 1962, spurred by Mal Hunt, Corning became interested in the company. "We were looking for ways to expand the business on a technological basis into electronics, which was rapidly growing at the time," recalled Tom MacAvoy, the chemist who rose to become Corning's president in the early 1970s. "Signetics was a tiny little company, but we thought integrated circuits was the wave of the future." Over the objections of Armistead, Corning acquired

Signetics in November 1962 for a relatively small investment, but one that would prove costly in time.[20]

The purchase of Signetics signaled a belief that Corning's future lay in new geographic areas and in areas that were tangentially related to its glass heritage. As if to further solidify that point, in late 1962, the Crystal City's last large remaining glass cutting shop, T.G. Hawkes, shut down, citing the inability to secure blanks. "Corning's pride no longer rested on its beautiful cut crystal," wrote Corning historians Dimitroff and Janes. "It was dependent upon space capsule windows and television tubes."[21]

Much as the Palomar telescope disc had in the 1930s, Corning's space capsule window business brought negligible revenues but inspired the popular imagination. In response to the 1957 launch of the Soviet satellite Sputnik, the federal government had created the National Aeronautics and Space Administration (NASA) in 1958. Under the leadership of James Webb, NASA worked closely with companies like General Electric to build spacecraft that could orbit the earth and, ultimately, reach the moon. Corning, of course, had a long tradition of supplying materials for various government and military projects, and it was involved with the American space program from the beginning. Still, Corning was never among the top rank of defense contractors. Complications in the Condon affair had underscored the dangers of depending too much on the government. And Corning relished its independence, its connection with commercial markets, and the ability to safeguard its own proprietary technology. Working more closely with the government and military would have undermined each of these values. As a result, Corning remained on the active periphery of the military–industrial complex, filling niche needs instead of becoming a major contractor. For example, it supplied the glass windows for Freedom 7, flown by Alan Shepherd on May 5, 1961, and Friendship 7, the first U.S.-manned orbital flight, flown by John Glenn. In 1963, it made glass panels for the two-man Gemini spacecraft. Each window consisted of three panels. The outside panel, a heat shield, was made of Corning's 96 percent silica glass, which could withstand temperatures up to 1,204C.[22]

Corning successfully leveraged its involvement with the space program to promote other products. On an NBC television program on May 16, 1963,

Corning's George McLellan told an estimated 15 million Americans about the window in Gordon Cooper's Mercury-Atlas 9 spacecraft. That spring, the consumer products division constructed mock Mercury space capsules, complete with rubberized astronaut mannequins, and displayed them in department stores such as J. Wanamaker in Philadelphia and Lazarus in Columbus alongside Corning Ware and Centura Ware.[23]

Television Glass

In the early 1960s, the increasingly pervasive medium of television was playing an important role in Corning's affairs. The company used it to advertise products like Corning Ware and to gain free publicity for products such as Chemcor and the space capsule panels. To a larger degree, the continuing expansion of television was even more integral to Corning's growth. Quite simply, glass for TV tubes had become Corning's major line of business, much as railway signals, Pyrex, and lightbulbs had been in previous generations. In the early 1960s, the profits from these high-volume lines, for which Corning had developed proprietary processes and compositions, helped fuel the company's continuing quest to produce new specialty products. In the early 1960s, as in the late 1950s, it was said that Corning had 125 percent of the market for the bulbs: it was the exclusive supplier for American television manufacturers and supplied an additional 25 percent to replace those broken in the manufacturing process. In a 1963 ranking of Corning's dozen-odd plants by their gross margins, the Albion, Michigan, TV bulb plant ranked first.[24]

Black-and-white television had long been established and was continuing to boom. In 1960, some 5.7 million sets were sold at the retail level, bringing revenues of $746 million. But at the beginning of the decade, color television began to catch on. Retail sales of color televisions rose from 147,000 in 1961 to 400,000 in 1962 to 800,000 in 1963. Corning, which had spent millions of dollars in research throughout the 1950s, first to develop the aperture masks and then to develop effective means of sealing the complicated bulbs, finally began to reap dividends on those investments.[25]

Overseas Thrust

With its aggressive expansion into consumer markets and efforts to associate itself with technology, cultural events, and education, Corning was intent on projecting itself onto a wider stage. A logical extension of this posture was to expand overseas aggressively. The 1960 *Annual Report* featured on its cover a photograph of Amory Sr. shaking hands with a French naval officer. The photo highlights the extent to which Corning viewed itself as a participant in a world economy that was growing more interconnected with every passing year. Of course, Corning had been dealing with foreign customers and strategic partners for decades. By the late 1950s, it had investments in Latin American glass companies, a factory in Canada, and affiliates and licensees in both England and France.

But in the 1960s international expansion reached places where the very idea of capitalism was considered dangerous. In 1959, for example, Arthur Houghton, a veteran of the U.S. intelligence service, was interested in having Corning scientists visit the Soviet Union. "I see nothing for us to lose by such a visit, except a few weeks' time and a few thousand dollars of travel expense. The gain might astonish us," he wrote Amo. In fact, William Belknap, Armistead, and Shaver were planning a trip "'as tourists' the last two or three weeks of May," visiting scientific institutes and manufacturing sites in Moscow, Leningrad, and Kiev.[26]

In 1959, the company decided to bring a greater focus to its foreign ambitions. In an inversion of Amory Sr.'s and Alanson's diplomatic service—the executive as diplomat—Corning decided to turn a career diplomat into an executive. In 1959, the company approached one of America's most distinguished and experienced diplomats: Robert Murphy. Murphy had joined the State Department in 1920 and went on to serve in a variety of posts. He was counselor in the Paris embassy in 1940, when the Nazis invaded and occupied France. During World War II, he served as President Roosevelt's personal representative on a variety of missions. "In Europe, in the Far and Near East, in Washington and at the United Nations, Robert Murphy eventually became America's foremost diplomatic troubleshooter," noted the *Saturday Evening Post*. After the war, he became the first postwar ambassador to Japan in 1952. For much of the 1950s, he served in Washington as a deputy secretary of state, helping put out diplomatic fires in the Suez crisis and Lebanon. In 1959, Murphy, who had come to know Am, was promoted to the third-highest slot in the department, undersecretary for political affairs.[27]

Amory Houghton Sr. believed that Murphy would help spur Corning's international expansion. At his suggestion, in early 1959, Amo, Arthur, and Bill Decker traveled to Washington to talk with the sixty-one-year-old diplomat about joining Corning as head of its international operations. "My ignorance of course is extensive," Murphy wrote to Am in February 1959. "We agreed that I would visit Corning and I am awaiting the moment when I can skip up there," Murphy wrote to Amory Sr. in February. Later that year, he signed on. Just as Lee Waterman had four years before, Murphy came to Corning with little knowledge of glass but with expertise in a discipline that would prove crucial to the company's future growth.[28]

Corning hoped to achieve several goals through international expansion. The first was simply to sell Corning's products in overseas markets. In the 1960s, any new product the company introduced was seen, almost instantly, as one that could be sold abroad as well as in the United States. After its successful U.S. introduction in 1959, for example, Corning Ware debuted abroad the next year. In September 1960, Corning Ware went on sale in the Takashimaya store in Tokyo. The first order sold out in twenty days, thanks largely to Americans stationed in Japan. And in early 1961, Corning Ware went Down Under. A buyer at the David Jones department store in Sydney called it "the biggest thing in housewares ever to hit Australia." CGW Australian sales representative Bryan Padman conducted a fifteen-minute presentation on a Sydney television station. The publicity surrounding Corning Ware helped fuel sales of other Corning consumer products. "We sold two whole carloads of Corning Ware and another two of Pyrex ware to a dealer in Puerto Rico just last month," George J. Wunderlich Jr., manager of sales and operation services, told the *Gaffer* in 1962. "And that's the first time that's happened here."[29]

The second goal was to extend Corning's influence by improving or forging new alliances and joint ventures, or by taking minority stakes in overseas firms. Such actions allowed Corning to leverage its resources while mitigating its risk. As it had done with its Latin American affiliates in the

1940s, Corning sought to supply companies in developing markets with the licenses, technology, or technical assistance necessary to manufacture Corning products. In 1964, Corning acquired a 49-percent stake in Borosil Glass Works, a Bombay, India–based company that made glass ampules and vials for the local pharmaceutical industry. As part of the investment agreement, Glenn Yeakey, a manager at the Bradford, Pennsylvania, plant, was sent over to manage the operation.[30]

The third goal was to set up Corning-owned fabrication facilities in more advanced economies, which would save the expense of shipping finished goods. Corning opened a TV-bulb plant near Sydney, Australia, in 1959. In late 1963, Corning announced the formation of a subsidiary in the Netherlands to make heat-proof glass ceramic cookware. Corning, Nederlandse Fabrieken N.V., the company's first wholly owned production facility in Europe, was based in Groningen and would market its products under the trademark Pyroflam. Through this range of expanding international activities Corning sought to boost its sales. In 1961, international sales accounted for less than 10 percent of overall sales. Over the course of the decade, international sales would grow at a 25 percent compounded rate.[31]

Imposing Discipline on Growth

Corning's rapid expansion in the early 1960s—in breadth, geographical scope, and product lines—posed new challenges to the company's top executives. To be sure, sales increased 44 percent between 1959 and 1963, a gratifyingly rapid pace. But the growth, in and of itself, was not wholly satisfying. The breakneck expansion meant that Corning was operating factories in many different locales and plowing millions of dollars into activities as diverse as fundamental research in Corning, national advertising for Corning Ware, and a new plant in the Netherlands. The introduction of Corning Ware and its affiliated products, including Centura Ware, required a rapid expansion in the size and depth of the company's sales operation.

Corning's scientists and managers had long mastered the demands of highly disciplined management of research and production processes. But in the general management of the company, Corning's executives had always favored a more informal, less rigid style. This had its advantages, particularly in making workers and managers feel a part of a coherent whole and encouraging communication and innovation. But there were periods in which Corning's financial controls and management lacked the rigor demonstrated by its research units. In a 1963 inventory of costs, for example, Decker found, to his dismay, that overall selling expenses rose 17.8 percent in 1962, to $22.1 million, or 8.5 percent of sales, up from 4.7 percent of sales in 1956. "I was amazed to learn from these figures that we are paying $332,000 annually for professional services in the sales departments."[32]

More troubling than such expenses was an apparent decline in return on equity after taxes. Between 1953 and 1962, the average return was 20.2 percent per year, Decker noted in a March 1963 memo. This was a strong performance, but the end of the period showed worrying signs of a dropoff: between 1958 and 1962 the average was 19 percent per year. Analyzing the decline, Decker found that sales of the consumer products division, which had higher selling expenses than other units, had increased relative to other sales. In response, he recommended that each division reduce its percent selling costs to below those in the 1963 budgets. On a broader level, he proposed controlling costs better by setting new standards for approving appropriation requests and establishing new standards for appraising the performance of operating divisions and plants.[33]

In other areas, controls seemed to have loosened. In 1962, over 90 percent of the newly hired staffers paid by the month (whose numbers grew 22 percent between 1961 and 1963) were started at salaries above scheduled rates on the basis of previous experience. Almost 30 percent were over thirty years of age, and only 30 percent came directly from college, compared with 46 percent for the company's 1959 monthly hires. "We must reverse this trend," personnel executive J. W. Fiske wrote. He suggested as a goal that 50 percent of 1963 hires be under twenty-five and that no more than 30 percent be hired above starting rates due to prior experience.[34]

Corning was running up against what had long been an informal management style. For the works was in some ways still very much a small-town company. "You not only work, but you play with your personnel," Decker told *Forbes* in 1962. "I play golf with some of our union guys." Indeed, Corning's very informality was appealing to many new employees.

In 1962, Roger Ackerman, a young engineer, was pursuing job opportunities at both Corning and General Electric. He had been put off by the atmosphere at GE, where he was not allowed to use an executive men's room on a visit. "At GE, everything was 'Mr. This, Mr. That,'" he recalled. Corning offered a marked contrast. "I got up here and it was totally informal... Everything was first name, the Chairman rode around in a Volkswagen Bug. Everything was 'Amo.'...There was no 'Mr. This, Mr. That.'"[35]

But Corning management was growing inexorably more formal and scientific, and some of the new arrivals began to bring a greater level of focus. Lee Waterman, for example, "started to professionalize strategic planning," recalled Tom MacAvoy. "We didn't do strategic planning before he came. Nobody did before about 1962 or 1963, except on the back of an envelope." Amo, Jamie, and an increasing number of executives had attended the Harvard Business School. And Amo began to instill the best practices learned at Cambridge in the company's Corning offices. "A unique program is the holding of monthly policy meetings," *Forbes* reported. "The first of each month's series is held in the president's office and, with one weeks' time, meetings have broadened to reach all supervisors including those in all domestic plants."[36]

In addition, top executives began meeting once a month, either at the Glass Center Club or elsewhere in Corning. Frequently, they would listen to presentations by company executives or guest speakers, like management guru Peter Drucker, GTE chairman Donald C. Power, or Douglas McGregor, a human relations expert from MIT. These Skytop luncheons were somewhat akin to pep rallies and were frequently followed by pointed memos from Amo. In an April 1963 "follow up on the theme of greater efficiency in the conduct of our business" he noted that while the company's sales had grown by $5.7 million in the first quarter of 1963, its profit margin had slipped from 11.2 percent to 10.5 percent. If the company were to meet its budgetary goals, "we must get the most out of the resources at our disposal. This means efficiency in operating, as well as effectiveness in gaining growth dollars."[37]

Even as it listened to management experts and developed new procedures, Corning continued to adhere to many of its homegrown, time-honored traditions, such as the annual service dinner. The company's 113th anniversary service dinner in 1964 was turned into a testimonial to Amory

Houghton Sr., who was retiring from active service after more than four decades at the company. To accommodate the 4,000 people who wanted to attend, Corning erected a tent at the municipal stadium. Decker spoke of the company's accomplishments during the ambassador's thirty-four years as chief executive or chairman: sales had risen from $9 million in 1930 to $289 million in 1964 while employment had risen tenfold to 18,000. Richard M. McElligton, the employee with the longest service record, presented Amory Sr. with a wooden toolbox, a traditional gift given by tradesmen to honor retiring master craftsmen. Clark Johnson, the president of AFGWU Local 1000, gave him an engraved Steuben vase and a letter. "You became a part of us and won the respect of every worker when you started your career with Corning Glass Works as a crack-off boy in A factory long before there was a union," it read. "Perhaps that gave you a better insight into the problems which the average worker faces and may have had some bearing on making you the thoughtful and considerate employer you have always been." Amory Sr. was momentarily overwhelmed and wiped tears from his eyes several times. "It is hard for one as choked with emotion as I am to make adequate reply," he said.[38]

The ambassador's retirement proved an active one, as he and Laura divided their time between residences in Corning, New York City, and California. They worked to maintain ties with their large family and network of friends, which included former president Dwight Eisenhower and his wife, Mamie. They exchanged visits in Corning and in Gettysburg, Pennsylvania, and engaged in Eisenhower's favorite leisure activity: golf. In 1965, an ailing Eisenhower sent a bow tie to Amory Sr., who promised he would wear it on their next trip to Augusta National Golf Club in Georgia. "I hope your progress continues so that you and I can play a game of golf when I am in the desert in March." By "the desert," he meant Palm Desert in California. In 1966, he and Laura built a house at the El Dorado Country Club, a private golfing community of 500 members that was referred to as "the Taj Mahal of the West." (The Eisenhowers were members as well.) That year, the Houghtons presented Ike and Mamie with a Steuben heart and gold key for their golden anniversary.[39]

Amory Sr.'s retirement dinner was the most visible single act of the larger drama that had played out at the company over the years: the changing of the guard. In 1964, William Decker formally retired after thirty-four years with the company. Amo was named board chairman and chief executive officer—a post he would hold for more than twenty years—and Lee Waterman was elevated to president. In the early 1960s, many of the scientists and executives who had been instrumental to the company's growth in the early and middle decades of the twentieth century retired or passed away. In 1960, both Hanford Curtiss and Arthur Day died. On May 12, 1962, Eugene Sullivan died at Corning Hospital after a short illness, at the age of ninety. The indomitable Frederick Carder celebrated his hundredth birthday on September 18, 1963, at a Rotary Club luncheon at which the mayor of Corning proclaimed Frederick Carder Day. He died in his sleep on December 18 and was buried in the Hope Cemetery Annex. "A part of Corning died last night," the *Corning Leader* wrote. "Mr. Carder lived as complete and meaningful a life as one could hope for," Amo said. Though Carder was a "distinguished citizen, a contributor to higher educational standards and a gifted artist," he continued, "I never thought of him solely in these terms. He was an ever-present legend, spanning almost five generations of glassmen—their designs and their technical skills."[40]

The passing of such figures was particularly poignant given that the company continued to rely on their innovations. In 1965, for example, the company marked the fiftieth anniversary of Pyrex, still a popular product. The 1965 *Annual Report* noted how much things had changed since the introduction of Pyrex. Back in 1915, the works had a single plant in Corning and sold mainly railroad signalware, lightbulb blanks, and glass tubing. "Today, in contrast, the company produces 43,000 different products in thirty-seven manufacturing plants located in fourteen states and three foreign countries. In addition, overseas associations have been formed with glassmaking companies in eight countries around the world."[41]

Indeed, Corning's international operations were already assuming greater importance. At the annual anniversary dinner in 1965, Amo spoke in a banquet hall festooned with flags from foreign countries. "Over 1,000 jobs in Corning Glass Works today are completely dependent on production of products for sale overseas," he said. He noted that Corning was exporting to eighty-six nations and was introducing its Corning Ware line abroad at the rate of one new country every ninety days.[42]

As a sign of the importance of the company's international operations, it became apparent that the next generation of Corning's management would need experience in the foreign arena. So in 1965, after having served as a financial analyst in the controller's division, twenty-nine-year-old Jamie Houghton went abroad. He was named vice president of the European area of the international division and moved to Zurich with his wife, Maisie, and their son, James.[43]

The Search for the New

While Corning deployed its executives and salespeople around the nation and the world in search of new markets and customers, the scientists in Sullivan Park pursued with equal vigor another activity for which Corning had long been known: basic research. In search of the next product or process that would boost the company's sales and efficiency, Corning continued to plow resources into its research efforts. In many ways, the 1960s proved to be a golden age for research at Corning. Scientists were given wide latitude and substantial resources, and they were encouraged to pursue their interest—regardless of the immediacy of a financial payback.

Scientists continued to find Corning, which *Dun's Review* dubbed "the acknowledged worldwide leader in glass research," a congenial and encouraging place to work. George Beall arrived in Corning 1962 and began working under Don Stookey on ways to make glass ceramics completely transparent. When he finally did so in 1966, Corning decided not to introduce the new product for fear it would cannibalize Pyrex sales. (The transparent glass ceramics would ultimately be introduced in France in the late 1970s under the trade name Visions.) Still, the effort was not deemed a failure. As Beall recalls, "That was the climate at the time. You should do some exploratory work. 'What ideas do you have?'"[44]

The sentiment was backed by financial resources. R&D spending was $18.3 million in 1946 and $19.9 million in 1965. This came at a time when research was enjoying a growth spurt generally in corporate America. In 1955, the United States spent $6.2 billion, or 1.6 percent of total gross national product (GNP), on research, with the government supplying about half of the funds. In the late 1950s, the percentage grew every year until 1964, when total spending was $18.9 billion, or 3 percent of GNP, with the government accounting for $14.7 billion of the total. In addition, Corning continued to build better facilities for its researchers at Sullivan Park. In 1963, work began on two new structures, a one-story rectangular development building and the fundamental research building, twin six-story towers that were completed in the spring of 1965. The company's growing labs tested 200 different kinds of glass a week and had compiled files on nearly 125,000 discrete glass formulas. As Amo proudly told *Dun's Review*, "R&D is our fastest growing activity."[45]

Apart from financial and logistical support, Corning's executives provided their scientists with emotional support, on occasion treating them like temperamental artists. Donald Stookey had a remarkably productive career at Corning. His most notable contribution was his development in the late 1950s and early 1960s of photochromic glass—glass that darkened during exposure to light at ambient temperatures. Several months after presenting his breakthroughs at the January 1964 of the American Physical Society, the fifty-year-old scientist was feeling low. "I ran out of research ideas and into a period of depression, feeling that I had nothing more to contribute," he later wrote. In addition, some personnel changes made him feel like "a has-been," and he tried to resign. His boss sent him to talk to Amo and Amory Sr. "All three were more sympathetic and complimentary to me than I deserved, and the upshot was that instead of resigning or being fired, I was given a paid leave of absence for a year." Stookey and his wife, Ruth, traveled for a year and cruised on his thirty-eight-foot motor cabin cruiser down the Atlantic coast. "That year really refreshed me in body, mind, and spirit. I came back to Corning eager to work and full of ideas," he recalled.[46]

The company could afford to be generous because of its extraordinary prosperity. "Everything was growing like mad, and we thought we were causing it," MacAvoy recalled. The television business in particular "was just raining money out of the sky." Retail sales of black-and-white and color televisions continued to boom. In 1965, when the new television plant at Bluffton, Indiana, opened, 8.4 million black-and-white and 2.7 million color televisions were produced in the United States, with Corning supplying virtually all the bulbs. Corning's television business was also growing overseas. In 1966, Corning constructed majority-owned television bulb facilities in Brazil and in Mexico, where it set up a new subsidiary: Productos Corning de Mexico. That year, aside from starting construction of a new plant in Canton, New York, Corning expanded its color television plants at Albion and Bluffton. By the end of 1966, fifty-one manufacturing plants were in operation or under construction, practically double the figure from 1959. Sales for 1966 rose a stunning 30 percent, to $444 million, and profits rose 40 percent, to $54 million.[47]

But there was a recognition that relying on television too much was unhealthy. And that was part of what fueled the growing investment in research. "We were very conscious of the idea that the real driving financial power of the corporation derived from a relatively short list of what I would call 'home runs,'" recalled MacAvoy, then the head of the technical products division. This lengthy list included lightbulbs, the Ribbon Machine, fiberglass, silicones, and Corning Ware. Consequently, executives were particularly interested in the efforts of the scientists at Sullivan Park. "Amo had a million ideas. If anyone came in with a good one, bang, he'd want to start working on it," said MacAvoy. It was this climate that led to the origins of products that would pay rewards in decades to come, such as fiber optics.[48]

Over the next five years, however, Corning would encounter an occasionally bewildering series of circumstances. While the scientists at Sullivan Park continued to make substantial breakthroughs in areas ranging from fiber optics to glass ceramics, the company would have difficulty parlaying them into profitable new lines of business. In addition, as the optimism so evident in the early 1960s gave way to the doubts of the turbulent late 1960s, Corning would face some fundamental challenges to its most established product lines. After a century of nearly continuous growth and breakthroughs, Corning Glass Works seemed to hit a wall.

CHAPTER TEN

International Growth and the Roots of Fiber Optics, 1966–1971

As THE TURBULENT 1960s wore on, many of the pillars undergirding American optimism began to erode. For the nation as well as the company, the years between 1966 and 1971 were full of frustration and turmoil. To a large degree, Corning and the other small towns that housed its factories were far removed from the unrest that rattled college campuses and inner-city neighborhoods. Still, as a company that took its corporate citizenship seriously and as a large, diversified manufacturer, Corning was deeply affected by the economic and social upheavals of the late 1960s—so much so that the ability of this large and established firm to continue to grow in its established markets came into question. Although Corning's researchers continued to churn out new discoveries that led to commercial products such as Corelle Livingware, each technical achievement seemed to be offset by an equivalent frustration. Several breakthroughs that appeared to have the potential to be big hits failed to bear fruit, and one of the company's longstanding jewels—its television business—suffered serious setbacks. As a result, between 1966 and 1971, sales would rise just 36 percent and, more troublingly, profits would fall 31 percent.

The Promise of Fiber Optics

The term "fiber optics" was coined in 1956 to refer to a class of products that used optical glass drawn in thin strands to transmit electrical impulses and light. In the early 1960s, when Corning began to look into them, fiber optics were being used as intensifiers in cathode ray tubes, computer circuitry, and high-speed printing, and in syringes that allowed doctors to view human tissue. When Corning conducted a study on fiber optics in 1965, it found that "more than 150 companies are doing work in this area." Competitors included small firms like Mosaic Fabrications, Inc., and large ones like Bausch & Lomb. In 1965, Corning was selling fiber optics for certain technical uses, although they constituted less than 1 percent of total sales.[1]

But it was a different use for fiber optics—as optical waveguides—that truly piqued the interest of Corning's scientists in the mid-1960s. In 1965, the British ministry of defense and the British post office began looking into technologies to forge a new communications infrastructure. They were concerned that the copper cable employed to carry voice traffic would eventually become outmoded and that it would be difficult to install more copper cable under the streets of Britain's densely populated cities. One solution would be to figure out a way to transmit voice via light beams. After all, cable composed of light pipes could carry a far greater volume of voice traffic than copper cable of a similar size. The logical material for such light pipes was glass.[2]

As early as 1880, Alexander Graham Bell, the father of telephony, harnessed light waves to send voice traffic by focusing sunlight with a mirror and then talking into a mechanism that made the mirror vibrate. A detector attached to another mirror picked up the beam and translated it into voice, just as a phone did with electricity. "I have heard articulate speech produced by sunlight," Bell wrote in his notebooks. "I have heard a ray of the sun laugh and cough and sing."[3]

Of course, the sun was an unreliable source of light. If light could really carry voices, scientists would need a highly focused beam of light that would maintain its intensity—like a laser beam. In 1960, Theodore Maiman demonstrated a working laser that could not only form but also modulate narrow beams of light. In the early and mid-1960s, Corning funded fundamental research on lasers at Sullivan Park, hoping that it would lead to commercial applications. By 1966, it hadn't. "The laser work led to nothing—no business," recalled Tom MacAvoy, head of the technical products division. "But the result was that we had about twenty people who understood quantum optics. We really understood it."[4]

In 1965, officials at the post office, who were familiar with Corning's British subsidiary, Electrosil, met with Corning researcher William Shaver to discuss possible areas of cooperation. Shaver ultimately invited his colleagues Gail Smith and physicist Robert Maurer to take part in the discussions. An Arkansas native who had degrees in physics from the University of Arkansas and MIT, Maurer had joined the company in 1952 and worked in optics alongside Stookey. Maurer had been a member of the team that developed fused-silica delay lines and investigated the phenomenon of light scattering. In 1964, his supervisor, Tom MacAvoy, called him "one of the best fundamental scientists employed by Corning." But he was also a manager, supervising fundamental physics research from 1963 to 1970. Maurer brought the idea to Bill Armistead, who approved the necessary capital to investigate optical waveguides. Although it was highly speculative, Armistead realized that the research project held a great deal of potential, and in some ways it seemed uniquely suited to Corning's capabilities. After all, spinning fiber-optic cable that could carry voice data effectively would require the talents of glass physicists, glass chemists, and engineers. And if the company could develop a product quickly, it could have a remarkably lucrative new global line of business to itself. In short, fiber optics had the potential to be the ultimate big hit.

There was something of a race to develop fiber optics, since Bell Labs and several companies in Europe and Australia were working on the same problem. Maurer quickly enlisted two colleagues in the effort: Pete Schultz, a Corning senior scientist hired from Rutgers University six months before, who specialized in creating new formulas for glass, and Donald Keck, an engineer and physicist who had recently joined Corning from Michigan

State University. They quickly devised a division of labor. Maurer worked on the physics, Schultz relied on his knowledge of chemistry to come up with different types of glass, and Keck used his expertise to draw the batch into a fine fiber.[5]

Corning's scientists faced daunting obstacles in devising a method of carrying voice by light. They would have to construct glass that was so clear that a sufficient amount of light could travel through it for up to a kilometer—the standard length of copper wire segments in telephone lines—without diffusing entirely. (At the time, the longest optical waveguides in use were about six inches.) The light pulse grew sufficiently weak (measured in decibels) over the distance that it needed to be amplified. They didn't need all the light from a concentrated laser beam to pulse through that distance. Rather, they concluded that if just 1 percent of a laser beam's light emerged from a kilometer-long pipe, that would be a sufficient amount to amplify and start the process all over again. A 1966 paper by two ITT scientists, M. C. Kao and G. A. Hockham, suggested that the light-carrying capability of glass would have to be improved to twenty decibels per kilometer—many millions of times the capability of existing fibers.[6]

Initial efforts to draw light-carrying fibers were discouraging. Keck devised an apparatus to measure the purity of the fiber they had made. It held a meter-long piece of fiber and aimed a laser beam from one end to a gauge at the other end. Keck then wrote a formula to extrapolate the results out to a kilometer. At first, the experiments fell remarkably short of the goal, with truly negligible amounts of light coming through.

The problem they faced was at once simple and complex. The tube couldn't be made of a single kind of glass. If the glass were uniform, the light would diffuse. Instead, the scientists quickly realized that the tube would have to consist of a glass core through which the light would travel and a glass skin—or cladding—that would reflect the light back into the core. Furthermore, the core would have to be as pure as possible, since any impurities in glass would absorb the light. Corning did have a remarkably pure glass it could use for the core—96 percent fused silica, which it had been making since the 1930s. But this material posed a few problems. Its melting level was 2,000°C, a temperature at which it was very difficult to spin fibers. A second problem was even more serious. The glass used for the cladding would have to possess a *lower* refractive index than that of the core, so the light would bounce back and remain in the pipe without diffusing. But fused silica had the lowest known refractive index. If it were to be used for the core, what composition should serve for the cladding?[7]

Confronted with such a dilemma, Maurer, in a counterintuitive move, decided to start with fused silica as a substance for the cladding, not the core. Now he needed a core glass that would have a *higher* refractive index. Optical glass fit the bill, but combining the two would be difficult in the manufacturing process. Instead, Maurer decided to mix chemicals into the core fused silica to increase its refractive index—in effect to make the purest possible glass somewhat less pure.[8]

The scientists next faced the challenge of how to spin the two glasses into fiber. The usual way of doing so was to create a large rod of core glass, and surround it with a sheath of cladding "like a bun around a hot dog," as authors Ira Magaziner and Mark Patinkin put it. The two pieces of glass would be held vertically in a furnace, and, as the heat rose, workers could stretch the melted end into a thin fiber. When the team tried this method on its new materials, air bubbles formed where the two masses of molten glass came together. Frustrated, they turned to other disciplines. "If all you do is think about what the industry's doing, you're locked in mentally," Maurer told Schultz and Keck.

Keck reasoned that if they got rid of the core and started with a hollow tube of cladding, they could sputter the glass on the inside until it formed the core. (When IBM coated its silicon chips, it used a technique called sputtering.) Schultz suggested a variation—spraying the inside of the tube with vaporized core glass. This process of "vapor deposition," pioneered by silicones inventor Franklin Hyde in the 1930s, would seal adequately without bubbles and allow for a thin core. Moreover, and perhaps more importantly, it would give Corning a patented manufacturing process. That would prevent other competitors from entering the field. The scientists began to experiment with the technique, but a breakthrough was still well off in the distance. They began to use many different formulas to make core glass and continually altered the many variables, raising the temperature and changing the cooking time. Every twelve months, Maurer presented his group's findings and argued for continued support, which Armistead steadfastly offered. By the end of 1967, the team was still reporting huge decibel losses. And the ambitious effort to send voice by light still seemed a fanciful dream.[9]

Getting through the 1960s

The Viet Cong's Tet offensive, launched at the beginning of 1968, set off shock waves that reverberated from Southeast Asia to the United States. The surprise attack opened a tumultuous year that would see the assassination of both Martin Luther King Jr. and Robert Kennedy, riots in America's inner cities, and student uprisings across the United States and Europe; the year closed with the launching of the moon-bound Apollo 11. In Corning, the year marked a milestone of a more peaceful sort—the twenty-fifth anniversary of the company's accommodation with the American Flint Glass Workers Union. Throughout the 1960s, the company generally enjoyed labor peace. George Parker, the national president of the Flints from 1961 through the 1980s, and Amo Houghton maintained an excellent and warm working relationship. And Corning's unionized workforce enjoyed a rising standard of living. The union reported that its members' average take-home pay in 1968 was $7,500, with eight paid holidays a year, four weeks' vacation, and a paid hospital and surgical health policy. Moreover, the Flints calculated that since 1943, its members had gained, on average, $5,775 in wages and fringe benefits—an increase of more than 270 percent.[10]

In the fall of 1968, the company also marked the centennial anniversary of the first glass melt in Corning by Amory Houghton. Looking back on the family enterprise's century in Corning, Amo believed the Houghtons should make some gesture to commemorate the event. "Most members of our family now live elsewhere, despite the fact that many were born in Corning, received their early education here, and continue to derive a substantial part of their income from the efforts of hundreds of men and women who live in and around Corning," he wrote Arthur Houghton on September 30, 1968. "Since this is the Centennial Year...may I be presumptuous for a minute and suggest that in this of all years, as we citizens struggle to improve the appearance of this community and attempt to give it new life, we as a family consider a significant gift to the city."[11]

By then, the Houghtons and the Glass Works were already involved in the "struggle to improve the appearance of this community." Indeed, one of the buzzwords of the 1960s was "urban renewal"—government-funded efforts to reconstruct blighted urban areas such as the Manhattan neighborhood that became Lincoln Center. As a small town of about 20,000 residents, Corning was not typically regarded as a candidate for urban renewal. But in the mid-1960s, the Glass Works became involved in efforts to revitalize Corning's business district and develop middle-income housing. In the earlier part of the decade, Corning's most prominent social contributions involved projects with national visibility, like Lincoln Center and the Corning Conference. In the latter half of the decade, however, the focus returned to upstate New York. As Amo put it in a radio interview, "Corning Glass Works is a country company, not a city company, and as a result we must concentrate our efforts where we are already established, which is primarily Corning, New York." In the mid-1960s the Glass Works established a community projects department under the direction of William Belknap. Even as it consistently sought out new markets and a wider stage, the company continued to focus its attention on its rural home base.[12]

The challenge for the company was to be helpful without appearing overly paternalistic. So it chose a sort of third way between charity and direct action. In an effort to improve the housing stock for Corning employees, for example, Corning in 1966 helped set up the Three Rivers Development Corporation (TRDC). TRDC raised money, acquired options on over 600 acres of land on U.S. Route 15 South near Sullivan Park and by June 1967 had completed some 200 units in the Spring Pond apartment complex, which was intended for middle-income workers.[13]

A second concern was the downtown area. By the 1960s, most of the area's residential and commercial development was taking place further and further from the historic core of Market Street—a process common in cities and towns of all sizes during this period. As a result, the century-old downtown area was withering. "Market Street is a mess," a Corning executive reported in a 1966 memo. "It has deteriorated for the past quarter of a century. Its buildings grow older and more dilapidated. Its merchants are dis-

couraged. It is beginning to look like, and to be, a slum." The writer realized it was fruitless to try to battle the long-standing development trends.
Instead, he proposed "that the entire Market Street area of Corning, New
York, be razed under Slum Clearance or other enabling legislation, and
rebuilt as a great pedestrian plaza" with office buildings, a municipal building, a library, and a hotel. Such a drastic and far-reaching solution did not
take place. However, in the coming decade the works would be intimately
involved in a series of projects that brought a new hotel, library, grocery
superstore, and other developments to the area around Market Street.[14]

A third set of concerns revolved around more generic issues of Corning's quality of life, which directly affected the company's ability to recruit
workers, including scientists, executives, and laborers. In the next decade,
company planners predicted that they would need to hire some 7,500 new
employees. "If we can't hire and keep, we're sunk," Belknap wrote in July
1967. As a result, he recommended that Corning not shrink from investing
money in a series of developments. He enumerated a list that included
Spring Pond, which Corning backed with a $1 million loan, a new library
($250,000), $1 million for various recreational facilities, and a contribution to
reduce $250,000 in debt for the health center. In all, area leaders had pro-
posed public and private projects worth $39 million over six years. And the
company would be on the hook for about $9 million of that total. "Seems
staggering!!" Belknap wrote. "But...so was the $10+ million tied up in Color
TV for 10 years. It paid off handsomely. THIS WILL TOO!"[15]

The Houghton family and the company also continued to participate in
social and political affairs outside of the Chemung Valley. In March 1967,
Vice President Hubert Humphrey wrote Amo thanking him for participat-
ing in the "closed circuit telecast which launched the 1967 Share in Freedom
Savings Bond Campaign." In a letter to Frank Wheaton of Wheaton Glass,
Amo defended his role in such projects. "I know how you can get 'fed up'
with the socialized state. You're not different from the rest of us. However,
the sale of 'E' bonds, I believe as a staunch Republican, is important to our
national security—currency, that is."[16]

In 1968, Frank Wheaton wasn't the only person reconsidering long-held
positions. While Amo remained a "staunch Republican," there were signs of
a crack in the family's GOP facade. "It is true that I am doing what I can to

help the Humphrey-Muskie ticket," Arthur Houghton Jr. admitted to Sidney Weinberg in the midst of the 1968 presidential campaign. "I have already made substantial contributions, through various committees, and shall do more if I can. As a Republican, I am supporting many candidates on the lesser levels, but I find the top of the ticket—Nixon and Agnew—indigestible."[17]

Race was one of the overriding issues of the 1960s, as the civil rights movement welled up from the South to break down segregation in educational institutions and public accommodations. As northeastern Republican moderates—prototypical Rockefeller Republicans—the Houghtons and their circle were progressive on this issue. In the 1960s, for example, the Corning Glass Works Foundation made substantial grants to the United Negro College Fund. Perhaps more importantly, the works made efforts to recruit more African Americans into the ranks of managers. In 1965, President Johnson issued an executive order that required corporations doing business with the U.S. government—the nation's largest buyer of goods and services—to set up affirmative action compliance programs. Corning responded with its first affirmative action program in 1968 and set its first goals for minority hiring in 1969, when there were sixteen blacks on the monthly salaried payroll. For each of the next several years Corning would double the number of blacks it hired, bringing the total number on the monthly salaried payroll to sixty-four in 1972. In addition, the company set up a community relations services unit, which was run by a black employee, Charles McGrady, out of an office at 65 East Market Street. In 1968, McGrady was given a year-long leave of absence to work in the Corning community on social problems.[18]

The problems that small-town Corning faced in 1968 were relatively tame, compared with the riots in places like Washington, D.C., Chicago, and Watts. Although the violence that punctuated the year remained at a far remove in 1968, the industrial and economic upheavals of the late 1960s began to penetrate the Chemung Valley.

A Retreat and Several Sallies

In previous generations, Corning had been forced to come to grips with the rapid maturation of products spawned by its proprietary breakthroughs.

And just as sales of Pyrex leveled off in the 1920s, Corning now confronted limited growth in core areas like Corning Ware and television. In the 1960s, revitalized and efficient Japanese producers, having finally rebuilt from the devastation of World War II, took advantage of America's comparatively low trade barriers and exported goods in growing volume. The penetration of Japanese television companies like Sony began to pick up the pace in the latter half of the decade. In 1965, Japanese firms had a 16-percent share of the U.S. black-and-white television market. That percentage increased every year in the latter half of the 1960s and ultimately caused serious trouble for Corning's single largest business.[19]

Ironically, Corning had helped establish the Japanese television industry. In the 1950s, when Asahi Glass inquired about starting a joint venture to manufacture television bulbs in Japan, Corning begged off and instead agreed to license its bulb-making technology to the Japanese firm. This decision ultimately deprived Corning of the ability to learn from its Japanese competitors. As future senior vice president—international Robert Turissini later put it, "We took the no-risk route in Japan" by licensing technology to Asahi "and by doing that we lost the knowledge we could have had of doing business in Japan directly when that knowledge would have done us some good." Asahi quickly developed its own expertise and was able to improve on Corning's processes. "Asahi was much more thorough about controlling the [manufacturing] process than we were," said Forrest Behm, president of Corning's international operations. "Although we had a few major breakthroughs, after a few years they were far ahead of us....We would work on the major breakthrough, and then resist any further changes to the process, whereas you could see them using our major breakthrough and adding constant improvements."[20]

During the mid- and late 1960s, with each passing year, Japanese television producers—who were supported by favorable government policies, operated in a well-protected market, and bought glass bulbs from a flourishing domestic industry—garnered a greater share of trade in the United States. Largely as a result of problems in the TV-bulb business, Corning's sales rose an anemic 3 percent to $455 million in 1967 as its net income fell 10 percent—the first time profits had fallen since 1960. That year, Corning's television sales were $128.7 million, 29.5 percent of the company's overall sales.

"In 1967, television volume was disappointing, particularly black-and-white bulbs," the *Annual Report* concluded. In 1968, market share of Japanese imports soared to 29 percent, nearly double the 1965 figure. Meanwhile, sales of Corning's TV bulbs fell to $125 million, or 27.5 percent of overall sales, and planners were projecting a further slump to about $115 million in 1969. In 1968, the company's overall sales rose 5 percent while profits slipped another 6 percent, to $46.7 million.[21]

Television wasn't the only problem. For several years, consultants had warned Corning that glass was a maturing technology with limited prospects for growth. And even though Corning's annual sales were approaching the half-billion mark, it was apparent that the company's existing products could only provide about half the expected 10 percent annual rate of sales increase. For the first time since the Great Depression, Corning was confronting serious obstacles to its century-long record of growth.

Corning wasn't alone in facing this challenge. Large American industrial companies operating in mature industries were grappling with the problems posed by a cooling stock market, a slowing economy, and the law of large numbers. Many companies sought to ensure continued growth by acquiring other companies, frequently in areas that were only tangentially related to their core businesses. Indeed, the 1960s witnessed a powerful wave of conglomeration as companies like ITT, Textron, and Gulf + Western purchased literally hundreds of smaller firms—sometimes indiscriminately.

Corning bucked this trend intentionally. "My belief is that corporate acquisitions can be extremely valuable when they hasten the logical extension and development of the company's business," Arthur Houghton wrote Amo in 1967. Examples would include a glass company in a country that Corning had yet to enter or a domestic producer of consumer products that would closely supplement existing consumer lines. "I would refrain from corporate acquisitions that are not related to our present or future business."[22] Bill Armistead echoed this view and even looked askance at Signetics because he believed its business was too far removed from Corning's.

Eschewing large-scale acquisitions for the moment, Corning sought growth through two areas that had brought it growth earlier in the decade: consumer goods and international. In 1967, consumer goods accounted for

$107 million in sales, nearly a quarter of Corning's overall revenues, and in eight years, Corning Ware had grown into a formidable line. By 1965, it was the largest single line of housewares on the market, and an integral part of the nation's consumer culture. A 1967 survey showed that 71 percent of all brides received Corning Ware cookware as wedding gifts, with an average take of five pieces. Indeed, that year an episode bore testimony to the product's durability. On January 16, 1967, just before the opening of the National Housewares Show in Chicago, a devastating fire tore through the convention hall, McCormick Place. The fire destroyed dozens of exhibits, caused some $150 million in damage, killed one person, and caused dozens of injuries. Wading through the rubble, Corning employees retrieved seventy-seven pieces of largely unblemished Corning Ware. Corning decided against publicizing this fact until 1971.[23]

In the late 1960s, however, the bloom had come off Corning Ware's rose. Like its experience with strengthened railroad lenses of the 1900s and with Pyrex in the 1920s, Corning found that producing glass products that resist breakage can reduce the potential for repeat business. Nearly a decade after the launch of Corning Ware, the company realized it would have to develop new consumer products to drive growth.

This time, it would fall to Jamie Houghton to roll out new products and manage existing lines. Jamie returned from Europe in 1968 as general manager of the Consumer Products Division and was elected vice president of Corning. (The following year he ascended to the board of directors.) His mandate was to boost sales, expand the lines of Corning Ware and Centura, and find new products to introduce. He brought a gung-ho enthusiasm to the task, proclaiming in an address to plant managers in 1968, "We're going to be the Saviors of the Company in 1969....We're going to make so damn much money they won't know what to do with it!"[24]

By the mid-1960s, Corning had figured out how to make large sheets of Pyroceram. And it reasoned it could make an entire stove top, "The Counter That Cooks," out of the product that would conduct heat and eliminate the need for burners. In 1965 it tested the product in ten households in the Corning area and employed a research psychologist to gauge people's feelings about it. After a test launch in Rochester in 1966, Corning rolled out The Counter That Cooks in the summer of 1968, with seventy distributors covering forty-six states and the District of Columbia pitching it in June 1968. In 1968, fueled in part by early favorable reception of The Counter That Cooks, consumer goods sales rose nearly 15 percent to $123 million. This in a year when Corning's overall sales rose just 5 percent.[25]

Consumer goods were also helping to spearhead growth in a second growth area: the international arena. In the fall of 1967, Corning Ware was rolled out in South America, Peru, and Venezuela. At the same time, Corning was conducting market tests of the product in Africa, the Near East, and Asia. "If the tests go well, Corning Ware products will be selling on six of the seven continents," the *Gaffer* reported. "That leaves Antarctica—but the market there is discouragingly small." Indeed, Corning was becoming a true multinational company in the late 1960s. By 1967, 14.3 percent of the company's sales came from outside the United States, up from 10 percent earlier in the decade. That figure would increase dramatically in each of the next three years, so that by 1970 some 27.4 percent of sales would come from outside the United States.[26]

Having made headway throughout Western Europe, Robert Murphy and his colleagues, including Forrest Behm, president of Corning's international operations, and Pierre Roederer, the area manager for Europe, began applying their diplomatic skills to push behind the Iron Curtain. On July 27, 1967, a Romanian delegation visited Corning. The American executives were appropriately suspicious. "There will be no plant visits," Amo told Behm. Ultimately, however, they struck a deal. Corning agreed to help the Romanians set up a factory to make black-and-white television bulbs, and General Electric would supply the electronics technology. The Romanian government would pay Corning $5 million over eight years for the know-how to construct the plant, plus $1.5 million for engineering and technical services and another $4.65 million for equipment. Corning gave the Romanians permission to sell bulbs to Bulgaria, Hungary, Czechoslovakia, Poland, the USSR, Mongolia, and East Germany.[27]

In addition, Corning's holdings in Western Europe continued to expand. Over the course of the decade, Corning had slowly increased its ownership of Sovirel, the French maker of TV glass, consumer, and technical products, until in 1969 it held a 73 percent stake. In 1968, Corning also set up a research laboratory in France, as Sovirel, the joint venture between Corning and St.

Gobain, combined various factory laboratories into one small research center in Avon. The following year, Sovirel expanded by building a consumer products ware plant in Chateauroux. In 1965, Corning and Asahi set up a joint venture—Iwaki—to make automotive sealed beam headlamp parts. Also in 1969, Corning acquired a company in Karachi, Pakistan, that was dubbed Corning Glass Pakistan, Ltd. It employed some 250 people making tubing and vials.[28]

In 1970, Corning continued to seek out new opportunities. Several executives had been invited by a Soviet bureaucrat to visit the USSR and talk about possible agreements. "The Socialist countries offer us excellent opportunity for royalty income. Such income could offset in part the anticipated drop in TV royalties from Europe and Japan," Behm wrote to Armistead on December 22, 1970. In March of that year, Corning had signed a deal with United Incandescent Lamp and Electrical Company, Ltd., Tungsram, of Budapest, Hungary, under which Corning would provide the know-how, technical assistance, and equipment (including a Ribbon Machine) for a lamp bulb factory in exchange for $6.75 million over three years.[29]

By 1970, Corning would have operations, subsidiaries or offices in nineteen countries, twenty-two plants in eleven foreign countries, fifteen subsidiary companies in ten countries, and six associated companies in six countries. The company was selling Pyrex in Japan, lab glassware in Lebanon, opthalmic lens blanks in the Philippines, and lantern globes in Iran. International sales rose from $65 million in 1967 to $110.9 million in 1969, $166.7 million in 1970, and $162.8 million in 1971. In the five-year period from 1967 to 1971, international sales would rise 150 percent while the company's overall revenues rose just 32.5 percent. "Corning's European business in 1970," Roederer told the *Gaffer*, "is approximately equal to the business of all the company in 1949." (That figure in nominal dollars was $73 million.)[30]

Worrisome Signs

Impressive as such performances were, they couldn't make up entirely for the decline in the TV bulb business. Japan's share of the black-and-white TV glass market surged to 43 percent by 1970. In 1969, the continuing difficulties of American television makers forced Corning to close one of its black-and-white television bulb manufacturing plants. Corning's executives viewed this as a temporary problem. They were, however, confronted by a far more troubling challenge to their seemingly dominant market position. Since the time it began making lightbulbs for General Electric, Corning had periodically been threatened with disintermediation, that is, the prospect of its largest customers simply trying to make their own products and cutting out Corning as a supplier. RCA had tried to do it with television bulbs in the late 1940s and early 1950s but ultimately failed. In the mid-1960s, however, the development Corning long feared finally came to pass. And it could not have come at a worse time.

Many companies grappling with the prospects of limited growth chose a means aside from conglomeration: forward integration. By assuming the functions formerly performed by suppliers, they reasoned they could increase sales and boost profits. In the late 1960s, Sylvania, one of Corning's most reliable television customers, was threatening to forward integrate its television business by starting its own glass production. Corning tried to convince Sylvania not to, and it even commissioned a study from consultants Arthur D. Little showing that such a move wouldn't save Sylvania much money. Ironically, Little had based its conclusion on data from RCA.[31]

At roughly the same time, RCA realized that Corning was making a huge profit on its television business. Corning, which was essentially the sole supplier to RCA, was reluctant to cut its prices on such a profitable line. Eventually, RCA determined it no longer wanted to deal with a sole supplier and in 1968 decided to build its own glass plant in Circleville, Indiana, to supply television bulb enclosures to its Lancaster tube plant as well as its television plant in Indianapolis. This move, long feared but nonetheless surprising, came as something of a shock. Corning's largest and most prominent customer in its largest line of business had suddenly disappeared.[32]

Other problems were cropping up too. On a broader level, Corning was finding its profit margins shrinking. Indeed, over the course of the 1960s, operating expenses rose faster than sales. The consumer goods division's gross margin between 1955 and 1967 (excluding the years 1960 and 1966) was 42.9 percent; for 1969, the margin shrank to 30.9 percent. This downward trend was evident in other divisions, such as lighting. There, the gross margin for the similar period was 42.4 percent while the projection for 1969 was 35.4 percent. For some within Corning, this long-term trend called for a fundamental reevaluation of the company's long-standing practices. "Since this longer term problem reflects the fundamental structure of the company, its policies and practices, its solution will require a basic departure in the business, and/or, in approach and thinking," J. W. Fiske wrote in 1968. It would be another decade before Corning would report the types of profits it had enjoyed in the early 1960s.[33]

While some units grappled with slipping margins, other units, from which Corning expected growth, continued to drain investment capital. Signetics, the integrated-circuit maker in California, had turned into something of a black hole. A follower rather than a leader, Signetics muddled along the first few years after the acquisition. After Corning named James Riley, a marketing manager from Raleigh, to run Signetics in 1964, it began turning a modest profit. But on the whole, Corning had proven unable to leverage its glass expertise with the skills of the technologists in Silicon Valley. Indeed, as Amo later put it, "we found we had nothing to give them."[34]

By the late 1960s, Signetics was expanding rapidly. In 1969 alone, it started a new plant in Utah, added a plant in Seoul, South Korea, and began work on facilities in Scotland and Portugal. While the semiconductor industry had grown rapidly, industry-wide sales soaring to $1.45 billion, the entire industry was entering a worldwide recession in 1970 and 1971. Meanwhile, market-leading firms like Intel were making important breakthroughs and leaping out ahead of the pack. In 1970, Signetics lost $6 million on revenues of $32 million.[35]

On a national level, the economy, stung by a rising budget deficit and the escalating costs of the Vietnam War, was slipping into a recession after nearly a decade of robust growth. The go-go stock market, raging for much of the decade, began to enter a long period of decline. By the spring of 1970, problems in television, declining margins in consumer business, social unrest, and difficulties in the economy at home began to take their toll on Corning. As Amo put it in a June 1970 memo, "The economy is in trouble.

We're part of it. Our net results have dramatically altered since the first quarter. The figures show we are neither meeting budget nor doing what we said we'd do in forecasts. We're banking on an unrealistic pick-up in the second half both in volume and in margin percentage."[36]

In May, amid what appeared to be a crisis atmosphere, Amo fired off a barrage of urgent memos to division heads. "Can we close Oneonta and Frederick—now? Also on a temporary basis either Leaside or Muskoka?" he asked Lee Waterman on May 15. "Can we reduce Albion's operations to a bare minimum?" he asked television head Al Dawson. He asked MacAvoy and Jamie to whittle down excessive inventories at specific plants. "Arthur," he wrote to his cousin, "Steuben inventories are scheduled to be $658 K over what they should be on a direct sales to budget ratio by the end of Period 7. Can we do anything to help bring them into line?"[37]

Like a large ship drifting off course, the Corning Glass Works appeared to be in need of a dramatic action to wrench it back in the right direction. Amo's prescription included a hiring freeze, a squeeze on merit increases, and delays on all appropriation requests not essential for the company. He also directed managers to seek ways to raise prices. "Each division manager ought to go through each class of product AGAIN —looking at—big items, low gross margin products, proprietary products, handmade glassware." Any class of product whose prices had not been raised by at least 6 percent since the beginning of the year should be raised 6 percent by August 1 "or else should be justified to either Mr. Waterman or me."[38]

The second quarter results—with earnings slumping 38 percent from the same period the year before—only confirmed the problems. "Our second quarter results were the poorest of any comparable period in many years— and substantially below budget and those of previous years. We not only encountered adverse conditions in many of our markets, we failed to adjust either expenses or production rates accordingly," Waterman wrote to Amo and others on July 2, 1970. In addition to changes at the margins, like adjusting production plans and overhead and reviewing prices, Waterman continued, "it is of utmost importance that the gravity and urgency of our situation be understood by everyone." Waterman mentioned places where the company could save $100,000 here or there. Noting that Corning had spent $17,900 on chartered aircraft for the year, he suggested executives fly commercial when possible. And with long-distance telephone bills up 10 percent from the previous year, to $479,000, he encouraged managers to send messages via the mail.[39]

The cost-cutting efforts did not produce immediate effects. For the year, sales rose about 10 percent, to $609 million, but net income fell some 20 percent to $40 million. The Corning Glass Works, for so many years identified in the public mind as a growth company, seemed to have hit a plateau.

Project Hercules Yields Results

There were some notable successes in 1970, however. Consumer and cookware continued to grow.

One of the outgrowths of Project Muscle, the early 1960s effort to create ultrastrong glass, was heightened activity in the area of glass lamination. Corning scientists grew proficient at using two or more glasses with different coefficients of expansion to create stronger glass. But James Giffen, the prolific and slightly eccentric inventor, wanted to take the work a step further. He believed Corning could make a new line of ultrastrong, ultrathin laminated glass in a continuous, reliable, and high-speed production line, as the company did with Corning Ware. It would be formed by using three sheets of glass layered in their molten state and delivered to a forming machine. The center layer would be thicker than the exterior skins, and each would have a different sensitivity to heat.

The project, officially begun in 1965, was dubbed Hercules, mostly because of the expected strength of the new product. But it was also a perhaps unwitting commentary on the type of labor that it would require. From the outset, Hercules was directed toward consumer ware. The goal was to produce a new line of dishes to complement the maturing Corning Ware line. Anticipating a potential big hit, Corning in 1966 retooled Pilot Plant 2. After settling on the appropriate glasses—an opaque opal glass sealed within layers of tougher, transparent glass—Corning's development specialists turned their attention to the production challenge. The trick was to figure out a means of layering but not mixing the streams of glass as they were formed. Once again, Giffen proved his mettle. In 1969, he developed a special platinum feeder—a conduit that shaped the two flows of glass into a multilayer laminate and proved to be the essential breakthrough. The glass would flow from two tanks through his platinum conduit, which shaped it into a laminated sheet and fed it into rollers that would ultimately convey the glass to the Hub Machine. Although the process worked in theory, it did not work in practice. The opal glass, used for the center part of the plate, was too stiff for the vacuum on the production-model Hub Machine to suck it in.

When this problem cropped up, Corning proved willing to deploy all possible resources to the problem at hand. Bill Armistead put together a task force to address the problem, effectively putting most other research tasks on hold. Within several months, by January 1970, Corning's scientists had developed glasses that worked for both the center and the skin. Later that year, they moved the process to the Pressware plant. Next, Corning had to choose a name for the product. A New York consulting firm that Corning had retained proposed Corever, but the company settled on Corelle.[40]

At its introduction, Corelle came in one basic white pattern—Winterfrost White—and four one-color rim designs, Spring Blossom Green, Butterfly Gold, Old Town Blue, and Snowflake Blue. It was tested in homes in April 1970 and soon was rolled out in New England. In July 1970, Corning installed new machines at Pressware to produce the ware in volume. With Lee Waterman's well-oiled marketing machine kicking into gear, Corelle made an immediate splash. The dishes—dubbed Livingware—came with a two-year warranty (a first for Corning). The company promised that if patterns were discontinued, it would keep pieces available for two years after that date. Large stores like Boston's Jordan Marsh displayed Corelle Livingware at a separate counter "island" on the first floor. "We expect to be taking Corelle ware to the West Coast early in the fall and will 'roll out' in the balance of the country one market at a time after that," said young product manager Van Campbell. The company made 425,000 pieces in 1970 and 38.9 million in 1971. Corning's habit of devoting resources to the patient investigation of the manifold means of mixing and processing molten glass had once again spun out another commercial success. In a period when it badly needed it, Corning had another big hit on its hands.[41]

Auto Windshield Failure

Development in another area highlighted both the frustration and the triumphs of the period. In the mid-1960s, with the success of books like consumer advocate Ralph Nader's *Unsafe at Any Speed*, momentum began to grow for federal safety and other regulations of the automobile industry. Corning had long been making sealed headlights, but it wanted a bigger presence in the massive automotive industry. In the mid-1960s, it thought that it had figured out a way to mass-produce a safer version of the biggest piece of glass used in the production of cars: the windshield. By developing an automotive windshield that wouldn't shatter into dangerous shards and cause injury, Corning believed it could find a lucrative new line of recurring business. After all, nearly 10 million cars were built and sold in the United States each year.

Corning believed it had a powerful crowbar that it could use to pry open the auto market: the Chemcor process. Traditionally, carmakers had not tried to strengthen windshield glass through tempering because thin pieces of glass were nearly impossible to temper. But the Chemcor process, which involved ion exchange, worked effectively on glass of any thickness. More importantly, glass thus strengthened would break into small, relatively harmless cubes. Meanwhile, in 1964 Corning researchers Stu Dockerty and Clint Shay had devised a means of making thin flat glass that did not need to be polished or ground, which was dubbed the "fusion process." By 1969, Corning's scientists believed the combination of tempering, ion exchange, and the fusion process would allow them to produce a superior, safe auto windshield. Optimistic, Corning spent several million dollars to revamp a furnace in the old Corning A Factory to melt the glass for the fusion process.[42]

Initially, the auto industry was enthused about the development. General Motors' Fisher Body Division tested the windshield in 1968 and found that "the head deceleration was significantly higher for the Corning windshields compared to production laminated plate glass. In addition, the chemically hardened outer layer of the Corning glass breaks, upon stone impact, in a pattern that might impair forward vision, although it was far better than the break pattern of other tempered glass." And in November

1968, American Motors announced it would include the windshields in its 1970 Javelin and AMX models.[43]

Soon after the announcement, Amo wrote Henry Ford II, the chairman of Ford Motor Company, making a pitch for Ford's windshield business. "We are now building a facility for production of windshields. This is planned to be in initial production in May, 1969, with full production by late June. Our people tell me that your Steve Sheridan in Ford Purchasing is already working with us to see if assembly modifications and tooling can be completed in time to put our windshields on the Thunderbird or Lincoln next year." Amory Sr. also touted the windshield to Ed Cole, the president of General Motors.

But even as Corning was refitting its Blacksburg, Virginia, plant to make the new windshields, other glass firms were adopting the revolutionary float method of making flat glass that had been developed by the British firm Pilkington Plc. This process allowed companies like Pittsburgh Plate and Libbey-Owens-Ford to draw windshield glass far more cheaply than it could using existing methods. Although they were less safe than Corning's offerings, these windshields were cheaper. And since no federal standards applied directly to windshields, the largest automakers had no incentive to switch to the Corning windshield. By 1971, Corning would terminate the windshield project. The windshield project turned out to be one of Corning's biggest and most expensive failures, and in many ways it typified the frustrations of the period. But the venture was not completely without redeeming returns. The technology developed to make the windshields—specifically the fusion process—would find an outlet in the future.[44]

Corning's efforts to provide a crucial component to automakers would also pay off in the short term. In 1970, after Amo demanded they try one more time, MacAvoy and other executives flew to Detroit to make a last pitch for the windshield business. "I knew we were dead; we were just having the wake as far as I was concerned," MacAvoy said. "But I was out there with my selling suit on." Before leaving, he asked GM's Cole for his opinion on another product Corning had been working on for years without much to show for: Cercor heat exchangers. These ceramic heat exchangers, intended for use in gas turbine engines, aimed to use the hot exhaust generated by a gas turbine engine to preheat the engine's air intake, thus improving efficiency. Light and highly resistant to heat, the honeycomb-shaped material had a vast amount of surface area, which maximized the transfer of heat.

Given Detroit's commitment to the internal combustion engine, the prospects for widespread adoption of the material seemed slim. Still, MacAvoy showed a sample to Cole and received an unexpected response. "When he saw it, he started talking about [an entirely new product], catalytic converters."[45] At the time, automakers were concerned with engine emissions. The recently passed Clean Air Act Amendments of 1970 set ambitious goals for reduction of hydrocarbons, carbon monoxide, and other emissions. By 1975, each was to be reduced by 90 or 95 percent of the average levels in 1968 automobiles. The main approach developed by the industry to reduce emissions was the catalytic converter. With these devices, engine exhaust passed through a catalyst and triggered a chemical reaction to convert pollutants into more benign substances. But the converter needed a substrate to hold the catalyst in place. The requirements for this substrate were resistance to exceedingly high temperatures and a high level of durability. A ceramic appeared to meet these requirements extremely well. In addition, to maximize the efficiency of the chemical reactions, the substrate should provide as much surface area as possible in a restricted volume of space.[46]

MacAvoy and his colleagues immediately believed that Corning's Cercor, with its honeycomb structure, would make an excellent substrate for the catalytic converter. And Cole seemed to agree. "Two days later, I was in GM laboratories in Flint, and six months later, we had 50 guys working on it in R&D," MacAvoy said. Back in Corning, all available resources were immediately committed to the project, which was called Emcon for emissions control. After all, other companies, including W.R. Grace and 3M, were racing to develop their own substrates.

The formal development of automotive substrates began during the second half of 1970 and quickly became the single largest project in the R&D labs, consuming at its peak 25 percent of the corporate lab's manpower. First, researchers settled on a ceramic material with the appropriate characteristics: cordierite, which was composed of magnesia, alumina, and silica. They quickly realized the profit potential was enormous. The raw material cost between $.50 and $.60 a pound and Corning could sell it for about $4 a pound, vice president and general manager of technical products division Dick Dulude reasoned.[47]

But Corning faced big obstacles in developing the new substrate into a commercial product. One of the most difficult problems was to produce the material in the huge volumes required by the automakers—hundreds of thousands, perhaps millions of units per year. The prospect of failing to deliver product on time and to specification was awful to contemplate. Engineer Rod Bagley made a promising breakthrough by developing a die that made it possible to extrude the honeycomb structure in large volumes. Corning received its first order for the new substrates, which it sold under trade name Celcor, in 1971. This order appeared to validate the company's crash effort, but it proved to be a harbinger of the explosive growth to come.[48]

Fiber Optics Revisited

Another triumph in the laboratories in 1970 failed to bear fruit as quickly. Corning's fiber-optics team was well into its fourth year of research on optical waveguides. And few researchers expected to commercialize the technology anytime soon. In 1969 Armistead warned that the project would not receive money much longer out of the general research budget, which was increasingly taxed by a variety of projects. But Chuck Lucy, an MIT-trained engineer who joined the company in 1952 and headed its fiber-optic business development group, persuaded Armistead to continue some funding until he could find partner companies to help with the financial load.

To do so, however, the team would need a breakthrough. One finally came in the summer of 1970. On a Thursday in August 1970, Keck and his colleagues drew yet another slew of fibers from the latest in a seemingly endless variety of batches. The next day, as per routine, Keck heat-treated the fiber. Although he was anxious to leave for the weekend, he decided to take one last measurement. As a recent book tells the story, "He put the fiber on the rig. He bent over his microscope and began to line up the laser. He watched as the pinpoint beam got closer and closer to the core. Suddenly, he got hit with a bright beam of light, right in the pupil." "Good grief, he said, "what do I have here?"[49]

Keck checked and rechecked the apparatus. The tightly focused laser beam had traveled down the core and bounced back. Startled, he nervously checked to see if a sufficient amount of light had coursed through the pipe. To his surprise and glee, the measurement was sixteen decibels, above the twenty-decibel threshold. By this time, it was 5:30 and his colleagues had left for the evening. So Keck had nobody with whom to share the gratifying discovery. He rushed out of the lab and saw Bill Armistead emerging from the elevator. Keck ushered him in to the laboratory and showed him what had happened. He noted the discovery in clinical language with a hint of excitement. "Attenuation equals 16 db it says. Eureka." Keck would later say that he could "just about feel the spirit of Edison" in the lab.[50]

The victory, satisfying as it was, appeared to be a giant leap forward on a long journey with many miles ahead. Demonstrating the feasibility of an optical waveguide was one thing; making it in commercial volumes was another. And attracting orders in a marketplace dominated by AT&T, which possessed its own waveguide development program and captive manufacturing facilities, would be still another. The team wrote a brief paper to be given at a conference in England. Buried near the end of the paper, as if an afterthought, was the statement that they had crossed the desired attenuation threshold. Not rushing to trumpet their discovery to the world gave Corning time to file the necessary patents without attracting other researchers into the same line of inquiry.

In short order, Lucy began to test the waters but found them remarkably cool. Officials at AT&T congratulated him on Corning's achievement but insisted it would be thirty years before the American phone system would be ready for optical waveguides. And by then, of course, AT&T would have developed its own technology. "There we were, all dressed with a technical breakthrough, and no place to go," said Lucy. Then Lucy started traveling all over the world, trying to interest telephone companies in Corning's breakthrough. In 1971 and 1972, he made fourteen trips to Europe and seven to Japan. But none of the companies he visited seemed interested. Most disappointing was the blasé reaction from the British post office, which had prompted Corning's research in the first place.[51]

Corning continued to explore ways to fund development of optical waveguides. One prospect that the company debated was to cross-license its waveguide technology to AT&T in return for Bell Labs patents required by Signetics. At the time, Signetics owed AT&T about $2 million in royalties and the cross-licensing arrangement seemed a good way to pay off the debt and avoid accruing more. As negotiations proceeded, Bell Labs essentially proposed that Corning swap the glass patents for the patents Signetics was already cross-licensing. But Bell Labs wouldn't, in return, cross-license its glass development. "It was a one-way street," said Armistead. "We had these optical waveguide patents and people were saying, 'that's not going to be worth anything until the year 2000, so let's exchange the license for the optical waveguide patents for the stuff we can use in Signetics today.'" Although Armistead and others were not enthusiastic about such a deal, this logic carried the day. For much of the next decade, Corning would have to find other and more creative ways to finance its continuing work on optical waveguides.[52]

One Step Back

The willingness to trade hard-won waveguide breakthroughs for access to AT&T's patents on integrated circuits also indicated difficult economic times at Signetics. In 1970, Signetics lost $6 million on $32 million in sales; in 1971 it lost another $3.4 million amid a worldwide recession for integrated circuits. In mid-1970, however, James Riley resigned and Charles Harwood, a longtime general manager of the electronic products division, took control. As Signetics began to demand larger injections of capital to stay afloat, Corning's hopes for making something out of its once promising acquisition began to unravel.

At the same time, another Corning foray into the emerging world of computers and electronics was also faltering. Researchers at Corning's electronics development lab in Raleigh, North Carolina, had been searching for distinctive, value-added products. One of the lab's products was a time-sharing computer terminal, the Corning 904, which was introduced in April 1970. But after an unsuccessful one-year market trial, the product was withdrawn and written off.[53]

Meanwhile, stalwart product lines like television glass and lightbulbs also showed signs of faltering. At the annual meeting in April 1971, Amo promised shareholders that Corning would exceed 1970s performance by year's end through improved plant efficiency, clamps on operating expenses, and quicker translation of development projects into the market. Amo also predicted that the television bulb business would improve due to relief from the Japanese practice of selling televisions at below-market prices in the U.S. market, and that Signetics would turn around through reorganization and tighter controls.[54]

But the difficulties continued throughout the year. Efforts by domestic television manufacturers to have the government sanction Japanese firms for dumping products on the U.S. market at below-market prices didn't produce quick results. Sales of Japanese sets in the United States in 1971 climbed to 6 million units, up from 5.5 million two years before. The Japanese companies, which had less than 1 percent of the American monochrome market in 1960, held a 72-percent share in 1972. In 1971, despite the advent of Corelle, Corning's overall sales declined slightly while earnings fell 7.8 percent. The company was forced to take $3.2 million in special charges to discontinue operations like the automotive windshield and the Corning 904 computer terminal. Even sales of one of Corning's growth machines—international— fell by $5 million because of poor results in Europe. "Certainly 1971 was not a year of growth for Corning Glass Works, and we are disappointed in its outcome," Amo wrote in the 1971 *Annual Report*.[55]

In another sign of transition, Lee Waterman and Robert Murphy, two of the executives who had spearheaded Corning's most successful drives of the decade—the push in consumer goods and international growth—retired in 1971. Upon Waterman's retirement, Amo said, "I could cite figures and facts about his accomplishments both as a division manager and as president— yet when it's all tallied, the answer says this: probably more than anyone else in my memory he has rebuilt and renewed not just the consumer name of Corning—but the consumer thinking inside Corning." MacAvoy, the self-described "chemist who came from nowhere," was elected Corning's new president. Jamie Houghton assumed Murphy's post as chairman of Corning Glass International.[56]

By the end of 1971, Corning had the team in place that would lead it through the next decade. And although they scarcely could have known it, the important development work on the next two generations of major growth products, fiber optics and Celcor, had already been completed. To be sure, the executives possessed a kind of congenital optimism and faith in the ability of Corning's scientists to spin ever new and profitable uses for glass. If anything, the difficulties it had faced in these years only reinforced the determination to push ahead. As the 1971 *Annual Report* put it, "This company must continue to probe, to take chances, to pursue the high potential of this extraordinary material with which we're dealing. Historically that has been our path to success, and we are convinced it will be so in the foreseeable future." The next decade would prove this faith well-founded. But the challenges and dislocations of the late 1960s would seem tame compared to the powerful manmade and natural forces that would be unleashed against the company and its small-town base in the coming years.

CHAPTER ELEVEN

Digging Out and Tough Economic Times, 1972–1975

IN THE Chemung Valley, the late spring of 1972 was hotter and steamier than usual.[1] Occasional thunderstorms punctuated the sultry weather and produced memorable downpours. Some old timers began to worry that the Chemung River, more or less quiet since "the flood of the century" in 1946, could soon overflow its banks again. They did not have long to wait.

On June 18, the first hurricane of the season, designated Agnes, hit Florida, triggering floods and tornadoes and causing nine deaths and millions of dollars in property damage. That was the first act and, as it turned out, a warm-up. As the storm worked up the coast, it showed signs of weakening. Then unexpectedly it bounced out to sea and gathered fresh strength. On June 21, the revived hurricane again veered inland, this time moving westerly across New Jersey, northern Pennsylvania, and the Southern Tier of New York state—an area already soaked by two straight days of rain. On Thursday, June 22, the storm hit a low-pressure front moving eastward from Ohio and combined with it to produce torrential rains. That evening, observers in Elmira, who had recorded 6.3 inches of water in twenty-four hours, lost track of the accumulation when their rain gauge was submerged; the total at Hornell, about fifty miles west of Corning, was a phenomenal 11.1 inches.

In the early hours of Friday, June 23, the Tioga and Conhocton Rivers, which meander through the tight valleys of the Southern Tier, had risen far above normal levels. When they merged to form the Chemung, they were already spilling over with angry, muddy water. At four A.M., the river broke through dikes in Painted Post, flooding much of that town, the neighboring village of Riverside, and northern parts of Corning. Minutes later, the New York Central railroad bridge gave way, despite being weighed down with loaded coalcars in a vain effort to stabilize it. At 5 A.M. alarms sounded in Corning's factories along the river. Onward the water surged, cresting in the city at about 9 A.M. On the south side of the Chemung, Main Plant, Fallbrook, and Pressware plants quickly went out of commission. Tons of muddy water poured onto Market Street, flooding basements and ruining first floors, rising to a height of more than four feet in some places. On the north side, the damage was even worse. The flood reached the second story of the Glass Center—a height of eighteen feet—and submerged the entire collection of rare books and thousands of pieces of precious art glass in the Museum of Glass next door. Employees who had rushed in to help as much as they could were forced to exit via the roof. Water rose well above the first floor of most of the the the buildings in nearby Houghton Park, not only sealing them off but also disabling the company's computer center in the basement of C Building. The Glass Works lost its ability to bill customers, track performance, and pay employees.[2]

The Chemung peaked at a record thirty-five feet above normal—more than ten feet higher than the terrible flood of 1946. It began to subside almost immediately, but not before it wrought staggering physical, economic, and human damage. In the city of Corning, eighteen people lost their lives, including Hobart A. Abbey, a senior designer in the forehearth development department of the Glass Works. Abbey had left work early on Thursday to serve as a volunteer fireman in Gang Mills. He was helping evacuate homes when the waters overtook his pickup truck and swept him to his death. In one of the cruelest incidents of the day, the emergency dispatcher who picked up his final call for help was his own daughter.[3]

The city lost electrical power and telephone service, and ham radio operators provided early reports on the devastation. More than 750 houses were severely damaged and 6,000 people—more than a third of the local population—became homeless. Houses, garages, and small buildings were lifted off their foundations and pushed downriver. Ruined automobiles, picnic tables, barbecue grills, yard furniture, bicycles, and small debris were strewn across the valley and everything was coated with slimy mud. The new director of the museum, Robert Brill, who was traveling in Asia, received a telegram bearing a curt message: "Museum destroyed. Return immediately."[4]

That dreadful Friday and the days and weeks that followed were filled with numerous acts of heroism and generosity, as the community rallied together to dig out and rebuild. Families living above the flood line opened their homes to less fortunate neighbors. People pitched in to provide extra food, clothing, and essentials. The National Guard, the Red Cross, and other public and private relief and service agencies arrived on the scene within hours. Some help came from unexpected quarters: a Glass Works retiree visiting Cleveland bought a dozen gasoline generators, loaded them in a rented trailer, and headed back to Corning to provide emergency power. Breweries in Rochester and Utica donated thousands of quart bottles filled with fresh water until the city's water supply could be restored. Amid the local devastation, the sight of people of both sexes and all ages chugging from brown beer bottles provided some welcome comic relief.

Rumors circulated that the disaster would force the Glass Works to relocate from the valley. Amo Houghton went on the local radio to deny the rumors and rally the company and community: "We are not only going to rebuild what we have lost," he said, his words carefully chosen,

> but we are going to add significantly to our manufacturing facilities in one of our plants....I want those of you who are employees of our company, to know that as long as we respond well to our customer's needs your jobs are secure. Not a flood, nor a hurricane, not any other act of nature is going to jeopardize this. You are the Corning Glass Works, particularly here in this city which is our home and our headquarters.[5]

Houghton pledged significant corporate resources to support the recovery. The company granted liberal time off to employees and advanced vacation pay. It provided immediate interest-free loans of $1,000 in cash to employees and retirees. It dispatched its personnel to photograph damage and assist with filing insurance claims. A handful of executives took temporary leaves of absence to assist public officials in running the city and providing essential services. The Corning Glass Works Foundation allocated $400,000 to fund a summer job program for 300 young people—the Youth Emergency Service (YES)—to assist with the cleanup. The head of Corning's office in Washington, D.C., Allan Cors, and local congressional representatives pushed hard and successfully for quick release of millions of dollars of federal emergency relief funds.[6]

With Houghton Park inaccessible, top officers relocated temporarily to the Corning Clubhouse, an old rolling mill at the corner of Market and Walnut Streets. The company met its payroll by writing checks literally by hand. Many employees were paid with scrip, which local merchants agreed to honor. With the computers down, recalled Van Campbell, who had just become corporate treasurer, "it was about a month [before we knew] what the real financials were." Several days after the flood, his colleague Bob Montgomery managed to get to New York, where he attempted to oversee financial dealings from Corning's midtown offices. The company drew heavily on the goodwill and understanding of the financial community. "I remember [Bob] calling me one day," Campbell recounted, "saying, 'Citibank just called and says we're $120,000,000 overdrawn, but that's okay!'"[7]

Meanwhile work crews worked long days and through the weekends to restore operations. Temporary barricades had kept the water away from the melting tanks at the plants, but most of the low-lying glass forming machinery and equipment was covered and clogged with gritty mud. Nonetheless, through round-the-clock effort and many astonishing displays of individual dedication, employees had Fallbrook and Pressware melting glass again and Houghton Park reoccupied by the July Fourth holiday. A temporary computer center, this time built on high ground, came on line at the end of the month. (In 1974 a new corporate data center was dedicated atop the hill at Sullivan Park.) On August 1, the Museum of Glass and Corning Glass Center reopened, although it would be years before the collection, especially the library, was fully restored. Fortunately, the flood had treated most glass objects gently. With the gradual ebbing of the waters, museum personnel found dirt and mud everywhere but little broken glass. Main Plant, the Glass Works facility the flood had hit hardest, resumed operation during the first week of August.

The total cost to the Glass Works of the downtime and cleanup reached about $20 million. Insurance covered the damage, although the company had not carried adequate flood insurance, despite the periodic ravages of the Chemung. What it did have, fortunately, was a large disaster insurance policy purchased for Signetics in the Silicon Valley, where earthquakes were an ever present danger. Although Signetics had yet to pay a direct return on Corning's substantial, sustained investment, its indirect contribution through its insurance provider in the summer of 1972 proved timely and welcome.

In the city, estimates of total property damage reached $175 million. Visible reminders of the disaster were all too evident, from the fine brown dust that gave the air a brownish hue to the commercial buildings that were slowly rebuilt, to the new homes that sprang up on cleared land on the north side. In one important respect, however, the flood worked to Corning's advantage: it drew the community together behind the process of urban renewal begun in the late 1960s. The first new building to open in the area east of Market Street was the new headquarters of Local 1000 of the American Flint Glass Workers Union, dedicated on May 4, 1974. Within a few years, it was followed by a civic plaza and an open-air ice skating rink, a new city hall, public library, and a housing block. A major boost to development was a new hotel bridging the new urban renewal area and Market Street. In the aftermath of the flood, as yet one more sign of its commitment to the area, the Glass Works announced plans to replace the antiquated Baron Steuben with a new hotel. The company formed a wholly owned subsidiary to develop the three-story, 130-room structure. The Hilton (now Radisson) Hotel opened in June 1974.[8]

The flood also hastened the renovation of Market Street. By the late 1960s, the street had deteriorated dramatically from its heyday, with new development occurring along Denison Parkway or east of the city in Horseheads, where a new shopping complex was in the works. Market Street still featured a record number of bars, but many shops were vacant or boarded up. "The street was a shambles," said Tom Buechner, who had been away for a decade, when he returned in 1971 as head of Steuben (where he took on the delicate task of succeeding Arthur Houghton Jr.), the Glass Center, and the Glass Works Foundation. Buechner and a group of like-minded local merchants and civic leaders believed that it would be futile for Market Street to compete with the shopping complex. They reasoned, however, that an authentically restored downtown area could support boutiques, specialty shops, and new restaurants and services to appeal to the thousands of tourists who visited the Corning Glass Center and other area attractions each year. The Downtown Restoration Committee was formed and then applied successfully to the state government for an architectural study. Early in 1972, the city government endorsed a comprehensive restoration plan developed with the help of the Glass Works Foundation.

Following the flood, interest in reviving Market Street redoubled. Federal disaster relief funds enabled the city to build new sidewalks and curbs and plant many trees. The Downtown Restoration Committee developed guidelines for renovation and provided assistance in research and grant applications. In the next few years, many architectural details, long obscured under layers of paint and haphazard remodeling, reemerged to public view. The ground floor of the Baron Steuben was redesigned to accommodate small shops and an ice cream parlor. Corning purchased the old city hall and renovated it, and local businessman Robert Rockwell donated his impressive collections of artwork and memorabilia of the American West and Carder glass as the basis of a new museum. By the mid-1970s, Market Street had a radically altered appearance, displaying the charm and eccentricity of a bygone America.

When the waters subsided and Corning employees could begin to reclaim their places of work, employees entering C Building at Houghton Park faced a particularly disturbing sight. A casket from a local funeral home had somehow floated into the lobby, where it remained for several days as a grim reminder of nature's devastation. During the following months and years, the reminder transmuted into an omen, and many veterans of the Glass Works later came to interpret the flood as the beginning of awful things to come. And what ensued for most big American industrial companies was terrible. The recession of 1970–1971 was a prelude to a deeper, nastier recession in 1974–1975. The Bretton Woods postwar monetary system ended when the United States abandoned the gold standard in 1971 and introduced new uncertainties in international trade and finance. The oil crisis of 1973 triggered seismic upheavals in energy markets, spurred inflation, and wrought havoc to the cost structures of most industrial corporations. Meanwhile, new economic powers abroad, most notably Japan, began to transform and escalate competitive rivalry in consumer electronics, metals and materials, automobiles, and many other big industries. It is no wonder that many Corning employees look back on the 1970s as "a tough time," "terrible years," and "a nightmare decade."

By the mid-1970s, many of Corning's major businesses operated in crisis mode, with lightbulbs and TV glass, both black-and-white and color, in severe distress. In spite of its travails, however, Corning also nourished several fledgling businesses—Celcor ceramic substrates, optical waveguides, and a collection of promising lines in medical diagnostic equipment and lab testing—that later blossomed into significant operations.

Twilight of Growth

Before the flood became a metaphor for Corning in the 1970s, the company was pushing ahead with a thorough reassessment of its businesses, a task undertaken with the optimism, vigor, and enthusiasm of young executives entering their prime years. The top-level reorganization in 1971 reenergized and redirected the company. Al Dawson, Paul Clark, and Forry Behm, the powerful general managers of the preceding decade, remained influential figures in the company, but the torch was passing to a new generation. Amo Houghton was only forty-five. Tom MacAvoy, the new president, was two years his junior. The third member of the top group, Amo's younger brother Jamie, was just thirty-five. During the next several years, the company accentuated the generational shift by naming five new vice presidents between the ages of thirty-four and thirty-eight; by then, the average age of all corporate officers was forty-four. Among the newcomers assuming significant responsibilities were Jack Hutchins as head of R&D (succeeding Bill Armistead, who became vice chairman), Van Campbell as corporate treasurer, Bill Ughetta as chief counsel and corporate secretary, Dick Dulude, as head of the Technical Products Division, Roger Ackerman as president of Corhart Refractories, and Marty Gibson as head of Corning's Medical Division.[9]

Most of the young executives were MBAs or graduates of executive education programs at elite business schools, where they had imbibed new concepts in strategic planning and management. Many of these young executives served on the Corporate Development Committee, which formed in the aftermath of the 1970–1971 recession to reassess the company's existing operations and its future opportunities. The committee drew on the assistance of outside consultants, especially Walker Lewis, a Harvard MBA and a former principal with the Boston Consulting Group. Lewis had recently left BCG, where he had made significant contributions to the firm's development of key strategic concepts such as portfolio management and the experience curve, to found his own firm, Strategic Planning Associates.[10]

Together, committee members and consultants plunged into the task of charting the company's future directions. Already Amo Houghton had gone on record as stating that the company need not limit its opportunities to glass, with its ventures in semiconductors and scientific instruments being the most notable signs.[11] In a letter to employees in 1971, he quoted the official statement of purpose developed a decade before: "The primary objective of Corning Glass Works is to pursue excellence in glass world-wide, making this family of materials, its related products, and its corollary technologies the most unusual and useful in our civilization." He went on to say that these words were "descriptive of the past, and reasonably directional for the future" and added that the mention of glass did not preclude pursuing "opportunities elsewhere which play to our real strengths, not fantasies."[12]

As they surveyed the company's operations, the new management team saw more cause for optimism than concern. Coming out of the 1970–1971 recession, there was a tendency to view declining sales in TV bulbs, incandescent lighting products, and sealed-beam headlights as cyclical phenomena. At the same time, results from several newer product lines were strongly encouraging. In all, the company fared well, with sales surging nearly 60 percent between 1971 and 1973 (from $603.4 million to $945.8 million) and net income more than doubled (from $33.9 million to $70.4 million). In 1973, the company reached the highest level of employment in its history, with a payroll of 45,900 people.[13]

Every product line contributed to this growth, but the most exciting were Corelle Livingware, a new, light-sensitive ophthalmic glass marketed under the trademark "Photo-Gray," and laboratory products. At the same time, the company pushed heroically to scale up its glass ceramic substrates for the automotive emissions market and to cultivate the market for optical waveguides.

A Hit and a Miss in Consumer Ware
(Corelle and the Counter that Cooks)

Introduced in 1970, Corelle Livingware remained a star performer. Despite repeated investments to expand the Pressware plant and several price increases, Corelle sold faster than Corning could make it and remained on allocation all but one year in the decade. Corelle was so successful, in fact, that it established a new segment in the marketplace: casual dinnerware. As baby boomers married and formed their own households in record numbers, the American middle class swelled disproportionately. Corelle proved ideal for this market: it was far more attractive and durable than most plastic dinnerware, while its light weight, translucency, and "ring of fine china" appealed even to well-heeled consumers. Corning further enhanced the product by offering an industry-first two-year warranty and guarantees that replacement patterns would remain in stock for at least two years after being discontinued. Another key innovation was packaging: Corelle came in twenty-piece sets, which included four place settings of dinner plate, salad plate, bowl, and cup and saucer. The inclusion of a bowl instead of a traditional bread-and-butter dish proved especially popular. Finally, Corning pushed Corelle through housewares channels with heavy promotion behind it. It was the first dinnerware to be backed by a national TV advertising campaign.[14]

Corning also continued to contemplate expansion by integrating forward from its base in materials into consumer appliances. The Hub Machine that Jim Giffen had pioneered proved useful for making large Corning Ware pieces such as platters, skillets, and serving trays. Another proprietary device, the escalator machine, could roll Pyroceram into flat sheets that were used first in skillets and then, in larger sizes, as cover sheets for drop-in electric ranges. The company combined these large Pyroceram sheets with specially made Corning Ware sets in a package called "The Counter that Cooks." Although consumer reaction to this drop-in range product initially was lukewarm at best, Corning saw in it the beginnings of an intriguing diversification opportunity. From drop-in range tops, it moved to drop-in ranges and then to freestanding ranges purchased from Kelvinator. The modest success of these lines spurred still more extensions, including frozen-food cookers and warming trays.[15]

Corning also pursued mergers and acquisitions in consumer products, but without much luck. In 1970, for example, it had acquired Salton, a producer of small kitchen appliances such as pizza warmers and yogurt makers that had also assembled Corning's electromatic skillets. In this instance, however, the acquirer and the acquiree failed to mesh. The businesses were very different, with Salton's business consisting of low-tech and low-margin assembly work, and its manner of operation still much influenced by founder Lou Salton's personality and distinctive management style. After three years, Corning abandoned the effort to integrate Salton and sold the business back to its founder. In the meantime, Corning held merger talks with Hobart, an appliance maker, and Rubbermaid, a producer of plastic household products, but could not close a deal. Nonetheless, throughout the early 1970s, management in the consumer products division continued to pursue growth through acquisitions and vertical extensions to complement Corning's core ovenware and dinnerware businesses.[16]

Creating New Photochromic Glass

Like Corelle Livingware, another big hit from the labs was Photo-Gray, the photochromic ophthalmic glass that, also like Corelle, established a new market segment—in this instance, comfort lenses. Containing light-sensitive chemicals, Photo-Gray lenses darkened and cleared in changing light conditions. When fitted into eyeglass frames, they were almost as effective as prescription sunglasses, but saved wearers the expense and hassle of keeping track of an extra set of glasses.

Photochromic glass had originated in Don Stookey's lab, but its eventual success reflected creative marketing as much as technological innovation.[17] As Stookey later recounted, the idea for the product sprang from some wishful thinking at a discussion between Bill Armistead and a customer for Corning's eyeglass blanks. The customer speculated that "spectacles that would turn dark in sunlight but clear again indoors" would make an appealing product. Armistead mused over the suggestion and directed Stookey to investigate. That research, in turn, led to the discovery that a precise formulation of transparent glass containing silver chloride crystals could darken and clear reversibly, depending on light conditions. The prototype lenses, however, had two drawbacks. First, the tint was a pinkish red color that was cosmetically unappealing. Second, the glass was harder and more difficult to machine—and hence more expensive—than conventional eyeglass blanks.[18]

To overcome these drawbacks, Dick Dulude and Marty Gibson crafted a clever strategy. First they persuaded researchers at Sullivan Park to develop alternative and faster-working tints, with a gray shade the most promising. Second, they test-marketed the product with eye doctors in Corning and Elmira and established that customers were willing to pay a hefty premium for the Photo-Gray lenses. Finally, the Corning marketers changed their traditional point of contact with the eyeglass makers. Instead of promoting the new product with technical and manufacturing personnel at their customers, they also lobbied the marketing staff. The prospect of premium pricing worked wonders. Corning charged four times more for Photo-Gray blanks than for blanks of standard ophthalmic glass, while the eyeglass makers and doctors passed along the higher costs plus a higher margin to their customers. As Dulude explained,

each part of the distribution system ended up making more money. [Our customers] were going to just take whatever the price was, if it was $3.00 a pound more, they were just going to add that on. We said, "No, no, no, no. You can get more for it than that. Don't just add on the material cost. This does something different. Instead of getting $3.00...for it, you might be able to get...$4.00 more for it." And I think that kept the lens manufacturers solvent for probably ten years because that was the only thing they made money on. They competed and knocked each other off on the clear lens business.[19]

In 1973, Corning introduced a new tint called Photo-Brown. Research on both Photo-Gray and Photo-Brown led to faster chemical response times to changing lighting conditions. In all, photochromic ophthalmic glass became an unusually profitable business for Corning and another affirmation of the value of its deep understanding of glass. Fresh off this success, Dulude and Gibson lent their talents to two other new businesses in the 1970s: automotive emissions control and medical laboratory equipment and services, respectively.

The Big Bet: Celcor

As MacAvoy's successor at the technical products division, Dulude assumed responsibility for the scale up of the new Emcon (emissions control) product line consisting of monolithic ceramic substrates. By 1972, Corning had already made the key technical breakthroughs in material composition and the extrusion process. (See chapter 10.) The big opportunity—and the big risk—was to ramp up production in time for the auto companies to meet the federal emissions control deadline for the 1975 model year. There were several dimensions to the challenge. First, Corning had to demonstrate conclusively that its product worked and performed better than the competition's. W.R. Grace, Monsanto, 3M, and the major auto companies were all working feverishly to identify alternative approaches. A particular source of concern was General Motors's decision to adopt a technology based on coated alumina pellets rather than a monolithic substrate. Corning's second problem was to ensure that it could produce millions of units each year reliably and at an affordable price for extremely demanding customers. The consequences of quality problems or disruptions in production would cost the company severely and perhaps cause customers to look elsewhere for suppliers. The potential liabilities so concerned Van Campbell, Corning's new treasurer, that he attempted to line up insurance coverage in case the company should fail to deliver. He found no takers.

The management team that rose to the challenge—Dulude, David Duke, Charles W. "Skip" Deneka, and (later) Roger Ackerman—made their careers with Emcon's success. Along the way, they developed techniques and processes for developing new products that Corning later applied successfully in optical waveguides and other areas.[20]

Corning gave the name Celcor to its Emcon product line. The honeycomb ceramic structure with 200 rectangular cells per square inch was roughly the size of a coffee can, and yet it provided the surface area of a football field. The manufacturing of such items in high volume posed formidable problems. The walls in the structure had to maintain their dimensions throughout the extrusion process so that the catalyst (in this case, the precious metal platinum) could be applied evenly and economically, and that the exhaust gases would flow through without meeting obstructions that could cause back pressure.

Corning poured abundant resources into the project. In the early days, according to some estimates, three-quarters of the personnel at Sullivan Park were engaged on Celcor development. Many moved over from the aborted automotive windshield project. Everything proceeded on an extraordinarily tight schedule with product and process development and sampling and testing moving ahead on concurrent schedules. Dulude, Duke, and their colleagues held daily meetings with Dave Leibson, head of corporate engineering, and Jack Hutchins, head of R&D. MacAvoy and Armistead usually attended as well. "The intent of these meetings," recalled Dulude, was that

> if there was any resource in the company that we needed, [this] group of people had it under their control. We would do whatever we had to, to make sure [that Celcor] worked. We'd run into unexpected things. The first time we fired up the ceramic kilns, we found out we were polluting the valley. We had this binder in there, and all of a sudden you fired up and at a cer-

tain temperature the binder vaporizes. We're polluting the whole valley. Thank God for Dave Leibson, who was the chief engineer. He said, "I know how to fix that." What we did was to recirculate the binder back through the furnace and it burned that second time through, or however many times was necessary, and got rid of it. But holy Toledo, we could have been shut down.[21]

It was a round-the-clock development effort. Manufacturing engineer Skip Deneka remembers working 100-hour weeks for a year or more.

In January 1973, with no confirmed orders, Corning broke ground on a a new plant in Erwin, New York, that would be dedicated to Celcor production. Dulude recalls delicate conversations with his bosses, who questioned the wisdom of going ahead without customer commitments. He had verbal assurances from Chrysler, however, and recognized that the company would have no hope of being able to produce Celcor in volume without pushing ahead rapidly. Meanwhile, Corning still did not know that its product would work reliably for the 50,000 miles that the customers had specified. An initial test of vehicles driven continuously for 35,000 miles by college students and volunteers was disastrous. When researchers opened up the metal containers housing the structure, they found them hollow: the substrates had disappeared with the exhaust. This caused a frantic search for better ways to mount ceramic materials in a metal exhaust system. The solution—a new adhesive—arrived just in time. The Erwin plant shipped its first product on schedule in April 1974—just months ahead of the automakers' introduction of their 1975 models. By then, Corning had big orders from Ford and Volkswagen, as well as Chrysler. Celcor proved an immediate hit, accounting for more than $100 million in profitable sales in its first year.

From Science Products to Medical Instruments and Services

Marty Gibson, meanwhile, was piecing together a fast-growing business in medical instruments—his assignment after the successful launch of Photo-Gray lenses. A Wharton MBA in marketing, Gibson had joined the company in the early 1960s after noticing in his job interviews that many young managers held positions of major responsibility. He started out as a sales rep in science products, which by then was following a strategy unconventional for Corning. "We were the only business in the company," Gibson said,

> that described itself or thought of itself in terms of a set of customers [scientific and medical laboratories]. We wanted to bring to those customers any product that they wanted. As opposed to every other business in the company, [which] thought of itself as a glass company—in other words, based on capabilities.
>
> On the other hand at Science Products, our approach was [to serve] a set of customers. We were well known to that set of customers. We had a strong distribution system to reach them…and so what we needed to do is broaden our product offering. And so we went into a variety of different nontraditional products. That really appealed to me and that's why I liked the lab business a lot.[22]

In the 1960s, the nonglass, nontraditional products were laboratory hot plates (featuring pyroceramic surfaces), pH meters, and blood-gas analyzers. Under Gibson—a nontraditional manager, Wharton, marketing, long hair, sideburns, and a modish dresser in a conservative company—more diverse offerings were soon to follow. In time, Corning Medical became the launching pad of the biggest diversification effort in Corning's history.

"First of all," said Gibson, reconstructing the story,

> we redefined our mission. We went from being scientific instruments to being specifically clinical instruments. We wanted to provide hospital laboratories with state of the art products to do blood testing. [Clinical] was by far the fastest growing part of the laboratory universe.…Medicare had been passed and technology was just exploding on the scene and the whole medical field as opposed to general scientific field was growing quite rapidly. We wanted to get in on that growth.[23]

The Scientific Instruments Division became Corning Medical Division, with a particular focus on equipment for "body-fluids analysis." The first steps were small but important ones. Corning's blood-gas analyzer, for example, featured "average technology." The company jazzed it up by packaging it in bright orange housing. This caught the eye of purchasing agents and appealed to technicians who welcomed something flashy into typically drab workplaces.

As the business began to grow, Gibson tapped into other expertise at Corning. The Raleigh electronics laboratory, for example, was eager to take on new assignments after the termination of the Corning 904 display terminal and jumped at the chance to develop medical instruments. "There were a bunch of electronic people down there looking for something to do," recalled Gibson, "and it was too tempting a target for us....It was love at first sight. We needed them and they needed us." The first joint project was a white blood cell-analyzer later known as LARC—leukocyte automatic recognition computer. The device used a small, specialized computer linked with a microscope and optical equipment to scan blood samples and count white blood cells. It thus automated and improved a slow process normally performed by hand and vulnerable to human error.[24]

Another independent Corning initiative also found a home fortuitously in the new medical division. In the mid-1960s, Ralph A. Messing, a biochemist at Sullivan Park who was experimenting with porous glasses as membranes, made an interesting discovery. Attempting to separate various organic solutions, he found that proteins bonded to the glass—a problem if that was an undesirable outcome. But Messing, whose specialty was enzymology, interpreted the result as an intriguing opportunity. Enzymes are proteins used to catalyze organic reactions of various kinds, including those used in the soap, textile, paper, beer, and dairy products industries. When enzymes are removed from their natural setting, however, they tend to be short-lived. Messing's research showed that the enzymes bonded to glass remained biologically active for six months or longer. The implication was that enzymes could be reused in many industrial applications with, at a minimum, significant manufacturing cost savings. Beyond that, Messing speculated, entirely new continuous processes eventually could be developed in a host of industries.[25]

In the long term, Messing's discovery raised the possibility of significant new business for Corning in industrial biotechnology. In the short term, it spurred additional research in biochemistry. In 1972, Howard Weetall, a biochemist recruited by Messing, broke away to focus on medical applications of immobilized-enzyme technology. Before long he developed a highly promising technique for body fluid analysis called radioimmunoassay (RIA) testing. The technique used biological, chemical, and physical processes to detect and measure extremely small quantities of antigens (foreign substances) in the blood stream. One part of the analysis relied on the bonding of antigens to small glass particles, which served as a separation agent and facilitated further testing and measurement. RIA provided several key advantages: it was faster and more reliable, and it enabled researchers to work with small blood samples. RIA would prove one of the most important technologies in medical testing in the 1970s and a major new business for Corning.[26]

The Medical Division also sought to grow via acquisition. In 1971 Corning acquired a start-up that made prefabricated kits for testing the presence of certain types of bacteria. Subsequently, it bought ACI, a small producer of electrophoresis products used in analyzing serum protein components to diagnose heart and liver diseases. Calling frequently on customers, Gibson and his colleagues also noticed the emergence of for-profit testing laboratories, many of which had formed in response to the health care programs of President Lyndon Johnson's Great Society. In 1973, Gibson and Ned Olivier, the newly hired director of corporate planning, began looking to acquire or invest in a for-profit lab. They called on the biggest and best of these and eventually targeted Teeterboro, New Jersey–based MetPath. Under founder Paul Brown, MetPath was attempting to process many tests from a single large facility and capture benefits of scale in competition with the many smaller and dispersed labs in the New York metropolitan area. Brown was reluctant to sell the company, but he agreed to part with 9 percent—the biggest stake Corning could acquire and still accomplish a later merger by pooling of interests. That eventuality was very much on Gibson's mind.

Through such measures, Corning Medical sales surged tenfold (from about $3 million to about $30 million) between 1970 and 1974. " We weren't very profitable," Gibson recalled. "In fact, the truth is I don't think we ever made a penny. We didn't lose much, but we were growing the top line and there was [increasing] interest in the business" among Corning's top management.[27]

Optical Waveguides at the Crossroads

During the recession of 1970–1971, Bill Armistead almost killed Corning's program in optical waveguides. The company was clamping down on costs and, although Armistead recognized the stunning achievements of Maurer, Keck, and Schultz and understood the enormous potential of the technology, payback seemed far off in the future, perhaps decades. And Corning faced major, perhaps insuperable obstacles in developing the technology: AT&T's commanding market position, its waveguide development program, its disinclination to acquire technology from outside sources, and the cross-licensing agreement that gave Bell Labs access to Corning's technology in any event. Although Corning was funding the program at a modest level and with part-time researchers, even small expenditures were called into question in a cost-cutting environment.

Lasers were too big, unreliable, and expensive to warrant everyday use. New passive technologies for cabling, splicing, coupling, and splitting would have to be developed, while new active technologies in switching, amplifying, and converting signals would have to be pioneered. Many companies working on these technologies, moreover, viewed Corning as a competitive threat and were not eager to collaborate. At the same time, the cable manufacturers and telecommunications companies had little incentive to change over. Expensive networks based on copper wires and cables were already in place. Engineers and technicians knew how to design, build, and maintain them, and they possessed tools and equipment for doing so. Electrical and electronic equipment was geared to the existing network. The advantages of optical waveguides would have to be overwhelming to persuade the telecommunications industry to convert. And Corning could affect only a small number of the variables necessary to influence the conversion.

And so, when Armistead seemed ready to pull the plug on optical waveguides, albeit reluctantly, Chuck Lucy, the business development manager for the program, thought fast on his feet for a way to keep it going. "Off the top of [his] head," he asked Armistead

> whether he would reconsider if I could get outside funding. This was kind
> of a novel idea. The lab had taken contracts before to do specific things, but

as far as I know, it was the first time anybody had proposed to get outside funding to cover an internal R&D budget item. Bill thought about it for a while, and I suspect he thought there was no way that that was ever going to happen, but he said, "Yes, if you can get enough funding."[28]

Armistead agreed to continue the program while Lucy looked around. Since AT&T was "the only game in town" and an unlikely partner in any event, Lucy decided instead to go "out of town." During 1971 and 1972, he made fourteen trips to Europe and seven to Japan, learning about the telecommunications and cabling industries and attempting to attract investors. The lifestyle was wearying, but on long trips Lucy propounded several observations about the risks of new business development that became famous in the company as "Lucy's Laws." The first one reflected a sardonic streak: "If there's a 50/50 chance of something going wrong, it will happen nine times out of ten." He explained: "That came to me one night in a hotel room somewhere in Europe, where I went to pull the drapes, as you usually have to do in European hotel rooms, and realized that nine times out of ten, when I went to do that, I was…grabbing the wrong one. It shouldn't have been. It should have been 50/50." Lucy's other laws were (echoing Intel's Andy Grove): "Just because you're paranoid doesn't mean that something's not out to get you," and, on a more serious note, "you haven't made a decision until you've said how much you're willing to pay to make something happen."[29]

In meeting with potential partners abroad, Lucy had had several goals in mind: first, to raise enough money to keep Corning's work moving ahead; second, to form alliances with "companies whose standing and credibility would be so impressive that Corning wouldn't consider pulling out" again; and third, to gain access to the cabling, electronic, and telecommunications technologies Corning would have to understand to develop operational fibers.

Lucy's entreaties often fell on deaf ears. "Most of the people who were in the [cabling] business didn't see this as an opportunity. They saw it as a threat. Their business was making copper cables. Most of them even owned their own copper mines." Many potential investors, including the national telecommunications monopolies, were disinclined to purchase such a significant technology from abroad. Still, Lucy pressed ahead, carry-ing new samples and the latest experimental results with him. Bob Maurer accompanied him on many of these trips to speak to the technical issues. A sample cable designed for battlefield use by the U.S. Army provided a par-ticularly convincing demonstration: here was an actual fiber-optic cable that had met operational requirements.

In 1972, Corning signed up its first partner: BICC in the United Kingdom, a major supplier to the British post office—the source of Corning's original stimulus to work on optical waveguides and now an indirect sponsor of its research. The deal, which Lucy and Corning International lawyer Peter Booth negotiated, committed BICC to pay Corning a fee of $100,000 per year for five years and agree to develop components and cabling technology to work with optical fibers. In return, BICC gained an option to license Corning technology to manufacture optical fibers in the United Kingdom under a fifty-fifty joint venture arrangement, if and when a market developed. To sat-isfy American antitrust law, the option also included BICC's right to license Corning's U.S. patents, should it decide eventually to sell there.[30] Once the first deal was signed, Lucy found, arranging others proved easier. By the end of 1973, Corning had optical waveguide development contracts with CGE in France, Pirelli in Italy, Siemens in Germany, and Furukawa in Japan.[31]

In the meantime, Corning made significant progress in waveguide research. The 20 db/km standard first achieved in 1970 demonstrated the eventual feasibility of optical fibers, but they were as yet far from practical and they were a long way from competitive with copper wire in telecom-munications applications. Shortcomings began with the fiber itself: the ini-tial samples were brittle and prone to break in normal use and under seasonal weather changes. Pete Schultz understood these fundamentally as problems in glass composition, and he began experimenting with alterna-tives to titanium as the dopant in the core glass. In June 1972—just days before the flood—he demonstrated a germanium-doped fiber that improved transmission capability by a factor of forty. This, in turn, meant that repeaters could be spaced much farther apart than previously assumed —as much as twenty kilometers (about 12.5 miles), as opposed to the four-mile standard for copper cable. And best of all, the new fiber resisted break-ing. "This was to my mind *the* breakthrough for fiber optics, because it was now a practical fiber," said Schultz. "It didn't break. . . .You could make fibers right off the draw with these nice low losses" [emphasis added].[32]

Aided by the funding agreements and technical interactions with its development partners, Corning made rapid progress toward meeting operational requirements for optical waveguides. In 1973, Siemens and Corning formed a fifty-fifty joint venture, Siecor GmbH, to produce optical fibers in Germany for Siemens cabling business. The other development partners proved more cautious, preferring to wait for more convincing demonstrations of the viability of fiber-optic cable.

Meanwhile, Corning set up a telecommunications development department at Sullivan Park under Maurer. The group worked not only on improving optical fibers but also on coatings and cabling. Its first samples were offered for sale in June 1974: fiber-optic cable in 500-meter spools at 30 db/km attenuation, costing from $25 to $57 per meter, depending on the size of the order. By mid-1975, Corning was selling an improved cable called Corguide, with 20 db/km attenuation at $13.50 per meter. Virtually all of this output went to Corning's development partners for experimental trials.[33]

Coping with Growth Abroad: Corning International Corporation

Between 1963 and 1972, Corning established factories in Holland, Brazil, Mexico, and Taiwan; built and licensed a plant in Romania; formed joint ventures in Japan and Australia; acquired an equity stake in a glass company in Pakistan and a scientific instrument company in the United Kingdom; and increased its ownership to majority positions in its long-time affiliates in Argentina, the United Kingdom, and France. Many of these initiatives, especially in TV glass, resulted from following Corning's customers abroad as they established operations around the world. Along the way, Corning's international sales soared tenfold from $35 million to $336 million and came to constitute a third of the company's total revenues.[34]

Jamie Houghton's election as vice chairman of Corning and chairman of Corning International Corporation (CIC), a wholly owned subsidiary, signified the importance the company attached to its international business as well as a new international strategy. During the early 1970s, CIC placed less emphasis on growth and more on consolidation and integration with Corning's business units. Both efforts were fraught with difficulty.[35]

The rapid growth of the international businesses created an abundance of administrative headaches. Corning possessed thirty-one distinct and separate legal entities in Europe; the decision-making processes, management systems, and standard operating procedures in most of these had to be brought in line with Corning's own way of managing. The biggest pieces of CIC—James A. Jobling in the United Kingdom and Sovirel in France—were old and proud companies, set in their ways and showing ambivalent feelings (at best) about American ownership. They were also barely profitable. Their businesses included Pyrex consumer products and labware, TV glass (in France), and ophthalmic glass, as well as a hodgepodge of items unrelated to Corning's interests. Jobling operated seven glass plants in the United Kingdom, two elsewhere in Europe, and one in Australia; Sovirel maintained four plants and an R&D lab, all in its home country. The two companies competed with each other in some lines, while Corning competed with both through exports to Europe.

Throughout CIC, there was a strong need for better information flows and tighter coordination of new product and marketing initiatives. And of course these initiatives also required tighter links with the business unit plans and activities of the parent corporation.

CIC initially carried forward the regional structure of Corning's previous international organization, with area managers responsible for Europe, Latin America/Canada, and Asia/Pacific. This organization had proved extremely effective in achieving growth, but less so in delivering profits or coordinating initiatives across area boundaries. As the number of plants and operations multiplied, for example, it became increasingly difficult to transfer technology across area boundaries. Many routine conflicts bubbled up to Forry Behm, president of CIC, for resolution, and the press of low-level operating decisions threatened to overwhelm him.

To address such problems, in 1972, Houghton and Behm appointed business managers for major product lines such as consumer, electrical and technical, and science and medical. These business managers shared power with the area managers in a matrix structure. As typical of such organizations, however, this matrix became a nest of tangled reporting channels and blurred responsibilities. Worse, neither the area managers nor the business managers in CIC succeeded in establishing their authority with the business unit heads in Corning Glass Works. The result was several years of administrative turmoil and tension atop CIC, friction between CIC and the Glass Works, and slow progress in the hard work of fashioning CIC's operations into a seamless, tightly run set of businesses.[36]

Meanwhile, CIC continued to grow at a more modest clip, with some churning of operations. In 1970, Corning retreated from Chile when the Allende government nationalized its operations. Although a right-wing coup three years later reversed the act, Corning decided against returning. In Europe, the joint development agreements in optical waveguides—especially the formation of Siecor GmbH—gave Corning a strong toehold in an exciting new industry with vast potential. Even Eastern Europe offered opportunity: in 1971 the company won a multimillion dollar contract to build a melting facility and high-speed lightbulb glass plant in Hungary.[37]

In Asia, Corning formed a new joint venture in 1973 with Samsung, a rising industrial power in Korea. Samsung was smaller than Corning but possessed enormous ambitions. It approached Corning for black-and-white TV glass technology because it wanted to take on the Japanese producers and expected to overtake them. Although Corning discussed involving Asahi and Philips in the venture, neither party wanted in. Samsung and Corning shared equal ownership but Samsung provided virtually all of the management. Corning furnished technology and know-how and participated in quarterly meetings of an "executive committee" to discuss business directions and address common concerns. Led by H. C. Shin, the venture launched on a fast-growth trajectory, beginning with a finishing operation on imported bulbs and evolving quickly into a full-scale TV glass plant near Seoul. Samsung-Corning turned profitable in its first year of operation.[38]

The Guns of August

A short, ugly war between Israel and its Arab neighbors in the fall of 1973 triggered massive changes in the world economy. Some signs were evident even before the war: incipient inflation and the restructuring of international trade as the United States went off the gold standard and (ominously for Corning) the rising success of Japanese consumer electronics companies. But the war in the Middle East did much more than worsen a darkening economic climate. In the span of a few months, the Organization of Petroleum Exporting Countries (OPEC), heretofore an ineffectual information-sharing association, suddenly became a militant cartel to control the price of oil. Energy prices around the world tripled, wreaking havoc with heavy industry, which couldn't pass price increases along to customers, and with consumers, who suddenly became aware that the costs of gasoline and heating oil amounted to a significant part of their household budgets. In the short term came a sharp recession that worked its way around the world in overlapping phases. Many American companies like Corning, which had believed international sales would shield it from depressed conditions at home, saw that belief shattered.

Although the Glass Works passed $1 billion in sales for the first time in 1974, its executives were hardly bullish about the future. Sales had begun to slump in the second half of the year and management noted a "severe contraction" in sales of integrated circuits and TV glass bulbs. The company's common stock, which had traded at a high of $126 5/8 in the first quarter of 1973, plunged to a low of $25 in the fourth quarter of 1974. The gloom persisted well into the following year, as the dimensions of a deep financial crisis became increasingly apparent. In mid-1975, Corning forecast a sales decline of 8–10 percent, a 30–35 percent drop in net income—on top of a 30 percent decline in net income the previous year.[39]

The timing of the recession proved especially awkward at Signetics. Although some Corning officers and board members had been quietly advocating divestiture of the unit for several years, it had powerful champions in the company, especially Al Dawson. He pointed to Signetics' robust recovery from the recession in 1971 and a rosy long-term forecast for semiconductors as reasons for patience. Although the bottom line results remained discouraging, in November 1973 Signetics managed to raise $20 million from the sale of 1.3 million shares of its common stock. This move was designed to repay Corning for loans and finance continuing expansion.[40]

As the recession hit, Signetics stock tumbled well below its initial offering price. Unhappy shareholders filed suit against Corning, while Corning itself was an unhappy shareholder. By late 1974, the company had had enough and Amo Houghton ordered Dawson to find a buyer for Signetics. Dawson protested the decision, which he believed Corning would regret in the next economic upturn. He took his time in looking for a buyer, but as Corning's fortunes continued to deteriorate, Houghton lost his patience. He summoned Dawson to a five-minute meeting in which he "made it very clear" that Signetics was to be sold as soon as possible. The message understood, Dawson accelerated talks with Philips, which in the spring of 1975 agreed to buy Signetics for $28 million. The transaction took place on June 10. The shareholder suit lingered much longer and constituted a significant distraction. Corning eventually prevailed, however, when its accusers failed to prove that the company had prior knowledge of the coming economic downturn and ensuing crisis in semiconductors.[41]

The divestiture of Signetics proved but the first step in a major restructuring of the Glass Works. By the summer of 1975, Houghton believed "the integrity of the company" was at stake. In August, he and MacAvoy convened Corning's top management for an off-site meeting at The Knoll. The agenda was to implement a sweeping reorganization and the biggest downsizing in the company's history.[42] The restructuring ultimately terminated many marginal or unprofitable product lines, including black-and-white TV bulbs, acid waste drain lines, and the major appliance initiative, and it resulted in the closing of five domestic plants. These measures, coupled with the sale of Signetics, slashed Corning's total employment by nearly 40 percent. After painful and painstaking deliberations on a case-by-case basis, the executives at The Knoll eliminated more than 1,200 management jobs—about a fourth of the total.[43]

Soon labeled "the Guns of August" (named after the title of Barbara Tuchman's best-selling book about the outbreak of World War I), the episode marked a major watershed in Corning's evolution. For many surviving employees, the company was never the same afterward. Few people continued to believe that the company would go to extraordinary lengths to avoid layoffs. In a small city like Corning—especially after the heroic efforts to rebuild after the flood—the effect of the downturn was magnified. Routine encounters in stores, churches, and public places between those let go and those still working made for awkward moments. For Amo Houghton and many other executives, the personnel cuts and plant closings were agonizing. Jack Hutchins found the need to terminate long-time employees hard to stomach. He nudged some veterans, including Jim Giffen, into retirement and finally cut employment at Sullivan Park by ten percent after receiving a blunt directive from MacAvoy. Hutchins vowed that he would never again put himself in such a position. The crisis even hit hard at Steuben, where Tom Buechner reluctantly cut the design staff and closed the business club atop the Corning skyscraper in New York.[44]

As it happened, the Guns of August coincided with the end of the recession in the United States and a general recovery of American industry. Much later, Van Campbell, who became Corning's chief financial officer in August 1975, speculated that the company need not have taken such drastic steps, but also pointed out that it became tougher, less patient, and more tightly managed as a result. Looking at the struggles of the TV-glass business, once the biggest contributor to the bottom line, top management concluded that it would henceforth seek to avoid becoming ever again so dependent on a single line of business. This lesson implied the need to extend the company's diversification, and Amo Houghton and Bill Armistead encouraged Sullivan Park to accelerate development of promising new technologies such as optical waveguides and industrial biotechnology. But the first order of business remained continuing vigilance about costs.

CHAPTER TWELVE

Cutting Costs and Changing Direction, 1975–1983

THE DIFFICULT times of the first half of the 1970s cast a pall over the entire decade for many Corning employees. Looking at the world around them, they saw continuing cause for concern in the aftermath of the Guns of August. The effects of the energy crisis lingered on during a period of low growth in the United States (less than 2 percent per year) and high inflation (well above 10 percent per year), and these conditions proved more or less characteristic of other developed countries in which Corning earned most of its revenues. The combination of low growth and high inflation culminated in a new economic condition—stagflation—and draconian monetary policies to combat it. The result was high costs, price sensitive customers, low margins, and disincentives to invest. And just when the economy finally showed signs of healing, a revolution in Iran in 1979 triggered another energy crisis and brought on the worst economic times for the industrial economy since the Great Depression.

For all the troubles outside of the company, however, on the inside the view was more hopeful, despite some hard feelings left over from the Guns of August. Corning's behavior was more decisive, its actions carried out with greater urgency. In the short term, tighter, more disciplined management restored the company to profitability, and hot products such as Corelle Livingware and Celcor helped move the company forward. The long-term prognosis was less encouraging, however. Assessing its portfolio, management saw serious problems with declining businesses such as light-bulb glass and black-and-white TV glass, as well as with suddenly mature businesses such as color TV glass and electronic components. There were even disturbing signs in consumer housewares. Despite the popularity of Corelle, changing patterns of distribution threatened Corning's margins. The company faced two strategic challenges. First, it needed to minimize damage from the decline of these businesses while simultaneously weaning itself from dependence on them and, second, Corning had to find, and find fast, new pathways to growth. The most promising opportunities were optical waveguides and industrial biotechnology. Corning possessed significant proprietary technological advantages in both areas, but in both areas the future direction of technology was anything but clear. In the telecommunications industry, moreover, Corning was a tiny competitor in industries dominated by huge and wealthy rivals; in biotechnology, it was a question of whether a glass company, a specialist in inorganic chemistry and materials, could succeed at the frontiers of organic chemistry and molecular biology. To open pathways into new areas, the company would require creativity, new ways of managing, and more than a little luck.

Bearing Down on Overhead

Many of his colleagues remark that the Guns of August exerted a transforming impact not only on the company but also on its chairman and CEO, Amo Houghton. He smarted from occasional references by business journalists and financial analysts who likened the company to "a country club" in which the genteel style of management seemed more appropriate to a bygone era than to the turbulent times at hand. Yet there was a decisiveness about Amo that his personal charm and outgoing nature sometimes masked, as Al Dawson found out when he dragged his feet in selling Signetics (see chapter 11). In the aftermath of crisis, Corning was becoming a different kind of company, and Amo a different kind of leader—less patient, more inclined to probe and prod. A similar change came over Tom MacAvoy, although it was perhaps less noticeable due to the unchanging nature of his blunt and occasionally earthy manner.

The new focus on cost control was evident in several new corporate programs and initiatives. One of the highest priorities was to reorganize Corning's international operations and integrate them more tightly with its domestic business units. Top management took a direct approach, retaining McKinsey & Company to help out. Throughout 1975 the consultants studied Corning's international operations, reporting back late in the year. Among their key findings and recommendations, the most important was to abolish the internal matrix at CIC and return it to a pure area structure that would form one side of a corporate matrix, with the business unit organization of the Glass Works as the other side. The relative authority of the area manager (from CIC) or the business manager (from the Glass Works) would differ according to the business or product line in question. In some businesses—medical products, for example—the business manager would take the lead because products were standardized around the world and required substantial central R&D investments. At the other extreme— in consumer products, for example—area and country managers assumed greater authority because of vagaries in local distribution channels and consumer taste. In between stood a host of businesses in which area managers and business managers would interact appropriately, depending on specific circumstances. McKinsey also proposed changes in information systems and new decision-making and conflict-resolution tools to help the new corporate matrix succeed.[1]

McKinsey recommended that Corning take advantage of the crisis environment of the Guns of August to make the changes quickly, and Corning's top officers were more than ready to accept the advice. They had already concluded that dramatic changes in CIC were necessary and that to become a major competitor on a worldwide scale it would be necessary to develop a broader and deeper cadre of international managers. To a reporter, Amo Houghton characterized (rather unfortunately) the kind of executives

Corning had sent abroad in the past as "people fluent in foreign languages, with social graces, and who were sometimes less ambitious and hard-driving than their domestic counterparts; the diplomatic type." The company would no longer make such choices, he declared, leaving, the reporter to infer that Corning intended to send "the most hard-driving, bottom-line-oriented SOBs" it could find. The careers of the new international managers had to be perceived in the company as at least equally attractive as careers in domestic assignments.[2]

By 1975, the need to restructure the European operations was particularly urgent. It was clear to Jamie Houghton that Corning had moved too slowly since acquiring full ownership of Jobling and Sovirel. "We tend to be too nice," he later said.

> We tend to say, in the case of James A. Jobling, "We now own 100 percent, but things are going to be about the same and you've got the same people, etc." I think in retrospect that's crazy. You ought to decide who you want to put in there and put them in on day one, whether it's the top person or the top financial person or whatever. But don't beat around the bush, because it's a hard cultural change, and you might as well get started at it, because it's going to happen. You might as well not waste two or three years being nice.[3]

When Dick Dulude, the new head of Corning Europe, arrived to sort out the situation, he found a region coping with the same recessionary and inflationary forces that were besetting the United States. The local institutional environment differed markedly, however. Although both Jobling and Sovirel were regarded in their respective homelands as excellent employers, they operated in larger contexts of militant labor unions, powerful socialist political parties, and strong legal restrictions on terminating employees (especially in France). Nonetheless, Dulude was well aware that Corning's European operations were significantly overstaffed and that plants and jobs would have to go. To leave no doubt about who was in charge, Jobling was renamed Corning Ltd., with former Corning controller Oakes Ames as chairman, and Sovirel became Corning France, SA.

Assisted by legal expert Peter Booth and other CIC staff, Dulude set about the downsizing with determination. The executives "kept pushing and kept pushing and kept pushing" government officials to obtain necessary permits and agreed to pay substantial severance packages, absorbing short-term losses to get long-term gains. By the end of the decade, several plants had been shuttered and Sovirel's R&D lab in Avon was downsized and transferred to the jurisdiction of Sullivan Park. Total employment in Europe plunged from about 11,000 to about 7,000 on rising volume of sales, with still meager financial returns. Along the way, Corning earned admirers in the European business community for toughness and pragmatism and a fearsome reputation with organized labor for ruthlessness. The big French company St. Gobain took notice and stole away one of Dulude's top assistants to help with its own efforts to downsize.[4]

As it was restructuring its European operations, Corning kept a close watch on general corporate expenditures, especially personnel costs. In January 1977, MacAvoy pulled Marty Gibson out of the Medical Division and placed him atop the corporate personnel division. Immediately, Gibson engaged McKinsey to analyze corporate overhead, make comparisons with peer companies, and help identify opportunities for savings. The findings showed Corning well out of step with its peers, its spending on overhead being about 20 percent higher than the norm.[5]

Armed with the study, Corning clamped down on hiring, redesigned jobs, and combined positions when openings occurred. Gibson instituted a personnel planning process to identify potential needs well before they materialized. Finally, he and his colleagues developed standards and procedures for personnel management across the company and implemented them over a two-year period.[6]

The determination to maintain tight controls on corporate overhead had significant implications at Sullivan Park. Jack Hutchins instituted many changes to forestall the possibility of another Guns of August. In the summer of 1976, he closed the electronics laboratory in Raleigh and relocated personnel to Sullivan Park. By then, most researchers in Raleigh were working on medical instruments and Hutchins reasoned that they could better serve the Medical Division from headquarters.[7]

Management at Sullivan Park also became more selective in choosing projects to pursue and sustain. Some long-standing projects were quickly terminated. A favorite of Ambassador Houghton's, for example, was a glass razor blade. Under the code name "Gaslight," a small group of engineers worked on it for years without much luck. Although glass blades held a sharp edge longer than metal, the razor companies were uninterested in changing over, and market research indicated considerable consumer skepticism. Gaslight spawned other projects, including a hemostatic glass ceramic scalpel for surgeons that would cauterize as it cut ("The Cutter That Cooks," as it was known around Sullivan Park). This too was a technical success and a marketing failure, as surgeons liked the concept but not the reality of learning to work with new, somewhat bulkier devices.[8]

It proved relatively easy to eliminate such projects as the glass razor blade and the hemostatic scalpel but much harder to slow down or terminate other promising work. Some researchers, for example, were well down the track on projects to make a transparent glass ceramic while another project on hydrated silica showed potential in optical lenses. Hutchins transferred the transparent glass ceramic project to the French laboratory in Avon, where it soon contributed to an exciting new line of range-top cookware that, with slight changes, was eventually marketed in the United States as Visions. The hydrated silica project simply languished.[9]

To help overcome the chilling effects of unpopular personnel and budgeting decisions, Hutchins and top assistants redesigned career paths at Sullivan Park. Early in 1978, they created a new position of Research Fellow to recognize accomplished researchers and give them room to pursue projects of special interest to them and to the company. The first such honor went to Dr. George Beall, holder of numerous patents in glass ceramics and, not coincidentally, a key figure in the development of transparent glass ceramics. Later that year, Hutchins followed up by announcing a major reorganization of the technical staffs into two new segments meant to improve coordination between the research and development functions and move projects more expeditiously from the lab to the factory floor. Harmon Garfinkel became director of research to oversee projects in glass, ceramics, and life sciences, and Ray Voss became director of product and process development.[10]

Continuities and Values

As painful as the Guns of August proved, Corning's management remained determined to show that the essential character and values of the company were unchanged. The company attempted to accomplish this in numerous ways. Amo Houghton gave a long interview about the crisis that was published in *Gaffer*, the employee newsletter. He explained the roots of the crisis and the basis on which the company had acted, but he dwelled on traditional strengths in research and projected "a great future—if we have the stomach to chase it."[11]

Employee communications shared extensive information about the company's plans while also celebrating historic achievements and stressing continuities with the past. The *Gaffer* featured a profile of Earl J. "Dutch" Hultzman Jr., who retired at Central Falls after forty-three years of service on the factory floor. He hailed from long-lived and loyal stock. Corning had honored his grandfather, "Yank" Hultzman, in 1956 for eighty years of service. His father, Dutch Sr., had sixty-five years with Corning when he died in 1962. Four of his siblings still worked at the company, with the youngest, Eileen, a thirty-three-year veteran. Not long afterward, the *Gaffer* took note when Louis Moschell eclipsed Yank Hultzman's service record by reaching the eighty-five-year mark. Amo Houghton flew to Indianapolis to present a service pin to Moschell in his home.[12]

As the personnel division was clamping down on headcount and redesigning jobs and career tracks, it was also promoting improved working conditions. Houghton and MacAvoy insisted that the company meet its obligations under the equal employment opportunity laws and also launched a special effort to recruit minorities and women into the workforce. One of the first female hires to the management ranks was Marie McKee, who joined the personnel division. On a plane ride with Amo Houghton, the two talked about problems in recruiting women and Houghton suggested that she investigate building a day care center in Corning. She did, and the center, which opened in 1979, was one of the first in the country to be sponsored by a major corporation. McKee also worked on a variety of assignments designed to address work/family issues in the company.[13]

Corning also continued to promote economic and cultural life in the Chemung Valley. As soon as the recovery was under way, the company signaled its ongoing commitment to its home by building a new corporate engineering center named in honor of Bill Decker. In 1979, Corning began sponsoring an annual Ladies Professional Golf Association tournament at Corning Country Club, with proceeds supporting area hospitals and medical institutions. At the same time, the company underwrote a major expansion of the Corning Museum of Glass. The new steel-and-glass building enabled the collection to escape cramped quarters and symbolized the museum's rebirth from the ravages of the 1972 flood.[14]

Such stories and initiatives helped restore the company's image among employees and citizens of the Chemung Valley. But the company illustrated even stronger commitments to its traditional values in two major business stories of the mid-1970s: a joint labor–management committee to protect jobs in the consumer electronics industry and a huge, expensive recall of a consumer product.

A Labor–Management Compact

Corning's most pressing business problem in 1975 was the color TV bulb business, which accounted for nearly three-quarters of the company's sales. Management had long recognized the cyclical nature of this business, tended to view the mid-1970s downturn as the painful part of a recurring pattern, and eagerly anticipated the next upward swing. But it was quickly apparent that the crisis masked more fundamental and (for Corning) distressing problems in the U.S. consumer electronics industry. Asian, especially Japanese, television manufacturers enjoyed substantial cost and quality advantages over their American rivals, and with the passage of time it seemed ever less likely that Corning's customers would rise to meet the challenge.

The sources of the Japanese success in consumer electronics naturally became a subject of hot debate. Initially attributed to a lead in converting to solid-state electronics (RCA was still putting vacuum tubes in TV receivers as late as 1973), the Japanese advantage was, on reflection, far more compelling.[15] It stemmed from many additional sources: the tight integration of R&D in semiconductors with consumer products manufacturing, aggressive automation, continuous cost reduction and quality improvement, an alliance with emerging mass retailers, and a strategy, wonderfully tailored to maturing baby boomers of wooing customers with small, inexpensive sets, establishing brand loyalty, and persuading them to trade up to more expensive models.

The U.S. producers responded in two ways that, in the long run, came back to haunt them. First, most American manufacturers set up offshore plants in low-wage areas of the world to assemble low-end products such as black-and-white TV receivers. They also began to source key electronic components from these same areas. These tactics saved money in the short run, but they locked the manufacturers into cost competition based on low wages while inhibiting new product development and the introduction of automation and other productivity improvements. Second, American manufacturers retained such a focus on their high-end, profitable products that they increasingly ceded the low end of the line to the Japanese. By the early 1970s, multinational manufacturers like RCA and Sylvania were sourcing whole sets, as well as components, from overseas. As the Japanese moved up to big color sets, the U.S. producers had no effective response, and casualties began to occur. In a single year (1975 to 1976), the Japanese share of the color-TV market surged from 19 to 40 percent. By then, Corning's customer base in color TV bulbs had plunged from twenty-eight to five. "It was," said Amo Houghton, "as if General Motors had lost Chevrolet."[16]

In a moment of belated introspection, Corning acknowledged its contributions to its customers' misfortunes. The same reluctance to cut prices that had prompted RCA in 1970 to integrate backward into TV bulb production persisted to the detriment of other American producers, whose Japanese competitors enjoyed lower prices from Japanese suppliers.[17] (See chapter 10.) By the mid-1970s, Corning's pricing was no longer tenable, even in an era of soaring inflation. Under Forry Behm's leadership, the company undertook a rigorous assessment of its manufacturing operations with a goal of achieving dramatic productivity improvements and cost reductions. Behm's work launched what eventually became in the 1980s a major corporate initiative in total quality (see chapter 13). But it was apparent to him at the outset that turning around Corning's operations would require systemic changes in management and organization over a sustained period.[18]

Corning also sought to lessen the effects of the TV-glass crisis through political action. The company formed an alliance with other suppliers, the Flints and other labor organizations, and Zenith, the lone U.S. set maker that still assembled virtually all of its TV receivers from American-made parts in American factories, in a plea for government protection. The allies formally created the Committee to Preserve American Color Television (COMPACT), with Corning's Al Dawson and Jacob Clayman, secretary-treasurer of the AFL-CIO industrial union department, as cochairs. In a petition to the U.S. International Trade Commission, COMPACT claimed that the Japanese were dumping sets in the U.S. market at prices well below those in Japan to gain market share. The committee further alleged that Japanese producers benefited from unfair trade practices such as government subsidies, low-interest loans, and tax incentives designed to enhance their international competitiveness. Unless these practices ceased, Dawson asserted, the color television industry in the United States was "threatened with extinction." Labor officials claimed that 65,000 American jobs were at stake.[19]

COMPACT delivered its petition to the ITC at the end of 1976, and early the following year, both Dawson and Amo Houghton testified on its behalf. The petitioners sought temporary quotas on Japanese color TV set imports to gain time for the U.S. industry to frame a competitive response. In March 1977, the ITC found that the U.S. industry had been injured by unfair foreign competition and recommended that tariffs on imported sets be raised from the existing 5 percent rate to 25 percent and gradually lowered to 15 percent over a five-year period. COMPACT hailed the finding but protested the solution as too lenient. The committee urged the new Carter administration to seek stiffer penalties, including quotas. Its intensive lobbying prevailed. In June, U.S. special trade representative Robert Strauss negotiated an orderly marketing agreement (OMA) with representatives of the Japanese government to roll back imports from 3 million units in 1976 to no more than 1.75 million units in each of the three subsequent years.[20]

In the end, the OMA did little to restore the competitiveness of U.S. set makers, which for the most part used the period of protection to reap profits and abandon domestic production of even large color TV models. But for Corning, the significance of the OMA was not the impact on its relationship with customers but rather its relationships with its workforce, the leaders of their unions, and the U.S. government. The company showed that it cared about maintaining an industrial employment base in the country and that it would become a national champion for labor-management cooperation to address problems of competitiveness. Both parties had to bend somewhat, with management conceding labor's interests in seeking protection, and labor recognizing the temporary nature of protection and the imperative to improve quality and efficiency in the factories. At the same time, Corning learned much about lobbying and the ways that labor-management cooperation and public affairs management could support its business interests. In 1980, Corning followed up COMPACT by helping to form the Labor Industry Coalition for International Trade (LICIT). Amo Houghton served as cochairman with senior officials from the AFL-CIO. LICIT's mission was to help reduce investment barriers abroad, especially in Japan.[21]

The Biggest Consumer Product Recall in History

The second business episode of the mid-1970s that tested Corning's values occurred in its consumer business. The problem stemmed from the 1974 model of the Electromatic percolator, the E-1210, which featured a Corning Ware base with a stainless steel collar and a hard plastic handle. The E-1210 was the best-selling product of its kind, with approximately 360,000 units on the market. With a selling price of $29.95 and a gross margin well over 50 percent, it was also one of Corning's most profitable consumer lines. Soon, however, the company began hearing complaints of collars breaking away from the base—a serious problem and a safety hazard when the percolator was full of hot coffee. By June 1976, 373 people had reported burns from the E-1210, with twelve requiring medical attention.

Product engineers Bruce Adams and Norval Johnston quickly traced the source of the problem. In its original design, the percolator's collar was made of Corning Ware, but it was prone to chip and crack if not handled carefully while washing. Corning substituted the metal collar, which was fitted to the Corning Ware base mechanically through overlapping joints and a rubber-adhesive sealing material. As new strong and quick-drying adhesives came on the market, Corning recognized potential cost savings and substituted an epoxy for the earlier rubber-adhesive sealer. At the same time, engineers modified the design to rely less on the mechanical joints. This solution lowered cost, enabled faster production, and seemed to work well—until it was discovered in the 1974 model that spills and repeated cycles of dishwashing could weaken the epoxy with disastrous consequences. The problem could be corrected, the engineers believed, with slight changes in product design and a different process for curing the epoxy.[22]

In June 1976, Corning announced a voluntary recall of the E-1210 and agreed to replace returned percolators with new units. The company spent about $1 million on the recall, furnishing display kits to some 90,000 retailers to inform shoppers of the problem and announcing the recall in newspapers and ready-to-run copy for local TV stations. About 15,000 percolators were returned and Corning believed that the matter had been closed. The Consumer Product Safety Commission (CPSC), however, believed differently. Although the head of the commission initially praised the company for mounting "an outstanding effort" in the recall, subsequent hearings concluded that Corning should have moved more quickly to notify consumers of potential hazard. The CPSC ordered Corning to pay a fine of $325,000—the largest civil penalty in the commission's history to that time. Although Corning's leaders believed the fine was unfair and considered an appeal, they reasoned that it would be more prudent to pay up rather than risk a more expensive outcome and the likelihood of damaging publicity.

Still, the matter would not go away. Complaints about percolators—not only the E-1210—continued to trickle in. By 1979, out of 18.5 million percolators of all kinds sold since 1960, Corning had more than 7,000 reports of failures. Some 1,250 people claimed injuries ranging from burns to cuts to blistered feet, and the company faced a handful of lawsuits. Internal analysis again identified the adhesives as the culprit: as they aged, they became more brittle and prone to failure. Although the failure rate on its percolators was less than 0.004 percent, some Corning engineers believed that the company should mount a general recall. "If you want to maintain a consumer franchise, and Corning had great credibility with the consumer, you don't have a product that is defective and people getting hurt in the marketplace," said engineer Johnston. MacAvoy remembers listening to legal advice to gather more facts and proceed deliberately before he and Houghton decided to act on the basis of simple criteria. "It gradually became apparent that our reputation, our integrity, was being questioned by some of our own key people," said MacAvoy, who found that intolerable.

> If you have half a dozen people who disbelieve that the company means what it says about quality and dealing with the customers, it's poison.
>
> So I remember I went next door and knocked on Amo's door, which happened to be closed. I opened the door and he was there with his secretary. I said, "I've just decided we're going to recall the Corning Ware Electromatic Coffee Pots." He was dictating a letter or something like that. He said, "How much is it going to cost?" I said, "I don't know, but it's probably going to be 10 million dollars or something like that." So he nodded his head and I went back and did it. It cost $14 million, but it was the right thing to do.[23]

In September 1979 Corning unveiled the recall. It ran advertisements in more than a thousand newspapers and women's magazines and again prepared announcements for the broadcast media. Since the company had discontinued its percolator line in 1978 due to the popularity of automatic drip coffeemakers, it instead invited consumers to choose between a cash payment (which varied with the age of the unit) or selected Corning consumer products from a special catalog.[24] In the end, the company preserved its reputation with consumers and employees, and it even won over some of its adversaries in the government. In 1982, Susan B. King, the former head of the CPSC, joined Corning as an executive, citing the effectiveness of the recall and the company's "very good reputation as a well-managed and responsible, ethical company with very good products.[25]

Accelerating Change

The Guns of August had the desired effect on the company's financial results in the short term: as the economy recovered from recession, the fortunes of the Glass Works also revived. In 1976, revenues again nudged past $1 billion, and net income reached an all-time high of $84 million. These results were the beginning of a six-year string of annual revenue increases and a four-year run of ever higher profits. Meanwhile, employment remained flat for the remainder of the decade.

This performance reflected not only a resurgent economy but also Corning's more focused strategy and tighter operating discipline. With the auto industry's return to health, Celcor became a big positive contributor under the leadership of Roger Ackerman. Under the respite that the OMA with the Asians provided, the color TV bulb business rebounded. Ophthalmic glass displayed renewed vigor after researchers in the Avon laboratory developed a new, faster photochromic glass that proved excellent for sunglasses. Several high-profile specialty-glass projects added to the bottom line and burnished the company's image as a source of high-tech materials. In the late 1970s, Corning supplied fused-silica windows and specialty glasses for the space shuttle. It also fabricated eight-foot mirror blanks for the new space telescope.

An unexpected opportunity in Poland proved a windfall. Early in 1976, UNITRA, the state-owned electronics company, approached RCA and Corning with a proposition. The Poles knew the American companies had licensed black-and-white TV-glass technology in Romania and that Corning had set up several glassmaking ventures in Hungary. They wondered whether the Americans would consider a deal for color-TV technology. Pierre-Louis Roederer, the cosmopolitan CIC veteran who had negotiated the company's earlier deals in Eastern Europe, represented Corning in the new discussions. In April, the parties concluded an agreement: UNITRA would pay $121 million for RCA and Corning to build and equip a color TV tube complex in Piaseczno, a suburb of Warsaw. Corning's share of the deal totaled $50 million and included not only construction and equipment but also engineering services for three years. [26]

From Corning's perspective, the Polish contract, settled soon after the Guns of August, was a lucrative, heaven-sent opportunity, and another step toward an accelerated licensing program in Socialist bloc and less developed countries in which direct foreign investment was difficult. Roederer remembers that when he explained the deal to Amo Houghton and his father, the

Ambassador exclaimed, "My God. Thanks to you [the company has] made a profit this year!"[27]

The deal in Poland was a prelude of similar ventures to come. In 1981, Corning reached agreement with Chinese officials to build a black-and-white TV glass plant in Shanghai. The company did not disclose the terms but acknowledged coyly that the deal was worth "many millions of dollars" and that the Chinese agreed to pay "a substantial amount in cash." Not long afterward, Corning announced a deal with P.T. Supreme Indo-American Industries of Indonesia to build a $26 million dinnerware plant in Surabaya. And in 1982, Corning formed a new unit, Corning Engineering, to license technology and provide engineering services in many new locations around the world. One of its first projects was a black-and-white TV glass plant in India.[28]

Corning's consumer products also continued to fare well, although disturbing signs of change also became apparent. To keep the momentum from the recovery going, the company pursued several strategies. A new brightly decorated, high-fashion line of dinnerware, Corelle Expressions, was targeted at upscale consumers and introduced with fanfare. Meanwhile, hundreds of thousands of sets of Corelle Livingware and Corning Ware were packaged each year as premiums for collectors of S&H Green Stamps and customers at banks and grocery stores. Even Pyrex received a makeover, as creative young marketing professionals including John Loose and Peter Campanella promoted new shapes and functions to go along with old standards like measuring cups and mixing bowls. The Un-Candle, a Pyrex vessel in which a wick floated on a layer of salad oil, enjoyed a fad-like boom. Corning had less luck with a Pyrex flower pot, however, as customers were unwilling to pay a premium for the benefit of seeing the root systems of their plants.[29]

The company's forced decision in April 1975 to discontinue "fair trade" practices in marketing its products was a source of long-term concern for Corning's consumer businesses. These practices had originated in the 1930s as a means of protecting merchants in rural areas by allowing manufacturers of consumer items to set the prices of their goods. A Pyrex pie plate cost the same at Sears in Chicago and at a general store in Montana. Fair trade obviously benefited manufacturers and distributors, since it effectively guaranteed them a profit. But some producers, including Corning, pointed out that it enabled them to afford investments in R&D and product improvements that otherwise would be difficult to fund.

Over the years, most states passed laws supporting fair trade practices, and federal law permitted manufacturers to apply them in states without legislation. In the late 1960s, however, an activist consumer movement began lobbying against fair trade practices as anticompetitive. Regional discount stores such as K-Mart (soon to be a national powerhouse) joined in the agitation, claiming that fair trade impeded their ability to offer consumers lower prices. By the mid-1970s, some states repealed their fair trade laws and the Federal Trade Commission challenged the traditional interpretation of federal law on the matter. These changes placed Corning in a difficult position: by sticking to fair trade, it controlled its margins and kept its traditional accounts happy, but it was losing the political and public relations battles and in danger of acquiring a reputation for profit mongering and hostility to consumer interests. Corning executives testified in favor of fair trade in many states but by the spring of 1975, the company ultimately had little choice but to give up and move on.

In the short term, Corning's decision to go off fair trade boosted its business. Volume soared as K-Mart and other discount houses, eager to shed their image as purveyors of cheap goods, placed huge orders for Corelle and Corning Ware and displayed them prominently. Some stores priced Corning's products below cost simply to attract customers. The longer-term implications were less positive, as the new pricing of Corning Ware and Corelle did less to raise the profile of the mass discounters than to lower consumer perception of Corning's consumer products. A set of Corning Ware as a wedding gift no longer signaled the generosity of givers or the rising status of the recipients. Meanwhile, Corning's wholesalers and traditional retailers were horrified, and sales through these channels began to dry up. In 1979, Corning created its first direct sales account—Sears—in an attempt to reduce its distribution costs. It followed soon after by setting up national accounts with K-Mart and other mass merchandisers. These moves were painful to a company that had partnered with its distributors for more than five decades. Worse, they portended a new balance of power between Corning and its retailing customers, with the latter increasingly in a position to dictate pricing and marketing strategy. In 1980, the company sought to mollify its traditional customers by launching Corning Designs, the first (as it turned out) of several efforts to package its glass and glass ceramic products with other upscale lifestyle housewares at fine department stores. Corning Designs purchased about four-fifths of its offerings, including crystal glassware, ceramic dinnerware, wooden salad bowls, and other items for resale.[30]

While waiting to see whether Corning Designs and other measures to cope with adverse trends in the distribution of consumer housewares would place its business on a better footing, Corning recognized that its long-term future lay elsewhere. During the late 1970s, it took advantage of its strengthening financial condition to fund the biggest bet in its history—that it could become a significant force in the telecommunications industry, one of the largest, wealthiest, and politically salient industries in the world economy.

Optical Waveguides: A Strategy for Breaking In

In 1975, Corning faced another critical decision about the future of its business in optical waveguides. For the second time in five years, it had to choose whether to push ahead with no certain return in sight or ease off and perhaps even exit altogether. Going forward would require big investments to scale up production. The safer, less expensive alternative was to back away and collect royalties on its technology. Given AT&T's dominance in the United States and the hard times at hand, the temptation to pursue the latter course was very real. Corning had invested in the business for nearly a decade with no payback and none in sight. Amo Houghton and Bill Armistead were steadfast in support but there were no meaningful commitments from customers. The development partners had placed small orders and were arranging field tests, but there were no assurances of big orders to follow. Meanwhile, AT&T remained a major threat and other big telecommunications companies had joined the race.

The stakes were high enough that the matter came to the attention of Corning's board of directors. One member, ordinarily quiet, was Dr. James B. Fisk, chairman of Bell Telephone Laboratories. Houghton asked him point blank for his assessment of Corning's research and its potential to play a significant role in the technology's future. "Fiber optics is going to be very big," Fisk replied. "Keep it going." With that remark, recalled Tom MacAvoy, Fisk "earned his director's fee for his entire tenure and beyond."[31]

As it recovered from the mid-decade recession, Corning not only sustained the waveguide program but also hastened development and commercialization. For by then other factors had come into play, creating an urgent need to push ahead. Rapid progress in laser research and development had yielded smaller, more reliable lasers that could operate at room-temperature conditions. A host of big companies and entrepreneurial ventures were making big strides in fiber coatings, cables, connectors, and alignment techniques. AT&T was now heavily committed to fiber optics for basic telecommunications applications (as opposed to its original interest in PicturePhone transmissions) and was readying its first field trial in Atlanta for January 1976. If that went well, the next trial would be a real installation in downtown Chicago. GTE, the British post office, and other players were likewise proceeding rapidly.[32]

In August 1975, MacAvoy had appointed Lee Wilson, formerly head of Corning Europe, as head of the electronic products division, which included responsibility for the optical waveguide program. With the full backing of his bosses, Wilson retained the Boston Consulting Group to help with a major study of the world telecommunications market and Corning's prospects for entry as a supplier of optical fibers. The study entailed extensive research and interviews at the leading telecommunications and cabling companies around the world to understand ownership arrangements, vertical integration, and customer–supplier relationships. The consultants concluded that for Corning to become a significant factor in the market it would have to achieve three objectives: first, it would have to develop and maintain an unassailable technical leadership position, including vigorous defense of its patents, to keep the cable companies from integrating backward into fiber; second, it would have to find a way to penetrate AT&T, which controlled four-fifths of the U.S. telecommunications market; and, third, it would have to move quickly to expand its position in international markets.[33]

With these objectives set, Wilson approached MacAvoy to launch the campaign in earnest. The initial challenge was to scale up capacity to make optical fibers in commercial volume. This required two things: a substantial financial investment, what Chuck Lucy termed "the real money-sucking phase,"[34] and a crackerjack team of engineers and manufacturing personnel. To head the team, Wilson asked for the best product development manager in the company. MacAvoy gave him three names, including that of Dave Duke, who had led the impressive crash development of Celcor and was now working on advanced materials in the ceramic products division. Wilson interviewed Duke and quickly hired him, although Duke himself saw irony in the situation. He was in a fast-track assignment with line responsibility for 1,000 employees and $100 million in revenues when he was invited to take on waveguides, a business with six employees and less than $1 million in revenues. Reviewing these numbers with MacAvoy, Duke asked with a smile, "Tom, what'd I do wrong?"[35]

Duke had done nothing wrong, and he signed up in the summer of 1976 to direct the building and operation of a full-scale pilot plant in Erwin with an annual capacity of 5,000 kilometers—more than double the capacity of the original development facility at Sullivan Park. He brought with him Skip Deneka and other colleagues who had worked on Celcor. By then, Corning was selling uncabled fiber, with attenuation ranging from 6 to 10 db/km, at prices between $1 and $1.50 per meter. Successful field tests at AT&T, Northern Telecom, and other installations had demonstrated the compelling technological advantages of fiber-optic cable and suggested that it would soon be cost competitive with traditional copper cable.[36] To succeed in an extremely high-stakes, competitive environment, Wilson, Duke, and their colleagues realized that Corning would have to move quickly and aggressively. A strategy "to merely stay even with the competition" wouldn't work, they believed. As Duke put it, "When your competition's bigger, matching it isn't good enough. 'I don't want to tie....If we tie we lose."[37]

Leadership in fiber optics meant leadership in research and manufacturing. To achieve it, Duke set exceedingly ambitious targets for all parties, starting with the research team. He asked them what it would take to get attenuation down from 5 or 6 db/km to 0.5 db/km within a decade and, over the same period, how they could expand bandwidth from 200 megahertz to several gigahertz? The answers to these questions suggested that

Corning take a fresh look at basic fiber design. There were two types: single-mode and multimode (or graded index). The original fibers produced by Corning in 1970 were single-mode, which meant that they had a tiny central core through which light traveled in a straight path. Single-mode fibers maximized speed, capacity, and distance between repeating stations, but aligning the light source with the core required extreme care and was believed to be impractical in the field. As a result, AT&T and most other telecommunications companies preferred multimode fibers, which featured bigger cores but compensated for the tendency of light signals to scatter by manipulating the index of refraction in the core glass. Multimode fibers were easier to make and use than single-mode fibers but at the cost of reduced capacity and shorter distances between repeating stations.[38]

By 1977, the development of new lasers that could operate at longer wavelengths sparked interest once again in single-mode fibers. Duke believed that single-mode fibers would eventually win out over multimode because of lower loss and wider bandwidth, and he dedicated a small team of researchers to single-mode technology. At the same time, however, Corning continued to work on multimode fibers to support its growing list of customers. However the market moved, the company would be prepared.[39]

Duke prodded the manufacturing team with another stretch goal: if fiber was selling for $1.50 a meter in 1976, how could Corning get the cost down to ten cents a meter within the next five to ten years? The answer was not only bigger blanks, faster speeds, and improved selections, but new generations of process technology, new equipment, and a fast learning curve. It also involved development of a fundamentally new process for making the blanks.[40]

At the time, there were two approaches to making fused silica. The first, derived from Frank Hyde's work in the late 1930s, was called the inside vapor deposition (IVD) process, because a pure, doped silica soot was deposited in successive layers inside a solid tube of glass. After consolidation at higher temperatures, the pure glass made from the deposited soot would become the core of the fiber, while the glass tube around it would form the outermost layer of cladding. Corning held key patents on the IVD process, which it—and all of its major competitors—used throughout the 1970s. The IVD process had certain drawbacks, however: impurities in the cladding that could affect optical properties and fiber strength, and constraints on batch sizes that could result in high manufacturing costs.[41]

An alternative process was the outside vapor phase oxidation (OVPO) process. Under this method, the silica soot was deposited on a rotating mandrill and built up in layers to required dimensions. The innermost layer became core glass, while subsequent deposits, with a different index of refraction, built up the cladding. The OVPO process resulted in superior fiber properties and also appeared to offer better manufacturing economics than the IVP process. Once again, Duke hedged Corning's bet, setting up an internal competition around both processes to determine which would win out.[42]

Another component of Corning's strategy entailed building capacity ahead of demand. When they had erected the pilot plant, which came on stream early in 1977, Duke estimated that it would not require expansion for several years. Within a year, however, Wilson and Duke saw that Corning would have to build sooner. Orders were pouring in, including a two-year commitment from Canada Wire & Cable for up to 20,000 km.[43] Corning decided that the next facility would triple the capacity of the pilot plant. Wilson and Duke chose land adjacent to Corning's electronics components manufacturing plant in Wilmington, North Carolina, as the site for the new waveguide plant. In addition to available space, Wilmington offered an existing workforce in a labor market the company understood and proximity to many cable manufacturers in the Southeast. Construction started early in 1978.

Another key component of Corning's strategy to break in to the telecommunications industry was a spirited defense of its intellectual property. "There are twelve basic patents in the field, and we have all twelve," Amo Houghton said. "It's *our* turf with our patents." The patents covered the fused-silica vapor deposition processes and the dopants used in the core glass, and the company was determined to enforce them. The first test case was a suit filed against ITT and its customer, the U.S. government, in July 1976. ITT had entered the optical waveguide race late, although its British R&D subsidiary, Standard Telecommunications Labs, made rapid progress on the basis of its own approach to inside vapor deposition. It patented its process in the United Kingdom and applied for patents in the United States.

Meanwhile, it won a competition to supply a U.S. military test program. That was enough for Wilson, who contended that it didn't matter whether ITT had developed its own vapor deposition process; what mattered, he believed, was that no one could make optical fibers in the United States without using a patented Corning process.[44]

Corning expected that ITT would negotiate a settlement but instead found itself embroiled in a prolonged and costly legal battle as ITT countersued. Discovery dragged on for five years, and "for much of the time," according to one account, "the battle was at a fever pitch, each side producing a thousand documents a week." Corning's top executives spent 210 days in cross-examination by ITT attorneys.[45] Finally, in July 1981, shortly before the case was to go to trial, ITT capitulated, admitting infringement and agreeing to pay a lump-sum penalty and license Corning's patents. The settlement caught many observers by surprise, but Corning's case was strong and the consequences of a loss for ITT were terrible to contemplate as the technology neared market readiness.[46]

Corning followed up its victory in the ITT case with another successful patent infringement suit against Valtec, a subsidiary of Philips. Valtec had made rapid progress in optical waveguides with the help of some former Corning employees who had been let go in the Guns of August. Corning also waged its patent defense around the world in Japan, the United Kingdom, Holland, Germany, and Canada. The process proved time-consuming and expensive, but the precedents of the ITT and Valtec more than justified the effort.

Another fundamental strategic question involved forward vertical integration. Although Corning had produced cable for experimental trials and sales samples, it faced a steep uphill climb to become a major cable supplier in the United States, given the size and market power of existing competitors. On the other hand, Corning was worried about backward integration by the cable companies into fiber production and the possibility that its foreign development partners might enter the United States. Among these, Siemens represented the biggest threat and the biggest opportunity. During the talks leading to the formation of Siecor GmbH, the joint venture to produce optical fibers for sale to Siemens in Germany, Lucy and his counterpart at Siemens, Dr. Berndt Zeitler, had discussed a longer-term prospect of establishing a second joint venture to manufacture cable in the United States. That prospect lay fallow until 1977, when Siemens approached Corning to revive it. Siemens was willing to take a minority position, but Houghton and Armistead insisted that a fifty-fifty deal would prove more stable and in keeping with Corning's traditional approach to operating joint ventures. The two parties agreed, and in December 1977 Siecor Optical Cables, Inc. (subsequently Siecor Corporation) was born. Corning would be Siecor's principal supplier of optical fibers and know-how in optical waveguides, while Siemens would contribute its technology and vast experience in making cable. Both parents agreed to make significant financial investments as well. The two parties held an equal number of seats on the board of directors, but Corning named the board chair (Lee Wilson) and hence controlled the management—just as, symmetrically, Siemens controlled the management of Siecor GmbH.[47]

The American Siecor established a temporary headquarters in a former men's clothing store in Horseheads (at the optimistic address of 631 Miracle Mile), with fewer than twenty employees. During its early months, the company began to hustle for customers while simultaneously improving ways to bundle optical fibers into cable. Siecor booked its first order from General Telephone Company of Fort Wayne, Indiana, in 1978. Most of its customers were independent telephone companies, and Siecor occasionally called on Siemens to provide turnkey installations linking cables and electronics. Siemens also contributed most of the technical support. For example, Dr. Peter Bark, a top cabling engineer, led the development of the loose tube cable design that became standard in the industry. Each optical fiber was given a color-coded, strippable polymer coating as additional protection. Bundles of the newly coated fibers were then gathered in layers with more protective and insulating materials in between. Finally, the resulting structure was enclosed in shielding and polymer materials that became a durable and protective outer layer. Automatic machinery coiled the cable onto large spools for delivery to customers.[48]

In 1979 the rising volume of business created an urgent need to expand Siecor's operations. Management began looking to merge with an existing cable company as the fastest way to satisfy demand, with the additional benefits of increasing market access and gaining an experienced workforce.

Using the services of an investment bank, Siecor identified several promising possibilities, including Superior Cable Corporation, a privately held cable manufacturing company based in Hickory, North Carolina. Once owned by Continental Telephone, Superior operated a modern cabling plant and a thriving business serving independent telephone companies such as its former parent. In 1979, Superior posted approximately $90 million in sales, operated four plants (including one devoted to cable equipment and attachments and another to specialty cables for elevators), and employed about 1,200 people. The deal was closed early in 1980. Soon afterward, Siecor relocated its headquarters to Hickory.

The immediate next step in Siecor's fast-growth trajectory was the decision to build a new fiber-optic cabling facility rather than attempt to retrofit a copper-cable plant. The company broke ground for its telephony cable plant in Hickory in October, and it came on stream the following summer. Siemens furnished most of the equipment and technology, while most of the 200 employees were drawn from Superior Cable.

Desperately Seeking the New

In the fall of 1980, Corning reorganized its top management group for the third time in a decade. In the biggest change, Tom MacAvoy and Jamie Houghton shifted and recombined assignments. MacAvoy assumed responsibility for all of Corning's operations on a worldwide basis and Houghton became chairman of the executive committee of the board and chief strategic officer with responsibility for all staff functions and the company's strategy for growth. In other changes, Al Dawson resigned as a Corning officer and board member to become chairman and chief executive of Siecor Corporation. Dick Dulude and Lee Wilson essentially swapped jobs, with Dulude returning to direct a new marketing and business division and Wilson going back to Paris as chair of Corning Europe. And Marty Gibson moved back from his staff position in personnel to resume leadership of the Medical Products Division, which was now combined with Science Products.[49]

There were several motives behind the reorganization: to position Corn-

ing for the coming decade, to complete Jamie Houghton's training to succeed his brother as chairman and chief executive of the Glass Works, and to
boost attention to newer businesses, including optical waveguides, industrial biotechnology, and medical equipment and services. And like comparable changes in 1971 and 1975, this reorganization occurred in the midst of
tough economic times. The Iranian revolution of 1979 had spawned another
energy crisis and plunged the industrial economies into yet another deep
and prolonged recession. Heavy industry, including the auto, steel, and
chemical industries—all big customers of Corning products—suffered especially severely. The company's sales peaked at $1.7 billion in 1981, but its prof-
its had started drifting downward a year earlier. The nadir was reached in
1982, when sales dipped more than 8 percent and net income reached its
lowest ebb since the Guns of August.

In this latest downturn, Corning's options were more constrained than
they had been earlier in the decade. There were fewer underperforming units
in the portfolio and little "extra" overhead to slash. The company resorted to
a spending freeze, offered early retirement incentives, and, at one point in
1982, cut salaries of administrtative personnel by 5 percent. Corning was
rumored to be an acquisition target of General Electric and itself in merger
talks with Owens-Corning Fiberglas. All parties denied the GE rumor, but
there was more to the Owens-Corning possibility. That company was suffer-
ing from the cyclical downturn and facing significant liability exposure stemming from the sale of asbestos products. Although Corning remained subject
to the 1949 consent decree that required the eventual divestiture of virtually
all of its interest in Owens-Corning—with the latest compliance date fixed
for 1986—it still held a 23.9 percent stake. The U.S. Department of Justice
indicated that it would not necessarily oppose a merger.

In September 1981, the talks between the companies broke down, how-
ever, and Corning announced its intention to sell its stake in Owens-
Corning. "We either wanted to get further in, or get out," said Amo
Houghton, but "they weren't terribly enthusiastic about a merger." Some
observers portrayed Corning's decision as "ungentlemanly," since it put
Owens-Corning in play, but they also applauded it as an "aggressive" move
that showed management would not allow a crisis of the magnitude of the
Guns of August to recur. Analysts forecast that the sale of Corning's interest

in Owens-Corning would fetch as much as $200 million to fund development of Corning's newer businesses. In fact, Corning chose not to sell its stake all at once and realized $66.6 million in 1982. The company simultaneously absorbed a $90 million (pretax) restructuring charge to help put the crisis behind it.[50]

Meanwhile, Corning divested several small businesses, including its European lab glassware operations.[51] Corning put another old business— glass bulbs for incandescent lighting—on the block more grudgingly. A lingering effect of the first energy crisis was reduced usage of traditional electrical lighting. At the same time, the lightbulb industry was undergoing a consolidation as the major producers began to reassess their strategies on a global basis. Primarily a domestic company, GE was looking to expand abroad, while Philips and other European producers were looking for better access to the U.S. market. Philips, which made its own glass envelopes, acquired Westinghouse's bulb business in 1980.

Decades of continuous cost reduction in the bulb plants in Wellsboro, Pennsylvania, Central Falls, Rhode Island, and Danville, Kentucky ironically increased Corning's vulnerability. By the late 1970s, transportation costs had become a relatively high proportion of total manufacturing cost. The lightbulb companies were wondering why they should continue to pay the freight and thinking about producing the glass envelopes themselves. For many years Corning had preempted that possibility by maintaining tight control of the Ribbon Machine by enforcing licenses and buying up used machines when they came on the market. In 1980, however, Sylvania acquired a used Ribbon Machine in the United Kingdom, and, as MacAvoy put it, "the game was afoot." Sylvania could reverse engineer the Ribbon Machine and undoubtedly find ways to develop the technology in ways beyond Corning's control. Sylvania was also now in the business of melting glass—bad news for Corning.[52]

With the inevitable end in sight, Corning negotiated the sale of its lightbulb plants to Sylvania and Philips in separate transactions. Wellsboro went first, in April 1981; the others followed within twelve months. The deals included provisions protecting workers' benefits and job security. Corning's exit was difficult for the Houghtons to contemplate, given the historical significance of the business to the company and its long stewardship of Wellsboro and Central Falls. Nonetheless, MacAvoy aptly characterized Corning's century in the business as "a pretty good run."[53]

Developing Area X

In his new assignment as chief strategic officer, Jamie Houghton directed a fresh study of Corning's entire portfolio of businesses. The work built on earlier plans and reached similar conclusions: the company would transfer resources from the industries of the past (lightbulb glass and refractories) to the industries of the future (optical waveguides and industrial biotechnology), while maintaining the "self-sustaining" and "cash-generating" industries of the present (consumer products, TV glass, automotive products, and ophthalmic glass).[54] Corning acted on these conclusions even as they were still forming. It proved willing to entertain small-scale ventures into new areas, approving a plan to integrate forward from its photosensitive glass lenses into the sunglass industry.[55]

The biggest new thrust came in optical waveguides and fiber-optic cable. As telecommunications companies around the world took a more active interest in optical waveguides, orders came thicker and faster. Although Corning had yet to earn a return in the business, it continued to make big investments, doubling the capacity of the Wilmington fiber plant in 1981 and tripling it again a year later. The company also helped underwrite the new Siecor cable plant in Hickory. At the same time, Corning converted its development deals in England and France into joint ventures to begin fiber production. It signed a fifty-fifty deal with BICC in 1980 to create Optical Fibers, Ltd.; a year later, it joined with St. Gobain and Thomson-CSF in France to form Fibres Optiques Industries. Corning held a 40-percent stake. Elsewhere, Corning licensed its technology to Pirelli in Italy and to several producers in Japan.[56]

By late 1981, Corning had invested more than $100 million in optical waveguides and related technologies. Not stopping there, the company maintained research and development programs in components like couplers and lasers to ascertain whether it would make sense to integrate forward. This new aggressiveness stemmed from lessons of the past: "We're looking at [optical fibers] internationally and nationally, vertically and horizontally," said Amo Houghton, "because we didn't do that with TV or lightbulbs."[57]

Although Corning's attention was focused on optical waveguides as a major growth opportunity, its leaders drew another lesson from the recent past, seeking to avoid dependence on any single business ever again. Relying too heavily on waveguides risked the same fate that befell the company when it all but lost the color TV glass business. Thus Houghton and MacAvoy prodded Sullivan Park to identify the next big opportunity in glass or, if necessary, another technology—even one unrelated to traditional Corning strengths.

When pressed for results, Hutchins could point with justifiable pride to Celcor and optical waveguides as major achievements. But his bosses would counter with, "That's all terrific, guys, but what's 'area x'"—Amo Houghton's code phrase for the next big opportunity. MacAvoy remembers that "after the recession of 1975, the drumbeat [to find "area x"] got louder."[58]

In the late 1970s, the most promising candidate for "area x" seemed to be industrial biotechnology. By 1975, Corning had acquired many patents on glass as a medium for immobilizing enzymes and was pushing additional research into recombinant DNA and the synthesis of enzymes. Although Hutchins killed basic research in biotechnology in the Guns of August, the company continued to pursue applications of immobilized-enzyme technology vigorously. For example, it could be used to facilitate conversion of glucose to fructose to make high fructose corn syrup, a sweetener increasingly attractive to the soft drink industry as an alternative to sugar. Another application involved converting lactose, a waste product in making cheese, to glucose, a general purpose sweetener. Howard Weetall championed still other applications in health care, including enzyme treatments for certain types of cancer.

With the support of top management, Hutchins authorized Weetall and Harmon Garfinkel to explore attracting outside funds—the financing strategy that had kept optical waveguides going just a few years earlier. The Corning representatives made the rounds of potential partners and attracted sporadic attention. The British Milk Processing Board proved willing to fund a small-scale research project to convert lactose to glucose. In the United States, the giant food chain Kroger wanted to explore using Corning technology to convert cheese whey into baker's yeast. Sebastiani, a California vintner, was interested in a biotechnological process to transform red wine into white. The fledgling biotech companies—Cetus, Genentech, and Biogen—were also receptive. Among these, Genentech showed the most interest and in 1979 agreed to work with Corning on the synthesis of enzymes for the production of fructose.[59]

By the early 1980s, several of these projects were beginning to bear fruit. In 1981, Corning acquired the fermentation enzyme business of Rohm & Haas and a controlling interest in a small Kansas City–based lab that produced animal blood serums and chemicals used in growing cells for vaccine production and biotechnological research. The following year, Corning and Kroger formed a small joint venture called Nutrisearch to process by-products from Kroger's dairy operations into sweeteners and additives for its bakeries. In that same year, Corning formed a more ambitious joint venture with Genentech called Genencor. As usual, the two parties held equal shares in the venture, which was capitalized at $40 million. Because Genentech was a cash-poor start-up, however, Corning put up all the money, including Genentech's share, in return for a 6.5 percent stake in Genentech and a seat on its board of directors. Genencor began its corporate life as a research and development entity drawing on its parents' capabilities to carry out contract research while also prospecting for new markets.

Corning also mounted a bigger push in medical equipment and services, attempting to build on the success of its blood gas and electrolyte analyzers and its radioimmunoassay technology. The biggest project in the mid-1970s was the leukocyte automatic recognition computer (LARC), a machine to classify and count white cells in human blood samples. The product of four years of development and millions of investment dollars, LARC attracted widespread interest in the business press. Unfortunately, the machine competed against not only traditional labor-intensive methods but also other machines and techniques pioneered by other medical equipment companies. And, doubly unfortunately for Corning, LARC was an expensive solution for its customers. Introduced in 1975, it sold for approximately $100,000. After three years and fewer than a hundred installations worldwide, Corning pulled LARC off the market.

Meanwhile the marketplace for Corning's scientific products and equipment continued to churn. More and more R&D labs were shifting from traditional "wet" chemical analysis that made use of beakers, flasks, and other conventional labware, to "dry chemistry," which relied on new, mostly digital instrumentation and equipment. This trend, moreover, was unfolding in a context very appealing to Corning. Medical research was projected to grow at a healthy clip well into the future, thus avoiding the cyclical downturns that afflicted most Corning businesses. At the same time, it seemed immune from foreign competition, at least the fierce variety the company had experienced elsewhere. With these considerations in mind, 1980 Corning's top brass grouped its Scientific Products and Medical Divisions together under Marty Gibson. MacAvoy handed Gibson a mandate to grow his businesses as rapidly as possible. He was free not only to capitalize on Corning's research but also to seek acquisitions.

Gibson wasted little time in getting started. Within months, he consummated his first deal, acquiring Gilford Instruments for approximately $40 million in cash and Corning stock. A privately owned company, Gilford came on the market when its owner and founder, Saul R. Gilford, was killed in a plane crash. Based in Oberlin, Ohio, the company posted annual revenues of $31 million and produced analytical instruments and diagnostic reagents used in conventional blood tests. Its business thus complemented Corning's more specialized equipment, although it also drew Corning into more hotly contested segments of the lab equipment market.[60]

Not long after, Gibson pushed for a much bigger deal, both in scale and extent, by negotiating to acquire the outstanding shares in MetPath, the blood testing laboratory in which Corning had first invested in 1973. The cost was $125 million in Corning stock, a sum that made it by far the biggest acquisition in the company's history to that point. The strategic rationale for acquiring MetPath was that it extended and completed Corning's forward integration from its traditional business in labware through lab diagnostic equipment and procedures to lab operation. Gibson had anticipated the move for years, and with the second energy crisis and second deep recession in a decade now upon the company, the Houghton brothers and MacAvoy agreed that there was little choice but to diversify into new, fast-growing areas that seemed impervious to the forces threatening to overwhelm its traditional businesses. Gibson later speculated that had he proposed the deal in the 1960s or in the late 1980s, his bosses "would have put me into a straightjacket." But, he pointed out, the 1970s and early 1980s were "a terrible time," and that, in retrospect, the MetPath merger was "an act of desperation" for Corning. "This was Tom and Amo saying we've got to find a new way to make our living because the old way isn't working."[61]

The MetPath deal propelled Corning along a path that led into entirely new directions—and one that would in time encounter serious obstacles. Soon after it was consummated, however, came an unexpected and enormous surprise: in January 1982, the U.S. Department of Justice announced a settlement in a long-standing antitrust case against AT&T. The agreement, which would take effect on January 1, 1984, called for AT&T to divest its telephone operating companies while retaining its long-distance telephone service and R&D and manufacturing units. The settlement also undermined AT&T's virtual monopoly in long-distance service by freeing it from regulation and introducing competitive pricing. In a single stroke, the major obstacle to Corning's advance in the U.S. telecommunications market was eliminated. The question was, how would—or could—Corning take advantage of it?

CHAPTER THIRTEEN

Emphasizing Performance, Quality, and Diversity, 1983–1989

IN THE LATE 1970s, Amo Houghton began thinking long and hard about the problem of succession. Although he was then in his early fifties, he had been a senior officer of the company for a quarter century and had served as chairman and CEO since 1964. The problem now was not that he lacked energy or enthusiasm. Rather, he recognized the need to create opportunities in the company for younger executives. In a series of conversations that Tom MacAvoy initiated, the two men reflected on how they had risen to the top at relatively young ages and remarked on the need to provide their successors with time to make an impact.[1] Amo was also intrigued by possibilities of finding new contexts in which to apply his talents. Of course, there was a family tradition of leaving early. His grandfather, Alanson B. Houghton, had embarked on his political and diplomatic career while in his mid-fifties. Amo's father, the ambassador, had begun his second career in public service at an even earlier age during World War II, then returned to the company, and left management for good at age 58. More immediately, Amo's younger brother Alanson had departed the company years before for the Episcopal ministry, a precedent of service that Amo much admired. To a handful of close friends and associates, he confided an interest in applying his leadership and organizational talents to humanitarian relief, perhaps in Africa.

Amo knew that if he were to leave that his brother Jamie, ten years younger, was the right man to take over the Glass Works. (Amo later quoted John F. Kennedy on the subject, after the president had named his brother Bobby as Attorney General: "Nepotism isn't too bad, as long as you keep it in the family!")[2] Jamie Houghton had worked his way up through the company, proving himself in a sequence of increasingly responsible assignments. After earning an MBA at Harvard in 1962, Jamie joined Corning, and with his bride Maisie, moved to Danville, Kentucky. He started as a process engineer, and then became a shift foreman with a crew working the Ribbon Machine.[3]

Within a year, Jamie and Maisie moved back to Corning, where he took a position as a financial analyst in the controller's office. He had already let it be known that he was interested in an international assignment, and in 1964, he got his wish, moving to Zurich as vice president of Corning International. Four years later, Jamie returned to Corning, New York as vice president and general manager of the consumer products division, a tenure that saw the hugely successful introduction of Corelle as well as a few stumbles. "'The Counter That Cooks' took a few years off my life!" he later exclaimed. In 1971, he was promoted to vice chairman and joined the top management team with Amo and Tom MacAvoy. Jamie's specific charge included Corning International Corporation (of which he was chairman) and the corporate staff departments concerned with external relations: law, finance, and public relations. He also served as chairman of the executive committee of the board of directors. As he climbed through the ranks, he developed a distinctive style: he usually wore bright ties and even brighter suspenders and smoked cigars constantly. Colleagues and subordinates admired his ability to combine a tough, no-nonsense focus on results and performance with the manners of a gentleman—a steel fist inside a velvet glove.

In the late 1970s, Jamie recalled, "I began to get whiffs in the air" that Amo might step down and that he would have the opportunity to lead the company. "I'm not clear on the exact sequence, but Amo and I began to talk about it." As a final step in his preparation, Jamie was asked by his brother in 1980 to undertake a thorough review of Corning's strategy and operations, a responsibility reflected in his new title as vice chairman and chief strategic officer. This assignment, of course, was not merely a finishing school for the next chief executive. Since the crisis in the mid-1970s, Corning had struggled to regain its footing, and another deep recession loomed on the horizon. The strategy study (discussed below) went on for about a year-and-a-half, during which Jamie relinquished his international line responsibilities to MacAvoy. The study recommended significant strategic and organizational changes for the company that the board of directors approved in February 1982. Later that year, Amo announced that he would retire the following April and that MacAvoy would succeed Bill Armistead as vice chairman with special responsibility for technology and R&D. While no further specifics were provided, it seemed likely to many observers that MacAvoy would retire when he reached the age of 60 in 1988.[4]

After stepping down as chairman, Amo remained on the board of directors for several more years. He no longer played an active role in the company's routine decision making, but as chair of the board's executive committee and with a growing interest in public service, he frequently represented Corning at ceremonies and in government contexts. He also helped to launch a new venture capital fund in which Corning became a minority partner. The goal of the fund was both to make money and to gain insights into new technologies, especially biotechnology that might be of interest to Corning.[5] In July 1986, Amo resigned from the board of directors after deciding to run as a Republican for the seat once occupied by his grandfather in the U.S. House of Representatives. He was elected in a close race and has been returned to office in every congressional election through 2000.

Amo Houghton's retirement as CEO was part of a broader set of changes in Corning's executive ranks during the late 1970s and early 1980s as many long-time veterans stepped down or (like MacAvoy) transitioned into terminal assignments. During the next several years, Oakes Ames, Bill Armistead, Forry Behm, Al Dawson, Jack Hutchins, and other top executives moved on, opening the door for younger colleagues. Henceforth, the company was in the hands not only of a new CEO but also of a new generation of management.

Troubled Times and Urgent Measures

When Jamie Houghton ascended to the top job at Corning Glass Works in April 1983, the fortunes of U.S. manufacturing companies were at their lowest ebb in fifty years. The recessions of the mid-1970s and early 1980s had rocked many manufacturers, exposing bloated headquarters, organizations, and out-moded work practices, and raising serious questions about conventional management tools such as portfolio strategies and discounted cash flow analysis of investments.[6] Worse still, the crisis in U.S. manufacturing reflected a shift of seismic proportions in the nature of competition. In industry after industry (including glass), the basis of competition became increasingly global, with U.S.-based companies facing not only their traditional domestic rivals but also competitors from overseas, especially Asia. And worst of all, it became abundantly clear that U.S. manufacturers in industry after industry (including glass) fell well short of world-class standards in cost and quality. Many U.S. companies thus competed at a devastating double disadvantage: foreign rivals offered better products *and* lower prices.

These distressing circumstances marked the beginning of a period of turmoil and dramatic change for most big American companies, which passed through repeated episodes of retrenchment, restructuring, delayering, and downsizing.[7] Hostile takeovers, leveraged buyouts, and huge mergers were in the air. Big companies such as Gulf Oil, Beatrice, Bendix, and RCA vanished in a climate characterized by a bull market, cheap debt, and the virtual collapse of antitrust enforcement. Voluntary asset restructurings became commonplace among highly diversified companies such as General Electric, Textron, and United Technologies. In the glass and materials industries, Owens-Illinois succumbed to a leveraged buyout and Owens-Corning Fiberglas restructured after a hostile takeover attempt. At Corning, the pressures of a hostile business environment prompted less dramatic but nonetheless sweeping changes in strategy, structure, and operations. Some of these changes were evident when Jamie Houghton took charge. Others emerged in the course of time as the company undertook a searching and thorough reexamination of its business.

The strategy study Houghton had directed in the early 1980s first hinted at the magnitude and direction of necessary changes. The study reaffirmed

Corning's traditional values and commitment to innovation, but also put fresh emphasis on achieving better financial results. The company set ambitious targets for profitability, measured by an average return on equity of 18 percent or better, a return on investment of 15 percent or better, and for growth, measured by real earnings-per-share growth of 5 percent or better. These goals, which Corning intended to meet by 1985, contrasted sharply with return on investment levels of about 12 percent and earnings per share growth that was essentially flat between 1973 and 1980.[8]

To achieve the twin objectives of profitability and growth, it was clear that Corning would have to change both its portfolio of businesses and its manner of operating. The company would transfer resources from the industries of the past to the industries of the future, while maintaining the "self-sustaining" and "cash-generating" industries of the present. Some measures took effect immediately, as the company followed the recent sale of its light bulb glass business by selling Corhart Refractories, a business with declining prospects, given the crisis in U.S. manufacturing. Corning also set about to prune marginal contributors and streamline operations. In 1983 and 1984, it closed plants in Indiana, Oklahoma, and Virginia, discontinued most operations in the main plant in Corning, and pared organization and staffing levels across the company. [9]

The strategy study also recommended that modify its organizational structure by creating larger, more autonomous business units, each responsible for its own portfolio and in control of its financial and technical resources. "The burden of profitable growth," Jamie Houghton argued, belonged on these units. In many instances, general managers of the units would have worldwide responsibility for their business, although Corning would maintain geographical units to support activity in some developing countries for a transitional period.[10]

Upon assuming the top office, Houghton proceeded to implement these structural changes and supported them by committing to a grueling schedule that called for him to visit at least ten company locations each quarter to listen to employees and explain the company's actions. He abandoned the top executive structure of which he had been part and replaced it with a new "chief decision-making unit" consisting of himself and five colleagues: vice chairmen MacAvoy (technology) and Van Campbell, 45 (finance and admin-

istration), and the heads of three operating groups: Dick Dulude, 50, at electronics and telecommunications; Marty Gibson, 45, at health and sciences;
and Bill Hudson, 53, at consumer and industry. The three operating executives were designated as presidents of their respective groups, titles that indicated Corning's commitment to decentralization. By making the titles of the
line executives equivalent—although Hudson's portfolio included most of
the traditional money-making parts of the company, while Dulude and Gibson presided over much smaller, barely profitable operations—Houghton
emphasized Corning's strategy to grow in new areas.[11]

Known formally as the management committee but more popularly as
"the six pack" or "the gang of six," the group served as a kind of internal
board of directors. (Each member also served on Corning's corporate
board.) The committee met formally every month to review operations and
progress against plans, discuss matters of concern, develop policies, review
strategic options, and make decisions. But the members met together in
informal settings much more often, by one estimate spending as much as a
quarter of their time together. Although the executives maintained some
genteel traditions of an earlier era (most notably, a shared fondness for fine
cigars and, after the meetings, fine wines), sessions were intense, spirited,
and demanding. These qualities reflected Houghton's personality, decisiveness, sense of urgency, and belief in teamwork. One executive later
remarked:

> From the day Jamie took charge, he maintained an incredibly punishing
> schedule to remain highly visible even in the outposts. He was very open in
> his decisions, relentlessly firm, and clear in his purpose. But he was almost
> Japanese in his attempts to get people to agree and commit. Teams and
> committees abounded. People who were not team players did not fit
> Jamie's style, and most of them soon departed—including some capable
> people.[12]

During its first year, the management committee set new performance
measures and proved serious about getting results. Once again, this
approach reflected Houghton's influence. The first goal ("Jamie's first stake
in the ground," as Van Campbell put it) was to improve operating margins,

then hovering at 2 percent, to 10 percent by 1985. This was clearly an ambitious target. Nonetheless, said Campbell, "It had the virtue of focusing significant attention on major changes having to be made. You just couldn't get there by incremental changes and hoping that growth would come back." But the management committee also focused on identifying and nourishing the core units that could contribute most toward reaching the goal. Campbell again: "If all else failed, we knew we could carve [Corning] down to a smaller company...[but] our preference was to have it be bigger when we reached the goal." That required "a lot of important changes, much more than if we had been trying to shoot for six percent."[13]

To help the business units strive toward the goal, Corning used both the carrot and the stick. Large bonuses would kick in as the company approached the goal. At the same time, the management committee, led by Houghton, would not accept halfway measures. "There had been a phase when we did not make a corporate budget for six years," recalled Roger Ackerman, who joined the committee in 1985. "Jamie quickly made it clear that such performance would not be tolerated. When people would take their budgets to the management committee and say they couldn't match corporate targets for the year, Jamie would tell them to come back when they had found ways to do it, then walk out of the presentation."[14] A few such episodes made the point.

The management committee also equipped the company with new management tools and techniques to help boost performance. One such technique was teamwork, which Houghton believed especially important as the company decentralized. The emphasis on teamwork started with the management committee itself. Incentive compensation for the members was based on performance of the corporation as a whole, and not on results at individual units. Consultants (first Bill Zierden of Dartmouth, then David Nadler of Columbia University and Delta Consulting Group) facilitated most of the Committee's gatherings. The point of these activities was to foster candor and trust and improve group processes to get better decisions. As Houghton recalled:

> The idea was that we were going to thrash things out together. I always said, "If at the end of the day we can't agree, I'll make up my mind. Make

no mistake about that, but I don't want to do it that way." Ninety percent of the time we didn't have to. . . .We had a lot of away meetings, a lot of wine at dinner. I mean seriously. A lot of dynamics happen if you get people after dinner yelling at each other with a bunch of wine. Most of that results in a head that doesn't feel so good the next day, but it gets people really interacting and getting rid of their inhibitions. We've always operated like that.[15]

In similar fashion—though perhaps without the wine—teamwork subsequently spread across Corning. In the mid-1980s, for example, Dick Sphon, corporate vice president of manufacturing and engineering, began meeting with the heads of manufacturing in various divisions (Bob Forrest, telecommunications; Ron Matthews, consumer; and Norm Garrity, glass and ceramic products) and with Dick Marks, corporate vice president of personnel (and industrial relations) in a group called "the gang of five." This group sought to coordinate manufacturing improvements and new labor practices throughout the company. Worker-management committees also spread to most facilities. These committees worked together on ways to improve performance—changing outmoded bumping practices, revamping grievance procedures, and tightening up observance of working hours. "By and large," recalled Sphon, these discussions weren't "combative. . . .Rather, both parties were, in essence, rewriting how we were going to work [together]. . . .The workers would get a lot more training. Our enemy was not each other, it was the competition, [and] we were all in this thing to win."[16]

Yet another set of teams formed around managing the process of innovation in a decentralized environment. Given the company's tradition of centralized research and engineering, decentralization posed thorny issues. Nonetheless, a high-level executive team headed by MacAvoy concluded that "a strong emphasis on product development [relative to basic research] is a desirable trend" and that the divisions should perform much of this work.[17] Once again, Corning relied on teams of R&D, engineering, and operating personnel to work out specific arrangements of research and engineering support to the respective operating units.

Toward Total Quality

Houghton recognized that the changes in strategy, structure, and high level teamwork, by themselves, would not enable the company to reach its objectives. He was receptive, then, to Forry Behm's suggestion to mount a major quality initiative. Quality management was believed to be at the heart of Japanese manufacturing success, and several prominent American corporations, including IBM, Motorola, Xerox, and Ford, had already achieved impressive gains through company-wide quality programs. A focus on quality, moreover, seemed a more positive and less threatening way to achieve significant performance improvements than, say, a productivity program.[18]

Behm had become a devotee of quality expert Philip Crosby, whose 1979 best-selling book, *Quality is Free*, had emphasized the "cost of quality" inherent in traditional American quality control methods that relied on detecting and fixing errors after the fact. Crosby demonstrated that setting up procedures and processes to do things right the first time could yield huge savings.[19] In the early 1980s, several Corning units had already begun applying Crosby's techniques with promising results. Houghton visited these units, as well as an IBM plant that had achieved a remarkable turnaround through a major quality initiative.

Intrigued by these examples, Houghton authorized further investigation. Corning sent out teams of managers and employees to study Japanese quality methods and American quality programs. The teams discovered, Houghton later wrote, "that successful companies were defining 'quality' in a framework much broader than product quality. They were demanding quality in every phase of their operations, from memo-writing to the conduct of meetings, from cost accounting to sales calls." The teams also found that companies that took quality seriously achieved superior results, while estimating the cost of poor quality as between 20 and 30 percent of sales.[20]

In October 1983, Houghton announced a major corporate quality initiative at a meeting of the company's top 130 managers. The initiative had four objectives:

- make Corning the world leader in quality
- institute a total quality plan in every unit, line, and staff, top to bottom, in the company

- eliminate surprise quality failures
- produce measurable results

As Houghton later put it, "We're talking about organizational and institutional quality affecting and motivating every phase of company operations. It is a new lifestyle, a whole new pattern of behavior, one which requires everyone to act differently—to face the true requirements of his or her job."[21]

Corning backed up the initiative with significant investments of time and money. Houghton himself began supporting the initiative with almost evangelistic fervor. Despite lean times, Corning allocated $5 million of corporate funds to the cause and named Behm as the company's first director of quality. The placement of a widely respected senior operating executive in the position was a deliberate signal of how serious the effort would be. A quality council consisting of representatives of each line and staff unit assisted Behm. To launch the training process, Corning established a Quality Institute with full-time instructors and planned to provide every employee with basic quality training, which would be offered in six languages. The first students in the institute were the members of the management committee. Operating and staff units each formed quality improvement teams and corrective action teams. Every employee in the corporation, top to bottom, was required to develop specific quality implementation goals. Progress against these goals became part of each individual's performance evaluation. Quality themes were stressed in management speeches and employee communications, including a daily "headlines" sheet, monthly issues of the *Gaffer*, posters, and slide and videotape presentations. This communication, moreover, was two-way, as Corning surveyed employees for their ideas and suggestions and managers met regularly with workers to discuss quality-related matters. A designer devised a logo that combined a cursive "Q" and an apple that became ubiquitous on Corning publications. Dubbed the "quapple," the symbol cropped up everywhere, from coffee mugs to pins to posters to T-shirts.

As the initiative proceeded, Corning employees generated many ideas and improvements that cumulatively added up to big savings. An employee whose job involved silk-screening measuring marks on beakers and flasks used his own time to design a machine to perform part of the work. The machine not only resulted in increased capacity but also cut setup time by 38 percent. To fend off Japanese competition, management and employees at a Celcor facility mounted a rigorous quality drive to reduce error rates to just 30 parts per million—one mistake per person in the plant every six weeks. Elsewhere, workers developed an adjustable mold that replaced a dozen different molds, an innovation that saved on changeover times as well as equipment. At another plant, the members of a quality circle reexamined inventory management and proposed changes that saved more than $500,000 and also reduced lead times for shipments from six weeks to two. At still another facility, employees discovered that they had been using a broken scale to weigh shipments and had essentially given away nearly 50,000 pounds of glass to customers. A new scale fixed the problem and yielded annual savings of at least $60,000. Such episodes, which Corning trumpeted through internal communications and made available to the national business press reinforced the company's progress toward superior performance.[22]

A Slingshot Effect

The new strategy, structure, and systems at Corning began to pay returns almost immediately. Although the company fell short of achieving a 10-percent operating margin by 1985, it hit 8.1 percent and during one heady 12-month stretch from the middle of that year into 1986, it did achieve the goal. Meanwhile, net earnings nearly doubled between 1982 and 1985 (from $72 million to more than $133 million) and earnings per share more than tripled (from $0.96 to $3.20).[23]

In achieving these results, Corning was helped by the resurgence of the U.S. economy. In August 1982, the stock market took off on a prolonged rise that would be checked momentarily in 1987 and somewhat longer in the early 1990s by bearish conditions. At the end of 1983, economic pundits pronounced the recession over and promised better times ahead.

But Corning also benefited from its own efforts at the corporate level and in each of the business units. As its markets recovered, these efforts propelled the company forward like a slingshot, and Corning outperformed the economy as a whole.

Optical Waveguides: Finally, the Payoff

From the perspective of what would become Corning's major growth business of the next two decades—optical waveguides—the transition to new management and the formalization of strategy occurred at a particularly opportune moment. In 1982, Corning recorded about $10 million in sales in optical waveguides, with experimental trials in Europe accounting for most of the volume. The business was not yet profitable, but that situation was about to change dramatically as a result of the sudden, unexpected restructuring of the U.S. telecommunications industry.

In January 1982, the U.S. Department of Justice announced a settlement in a seven-year-old antitrust suit against AT&T. The terms called for the breakup of the integrated Bell System by January 1, 1984, and opened up long-distance telecommunications to intense competitive rivalry. The nation's second-largest long-distance carrier, MCI, was number two by a long distance. Its network relied on microwave technology, but the company was dissatisfied with both the tinny quality of communications via microwave and constraints on capacity. The imminent breakup of the Bell System seemed a heaven-sent opportunity to install new technology and gain ground on AT&T. MCI began raising money for a big capital investment, much of it coming from junk bonds syndicated though Michael Milken at Drexel Burnham Lambert.[24]

In the fall of 1982, MCI was ready to move. The company contacted Corning and Siecor to discuss a major order. Dave Duke, general manager of Corning's telecommunications products division, and Al Dawson, chairman and CEO of Siecor, met at MCI's headquarters in Washington and listened with growing astonishment as MCI placed an order of breathtaking dimensions: 100,000 kilometers of fiber-optic cable, with delivery in twelve months. Corning lacked both the capacity to make this volume (ten times the size of any previous order) and experience in manufacturing the type of fiber MCI wanted (discussed below), and Siecor faced similar challenges. However, Duke and Dawson understood opportunity when they saw it and they accepted the business on the spot.[25]

Fulfilling the MCI order called for R&D and manufacturing achievements of heroic magnitude in an environment of great uncertainty and pressure. At Sullivan Park, a team led by Don Keck mounted a round-the-clock effort to develop single-mode fiber tailored to MCI's needs. Most of the company's previous experience had been based on multimode fiber. The difference between the two types was significant. In multimode fiber, the ratio of core transmission glass to cladding glass was much higher than in single-mode fiber. Given laser technology in the late 1960s and early 1970s, when optical waveguides were first developed, multimode was suitable for most applications. Smaller, more precise lasers became available in the early 1980s, however, and were better matched to single-mode fibers, which had superior transmission qualities—faster, more capacity, less attenuation. But single-mode fiber had to be manufactured to a much higher level of precision than multimode. While Corning had made single-mode fiber in experimental quantities, it was far from capable of producing the quantities that MCI required.

Building on a decade of experiments with single-mode fiber, Keck's team quickly developed a workable prototype. Next the challenge became to scale up in time for delivery to MCI. This step too required breakthroughs in processes for making fused silica and drawing fiber. In the months following MCI's placement of the cable order, debates raged inside Corning on whether to fulfill the order with the inside vapor deposition process—a proven technology, well understood by Corning and its competitors, and the safe course—or pursue the potentially greater rewards of the outside vapor phase oxidation process. In the end, Dave Duke made the call, committing to the outside process. As he later recounted his reasoning:

> I don't want to be in a business where I'm just one of five guys doing the same thing," he said. He again made the point about how it wouldn't be good enough to tie. As competitive as waveguides were now, he said, the business would be triply so in the future. This was like color TV in the sixties. If American companies had redesigned their products and factories

then, while they were ahead, they'd have kept in front of the Japanese. That's what was needed now—a factory leap.[26]

Scaling up to fill the MCI order also required Corning to install new systems and equipment to speed up throughput: longer draws, faster spooling, and computers to control it. Meanwhile, activity was similarly feverish at Siecor, where the Hickory, North Carolina, cable plant acquired in 1980 was retooled to make fiber-optic cable.[27]

In the fall of 1983, Siecor made its first delivery to MCI—on time and to specification. The MCI-Corning-Siecor success sent shockwaves throughout the telecommunications industry. That fall, U.S. Sprint Communications, Inc., a joint venture between GTE and United Telecommunications, placed another 100,000 km order with Siecor and, by extension, Corning. To accommodate this business—and in anticipation of more to come—Duke prepared a $94 million appropriation request to boost plant capacity to 1.2 million km annually and install yet another new generation of process technology. Although the request was the biggest in the company's history, it was approved quickly. By 1986, despite the heavy investments, optical waveguides accounted for profitable growth, with more than $220 million in sales (up from $10 million in 1982) and an operating margin of well over 25 percent.[28]

In addition to its capital investment, Corning supported its booming waveguide business in other ways. For example, it continued to defend its patents vigorously, in 1985 winning a preliminary decision against Sumitomo, which had violated its license agreement by exporting fiber from Japan to the United States via Canada. The final verdict in 1987 confirmed the decision.[29] At the same time, Corning became a font of ongoing product and process improvements. Researchers at the waveguide product engineering laboratory at Sullivan Park, for example, developed new "dispersion-shifted" fibers for use in especially long links, introduced a new multimode fiber designed specifically for data communications, and produced experimental quantities of shortwave single-mode fibers, a technology with promise to supersede conventional single-mode fibers in long-haul applications.[30]

Finally, Corning explored related technologies through acquisitions and joint ventures. In 1984, the company formed a small joint venture with

Plessey Company PLC, a British electronics concern, called PlessCor Optronics, Inc., to exploit new technology to convert electronic signals into light and back again. A similar investment was Corning's 1985 purchase of a minority stake in Raycom Systems, Inc., a Boulder, Colorado-based maker of modems, couplers, and multiplexers.[31]

Sorting through Health and Sciences

The health and sciences group that Marty Gibson oversaw consisted of a diverse set of operations and ventures ranging from laboratory glassware, to the medical diagnostic instrumentation equipment, to MetPath, the recently-acquired clinical laboratory testing company, to Nutrisearch and Genencor, two small biotechnology joint ventures. During the mid-1980s, the units in the health and sciences group underwent dramatic changes as Gibson and his colleagues gained deeper understanding and control of the respective businesses.[32]

Gibson's immediate challenges began with MetPath. Under founder Paul Brown, the company had grown swiftly through a combination of internal means and acquisitions, including some overseas. Brown, however, was an entrepreneur and not a manager, and the company's internal administrative systems proved woefully inadequate to support this growth. Worse, the assumptions behind Brown's original strategy seemed suddenly outmoded. MetPath had surged ahead of its many local rivals by investing in state-of-the-art equipment and quickly processing a large quantity of tests in a central facility in Teterboro, New Jersey. By the late 1970s, MetPath proclaimed that its facility in Teterboro was "the world's largest clinical lab."

So far, so good. But Brown attempted to replicate this success by establishing three more "mega-labs" across the country, first in Chicago and later on in Dallas and Los Angeles. He also sought to feed these labs by acquiring a series of small labs around the United States, where technicians would collect specimens and ship them to the closest mega-lab for processing. The plan, quipped a reporter, amounted to transforming MetPath into "a kind of medical Federal Express." In 1980, the company invested $30 million in its new mega-lab in Chicago.

Almost immediately, however, MetPath ran into big trouble. Logistical problems became nightmarish. Said one executive, "We had cases where one of our drivers would drive 200 miles a day to pick up four specimens and put them in a box for air-freighting to Teterboro. While revenues on the tests were $60, air shipment alone cost $50." Meanwhile, many personnel from the small labs MetPath had acquired defected, taking their accounts with them. MetPath's foreign labs in the United Kingdom and Switzerland were subject to very different market and regulatory environments and faced limited prospects for growth or earnings. Finally, the scale economies simply evaporated as new technology and PC-based systems made small labs competitive. At the very moment of its completion, MetPath's new mega-lab in Chicago proved nearly worthless.[33]

To bring MetPath in line, Corning dispatched 45-year-old Roger Ackerman, one of its most promising young managers, and a close friend of Marty Gibson's, to Teterboro. A past president of Corhart Refractories, vice president and general manager of the ceramics products division during the ramp-up of Celcor, and head of Engineering when it occupied the Decker Building and supported the massive buildup of the Wilmington optical fibers plant, Ackerman greeted his new job with ambivalence: he was smarting at being passed over for the management committee, concerned about the magnitude of the differences between Corning's traditional business and MetPath's, and yet also intrigued and excited about the challenge ahead. The move, he recalled, represented

really a wrenching change. There's no way to call [MetPath] a high-tech, materials-oriented business. It's a service business. The primary issue there was getting the information to doctors and keeping your prices low enough that you could compete. It really amounted to a down-and-dirty business. Blood testing laboratories are important, but it's a totally different business than high-technology, patent-oriented, and intellectual property-oriented business. The only commonality was that you had to find people you could trust and work with.[34]

During the next two years, Ackerman engineered a thorough overhaul and turnaround of MetPath's operations. He replaced most of the company's management team with a combination of promotions, new recruits, and a sprinkling of Corning veterans. The new management team, in turn, upgraded the company's management systems and subjected its operations to the same rigorous TQM disciplines as Corning's other businesses. The team also worked with Gibson to develop a new strategy based on building a decentralized network of small regional labs across the United States to process routine tests, while using Teterboro as a central facility to handle more sophisticated and expensive tests such as determining the malignancy of tumors or detecting Down's syndrome. To help pay for these changes, including a $30 million write-off on the Chicago mega-lab, MetPath sold its European labs. The results of these changes were dramatic. MetPath continued to grow rapidly, approaching $250 million in sales by 1985, while also beginning to show signs of becoming profitable soon, and in a big way.

Meanwhile, Gibson addressed a different set of challenges in the $160 million diagnostic equipment business. Corning's original product had been a blood-gas analyzer, while later offerings included electrolyte analyzers and diagnostic reagents. The 1980 acquisition of Gilford Instruments had added other analytic instruments, including low-throughput equipment for chemical analysis designed specifically for small laboratories. In the mid-1980s, Corning's diagnostics business was growing at a healthy clip, although heavy R&D and capital requirements kept it from attaining profitability goals. Gibson became increasingly worried by the magnitude of the investments necessary to remain a viable long-term competitor. "Basically, we looked at the resource needs" of the business, he recalled, concluding that it "needed a massive infusion of new technology, biotechnology and what have you, new sensors, new immunoassay techniques, etc. This was going to take a lot of money."[35]

In these circumstances, Corning resorted to a time-honored tactic and sought a joint-venture partner. The company held discussions with several potential partners and eventually settled on the Swiss pharmaceutical giant Ciba-Geigy, which, like other pharmaceutical companies, was interested in establishing a position in diagnostics. From Corning's point of view, said Gibson, the rationale for the deal was "access to fundamental biotechnology" at Ciba-Geigy. He added that until recently "diagnostics was primarily a product-development game—you take existing technology and repackage it. But the drivers in diagnostics are changing from packaging to basic life science. We didn't have basic life science, and it's too late in the day to build it from scratch." In July 1985, the parties agreed to terms, forming Ciba Corning Diagnostics Corp., a 50/50 joint venture based in the United States. Corning contributed the assets of its diagnostic equipment business, with Ciba-Geigy investing financial capital.[36]

The third set of businesses in Gibson's domain were Genencor and Nutrisearch, the biotechnology joint ventures formed in the early 1980s. By mid-decade, neither venture was paying a return. Although Nutrisearch added an infusion of capital by selling a one-third interest to Eastman Kodak Co., Gibson admitted "the technology never worked the way we thought it would."[37] In 1987, the parties dissolved the business. Genencor initially showed greater potential, although it proved slow to get off the ground. In part the problems reflected Corning's deviation from a long-standing policy that called for personnel assigned to joint ventures to resign from their original companies and commit themselves fully to their new undertaking. Genentech resisted this approach, however, believing that its personnel would be reluctant to abandon a company with such tremendous upside prospects. During the first few years, Corning's apprehensions were realized, as Genencor made little headway.[38] In 1985, however, the two parties finally agreed that employees of the venture should resign from their parent corporations. At about the same time, the venture added a new partner, A. E. Staley Manufacturing Company, which bought in for a one-third share.

By the mid-1980s it was evident to both Gibson and Dulude that the biotechnology business, like the diagnostics business, would require bigger investments to create a secure leadership position than Corning could reasonably afford. Dulude estimated that it would take a half billion dollars simply to stay competitive and noted that Corning could not come up with such an amount while also scaling up to make waveguides.[39]

Revamping the Core

The consumer and industry group under Bill Hudson included the businesses that had been Corning's strongest performers historically: specialty glass and glass ceramics (especially Celcor), and consumer products, which included not only housewares but also a new venture in sunglasses. Each of these businesses posed different issues for Corning in the mid-1980s.

As part of an earlier restructuring that saw the sale of the light bulb glass operations, Corning had also retrenched in TV glass. The big decision in 1983 was the consolidation of its two remaining color TV tube factories—Bluffton, Indiana and State College, Pennsylvania—into a single operation. Although the Bluffton plant was the younger and larger of the two facilities, Corning chose State College for the consolidated operation primarily because its labor force seemed more responsive to the need to make significant changes in work practices. Certainly, the workforce at State College seized on the corporate quality initiative with unusual zeal. "We were at the brink, peeking over," said plant manager Mark Mitchell. "We knew we wouldn't survive unless we became competitive." Bob Rusnak, a supervisor in the forming area, put it another way: "We just felt we had to really go and show [the Corning executives that] they made the right decision."[40]

Employees contributed many ideas and suggestions that added up to big performance improvements. These in turn fed into a bull market for TV sets in the United States. Sales of color TV sets climbed 35 percent between 1982 and 1985, as many new models and bigger rectangular screens were developed. Other factors contributing to this growth included the rising popularity of VCRs and the expansion of cable and satellite services.[41] These same forces also boosted results at Samsung-Corning Company, Ltd., which also enjoyed an apparent cost advantage over Japanese manufacturers. In 1986, the joint venture announced a $100 million expansion of production facilities in Korea.[42]

The fortunes of Corning's specialty materials businesses—scientific and industrial glass and glass ceramics—had always risen and fallen with the industrial economy. This pattern particularly applied to Celcor, the star performer in the group when the automobile industry was healthy and a problem child when it wasn't. Fortunately for Corning's new management team, the automobile industry roared back from recession in 1983 and began a seven-year boom. This was good news for sales of Celcor and sealed-beam headlights. As demand picked up, the cost control and quality initiatives

Corning had embarked upon paid handsome dividends: the company reported a 20-percent surge in segment sales between 1983 and 1984 and a 15-percent rise in operating income.[43]

To help offset its dependence on the U.S. auto industry, Corning sought to penetrate foreign automakers and develop new applications of cellular ceramic technology.[44] The company proved successful in both undertakings. The European auto industry seemed an especially attractive prospect. In the early 1980s, Switzerland, Sweden, Austria, and Norway had adopted emission standards similar to those in the United States. West Germany was expected to follow soon, and on the horizon the European Community seemed likely to adopt a common standard. In 1985, Corning announced plans to build a ceramic substrates plant in Kaiserslautern, West Germany, near the heart of the powerful German auto industry. The new plant constituted Corning's biggest single investment in Europe to date. At the same time, Corning R&D personnel investigated other environmental applications of ceramic substrates: a filter to capture soot emitted by diesel engines; a catalytic combustor to reduce pollution (and increase the heating efficiency) of wood stoves; and an industrial product called MetalFilter to remove impurities from molten metal during foundry operations. Of these, the MetalFilter proved a big hit, with sales of 150,000 units in 1983 and an annual growth rate during the next few years exceeding 100 percent.[45]

Meanwhile, Corning's most visible business—consumer products—was struggling against forces that would eventually cause the company's leaders to place it on the block. At first, general economic conditions masked these forces. The recession of the early 1980s hammered the business, and volume dropped by 30 percent. As the economy recovered, however, the business failed to follow suit, and structural problems became apparent. First, the strong dollar had added to the already significant cost advantages of Asian producers, and imports flooded the American market. Some of these imports—Mikasa, for example—succeeded in establishing valuable brands and loyal customers. A second problem was changing uses of housewares, especially due to the growing popularity of microwave ovens. Although Pyrex and Corning Ware products were suitable for microwave use, the company proved slow to tout the capability.

Corning's third and most serious problem was profound change in the distribution channels for housewares. For decades, the company had prospered by focusing on the ultimate consumer and offering a very broad product line. Corning's brands had become very powerful. Van Campbell, who ran the consumer business in the early 1980s, remembered that "we were the captain of the channel, because we sold through wholesalers who then sold through retailers, mostly department stores. We talked directly to the consumer and everybody in between did what we wanted them to do."[46]

That situation began to change, starting in the mid-1970s, with modifications to fair trade practices across the country. The ensuing phenomenal growth of mass discounters such as K-Mart and then Wal-Mart meant that Corning lost control of its pricing and distribution, with disastrous effect. As Campbell put it, as

> the major retailers became more and more powerful [and gained] substantially higher market share, then they became captains of the channel. They only wanted to devote so many feet to display, and they only wanted to have 15 items instead of 500. Meanwhile, we had a whole manufacturing setup that was geared around many varieties of decorations and shapes, and a mindset that went back to the department store days. When I [grew up] in the business, department stores were the most important outlet. At Macy's and Bon Marché, the product was out there on velvet with flowers sticking in it. So we had this glamorous feeling about the products and how they should be presented. Now, however, we'd walk into Wal-Mart or K-Mart and see 30 feet of boxes with pictures on them.[47]

The pricing policies of mass retailers, which traded off low unit margins for high sales volume, also eroded Corning's profits.

To address these challenges, Corning recruited its first senior outside hire since Lee Waterman three decades earlier. The new senior vice president and general manager of consumer products was Ed Fogarty, a Harvard MBA and former brand manager with Colgate-Palmolive, Clairol, and International Playtex. Fogarty proved a source of copious fresh ideas to rejuvenate aging brands such as Pyrex, Corning Ware, and Corelle and promote new ones such as Visions and Microwave Plus.

During the next two years, Corning attempted to refashion its existing consumer product line. In 1985, for example, the company introduced the first new Corning Ware decoration in a decade. Called Pastel Bouquet, the new design was also the first to wrap around the outside of the casserole. Meanwhile, Corning attempted once more to reposition Pyrex from a replacement product to a growth product. The vehicle was Pyrex Designs, a new line of decorated and colorful Pyrex bowls and ovenware, as well as simple redesigns of familiar products. When Pyrex measuring cups were offered with open handles—a feature that enabled the cups to be stacked in sets—sales of this most familiar product enjoyed a sudden surge. Corelle also underwent a facelift. Under brand manager Peter Campanella, Corning developed a new strategy to differentiate offerings in categories of good, better, and best. The segmentation was based on features clearly identifiable to consumers: the shape and weight of the pieces, the quality of the design, and set size and packaging. Corning also developed new decorating technology to enable mechanical decoration not only on the centers and rims of pieces but anywhere on them. The top-of-the-line Occasions products featured five intricate full-color patterns that flowed across the entire surface of the plate.[48]

These measures helped stem losses of market share and portended an imminent turnaround. A much bigger hit was a "new" product: the stove-top Visions line of glass ceramic pots and pans. Essentially a transparent form of Corning Ware that was developed and promoted in France, the amber-tinted Visions became one of the hottest products in the American housewares market during the mid-1980s. At first, Corning imported Visions from its French factories. By 1985, however, demand was so great that the company retooled its factory in Martinsburg, West Virginia so that it could produce both Visions and Corning Ware from the same melting tank. The plant's capacity was increased by a third, and the workforce proved adept at managing changeovers and also producing the new shapes, including many with handles, that Visions required. In its first year, Visions achieved a 10-percent penetration of American households, a fraction that would surge to 30 percent in the next two years. Best of all, as a stovetop product, Visions did not cannibalize sales of Pyrex or Corning Ware.[49]

Other ventures in consumer housewares proved less promising. Corning sought to tap into the microwave revolution, for example, introducing a new line called Microwave Plus. The line included not only cook-and-serve bowls and dishes but also divided plates, microwave steamers, and even a bacon rack. By then, however, Corning was perceived as a latecomer, and faced an uphill battle against Anchor Hocking, Rubbermaid, and other competitors, which had already developed low-cost yet fashionable plastic products for microwave use.[50]

Another struggling venture was Crown Corning, an organization formed by Corning's 1984 acquisition of the U.S. distribution arm of an old Australian partner in housewares and focused on the department store channel. Crown Corning's charter enabled it to resell products from a variety of sources to complement Pyrex, Corning Ware, and Visions: solid-color dinnerware, lead crystal glasses, fashion glass florals, "fun/fashionable color-handled stainless, high-style thermal products," and fashion plastics. Sales of the venture soared from zero to more than $50 million in its first two years.[51] Unfortunately, this was not profitable growth as the company struggled to develop logistical and management systems to support efficient distribution from many different vendors.

The final component of Corning's consumer products businesses was another new venture: sunglasses. After fits and starts, this would prove an exciting and attractive business later in the 1980s. Corning had sold eyeglass blanks to eyeglasses manufacturers for many years. Following the proprietary development of photochromic glasses in the early and mid-1960s, the company also became a major supplier of sunglass blanks. In 1982, the company launched a new operating unit, Corning Sunglass Products, with the express purpose of capturing a bigger slice of profits from the downstream business.[52]

Corning's initial efforts to market sunglasses proved disastrous. Emphasizing the business as fashion (and to avoid further alienating customers for sunglass blanks), the company downplayed its own name and proliferated new styles and models. The result was failure to establish a clear position in the marketplace, as well as serious difficulties in supporting 230 different items for sale. Problems cropped up everywhere, in manufacturing, quality, and distribution. The division racked up heavy losses, and in the summer of 1984, corporate management decided to shut it down, absorbing a write-off of $24 million. At this point, however, the division's operations manager, S. Zaki Mustafa, lobbied Bill Hudson for a reprieve. Betting his career on the opportunity, Mustafa persuaded Hudson to allow Corning one more year to execute a turnaround. Mustafa negotiated a free hand to make radical changes in the business, including the opportunity to relocate the division into its own facilities in Horseheads, New York, near Corning.

Supported by a handful of dedicated colleagues, Mustafa made the most of his freedom and repositioned the company's product line, abandoning low-end and middle-market products and focusing instead on the top end, which bore the "Serengeti" brand. Corning Sunglass Products was renamed Serengeti Eyewear. At the same time, Mustafa and his colleagues further repositioned the product line to capitalize on Corning's image as a technology-based company. Rather than a fashion accessory for any customer with money to spend, Serengeti sunglasses would become "high-tech, high-end, functional products" targeted specifically at male buyers.

The Serengeti line was relaunched in January 1985, supported primarily by word-of-mouth advertising. Mustafa and his colleagues donated hundreds of pairs of sunglasses to high-profile athletes—skiers, yachtsmen, race-car drivers, and the like—as well as to individuals in occupations in which optical performance seemed important—ski patrolmen, pilots, and state troopers. As demand began to build, Serengeti followed up with print advertising that emphasized innovative design and technological features engineered into the product: photochromic glass, blue-shift correction, full ultraviolet protection, and polarizing qualities to reduce glare.

These measures proved effective. In 1985, sales reached $5 million, although losses remained heavy at $3 million; a year later, sales surpassed $11 million, with losses down to $900,000. At the end of 1986, Serengeti seemed poised on the verge of significant growth.

The Strategy Wheel

During the winter and spring of 1984–1985, Corning instituted several changes in management. Bill Hudson retired and the consumer and industry group was restructured into two pieces. Roger Ackerman returned to Corning as senior vice president and head of a new specialty glass and ceramics group, and as a member of the management committee and board of directors. At the same time, Marty Gibson assumed oversight of the consumer products businesses, as well as the health and sciences group. In the meantime, Jack Hutchins had moved from leading the R&D organization at Corning to become executive vice president at Siecor. He was succeeded by Dave Duke, who also became heir apparent to Tom MacAvoy, who was scheduled to retire as vice chairman in the spring of 1988.

As these changes took effect, the management committee worked on revising the company's statements of mission, objectives, strategy, and values last updated in 1978. Printed in 1985 as *Corning Values*, the new document endorsed Jamie Houghton's emphases on performance and quality and spelled out additional values: independence, integrity, technology, the individual, and leadership. *Corning Values* also proclaimed a new set of financial goals: in the top 25 percent of the *Fortune* 500 in terms of ROE; an average annual real growth rate in excess of 5 percent; a debt-to-capital ratio of approximately 25 percent and a long-term dividend payout of 33 percent. Finally, the document also provided a fresh definition of the company's strategy:

> Corning is an evolving network of wholly owned businesses and joint ventures. We choose to compete in four global business sectors: *Specialty Materials, Consumer Housewares, Laboratory Sciences,* and *Communications.* Each segment is composed of divisions, subsidiaries and alliances. Binding the four sectors together is the glue of common values, a commitment to technology, shared resources, dedication to total quality, and management links.[53]

This manner of thinking was rendered visually as "The Strategy Wheel of Corning," a circle divided into four equal shares, each representing one of the four global business sectors.

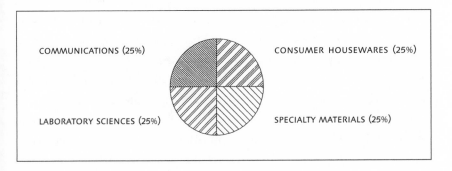

COMMUNICATIONS (25%)   CONSUMER HOUSEWARES (25%)

LABORATORY SCIENCES (25%)   SPECIALTY MATERIALS (25%)

Almost as soon as the strategy wheel was envisioned, however, it was already spinning and beginning to wobble. In the short term, a sudden, sharp downturn in the market for fiber optics triggered another probing examination of the company's strategy, as well as a new organizational restructuring. In the longer term, Corning began to rethink prospects for its major business segments and to take steps to manage them in different ways.

The problems in the fiber and cable businesses were not unexpected, although they proved unexpectedly severe. By late 1986, the major trunk lines for transcontinental telecommunications had been built and orders for cable at Siecor and for optical fiber at Wilmington plummeted. At about the same time, AT&T brought a new cable plant on stream and new entrants such as Pirelli and Fitel (subsequently Alcatel) contributed to a sudden glut of cable capacity. Cable prices tumbled by half during a nine-month period stretching into the third quarter of 1987. Siecor was forced to lay off about a third of its employees, while 40 percent of its executive team retired or took an early retirement option. "We went from making a lot of money to wondering if there was ever going to be a way to make money again," recalled Joe Hicks, then general manager of the optical fiber cable business. At Wilmington, the effects of the downturn also proved dramatic and painful: sales volume plunged 20 percent and more than 200 jobs (out of 870) were eliminated. "This was the first sign," recalled Jerry McQuaid, the plant manager at the time, "that trees won't grow all the way to the sky."[54]

Corning's leaders recognized that the fiber and cable businesses would pick up again soon, and they portrayed the event as nothing more than a "pause" along a trajectory of rapid growth. Nonetheless, as the effects of the downturn propagated across the company, management took strong actions in response: a program to streamline costs that included removing unnecessary positions and layers of organization, a hiring freeze, and an early retirement plan that induced, among others, a half dozen longtime senior executives to depart. Total corporate staff was reduced by nearly a quarter. The last vestiges of the geographical structure of the old Corning International Corporation disappeared, leaving the business unit general managers in full control of their organizations worldwide. Another significant step involved decentralization of responsibility for manufacturing and engineering, with personnel who had worked in the central corporate department reassigned to the business units or to corporate R&D. Other responses to the business downturn included postponing previously announced plans to build a new headquarters facility in Corning, New York (discussed below) and selling the electronic components business.

Proceeds from the electronics transaction as well as from the sale of its residual interest in Owens-Corning Fiberglas as it underwent a buyout in 1986 helped Corning company absorb the costs of restructuring without significant damage to the bottom line or the share price. The waveguide pause nonetheless caused the company's top management to reevaluate its entire portfolio of businesses, starting with its products for the telecommunications industry.[55]

New Fibers and the New Field of Photonics

Although management recognized that the fiber and cable businesses would quickly resume booming growth, the experience of the pause prompted new strategic initiatives. Both Siecor and Corning sought ways to add value by extending their product lines. At Siecor, Al Dawson and his eventual successor, Joe Hicks, sought to grow hardware and equipment sales to help offset the company's heavy dependence on cable. When Siecor had acquired Superior Wire & Cable in Hickory, North Carolina, in 1980, it had bought not only a producer of cable and related equipment such as wiring cabinets, junction boxes, connectors, splicers, test equipment, and cables for specialized uses such as elevators. In 1987, Dawson and Hicks saw the potential of these lines to constitute a major business for Siecor. By investing in these lines and developing new ones—such as network interface devices to centralize and simplify telephone, electrical, cable, and other kinds of wiring at the point of entry to a building, and cable wiring systems of packaged components—Siecor grew hardware and equipment into about 40 percent of its total sales by the early 1990s.[56]

Another major Siecor initiative involved expansion overseas. Although its founding covenants prohibited it from competing with Siemens in most of the world outside of North America, Siecor was free to sell in Japan—if it could. Both corporate parents were skeptical of the ability of an American company to penetrate the Japanese market, but Siecor chose to respond to a request from Nippon Telephone and Telegraph, the Japanese telecommunications monopoly, to develop a new generation of densely packed cables. In the late 1980s, most cables in the United States strung together 216 fibers; the Japanese wanted a cable with 4,000 fibers. Drawing heavily on engineering support from both its parents, Siecor prepared its bid and, benefiting from U.S. government pressure on Japan to open its markets, was chosen as one of four suppliers to NTT and the only foreign company in the mix. Although NTT eventually decided against buying 4,000-fiber cable, it placed significant orders for 1,000-fiber cable from Siecor. By the early 1990s, Siecor had become a major factor in the Japanese market, accounting for nearly a quarter of all shipments.

In Corning's Telecommunications Products Division, strategy also shifted in the wake of the waveguide pause. Management remained confident that demand for optical fiber would recover soon enough, and it did. Regional and local telephone companies began buying fiber cable to connect central offices and then to build new "feeder" networks to link central offices to the "remote terminals" that served as penultimate points of distribution before branching to homes, offices, and individual telephone users. Total volume of feeder networks was projected to exceed that of the long distance market and to grow fast for many years into the future. Local telephone companies replaced the long-distance providers as the biggest segment of the market. At the same time, cable TV operators resorted to fiber optic cable to build their core distribution networks. To meet the different requirements of buyers in new segments, Corning pushed hard to develop new fibers and new coatings to protect them from more intensive handling and mechanical strain. It also continued to invest aggressively in capacity expansions and process improvements in Wilmington.

Corning also mounted a more focused effort to develop ancillary products to spur the usage of fiber optic cable by making it easier to install and maintain and cheaper to operate. Fiber optic cable offered significant economic advantages in cost and quality over copper in long-haul applications. In short-haul markets, the much greater capacity of fiber was less compelling. Conventional electronics and equipment required to manage infor-

In June 1972, Hurricane Agnes rammed into a weather front moving from the West and dumped extremely heavy rains on the Chemung Valley. Despite desperate precautions, the river overflowed its banks and caused tens of millions of dollars in damage in the Valley and nearly destroyed the Corning Museum of Glass. The high water mark on Market Street reached four feet.

As the city of Corning and the Glass Works began the recovery process from Hurricane Agnes, Amo Houghton quickly went on the radio to reassure citizens the company would remain rooted in the community.

Corning listened to all your problems about everyday dishes... and did something about it.

New Corelle Livingware

Corelle Livingware—a lightweight, everyday tableware—became one of Corning's hottest products after its introduction in 1970, and it remained on allocation for the following decade.

Eyeglass to sunglass in less than 60 secs.

Another hot product of the 1970s was Photogray eyeglass lenses, which lightened or darkened within minutes depending on light conditions. Photograys created a new market segment in fashion eyewear: comfort lenses. The technology originated in Corning's R&D labs, but the success owed much to creative marketing.

Tom MacAvoy succeeded Lee Waterman as president of Corning and worked closely in tandem with Amo Houghton during the last dozen years of his tenure. A former research scientist, MacAvoy retired in 1987 as vice chairman with responsibility for technology.

In the late 1970s and early 1980s, Corning's leaders worried that the company's core glass businesses would not generate enough growth or cash flow to fund development of expensive and risky new lines like fiber optics. They decided, therefore, to diversify into wholly new areas, including biotechnology and laboratory services. One of the most successful of these new ventures was MetPath, a blood testing laboratory in the New York City metropolitan area that became the anchor of a new subsidiary, Corning Life Sciences, Inc. The strategy worked, although Corning later divested most of its diversified units in the 1990s with the boom in optical communications business.

As chairman and CEO between 1983 and 1996, Jamie Houghton (Amo's younger brother) demanded—and got—breakthrough results in performance, quality, and workforce diversity. In all areas, Corning worked in close partnership with the American Flint Glass Workers, led by longtime president, George Parker (right).

Jamie Houghton (center) and members of the Management Committee—the "Six Pack"—meet with employees at Corning's innovative, high-performance factory in Blacksburg, Virginia. The Six Pack included Dick Dulude and Marty Gibson (at left), Van Campbell (with Houghton, center), and Dave Duke and Roger Ackerman (far right). The group stands behind a trays of Celcor—honeycombed glass ceramic substrates used in automotive catalytic converters.

The optical shot heard round the world: in 1970, the team of Peter Schultz, Donald Keck, and Robert Maurer demonstrated the technical feasibility of optical communications. Schultz worked on glass composition; Keck developed key metrics and measurements; and Maurer designed the fiber structure.

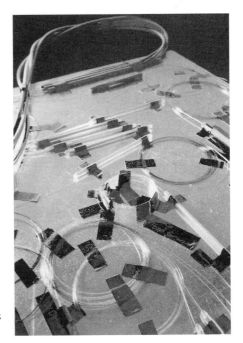

"Photonics"—a technology that moves and manipulates information as pulses of light holds promise of revolutionizing electronics as we know it. As early as 2020, an all-optical computer may run at speeds thousands of times faster than today's fastest supercomputers. Corning began making passive photonic devices—splitters, couplers, optical amplifers—to extend its sales of optical fibers and cables. With the 2000 acquisition of Lasertron, Corning became a factor in active photonic devices such as semiconducting lasers.

Roger Ackerman (center) became chairman and chief executive officer of Corning in 1996. Under his leadership—with help from top executives Van Campbell, Norm Garrity, and John Loose (l to r)—Corning divested its consumer products business and poured resources into new businesses such as fiber optics and photonics.

With the opening of its Celcor plant in Kaiserslautern, Germany, Corning became a leading supplier of environmental products to the European auto industry. The company successfully transferred not only its technology and product lines, but also its disciplined approach to management. Note the "quapple" on this German technician's T-shirt.

A joint venture of the 1970s mushroomed into a huge global business. Samsung Corning started modestly in Korea but now makes TV glass and other products sold all over the world.

A technology thought to be a failure in the 1960s because it wasn't economical in fabricating automotive windshields, the fusion process for forming perfectly smooth glass later paid dividends in other applications. Today it is the basis of a fast-growing business in glass for liquid crystal displays. Corning supplies the leading makers of laptop computers and handheld electronic devices with fusion glass from its factories in Harrodsburg, Kentucky, and Shizuoka, Japan (above).

In the late 1990s Corning placed yet another major bet on its future by doubling the capacity of its research complex at Sullivan Park, at the same time expanding many of its satellite laboratories in North America, Europe, and Asia. The company's leaders are convinced that its future, like its past, will depend on mastering the still-vast untapped potential of glass.

mation traffic along the cable impeded the adoption of optical fibers. To address this problem, Corning retreated from an old approach and explored a new one. By the late 1980s, it was clear that Corning lacked the scale, capital, and technological expertise to keep up with much bigger rivals in active components such as those in development at PCO (formerly PlessCor Optronics) and Raycom Systems. Accordingly, Corning wound down its work on active components and redirected its attention to passive "photonic" devices such as splitters, couplers, and optical amplifiers. Such devices enabled light signals to be split, combined, and boosted passively, without the intervention of microprocessors and electronic equipment. Indeed, the passive devices offered the potential to cut the installation and maintenance costs of fiber-optic cable to levels competitive with copper cable in many short-haul applications—including the last frontier, the local telephone loop.[57]

Early photonic couplers were fairly primitive devices and costly to make. They featured only two ports, enabling the signal from one fiber to split into two fibers, or, alternatively, the signals along two fibers to merge into one. Researchers at Corning's Avon (France) laboratory, however, developed couplers that possessed many more ports and could be manufactured cost-effectively in volume, using planar fabrication techniques similar to those for integrated circuits. Although the French program was eventually terminated, Corning continued to work on passive components at Sullivan Park. In 1990, the company developed a reliable and cost-effective coupler for single mode fiber that was ready for field tests.[58]

The new couplers became part of a major Corning initiative in photonics. In 1988, Dr. Gitimoy Kar, director of new development in the telecommunications products division, joined Skip Deneka at a conference in England that addressed the need for optical amplifiers to boost light signals at stated intervals—in long distance transmission, approximately every 100 kilometers. The telecommunications companies typically resorted to electronic "regenerators" to solve the problem. These devices converted a light signal into an electronic form, pumped it up, converted it back into light, and then sent it on toward its destination or the next regenerator. This was an expensive and inefficient way to boost signals, and several big telecommunications companies were looking at alternatives.

Upon his return to Corning, and with Deneka's strong support and encouragement, Kar formed a small project team to work on optical amplification. Despite the skepticism of some senior lab personnel, including Don Keck, the team made steady progress, drawing on the company's knowledge of fiber and its work in doping glass with rare-earth minerals. The final, risky move was to employ an unproven, experimental laser chip made by IBM. In 1990, the Corning team assembled an amplification module using the IBM laser that demonstrated a 10 db gain. By then it seemed clear that continued work on optical amplifiers would soon yield a device that could replace regenerators at one-tenth of the cost.[59]

Changes and Opportunities in Specialty Glass and Ceramics

In Specialty Glass and Ceramics, Roger Ackerman focused on managing a portfolio of diverse businesses with diverse needs. The problem was to maintain the health of older contributors such as automotive headlamps and TV bulb glass, while funding the rapid growth of young businesses like Celcor substrates and other environmental products. At the same time, Ackerman had to target other new investments for only the most promising of the hundreds, if not thousands, of potential new applications.[60]

The most pressing need was to ramp up production of Celcor substrates to keep up with soaring demand. As car and truck production in the United States revived and Asian automakers transplanted assembly operations into the country, Corning's capacity was sorely strained. The Erwin works ran around the clock and still fell behind. As Ackerman put it, "We can sell everything we make—and if we could make more, we'd be selling it." To make more Celcor substrates, in 1988 the company poured $40 million into retooling a mothballed flat-glass facility in Blacksburg, Virginia.[61]

Meanwhile, other investments in growth businesses demanded management attention and investment dollars. The big new ceramic substrate facility in Kaiserslautern, West Germany, built to supply the European auto industry, came on stream in late 1986 and was soon running full tilt. Nonautomotive applications of ceramic materials also continued healthy growth.

To make more MetalFilters and other foundry products, substrates for use in wood stove catalytic combustors, and other nonautomotive products, in 1988 Corning undertook a major capacity addition at Erwin. The following year, it formed a new joint venture called Cormetech with Mitsubishi Heavy Industries, Ltd. and Mitsubishi Heavy Petrochemical Company,Ltd. as its partners. Cormetech sold ceramic devices to control emissions from stationary power-generating systems.[62]

Among the older businesses in the specialty glass and ceramics group, automotive headlamps, a business that ebbed and flowed with the cycle of production in the automobile industry, experienced good times in the late 1980s. Times were less good for the TV bulb business. Although it had achieved significant operating improvements under total quality management, top executives remained concerned about Corning's market position and ability to remain at the forefront of new technology. Japanese consumer electronics manufacturers continued to thrive in the U.S. market, introducing new models and bigger screens at prices and paces domestic competitors were hard pressed to match. Only the intense lobbying of U.S. trade negotiators induced the Japanese to assemble television sets in the United States. In the mid-1980s, Sony, Toshiba, and Mitsubishi opened plants in the United States and Canada, and Matsushita announced plans to follow suit. The prospect of direct investment in the United States by the Japanese TV bulb suppliers loomed as a serious threat. Early in 1988, Corning's long-time rival Owens-Illinois announced the formation of a joint venture with Nippon Electric Glass, one of the biggest Japanese TV bulb suppliers.

In these circumstances, Corning sought an alliance with Asahi, its long-time partner in Iwaki. In July 1988, the parties reached agreement, announcing the formation of Corning Asahi Video Products Company (CAV). The venture's principal assets consisted of Corning's operations in State College, Monterrey, Mexico, and Bagneaux, France. Ashai purchased a 33-percent stake in CAV along with the prospect of eventually increasing its ownership to 49 percent. Corning supplied management to CAV, while Asahi agreed to furnish technology and engineering support (especially for making large bulbs) and facilitate access to Japanese set manufacturers with operations in the United States.[63]

John Loose, first chairman of CAV, recalled an almost instantaneous boost from the formation of the deal. Previous attempts to win Japanese business had met with repeated frustrations.

> Every time we'd go call on these customers it was like [there was a] veil in front of them. We could just never work with them. We could just never get through. [We negotiated in] very private interview rooms. We never got out on the factory floor to work with them. It was very awkward. We just couldn't seem to crack them.
>
> I swear the day we did the deal and we were now Corning Asahi Video, we'd walk into the Japanese customer and the veil was completely lifted. "Work with us. Bring your applications engineers out on the factory floor. We've got this problem. Work with us on this. We want to come to your factory. Let's solve this. Let's do joint projects together." It was just amazing to break into the Japanese club.[64]

Funds from Asahi helped underwrite a major expansion at State College in the late 1980s, as the plant was retooled for fabrication of bigger tubes. The expansion included installation of a huge new melting tank—the biggest in the world for TV glass—and Asahi technology to press large funnels, a development that brought an end to the service of the marvelous centrifugal casting machines that Jim Giffen had designed decades before.[65]

The revival of State College under CAV caused top management to view the TV bulb business in a new light. Once a candidate for divestiture, the business became again a reliable source of positive cash flow. It also offered attractive growth prospects in the developing world, especially in Asia. Meanwhile, the fortunes of Samsung-Corning soared with the remarkable rise of the Korean consumer electronics industry as a global rival to the Japanese. In 1989, when Corning began disclosing Samsung-Corning's financial results, the venture posted net income of $52 million on sales of $338 million. Not only did this represent enviable profitability, but Samsung-Corning was also growing at 20 percent per year. During the late 1980s, Corning also formed joint ventures with local partners in China (1987) to transfer TV glass technology and in India (1990) to manufacture black-and-white TV glass, with a plan to add color TV glass within five years.[66]

Corning management also began to view the rejuvenated TV glass business as related to an intriguing new area of opportunity in information displays. From a revenue standpoint, TV glass represented by far Corning's biggest activity in this area. But it was not the only activity. In 1986, Corning acquired U.S. Precision Lens Inc. Founded in 1930 on the outskirts of Cincinnati, USPL had grown into a $30 million company on the strength of camera lenses and light-emitting diode (LED) displays for calculators and other devices and appliances. In the mid-1980s, it was "the world's largest manufacturer of lenses for large-screen projection TVs and video systems" and exported a third of its products to Japan. Looking ahead to a future of rapid growth, the ownership group of USPL recognized the need for new investment capital and put the company up for sale. To Corning, the business seemed a good fit, and the deal was quickly consummated. Taking note of USPL's success in Japan, President Ronald Reagan stopped by for a visit in August 1988 and proclaimed the company an example of "America's economic expansion and manufacturing boom."[67]

Corning also mounted a major effort to bolster its position in glass substrates for liquid crystal displays (LCDs). The company made LCD glass at its plant in Harrodsburg, Kentucky using fusion technology originally developed for the automotive windshield (discussed in Chapter 10) and later adapted for applications as diverse as aircraft and spacecraft windows, eyeglass blanks, and self-cleaning ovens. In the mid-1980s, although cathode ray tubes dominated the market for information displays, use of LCD displays in notebook computers and portable electronic devices was projected to skyrocket. In preparing to meet this growth, Corning also sought to increase its technological lead by focusing on refinements to glass composition and improvements to the fusion process to make it more efficient. Bill Dumbaugh spearheaded an R&D effort that made significant progress on both fronts.

The company's principal marketing challenge in the LCD glass market was to penetrate further the powerful Japanese consumer electronics manufacturers. Rising to that challenge led Corning to make a bold decision. In 1988, it invested in a greenfield operation in Shizuoka Prefecture, about 150 miles southwest of Tokyo and placed it under the management of Corning Japan K.K., a subsidiary created in the 1970s to market specialty glass and ceramic products. Thus Corning Japan was transformed from a staff organization into an operating unit. The new facility not only constituted Corning's first full-scale manufacturing operation in Japan but also housed personnel and activities relocated from the R&D lab acquired earlier from RCA. Led by Peter Booth, Corning Japan steadily gained ground in Japan despite fierce competition from entrenched rivals Asahi Glass and Nippon Electric Glass.[68]

Beyond the automotive, environmental, and information display markets, Corning identified one other intriguing growth area for specialty glass and ceramics: substrates for computer memory disks. As the capacity of disk drives expanded in quantum leaps, the physical stresses on the disks themselves also increased. They spun faster, packed information more densely, and demanded tighter specifications for surface properties. Marveled research scientist George Beall, the requirements for future disks seemed "incredible...like flying a Boeing 747 full speed down a valley at the height of a row of corn. . . .In order to produce [such a result], especially at high speeds like 5,000 rpm, you have to have an extremely smooth material. So this is why glass and glass ceramics were considered." With Deneka as the project's champion, Corning eventually settled on a glass ceramic material that offered superior strength, reliability, and durability over conventional substrates made of aluminum. During the late 1980s and early 1990s, Corning poured millions of dollars into development of the memory disk substrate, chasing accelerating performance targets while attempting to drive manufacturing costs down. Dubbed Memcor, the product was pronounced ready for field trials in the early 1990s.[69]

From Health and Sciences to Laboratory Services

The sales of Corning's interests in Nutrisearch, Genencor, and Ciba Corning left the health and sciences group focused on MetPath as the foundation of a mushrooming business in laboratory services. Marty Gibson's strategy featured three dimensions. First, he continued to decentralize MetPath while also applying total quality principles to improve operations. In 1986, MetPath delivered 88 percent of its lab test reports to customers in 24 hours or less; four years later, that rate had jumped to 98.5 percent. As a result, said Jamie Houghton, MetPath became "a very, very high producer of profit."[70]

Second, Gibson saw an opportunity for Corning to play a consolidating role in the lab services industry. In 1987, medical testing was estimated to cost as much as $27 billion per year in the United States, about 6 percent of the nation's total health care bill. Yet the six biggest companies—SmithKline Clinical Laboratories, Roche Biomedical Laboratories, MetPath, International Clinical Laboratories, National Health Laboratories, and Damon Corporation—accounted for less than 10 percent of the market, which remained fragmented among more than 7,000 competitors.[71] Feeling urgency to move, Corning embarked on a buying spree that included numerous small labs along the East Coast as well as a joint venture with Swiss-based UniLab Holdings that established a presence in the western part of the country. By 1989, Corning operated fourteen regional labs, claimed a market share of about 7 percent, and posted revenues of $440 million. But as Gibson had foreseen, Corning's major competitors also pursued similar strategies. In 1988, Corning lost out in a bidding war for International Clinical Laboratories when SmithKline Beckman topped its final offer of $360 million by another $40 million. As a result of this and other deals, SmithKline rose to about twice Corning's size in the industry.[72]

The third dimension of Gibson's strategy was to complement MetPath's position in clinical testing with acquisitions in the other major segments of the laboratory services industry, which he identified as life sciences (especially biotechnology, pharmaceuticals, chemicals, and agriculture) and environmental testing. In 1987, Gibson arranged for Corning to purchase Herndon, Virginia-based Hazleton Laboratories, "the world's largest independent supplier of biological and chemical research services," with 1,700 employees and annual revenues of $77 million. The deal was worth approximately $115 million and it signaled for Corning, said Houghton at the press conference announcing it, "a swing even more heavily into technology-intensive services."[73]

Two years later, Corning acquired G. H. Besselaar Associates, a company based in Princeton, New Jersey, and specializing in clinical tests and evaluations of new drugs. The company appeared to offer a strong complement to Hazleton Laboratories, which focused on preclinical drug development, and it enabled Corning to provide "a complete resource for new drug development." Another deal followed just months later, when Corning merged with Somerset, New Jersey-based Enseco Inc., which maintained a network of laboratories to test for industrial pollutants, for considerations worth approximately $125 million.[74]

Struggles in Consumer Housewares

Among the segments in the Corning strategy wheel, only the consumer business faced a future fraught with difficulty. Although a few small product lines like Serengeti Eyewear continued to rocket upward in the late 1980s, the much bigger housewares businesses continued to struggle. At first, it appeared that the flurry of new initiatives and products that Fogarty had launched would turn the business around. During 1986 and 1987, consumer revenues grew 30 percent, with products introduced since 1983 accounting for two-thirds of sales. New designs of Corning Ware, Corelle, and Pyrex fared well, but Visions accounted for most of the surge. To maintain this momentum, Corning built a new Visions factory in Brazil. Unfortunately, nearly coincident with the turning of the first spade of earth, Visions displayed the alarming indications of a fading fad. Although the product served well enough for making soups and boiling pasta, it failed miserably in frying, where hot spots caused sticking and poor temperature distribution yielded unevenly cooked food. In 1988, growth slackened, leveled off the following year, and then began a disastrous plunge.[75]

Meanwhile, Crown Corning's efforts to penetrate the upscale department store trade bogged down in the face of low-cost competition and massive logistical problems. Corning began a retreat but sought to protect its position in the department store channel by acquiring Clinton, Illinois-based Revere Ware Inc., a company that claimed Paul Revere as its founder in 1801. Revere Ware was the second-biggest maker of stovetop cookware in the United States. Unfortunately, the company arrived in troubled condition. Its antiquated facilities and outmoded production practices were depleting the value of the Revere brand, which was squeezed by cheap imports at the low end and expensive imports at the top of the line, as well as tough competition in the middle from archrival Farberware. The company's inability to deal with these forces had forced it into bankruptcy in 1982. Thus when Corning bought it, Revere Ware was in the midst of a protracted turnaround. And it was far from clear that Corning would manifest the patience to see the unit all the way back.[76]

In 1989, Fogarty announced his decision to return to International Playtex, whence Corning had recruited him. The challenge left behind was whether Corning could reverse the decline of the housewares business relative to faster-growing units and, if not, whether the strategy wheel could long tolerate an unbalanced load.

Corning Values

Corning's aggressive response to the waveguide pause, its narrowing strategic focus, and continuing improvements in operations combined to produce strong financial results in the late 1980s. The company enjoyed steady growth and high profitability, and in 1989 it split its stock for the second time in five years. Annual revenues neared $3 billion and return on equity in 1990 hit 16.3 percent—about twice its level in 1983. Income from the equity companies, especially Dow Corning and Samsung-Corning, accounted for about 40 percent of the corporation's net income.[77]

The national business press took increasing notice of Corning in the late 1980s, acclaiming not only its performance, but also its values. Corning attracted widespread interest and praise for its relentless emphasis on quality, innovation, widespread use of teamwork, success in joint ventures, commitment to diversity, and responsibility to the communities in which it operated, especially Corning, New York. The company began to appear and then rise on lists of "most admired" corporations. It was even profiled (and celebrated) in a top-selling management book by consultants Ira Magaziner and Mark Patinkin, *The Silent War: Inside the Global Business Battles Shaping America's Future*.

Corning's front-rank position in the total quality movement stimulated much of the favorable press. During the late 1980s, Jamie Houghton continued to champion quality with the same zeal that he showed in his first year as chairman and CEO. The difference was that Corning could now point to tangible benefits from its efforts, a circumstance that reinforced employee commitment to the quality initiative. And that initiative moved into a new phase. No longer an awareness program, it was becoming engrained as a way of life. Indeed, Houghton's usual message about quality was that it was "an endless journey" with no destination and that no matter how much the company improved, it could always improve more.[78]

Corning employees were expected to spend at least 5 percent of their working time—more than two weeks each year—in training on quality and related matters such as group dynamics, problem solving, and statistics. More than 3,500 quality teams were at work. In 1990, they generated nearly 15,000 corrective action ideas—as compared to the approximately 200 ideas contributed under an employee suggestion program in 1982. Corning regularly conducted formal surveys of employees, customers, and suppliers to ensure understanding of quality related issues. It tracked key results indicators (KRIs) to measure customer deliverables and the efficiency of key processes and instituted a customer action planning system across the company to better understand customer needs and their level of satisfaction.[79]

Corning's success in quality management won increasing notice and respect in national business circles. In 1984, the company won its first major quality award from a major customer; in 1987 it won two more awards; in 1989 six more; and in 1990, 25. In 1987, Houghton served as chairman of National Quality Month on behalf of the American Society of Quality Control. Houghton and other officers spoke frequently to business groups and penned dozens of articles about quality. Mike McDonald, who hired into Corning as a janitor in 1957, rose through the ranks to become a ceramics engineer, and became a popular instructor in the quality program, was much in demand as a speaker to groups inside and outside the company.[80]

In 1989, Corning's telecommunications products division became a finalist for the Malcolm Baldrige Award. The fact that the unit failed to win caused Corning to redouble its efforts for the next round. The company adopted the Baldrige evaluation criteria as its own internal standard for assessing quality performance. Once again, training proved a powerful vehicle for change: 1,200 managers attended Baldrige seminars; a Baldrige awareness program was made available to all employees throughout the company; and every year, under a process called the Corning Quality Cycle, each business unit was required to track its performance against the 33 criteria evaluated in the Baldrige competition. Each business unit again surveyed its customers and suppliers to develop more new performance standards. At MetPath, for instance, KRIs shifted from productivity measures like tests run per hour to customer-oriented standards like error-free lab reports delivered on time. Each unit was also expected to benchmark its results against the best performance in the world. Finally, each unit was required to develop specific plans for closing the gap between actual and desired performance. To stimulate internal quality competition, in 1990 Corning reconceived its internal recognition program. The Houghton Award, for example, had been established a decade earlier in the name of Amory Houghton Sr. and Arthur A. Houghton Jr. and was bestowed annually on the individual best exemplifying Corning's standards of excellence. It was renamed the Houghton Quality Award and could honor individuals or groups. The initial award went to Telecommunications Products Division.[81]

The drive toward total quality affected Corning's organization and operations in many ways. The most significant included the proliferation of teams across the company and the increasing autonomy of employees. When the company reopened the Blacksburg, Virginia plant to make Celcor, for example, it followed "a partnership process" designed to create a "high-performance work environment." Guided by Norm Garrity, senior vice president for manufacturing, the plant featured many innovations. Although it was unionized, work assignments were designed around process flows rather than job descriptions or traditional labor contracts. There were no supervisors or time clocks and only four job classifications, as compared to 47 at Corning's Celcor facility in Erwin, New York. Blacksburg employees were paid a salary, were eligible for performance bonuses, and were afforded increased job security protection. In return, they agreed to work shifts as long as 12.5 hours, with alternating three- and four-day weeks. Each employee was also required to master three skill "modules"— that is, families of skills. Employee teams planned, carried out, and controlled the work itself. They also possessed authority to hire and fire their members, and they reported directly to the plant manager. Thus Houghton could claim that there were just two levels of management in these operations: the plant manager and everyone else.[82]

The results at Blacksburg exceeded Corning's expectations by a wide margin. Employee teams analyzed each of the 235 manufacturing steps involved in a conventional process for making Celcor and eliminated 115 of them. A product line changeover that took an hour at the older Celcor facility in Erwin was accomplished in ten minutes at Blacksburg. Before the plant opened, Garrity had estimated that it would lose $2.3 million in its start-up phase; instead, the plant earned a $2 million profit in its first eight months. A reporter from *Business Week* who toured the factory found workers talking like managers. As one, Robert Hubble, put it, "Everybody that works here is competitive. We're willing to work long hours. We want to be multiskilled and learn how we can make the product better so we can be the best in quality and service to the customer. And if we do all that, this plant will be around a long time."[83]

Lessons learned from Blacksburg were used to restructure operations in facilities across the company. The extent of change depended on local circumstances. Nonetheless, at both national and local levels, Corning collaborated with the American Flint Glass Workers Union to include pay-for-performance incentives in contracts and to form labor-management committees to work together to simplify work processes and redesign jobs. Corning also pursued a more rigorous approach to recruiting, adopting higher minimum requirements and using tests to ensure ability to thrive in a high-performance work culture. Most new factory employees had completed at least one year of college in addition to a high school diploma. When added to the ongoing quality initiative, the new incentives and human resource practices yielded significant operating improvements throughout the company.[84]

Still another result of Corning's focus on total quality was heightened emphasis on recruiting and developing a more diverse workforce. [85] In the mid-1980s, the company was alarmed by trends showing high attrition rates among female, African-American, and other minority employees. Between 1980 and 1987, an average of 7.8 percent of the company's white male employees left each year; the rates for women and African Americans over the same period were 13.1 percent and 15.3 percent, respectively. An internal study found these results "unacceptable" and amounted to "a high cost of quality—an average of nearly $3.5 million per year." When such numbers were set against a U.S. Bureau of Labor Statistics forecast that in the year 2000 white males would account for only 39 percent of the workforce (down from 50 percent in 1975) and that 80 percent of new jobs would be filled by women and minorities, Houghton perceived a serious problem emerging. In 1986 he declared that increasing the diversity of Corning's workforce, especially in management, was a corporate priority on a level with its emphases on financial performance and total quality.[86]

The new initiative differed from earlier efforts under Affirmative Action in two important respects. First, the focus in the late 1980s was on retention rather than hiring, although hiring women and minorities remained an important priority. Corning sought to smash the "glass ceiling" that women and minorities believed stood in the way of their advancement. Second, instead of assimilating nontraditional groups into the Corning culture, it attempted to honor the differences in the mix. The metaphor Houghton applied to the company was a salad, not a melting pot—"blacks who are proud to be black and women who are proud to be mothers and engineers."[87]

Corning approached its diversity challenge as it had approached quality—as a change management initiative. It set ambitious goals, seeking to beat average employment numbers among big American corporations generally. Between 1988 and 1991 Corning aimed to lift the percentage of women in management from 17.4 percent to 23.2 percent and the number of African Americans from 5.1 to 7 percent. It formed high-level teams to plan how to meet the targets. It commissioned women's issues and black progress quality improvement teams to help with the challenge and serve as support groups. It appointed an African-American woman, Dawn Cross, as director of cultural diversity and had her report regularly to senior management. It retained consultants and invested heavily in training, requiring all employees to attend workshops on racism, sexism, cross-cultural communications, and other diversity-related matters. It expanded day care facilities and accommodated flexible working arrangements. It modified incentives and performance appraisals to encourage senior personnel to develop younger managers from nontraditional backgrounds. It communicated frequently and intensively on the subject. It reported on progress regularly to the board of directors. It promoted champions. And it identified success stories and celebrated them internally and in the business press. All this added up to what a front-page story in the *New York Times* called "one of corporate America's most ambitious experiments in cultural engineering."[88]

Corning made significant progress toward its goals during the late 1980s. Between 1987 and 1990, 52 percent of the people moving into the salaried ranks were female and 16 percent were African American; overall, in 1990, women constituted 33.6 percent of all salaried personnel and African Americans, 5.5 percent.[89] For its efforts Corning won recognition from *Working Mother, Black Enterprise*, and other publications, and it received high ranking on lists of desirable employers for women and minorities.

Yet for all its progress, Corning faced continuing challenges in striving to achieve its stated diversity goals. Diversity was not an issue like quality that everyone could readily embrace, and the company noted backlash among some white males who resented what they saw as a new quota system for hiring and promotions. Corning did not tolerate foot-dragging when it could prove it, but in many instances it was hard to prove. Second, success in diversity did not show up automatically or quickly on the bottom line. To many employees, the case for diversity seemed less urgent and more politically charged than, say, the imperative to improve performance in 1983 or the drive for world-class quality a few years later. And third, increasing the diversity of management entailed overcoming some obstacles that Corning could affect only indirectly. Some promising African-American candidates for management, for example, proved reluctant to live in a small city like Corning, where the indigenous black population was relatively small. Facing a choice between a job offer at Corning and one with another good employer in, say, New York City, many candidates preferred the latter. The company could alter the odds in small ways by a variety of means—working with the public schools to increase minority representation and develop more inclusive curricula, encouraging the local cable TV provider and radio stations to offer programming catering to African Americans, or wooing black hairdressers to Market Street—all of which it did. Nonetheless, Corning faced an uphill fight in raising the number of African Americans in management. (For similar reasons, it had always proved a struggle to recruit and retain single people of both sexes and all races to Corning.)

Corning's willingness to promote change in its local environment in the cause of diversity was consistent with its long-standing sense of corporate responsibility, especially in Corning, New York, and its environs. During the 1980s, Corning continued to make significant contributions to its hometown. The most visible was the decision, announced in 1986, to build a new corporate headquarters facility in Corning on the site of the old Main Plant. Although construction was postponed in the aftermath of the waveguide pause, the announcement and eventual follow-through once more emphasized the company's enduring commitment to the city. Given its investment and employment in the region and the advantages of locating management, research, and production facilities in close proximity, Corning did not seriously entertain thoughts of moving elsewhere.[90]

Corning Enterprises, a wholly owned subsidiary that Amo Houghton had established in 1983, sponsored many contributions to the region. Funded by the sale and management of real estate and subsidies from its corporate parent, Corning Enterprises acted as a kind of economic development agency for Corning and the surrounding area. In the mid-1980s it facilitated the arrival of Wegman's, a giant grocery located at the west end of Market Street, the sale and renovation of the hotel complex at the other end of Market Street, the construction of a new parking garage, and other civic improvements to the downtown area. Corning Enterprises also sponsored the annual LPGA tournament in Corning and rescued the racetrack at nearby Watkins Glen from bankruptcy. It worked with government and civic agencies to construct the $127 million Route 17 bypass north of Corning. It helped attract employers and services to the region and promote the southern tier of New York as a "ceramic corridor" modeled on California's Silicon Valley.[91]

During the 1980s shareholder activists occasionally criticized Corning for its investments in community affairs and wondered whether the company was spending its money wisely. Jamie Houghton showed little patience for such views. "I happen not to be a great fan of Milton Friedman, who says that the corporation must only make money and give it to the stockholders and let them decide what to do with it," he said in an interview on

CNN. "To me, that's ludicrous. A corporation today is too important in our society. A corporation has to participate."[92] Corning's determination to be a good corporate citizen went well beyond altruism. It believed that providing a supportive environment in which to attract and retain high-quality employees was a business imperative. As Houghton looked ahead to the 1990s, he saw signs of a looming recession, and he knew that the company would have to draw on all of its resources and assets to navigate through a period of accelerating change.

CHAPTER FOURTEEN

Refocusing and Reengineering, 1990–1996

AT THE ANNUAL meeting in April 1989, Corning's stockholders voted to approve a new identity for the corporation, replacing the 114-year-old name, Corning Glass Works with the simpler, more contemporary, and less specific, Corning Incorporated. Jamie Houghton announced several reasons for the change. First, the growth of its diversified interests, especially lab services, meant that Corning was no longer accurately called a glass works. Second, the company sought to recognize something fundamentally new in its own nature. Corning was not a traditional manufacturing corporation, explained Houghton, but rather "a global network...a closely knit web of businesses tied together by common interests." In 1989, the network consisted of six operating divisions, 21 subsidiary companies, and 20 joint ventures. The new Corning spanned geographical and industry borders, mixed manufacturing and services, concerned itself with horizontal processes rather than hierarchical control, and managed itself through teams, partnerships, and alliances. Together with the strategy wheel, and the disciplines and values of total quality management, the global network organization structure was making Corning a different sort of company, one that seemed "poised to lead" into the 1990s and beyond.[1]

At the end of 1990, Houghton announced a major corporate reorganization. Roger Ackerman was promoted to a new position as president and chief operating officer, with responsibility for Corning Incorporated operations. These operations now included three groups: Specialty Materials under Norm Garrity; Information Displays under John Loose; and Opto-Electronics under Jan Suwinski. At the same time, Dick Dulude was elected vice chairman of Corning and handed special responsibility for the consumer products businesses worldwide. (Van Campbell and Dave Duke remained vice chairmen with responsibilities for finance and technology, respectively.) Finally, the lab services businesses were grouped into a separate subsidiary, Corning Laboratory Services Inc. (CLSI), with headquarters in Teterboro, New Jersey, and its own board of directors. Marty Gibson was named chairman and CEO of CLSI, an assignment in which he continued to report to Houghton.[2]

Behind the reorganization lay Houghton's plan for an eventual transition in the top job. Previously, he had told the board that he would step down either in 1993, after ten years on the job, or at the latest, in 1996, when he turned 60. It was time, then, to identify a likely successor—Ackerman—and allow time for him to manage a bigger entity than a group while learning and being tested. Although Ackerman was given no assurances, it appeared that if he performed well in the number-two job, the number-one job would eventually be his. Other factors also contributed to Houghton's thinking about top-level decision making. Since his brother Amo had left the board in 1986, Jamie had been stretched in many different directions by the demands of his office. He needed a strong president to attend to strategy and operations, so that he himself could devote more time to dealing with internal and external constituencies—to leading. Finally, the reorganization reflected Houghton's sense that the lab testing businesses were better off distanced from Corning's traditional glass-related businesses. There was little synergy between CLSI and the traditional core, and it made sense both strategically and organizationally for CLSI to move nearer to its customers in the New York City metropolitan area while pursuing its own plans for growth. In the back of everyone's mind was the possibility that the lab businesses might eventually be sold or spun off.[3]

The corporate reorganization prepared Corning, its top executives believed, for the challenges of the 1990s. They anticipated the needs to cope with an imminent recession, develop strategies to penetrate the newly opened markets of eastern Europe and Asia, address bright long-term opportunities in telecommunications products, specialty materials, and laboratory services, deal with longstanding issues in consumer housewares, and prepare for an orderly change in leadership. And they understood that, no matter how well prepared the company was, even the best-laid plans were unlikely to proceed without a hitch.

Rethinking the Portfolio in Another Difficult Period

In 1990, the Quality Council, an informal group of quality executives from leading corporations (including Corning), developed guidelines for how CEOs should spend their time to ensure the "health" of their office. The guidelines were framed as a checklist of seven responsibilities, with suggested allocations of time for each: (1) provide strategic direction, 10–20 percent; (2) assess operations, 5–20 percent; (3) lead the management team, 10–15 percent; (4) create the environment and value system, 5–15 percent; (5) provide external representation, 5–20 percent; (6) work with board of directors and shareholders, 5–10 percent; and (7) promote personal growth and health, 5 percent. Houghton decided to assess his own schedule against the checklist, and he pored over his diaries and calendars. He found significant departures on two points: he spent only about 10 percent of his time on strategic direction, and he spent 30 percent of his time on values, especially quality and diversity. He was not troubled by either discrepancy, pointing out that the corporate strategy had been set early in his tenure and that his job as chairman demanded a commitment to "beating the drums. . . . This is where leadership is important, and I have no intention of stopping or slowing down this part of my activities."[4]

While Houghton continued his rounds, visiting forty to fifty company locations each year, Ackerman took a fresh, hard look at the units in his charge, assisted by the Strategic Leadership Team, which included the three vice chairmen (Campbell, Duke, and Dulude) and the three group general managers. This team modified an old planning tool from the Boston Consulting Group to help—a two-by-two matrix, in which the vertical axis measured return on equity and the horizontal axis, rate of growth. The midpoint or crosshairs of the matrix was set at the average ROE of the company (about 15 percent) and the rate of GNP growth plus inflation (about 8 percent). Once the company's various businesses were sorted into the four boxes, it became clear what had to be done. Units not earning the company's average ROE and growing at less than the rate of the U.S. economy occupied a "no parking zone" and became candidates for dramatic improvement or disposal. The high ROE and low-growth ("mature") businesses were managed for cash to fund development of the fast-growing but not yet sufficiently profitable businesses. The overall goal was to move a bigger fraction of the company's businesses into the high return, high-growth quadrant—the space occupied by the company's best communications, display, and environmental products businesses.[5]

GOOD RETURN	Lighting Optical Materials P.C.	Optical Fiber / Cable NIDS Projection TV Clinical Testing Pharmaceutical Testing Platic Labware Auto Substrates Dow Corning
POOR RETURN	CRT Lab Glass Consumer Materials	LCD Opto Components Memory Disks Biosym Enseco Diesel / Other Substrates
	LOW GROWTH	**HIGH GROWTH**

The Strategic Leadership Team's analysis led Corning to put some businesses on the block. In 1993, for example, the company sold its industrial process systems business to a management group, and the following year, it sold its World War II era glass tubing plant in Parkersburg, West Virginia, to longtime rival Schott. In other instances, the portfolio analysis inspired managers to reposition their units in search of new growth opportunities. In science products, which made beakers, flasks, and other labware, Corning suffered when its traditional customers shifted from "wet" analytical chemistry to "dry" methods using electronic diagnostic equipment. Corning considered exiting labware altogether but finally chose in June 1993 to acquire Costar Corporation, a maker of disposable plastic products, membrane filters, cartridges, and filtration devices used in laboratories and industry around the world. The deal, which Ackerman characterized as "a logical expansion of our laboratory products business," was accomplished through an exchange of shares valued at approximately $180 million.[6]

The portfolio analysis also laid bare the seemingly intractable strategic challenges in consumer housewares. Despite a parade of new schemes for promotion and distribution, the company's traditional glass products—Pyrex, Corning Ware, Corelle, and Visions—continued to show signs of maturity and decline. The vast purchasing power of K-Mart and Wal-Mart ("the Mart brothers," as Houghton called them) continued to rise, and Corning's attempts to regain control of pricing were repeatedly thwarted. The situation went from bad to worse after 1989, when Visions, the last hot new product in the business, suffered an abrupt and apparently irreversible downturn in sales. Consumer research showed that the cosmetic appeal of the product line could not offset its shortcomings in performance: Corning's new Visions factory in Brazil quickly became an expensive write-off. Meanwhile, Corning's 1988 acquisition of Revere did little to help the company's bottom line, although it added a venerable brand name and allowed Corning to expand its retail offerings to include metal cookware as well as traditional glass products.

As vice chairman with responsibility for the consumer housewares business, Dick Dulude grappled with ways to achieve a turnaround. Late in 1991, with the North American Free Trade Association on the horizon, Dulude negotiated a promising agreement with Vitro, Sociedad Anonima, Mexico's largest glass manufacturer. The deal called for the formation of two new joint ventures, Corning Vitro Corporation in the United States, and Vitro Corning S.A. de C.V. in Mexico, which would combine the worldwide consumer glassware businesses of the parent corporations. Corning's respective shares in the two new joint ventures came to 51 and 49 percent, with Vitro's interest the complement.[7]

At first glance, the partners seemed an ideal match, with few overlapping product lines or markets and long histories in the industry. Vitro's major products included stemware and crystal glassware, while Corning contributed its well-known brands of cookware and dinnerware. But serious problems quickly became apparent. In 1990, the year before the deal, recalled Dulude, the respective partners had earned approximately $12 million in profits. In the first year after the deal, the profits disappeared, and in the second year, the ventures reported a $12-million loss. The parties shared equally in producing these results. Corning absorbed the write-off of the Brazil Visions plant, while its North American product lines continued to languish; Vitro, it turned out, had a high cost structure that made it vulnerable to Asian imported glass. The cross-ownership agreements also proved unwieldy, making it difficult to assign accountability for problems and achieve consensus on remedial actions. After the second year, both parties decided they had had enough, and the deal was unwound, amicably, early in 1994.[8]

The disintegration of the Vitro partnership left Corning back where it had started three years before. Now in the hands of John Loose (Dulude had retired in 1993), the Corning Consumer Products Company remained a problem in search of a solution, with low growth prospects and a string of annual losses. Corning's top officers were reluctant to sell it, although some directors and executives were becoming increasingly vocal advocates of that course, and it was far from clear that Corning would realize much for it in its current state. Accordingly, Loose took the unit through an extensive redesign of its basic processes—a reengineering program. In 1994, full-time teams "took out tremendous amounts of costs, 20 percent of the people, redesigned the product development process, [and] how we went to market." At the same time, Corning invested heavily in new information systems to gain a better understanding of its costs and identify winners and losers among its products and accounts. Loose compared the effort to rehabilitating an old house: it could be done superficially with a coat of new paint or it could involve hard-to-see improvements in plumbing and wiring. Corning chose the latter course, despite its high cost. But the company also signaled that it was nearing the end of its patience in October 1994 by selling the consumer glass operations in Europe, including manufacturing facilities in England, France, and Germany, to Newell Company for $90 million in cash.[9]

Meanwhile, at CLSI, the move from Corning to MetPath's old head-quarters at Teterboro, New Jersey, in sight of Manhattan, sparked a new round of acquisitions. Between 1991 and 1994, Gibson and his successor, Randy Thurman, closed deals on nine large clinical testing businesses and many other smaller ones, in the process raising CLSI's revenues to more than $1.5 billion and its total employment to approximately 20,000. By the mid-1990s, CLSI accounted for a third of Corning's revenues and profits and half of its total employment. The unit had a nationwide presence in blood testing and was vying with SmithKline Beecham to become the biggest competitor in the industry. Among the new arrivals were MetWest and Damon Corporation (1993), and Maryland Medical Laboratory, Inc., Nichols Institute, and Bioran Medical Laboratories (1994). The deal for Damon, which cost Corning nearly $400 million following a bidding war, constituted the biggest acquisition in the company's history.[10]

Yet even as these deals were closing, adverse forces were gathering to batter clinical testing labs in general and CLSI's units in particular. Although the Clinton administration failed to enact a comprehensive national health care plan, its attempt nonetheless heralded a new era of cost-conscious reg-ulation of the health care industry. The rise of HMOs and managed care programs cut deeply into the profits of lab testing companies. Between 1984 and 1994, the market share of HMOs surged from 6 to 40 percent of all health insurance plans in the United States. They got there by offering sig-nificantly lower prices to employers and employees, which in turn were based on tight management of costs. The HMOs bought testing services in bulk and used their purchasing power to drive down prices—more than 90 percent in some instances. A test priced at $100 under a fee-for-service plan in New York might fetch as little as $1.20—well below cost—under an HMO in Baltimore. The effect was devastating at CLSI. Operating margins that had averaged more than 25 percent for a decade fell to an average between 7 and 8 percent.[11]

What the HMOs left behind, reforms in Medicare purchasing threat-ened to take. In 1992, the U.S. Department of Justice, which had been inves-tigating billing and marketing practices in the lab testing industry, reached a

$111.4 million settlement with National Health Laboratories after that company pleaded guilty to fraudulent billing of Medicare and its former president earned a short prison term. The specific complaints against National Health Labs concerned overcharges for tests and inducements to perform unnecessary tests. The following spring, with investigative reporters from the TV newsmagazine *60 Minutes* probing into the lab testing industry's practices, the government turned its focus to MetPath, alleging that the company systematically and over a period of years had billed Medicare for unnecessary tests. Management denied the charges, but in September 1993 nonetheless agreed to pay a $35 million settlement with the government. MetPath refused to admit guilt but asserted that the settlement was "a business decision to engage in no further debate or prolonged litigation with our largest payor, but to accept the government's and regulators' current interpretations of the rules...and move on."[12] Two years later, MetPath paid another fine of $8.9 million, and a year after that, Damon was obliged to pay a whopping $119 million in penalties for fraudulent practices in the years before Corning acquired it.

In the midst of these scandals, Congress revised Medicare's policies for reimbursement, significantly lowering fee schedules for particular kinds of tests. At the same time, Medicare administrators adopted "anti-utilization" guidelines to discourage the practice of some for-profit labs, including those in CLSI, of promoting additional services for additional fees. These guidelines, Gibson pointed out, struck at the heart of CLSI's strategy:

> The definition of marketing is to do things to make the utilization of your product or service increase.....[But] anything MetPath did to market its service, i.e. to increase the utilization of its service, is defined by Medicare as fraudulent. So what Medicare basically said, to put it in its simplest terms, is marketing is fraudulent. You, the provider of this service, can do nothing to increase the utilization of that service. In fact we expect you to go out of your way to decrease the utilization of that service. Now, how can you run a business that way? It was just impossible.

The rise of managed care and the new Medicare rules combined to wreak a fundamental change in CLSI's business. "It was the scariest thing I ever saw," said Gibson. Almost overnight, CLSI "went from a great business to a very garden-variety, mediocre kind of business."[13] At the same time, the scandals sapped morale absorbed disproportionate amounts of management time and legal services, and raised fresh questions atop Corning as to whether the blood testing labs any longer belonged in the corporate portfolio.

With its clinical labs under siege, Corning scaled back its plans to build a diversified lab testing services company. Although its pharmaceutical and environmental testing units were profitable, they were also small, and Corning lacked the inclination and resources to build them up simultaneously. In 1993, Corning pulled three recent acquisitions—Hazleton (1987), G. H. Besselaar (1989), and SciCor (1991)—out of CLSI to form a new, autonomous organization, Corning Pharmaceutical Services. This entity provided a range of services from plan development to drug testing to marketing support. At about the same time, Corning shifted Enseco, the environmental testing unit, from CLSI to the specialty materials group, where it seemed a better fit with Celcor and other environmental products businesses. In 1994, Corning placed Enseco's assets into a fifty-fifty joint venture with International Technology Corporation called Quanterra Incorporated. CLSI, meanwhile, changed its name to Corning Clinical Laboratories.[14]

Step by step, the strategy of diversification into services that Corning had pursued since the early 1980s to offset its complete dependency on glass and related technologies was coming undone. But the reasons for the change only partly reflected problems and challenges in the lab testing businesses. The other side of the story was the rejuvenation of the older core businesses.

The Core Businesses Pay Dividends

In the early 1990s, another sharp recession hit the American economy and triggered a wave of corporate restructurings, shareholder revolts, and process reengineering initiatives. At first, it seemed that Corning would escape the turmoil that beset many American industries because most of its international operations remained healthy and especially because the company's revamped core businesses continued to deliver impressive results.

The environmental products and specialty materials lines, for example, recorded excellent results. In the United States, new environmental standards for air quality actually boosted Corning's Celcor business despite the decline of automobile production during the recession. Detroit was making fewer cars, but a higher proportion of these cars included Corning's substrates in their catalytic converters. Meanwhile, Corning pushed hard to lower its costs and raise its quality, helped by the high-performance work systems in the Blacksburg, Virginia, plant. The story was similar in Europe, where Corning's decision in the mid-1980s to build a Celcor facility in Kaiserslautern, Germany, paid off handsomely. During the late 1980s and early 1990s, the leading auto-producing nations in Europe, and then in the European Community as a whole, adopted clean air standards comparable to those in North America. As these standards took effect, the Kaiserslautern plant operated at full bore.[15]

Meanwhile, lessons from the Blacksburg experience were spreading to other Corning plants, including a new facility in Erwin, New York, that was designed to make glass ceramic filters for molten metal and substrates for various industrial uses. The plant was also designed to introduce Local 1000 of the Flints to high-performance work systems, including fewer job classifications. Given the Flints' long history in the Chemung Valley, Norm Garrity pointed out, these were tough negotiations. But because Corning could decide to build the plant elsewhere, the company held the upper hand. In the end, the Flints cooperated, and the Erwin plant, like Blacksburg, became a highly productive facility.[16]

By the mid-1990s, as they contemplated the future of catalytic converters, Corning's leaders saw ample reason to be optimistic. For one thing, it was likely that standards for air quality in North America and Europe would become tougher—a scenario that created opportunities for innovative suppliers. California, for example, adopted emissions control standards for the 1997 automobile model year and beyond that were stricter than those in place across the nation. In anticipation of the new standards, Corning engineers introduced an electrically heated substrate that enabled cold engines to start with less pollution. Approximately 80 percent of an automobile's total emissions occur in the first few minutes after the engine starts, before the catalysts in the catalytic converter heat up. Corning's new system promised to work so well that automobiles would not only cease polluting but would actually clean the surrounding air as they passed through it.[17]

Opportunities on a global scale also seemed extraordinarily bright. It appeared inevitable that nations around the world—including huge, populous countries like China, India, Russia, and Brazil—would eventually gravitate toward air quality standards similar to those in Europe and North America. The projected demand for Celcor substrates alleviated the fear once felt by the product's original developers that alternative pollution control technologies or improvements in internal combustion engines would render catalytic converters obsolete.

Corning also continued to develop new specialty items from glass and ceramics. Some recalled the company's earlier technical triumphs—and failures. In August 1991, the Mitsubishi Electric Corporation selected Corning to manufacture the world's largest monolithic mirror blank for the Japan National Large Telescope project on Mauna Kea, Hawaii. This 327-inch behemoth dwarfed the 200-inch Mount Palomar blank in surface area. A new fabrication technique—the "hex-seal" process—enabled the disk to be fabricated by forming boules of high-purity fused silica that could be bonded together to form the monolith. Corning delivered the mirror blank to Mitsubishi Electric Corporation for the Suburu telescope on schedule in 1994. At the same time, Corning took orders for a pair of 8.1-meter mirror blanks for the multinational Gemini project telescope in Chile. In that same year, Corning also revisited a former failure by forming EuroKera-North America, a joint venture with St. Gobain Vitrage SA to manufacture glass ceramic cook tops. Undeterred by the dismal history of The Counter That Cooks (discussed in chapter 11), EuroKera committed $10 million to build a new production facility near Greenville, South Carolina, to serve "rapidly rising demand" in the United States.[18]

Other specialty glass products were genuinely new—or at least of recent vintage. U.S. Precision Lens, the subsidiary that produced lens systems for projection television, enjoyed strong growth in the early and mid-1990s. A flurry of recent orders for huge mirror blanks notwithstanding, Garrity and his colleagues understood that "not too many people need 40-foot mirrors. There are only so many in the world you can make." Accordingly, Corning cultivated new markets for its high-purity fused silica. One of the most promising involved "stepper lens systems" for the machines that etched circuitry on computer chips. The lasers that performed this work operated at microscopic and ever diminishing tolerances and had to be focused with extraordinary precision. Lenses of high-purity fused silica filled the bill because of their exceptional quality and high durability. Once again, Corning projected robust growth for its lens systems well into the future.[19]

Not every specialty materials initiative met with success, however. A particular disappointment was Memcor, a glass ceramic substrate for computer memory disks. The product possessed apparent technical advantages over conventional aluminum substrates: it was stronger, smoother, and more stable when spinning at high speeds—up to 5,000 rpm in some disk drive models. In 1993, Corning announced a partnership with Seagate, a leading manufacturer of drives, to market disks based on Memcor. Unfortunately, by then, metallurgists had found ways to strengthen aluminum substrates, which made them competitive in performance with the higher-priced Memcor. After about a year, Corning reluctantly withdrew the product, although some scientists insisted that it would eventually make a comeback in ever faster disk drives.[20]

The news for Corning was much better in its fast-growing optical fiber and (via Siecor) fiber-optic cable businesses. Corning's fiber sales surpassed $1 billion in 1992, while Siecor's revenues were fast approaching $500 million. Fundamental market and technological forces worked to the company's advantage. Telephone companies pushed fiber links deeper into their networks, moving from long-distance applications to regional and local services, which accounted for nearly 90 percent of all cable installations. The cable TV services also converted their central networks to fiber optics. Photonic devices continued to dislodge electronic devices in managing information flows on fiber networks. The phenomenal growth of the Internet, especially after the introduction of the Mosaic graphical browser (ancestor of today's Netscape browser) in 1993, showed the attractions of high-bandwidth, interactive communications to households and offices around the world. Many nations privatized telecommunications, opening the door to competition and accelerated innovation, much of it relying on fiber optics and photonics. And densely populated developing countries—China, India, Russia, and the countries of Southeast Asia—planned massive telecommunications infrastructure projects, including state-of-the-art fiber-optic networks. With demand growing at 30 percent per year during the early 1990s, Corning could not make fiber fast enough, and Siecor sold as much cable as it could make.[21]

Corning continued to push the frontier in fiber design and manufacturing. A specialty fibers unit customized fibers for specific applications, such as short-haul data transmission and service in specific environments such as in oil wells, chemical plants, aircraft, under water, or on the battlefield. Corning commanded premium prices for these specialty fibers. At the same time, the company was adding to its expanding base of knowledge in optical communications and photonics. At Sullivan Park, Donald Keck, one of the founding fathers of fiber optics, developed a fiber doped with erbium that led to a new way to boost optical signals without converting them in electronic form and back again. Keck and his colleagues shifted their focus from developing fibers to the new "fiber gain modules" that became a hot-selling product line.[22]

Siecor also continued to make rapid strides in the early 1990s. The company established itself as a leader in not only fiber optic cable but also associated hardware and attachments. In 1993, Siecor acquired Northern Telecom's fiber-optic cabling facility in Saskatchewan, thereby gaining a commanding market share position in Canada. During the next several years, Siecor added Northern Telecom's hardware and equipment businesses, as well. At the same time, Siecor continued to make headway in Japan, where it remained the only foreign cable supplier authorized to sell to the national telecommunications service.[23]

As healthy as Corning's businesses in optical fibers and cables were, its operations in LCD glass and information displays were even healthier, with markets expanding at 50 percent per year. The development of bright, colorful active-matrix displays spurred sales of laptop computers, which in turn boosted demand for Corning's LCD glass. Displays in new digital electronic devices and applications—cameras and camcorders, onboard navigation systems, kiosks, and video games and other portable units—relied on

Corning's lightweight and inexpensive precision flat glass. In 1994, Corning sold 70 percent of the glass used in active-matrix displays worldwide. With its Harrodsburg, Kentucky, plant operating at full capacity, the new melting facility in Shizuoka, Japan, came on stream early in 1994 to serve the powerful Japanese consumer electronics industry. In Korea, Samsung announced plans to begin mass production of active-matrix displays using LCD glass provided by a new joint venture with Corning that was outside the boundaries of the original Samsung-Corning covenants.[24]

Corning Competes

Early in 1993, Jamie Houghton held a private meeting with the Corning board and announced his desire to remain as chairman and CEO for three more years, until he reached age sixty. He also indicated his choice of Roger Ackerman to succeed him in 1996. "By that time," Houghton recalled later,

> I was even telling Roger...in my personal reviews with him that I...thought that he was the logical person to succeed me.
> I frankly asked him if he wanted to. I remember the first conversation. He said, "I want to think about that, because I'm not sure." But he came back pretty quickly. I liked that about him—that it wasn't a slam dunk.[25]

During the interim, the two men planned to work together closely to prepare for the eventual transition. Houghton intended to offload increasing responsibilities to Ackerman, while he himself expected to devote more attention to dealing with outside constituencies. He remained a high-profile national spokesperson on quality and diversity issues, and, as the leading citizen of the city of Corning, he was involved in many local and regional organizations and initiatives. Houghton also began to focus more on promoting research and development and long-range new product opportunities. Corning's work at the frontiers of organic and inorganic chemistry particularly intrigued him. He planned to help promote a new composite of glass and plastic called Placor. Developed at Sullivan Park, the composite possessed an unusual combination of strength, durability, and resistance to fire and high temperatures that made it potentially suitable for a wide range of industrial applications.[26]

After a few months, however, Houghton's plans were suddenly interrupted, and Ackerman's preparation for the top job quickly accelerated. While in Williamsburg, Virginia, where he was attending the annual meeting of The Business Council, Houghton was hit by a car and suffered multiple fractures to his lower right leg, as well as injuries to his head. The accident occurred late in the evening on May 7, as he was returning to his hotel and conversing with a colleague. He stepped off the sidewalk onto a poorly-lit street and failed to see an oncoming car. The driver slammed on the brakes but couldn't stop in time. Houghton was hospitalized or housebound for several months while Ackerman and Executive Vice Chairman Van Campbell ran the company. Following his return to the office, Houghton worked reduced hours for several more months and was fully reengaged by fall. During his absence and recovery, said David Nadler, a consultant who worked with Corning's top executives over the years, "the rest of the management team had to grow up." Ken Freeman, the chief controller, noted that when Houghton was gone, "Roger and Van filled the void, calming the troops. When he returned, they kept their stepped up role."[27]

Houghton's accident became the first indication of the unexpectedly eventful nature of the transitional period to new leadership. The extraordinarily strong performance of Corning's core glass and related businesses had carried the company through the U.S. recession of the early 1990s with hardly a pause. But as the rest of the U.S. economy began to recover, serious problems for Corning were beginning to unfold. The troubles in CLSI were showing up on the bottom line, while poor performers such as consumer housewares continued to drag earnings. And then came two unpleasant surprises. First was another momentary pause in the optical fibers business resulting from a temporary glut in capacity. In 1993, prices tumbled by 10–15 percent.[28]

Most observers recognized the short-term nature of the problem, but for Corning it occurred at a particularly inopportune moment, as a much bigger and much nastier surprise was unfolding at Dow Corning. "If you had asked me in 1992 to list the top 20 things that could go wrong for

Corning," said Houghton, "trouble at Dow Corning would not have been one of them." Yet in 1992, Dow Corning was about to confront a crisis of overwhelming proportions that would have a severe impact on the finances of its corporate parents.[29]

By the early 1990s, Dow Corning had evolved into an extremely valuable financial asset to Corning. Dow Corning posted revenues of $1.8 billion in 1991, with net income of $154 million, and half of that net income flowed directly to Corning's bottom line. Together with Samsung-Corning— another solid contributor—income from equity investments accounted for as much as a third of Corning's overall earnings. Dow Corning was well managed and had grown steadily as its silicone-based products penetrated an expanding variety of industrial applications. But Dow Corning also included a unit that since 1964 had manufactured silicone implants for human patients, with the most prominent of these products female breast implants. During the 1970s and 1980s, the U.S. Food and Drug Administration registered an increasing number of complaints of leakage and other complications from the breast implants, but it took little heed until allegations linked the implants with breast cancer. Although the scientific basis for such a linkage was far from clear and initial studies were inconclusive, in February 1992, FDA Commissioner David Kessler called for a moratorium on the use of silicone breast implants. That action opened the door to thousands of lawsuits from patients against physicians and implant manufacturers—a wave of tort litigation with potential settlement costs in the billions of dollars and a ominous threat to Dow Corning's continuing solvency. During the next few months, approximately 3,000 federal lawsuits and a roughly equal number of state lawsuits targeted Dow Corning and its corporate parents.

From Corning's perspective, the first critical response to the crisis was to ensure that it could not be found liable for the troubles—that the corporate veil of ownership could not be penetrated. Corning and Dow alike took the positions that they were passive investors in the joint venture, that neither party exerted a controlling interest, and that their involvement in Dow Corning was confined to the boardroom. This was a high-stakes argument, especially since the government announced a preliminary settlement with the implant manufacturers of $4.25 billion in September 1993. Dow

Corning's share was $2 billion and, in a worst-case scenario, Corning could conceivably be liable for half of that amount. Two months later, however, a federal judge absolved both corporate parents of any liability stemming from the implant lawsuits, finding no evidence that they had participated in decisions involving the manufacture of silicone breast implants. Meanwhile, the lawsuits against Dow Corning continued to multiply.[30]

But that left a second, longer-term challenge to Corning: how to offset the loss of what had been a lucrative financial asset. The impact of Corning's lost earnings was substantial, and in 1993 the value of the company's stock plunged by a third, from about $40 per share to about $25 per share. Corning absorbed restructuring charges of $203 million due the troubles at Dow Corning and took another $76 million hit the following year. These charges foreshadowed much worse to come: a staggering $365.5 million write-off—the entire value of Corning's investment—after Dow Corning filed for bankruptcy protection on May 15, 1995.[31] This was a bitter pill to swallow, especially since Corning's leaders maintained that the case against Dow Corning was based on bad science and that demand for its core product lines remained strong and rising.

As the full measure of the financial disaster at Dow Corning gradually became apparent, the restructuring charges contributed to modest overall losses at Corning in 1992 and 1993. With the stock price in the doldrums and storm clouds on the horizon, the company's top officers reached the inevitable conclusion late in 1993 that Corning should undergo a fundamental reengineering of its processes and operations. They had in mind not only large-scale reengineering initiatives throughout American industry during the early 1990s but also their own experiences in Corning Asahi Video and the consumer housewares business, which had begun to show significant improvement in results.[32]

Corning took pains, however, to avoid calling the new corporate initiative a "reengineering" program, which had become a code word throughout much of American industry for massive downsizing, with debilitating effects on employee morale. Given the likely perception of the program in the city of Corning, still haunted by its memories of the Guns of August in 1975, Houghton avoided any suggestion that the changes in the company would disrupt the larger community. In bars and coffee shops around town, concerns were manifest, and the Flints argued that the specter of reengineering hung over the Chemung Valley "like a skull and crossbones."[33]

To allay such fears, Corning named the initiative Corning Competes to emphasize the need to make the company more competitive rather than simply leaner. That symbolic change hardly overcame all skepticism, however, as some employees dubbed the program Corning Deletes. But at the outset, Corning's leaders insisted that changes would be gradual and evolutionary, and they would not institute massive layoffs at any point. Ackerman pointed out that the program would primarily affect managerial ranks and added that he did not expect significant employment effects among hourly workers.

The company approached its redesign much as it had tackled the total quality and diversity initiatives of the previous decade: it asked employees to take charge of the process. Coordinated by Ken Freeman, Corning Competes formed a series of task forces that included managers of various ranks and perspectives in each area of business or operations and provided assistance of consultants from Booz-Allen & Hamilton. Task force members took time off from their regular jobs and plowed into the assignment, concentrating on reducing the complexity of the company's operations and finding ways to spread "best practices" across the units. Throughout the process, which proceeded through four distinct phases and lasted for nearly two years, Ackerman and Freeman presided over frequent town meetings of employees, while employees received a stream of publications and bulletins about progress and findings.

The results of Corning Competes evidently justified the effort and the approach. In the end, Corning thinned about 10 percent of its managerial ranks but without incurring the lasting rancor that had accompanied the Guns of August two decades before. The company's financial results showed noteworthy gains in the form of lower costs and higher sales and profitability (excluding the impact of Dow Corning's troubles) in 1994 and 1995. The Corning Consumer Products Company even recorded its first annual profits in several years. Corning pegged the overall savings from Corning Competes at more than $300 million and calculated that the program improved return on equity by at least 3 percent.

As Jamie Houghton approached his sixtieth birthday and his impending retirement, the company seemed poised again for a burst of renewed growth. Its portfolio of businesses had been freshly evaluated, and new business unit strategies were in place. Across the company, operations and organizations were streamlined, and factories enjoyed the benefit of more than a decade of disciplined total quality management. Key lessons in work-force management were spreading from the new high-performance facili-ties to older locations. The optical fibers business picked up from its momentary pause and prompted another major expansion at Wilmington, as well as a decision to build an entirely new optical waveguides plant in Concord, North Carolina, near Charlotte. Even some older businesses showed renewed vigor. In November 1994, Corning, Asahi Glass, and Sony joined forces to create a new company, American Video Products, to manu-facture TV glass at a revamped factory near Pittsburgh.

The outlines of key strategic decisions for the corporation as a whole also became clearer. Dow Corning's fate hastened Corning's decision to put its clinical laboratory businesses on the block. Some directors and execu-tives began to wonder about the legal risks and potential liabilities of deal-ing so intensively with matters affecting human life and health. Given its challenges, Corning Clinical Labs could no longer be expected to serve as a cash machine and, in any event, Corning's optical fibers business could now generate its own funds for development and expansion. Advocates of selling CCL—which included some CCL executives as well as Houghton and Ack-erman—argued that Corning would achieve a higher valuation on the basis of its core manufacturing operations. In the fall of 1995, such reasoning car-ried the day. According to Campbell, the "small decision" to explore divest-ing CCL was made in October, when the Corning board agreed to hire investment bankers to shop the properties.[34]

Other factors contributed to an upbeat mood in the mid-1990s at Corn-ing. In April 1994, it dedicated its new headquarters building on the south bank of the Chemung, where Main Plant and the original general offices once stood. Designed by noted architect Kevin Roche, the building com-bined cosmopolitan style, functionality, and the latest technology in a prize-winning package. The exterior showed pronounced Asian influence but also featured an abstract representation of the Robinson ventilators familiar in every hot-glass manufacturing plant, including the Steuben facility across the Chemung. In addition to the offices, meeting rooms, cafeteria, and auditorium, there were seven two-story atriums featuring commissioned glass sculptures from such renowned artists as Peter Aldridge, Dale Chihuly, and the Czech husband-and-wife team Stanislav Libensky and Jaroslava Brychtova.[35]

The lobby in the new headquarters displayed two remarkable awards. In 1994, President Clinton bestowed on Corning the National Medal of Technology, a sort of lifetime achievement recognition for a handful of companies that have made fundamental contributions to industry and society through the years. The next year the telecommunications products division won the prestigious Malcolm Baldrige National Quality Award. Coming in the final year of Jamie Houghton's tenure, it was a fitting tribute to a company and a leader so dedicated to total quality management. The awards and Corning's robust performance in 1995 augured well, Houghton and Ackerman believed. Looking ahead, they also believed that the company was poised for a new era of growth. Little did they know how right they were.

VI

NEXT GENERATION

CHAPTER FIFTEEN

Growing in the New Economy, 1996–

IN APRIL 1996, fifty-seven-year-old Roger Ackerman succeeded Jamie Houghton as chairman and chief executive of Corning Incorporated. For the first time in the company's history no member of the Houghton family served as chairman or president, or seemed likely to in the foreseeable future. Ackerman was just three years younger than his predecessor and had spent his entire career with the company, starting in research and development. Yet his ascendancy foreshadowed changes as profound as any produced by earlier generational shifts of leadership. During his first four years, Ackerman presided over the spinoff of Corning's lab testing businesses, the sale of the consumer housewares business, the doubling of investment in the company's science and technology (R&D) organization, and two blockbuster acquisitions that catapulted Corning to global leadership in optical fiber, cable, and related components and systems. The change atop the company in 1996, then, marked both the end of one era—of nearly 150 years of Houghton family leadership; of Corning as a diversified company after nearly twenty years; of Corning as a familiar name to consumers after nearly forty years—and the beginning of another.[1] In its 150th year, Corning

faced bright opportunities as a high-tech company with advanced knowledge and expertise in glass and related materials and global leadership positions in its major markets.

At the turn into the third millennium and twenty-first century, momentous events at the company played out in an environment of breathtaking
changes in the world around it. The liberalization of many once centralized
economies, the progressive, piecemeal unification of Europe, the collapse
of the Asian growth economies, and a resurgence of U.S. industrial competitiveness marked a new stage in the global economy. Assumptions accepted
and engrained for decades—about nation-based economic competition,
Japan as number 1, Europe and North America in rusty, irreversible decline,
the transition from a manufacturing into a service economy—no longer
seemed to explain the ways of the world. The relentless rise in power of
information technology, coupled with the equally relentless fall in its prices,
portended economic and social changes of a staggering order. The arrival of
the Internet as a tool for nonspecialists—especially after the introduction of
the Mosaic graphical browser for the World Wide Web in 1993—and phe-
nomenally popular information networks like America Online were rewriting the rules of commerce and dramatically altering the strategies and
behaviors of organizations. In a wired world, boundaries between companies and their customers and suppliers were shifting and eroding; organization structures were becoming more fluid, permeable, and even virtual; ties
of loyalty between employers and employees were dissolving or taking on a
temporary cast; time zones were disappearing; distinctions between work
and home life were blurring; and everything, it seemed, was happening at
an accelerating pace. Pundits, perhaps influenced by the approaching turn
of millennium, proclaimed the advent of a new economy in which networks and knowledge were the only true sources of sustainable advantage.[2]

In 2001, Corning showed signs not merely of adapting to the new economic order but of thriving in it—quite a claim for a 150-year-old company.
Its technologies remained in high demand, and its capabilities and experience seemed well suited to an economy founded on knowledge, networks,
and alliances. In a world of rapid, dramatic changes, Corning drew strength
from key continuities, starting at the top.

A New CEO and a New Operating Environment

Roger Ackerman joined Corning in 1962, just after leaving Rutgers with a master's degree in ceramics engineering. Initially interested in high-tech products such as missile nosecones, he was attracted to the informal and collegial environment of Corning's R&D labs, and he had no complaints when he began working instead on improving the rim impact strength of Centura teacups. When Sullivan Park opened in 1964, he moved up the hill to the new Process Research Center (PRC), where he established himself as an excellent researcher and became, at age twenty-five, one of the youngest managers in the company. A trim, vigorous man, he was also a ferocious competitor in intramural softball and basketball games. Ackerman recalls this period in his life fondly. In fact, the sylvan setting and bonhomie of the PRC led those envious of working there to dub it "the Ponderosa."[3]

In 1969, Corning sent Ackerman to Harvard Business School for a sixteen-week program for promising young managers. Afterward, the company decided to continue his rounding at Corhart Refractories in Louisville, where he became vice president of sales and marketing. When his boss left abruptly, Ackerman, at age 32, became Corhart's acting president. It proved to be baptism by fire and an experience without precedent for a Corning-bred executive. Corhart was embroiled in a long and bitter strike over wages and work rules, with management faced off against a militant local union of the United Mine Workers. Corhart had seen the strike coming and had prepared for it by building up inventories and training managers and support staff to operate the factory. As the strike dragged on, however, the company hired replacement workers and engaged off-duty Louisville policemen to provide security. The dispute turned ugly one morning when the strikers attacked the caravan bringing in the replacement workers. A brawl broke out and people on both sides suffered injuries. This was too much for the citizens of even a prolabor city like Louisville, and public opinion shifted strongly toward management. A short while later, the strike was settled on Corhart's terms, and most of the strikers were eventually rehired. Looking back on the experience, says Ackerman, "everything has seemed easy since then."

Ackerman remained president of Corhart for four years until, following the Guns of August, the company was combined with other Corning operations into the ceramic products division. He took over this unit during a strong burst of growth and the establishment of Celcor as a major product line. Next came a headquarters assignment as head of corporate engineering during the ramp up of the Wilmington optical fibers plant. In 1983, he almost left Corning when he was passed over for the management committee (Jamie Houghton's "Six Pack") but stayed when Marty Gibson talked him into becoming president of MetPath. It didn't take long for him to start a turnaround (see chapter 13). In 1986, Ackerman returned to Corning as president of the specialty glass and ceramics group and joined the management committee. His distinguished record there encouraged Jamie Houghton in 1990 to tap him as president and chief operating officer of Corning, the last rung on the ladder before the top job.

Ackerman's biography revealed important details not only about him as an individual and a leader but also about the company he led. His education and early training gave him a firm grasp of technical issues and great credibility with the R&D establishment; his executive experience leading growth businesses afforded him insights into the concerns of customers and shareholders; and his toughness and competitiveness were evident to those negotiating with Corning, and competing against it. Ackerman, moreover, was through and through a company man who believed devoutly in its traditional values. These, he wrote, "are the unchanging moral and ethical compass of this organization, and they guide us every day. We can be thankful that those who came before us instilled in us their importance and their permanence."[4]

As chairman and CEO, Ackerman proved quick to make his mark, in small ways by relaxing company policy to allow casual dress in offices and labs, and in large ways by making significant changes in organization and management. The new top executive group included holdover Van Campbell as CFO, Skip Deneka as the retired Dave Duke's successor as chief technical officer, Ken Freeman as head of Corning Clinical Laboratories, and two chief operating officers: John Loose as president of Corning Communications (optical fiber, cable, photonic devices, LCD glass, and TV glass) and Norm Garrity as president of Corning Technologies (environmental products, consumer products and specialty materials). Working closely with these executives, Ackerman dedicated many hours to reviewing once again the company's formal statements of objectives, philosophy, and values. The result, published in January 1997, was a revised Blue Book (see chapter 13 for an account of the original edition).[5] The content of the new version reaffirmed similar statements from earlier years but it also differed in several significant respects. Earlier strategy statements, for example, had emphasized that Corning would invest in "traditional businesses" to generate cash and in growth markets for growth. In the new version, there was no mention of traditional businesses but rather a declaration that Corning would "invest carefully" in "mature markets" and "invest aggressively" in growth markets. The clear implication was that Corning would not be wedded to the businesses of its past and that it would push vigorously ahead into new areas.

Another key difference from earlier corporate statements was a new section called "Our Operating Environment," which followed the statement of corporate values (quality, integrity, performance, leadership, innovation, independence, and the individual). The new section was designed to help Corning employees translate the values into specific, measurable behaviors. The operating environment had eight dimensions: the first five (customer focused, results oriented, forward looking, entrepreneurial, and rigorous) described how Corning sought to run its businesses; the last three (open, engaging, and enabling) depicted how employees should work together. Giving teeth to the document, Corning modified its performance appraisal and compensation policies to take account of performance along the eight dimensions. Employee reviews, for example, also included peers and subordinates as well as individuals and bosses—"360 degree" appraisals that took account of how open, engaging, and enabling these individuals actually were. To demonstrate customer focus, general managers and sales personnel were required to document not only how often they met with customers but also how much they *listened* to them.[6]

The Spin-Spin and a Sale

On the strategy front, Corning once again displayed a willingness to embrace dramatic change. The first moves involved the divestiture of Corning Clinical

Laboratories (CCL) and other lab testing units and the sale of the housewares business. The company had debated the merits of selling these businesses for several years, and the reasons in both instances were abundantly clear (see chapter 14).

Shrinking margins, tighter regulation, and the costs and embarrassment of recent scandals combined to make the future of CCL especially problematic for Corning. Investment bankers had begun shopping the property in the fall of 1995, but few buyers stepped forward. One tack was to sell to a leading competitor—SmithKline Beecham or National Health Laboratories, for example—to accelerate the consolidation of the lab testing business. That move seemed aggressive, however, and some Corning executives worried that it was bound to raise antitrust concerns and delay the disposition of CCL. Corning also considered retaining or selling separately its Pharmaceutical Services businesses. That course, however, would require a favorable ruling from the IRS to permit the tax-free transfer to Corning of the pharmaceutical services units, which were legally still owned by a shell corporation, Corning Life Sciences, Inc., which also owned CCL. Such a ruling was far from a sure thing. Still another option was to spin off CCL and perhaps other units as a tax-free dividend to stockholders. AT&T, Hewlett Packard, and other companies had recently used similar spin-offs to restructure their portfolios. One of the divested units of AT&T, Lucent Technologies, was a major customer and competitor of Corning's, and the example was thus fresh in mind.[7]

After months of what Ackerman described as "actively pursuing every imaginable alternative other than business as usual," Corning reached the "big decision" to act in May 1996. It announced that it would spin off CCL and the pharmaceutical services business into two separate companies whose stock would transfer tax-free to Corning shareholders. For every eight shares of Corning stock they held, owners received one share of Quest Diagnostics, Inc., the blood testing unit, and two shares of Covance, Inc., the pharmaceutical services unit. The so-called spin-spin took place on December 31, 1996. The next day, two new companies were born, and Corning shed itself of $2.1 billion in revenues and 22,500 employees—about 40 percent of its total revenues and more than half of its total employment. Ken Freeman, whom many had expected eventually to succeed Van Campbell as Corning's CFO, went with Quest Diagnostics as its chairman and chief executive.[8]

The sale of the consumer housewares business proved more complicated and required more time. It had been apparent to top management for nearly a decade that the housewares business faced serious, perhaps intractable, structural problems that would prevent it from attaining corporate objectives for growth and profitability. The company tried many solutions—the ill-fated Corning-Vitro joint venture, downsizing, price cuts, tighter cost controls, new management, and ultimatums—but still performance and projections remained unsatisfactory. At the same time, a consensus grew in the top ranks that the business no longer fit Corning's emerging strategic profile as a high-tech specialty materials company.

The decision to divest the consumer business faced several hurdles. First, much of Corning's identity was bound up with consumer housewares—to the extent that the company was known among the general public, it was because of Corning Ware and the Corning-Revere stores. The company did not do much institutional advertising, and its consumer business gave it exposure to small investors. "These were average people who bought our products and our stock, so that we could avoid the 'black box syndrome' of companies known only to the investment community," said Jamie Houghton. "Our consumer products business gave us access to the small shareholders in the country, and we thought there was great value in that."[9]

A second hurdle involved emotional connections. Many of Corning's top executives had worked in the business on their way up. Jamie Houghton and Van Campbell had been general managers; John Loose had spent the first two decades of his career in the business and had recently been its acting general manager. Ackerman had an emotional attachment to the housewares from his initial assignment with the company in the early 1960s. Divesting consumer also proved difficult for rank-and-file employees to consider. Although most of the company's consumer operations were in West Virginia, Ohio, Pennsylvania, Illinois, or overseas, the Pressware plant, which made Corelle, was in Corning. Thus local jobs and professional relationships were at stake. At the same time, many employees viewed the discount they received at the Corning-Revere outlet stores as a significant fringe benefit and were not eager to lose it.

In May 1997, with its housewares business on a modest upswing, Corning went public with the decision to sell, retaining Goldman Sachs to shop
the property. In recognition of its long involvement in the business and its
emotional attachments, Corning stipulated certain conditions for any buyer.
It insisted that the business remain headquartered in the Corning–Elmira
area for at least five years; that employees be offered salaries, wages, and
benefits of "substantially equivalent value" to those offered by Corning; and
that the buyer assume existing labor agreements and contracts. Despite
these terms, analysts figured that Corning might reap as much as $650 mil-
lion (about twenty times 1996 earnings) from the sale.[10]

During the next few months, Corning entertained bids from several parties. The restrictions imposed on the deal tended to favor financially motivated buyers over strategically motivated buyers, who might have wished to
consolidate Corning's operations into their own, relocate the headquarters,
or revamp the compensation policies. In August, Corning announced a high
bid from AEA Investors, Inc., an investment vehicle for some leading industrial families and CEOs. AEA Investors agreed to pay $975 million for 89 per-
cent of the equity in the new Corning Consumer Products Company, with
Corning holding the remaining equity stake. Corning expected the transaction to close by the end of 1997.

Soon, however, signs of trouble began to appear. An economic crisis in
Asia devastated the housewares business, dragging down both sales and
projected earnings. In October, the terms of Corning's deal with AEA
Investors were renegotiated, and the total price dropped by $150 million. As
the misfortunes of the consumer business compounded (1997 sales were 15
percent below those of a year earlier), AEA Investors decided to drop out.
That touched off a scramble for another suitor. In March 1998, Corning
found another financial buyer, an affiliate of Borden, Inc., which in turn was
owned by the leveraged buyout firm Kohlberg Kravis Roberts & Company.
Borden accepted Corning's conditions and agreed to buy 92 percent of
Corning Consumer Products Company for considerations of approximately $603 million. Borden further agreed to retain the existing manage-
ment team headed by Peter Campanella and allow the consumer company
to operate as an autonomous unit. These decisions fueled speculation that,
like other KKR properties, Corning Consumer Products would eventually

be resold to the public. This time, the transaction closed quickly, and the sale was concluded on April 1, 1998.[11]

From Corning Competes to Growing Corning

The sale of the consumer housewares business concluded efforts started in the early 1990s to streamline Corning's operations and shift its portfolio toward its most promising opportunities. "Corning Competes" gave way to a new corporate thrust called "Growing Corning." The result was a tighter, leaner company based on a deep understanding of glass and closely related materials. At the same time, Corning's strategic focus narrowed to an attractive mix of high-tech and mostly high-growth markets in communications, environmental protection, displays, and a host of specialty-materials applications.

In announcing the Growing Corning initiative, Ackerman stated that the company's business strategy "at the most basic level is to focus on attractive global markets where Corning's leadership in materials and process technology will allow us to achieve and sustain competitive advantage and superior growth over time." At the same time, he went public with the goal of doubling the size of the company by 2001.[12]

The most visible signs of growth were new facilities. In 1996 and 1997, Corning announced a flurry of major construction projects: a $75 million high-purity fused silica plant near Charleston, South Carolina, to manufacture glass for use in high-tech optical components; a $300 million TV glass plant in Pennsylvania (in partnership with Asahi and Sony); a $300 million optical fiber plant near Charlotte, North Carolina (and coming on the heels of a $250 million expansion at Wilmington in 1995); and a new $40 million photonics component plant in Erwin, New York, on the hillside below Sullivan Park.

Many of these investments reflected the company's assessment of tremendous growth opportunities in communications and photonics, as well as a hard-nosed attitude about its competitive cost position. Unlike its facility in Wilmington, for example, the new North Carolina fiber plant would not be unionized. In agreeing to build the new photonics plant in

Erwin, Corning negotiated attractive incentives from state and local government agencies, as well as a separate bargaining agreement with the Flints.
The new labor agreement, which officials of Local 1000 approved unani-
mously, featured entry-level wages below those typical of Corning's other
plants in the Chemung Valley, as well as fewer job classifications, more flexible work rules, team-based work systems, and protections against layoffs.
Corning placed the plant under a new photonics products division directed
by thirty-eight-year-old executive Wendell Weeks and assigned Marc
Giroux, who had presided over the expansion of the Wilmington fiber
plant, as the new plant manager.[13]

Corning followed news of the new photonics plant closely with another
blockbuster announcement: a five-year expansion plan to double the capacity of its science and technology (R&D) organization. The plan included
new facilities, the hiring of several hundred new professionals, and a hike in
R&D spending from 5 percent to 6 percent of annual revenues. The most
dramatic change was the doubling of capacity at Sullivan Park, but Corning
also expanded its satellite labs elsewhere in the United States, France, and
Japan into a global R&D network.[14]

The decision to invest so heavily in R&D was hardly a matter of faith:
rather, it emerged from a rigorous assessment and analysis of Corning's
technologies and their potential markets. In May 1997, senior managerial
and technical personnel participated in a "deep dive" (a two-day offsite
meeting of detailed presentations and discussions) on the company's R&D
capabilities and possibilities for internally generated growth. The Science &
Technology organization under Skip Deneka laid out a future in Corning's
core businesses—opto-electronics, display, environmental, and advanced
materials—that was ripe with "huge opportunities."[15]

The very brightest prospects appeared to be in opto-electronics, including optical fibers, cable, and photonic components. Corning was pursuing
exciting developments in all of these areas, with the continued blurring of
once distinct lines between telecommunications, computing, media transmission, and display technology. The spectacular growth of the Internet,
with traffic doubling every three months, accelerated these changes and
generated an insatiable demand for bandwidth to move ever larger volumes
of information more quickly from a multiplicity of sources in a multiplicity

of formats to a multiplicity of destinations. And in the battle for bandwidth, optical fibers possessed enormous speed and capacity advantages over souped-up copper phone lines, coaxial cable, and wireless transmission. And these advantages were bound to become more pronounced as researchers developed fibers with almost unimaginably huge capacity and cheaper ways to manipulate optical signals. Fibers on the drawing board could carry as much as a trillion bits per second, roughly equivalent to the entire long-distance traffic in the United States. Clamors for local access and high bandwidth connections promised to open the last frontier in optical communications—fiber links between local exchanges and homes and commercial buildings around the world.

By the late 1990s, moreover, it was increasingly clear that conventional electronics would ultimately constitute a bottleneck in the delivery of high-bandwidth information because it was too inefficient, expensive, and slow to convert electronic signals from the source to light pulses for transmission and then reconvert at the destination—and perhaps multiple times along the way to boost signals. Eventually, it would become more economical to generate the information as optical signals and manipulate it in that format. Corning forecast that communications networks would become "all optical" before 2020 and that before then, "optical solutions" would launch revolutions in information generation, display, storage, and processing technology, as well as transport. The "all-optical computer"—the next quantum leap in information processing—was no longer a fantasy but a realistic possibility in the next two decades. Photonics could become one of the most significant new technologies of the first half of the twenty-first century—perhaps with as much impact as electronics had manifested during the second half of the twentieth century.[16]

Meanwhile, in the near-term future, Corning pursued rapid growth through new fiber designs that permitted greater capacity and faster transmission, fibers with multiple cores, new multiple-fiber structures such as ribbons, and passive photonic components such as signal splitters, couplers, and amplifiers (fiber gain modules). From there, it seemed but a short step into active components such as lasers and switches and from there, to subassemblies that combined components into network modules—if the company could find the right point of entry and pathway in.

Corning's prospects in other glass-related businesses seemed only slightly less dazzling. The market for ultrathin sheets of glass for flat panel displays was projected to grow 50 percent per year into the foreseeable future, finding applications in notebook computers, slimmed-down desktop computers, wall-mounted TV sets, instrumentation in automobiles and aircraft, handheld digital video display (DVD) units, and many small consumer electronic products. Possibilities in advanced materials also seemed highly attractive. Although several new telescope mirror blanks garnered press attention in the mid-1990s (see chapter 14), Corning researchers were more excited about new applications of high-purity fused silica on the horizon, including new "deep ultraviolet" microlithography systems in development for etching the circuitry of ever faster, ever tinier, ever more capable chips. Corning's 1997 acquisition of Optical Corporation of America, a small company with valuable technology and patents in optical filters and coatings, added capability to finish and coat lenses and assemble them into components and subsystems. Corning also foresaw that glass ceramic sheets could be molded around gas burners to form modular range tops—a complement to Eurokera's popular, easy-to-clean electric range-top units. Still more intriguing possibilities involved new photochromic polymers for sale to lens casters and new biomedical applications of Corning's polymer labware and know-how in surface chemistry and cellular analysis.

The future of the environmental businesses was tied to mobile emissions standards, which were expected to converge worldwide and apply to a wider range of popular vehicles, including light trucks, sport utility vehicles, and even motorcycles. Corning also depicted attractive possibilities for thin-walled substrates that would make catalysts significantly more efficient. Another project was the environmental industry's "holy grail": a more efficient way to scrub nitrous oxide from automotive and industrial processes. Corning scientists believed that the quest for this grail could involve ceramic substrates. Yet another major opportunity involved stationary power source pollution control, and Cormetech, the company's joint venture with Mitsubishi Heavy Industries, Ltd. and Mitsubishi Petrochemical Company Ltd., seemed poised to take advantage. And still another promising area was uses of glass and related materials in future batteries and fuel cells—areas of enormous opportunity in the twenty-first century as new electrical, electronic, and photonic devices continued to proliferate and fossil fuels were expected to become depleted.

In the aftermath of the Science & Technology deep dive, Corning further increased its R&D spending, to more than 8 percent of sales, and went public with bullish messages to the financial community. The company trumpeted not only its specific capabilities but also its global network of R&D facilities, to which it added, in 1998, a new facility in St. Petersburg, Russia. Corning commenced hiring several hundred new scientists and technicians, many with skills in frontier areas such as micro-optics, plasma deposition, and surface chemistry. The divestitures of the lab testing and consumer housewares businesses, combined with the surge in photonics and the expansion of R&D spending, wrought a qualitative change in Corning's workforce. It was younger, better educated, and more diverse than ever before.

Two Blockbuster Transactions

Investors and financial analysts applauded Corning's repositioning in 1996–1997. "Wall Street Shouts 'Eureka!' as a New CEO Boosts the Wattage of a Once-dim Bulb," headlined the *Wall Street Newsletter* in picking Corning as its stock of the month in April 1997.[17] Corning stock, which had traded in the mid-$30 range during the previous year-and-a-half, surged to above $60 in August 1997, with most analysts still rating the company as a "strong buy."

Soon, however, the economic crisis in Asia—the so-called Asian flu that had caused the initial sale of Corning Consumer Products Company to collapse—also caused Corning to miss its forecasts and its stock price to tumble. Several big telecommunications infrastructure projects in Thailand and Malaysia were canceled, and optical fiber prices plunged rapidly. Corning tightened its belt, put a freeze on hiring, instituted another round of early retirement offers, and delayed completion of the new facilities for optical fibers in North Carolina and for new high-purity fused silica in South Carolina.

Corning's leaders never viewed the company's troubles as anything other than momentary, and by the middle of 1998, the stock rebounded more strongly than ever as the fast-growth markets Corning had projected sprang to life. The company recorded significant gains in volume and market share in telecommunications and cable TV markets around the world. The explosive growth of the Internet remained unchecked, while cries for more bandwidth grew ever louder. In February 1998, Corning introduced a new large effective area fiber (LEAF) designed for data transport applications. LEAF technology dramatically increased the capacity of individual fibers as well as the distance optical signals could travel without amplification. LEAF became the hottest fiber product in Corning's history, with more than a million kilometers being sold in its first year.[18] And LEAF was hardly the only star of the late 1990s. A new fiber-gain module increased usable bandwidth in certain types of optical amplifiers by 50 percent. Late in 1998, Corning strengthened its position in Europe by acquiring for $70 million BICC's 50-percent interest in Optical Fibres, the joint venture founded in 1981 to produce optical fibers in the United Kingdom.

Other lines also contributed strong growth and earnings. Corning broke ground on a new ceramic substrates plant in China to serve Asian automakers and industry and another new environmental products plant in South Africa. The company added capacity in Taiwan for flat-panel display glass and doubled the size of its Japanese plant making the same products. By late 1999, Corning's stock had surged past $125 per share.

Bigger things were yet to come in communications products. Despite the company's bullish prospects, some insiders worried that LEAF notwithstanding, optical fiber was becoming a commodity business and that Corning would ultimately prove vulnerable to much bigger companies such as Lucent Technologies, Siemens, and Fujitsu, which possessed capability to make the full range of communications products, from fiber to lasers, electronics, active photonic devices, cable, switches, modules, subassemblies, and network systems. The risk for Corning in the long run—or perhaps in the not-too-distant future—was becoming boxed in and excluded from the higher-value applications of optical communications.

Another concern was Corning's relationship to the much bigger Siemens. In Siecor GmbH the partners operated a very successful optical fiber plant in Germany, but it primarily served the captive needs of Siemens. Siecor Corporation in the United States faced limited growth opportunities outside of North America and Japan because of covenants that restricted its ability to compete with Siemens's cable-making operations. For Corning to take full advantage of its opportunities in optical fiber and cable on a worldwide basis, it would need to restructure its deal with Siemens.[19]

In late 1999, Corning resolved these issues with two blockbuster transactions. The first, announced on November 14, was a merger with Oak Industries, a deal valued at $1.8 billion and accomplished by an exchange of shares that yielded owners of Oak Industries stock a premium of about 51 percent over a market price of just under $50 per share. The corporate parent of several operating units that manufactured equipment and components primarily for the communications industry, Oak Industries employed 3,900 people and reported net income of $28 million on revenues of $348 million. From Corning's perspective, the jewel in Oak's portfolio was Lasertron, Inc., a pioneer in the development of semiconducting lasers for optical amplifiers and transmission. Lasertron also possessed its own chip-making and packaging capabilities. The merger closed early in 2000 and significantly extended Corning's capability to provide its customers with active photonic components. "The addition of Oak Industries," said Ackerman, "demonstrates the strength of [Corning's] commitment to being the world's leading supplier to system houses in all areas of optical communications, including amplifiers, optical components, modules, fiber, cable and hardware."[20]

A few weeks later, Corning dropped another bombshell, announcing agreement to acquire Siemens's 50 percent interests in Siecor Corporation, Siecor GmbH, and other Siemens properties related to optical fibers and cables. This deal, funded by a new issue of equity and loans, was valued at $1.4 billion. It increased Corning's revenues by approximately $780 million (DM 1.5 billion), its employment by 3,300, and added facilities in Germany, France, Italy, Turkey, Argentina, and Australia. With consummation of the deal, Corning became, on its own, a vertically integrated supplier of optical communications products and systems, operating on a global scale. As Ackerman put it, "Corning is poised to be the leading supplier into what is referred to as the 'optical layer'—where optical fiber and photonic devices join with optical cable, hardware and equipment to leverage the full potential of today's state-of-the-art communications networks."[21]

The merger with Oak Industries and the acquisition of Siecor triggered another reorganization atop Corning, effective in January 2000. John Loose became president and chief operating officer and assumed charge of all of the company's operations worldwide. Norm Garrity became vice chairman with responsibility for the nonfinancial corporate staffs and a company-wide initiative to strengthen core business processes. Skip Deneka, chief technology officer, and Jim Flaws, chief financial officer, also were promoted to executive vice president positions. The company planned to combine Siecor GmbH and Optical Fibres into a new operating unit, Corning Communications Europe, with headquarters in London. At the time of its creation, the unit was by far the biggest manufacturer of optical fiber and cable in Europe. Meanwhile Corning continued to add more companies and capabilities in 2000. These included a lab acquired from British Telecom, Net Optics, and Willow Systems.

150 Years in Glass

If the early generations of Corning's leadership could somehow come back to life to visit the company in 2001, they would find essential aspects of the company familiar. It was still making glass, still in Corning, New York, with offices still located on the site occupied by the original plant in 1868. They would find a fifth-generation Houghton as a member of the board of directors and a sixth-generation descendant working in management. They would see a smooth-running company that remained proud of its heritage and continued to honor many traditions instituted in its earliest years.

But after 150 years in the business, the early leaders would surely note, Corning Incorporated was anything but an old company. Still making glass, it was doing so by very sophisticated processes, and the materials it made found their way into the most advanced and essential of industrial applications. Still in Corning, but the city had become an attractive center of culture and tourism in the Finger Lakes region. The company's influence was apparent throughout the city, from the prosperous boutiques along Market Street to the complex of buildings at Houghton Park on the north bank of the Chemung, to the freshly pointed and painted thermometer tube drawing tower displaying Little Joe, the old logo of the Corning Glass Works (and before that, Macbeth-Evans), at 187 feet, still the tallest structure in the city. Still on the banks of the Chemung River, the corporate offices were housed in an ultramodern office building with pronounced Asian influences and a cosmopolitan feel reflecting the global scale of Corning's operations and the diverse mix of employees inside.

With its stock soaring to record highs—over $300 per share before a 3-for-1 stock split in October 2000—Corning seemed less a traditional industrial-age manufacturing enterprise than a nimble creature of the new global, information age economy. In 1999, *Wired* magazine, one of the most distinctive contemporary voices of business and technology, included Corning in its index of forty companies "driving the new economy." Corning was by far the oldest member and one of the few manufacturers in the group.[22] Meanwhile, Corning continued to rank high on independent lists of "most admired" companies, "best places to work," and employers of working mothers and minorities.

Much of the attention lavished on Corning naturally focused on the big news in its optical communications business, as well as the extraordinary impact of that business on modern life. Some analysts were eager for the company to become a "pure-play" telecom stock and urged management to deemphasize or even exit other lines. Corning's leaders clearly were not much interested in such views, however. "Our history indicated that [becoming a pure-play stock in any particular business] would be a mistake," said Jamie Houghton. "We've had many different opportunities. Who would have dreamed in 1966 that in 20 years or so our largest business would be glass fiber for telecommunications use. Today, we have a huge pallet of opportunites, not only in telecommunications, but also in flat-glass displays, emissions control, and in life science products for biomedical research."[23] Corning's leaders maintained steadfastly that the company's future, like its past, would continue to depend on its mastery of materials, its technical capabilities, and its ability to penetrate the big growth markets of tomorrow.

The determination to make its way as a specialist in materials, especially glass and its close relations, was a theme that echoed from Corning's very early years. So, too, other themes in the company's history still resonated at the 150th anniversary. The purchases of Oak Industries and Siecor indicated Corning's willingness to place big bets, as well as its sense of urgency and vulnerability when competing with much bigger rivals. Corning's investments in developing its scientific and technical capabilities on a global scale illustrated the ongoing quest—and commitment to find—the next big hit. Its sixty-five-year-old joint venture with Pittsburgh Plate Glass, other joint ventures with Samsung, Asahi, and Sony in TV glass, with Mitsubishi Heavy Industries and Mitsubishi Petrochemical in environmental products, and with St. Gobain in range countertop units, as well as other business alliances, highlighted its continuing willingness to leverage its capabilities and resources in partnership with others. The imminent emergence of Dow-Corning from federal bankruptcy protection portended renewal of another long-standing relationship, as well as the restoration of an extremely valuable asset.

Although the Houghton family's investment and involvement in the company had waned in recent years, its influence was still felt in the values and culture of the company—as the Blue Book and other key documents of the Growing Corning initiative demonstrated. The links between the company and its hometown community, moreover, remained as strong as ever— as symbolized by the new headquarters building, the new photonics plant, the new facilities at Sullivan Park, and the freshly refurbished Little Joe tower. Still another sign of commitment was a $62 million expansion and renovation of the Corning Museum of Glass, with support from the Corning Foundation and the company. The project began in 1994 and was designed to attract new visitors, renew interest in the collection among artists and scholars, and simultaneously commemorate the museum's fiftieth anniversary and the company's one-hundred-fiftieth.

In June 1999, a major phase of the project concluded with the opening of the new Glass Innovation Center, a new glass sculpture gallery, and an expanded retail area and café to popular and critical acclaim. The Glass Innovation Center featured engaging multimedia displays of "world-changing technological breakthroughs" in glass, with galleries devoted to windows, optics, and vessels, and linked by a 300-foot bridge. Artifacts and stories highlighted not only Corning's key contributions—Pyrex, fiberglass, silicones, TV glass, glass ceramics, optical fibers, and the still-astonishing 200-inch telescope mirror blank—but also significant innovations by Pilkington, Owens-Illinois, and other glassmakers. Other phases of the museum project included renovated art and history galleries—a renewed exhibition of the renowned glass collection, a new regional visitors center designed to welcome and introduce tourists to the Finger Lakes region, and *Crystal City*, a new exhibit devoted to the history of glassmaking in the city of Corning.

In 1851, when hardware merchant Amory Houghton Sr. bought an interest in a glass company in Somerville, Massachusetts, no one could have predicted that glass would become one of the building blocks of an industrial (much less a postindustrial) economy. In 1868, when the Brooklyn Flint Glass Works moved to Corning, no one could have predicted that the company would become what an analyst in *Fortune* magazine (one of the most distinctive voices of the "old" industrial economy) would cite as "a scientific powerhouse, a national treasure."[24] Yet these outcomes are what the marriage of the material and the company so far has produced. As it moves beyond its major anniversary, Corning Incorporated faces daunting challenges ahead—managing growth, integrating big acquisitions, expanding and defending its position in telecommunications, justifying the new investment in Science & Technology, finding the next big opportunity, developing the next generation of leadership—but there is ample reason for optimism. Addressing to the International Congress on Glass at the end of the twentieth century, Roger Ackerman expressed the company's core beliefs about glass and sounded eerily like his distant colleagues, the first Amory Houghton Jr., Eugene Sullivan, and George Macbeth among them:

> When we look at all that has happened in photonics and fiber optics it's a bit sobering to hear the world's leading technologists say that we haven't even hit our stride. In fact, we are just starting to walk.
>
> There is more progress still to come in the application of light to information than we've made since the Mesopotamians first saw that interesting things happened in the combination of fire and sand.

In all rich and diverse areas of research and applications that are pushing the frontiers of glass, we are part of a continuum that began with the ancients, and progressed through history.

We are an extension of the early artisans of Alexandria and Rome, the cristallo makers of Venice, the cathedral glaziers of Europe, the innovators in sheet glass, fiberglass and containers, and the pioneers of the information age.

We are still learning, changing and growing.

. . . We may not be able to predict with precision what is to come twenty or thirty years from now.

But what we do know is that glass offers us possibilities beyond our imaginations.[25]

Notes

Chapter One

1. Useful introductions to glass include Stephen L. Sass, *The Substance of Civilization: Materials and Human History from the Stone Age to the Age of Silicon* (1988), which deals with glass as a useful material; and Chloe Zerwick, *A Short History of Glass* (1980), which focuses on art glass.
2. For the development of modern engineered materials, see Philip Ball, *Made to Measure: New Materials for the Twenty-First Century* (1997), esp. chap. 1.

Chapter Two

1. *Corning Journal*, May 21, 1868; ibid., June 11, 1868.
2. *Corning Journal*, May 21, 1868.
3. Arthur A. Houghton Jr., *Remembrances* (1986), pp. 1–15; Beatrice Houghton, *The First American Houghtons* (n.d.); Rosamond Houghton VanNoy, *A Houghton Family: From Ralph Houghton of Lancaster, Ma. 1652 to Rosamond Houghton VanNoy of Conover, Wi., 1992* (1993), pp. 1–2; John W. Houghton, *The Houghton Genealogy: Descendants of John and Ralph Houghton* (1912).
4. Houghton, *Remembrances*, pp. 141, 19ff.; *Corning Leader*, November 6, 1909; letter from Andrew Cox of Ropes, Gray, Best in Boston to Howard E. Bahr, manager of Corning public relations department, July 3, 1947, Corning Incorporated Department of Archives and Records Management (hereafter CIDARM) 34-6-2.
5. George Buell Hollister, *Historical Records of the Corning Glass Works, 1851–1930* (1951), p. 8A.
6. Sources on the early American glass industry include Kenneth M. Wilson, *American Glass, 1760–1930*, 2 vols. (1994); Lura Woodside Watkins, *American Glass and Glassmaking*, Warren C. Scoville, *Revolution in Glassmaking* (1972); Rhea Mansfield Knittle, *Early American Glass* (1927); George S. McKearin and Helen McKearin, *American Glass* (1941).
7. Wilson, pp. 56–57; Watkins, pp. 28–31.
8. Scoville, pp. 1–11.
9. Lura Woodside Watkins, *Cambridge Glass: 1818–1888, The Story of the New England Glass Co.* (1930), p. 3.
10. Watkins, *Cambridge Glass*, p. 18; Henry C. Binford, *The First Suburbs: Residential Communities on the Boston Periphery: 1815–1860* (1985), pp. 156–157.
11. Edward A. Samuels and Henry Kimball, eds., *Somerville Past and Present* (1897), p. 94; Lura Woodside Watkins, "Union Glass Co.," *Antiques*, November 1937.
12. Houghton, *Remembrances*, p. 21.
13. Ibid.; John H. Munier, "A Perspective of the Role of Research, Development, and

Engineering in the Corning Glass Works: The First Hundred Years," pp. 1–2, history folder, CIDARM 34-3-2; *Corning Leader*, November 6, 1909; Lillian G. Pattinson, "The Union Glass Company, Somerville, Mass., 1854–1927," Dorchester, Mass., CIDARM 34-6-2.

14. Broadside, November 1860, Union Glass Co. folder, CIDARM 34-6-2.

15. *Preliminary Notes toward a History of the Brooklyn Flint Glass Company*, The Long Island Historical Society, Brooklyn, New York (1968), p. 3-D; Knittle, p. 411.

16. Ibid., pp. 2A–3F: "The Brooklyn Flint-Glass Company," *Home Journal*, March 20, 1852; Brooklyn Flint Glass Company notes, p. 2; Joshua Brown and David Ment, *Factories, Foundries, and Refineries: A History of Five Brooklyn Industries* (1980); Wilson, p. 520.

17. Brown, pp. 1–12; Knittle, p. 411.

18. Light to Houghton, May 23, 1861, Union Glass Co. folder, CIDARM 34-6-2.

19. Amory Houghton Jr. to Ellen Houghton, February 24, 1862, Union Glass Co. folder, CIDARM 34-6-2.

20. Light to Amory Houghton Jr., January 29, 1864, CIDARM 34-6-2.

21. *Lain's Brooklyn, New York, Directory*, 1865–1868.

22. "Certificate of Incorporation and By-Laws of the Brooklyn Flint Glass Co. of Long Island, New York" (1865), CIDARM 34-5-2; Dun Papers, Harvard Business School, 126: 232.

23. Estelle Sinclaire Farrar and Jane Shadel Spillman, *The Complete Cut and Engraved Glass of Corning* (1979); "Office of Brooklyn Flint Glass Works," broadside, December 1867; minutes of Brooklyn Flint Glass Works Board of Trustee Meetings, March 10, 1866, April 10, 1866, Brooklyn Flint Glass Co. folder, CIDARM 34-5-2.

24. Charles Houghton to Amory Houghton Jr., January 28, 1867, Brooklyn Flint Glass Works folder, CIDARM 34-5-02.

25. Wilson, pp. 519–520.

26. Wilson, p. 522; Watkins, p. 29; Josephine Jefferson, *Wheeling Glass* (1947).

27. *Corning Leader*, May 21, 1868.

28. Regina Lee Blaszczyk, "Imagining Consumers: Manufacturers and Markets in Ceramics and Glass, 1865–1965" (unpublished Ph.D. diss., University of Delaware, 1995), p. 446; Hollister, p. 9; Brown, p. 12.

29. Dun Papers, 16:1.

30. Thomas P. Dimitroff and Lois S. Janes, *History of the Corning-Painted Post Area: 200 Years in Painted Post Country* (1977), pp. 1–7; Uri Milford, *Corning and Vicinity, 1789–1920* (1922).

31. Alexander Flick, *History of the State of New York* (1933–1937), 4: 194–220.

32. Dimitroff and Janes, pp. 1–24.

33. Carter Goodrich et al., *Canals and American Economic Development* (1972), pp. 55–59; 169–179, 218; Scoville, p. 49.

34. Dimitroff and Janes, pp. 24–27.

35. Ibid., p. 29; John F. Stover, *The Life and Decline of the American Railroad* (1970), pp. 7–25.

36. Irene D. Neu, *Erastus Corning: Merchant and Farmer, 1794–1872* (1960); Dimitroff and Janes, pp. 29–42; John F. Stover, *American Railroads* (1961), p. 41.

37. Dimitroff and Janes, p. 27.

38. Ibid., p. 12; Neu, pp. 115-116.

39. Dimitroff and Janes, p. 41.

40. Ibid., p. 38; Robert F. McNamara, *A Century of Grace: St. Mary's Church, Corning, New York, 1848–1948* (1948), pp. 21–22, 33ff.

41. Dimitroff and Janes, pp. 34–36, 44–48.
42. Ibid. p. 60; *Corning Journal*, October 28, 1868; *Corning Journal*, April 30, 1868.
43. Brooklyn Flint Glass Works minutes of trustees meeting, May 18, 1868, Hilbert Collection.
44. *Corning Journal*, May 21, 1868.
45. *Fortune*, July 1945; *Brooklyn Flint Glass Co.*, p. 4.
46. *Corning Journal*, June 11, 1868; Hollister, p. 10; *Corning Journal*, September 10, 1868.
47. *Corning Journal*, November 5, 1868; Hollister, pp. 10ff.
48. *Corning Journal*, October 22, 1868.
49. *Corning Journal*, November 5, 1868; *Elmira Advocate*, November 12, 1868.
50. Hollister, p. 11; Corning Flint Glass Works cash book, 1868–1872, CIDARM 24-5-10.
51. Hollister, pp. 12–13; *Corning Journal*, April 29, 1869.
52. Cash book, pp. 62–65.
53. *Corning Journal*, January 20, 1870.
54. Cash book, pp. 205, 214–215; *Corning Journal*, September 18, 1870.
55. *Corning Journal*, November 10, 1870, p. 2.
56. *Corning Journal*, April 27, 1871.
57. Milford, p. 258; Blaszczyk diss., p. 449.
58. *Corning Journal*, April 27, 1871; March 30, 1871, p. 4.
59. Cash book, pp. 94–112; Hollister, p. 12; *Corning Journal*, September, 15, 1870.
60. Amory Sr. letter to Amory Jr., September 21, 1871; Cushing letter to Amory Jr., September 29, 1871; Amory Sr. letter to Amory Jr., October 22, 1871; Amory Sr. letter to Amory Jr., October 25, 1871; Cushing letter to Amory Jr., October 30, 1871; Cushing letter to Amory Jr., December 13, 1871; Pomeroy letter to Amory Jr., December 23, 1871; Amory Jr. letter to Amory Sr., n.d., folder VI, CIDARM 22-4-8.
61. Dun Papers, New York, p. 131, Brooklyn, p. 177; Barbara Leaming, *Katharine Hepburn* (1995), p. 5.
62. Dun Papers, Steuben County, 1:380.
63. H. C. Fry letter to Amory Jr., January 11, 1871; Cushing letter to Amory Jr., July 12, 1871, folder VI, CIDARM 22-4-8.
64. Henry Libbey to Amory Jr., August 15, 1871, folder VI, CIDARM 22-4-8.
65. John Leighton to Amory Jr., November 1871, folder VI, CIDARM 22-4-8.
66. *Corning Journal*, May 16, 1872.
67. Milford, pp. 257–261; Dimitroff and Janes, p. 33; *Corning Journal*, March 28, 1873.
68. *Corning Journal*, May 9, 1872; August 20, 1872; January 31, 1873, p. 3.
69. Hollister, p. 17; *Corning Leader*, November 6, 1909.
70. Hollister, pp. 13–15.
71. Hollister, pp. 13–15; Blaszczyk, diss., p. 449.

Chapter Three

1. Corning Glass Works cash book, Dun Papers, and Amory Houghton Jr.'s cash book.
2. George Buell Hollister *Historical Records of the Corning Glass Works, 1851 to 1930 (1951)*, p. 21; Thomas P. Dimitroff and Lois S. Janes, *History of the Corning-Painted Post Area: 200 Years in Painted Post Country* (1977), p. 65.
3. Hollister, p. 22.

4. Hollister, pp. 23–24; Blaszczyk diss., p. 451; patent application, Railroad Ware folder, CIDARM 33-6-2.

5. Leonard S. Reich, *The Making of American Industrial Research: Science and Business at GE and Bell, 1876–1926* (1985).

6. Ibid., p. 19.

7. Hollister, p. 25; Blaszczyk diss., 452–453; correspondence in Railroad Ware folder, CIDARM 33-6-2.

8. Reich, pp. 132–135; Uri Milford, *Corning and Vicinity, 1789–1920* (1922), p. 275.

9. David F. Nobel, *America by Design: Science, Technology, and the Rise of Corporate Capitalism* (1977), pp. 7–8; W. Bernard Carlson, *Innovation as a Social Process: Elihu Thomson and the Rise of General Electric, 1870–1900* (1991), p. 134.

10. For Edison, see Matthew Josephson, *Edison: A Biography* (1992).

11. Correspondence in Bulbs Incandescent folder, CIDARM 33-5-2.

12. Blaszczyk diss., pp. 453–454; Robert Friedel and Paul Israel, with Bernard S. Finn, *Edison's Electric Light: Biography of an Invention* (1986), p. 164. According to historians Robert Friedel and Paul Israel, "Holzer may have been responsible for urging Edison to contact the Corning Glass Works, which sent a representative to Menlo Park, according to Mott, on June 21 [1880].

13. Hollister, pp. 29, 90; Blaszczyk diss., p. 454; Diane Vogt O'Connor, "Origins of Lighting Time-line," Edison, T. A. folder, CIDARM 34-1-3.

14. Correspondence in Edison, T. A. folder, CIDARM 34-1-3; *Corning Leader*, October 21, 1968, p. 11; correspondence in Bulbs—Incandescent folder, CIDARM 33-5-2; Dimitroff and Janes, p. 65.

15. Edison, T. A. folder; Dun's Papers, Steuben County, 1:380, June 27, 1881.

16. *Corning Journal*, August 18, 1880; Warren Scoville, *Revolution in Glassmaking* (1960), pp. 22–70; Blaszczyk diss., p. 447.

17. Hollister, p. 18; Scoville, pp. 76–77, 176–77; R. W. Devillers and F. E. Vaerewyck, "Glass Tank Furnaces," trans. Samuel R. Scholes (1950), Furnaces folder, CIDARM 35-5-X; Department of Commerce, Bureau of Foreign and Domestic Commerce, *The Glass Industry*, Miscellaneous Series, no. 60, "Report on the Cost of Production of Glass in the U.S." (1917).

18. Scoville, p. 241; Harlo Hakes, *Landmarks of Steuben County* (1896), p. 65.

19. Pearce Davis, *Development of the American Glass Industry* (1949), p. 157; Scoville, p. 235.

20. Dimitroff and Janes, p. 65.

21. Blaszczyk diss., p. 454; Reich, p. 44; Robert Conot, *A Streak of Luck* (1979), p. 177.

22. Carlson, pp. 174–217.

23. Dun Papers, Steuben County, 580:245; Harold C. Passer, *The Electrical Manufacturers, 1875–1900: Studies in Entrepreneurial History* (1953), p. 95.

24. Milford, p. 274; Hakes, p. 65; *Cambridge Chronicle*, February 25, 1882, Amory Houghton folder, CIDARM 34-1-2; correspondence in Charles F. Houghton folder, CIDARM 34-1-2.

25. Hollister, p. 19; R. H. Dalton, "A Century of Chemistry at Corning." Research Laboratory General folder, CIDARM 33-6-1; Dimitroff and Janes, p. 101; Hakes, p. 65; Document in Charles Houghton Folder, CIDARM, 34-1-3.

26. Dimitroff and Janes, pp. 82–98.

27. Robert F. McNamara, *A Century of Grace: St. Mary's Church, Corning, New York, 1848–1948* (1951), pp. 100–116.

28. Milford, p. 303; T.G. Hawkes folder, CIDARM 34-1-2 ; Farrar and Spillman, pp. 5–12; Dimitroff and Janes, p. 72.

29. Farrar and Spillman, pp. 12, 28, 53–55.

30. Alanson B. to Amory Houghton Jr., December 1, 1885, folder H, CIDARM, 9-3-4.

31. Ibid.

32. Hollister, pp. 41–42; Arthur A. Houghton Jr., *Remembrances: Arthur A. Houghton Jr.* (1986), p. 35; Dimitroff and Janes, p. 306; Alanson B. Houghton folder, CIDARM 34-1-2.

33. Houghton, *Remembrances*, pp. 35–37; anonymous biography of A. A. Houghton, A. A. Houghton folder, CIDARM 34-1-2. There is some question as to why Arthur Houghton didn't attend Harvard. His son recalled that "there was not enough money to send both Uncle Alan and my father to college." But given the entries in Amory Houghton Jr.'s personal cash ledger in the 1880s, this explanation doesn't seem credible.

34. Dimitroff and Janes, p. 65; Milford, pp. 312–317; folder E, 65; Passer, p. 149; folder M 46–51, CIDARM 2-4-2.

35. Reich, pp. 46–51; André Millard, *Edison and the Business of Innovation* (1990), pp. 88–102; Blaszczyk diss., p. 455.

36. Correspondence in folder G, CIDARM 2-4-2; Milford, p. 317.

37. Lura Woodside Watkins, *Cambridge Glass: 1818–1888, The Story of the New England Glass Co.* (1930), p. 36; Passer, p. 197.

38. Scoville, p. 91.

39. Correspondence in folder G, CIDARM 2-4-2.

40. Hollister, pp. 34–35; Dimitroff and Janes, pp. 66–70; AFGWU convention report, 1890.

41. Hollister, pp. 35–36; Dimitroff and Janes, pp. 66–70.

42. Dimitroff and Janes, pp. 66–70; Higgins testimony in folder 3, CIDARM 24-2-6.

43. Correspondence in folder G, CIDARM 2-4-2.

44. *Elmira Advertiser*, June 7, 1891; Buildings folder, CIDARM 33-5-3.

45. Corning Glass Works cash book, CIDARM 24-5-10, pp. 15-22.

46. Amory Houghton Jr., Trial Balances ledger, CIDARM 26-2-2; Thomas J. Watson Jr. and Peter Petre, *Father, Son & Co.: My Life at IBM and Beyond* (1990).

47. *Corning Daily Journal*, June 26, 1891.

48. Hollister, p. 37; Robert B. Shaw and P. R. MacMillan, *Down Brakes: A History of Railroad Accidents, Safety Precautions, and Operating Practices in the United States of America* (1961), p. 115.

49. Hollister, pp. 36–37.

50. Carlson, pp. 203, 217, 277–280; Passer, p. 206.

51. Carlson, pp. 277–280; Nobel, p. 9; Reich, pp. 46–51; Millard, pp. 102–133.

52. Scoville, pp. 93–108; 153–154.

53. Blaszczyk diss., p. 462.

54. Owens-Libbey folder, CIDARM 34-6-3.

55. Reich, pp. 52–58.

56. Owens-Libbey folder, CIDARM 34-6-3; "Bulb Price," Bulbs—Incandescent folder, CIDARM 33-5-2.

57. *Corning Daily Journal*, September 4, 1895; Farrar and Spillman, pp. 6–18, 125–133.

58. *Elmira Daily Gazette*, January 21, 1895; Dimitroff and Janes, pp. 58–59, 99; Milford, p. 331.

59. *Corning Daily Journal*, November 21, 1895.

60. Hollister, p. 43.

61. Arthur A. Houghton folder, CIDARM 34-1-2; Houghton, *Rememberances*, p. 37.

62. Hollister, p. 44; correspondence in untitled folder, CIDARM 22-4-8.

63. Correspondence in untitled folder, CIDARM 22-4-8.

64. Hollister, p. 31; "Thermometer Tubing Chronology," Tubing-Thermometer folder, CIDARM 33-7-1.

65. Pierce and Bickford statement and correspondence in Houses folder, CIDARM 20-4-9, and folder IV, CIDARM 20-4-10; Alanson to Amory, July 27, 1899, untitled folder, CIDARM 9-3-4.

66. Houghton, *Remembrances*, pp. 40–50; Milford, p. 373; Pierce and Bickford statement, Grace Church Parishioners, 1903, CIDARM 21-5-8.

67. Passer, p. 206; Scoville, p. 77; Hollister, p. 18; Carlson, pp. 110–111.

68. George Wise, *Willis R. Whitney, General Electric, and the Rise of U.S. Industrial Research* (1985).

69. Reich, p. 1.

70. Correspondence and agreements in Bulbs folders, CIDARM 33-5-2.

71. Alanson to Arthur Houghton, in untitled folder, CIDARM 9-3-4.

72. Blaszczyk diss., pp. 467-471ff.

73. Ibid.

74. R. C. Richards, *Railroad Accidents: Their Cause and Prevention* (1906), pp. 466–479.

75. Hollister, p. 59; Blaszczyk diss., pp. 462–464.

76. Blaszczyk diss., p. 472; Houghton, *Remembrances*, p. 89.

77. Blaszczyk diss., pp. 473–474; Contract between CGW and Churchill in William Churchill folder, CIDARM 34-1-3.

78. Correspondence from Joseph A. Deghuee, Ph.D., to Arthur A. Houghton and George B. Hollister, folder 1, CIDARM 33-5-3.

79. Farrar and Spillman, pp. 1–77, 125–173, 187–200.

80. Paul V. Gardner, *Frederick Carder: Portrait of a Glassmaker* (1985), pp. 5–18; Paul V. Gardner, *The Glass of Frederick Carder* (1979), pp. 1–23.

81. *Corning Evening Leader*, March 11, 1903; Gardner, *Frederick Carder*, p. 18; Farrar and Spillman, pp. 192–200.

82. Gardner, *Glass*, p. 28; *Brierley Hill Advertiser*, June 20, 1903.

83. Gardner, *Glass*, pp. 29–31; Gardner, *Frederick Carder*, pp. 15–21; Dimitroff and Janes, pp. 138–142.

84. Gardner, *Glass*, pp. 29–31; Gardner, *Frederick Carder*, p. 31.

85. Hollister, pp. 99–103.

86. Hollister, p. 66; Blaszczyk diss., pp. 479–481; Dimitroff and Janes, p. 66.

87. Blaszczyk diss., pp. 482–483; Correspondence from Joseph A. Deghuee, Ph.D. to Arthur A. Houghton and George B. Hollister, Batch Folder no. 1, CIDARM 33-5-3.

88. Correspondence and material in Railroad Ware folder, CIDARM 33-6-2; Hollister, p. 50.

89. Blaszczyk diss., pp. 486–487; Hollister, pp. 50–51.

90. Blaszczyk diss., pp. 473–485; Hollister, p. 55.

91. Sales of CGW in Globes and Lenses folder no. 1, CIDARM 33-6-2; "Bulbs as Portion of Total Sales," Bulbs folder, CIDARM 33-5-2.

92. Hollister, p. 78.

93. Niles and Niles, Certified Public Accountants. "Report on Cost of Bulbs and Tubes,

Manufactured by the Corning Glass Works, Corning, NY, 1907," Bulb Costs folder, CIDARM 33-5-3.

94. Blaszczyk diss., p. 493.
95. Houghton, *Remembrances*, p. 26, Anna Haar folder, CIDARM 34-1-2.
96. Blaszczyk diss., p. 493; Hollister, p. 79.
97. Blaszczyk diss., pp. 487–488; Hollister, pp. 66–67.

Chapter Four

1. Amory Houghton Jr. obituary, *Corning Evening Leader*, November 6, 1909; "The Houghtons of Corning," *Fortune*, July 1945, pp. 129–133; 253–260.
2. Reich, pp. 74–82; Naomi R. Lamoreaux and Kenneth L. Sokoloff, *Location and Technological Change in the American Glass Industry during the Late Nineteenth and Early Twentieth Centuries*, Working Paper 5938, National Bureau of Economic Research (1997), pp. 3, 6–7, 121–122; John Winthrop Hammon, *Men and Volts: The Story of General Electric* (1941), pp. 340–343.
3. Chamberlin to Arthur Houghton, March 24, 1908, CIDARM 14-3-2; "CGW Historical Project Machinery V-B-1," Hilbert folder 12, CIDARM.
4. Hilbert files, Empire Machine section; Chamberlin to Alanson, February 13, 1910, "CGW Historical Project Machinery V-B-1," Hilbert folder 12, CIDARM.
5. Hollister, p. 101.
6. Hollister, pp. 79–82; Hilbert folder, Empire Machine material; Day to Chamberlin, 1911, Empire Machine Co. letter book, CIDARM 14-3-2.
7. Chamberlin to Alanson Houghton, June 13, 1913, Empire Machine Co. letter book, CIDARM 14-3-2; Arthur Bright, *The Electric Lamp Industry* (1949), p. 353.
8. Margaret B.W. Graham and Alec T. Shuldiner, *Corning and the Craft of Innovation* (2001), chapter 2; Day to Alanson Houghton, and other correspondence in 1911, Arthur L. Day folder, CIDARM 34-1-3.
9. Biographical sketch of Gage; Churchill to Gage, August 9, 1911, Henry Gage folder, CIDARM 34-1-3.
10. "Relation of Laboratory to Plant," handwritten notes by H. P. Gage, 1912 or 1913, CIDARM 12-3-4.
11. Hollister, pp. 105–106.
12. Accounts of this episode vary in detail but agree on essentials. See Regina Lee Blaszczyk, *Imagining Consumers: Manufacturers and Markets in Ceramics and Glass, 1865–1965* (diss., 1995), pp. 498–500; "Statement dated July 29, 1919: William Churchill to Vernon Dorsey," "Pyrex" Hilbert files; Joseph Littleton interview by Davis Dyer, December 18, 1997.
13. There are varying accounts of the origin of the Pyrex name, but this one, which rests on near contemporaneous sources (Churchill) seems most authoritative. See Blaszczyk diss., pp. 510–511; Sullivan quote in "Notes Written by Dr. Sullivan 11/6/57," and Churchill statement, July 29, 1919, Hilbert folder 15.
14. Blaszczyk diss.; "Notes Written by Dr. Sullivan."
15. "Pyrex," Hilbert Files; Blaszczyk diss., pp. 504–505; Rorer to Churchill, January 23, 1915, in S&E 3, CIDARM; Churchill to Alanson, May 29, 1915.

16. Advertisements in *Good Housekeeping* for October 1915, September 1916, March 1917; in Wright Files, CIDARM.

17. Blaszczyk diss., p. 511; statement of Pyrex sales in Sales Statement folder, CIDARM 22-5-3.

18. W. H. Curtiss, "Pyrex: A Triumph for Chemical Research in Industry," *Journal of Industrial and Engineering Chemistry* 4 (1922): 336–337.

19. *The Glass Industry as Affected by the War* (1918), pp. 20, 32–36, 63, 126; William Leuchtenburg, *The Perils of Prosperity* (1958), pp. 16–17.

20. Hollister, p. 130; sales statement in sales statement folder, CIDARM 22-5-3; George Wise, *Willis Whitney, General Electric, and the Origins of U.S. Industrial Research* (1985), p. 123.

21. Scoville, p. 314; *Glass Industry as Affected by the War*, p. 29.

22. "Ribbon Machine," Hilbert folder; Alexander Falck, "Outline of History of Empire Machine Company," in Hilbert folder.

23. Falck's 1925 book, CIDARM 14-3-4; *Cullet*, October 1918, p. 8, CIDARM 13-4-8.

24. Hammon, p. 302.

25. Hollister, p. 84.

26. *Glass Industry as Affected by the War*, p. 10.

27. Leuchtenburg, p. 40; Robert D. Cuff, *The War Industries Board: Business–Government Relations* (1973), pp. 1–222.

28. Bernard Baruch, *American Industry in the War: A Report of the War Industries Board* (1941), pp. 287–288.

29. Graham and Shuldiner, chap. 6.

30. *Cullet*, October 1918; Blaszczyk diss., p. 517; Hollister, pp. 128–133.

31. "War Zone Headlamp Test" and other correspondence, folders 69–71, CIDARM 11-4-10.

32. Day to Houghton, November 8, 1917; Summer 1917 in Arthur L. Day folder, CIDARM 34-1-3

33. Dimitroff and Janes, pp. 139–140.

34. Corning Sales document in sales document folder, CIDARM 22-5-3.

35. Leuchtenburg, pp. 1–84.

36. Reich, p. 251; Bright, pp. 353–355.

37. Blaszczyk diss.; Pearce Davis, *The Development of the American Glass Industry* (1949), pp. 279–281; Scoville, p. 68.

38. Correspondence about Alanson's house in house folder, CIDARM 20-4-1; in folder CIDARM 18-4-1; Alanson Houghton campaign material, folder 18, CIDARM 19-5-2; Cites for Knoll material.

39. Alanson Houghton, biographical sketch, folder 19, CIDARM 19-5-2.

40. *Cullet*, August 1921, pp. 25–28; Houghton, *Remembrances*, pp. 42–51.

41. Falck obituary, *Corning Evening Leader*, April 5, 1950.

42. Falck to the Houghton brothers, January 13, 1920, Falck folder, CIDARM 6-5-6.

43. Development plan, August 1920, in Arthur L. Day Report folder, CIDARM 6-5-6.

44. Ibid., p. 24; Falck to Arthur Houghton, January 1920, Falck to Arthur and Alanson Houghton, January 13, 1920, Falck folder, CIDARM 6-5-6.

45. Day development plans, p. 29 in financial figures folder, CIDARM 6-5-6.

46. *Gaffer*, July 1946; Hollister to A. B. Houghton, January 31, 1919, Hollister folder, CIDARM 14-3-4; CIDARM 7-3-1; Earl Lifsheyk, *The Housewares Story: A History of the American Housewares Industry* (1973); Otto Hilbert, "Information to Employees and Outsiders," Hilbert folders, CIDARM 7-3-1.

47. "1918–1924," sales document, April 26, 1921, CIDARM 14-3-4.

48. "The 1922 Pyrex Story for Store People," in Pyrex folder, CIDARM 14-5-1; advertisements in Wright folders.

49. Hollister, pp. 144–145.

50. *Cullet*, April 1922, pp. 9–11.

51. Sander A. Diamond, *An American in Berlin: Alanson B. Houghton Reports from Germany, 1922–1925* (1978), CIDARM; "Abroad with Our Ambassador," Alanson B. Houghton folder, CIDARM 34-1-2.

52. Alanson Houghton biographical sketch, folder 18, CIDARM 19-5-2.

53. Falck memo, Falck folder, CIDARM 6-5-6.

54. Falck memo; Falck to Alanson, 1923, Financial folder, CIDARM 6-5-6.

55. Leuchtenburg, pp. 178–201.

56. Ibid, pp. 179ff.

57. *Cullet*, October 1918; *Cullet*, February 1921, p. 38.

58. Wright memo, April 1927; HN-K folder, CIDARM 14-3-4.

59. Graham and Shuldiner, p. 147.

60. Memo on bulb production, April 1925, in Bulbs folder, CIDARM 33-5-3; memo, February 7, 1925, folder, CIDARM 14-3-4; Hilbert folders, documents called "machine development historical," pp. 6–7; Wise, p. 212; number in "Outline of History of Empire Machine Co.," Hilbert folder 12.

61. Falck to A. B. and A. A. Houghton, August 29, 1924, in 1918–1924 folder, CIDARM 14-3-4.

62. Machine development historical memo, Hilbert files; Ribbon Machine, Hilbert folders.

63. Hollister, pp. 84–86.

64. Hollister, p. 87; "399 Corning Machine—Ribbon Machine," Hilbert folder 12.

65. Hollister, p. 88; "399 Corning Machine."

66. Hollister, pp. 88–91; "399 Corning Machine."

67. Hollister, pp. 94–95; Bright, p. 355; "399 Corning Machine." Ribbon Machine; Sullivan daybook, CIDARM 22-5-3.

68. Hollister, p. 147; Graham and Shuldiner; Hilbert folders.

69. Hollister, pp. 149–150; Hilbert folders.

70. Material on wedding in CIDARM 19-5-2; "Abroad with Our Ambassador," Alanson B. Houghton folder, CIDARM 34-1-2.

71. Amory to Alanson correspondence in the 1920s in folder 24, CIDARM 19-5-2.

72. *Cullet*, July 1920, p. 8; Falck memo to the Houghton brothers, 1927, ABH Files Folder, CIDARM 6-5-6; Arthur Houghton quote in unsigned biographical sketch, Arthur A. Houghton folder, CIDARM 34-1-2.

73. Falck to Alanson, August 29, 1924, in 1918–1924 folder, CIDARM 14-3-4.

74. Amory to Alanson, October 1927 folder 24, CIDARM 19-5-2; April 24, 1928, folder 26, CIDARM 19-5-2.

75. Amory Houghton biographical sketch, folder 18, CIDARM 19-5-2.

76. Blaszczyk diss., pp. 644–650.

77. Amory to Alanson, September 27, 1928, folder 26, CIDARM 19-5-2.

78. Leuchtenburg, p. 202.

Chapter Five

1. The account of this event is drawn from "Corning Glass Works Pays Tribute to Veterans at Testimonial Banquet," *Corning Evening Leader*, September 14, 1928, p. 12.
2. Donald Bonnell, "History of Employee Service Dinners and Service Pins," undated typescript, n.d. [1954?]. Copy furnished by Donald Bonnell.
3. For an overview of Williams's fascinating career, see Daniel A. Wren, *White Collar Hobo: The Travels of Whiting Williams* (1987).
4. Amory to Alanson Houghton, September 17, 1928, CIDARM 19-5-02.
5. Anna Haar (Mrs. Hin) interview by Ralph C. Epstein, 1956, Biographical files, CIDARM.
6. J. C. Hostetter to Board of Directors, June 13, 1929, in Fallbrook folder, CIDARM.
7. Ibid.
8. Ibid.
9. Fallbrook folder, CIDARM.
10. "Summary table of Pyrex sales figures, 1924 to 1950," Ovenware folders, CIDARM. See also, Regina Lee Blaszczyk, *Imagining Consumers: Design and Innovation from Wedgwood to Corning* (2000), chap. 6.
11. On Copeland, see Jeffrey L. Cruikshank, *A Delicate Experiment: The Harvard Business School, 1908–1945* (1987), pp. 133–134; and Jonathan A. Silva, "The Development of American Marketing Thought and Practice, 1902–1940" (Ph.D. diss., Ohio State University, 1998), p. 7.
12. Ovenware folders, CIDARM. The following paragraph draws on several sections of Copeland's 20-page typescript report.
13. LaFollette biographical folder, CIDARM.
14. Ibid.
15. *Corning Evening Leader*, September 10, 1928.
16. Thomas P. Dimitroff and Lois S. Janes, *History of the Corning-Painted Post Area: 200 Years in Painted Post Country* (1976), pp. 222–223 and 226–227.
17. Corning Glass Works, "Eugene Cornelius Sullivan—Glass Scientist, 1872–1962," unpaginated section entitled "Vice Chairman, 1930–1936."
18. Amory to Arthur A. Houghton Jr., August 7, 1930, CIDARM 19-5-02, f. 22.
19. "CGW—History—Gen'l," in Hilbert notebooks, 9A; Fallbrook folder, CIDARM; "Central Falls Chronology," Hilbert notebooks 3.
20. Margaret B. W. Graham, "New Forms of Information and New Users in the Vacuum Tube Era," in Alfred D. Chandler Jr. and James W. Cortada, eds., *A Nation Transformed by Information* (2000); "Television" (1983), in Television folder, CIDARM; Jeffrey L. Meikle, *Twentieth Century Limited: Industrial Design in America, 1925–1939*, (1979), p. 97.
21. "Discounts on PYREX Baking Ware, Teapots and Nursing Bottles (from 1920 to April 17, 1935)," and "Summary table of Pyrex sales figures, 1924 to 1950," Ovenware folders, CIDARM; *Gaffer*, July 1946, p. 6. For Maltby, see Blaszczyk, pp. 243–245; Regina L. Blaszczyk, "Imagining Consumers: Manufacturers and Markets in Ceramics and Glass, 1865-1965" (Ph.D. diss., University of Delaware, 1995), chap. 9.
22. This section is based on material found in Telescope folder, CIDARM, especially George McCauley's chronological narrative of Corning's development of Pyrex mirror blanks. Other general sources include Ronald Florence, *The Perfect Machine:*

Building the Palomar Telescope (1994) and Richard Rhodes, "Reflected Glory: How They Built Palomar," *American Heritage of Invention and Technology* (1985), pp. 13–21.

23. G. V. McCauley, "Some Engineering Problems Encountered in Making a 200-inch Telescope Disk," *Bulletin of the American Ceramic Society*, 14, no. 9 (1935), p. 301; Florence, chap. 14.

24. H. R. Kiehl, "Survey of Technical Progress, Corning Glass Works, Part 36, Reflecting Telescope Disk Manufacture—A Résumé of Dr. McCauley's Report," February 11, 1966, Telescope folder, CIDARM.

25. Florence, pp. 166–168; quotation from Day on p. 166.

26. Rhodes, p. 17.

27. Kiehl, "Résumé of Dr. McCauley's Report," p. 5.

28. Florence, chap. 17; Donald Bonnell video interview by Davis Dyer, March 17, 1999. Bonnell later joined Corning as a member of the public relations department and edited the *Gaffer*.

29. Rhodes, pp. 17–18; Bonnell video interview, March 17, 1999.

30. Alanson B. to Amory Houghton, September 24, 1934, in folder 24, CIDARM 19-5-02.

31. W. C. Decker to Dr. Sullivan, April 29, 1938; copy in Telescope folder, CIDARM. The discrepancy in the cost-plus ten percent fee arrangement was due to accounting for equipment charged as expense that became the property of the customer.

32. Alanson B. Houghton to Harlow Shapley, April 22, 1939, folder 19, CIDARM 19-5-02.

33. Steuben notebook, CIDARM. See also tables reproduced in Blaszczyk diss., pp. 600–601. See also Silva diss., pp. 281–284.

34. Autobiography of Fred E. Schroeder (copy at CIDARM), p. 13.

35. R. C. Vaughn, "Report on the Steuben Division of Corning Glass Works," April 11, 1931, Steuben notebook, CIDARM. See also summary in "Steuben—1924–1933," in folder 24, CIDARM, 33-6-01.

36. On Teague, see Blaszczyk diss., pp. 590–605.

37. Teague to Houghton, Steuben notebook, CIDARM.

38. E.g., Arthur Houghton's recollections, Steuben file, CIDARM; and Mary Jean Madigan, *Steuben Glass: An American Tradition in Crystal* (1982).

39. W. D. Teague to Amory Houghton, April 5, 1932, in Steuben notebook, CIDARM.

40. W. W. Oakley to Dr. W. H. Armistead, Development of Steuben Crystal Glass, March 16, 1966, pp. 1–3; H. P. Hood to Dr. W. H. Armistead, June 14, 1966. Both documents in folder 24, CIDARM, 33-6-01. See also Blaszczyk diss., p. 596.

41. Blaszczyk diss., pp. 600–601; "Steuben—1924–1933," folder 24, CIDARM 33-6-01.

42. Madigan, p. 310. Houghton had the remaining undamaged pieces put into storage. In 1975, Corning donated the whole lot, about a thousand items, to the Corning Museum of Glass.

43. Blaszczyk diss., pp. 605–610; "Corning in the '30s. A Personal Reminiscence," CIDARM.

44. Conversation with Arthur A. Houghton Jr. and John M. Gates, May 14, 1969, p. 5. Document in Arthur A. Houghton Jr. biographical folder, CIDARM.

45. Thomas Buechner video interview by Davis Dyer, June 11, 1998; Sally Walker video interview by Davis Dyer, October 9, 1998.

46. Elsewhere in the joint Houghton–Gates interview (see n. 44) Arthur Houghton stated that "we wanted to make some of the greatest objects that have ever been made in the history of the world including the Renaissance."

47. Houghton–Gates interview.

48. Houghton–Gates interview.

49. Autobiography of Fred E. Schroeder, p. 16.

50. Blaszczyk diss., pp. 622–623.

51. Houghton–Gates interview. Steuben mounted other exhibitions in New York and Cambridge, Massachusetts in 1935. See "The Evolution of Steuben Glass," Steuben folder, CIDARM.

52. Eugene C. Sullivan, "The Many-Sidedness of Glass," *Industrial and Engineering Chemistry*, Vol. 21 (February 1929), p. 5; see also Margaret B. W. Graham and Alec T. Shuldiner, *Corning and the Craft of Innovation* (2001), chap. 1.

53. David A. Hounshell and John Kenly Smith Jr., *Science and Corporate Strategy: R&D at Du Pont, 1902–1980* (1988), chap. 5. Other chemical companies followed Du Pont's lead. See Davis Dyer and David B. Sicilia, *Labors of a Modern Hercules: Evolution of a Chemical Company* (1990), chap. 7. Hercules and Corning were about the same size in the 1930s and evolving in similar directions.

54. Dyer and Sicilia, pp. 183–184.

55. W. W. Shaver to Dr. G. P. Smith, "Strong Glass," Hilbert notebooks, CIDARM.

56. Ibid.

57. W. W. Shaver to Dr. G. P. Smith, "Top-of-Stove Ware," May 22, 1974; H. R. Kiehl, "A Historical Summary of the Development of Tempered Top-of-Stove Ware," June 1, 1965, Hilbert notebooks, CIDARM; Blaszczyk, p. 246; Blaszczyk diss., pp. 657–660.

58. Kiel, p. 1.

59. W. C. Taylor to C. H. Kruidenier, August 8, 1945, CIDARM 33-5-01.

60. Leon V. Quigley, "To Editors and Correspondents: Information on Top-of-Stove Glass Ware," January 14, 1936, CIDARM; "The Battery Jar That Built a Business: The Story of Pyrex Ovenware and Flameware," *Gaffer*, July 1946, p. 6; Taylor to Kruidenier, August 8, 1945; Blaszczyk diss., pp. 657–659.

61. "Architectural Glass," Hilbert notebooks, 1, CIDARM.

62. W. W. Shaver to Dr. G. P. Smith, "Glass Building Blocks," December 3, 1973.

63. J. Franklin Hyde biographical file, CIDARM; Graham and Shuldiner, chap. 3.

64. J. Franklin Hyde, video interview by Davis Dyer, February 9, 1999.

65. Earl L. Warrick, *Forty Years of Firsts: The Recollections of a Dow Corning Pioneer* (1990); Dorothy Langdon Yates, *William R. Collings: Dow Corning's Pioneer Leader* (1985); Graham and Shuldiner, chap. 3.

66. Harry Hosier biographical folder, CIDARM, Hilbert notebooks, 8, "Employee Relations"; Board Minutes, 2/9/37 and 6/15/37.

67. Alanson B. to Amory Houghton, March 2, 1931, CIDARM 19-5-02, f. 24.

68. Lonnie Bennett video interview by Davis Dyer, February 26, 1998; Ed Wellech Recollections, February 12, 1973, Wellech biographical file, CIDARM. Wellech gave a slightly different account of the same story in a 1965 memorandum. See also, "History of the Fall Brook Plant," 1946, typescript, Fallbrook folder, CIDARM.

69. Wellech Recollections, 1973; Bonnell video interview, March 17, 1999.

70. Wellech Recollections, 1973.

71. Wellech Recollections, 1973; "Corning Managers Meeting, Corning— January 1958," Fallbrook folder, CIDARM.

72. Pittsburgh Corning folder and notebook, CIDARM; William C. Decker interview by Ralph L. Epstein, 1958, Decker biographical folder, CIDARM.

73. Amory Houghton Jr. interview by Margaret Graham and Davis Dyer, May 5, 1997; James Houghton interview by Davis Dyer, June 3, 1997.

74. Wellech Recollections, 1973; "Fiberglas," *Fortune*, 35 (January 1947), p. 91.
75. Hyde video interview, February 9, 1999; J. Franklin Hyde interview by Margaret Graham, April 28, 1997.
76. "Owens-Corning Fiberglas" in Hilbert notebooks, 13, CIDARM.
77. Remarks and conversations with Mr. George T. Macbeth, February 28, 1968, Macbeth biographical folder, CIDARM; Decker interview, 1958.
78. Amory Houghton Jr. interview, May 5, 1997.
79. Pressware and Macbeth-Evans folders, CIDARM.
80. Graham and Shuldiner, chap. 3.
81. Otto Hilbert, "Television," June 17, 1971, Hilbert notebooks, 2, CIDARM; C. J. Parker, "Applied Optics at Corning Glass Works," *Applied Optics*, 7, no. 5 (1968), p. 739.
82. Graham and Shuldiner, chap. 6.

Chapter Six

1. Kenneth T. Jackson, ed, *Encyclopedia of New York City* (1995), p. 1276; document dated September 23, 1938, in Fiberglass folder, CIDARM 33-5-1; *Time* advertisement, September 1939.
2. Shaver to Littleton, "Possible New Applications for Glass," August 26, 1940, War Products Folder, CIDARM 34-4-1; Amory to Hollister, March 21, 1940, folder 21, CIDARM 19-5-2; "Corning Sales, 1906–1960."
3. Alanson to Amory, June 13, 1940, folder 21, CIDARM 19-5-2.
4. Amory to Alan Lake Childsey, A-B folder, CIDARM 19-3-8.
5. *New York Times*, March 31, 1940; Arthur Houghton correspondence, CIDARM 24-4-1; Arthur to Claflin, August 16, 1940, CIDARM 24-4-1; Perry, Shaw and Hepbrun, architects to Arthur, September 27, 1940, folder 10, CIDARM 20-4-4.
6. Richard Polenberg, *War and Society* (1972), p. 6; O'Neill, *Democracy at War*, p. 9; Arthur to Amory, September 23, 1940, folder 21, CIDARM 19-5-2; Arthur, correspondence, CIDARM 24-4-1; *New York Times*, March 31, 1940.
7. Cole personnel file, CIDARM 34-1-3; Amory to Kaye Martine, March 28, 1941, folder 15, CIDARM 19-5-3; Corning Glass Works time book entries, folder 10, CIDARM 34-3-2.
8. *New York Times*, September 17, 1941; September 18, 1941.
9. Amory Jr. to Alanson correspondence, folder 17, CIDARM 20-4-4.
10. Polenberg, pp. 13–35; Elliot Janeway, *The Struggle for Survival* (1951), pp. 40–202; Gregory Hooks, *Forging the Military–Industrial Complex: World War II's Battle of the Potomac* (1991), pp. 80–125.
11. Amory to Reed, November 20, 1939, folder R, CIDARM 19-4-4; Amory to Head, December 6, 1941, War Production Board no. 2 folder, CIDARM 19-3-6; Dodge to Amory, November 17, 1941, in War Production Board, no. 2 folder, CIDARM 19-3-6.
12. Sheldon, *A History: Corning's Role in the First 101 Years of Television*, Television Bulbs folder, CIDARM 33-7-1; *Gaffer*, September 1945, pp. 8–9; Polenberg, pp. 7–8.
13. Shaver to Littleton, December 16, 1941, Research Laboratory Physical Quarters folder, CIDARM, 33-6-1; Corning Sales document; Corning *Annual Report*, 1945.
14. Polenberg, pp. 8–9; J. S. Knowlson, "The Conclusions of a Dollar-A-Year Man," *Atlantic Monthly*, May 1943.
15. Amory to H. S. Rogers, June 5, 1942; Amory to Carroll Morgan, June 13, 1942, WPB

Chronological File folder, CIDARM 19-3-6; Amory to Lt. Col Quincy Adams Shaw Jr., July 31, 1942; March 17, 1942, inventory of items moved from Marion to Washington, March 17, 1942, folder 17, CIDARM 20-4-4.

16. Polenberg, p. 11; Knowlson, pp. 8–9; Bill Flannery to Amory, September 8, 1942, in Mission for Economic Affairs folder, CIDARM 19-3-12; Amory and Reed to Robert Nathan, June 25, 1942; War Production Board, no. 2 folder, CIDARM 19-3-6.

17. Nathan to Reed and Houghton, May 29, 1942, in War Production Board, no. 2 folder, CIDARM 19-3-6.

18. "Information Concerning Production Requirements," War Production Board, no. 2 folder, CIDARM 19-3-6.

19. Hilbert recollection, War Products folder, CIDARM 34-1-1.

20. Harvey Anderson, Bureau of Industrial Conservation, to Amory, April 11, 1942, War Production Board, no. 2 folder, CIDARM 19-3-6.

21. Amory to John Sessions, July 1, 1942, folder: WPB Chronological File—Jan. 30, 1942 to Sept. folder, CIDARM 19-3-6.

22. *New York Times*, July 8, 1942; Amory to Cary, July 22, 1942, and Amory to Ryerson, July 20, 1942, War Production Board, no. 3, WPB Assignment Congratulatory Letters: 1942 folder, CIDARM 19-3-6.

23. *Business Week*, August 15, 1942; *PM Daily*, July 13, 1942.

24. *Wall Street Journal*, August 26, 1942; Amory to Nelson, August 28, 1942, in War Production Board, no. 1 folder, CIDARM 19-3-6; Amory to Nelson, September 10, 1942, in War Production Board, no. 2 folder, CIDARM 19-3-6.

25. WPB release, November 2, 1942, in War Production Board, no. 2 folder, CIDARM, 19-3-6.

26. Reed to Amory, September 9, 1942, in WPB Resignation folder, CIDARM 19-3-6.

27. W. W. Shaver to J. T. Littleton, "Glass Bullets," November 10, 1942; Shaver to Littleton et. al., September 1, 1942; Shaver to T. J. Thompson, September 21, 1942; Shaver to Littleton, March 5, 1942; Shaver to Littleton, October 27, 1942; all in War Products folder, CIDARM 34-4-1.

28. "Laboratory Estimate Report by Men and Their Participation on National Defense Work," War Product folder, CIDARM 34-4-1. *Multiform-Gaffer*, April/May 1943.

29. "Optical Glass Development," Hilbert files, no. 14; *Applied Optics*, May 1968.

30. Leon Fourvel-Rigolleau to Arthur, June 4, 1940, folder F, CIDARM 20-4-4; "Translation of 85 Anos Rigolleau, Cristalerias Rigolleau, SA, 1967, in Hilbert folder 7.

31. Sullivan to Amory, April 14, 1942, folder S, 1931–1945, CIDARM 19-5-4; South America folder, CIDARM 34-6-1; correspondence and material on South American investments in Cristalerias Rigolleau folder, CIDARM 14-4-4.

32. Ibid; South American Investments, Hilbert folder, 10; "License to Use Patents," February 27, 1943, Cristalerias Rigolleau folder, license folder, CIDARM.

33. *Gaffer*, June-July, 1943, p. 4; *Corning Leader* article about war preparations, 1972.

34. *The Conference Board Management Record* 8, no. 3 (1946); *Corning Evening Leader*, February 4, 1943; *Gaffer*, April-May, 1943; War Products World War Two Production and Awards folder, CIDARM 34-4-1.

35. *Gaffer*, April-May 1943, p. 13; *Time*, June 14, 1943.

36. "Dr. James Franklin Hyde," Silicones folder, CIDARM 33-6-1.

37. "History of the Present Business of Dow Corning," Dow-Corning-folder, CIDARM 34-5-1.

38. Collins to Cole, September 9, 1944, in Hilbert folder, 8; Collins to commanding general, air service command, "History of Dow Corning–4. Ignition Sealing Compound," Silicon folder, CIDARM 33-6-1; "History of the Present Business of Dow Corning," Dow Corning–1 folder, CIDARM 34-5-1.

39. *Compressed Air*, August 1945; "Net Sales: Owens-Corning Fibreglas Corp., Hilbert files, no. 14; *Fiberglas: A New Basic Material*, 1943, in folder 6, CIDARM 7-4-8.

40. Rayback, pp. 375–380; Wages, annual folder, CIDARM 34-4-1; "Five Years of War-Time Service: Some of the Problems of War Expansion and How Corning Glass Works Met Them," War Products folder, CIDARM 34-4-1.

41. *Gaffer*, August-September 1943; May 1944.

42. *Gaffer*, May 1944.

43. Rayback, pp. 373–383.

44. Thomas Waaland interview by Margaret Graham, April 1997; Richard Marks video interview, November 1998.

45. Waaland interview.

46. History—Timeline, Hilbert folder 4; Cole to Amory, February 18, 1944, folder 14, CIDARM 19-3-7; W. C., "While You Were Away," *Gaffer*, War Products folder, CIDARM.

47. Cole to Amory, February 18, 1944 and telegram in folder 15, CIDARM 19-3-7; Amory's itinerary; Reed to Amory, October 8, 1943, Mission for Economic Affairs folder, CIDARM 19-3-12.

48. *Business Week*, January 29, 1944.

49. Amory to Samuel Boykin, November 11, 1943, Mission for Economic Affairs folder, CIDARM 19-3-12; press bulletin, October 30, 1943; Levis to Amory, February 18, 1944, folder L, CIDARM 19-5-3.

50. Falck to Amory, February 9, 1944, and attached memo, folder E, 1940–1948, CIDARM 19-4-8; South American Investments, Hilbert folder, 10.

51. Folder H, CIDARM 19-5-2; *Gaffer*, September 1944; *Annual Report*, 1945.

52. Curtis K. Oakley folder, CIDARM 34-1-1.

53. *Gaffer*, April-May 1943, p. 13; *Gaffer*, September 1944, p. 12; *Gaffer*, May 1945.

54. *Gaffer*, October 1944, p. 6; *Gaffer*, August 1944.

55. *Saturday Evening Post*, August 14, 1944, p. 26. Hood was not exactly young at the time—he was forty-eight.

56. *Applied Optics*, May 1968; Charles DeVoe folder, CIDARM 34-1-3; *Corning Leader*, March 18, 1991.

57. *Gaffer*, September 1945, pp. 8–9; *Gaffer*, November 1944; *Gaffer*, February 1945, p. 8.

58. *Gaffer*, May 1944; *Gaffer*, August 1946.

59. *Gaffer*, April 1945.

60. "Mission for Economic Affairs: Index to Progress Report, March 29, 1944, Mission for Economic Affairs folder, CIDARM 19-3-12.

61. Reed to Winant, November 7, 1944; Amory to Leo Crowley, November 30, 1944; Amory's itinerary; all in Mission for Economic Affairs folder, CIDARM 19-3-12.

62. Amory Houghton, December 9, 1944, "Corning Glass Works" [little booklet with American flag on it], in War Products folder, CK; *Gaffer*, January 1945.

63. T. Waaland, "Post War Plans Product Engineering Department," December 14, 1944; "Post War Vycor Program," March 12, 1945, Vycor folder, CIDARM 33-7-1.

64. *Gaffer*, November 1944; *Gaffer*, May 1945; South American Investments, Hilbert files, no. 10; documents, July 3, 1945, April 27, 1944, folder 7, CIDARM 14-4-4.

65. *Annual Report*, 1945.

66. Amory Houghton Jr. interview by Davis Dyer and Margaret Graham, May 1997.

67. *Fortune*, July 1945, pp. 129–133, 253–260; *Annual Report*, 1945; CIDARM 17-5-5.

68. *Gaffer*, May and July 1945.

69. *Gaffer*, October-November 1945, p. 10; *Gaffer*, April-May, 1945.

70. Cole to shareholders, October 1, 1945, folder 2, CIDARM 34-2-3; Cole to shareholders, December 31, 1945, War Products folder, CIDARM 34-4-1.

71. "The Operating Results of Corning Glass Works for 1946," folder 2, CIDARM 34-2-3; "The Houghtons of Corning," *Fortune*, July 1945, pp. 129–133, 253–260.

72. *Fortune* article, 1945, p. 129.

Chapter Seven

1. *Annual Report*, 1946; D. T. Bonnell, *Report on Optical and Ophthalmic Glass Operations at Corning Glass Works, June 1948, and Outline of Parkersburg Plant Development*, April 9, 1956, Parkersburg folder, CIDARM 34-6-3.

2. Dimitroff and Janes, *History of Corning*; Corning Glass Works *Annual Report*, 1946, p. 4; Behm interview.

3. Leighton to Amory Houghton Sr., October 10, 1946, folder H 1946, CIDARM 19-5-2.

4. Quote from document in Decker folder, CIDARM 34-1-3.

5. *Annual Report*, 1947; *Report on Optical and Ophthalmic Glass Operations at Corning Glass Works*, in Parkersburg, W. Va. folder, CIDARM 34-6-3; Donald Stookey, *Journey to the Center of the Crystal Ball* (1985).

6. Stan Fairman to Otto Hilbert, June 6, 1973; E. W. Smartt Jr., general secretary of chamber of commerce in Muskogee, to W. H. Curtiss, 1920, "Facts about Muskogee Plant"; all in Muskogee folder, CIDARM 34-6-3; Decker to Amory Sr., February 10, 1948, folder 24, CIDARM 19-3-7.

7. Dimitroff and Janes, pp. 255–265.

8. *Corning Leader*, Sunday, September 13, 1948, pp. 1ff.

9. Amory Sr. to Eisenhower, September 14, 1948, folder E, CIDARM 19-4-8.

10. *Annual Report*, 1947; "Television," Television Bulbs folder, 2, CIDARM 33-7-1; Development expense: Chart, Television Bulbs folder, 2, CIDARM 33-7-1.

11. "Television," p. 2; Margaret B. W. Graham and Alec T. Shuldiner, *Corning and the Craft of Innovation* (2001), chap. 7; Dimitroff and Janes, pp. 282–283. *Annual Report*, 1947, 1948; Decker to Amory Sr., February 10, 1948, folder 24, CIDARM 19-3-7.

12. Graham and Shuldiner, chap. 7.

13. Ibid; Robert Sobel, *RCA* (1986), p. 151.

14. Forrest Behm interview by Margaret Graham, May 13, 1997.

15. "Television," Television Bulbs folder 2, CIDARM 33-7-1.

16. Graham and Shuldiner, chap. 7.

17. Graham and Shuldiner, chap. 7.

18. Memo from A. W. Weber to W. C. Taylor, April 18, 1949; Decker to Sullivan, April 28, 1949; both in Centrifugal Casting folder, CIDARM 6-5-6; Charles F. Devoe to Otto Hilbert, March 6, 1979, Pilot Plant folder 1, CIDARM 34-6-3.

19. Christopher Sterling and John Kittros, *Stay Tuned: A Concise History of American Broadcasting* (1978), pp. 232–280.

20. *Annual Report*, 1950; Graham and Shuldiner, p. 9; Robert Sobel, *RCA* (1986), p. 101.

21. Agreement between Corning and His Majesty the King in Right of Canada, June 15, 1945, Leaside folder, CIDARM 34-6-1; "Gaffer Goes to Leaside," *Gaffer*, October 1947.

22. "Corning Project Sun," Jobling folder, CIDARM 34-6-1; Hans Schott to Amory Sr., September 20, 1955, folder S 1953–1957, CIDARM 19-5-4.

23. "Cristales Mexicanos," Cristales Mexicanos, Monterrey, Mexico folder, CIDARM 34-6-1.

24. Graham and Shuldiner, chap. 7.

25. Dimitroff and Janes, pp. 268–270.

26. Dimitroff and Janes, p. 273.

27. Newspaper article, in Ambassador folder, CIDARM 34-1-2.

28. Corning Conference, Hilbert folder 5, CIDARM.

29. *Gaffer*, October 1954.

30. Folder F, CIDARM 19-4-8; 2-5-8; Yacht Charter folder, Amory Sr. to Gentil, October 13, 1952, folder 20, G, 1949–1952, CIDARM 19-4-8; Bill, March 7, 1952, Amory Houghton—Illness folder, CIDARM 19-5-2; Dr. Edgar Lawrence to Am, April 3, 1952, folder L 1950–1952, CIDARM 19-5-3, Julia Peck to Ralph Epstein, November 28, 1951, folder E 1949–1952, CIDARM 19-4-8.

31. August 28, 1949, clipping in folder 12, C 1949–1950, CIDARM 19-4-8.

32. Decker to Am, March 6, 1952, folder 22, CIDARM 19-3-7.

33. Lacy to Amo, Amo to Lacy, December 9, 1954, folder L, 1954–1979, CIDARM 9-5-8; *Gaffer*, May-June 1953; *New York Herald Tribune*, June 28, 1950; *New York Herald Tribune*, April 19, 1953; *Annual Report*, 1950; document, in folder 5, H 1953, CIDARM 19-5-2.

34. *Annual Report*, 1951; material and correspondence in Television Bulbs folders 1 and 2, CIDARM 4-4-2.

35. Sobel, p. 166; *Annual Reports*, 1952, 1953; Decker to AM, May 18, 1953, folder 22, CIDARM 19-3-7.

36. Decker to Am, May 18, 1953, folder 22, CIDARM 19-3-7.

37. Decker to Am, March 6, 1952, folder 22, CIDARM 19-3-7.

38. Decker to Am, May 25, 1953, folder 22, CIDARM 19-3-7; *Moody's Industrial Manual* (1954), pp. 1209, 1954.

39. *Gaffer*, May-June 1954, p. 7; *Annual Report*, 1952, p. 11; Graham and Shuldiner, chap. 6.

40. *Techniques of Chemistry*, vol. 4, *Elucidation of Organic Structures and Physical and Chemical Methods* (1972); document in Edward Condon folder, 19-2-1974, CIDARM 34-1-3.

41. Condon to Am, March 3, 1952, Edward Condon folder, CIDARM 19-3-7; hearing before the Committee of Un-American Activities House of Representatives, Eighty-second Congress, second session, September 5, 1952.

42. *Techniques of Chemistry*, pp. x–xv.

43. Graham and Shuldiner, chap. 6; Condon to Armistead, 1961.

44. *Elmira Advertiser*, September 26, 1952; HUAC transcript; *Techniques of Chemistry*, pp. i-xviii; *Daily News*, April 20, 1954. Ellen Schrecker, *No Ivory Tower: McCarthyism and the Universities* (1986) pp. 1–165. Harlan Logan to William Decker, CC: Amory Houghton, December 30, 1952, Condon folder, CIDARM 34-1-3.

45. *Techniques in Chemistry*, p. xiv–xx; HUAC transcript; handwritten notes, apparently by Sullivan on Condon, Edward Condon folder, CIDARM 34-1-3.

46. Condon to Am, January 4, 1954, Edward Condon folder, CIDARM 19-3-7; *Techniques in Chemistry*, pp. i–xviii.

47. *New York Times*, October 22, 1954; *Washington Post*, October 29, 1954; Condon to Henry T. Heald, chancellor of NYU, March 1, 1955, CIDARM 34-1-3.

48. Press release, in Edward Condon folder, CIDARM 34-1-3; *Techniques in Chemistry*, xvii; document, Edward Condon folder, CIDARM 34-1-3; Sullivan handwritten notes, 11/6/54, CIDARM.

Chapter Eight

1. Graham and Shuldiner, *Corning and the Craft of Innovation* (2001), chaps. 2,7.

2. "Color TV Comes of Age," *Corning Today*, December 1964.

3. Document in folder 5, H 1953, CIDARM 19-5-2; *Gaffer*, December 1954, p. 10.

4. "Color TV Comes of Age"; *Concise History of American Broadcasting*, p. 298; Robert Sobel, *RCA* (1986), p. 164.

5. "Trip to France," June 1955, Sovirel folder, CIDARM 34-6-1; *Gaffer*, November 1955.

6. *Annual Report*, 1954; Prospects, March 29, 1955; Stock folder, CIDARM 34-2-3.

7. *Gaffer*, May-June 1955; *Gaffer*, October 1954; W. Earl Weller, "Government of the City of Corning in the Country of Steuben," July 16, 1957, City Government folder, CIDARM 1-5-9; Dimitroff and Janes, *History of Corning* (1976), p. 262.

8. Graham and Shuldiner, chap. 7; *Gaffer*, July 1954, p. 12.

9. Graham and Shuldiner, chap. 7; Decker to Am, February 15, 1955, folder 22, CIDARM 19-3-7.

10. Decker to Am, February 9, 1955, folder 22, CIDARM 19-3-7; Sylvania *Annual Report*, 1955; Decker to Am and Sullivan, January 25, 1956; Decker to Am and Sullivan, August 21, 1956, Sylvania Electric folder, CIDARM 3-6-2.

11. Am to Frank Hultzman, January 24, 1957, and Eisenhower letter in folder no 1, CIDARM 19-5-2; *Annual Report*, 1956, p. 12.

12. *Gaffer*, November 1955.

13. Amo to Am, April 29, 1957, Amory Houghton folder, CIDARM 2-5-5.

14. Folder 3, N 1953–1959, CIDARM 19-4-4; *U.S. News & World Report*, September 23, 1955; Eisenhower to Am, January 5, 1955, folder E, 1953–1960, CIDARM 19-4-8.

15. Political Contributions, 1956—disclosure document from United States Senate, Political Contributions folder, CIDARM 20-5-8; Eisenhower to Am, November, 13, 1956, CIDARM 19-4-8; folder E, 1953–1960; folder 22, R 1953–1956, CIDARM 19-4-4; folder 8, CIDARM 19-3-7.

16. Am to Amo, May 11, 1957, Amory Houghton folder, CIDARM 2-5-5.

17. Amo to Am, November 19, 1957, folder H, 1957, CIDARM 19-5-2; Amo to Am, April 29, 1957, Amory Houghton folder, CIDARM 2-5-5.

18. "The Idea Mills: Glass Scientists Seek New Knowledge, New Products," *Wall Street Journal*, March 19, 1957; "The Fifty-Million-Dollar Man," *Fortune*, November 1957.

19. Peck to Am, May 27, 1957, folder 1, CIDARM 19-5-2.

20. *Gaffer*, June 1957, pp. 1–8; Peck to Am, May 27, 1957.

21. M. G. Britton, "Case History of the Development of PYROCERAM Brand Glass-Ceramics" (1966), p. 15 in Pyroceram folder, CIDARM 4-3-8; R. L. Waterman, address to

the Stanford Marketing Club, 1965, p. 1 in folder no. 5, CIDARM 16-4-6; *Business Week,* July 16, 1960.

22. Decker to Am, June 29, 1956; Decker to Am, July 16, 1956, Decker to Am, July 27, 1956; all in folder 22, CIDARM 19-3-7; *Annual Report,* 1956.

23. *Corning Leader,* November 21, 1961.

24. *Corning Business in Glass,* October 1957, pp. 5–6; Waterman, address to the Stanford Marketing Club, p. 7.

25. Stookey, p. 17; "Glass Chemistry as I Saw It," *Chemical Technology,* August 1971, p. 463; Stookey, pp. 1–25.

26. Graham and Shuldiner, chap. 7; Stookey, pp. 17–19; "Still the Cookware of the Future," timeline in Hilbert folder 7.

27. Stookey, p. 21; case study, p. 6.

28. Stookey, p. 23; "Still the Cookware of the Future," CIDARM.

29. Case History, A.M.A. Seminar—New York—Thursday, 10-13-60 and 1-19-61 folder.

30. Harland W. Warner, "Still the Cookware Material of the Future" (1977) in Hilbert folder 7; Lee Waterman, "Anatomy of Growth," folder 8, CIDARM 16-4-6.

31. Stanford Marketing Club speech, Hilbert folder 7, LaFollette to Am—August 29, 1958, Correspondence with Charles LaFollette folder, CIDARM 20-5-10.

32. *Product Development News,* December 1958, pp. 5–6; Warner.

33. "The New Dimensions," Waterman speech to the Marketing Club, July 1959, Pyroceram folder, CIDARM 4-3-8; *Gaffer,* June 1959, p. 2.

34. Waterman speech to Dow-Corning Executives, Pyroceram folder, CIDARM 4-3-8.

35. Waterman, Dow-Corning speech, *Gaffer,* December 1958.

36. Waterman presentation to Advertising Managers Bureau of the New York State Dailies, May 18, 1959, Pyroceram folder, CIDARM 4-3-8.

37. Ibid; *Gaffer,* September 1959, p. 2.

38. Waterman Stanford Marketing Club speech; Consumer Advertising Binders, CIDARM.

39. Consumer Advertising binders.

40. *Gaffer,* December 1959; 1959 *Annual Report,* pp. 12–13. *Forbes,* February 1, 1962, pp. 20–23; Duff, Anderson and Clark, "Basic Study: Corning Glass Works. September 8, 1961," p. 16 in the untitled folder, CIDARM 22-5-3; Martinsburg plant history at Martinsburg plant, West Virginia.

41. "Corelle and the Impossible Dreams of Jim Giffen," 10 June 1996, Glass Innovation Center papers, Hub Machine/Corelle folder; *Gaffer,* April 1960, p. 12; *Gaffer,* December 1959.

42. Ibid; Corning *Annual Report,* 1963; Waterman, "The Anatomy of Growth," July 1967, p. 9.

43. *Business Week,* July 16, 1960; *Forbes,* February 1, 1962, p. 22; *Gaffer,* August 1960, p. 3; Duff, Anderson and Clark, p. 15.

44. Decker to Am, October 3, 1958, folder 22, CIDARM 19-3-7; *Annual Report,* 1958; folder Budget-Wages, table on sales, CIDARM 34-2-1.

45. *Elmira Advertiser,* November 14, 1958.

46. Graham and Shuldiner, chaps. 3 and 7.

47. Sally Walker video interview by Davis Dyer, October 9, 1998.

48. Press release, New York folder, CIDARM 34-5-3; *Annual Report,* 1958.

Chapter Nine

1. Amory Jr. to Amory Sr., May 31, 1960; July 14, 1960, Amory Houghton folder, CIDARM 2-5-5.

2. Amory Jr. to Amory Sr., May 31, 1960, Amory Houghton folder, CIDARM 2-5-5; *Corning Leader*, September 23, 1959; folder W, CIDARM 9-5-1; *New York Times*, March 9, 1962.

3. Jamie to Robert McGarrah, June 16, 1961, folder H, CIDARM 19-4-7; Jamie's papers, CIDARM 26-2-7; James R. Houghton interview by Davis Dyer, February 3, 1997.

4. David Rockefeller to Amo, July 22, 1960, folder R, CIDARM 1-5-9; August 22, 1960— radio commentary, folder W, CIDARM 9-5-1; folder T, CIDARM 9-5-1.

5. Amory Jr. to Amory Sr., July 14, 1960, in Amory Houghton folder, CIDARM 2-5-5.

6. *Gaffer*, March 1961, p. 11; *Corning Leader*, January 28, 1961.

7. "Highlights in the Evolution of Science at Corning" Corporate Communications document, undated.

8. *Annual Report*, 1961, in Amory Houghton Jr. folder, CIDARM 34-1-2.

9. *Gaffer*, July 1962; Corning Conference brochure, Hilbert folder, 5.

10. Edgar Young, *Lincoln Center: The Building of an Institution* (1980), pp. xii–xiv, 61–62, 76–77; Amo to Alice Tully, October 17, 1958, folder T, CIDARM 9-5-1; *New York Times*, May 10, 1966.

11. *Annual Report*, 1962; *Gaffer*, August 1962, November 1962; *Lincoln Center*, pp. 168–170.

12. Biographical material in Arthur A. Houghton Jr. folder, CIDARM 34-1-2.

13. *Gaffer*, November 1962 and April 1963.

14. Duff, Anderson and Clark, pp. 4–5; "Decker of Corning Glass," *Forbes*, December, 1962; Decker document, 1963.

15. *Time*, September 28, 1962.

16. William Armistead interview by Margaret Graham, August 1, 1997.

17. *Time*, September 28, 1962.

18. *Annual Report*, 1962; *Gaffer*, April 1963, November 1963.

19. Daniel I. Okimoto, Takuo Sugano, and Franklin B. Weinstein, eds. (1984), pp. 10–22; 80–84.

20. Joseph Morone, *Winning in High-Tech Markets: The Role of General Management: How Motorola, Corning, and General Electric Have Built Global Leadership through Technology* (1993), p. 138; Thomas MacAvoy interview by Margaret Graham, July 31, 1997; MacAvoy video interview by Davis Dyer, July 10, 1998; "A Big Industry That Thinks Small," *Corning Glass Magazine*, March 1967.

21. Dimitroff and Janes, pp. 277–282.

22. Walter A. MacDougall, *The Heavens and the Earth: A Political History of the Space Age* (1985), p. 344.

23. *Gaffer*, April 1963, p. 4; June 1963; "Corning Glass Works' Mercury Capsule Program," folder 22, CIDARM 33-6-1.

24. Amo to Decker, March 12, 1963, Accounting folder, CIDARM 34-2-3.

25. Robert Sobel, *RCA* (1986), p. 166; *Gaffer*, June 1964, "Color TV Comes of Age," *Corning Today*, December 1964, Television Bulbs folder 2, CIDARM 33-7-1.

26. Arthur to Amo, July 28, 1958; Belknap to Arthur, General Services Dept. folder, CIDARM, 7-5-8.

27. *Advertiser*, November 5, 1959; *Saturday Evening Post*, February 22, 1964.

28. Murphy to Amory Sr., Amory Houghton folder, CIDARM 2-5-5.

29. *Gaffer*, January 1961, p. 12; *Gaffer*, April 1962.
30. Corning Glass Works *Annual Report*, 1964.
31. "Corning to Construct Plant in Netherlands," *Gaffer*, November 1963; James Houghton, talk before financial analysts' meeting, December 16, 1971, in folder 1971, CIDARM 26-4-7.
32. Decker to Amo, March 28, 1963, Accounting folder, CIDARM 34-2-3.
33. Decker to Amo, March 28, 1963, Corporate Finance folder, CIDARM 1-5-8.
34. J. W. Fiske to Amylon, Behm, Dawson, Hunt, Clark, Waterman, and others, March 20, 1963, folder cost, CIDARM 7-5-8.
35. *Forbes*, February 1, 1962; Roger Ackerman, interview by Margaret Graham and Davis Dyer, March 5, 1997.
36. "Decker of Corning Glass," *Forbes*, February 1, 1962.
37. Amo memo, Staff General folder, and Skytop folder, CIDARM 12-3-11.
38. *Corning Leader*, September 14, 1964.
39. Amory to Mrs. William P. Carley, July 29, 1966, folder H, CIDARM 19-4-7; Am to DDE, December 6, 1965, folder II, CIDARM 19-4-8; DDE to Am, August 31, 1966, Folder I, CIDARM 19-4-8.
40. *Gaffer*, April 1960, May 1962, February, 1964; Carder material in Hilbert folder 3, Carder, *Corning Leader*, December 11, 1963.
41. *Annual Report*, 1965.
42. *Gaffer*, November 1965.
43. "Zurich: Hub of Corning's European Markets," *Gaffer*, November 1966.
44. George Beall interview by Margaret Graham and Kathleen McDermott, March 28, 1996.
45. *Gaffer*, November 1964; *Dun's Review*, September 1965; Walter A. MacDougall. *The Heavens and the Earth: A Political History of the Space Age* (1985), p. 461.
46. C. J. Parker, "Applied Optics at Corning Glass Works," *Applied Optics*, May 1968, pp. 735–743.
47. *Annual Report*, 1966.
48. Morone, pp. 130–132.

Chapter Ten

1. F. B. Leibold Jr., "Fiber Optic Market Study," March 22, 1965, Fiber Optics folder 1," CIDARM 33-5-1; Fritz O. Kahl, "Fiber Optics in Electronic," *Electronics World*, May 1965; Morone, pp. 134–135.
2. Ira C. Magaziner and Mark Patinkin, *The Silent War: Inside the Global Business Battle Shaping America's Future* (1986), p. 266.
3. Ibid.
4. Morone, p. 135.
5. *Corning Leader*, December 9, 1986; August 5, 1989; Magaziner, p. 268.
6. Magaziner, p. 265; Morone, pp. 134–135; Margaret B. W. Graham and Alec T. Shuldiner, *Corning and the Craft of Innovation* (2001), chap. 8.
7. Magaziner, pp. 267–270; Graham and Shuldiner, chap. 8.
8. Magaziner, p. 271; Don Keck interview by Margaret Graham, May 17, 1997.

9. Magaziner, pp. 272–274; Keck interview by Margaret Graham, May 17, 1997.
10. Dimitroff and Janes, pp. 288–300; Richard Marks video interview by Davis Dyer, November 12, 1998.
11. Amo to Arthur, 9/30/68, folder H 1968, CIDARM 19-4-7, *Fortune*, May 1968.
12. Amo's talk "Industry's Responsibility to Society," ran January 14, 1968; folder H 1968, CIDARM 19-4-7; *Gaffer*, January 8, 1968.
13. Belknap to Amo Jr., 5/5/66, CIDARM 1-5-9; Belknap to A. W. Weber, community projects department annual report, Community Development folder, CIDARM 1-5-9.
14. "A Proposal for the Renovation of Market Street," memo, October 3, 1966, Community Development folder, CIDARM 1-5-9; Thomas Buechner interview by Davis Dyer, May 1997.
15. From Belknap to Weber and Amo, July 27, 1967, Community Development folder, CIDARM 1-5-9.
16. Humphrey to Amo, 3/10/67; Wheaton letter; both in Savings Bonds folder, CIDARM 12-3-11.
17. Arthur to Sidney Weinberg, October 7, 1968, folder H, 1968 CIDARM 19-4-7.
18. *Gaffer*, July 1973; *Gaffer*, June 26, 1968.
19. Morone, p. 140.
20. *Annual Report*, 1967; Morone, pp. 125–126.
21. Arthur to Amo, September 6, 1967, folder H, CIDARM 19-4-7.
22. Harland Warner, "Giant Corporation Is Humanistic in Time of Tragedy," January 1971, Hilbert folder 7; M. G. Britton, "A Case History of the Development of Pyroceram Brand Glass-Ceramics," CGW, May 15, 1966.
23. James Houghton, speech to plant managers, December 9, 1968, folder 1968, CIDARM 26-4-7.
24. Jerry Wright to Tina Vants, October 11, 1974, Smooth Tops folder, CIDARM 33-6-1; *Gaffer*, June 26, 1968; Jerry Wright to Tina Vants, October 11, 1974.
25. "Corning Ware Abroad: They Like It There, Too," *Gaffer*, August 1967, 1960s table.
26. From W. H. Dana to Forrest Behm, September 29, 1967, Romania folder, CIDARM 7-4-11; To Amo from Forrest Behm, July 27, 1967, Romania folder, CIDARM 7-4-11; Pierre-Louis Roederer interview by Margaret Graham, August 28, 1997.
27. Corning Glass Works *Annual Reports*, 1968–1970.
28. USSR folder, CIDARM 7-4-11; Bulbs-License Agreement CGW Incandescent Lamp & Electric Co. folder; memo to C. H. Schuckers from W. H. Dana, April 1, 1970; *Annual Report*, 1970.
29. *Gaffer*, June 26, 1970; *Gaffer*, August 7, 1970; *Annual Reports* 1970, 1971.
30. Oakes Ames to Houghton and Waterman, memo on Sylvania and ADL report on Sylvania and the structure of the television industry.
31. Morone, p. 140; Keck interview, May 17, 1997.
32. J. W. Fiske to R. W. Foster, November 22, 1968, Consolidated CGW-Gross Margins, Operating Expenses, Operating Margins folder, CIDARM 34-2-1.
33. Quoted in "Signetics Shows How in Semiconductors," *Business Week*, July 26, 1969, p. 41.
34. *Business Week*, July 26, 1969.
35. Amo to Ames, Armistead, et. al., June 24, 1970, Cost folder, CIDARM 7-5-8.
36. Amo to Waterman, May 15, 1970, Cost folder, CIDARM 7-5-8.
37. Amo to Ames, Armistead, et al., June 24, 1970, Cost folder, CIDARM 7-5-8.

38. Waterman to Amo, et. al., July 2, 1970, Cost folder, CIDARM 7-5-8.

39. See Rumrill-Hoyt, Inc., "Preliminary Merchandising Plan, Corelle Livingware Intro-duction, 1968," November 22, 1967, p. 4; and Rumrill-Hoyt, "Recommendation for Names for Corning's New Hercules Product," 24 May 1967, p. 4; both box C.A. 1124, Miscellaneous (Corelle Livingware) folder, CIDARM.

40. Corning Livingware: "American Marketing Miracle," *Gaffer*, August 7, 1970, p. 2. From Group 4, to Dr. James G. Bennett, "Principles of Marketing," March 27, 1985, p. 13, Hilbert files, no. 5.

41. Morone, pp. 142–146.

42. Memo on windshield testing, from C. A. Crawford to Amo, October 25, 1968, folder 14 G 1968, CIDARM 19-4-8; also Am to Cole, November 7, 1968, folder 14 G 1968, CIDARM 19-4-8; Morone, pp. 133, 142–146; *Corning Annual Reports*, 1969 and 1970.

43. Amo to Henry Ford II, Automotive Windshield folder, CIDARM 4-3-3; Morone, p. 133.

44. Morone, p. 142.

45. Morone, pp. 142–145; Robert W. Crandall, *Regulation of the Automobile* (1986), pp. 3–11.

46. Richard Dulude interview by Davis Dyer, September 21, 1998; David Duke interview by Davis Dyer, April 18, 1997; Thomas MacAvoy video interview by Davis Dyer, July 10, 1998.

47. *Annual Report*, 1970; Morone, pp. 142–145.

48. Keck interview, May 17, 1997; Magaziner and Patinkin, p. 274.

49. Magaziner, p. 275.

50. Magaziner and Patinkin, pp. 275–277.

51. William Armistead interview by Margaret Graham, August 1, 1997; Morone, p. 138.

52. Morone, pp 138–139.

53. *Gaffer*, May 1971.

54. *Annual Report*, 1971, p. 914; Robert Sobel, *RCA* (1986).

55. *New York Times*, June 27, 1971; Waterman, obituary, Waterman folder, CIDARM 34-1-1.

56. *New York Times*, June 27, 1971; Waterman biographical folder, CIDARM 34-5-1.

Chapter Eleven

1. The following account of the 1972 flood is based on Thomas P. Dimitroff and Lois S. Janes, *History of the Corning Painted Post Area: 200 Years in Painted Post Country*, rev. ed. (Corning, N.Y.: Bookmarks, 1991); *Gaffer*, special flood edition, July 1972; Marvin W. Copp, *Floods of the Chemung Watershed, 1794–1972* (1975); and an anonymous typescript, "A Letter from Corning" folder 2, CIDARM 34-3-02.

2. Van Campbell video interview by Davis Dyer, January 20, 1999.

3. "Volunteer Who Lost Life in Flood Cited in Board Chairman's Talk," *Gaffer*, November 1972.

4. Robert Brill, telephone message, November 1, 2000.

5. Houghton's radio talk was reprinted in the *Gaffer*, July 1972, p. 15.

6. *Gaffer*, July 1972, p. 15; Allan D. Cors, video interview, by Davis Dyer, May 13, 1999, Jamie Houghton comment to authors, October 15, 1999.

7. Campbell video interview, January 20, 1999.

8. *Corning Leader*, June 1, 1974; "Subsidiary Builds Corning, N.Y., Inn," *Gaffer*, March 1974,

p. 7. Thomas Buechner interview by Davis Dyer, April 25, 1997; Dimitroff and Janes, pp. 295–298.

9. "Corning Reflects New Colors," *Financial World*, December 5, 1973, p. 10.

10. Thomas MacAvoy papers, Objectives folder, ARV 25-E-2, CIDARM; Graham and Shuldiner, *Corning and the Craft of Innovation* (2001), chap. 7; William Ughetta interview by Davis Dyer, June 10, 1998.

11. Amory Houghton Jr., "Strategy for the 1970s," speech to Corning Glass Works Management Conference, April 23, 1968.

12. Amory Houghton Jr., letter to employees, the *Gaffer*, March 1971, p. 2.

13. Corning Glass Works, *Annual Report*, 1973.

14. "The Corelle Livingware Story," September 20, 1978; Hilbert notebook 5, CIDARM.

15. Norval Johnston video interview by Davis Dyer, December 11, 1998.

16. Johnston video interview, December 11, 1998; James R. Houghton interview by Davis Dyer, February 3, 1997.

17. S. Donald Stookey, *Journey to the Center of the Crystal Ball* (1985), pp. 13–14.

18. Richard Dulude interview by Davis Dyer, September 21, 1998; E. Martin Gibson video interview by Davis Dyer, February 8, 1999.

19. Dulude interview, September 21, 1998.

20. The following account is based on Dulude interview, September 21, 1998; David Duke interview by Davis Dyer, April 18, 1997; Charles W. "Skip" Deneka, interview by Margaret Graham and Davis Dyer, December 10, 1998.

21. Dulude interview, September 21, 1998.

22. Gibson video interview, February 8, 1999.

23. Gibson video interview, February 8, 1999.

24. "Research Adds to CGW Strength," and "LARC System Gets First Viewing," *Gaffer*, March 1973, pp. 13, 15.

25. "Sullivan Park Biochemist Discovers Way to Bond Enzymes," *Gaffer*, February 1971, p. 9; "Discovery Leads to Enzyme Economy," *Gaffer*, October 1973, p. 4; J. R. Hutchins interview by Davis Dyer, November 1997; Harmon Garfinkel video interview by Davis Dyer, February 9 1999.

26. "Research Adds to CGW Strength," *Gaffer*, March 1973, p. 13; "RIA Procedure Speeds Testing," *Gaffer*, March 1975, p. 5.

27. Gibson video interview, February 8, 1999.

28. Charles Lucy interview by Alec Shuldiner, October 29, 1998.

29. Charles Lucy video interview by Davis Dyer, January 9, 1999.

30. Lucy interview, October 29, 1998; Lucy, "Fused Silica and Me"; Peter Booth video interview by Davis Dyer, January 20, 1999; Lee Wilson interview by Margaret Graham, November 27–28, 1998.

31. Lucy interviews; Lucy, "Fused Silica and Me"; Magaziner and Patinkin, *The Silent War*, pp. 278–279; Hecht, *City of Light*.

32. "Research Adds to CGW Strength," *Gaffer*, March 1973, p. 13; Hecht, pp. 144–146; Magaziner and Patinkin, pp. 279–280.

33. Morone, p. 149.

34. *Corning Glass Works: International (A)*, Harvard Business School Case Services, 9-379-051, pp. 5–6.

35. James R. Houghton interview by Davis Dyer, June 3, 1997; James R. Houghton video interview by Davis Dyer, May 10, 1999.

36. Roy Hill, "Corning Glass Reshapes Its International Operations," *International Management*, October 1974, pp. 32–38.

37. Dan Morgan, "Pioneers in Economic Cooperation," *Washington Post*, May 3, 1973.

38. Robert Turissini video interview by Davis Dyer, June 11, 1998.

39. Corning Glass Works, *Annual Report*, 1974; *Corning Glass Works International (B-1)*, Harvard Business School Case Services, 9-381-162, p. 4.

40. Signetics Corporation, prospectus, November 1, 1973.

41. Ughetta interview, June 10, 1998.

42. Thomas MacAvoy video interview by Davis Dyer, September 15, 1998, Campbell video interview, January 20, 1999.

43. Campbell video interview, January 20, 1999.

44. MacAvoy video interview; Hutchins video interview; Thomas Buechner video interview by Davis Dyer, June 11, 1998. Most people who lived through this period and were interviewed for this book remarked on the downsizing as a watershed. Two who did not—Marty Gibson and Dave Leibson—pointed out that there are no guarantees in business and argued, from their perspective, that Corning recovered quickly from the episode: Gibson video interview, February 8, 1999; David Leibson video interview by Davis Dyer, February 9, 1999.

Chapter Twelve

1. The study is summarized in *Corning Glass Works International (B-1)*, Harvard Business School Case Services, 381–161; and *Corning Glass Works International (B-2)*, Harvard Business School Case Services, 381–162.

2. Quoted in "The Trials of Amory Houghton, Jr.," *Forbes*, August 1, 1977 and in *Corning Glass Works International (B-2)*, p. 3.

3. James R. Houghton video interview by Davis Dyer, May 10, 1999.

4. Richard Dulude interview by Davis Dyer, September 21, 1998, Corning Glass Works, *Annual Report*, 1979. Charles Wakeman interview by Margaret Graham, July 11, 1997; Peter Booth video interview by Davis Dyer, November 24, 1998.

5. E. Martin Gibson video interview by Davis Dyer, February 8, 1999; "Gibson Directs Major Review of Worldwide Personnel Policies," *Gaffer*, February 1977, p. 2.

6. E. Martin Gibson, "Employee Policies Defined Worldwide," *Gaffer*, March 1978, p. 3.

7. J. R. Hutchins video interview by Davis Dyer, November 10, 1998; Harmon Garfinkel video interview, February 9, 1999; John MacDowell video interview by Davis Dyer, February 10, 1999; "Biomedical Work to Be Consolidated," *Gaffer*, March 1978, p. 11.

8. Hutchins video interview, November 10, 1998; Garfinkel video interview, February 9, 1999; MacDowell video interview, February 10, 1999.

9. Garfinkel video interview, February 9, 1999; MacAvoy video interview by Davis Dyer, September 15, 1998; Margaret Graham and Alec Shuldiner, *Corning and the Craft of Innovation* (2001), chap. 7.

10. Hutchins video interview, November 10, 1998; George H. Beall video interview by Davis Dyer, June 11, 1998; MacDowell video interview, February 10, 1999; "George H. Beall Is Company's First Research Fellow," *Gaffer*, March 1978, p. 3; "Reorganization Is Announced for Technical Staffs Division," *Gaffer*, November 1978.

11. "What We Did Was Essential...Houghton," *Gaffer*, December 1975, p. 10.

12. "Hultzman Retires at Central Falls," *Gaffer*, May 1975, p. 13; "Corning Honors First Employee Ever to Receive 85-Year Pin," *Gaffer*, November 1976, p. 1.

13. Marie McKee video interview by Davis Dyer, September 15, 1998.

14. Rita Reif, "A New Setting for Corning's Glass Collection," *New York Times*, June 5, 1980, p. C1.

15. James E. Millstein, "Decline in an Expanding Industry: Japanese Competition in Color Television," in John Zysman and Laura Tyson, eds., *American Industry in International Competition: Government Policies and Corporate Strategies* (1983), chap. 3.

16. "The Trials of Amory Houghton Jr.," *Forbes*, August 1, 1977; Morone, p. 141.

17. Morone, p. 140.

18. Forrest Behm interview by Margaret Graham and Davis Dyer, March 6, 1997; Behm video interview by Davis Dyer, December 18, 1997.

19. Allen Dawson interview by Margaret Graham, January 29, 1998; Houghton and Dawson testimony; "CGW Seeks Color TV Import Relief," *Gaffer*, November 1976, pp. 1–2.

20. "CTV Industry Awaits Carter Action as ITC Rules Injury by Imports," *Gaffer*, April 1977, p. 1; "If Properly Implemented President Carter's Agreement with Japan on Color TV Imports Can Save Our Jobs," Corning advertisement featured in local newspapers, June 15, 1977.

21. Allen Dawson interview by Margaret Graham, May 1, 1997; Dawson interview, January 29, 1998; Allan Cors video interview by Davis Dyer, May 13, 1999, *New York Times*, May 5, 1980, p. 2.

22. "How to Turn a Recall into a Sales Pitch," *Business Week*, August 30, 1976, p. 21; Norval Johnston video interview by Davis Dyer, December 11, 1998; Tom MacAvoy video interview by Davis Dyer and Margaret Graham, July 10, 1998, Corning, New York; "Percolator Recall Under Way; Effort Praised by CPSC," *Gaffer*, August 1976, pp. 1–2.

23. Thomas MacAvoy video interview by Davis Dyer, September 15, 1998.

24. Jane Seaberry, "Corning Tells Consumers of Defects in Percolators; Corning Warns Consumers Percolators May Fall Apart," *Washington Post*, September 5, 1979, p. F1.

25. Susan King video interview by Davis Dyer, November 9, 1998. Johnston video interview, December 11, 1998.

26. *New York Times*, April 24, 1976, p. 35; Pierre-Louis Roederer interview by Davis Dyer, December 11, 1997.

27. Roederer interview, December 11, 1997.

28. "Corning Glass, China Sign Pact for TV Picture Tube Development," *Dow Jones Newswire*, September 15, 1980; "Corning Glass to Build Shanghai TV Tube Plant," *Dow Jones Newswire*, February 20, 1981; "Corning Glass, World Bank Arm to Finance Indonesian Plant," *Dow Jones Newswire*, July 8, 1981; "Corning Engineering Gives New Profit Center to Company," *Gaffer*, April 1983.

29. John Loose video interview by Davis Dyer, November 24, 1998; Peter Campanella video interview by Davis Dyer, March 8, 1999.

30. Campanella video interview, March 8, 1998; MacAvoy video interview, September 15, 1998, Van Campbell video interviews by Davis Dyer, January 20 and March 18, 1999; "CGW Stops Fair Trading Products," *Gaffer*, May 1975, p. 5; "Corning Designs to Sell Product Concept through Ready Retailer to 'Waiting' Market," *Merchandising*, November 1980, pp. 70–71.

31. Tom MacAvoy video interview, September 15, 1998; J. R. Hutchins interview by Davis Dyer, November 20, 1997.

32. Hecht, pp. 168–174.

33. Leroy Wilson interview by Margaret Graham, November 27–28, 1997. Wilson's account of the BCG study is very different from that in Magaziner and Patinkin. These authors, members of a rival consulting firm, say that Wilson and Duke ignored the study, which had concluded that the telecommunications market would not welcome optical waveguides anytime soon. Wilson, in contrast, cites the study as instrumental in increasing Corning's understanding of the telecommunications industry and outlining Corning's basic strategy to penetrate the telecommunications market through aggressive technical leadership.

34. Quoted in Magaziner and Patinkin, p. 282.

35. David Duke interview by Davis Dyer, April 18, 1997; Magaziner and Patinkin, p. 281.

36. Morone, p. 150.

37. Quoted in Magaziner and Patinkin, p. 283.

38. Hecht, p. 127.

39. Duke interview, April 18, 1997; Hecht, p. 186.

40. "Full Production at Pilot Plant for Waveguides Due by Summer," *Gaffer*, May 1977, p. 2; Morone, pp. 151–152.

41. David Duke interview by Davis Dyer and Margaret Graham, July 17, 1997, Corning, New York.

42. Duke interviews, April 18 and July 17, 1997.

43. "Waveguide Order Is Largest Ever," *Gaffer*, March 1978, p. 1; Duke interview, April 18, 1997.

44. "The Trials of Amory Houghton Jr.," *Forbes*, August 1, 1977, p. 37; See Graham and Shuldiner, chap. 6; Hecht, pp. 198–199; Magaziner and Patinkin, pp. 290–291; Wilson, interview November 27 and 28, 1997; Al Michaelsen interview by Margaret Graham, February 17, 1998.

45. Magaziner and Patinkin, p. 219.

46. "ITT Concedes It Infringed Corning Glass Works Patents," *Dow Jones Newswire*, July 28, 1981; Hecht, pp. 198–199.

47. "Optical Cable Firm Formed," *Gaffer*, January 1978, p. 1; Charles Lucy interview by Alec Shuldiner, October 29, 1998, Peter Booth video interview by Davis Dyer, November 24, 1998; Wilson interview, November 27 and 28, 1997; Joseph Hicks interview by Davis Dyer, November 18, 1997; Joseph Hicks video interview by Davis Dyer, November 10, 1998.

48. Hicks interview, November 18, 1997; Hicks video interview, November 10, 1998; Siecor Corporation, *Visions of Yesterday, Today and Tomorrow* (1993), pp. 1–2; Siecor Corporation, *Siecor Firsts* (1998).

49. Leonard Sloane, "Top Management Roles Change at Corning," *New York Times*, June 16, 1980, D-2.

50. "Corning Glass to Sell Its Stake in Owens-Corning," *Dow Jones Newswire*, September 3, 1981; Barnaby J. Feder, "Corning Seeks to Sell Owens-Corning Interest," *New York Times*, September 4, 1981, p. D-1.

51. Charles Batchelor, "J. Bibby in 10M Deal with Corning Glass," *Financial Times*, July 21, 1982, p. 21.

52. MacAvoy video interview, September 15, 1998.

53. Myron Magnet, "Corning Glass Shapes Up," *Fortune*, December 13, 1982, p. 90.

54. *CGW Strategies for the 1980s* (presentation to board of directors, February 2, 1982), pp. 53–61.

55. "Corning to Enter Sunglass Market," *New York Times*, March 9, 1982, p. D-4.

56. *Dow Jones Newswires*, July 21, 1980; *Dow Jones Newswires*, November 20, 1981.

57. Morone, pp. 154, 163–64; Myron Magnet, "Corning Glass Shapes Up," *Fortune*, December 13, 1982, p. 94.

58. Quoted in Morone, p. 155.

59. Howard Weetall interview by Margaret Graham, March 4, 1999. The Sebastiani relationship soured when it turned out that the enzymatic process "deflected the flavor" of the wine. See also, Gary Taylor, "Genentech Plus Corning Equals Genencor," *Business Week*, July 1989, pp. 40–41.

60. Dow-Jones News Service-Wall Street Journal Combined Stories [electronic database], May 30, June 12, July 11, 1980; E. Martin Gibson, video interview, February 8, 1999.

61. Gibson video interview, February 8, 1999.

Chapter Thirteen

1. Thomas MacAvoy interview by Margaret Graham, July 31, 1997; MacAvoy interview by Davis Dyer, September 15, 1998; Jeffrey Sonnenfeld, *The Hero's Farewell: What Happens When CEOs Retire* (1988), pp. 246–251.

2. Sonnenfeld, pp. 248–249.

3. James Houghton interview by Davis Dyer, February 3, 1997. Information in this and the following two paragraphs is drawn from this interview.

4. MacAvoy interview, July 31, 1997.

5. Oakes Ames video interview by Davis Dyer, March 30, 1998; James Houghton interview by Davis Dyer, June 3, 1997.

6. One of the most influential statements of the problem was Robert H. Hayes and William J. Abernathy, "Managing Our Way to Economic Decline," *Harvard Business Review*, July-August 1980.

7. Alfred D. Chandler Jr., "The Competitive Performance of U.S. Industrial Enterprise since the Second World War," *Business History Review*, 68 (Spring 1994): 1–72; George David Smith and Davis Dyer, "The Rise and Transformation of the American Corporation," in Carl Kaysen, ed., *The American Corporation Today: Examining the Questions of Power and Efficiency at the Century's End* (1996), pp. 28–73; Nitin Nohria, "From the M-form to the N-form: Taking Stock of Changes in the Large Industrial Corporation," Harvard Business School Working Paper 96-054.

8. *CGW Strategies for the 1980s* (presentation to Board of Directors, February 2, 1982), pp. 12–13, 51.

9. *CGW Strategies for the 1980s*, pp. 53–61; Corning Glass Works, *Annual Report*, 1982; Roger Ackerman video interview by Davis Dyer and Margaret Graham, June 17, 1999.

10. James Houghton, "Strategy 'Update' to CGW Board of Directors," July 27, 1981.

11. Corning Glass Works, *Annual Report*, 1983.

12. Quoted in *Corning Incorporated: A Network of Alliances*, Harvard Business School Case Services 9-391-102, p. 3.

13. Van Campbell interview by Davis Dyer and Margaret Graham, May 27, 1997.

14. *Corning Incorporated: A Network of Alliances*, p. 3.

15. James Houghton interview, February 3, 1997.

16. Richard Sphon interview by Margaret Graham, August 1, 1997. Cf. Richard Marks interview by Davis Dyer, November 17, 1997.

17. T. C. MacAvoy, "Technology Assessment and Strategy," April 10, 1984, pp. 11–13 (copy furnished by Dr. MacAvoy); MacAvoy interview, July 31, 1997.

18. MacAvoy interview, July 31, 1997.

19. Philip B. Crosby, *Quality is Free: The Art of Making Quality Practical* (1979).

20. The following paragraphs are based on James Houghton interview, February 3, 1997; James R. Houghton, " 'The Old Way of Doing Things Is Gone,' " *Quality Progress*, September 1986, pp. 15–18; Forrest Behm interview by Davis Dyer and Margaret Graham, Corning, New York, March 6, 1997; Behm interview by Margaret Graham, May 13, 1997; Behm interview by Davis Dyer, December 18, 1997; and Joseph G. Morone, *Winning in High-Tech Markets* (1993), pp. 159–161.

21. Houghton, " 'The Old Way of Doing Things Is Gone,' " p. 16.

22. David B. Luther, "Closing the Quality Gap," *Syracuse University Magazine*, August 1987, p. 3; Maggie McComas, "Cutting Costs without Killing the Business," *Fortune*, October 13, 1986, p. 72; Barbara Buell, "Smashing the Country Club Image at Corning Glass," *Business Week*, May 5, 1986, p. 95.

23. "CGW Net Operating Margin 7.1% in 1987," *Corning Leader*, January 25, 1988; Campbell interview, May 27, 1997; Corning Glass Works, *Annual Report*, 1985.

24. E. Martin Gibson interview by Margaret Graham, April 30, 1997.

25. Ira C. Magaziner and Mark Patinkin, *The Silent War: Inside the Global Business Battles Shaping America's Future* (1989), pp. 285–287.

26. Quoted in Magaziner and Patinkin, p. 288.

27. Joseph Hicks interview by Davis Dyer and Stuart K. Sammis, November, 18, 1997.

28. Analyst's estimate, quoted in Morone, p. 165.Other estimates placed Corning's revenues from waveguides in 1985 as high as $290 million. See "Corning's Strategy of Diversification," *Lightwave*, April 1986.

29. Calvin Sims, "Corning Wins Case on Patents," *New York Times*, October 14, 1987; Al Michaelsen interview by Margaret Graham, February 17, 1998.

30. "Corning's Strategy of Diversification," *Lightwave*, April 1986.

31. "How Corning Glass Spawns Tech Firms," *Lightwave*, July 1988. In 1986, Plessey sold its share of PlessCor Optronics to Corning, which renamed the unit PCO, Inc. In 1989, Corning sold PCO to IBM.

32. Gibson interview, April 30, 1997; Roger Ackerman interview by Davis Dyer and Margaret Graham, May 27, 1997; Morone, pp. 155–158 and 169–172; "Corning Glass Works' Marty Gibson: Forging an Industry Position in Laboratory Services," *Medical Business Journal*, January 31, 1988, cover story.

33. "Corning Glass Works' Marty Gibson"; Ignatius Chithelen, "Clinical Case," *Forbes*, March 20, 1989, pp. 178–179; David Cassak, "Managing Through the Storm," *In Vivo*, June 1989, pp. 15–19.

34. Ackerman interview, May 27, 1997.

35. "Corning Glass Works' Marty Gibson," p. 1; cf. James Houghton interview, June 3, 1997.

36. "Mixed Marriages, Mixed Blessings," *In Vivo*, July-August 1986, p. 12. Around the same

time that Corning and Ciba-Geigy linked up, Eli Lilly and Bristol-Myers also entered the diagnostics business. See also James Houghton, interview, June 3, 1997; Corning Glass Works, *Annual Report*, 1985; Constance Mitchell, "Partnerships Have Become a Way of Life for Corning," *Wall Street Journal*, July 12, 1988, unpaginated reprint.

37. "Corning Glass Works' Marty Gibson."
38. Mitchell, "Partnerships."
39. Quoted in Morone, p. 169; Gibson interview, April 30, 1997.
40. Bob Rusnak interview by Davis Dyer, September 19, 1997; Gerald J. Barry, "Stay Tuned," *Quality Review*, Spring 1998.
41. D. H. McConnell, "Planning Manufacturing Expansion in the Television Glassware Sector," photocopy in public relations files, Corning Incorporated.
42. Robert Turissini interview by Davis Dyer and Margaret Graham, March 5, 1997; Turissini video interview by Davis Dyer, June 11, 1998; "Nothing but Smiles and Handshakes," *Business Korea*, April 1986, p. 13.
43. Corning Glass Works, *Annual Report*, 1985, p. 31.
44. This paragraph draws on George Beall video interview by Davis Dyer, June 11, 1997 and the account in Morone, pp. 161–164.
45. Morone, p. 163.
46. Campbell interview, May 27, 1997.
47. Campbell interview, May 27, 1997.
48. "Corning Renews Established Brands, Launches New Ones," *Housewares*, April 14, 1986, pp. 50–52.
49. Paul Miczuzak interview by Davis Dyer and Margaret Graham, September 17, 1997; "Corning Renews Established Brands," pp. 50–52. For the French origins of Visions, see Jacques Lemoine, Avon Laboratory, OPCOM Review, May 13, 1993.
50. "Corning Renews Established Brands," pp. 50–52.
51. Terrence Murphy, "Crown Corning," *Entrée* (1986), unpaginated reprint.
52. Information in this and the following paragraphs is based on Jonathan West and David A. Garvin, *Serengeti Eyewear: Entrepreneurship within Corning Inc.*, Harvard Business School Case 9-394-033 and "Back from the Brink," *Corning Leader*, February 22, 1988.
53. *Corning Values*, 1986 edition; Nanda and Bartlett, *Corning Incorporated: A Network of Alliances*, pp. 5, 19.
54. Joseph Hicks video interview, November 10, 1998; Jerry McQuaid, telephone interview, November 17, 1997. Statistics furnished by plant manager's office at Wilmington, November 18, 1997.
55. Corning Glass Works press releases, November 19, 1986, November 10, 1987; *Corning Incorporated: A Network of Alliances*, p. 5.
56. Hicks interview, November 18, 1997; Hicks video interview, November, 10, 1998.
57. John Hutchins video interview by Davis Dyer, November 10, 1998; Charles "Skip" Deneka video interview, December 10, 1998; Morone, p. 168; Gitimoy Kar video interview by Davis Dyer, August 13, 1998.
58. Robert Green and Luc Dohan, "The Case for Integration," *Communications International*, January 1990, pp. 64–65; Kevin W. Murphy, "Couplers Let Fiber Phone Home," *Transmission*, April 1, 1990, pp. 60–65; Deneka video interview, December 10, 1998.
59. Kar video interview, August 13, 1998; Loose video interview, November 24, 1998; Deneka video interview, December 10, 1998.

60. Ackerman interview, May 27, 1997; Telesis, USA, Inc., "An Outsiders View of Corning's Special Glass and Ceramics Businesses," December 14, 1987.
61. Morone, p. 162; "Corning Plant to Reopen in '88," *Roanoke Times & World News*, October 9, 1987, unpaginated photocopy.
62. Corning Glass Works, press release, June 7, 1988; Corning Incorporated, *Annual Report*, 1989.
63. Ron Kovalcin interview by Davis Dyer, September 18, 1997; Loose video interview, November 24, 1998; Corning Glass Works, "Corning/Asahi TV Joint Venture, Questions and Answers," July 11, 1988; Cristina Lee, "Corning Glass, Japan's Asahi Agree to Form Joint Venture," *Journal of Commerce*, July 12, 1988; Mitchell, "Partnerships Have Become a Way of Life."
64. Loose video interview, November 24, 1998.
65. Ernie Lucas, Steve Wertz, Nate Summers, video interview by Davis Dyer, September 19, 1997.
66. Corning Incorporated, *Annual Report*, 1989, p. 33; "Transferring TV Glass Technology Is Heart of Corning Glass's JV," *Business China*, July 13, 1987, pp. 97–98; Corning Incorporated, press release, March 16, 1990.
67. Richard L. Gordon, "Corning Glass in Deal to Buy Precision Lens," *Cincinnati Post*, August 16, 1986; "Rustbelt Renaissance," *Business Tokyo*, Summer 1989, pp. 53–55.
68. Corning Glass Works, press release, October 6, 1988; Peter Booth video interview by Davis Dyer, November 24, 1988; Morone, pp. 172–173.
69. Beall video interview, June 11, 1998; Deneka video interview, December 10, 1998.
70. Gibson interview, April 30, 1987; Keith H. Hammonds, "Corning's Class Act," *Business Week*, May 13, 1991, cover story; Morone, p. 171; Marci Toback, "Houghton: 'We're in Pretty Good Shape,'" *Corning Leader*, May 14, 1988.
71. Milt Freudenheim, "Debate Widens over Expanding Use and Growing Cost of Medical Tests," *New York Times*, May 30, 1987.
72. David Cassak, "Managing through the Storm," *In Vivo*, June 1989, pp. 15–19; Laurie Hays and Gregory Stricharchuk, "International Clinical Bidding War Intensifies," *Wall Street Journal*, March 29, 1988.
73. Corning Glass Works, press release, January 2, 1997.
74. Corning Glass Works, press release, February 21, 1989; "Corning Glass to Buy Enseco in Transaction Valued at $125 Million," *Wall Street Journal*, March 23, 1989; Corning Incorporated, press release, June 2, 1989; Morone, p. 171.
75. Norval Johnston video interview by Davis Dyer, December 11, 1998.
76. Constance Mitchell, "Corning's Purchase of Revere Expected to Broaden Sales," *Wall Street Journal*, May 2, 1988; "Corning Will Acquire Revere Ware to Boost Consumer Product Sales," *Investor's Daily*, May 2, 1988.
77. Corning Incorporated, *Annual Report*, 1990.
78. James R. Houghton, Journey without End," keynote address to GOAL, November 8, 1991.
79. "Corning Glass Works: Putting Money Where Its Mouth Is," *Industry Week*, September 19, 1988, p. 58; David A. Garvin, "How the Baldrige Award Really Works," *Harvard Business Review* (November-December 1991), p. 90; Houghton, "The Endless Journey."
80. Michael McDonald video interview by Davis Dyer, October 15, 1998.
81. Houghton, "Endless Journey"; Corning Incorporated, press release, February 1, 1990.

82. Houghton, "Endless Journey"; Norman E. Garrity, "People, Partnership, and Productivity," *PI Quality*, Fourth Quarter, 1991, unpaginated reprint; "Corning: The Search for Flexibility on the Line," *New York Times*, July 16, 1989; "Sharpening Minds for a Competitive Edge," *Business Week*, December 17, 1990, pp. 44–46.

83. Timothy D. Schellhardt and Carol Hymowitz, "U.S. Manufacturers Face Big Changes in Years Ahead," *Wall Street Journal*, May 2, 1989, p. 1; "Sharpening Minds for a Competitive Edge," pp. 44–45.

84. Richard Marks video interview by Davis Dyer, November 12, 1998.

85. Houghton drew the connection between total quality and diversity in "Endless Journey": "you simply cannot achieve World Class Quality unless you use the talents of all employees. The most obvious examples of this are the culturally diverse U.S. Olympic team and our armed forces." See also, Marie McKee video interview by Davis Dyer, September 15, 1998.

86. James R. Houghton, "To Add Corporate Value, Break the Glass Ceiling," *Financier*, July 1988, pp. 32–36; McKee video interview, September 15, 1998.

87. McKee video interview, September 15, 1998; Susan King video interview, November 9, 1998; Houghton interview, August 10, 1998; Peter T. Kilborn, "A Company Recasts Itself to Erase Decades of Bias," *New York Times*, October 4, 1990, p. 1.

88. McKee video interview, September 15, 1998; Loughran, "Corning Tries to Break the Glass Ceiling," p. 52; Kilborn, "A Company Recasts Itself."

89. Kilborn, "A Company Recasts Itself."

90. Amory Houghton Jr. interview by Margaret Graham and Davis Dyer, May 5, 1997; James Houghton interview, August 10, 1998.

91. "Corning Enterprises Sees Endless Horizons for Area," *Corning Leader*, October 28, 1989; Cindy Skrzycki, "Company Town," *Washington Post*, August 12, 1990; "Ceramic Corridor May Bring Prosperity," *Sunday Democrat and Chronicle* (Rochester, New York), May 17, 1987.

92. "CNN Provides a Rare Glance at Jamie Houghton," *Corning Leader*, August 18, 1986; James Houghton interview, August 10, 1998.

Chapter Fourteen

1. Corning Incorporated, press release, April 27, 1989; *Annual Report*, 1989; *Corning Incorporated: A Network of Alliances*, Harvard Business School Case 9-391-102.

2. *Corning World* [successor to *Gaffer*], November 1990.

3. James Houghton interview by Davis Dyer and Margaret Graham, August 10, 1998; James Houghton video interview by Davis Dyer, May 28, 1999; Roger Ackerman video interview by Davis Dyer and Margaret Graham, June 17, 1999; E. Martin Gibson video interview by Davis Dyer, February 8, 1999, Robert Stone video interview, October 27, 1998.

4. J. R. Houghton, "I Do What I Value: How Do I Spend My Time," *Presentation Graphics*, January 31, 1992; David A. Garvin, "How the Baldrige Award Really Works," *Harvard Business Review*, November-December 1991, p. 90.

5. Ackerman video interview, June 17, 1999; Van Campbell presentation to analysts, April 23, 1994, Corning Incorporated.

6. Corning Incorporated, news release, June 23, 1993; Peter Campanella video interview by Davis Dyer, March 18, 1999.

7. Corning Incorporated, news release, January 2, 1992; Richard Dulude interview by Davis Dyer, October 19, 1998.

8. Dulude interview, October 19, 1998; James Houghton video interview, May 28, 1999.

9. John Loose video interview by Davis Dyer, November 24, 1998; Loose video interview, November 24, 1998; "Corning Plans to Sell European Operations for about $90 Million," *Wall Street Journal*, October 17, 1994.

10. Corning Clinical Laboratories, "Facts About Corning Clinical Laboratories," n.d. [1996?]; Joan E. Rigdon, "Corning Tops Competing Bid to Buy Damon," *Wall Street Journal*, June 29, 1993; Gibson video interview, February 8, 1999.

11. Gibson video interview, February 8, 1999.

12. Corning Incorporated, news release, September 13, 1993; Rhonda L. Rundle, "Corning Unit, Unilab Pay $39.8 Million to Settle Allegations of Medicare Fraud," *Wall Street Journal*, September 14, 1993; Houghton interview, August 10, 1998.

13. Gibson video interview, February 8, 1999.

14. Corning Incorporated, *Annual Report*, 1993 and 1994.

15. Norman Garrity video interview by Davis Dyer, January 20, 1999.

16. Garrity video interview, January 20, 1999.

17. Ibid, "Smog-Busters' Invention Still the Catalyst for Clean Air," *Detroit News*, May 4, 1994; "Cold Calculation," *Scientific American*, May 1994.

18. "Corning Produces Monolithic Mirror Blank," *Ceramic Industry*, October 1994, unpaginated reprint; Corning Incorporated, *Annual Report*, 1994; "Corning-St. Gobain Venture to Make Cooktops in U.S." *Dow Jones News*, October 11, 1994.

19. Garrity video interview, January 20, 1999.

20. Terry Costlow, "Seagate's Ceramic Drive," *Electronic Engineering Times*, April 26, 1993, unpaginated photocopy; Houghton interview, August 10, 1998; George Beall video interview by Davis Dyer, June 11, 1998; Charles Skip Deneka, video interview by Margaret Graham and Davis Dyer, December 10, 1998.

21. Andrew Kupfer, "The Race to Rewire," *Fortune*, April 19, 1993; Jan Suwinski, "Photonics Shifts into High Gear," *Photonics Spectra*, January 1994; John Loose, Corning Communications, presentation to analysts, November 1997; Jan Suwinski video interview by Davis Dyer, January 21, 1999; Loose video interview, November 24, 1998.

22. Suwinski video interview, January 21, 1999.

23. Joseph Hicks video interview by Davis Dyer, November 10, 1998; Suwinski video interview, January 21, 1999; "Corning Plans to Buy Northern Telecom's Optical Fiber Unit," *Wall Street Journal*, December 16, 1993.

24. Corning Incorporated, investor presentation, November 3, 1998; "Japan's Liquid-Crystal Gold Rush," *Business Week*, January 17, 1994; Andrew Pollack, "From Korea, a Challenge to Japan," *New York Times*, May 12, 1994; Loose video interview; Peter Booth video interview by Davis Dyer, January 20, 1999.

25. Houghton video interview, May 28, 1999.

26. Houghton video interview, May 28, 1999; Joseph G. Morone, *Winning in High-Tech Markets: The Role of General Management* (1993), p. 175; Corning Incorporated, *Annual Report*, 1992.

27. Richard D. Ringer, "Corning Chief Recovers after Being Hit by Car," *New York Times*, May 8, 1993; Wendy Bounds, "A Near Fatal Accident Changes a CEO's View of His Life and His Job," *Wall Street Journal*, February 2, 1996.

28. "Corning Says Outlook Is Bright Despite Low Stock Price," *Wall Street Journal*, November 11, 1993.

29. Houghton video interview, May 28, 1999. The following narrative is based on a series

of accounts by Gina Kolata in the *New York Times* in 1995; Marcia Angell, *Science on Trial: The Clash of Medical Evidence and the Law in the Breast Implant Case* (1996); Richard Hazleton interview by Davis Dyer, June 12, 1997, and William Ughetta interview by Davis Dyer, June 10, 1998.

30. "Judge Absolves Dow Chemical, Corning of Liability in Breast-Implant Cases," *Wall Street Journal*, December 6, 1993; Ughetta interview, June 12, 1997.

31. Corning Incorporated, *Annual Report*, 1994, 1995.

32. Roger G. Ackerman and Gary L. Neilson, "Partnering for Results: A Case Study of Re-Engineering the Corning Way," *Strategy and Business*, second quarter 1996; "Re-engineering, with Love," *Economist*, n.d. [unpaginated reprint, 1995]; Ackerman video interview; Ken Freeman video interview by Davis Dyer, October 9, 1998.

33. "Reengineering with Love."

34. Van Campbell interview by Davis Dyer, May 27, 1997; Houghton interview, August 10, 1998.

35. "A Look Inside the New HQ," *Corning Leader*, December 15, 1993.

Chapter Fifteen

1. When Jamie Houghton stepped down, his son James was on a fast track to senior management at Corning. In 1997, however, James left the company to pursue a career in financial services and venture capital in Boston. As noted in the introduction, Carter Houghton, a nephew of Amo's and Jamie's, joined Corning's management ranks in 1999. Although Corning had produced consumer housewares since introducing Pyrex in the 1910s, its products were known by its corporate name only after the introduction of Corning Ware in the late 1950s.

2. See, for example, the special edition of *Fast Company*, September 1999, for a review of "the state of the new economy."

3. Roger Ackerman interview by Davis Dyer and Margaret Graham, May 27, 1997, Corning, New York; Roger Ackerman video interview by Davis Dyer and Margaret Graham, June 17, 1999, Corning, New York.

4. Corning Incorporated, *Growing Corning: Our Purpose, Our Strategy, Our Values, Our Operating Environment, Our Financial Goals* (1997).

5. Ibid.

6. Ackerman video interview.

7. Van Campbell interview by Davis Dyer, May 27, 1997, Corning, New York; Ken Freeman video interview by Davis Dyer, October 9, 1998, New York City; Steven Lipin and Wendy Bounds, "Corning Seeks to Shed Lab-Testing Unit," *Wall Street Journal*, January 31, 1996.

8. "Corning Decides It's Not Business as Usual," *Financial Times*, March 20, 1997; Campbell interview, May 27, 1997; Larry Wilson, "Corning Spins Off 2 New Companies," *Star-Gazette*, May 15, 1996.

9. James R. Houghton to Davis Dyer, March 17, 2000.

10. Corning Incorporated, press release, May 6, 1997; Emily Nelson, "Corning Aims to Sell Off Its Pots and Pans," *Wall Street Journal*, May 6, 1997. Corning also sold off its Serengeti sunglasses business in the spring of 1997 to Solar-Mates, Inc., for $27 mil-

lion. (The sale was announced in October 1996.) "Corning Finishes Serengeti Sale," *Corning Leader*, February 14, 1997.

11. Peter Campanella video interview, March 18, 1999; Corning Incorporated, press release, October 15, November 20, 1997, March 2, April 1, 1998.

12. *Growing Corning*, inside front cover; "Corning Tackles the World from Our Little Home Town," *Corning Leader*, February 9, 1997.

13. "Erwin Gets Plant," *Corning Leader*, February 13, 1997, p. 1; "Union Made Concessions to Land Jobs, Erwin Plant," *Corning Leader*, February 15, 1997.

14. "Sullivan Park Expansion Means Research Growth," *Corning Leader*, February 14, 1997.

15. Ackerman video interview; Corning Incorporated, Science and Technology Deep Dive, May 12–13, 1997; Skip Deneka video interview by Margaret Graham and Davis Dyer, December 10, 1998.

16. Jeff Hecht, *City of Light* (1999); George Gilder, *Telecosm: How Infinite Bandwidth Will Revolutionize Our World* (2000); Cary Lu, *The Race for Bandwidth: Understanding Data Transmission* (1998); Brian Winston, *Media Technology and Society: A History: From the Telegraph to the Internet* (1998); Philip Ball, *Made to Measure: New Materials for the 21st Century* (1997).

17. *Wall Street Newsletter*, April 14, 1997.

18. William C. Symonds, "Has Corning Won Its High-Tech Bet?" *Business Week*, April 5, 1999.

19. Joseph Hicks video interview by Davis Dyer, November 10, 1998.

20. Corning Incorporated, press release, November 14, 1999; information on Oak Industries gleaned from its Web site: www.oakind.com. The terms of the deal called for 0.83 shares of Corning stock to be exchanged for each share of Oak Industries stock.

21. Corning Incorporated, press release, December 8, 1999; Siemens A. G., press release, December 8, 1999.

22. *Wired*, June 1999, on-line edition.

23. James R. Houghton to Davis Dyer, March 17, 2000.

24. Ronald B. Lieber, "Why Wall Street Won't Buy the New, Improved Corning," *Fortune*, September 7, 1998, on-line edition, quoting T. Rowe Price analyst Hugh Evans.

25. Roger G. Ackerman, "The Role of Glass in the 21st Century," speech before the International Congress on Glass, San Francisco, California, July 6, 1998.

Index